Neighbors
at
WAR

Map 1   The Former Yugoslavia

Edited by Joel M. Halpern and David A. Kideckel

Neighbors at WAR

Anthropological Perspectives
on Yugoslav Ethnicity,
Culture, and History

The Pennsylvania
State University Press
University Park,
Pennsylvania

Photos by Joel Halpern have previously appeared in *The Thin Veneer: The Peoples of Bosnia and Their Disappearing Heritage* (University of Massachusetts Gallery, Amherst, 1997).

Library of Congress Cataloging-in-Publication

Neighbors at war : anthropological perspectives on Yugoslav ethnicity,
    culture, and history / edited by Joel M. Halpern and David A.
    Kideckel.

        p.   cm.
    Includes bibliographical references and index.
    ISBN 0-271-01978-6 (cloth : alk. paper).
    ISBN 0-271-01979-4 (pbk. : alk. paper).
    1. Former Yugoslav republics—Ethnic relations. 2. Nationalism
—Former Yugoslav republics. 3. Yugoslav War, 1991–1995—Causes.
I. Halpern, Joel Martin.   II. Kideckel, David A., 1948–   .
DR1229.N45   2000
305.8′009497—dc21   99-26976
                                                                CIP

It is the policy of The Pennsylvania State University Press to use acid-free paper for the first printing of all clothbound books. Publications on uncoated stock satisfy the minimum requirements of American National Standard for Information Sciences—Permanence of Paper for Printed Library Materials, ANSI Z39.48–1992.

Contents

Acknowledgments

Joel M. Halpern appreciates the patience and understanding of his wife, Barbara Kerewsky-Halpern. He also wishes to express appreciation to Dejan Tričković of New York for his help in editing the bibliography and also to his colleagues at the Institute of Southeast European Studies in the Department of History at the University of Graz for their interest and support.

David A. Kideckel wishes to thank his wife, Judith, and children, Zachary and Caitlin, for their forbearance with his time spent on this project. He also wishes to thank Carol Sessions, secretary at the Department of Anthropology, for her extensive efforts on behalf of this project, and June Higgins, dean of the CCSU School of Arts and Sciences, for the various types of support she offered as well. Thanks also to John Harmon and Randi Veklund of the CCSU Department of Geography for their assistance with the preparation of the maps.

Both editors express their appreciation to the unnamed readers of the manuscript and to Peter Potter, Cherene Holland, Shannon Pennefeather, and others at Penn State Press for both their encouragement and assistance. For the photographs of Kosovo we appreciate the aid of Janet Reineck, Andrei Simić, and Albanian colleagues who are named in the captions. We also wish to mention our appreciation of publishing an initial version of many of the papers presented here in a special issue of the *Anthropology of East Europe Review*. Finally, and most crucially, we are indebted to our twenty-two authors, who patiently bore their responsibility for preparing this extensive manuscript, and who articulately expressed their points of view.

PART I

CULTURE, SOCIETY, AND HISTORICAL CONTEXT IN FORMER YUGOSLAVIA

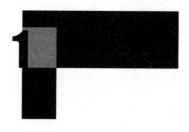

Introduction

The End of Yugoslavia Observed

Joel M. Halpern and David A. Kideckel

Why This Book?

How can we understand the war in former Yugoslavia and, most particularly, its violent nationalisms? Enormous amounts of information have been generated about the war. Scholars, journalists, and diplomats have produced many diverse analyses of the region. There is also a plethora of information available through the Internet. Some sources are either explicitly or implicitly partisan, while others view matters from a greater geographical, emotional, or intellectual distance. Still, these scholars, journalists, and diplomats have done little to ameliorate the conflict. Nor has the rest of the world, working through the UN, NATO, and the European Community, brought an end to the violence. Kosovo still burns. Indicted war criminals remain free. Many of the provisions of the Dayton Accord are honored only when external pressure is applied. In Bosnia many observers predict renewed fighting if NATO forces are withdrawn.

Given that more knowledge and improved understanding will not necessarily lead to peace, what can justify another book on the conflicts in former Yugoslavia? Here we do not claim total objectivity or some hitherto undiscovered source of enlightenment. Rather, in this volume we present certain alternative perspectives, some of which have not received much attention. We do not analyze the politics of the region as such. Rather, we focus on sociocultural processes directly related to the causes and nature of the conflict. The contributors, principally anthropologists, probe local and particularistic dimensions of the war, the related destruction of a common nation-state, and the reconstruction and emergence of separate national identities through both direct and implicit cross-cultural analysis. While the chapters deal with regional developments, they are not so much focused on politics as they are concerned with how values and attitudes are altered and new identities formed, albeit on the bases of preexisting ones.

The contributors to this volume recognize that for social science generalizations to be heuristic they must account for local complexity and historical variation, which includes intraethnic diversity and conflict as well as interethnic warfare. This perspective is lacking in many accounts of Bosnia, Kosovo, and former Yugoslavia, where observers assume too often that ethnic-religious categories are fixed, homogeneous, and predictive of both historical and present behavior. Thus these chapters describe how historical models shape the policies implemented by new national elites in their construction of emergent, mutually antagonistic nationalisms and influence their prosecution of war. Those responsible for political decision making lead societies where the definition of a desired future is based on an idealized past of one's own group. This is often strengthened by simultaneously demonizing the "Other," whether that Other is the former secular, multinational state, the "religious/national" groups in now-neighboring states, or even dissident groups within one's own nation.

Anthropologists have long focused on how cultures emerge and develop. Recently some of them have turned their attention to how cultures decay and end. These essays suggest that these must be considered complementary processes. Linking destruction to creation is not a new theme, whether in political ideologies such as Marxism or in religion. Such opposition underlies the revolution that created communist Yugoslavia. Its basic rationale followed directly from the destruction of World War II. The new communist state sought to negate that history and that of the preexisting Yugoslav state through the construction of monuments, the production of socialist-realist art, the creation of state holidays and state folklore, the obsessive chronicling of the Partisan struggle, and the publication of biographies of the leaders of the struggle, especially Tito.

The current conflict in former Yugoslavia recalls earlier conflicts in other areas where new national identities and states were created on the ruins of preexisting, more inclusive polities. This was also the case for the first Yugoslav state following World War I. However, as the current Balkan conflict has produced no definitive winners or acknowledged losers, the new state structures and identities must necessarily be viewed as tentative. Unfortunately, the trends that can be discerned are not salutary. They include increased factionalization, the persistence of authoritarianism, continued retributive conflict, and the intensification of fundamentalist religious beliefs. The future may be open, but in some ways seems ominously foreclosed.

Background to the Book

This book began in 1993 as a special issue of the *Anthropology of East Europe Review* edited by David Kideckel and Joel Halpern, with initial cooperation from Sam Beck. Most of the contributors to that issue revised their chapters for this collection. We also invited contributions from scholars with kindred interests—social historians (Hannes Grandits and Christian Promitzer), a sociologist of graphic media (Goran Jovanović), an ethnomusicologist (Mirjana Laušević), a psychiatrist (Stevan Weine), and a specialist in international law (Julie Mertus). Each contributor has extensive firsthand experience in former Yugoslavia. In order to facilitate a diversity of understandings about the conflict we insisted only that the essays focus on the conflict's diverse meanings, how they played out, and where appropriate and feasible, their implications for the long term, made more acute by the war in Kosovo and Yugoslavia and its consequences. Our ultimate hope is that insight into cultural processes can help build peace. But building peace requires more than knowledge or offers of external assistance. The participants must also be willing.

In the original *Review,* as well as in this volume, we purposely sought contributors representing diverse, even conflicting, points of view. Some of the essays focus on particular groups. Others look at the conflict from a variety of cross-national perspectives. Even these categories are, however, much too rigid to encompass the ways in which methodological and regional perspectives overlap even as conceptual approaches may vary. Whatever their focus, as editors we sought not only to present these diverse perspectives as independent analyses, but also to point out their common themes and shared perspectives.

It has not been easy to put this collection together. Political passions surrounding the breakup of Yugoslavia run high. It would be disingenuous not to acknowledge some of the criticisms we received about the *Anthropology of East Europe Review* special issue. Maja Povrzanović contributed to the original volume, but later wrote that "the readings of the articles . . . by foreign anthropologists (as well as many journalists) who tried to explain the war in Croatia (and sometimes justify the reasons for Serbian military aggression) should not be based on an a priori positioning of the authors . . . the readership should question the foreign authors' partiality in political terms" (Povrzanović 1995). Further, she continues in a footnote: "Croatian readers were rather irritated by the [sub]title of the 1993 special issue of *The Anthropology of East Europe Review: War Among the Yugoslavs,*" because, as she reminds us, "Yugoslavia officially ceased to exist on January 15, 1992, when the UN recognized Slovenia and Croatia. Therefore, such a title inevitably provokes interest in the political positions of the editors" (Povrzanović 1995: 102).

Although "Yugoslavs" was the appropriate official as well as generic term for the diverse South Slav peoples, Povrzanović apparently assumes that our use of it implies a pro-Serbian bias. But her attitude, while (clearly) debatable, is at least straightforward. We were more surprised by Dunja Rihtman-Auguštin, a senior, influential Croatian ethnologist. In a 1995 article she writes as "an elderly Croat lady" who has lived through World War II and the recent war in Croatia in 1991–92. She goes on to say "my views necessarily are biased" (Rihtman-Auguštin 1995: 61–67). Like Povrzanović, she was also offended by the title: "Skepticism is due to my recent reading of [the] text published in the special issue of . . . ' "War among the Yugoslavs' (as if ever Yugoslavs had been a nation)." This statement is then followed by a footnote: "Joel Halpern's own inaccurate quotation in a letter published in *Anthropology Newsletter* (1994: 6) is also worth noting: 'As a long-term researcher in the Balkans and editor of the "Yugoslav Conflict". . . I would like to respond. . . .' 'Yugoslav Conflict' thus appears instead of the original title. . . . Are there two special issues or does it mean a lapsus, a mistake or a change of the approach of the editor?" Rihtman-Auguštin continues,

> The papers have been written by non-Yugoslavs, mostly American anthropologists who did considerable research in former Yugoslavia. Some of those writing have been partial (not to say prejudiced). What is common to all of them is the lack of the presumption that their authors, non-native anthropologists, might be biased too. Reading some of those texts the native anthropologist has an impression that the authors have been confused and shared the same or even greater difficulties as we, the native(s) have, when discerning between fact and political propaganda of the parts in conflict.

While concern for any author's analytic perspective is legitimate, Rihtman-Auguštin's blanket condemnation is more puzzling. Though she wrote, "The papers have been written by non-Yugoslavs," this remark is manifestly untrue. Anyone who looked at the contents page would find not only Rihtman-Auguštin's colleague, Povrzanović, but also Prošić-Dvornić then of the University of Belgrade. Further, considering works that "have been partial (not to say prejudiced)," would she include Elinor Despalatović's articulate defense of Croatian independence or Brian Bennett's evocative portrait of a Dalmatian community?

We deal with these matters in detail because analysis of Rihtman-Auguštin's complaints reveals how this struggle is now waged rhetorically, if not at the moment militarily, in this part of the Balkans. Apparently it is our use of the terms "Yugoslavs" and "Yugoslavia" that inspires the most passion. In her comment Povrzanović notes that "(ex)Yugoslavia ceased to exist on 1/15/92." Clearly this is true, in a (formal) sense. As of that date there were no longer six republics but two. Serbia and Montenegro remained in a union that continues to use the name Yugoslavia. But Rihtman-Auguštin implies that the "Yugoslavs" never were a "nation." This is, of course, not true in a structural political sense.

The current Croatian state was part of the socialist Yugoslav polity for almost a half century after World War II and part of the Yugoslav kingdom for a quarter century after World War I. We suppose that she refers more to perceptions; namely, did the Croats ever feel that they were Yugoslavs? Still "Yugoslavs" evidently existed as a reference group to her in 1993 or else she could not have spoken of "non-Yugoslav" authors of questionable objectivity.

In analyzing such convoluted arguments, we don't mean to disparage obviously conflicted scholars living new political identities. Leaving aside purposeful distortion and *ad hominem* critique, we see these tortured ambiguities as central to the tragedy of the Yugoslav (yes, the term is still useful) conflict. These ambiguities partially grow from a condition discussed by many of the contributors; namely as already noted, the frequent reversal of victim and victimizer roles. Using an arbitrary historical base line there was the victimization of the Serbs in World War II and the Croats at the end of World War II. In the 1990s there were first the brutal depredations of the Yugoslav army and Serbian militias on Croatian territory. This was followed by the sometimes-violent expulsion by the newly formed Croatian military of many of the Serbian minority from Croatia. There were the subsequent wars in Bosnia and Kosovo with NATO involvement. The lack of decisive victories or defeats by the Serbs or their opponents has thus contributed to an atmosphere in which wounds, both real and imagined, fester. Clearly any foreigner venturing to examine such matters can expect hostility from one group or another.

We dwell on this matter at length here because one consequence of the conflict has been a serious polarization of scholarly researchers involved with former Yugoslavia, whether resident in the Balkans, Western Europe, or North America. Understandably some may have disliked the title of the earlier collection. However, to conflate that title with an alleged "pro-Serbian" bias or a wish for the reinstatement of Yugoslavia as a political entity seems symptomatic of the deep emotional passions inherent in this conflict.

A fundamental purpose of this book is to show the Yugoslavs as peoples who inhabit an area with overlapping borders, and who possess a significantly shared, but differentially experienced history. Our hope is that understanding what drove these peoples apart will help us discover ways for them to coexist in peace within their geographically circumscribed space. That said, to place Povrzanović's and Rihtman-Auguštin's comments in proper perspective, we also need to stress some obvious facts. It was Croatia, not Serbia proper, that suffered killing, rape, and destruction in the early 1990s. The Croatian people feel violated, notwithstanding the horrors visited on the Serbs by the Croatian state in World War II or, more recently, in Krajina (see Grandits and Promitzer, Chapter 8). Hostile feelings toward foreigners perceived as unsympathetic or critical toward one's particular nation is a sad consequence of this recent history, unfortunately shared by all the peoples of what was once a common homeland.

Organization of the Chapters

This volume is divided into five sections. Part I consists of overviews of the history of former Yugoslavia and the origins, development, and persistence of its diverse national groups. Part II deals with general issues of ethnicity and nationalism as they relate to events preceding the current armed conflict. Part III considers some specific cases of social and political processes in the area and how conflict affected and affects each. Part IV evaluates the role of expressive culture, partly as manifested in the arts, in the actual conduct of hostilities. Part V consists of studies of the consequences of conflict and the attempt to build viable new polities.

In Chapter 2, Eugene Hammel defines some critical conceptual problems about objectivity in the analysis of these conflicts. Following Ernest Gellner, he suggests that "objectivity is not a misguided aspiration, still less a form of domination, and subjectivism and obscurity are not forms of liberation." He goes on to say that "I seek objective truth here, knowing . . . new information will oblige me to revise my views." Given the diversity of voices in this book, Hammel's demand for objectivity might lead us into a complex discussion beyond our immediate objectives. However, the question must be faced. In our concern for objectivity we recognize that observers producing texts on the "Other" form a critical part of the process of the creation of knowledge. But we also realize that we must try to understand not only the historical context of the conflicts in the Balkans but also the complex relationships between observation and moral evaluation, recognizing the analytical utility of the former without distancing ourselves from the latter. To effect that goal in this volume, we solicited divergent views based on the recognition that there can exist such multiple legitimacies. Still, we must not permit the examination of multiple legitimacies to prevent us from identifying those responsible for the destruction of lives and property and the trampling of human rights.

We need to know exactly what transpired on the killing fields of Srebrenica, in the siege of Sarajevo, during the destruction of Vukovar, the expulsions from Krajina and Eastern Slavonia, and with murders in Kosovo. All these depredations must be examined and their perpetrators identified and the roles of the UN, NATO, and other powers evaluated. Multiple legitimacies cannot obscure—and tensions between verifiable observation and moral evaluation pale next to—the actual realities of grave sites, skeletal remains, forced pregnancies, and the massive destruction of religious and cultural sites and other property. It is necessary that those responsible for such violations of human rights be brought before the International War Crimes Tribunal in The Hague (see Physicians for Human Rights 1996) and a basis for a lasting peace be established. This cannot be done without careful consideration of how these deadly conflicts came about.

In Chapter 3, Bette Denich approaches the problem by defining some of the political processes that speeded Yugoslavia's dissolution. She describes how the various elites dominating the republics of the Yugoslav Federation used mass media to present opposing interpretations of the same events. Such contrasting narratives of victimization and threat had a powerful effect on publics whose nationalist ideals had been suppressed. According to Denich, the development of opposition to the multiethnic Yugoslav state coalesced along ethnic lines as national slogans replaced the official theme of "brotherhood and unity."

In presenting a Slovenian perspective on the conflicts, Rajko Muršič emphasizes, in Chapter 4, the role of Serbian hegemony. He notes that the wars in the former Yugoslavia were not ethnic, but fought for territories between Serbia, under the cover of Yugoslavia, and other newly established states. Muršič also suggests the essential cause of the dissolution of Yugoslavia was the impossibility of its democratization after the collapse of the dominant socialist ideology, and the parity of its constituent federal units. He also examines Western anthropological contributions to analyses of the wars in former Yugoslavia and considers how "insider-outsider" interpretations of data vary and how such different perceptions may obscure understanding.

Part II explores relationships among ethnic identity, nationalist ideology, and cultural practice. Chapters 5 and 6, by Elinor Despalatović and Andrei Simić, respectively, both writing from the United States, should be read together, since they respectively treat Croatian and Serbian perspectives. Despalatović, reflecting on her decades-long research in Croatia, considers Croat interpretations about the former Yugoslav state. As she notes, the collapse of communist Yugoslavia was as unexpected as Croatian independence. In part, the depth of nationalist feeling was hard to assess, since it had long been a forbidden topic. She also considers Croat views that their national identity and interests were exploited in the Yugoslav state from the time of its founding in 1918. Despalatović also critiques others' views of Croatia subsequent to the collapse of former Yugoslavia in 1991–92. Like Muršič, she sees the Serb-dominated federal government as "the instigator of war." Writing prior to the conflict in Kosovo, she observes that their Serbian homeland was physically untouched while countless men, women, and children have died in Croatia and Bosnia-Herzegovina.

In contrast to Despalatović, Simić identifies a complex of specific South Slav ideologies that he posits underlie a common belief system and contributed to a generation of conflict. These include national identity as a product of kinship-writ-large, a common culture that "ultimately defines the boundaries of the nation," co-nationals united by "quasi-mystical bonds," the assumption that each nation has a "natural" or "God-given" right to its territory, and the perception of nations as "objective categories." To Simić the Serbian case differs little in its basic characteristics from that of the Croats or Muslims. Though he emphasizes different causes, he and Despalatović agree that the strains in the South Slav state were present from its beginnings in 1918. Simić also points to "internal ethnic and religious division and separatist aspirations." Referring to the civilizational divides separating Catholic, Orthodox, and Muslim, he says, "The Serbs, Croats,

Slav Muslims, Slovenes and Macedonians were . . . separated by dialect, religion, historical tradition, worldview, and ties to different civilizations and allies." He notes that with the collapse of the Yugoslav state that which divided people became more emphasized than that which united them, such as the multiethnic Partisans, now fading in historical memory. As symptomatic of variations in interpretations Simić cites estimates that the Ustasha and its Muslim allies killed between 800,000 and one million Serbs during World War II. Despalatović, on the other hand, cites estimates that during the same period the death toll for all Yugoslavia was approximately 487,000.

In Chapter 7, Robert Hayden is concerned about "the labels imposed on Bosnian Muslims by their Serb and Croat opponents" and notes that both Serbs and Croats allege a non-European cultural orientation for Bosnian Muslims. Politically such a distinction seeks to delegitimize them and limit their access to power. Ironically, however, it has caused many, formerly nonobservant Muslims to see Islam as central to their identity. Other essays in this section also challenge Serb and Croat perceptions. In Chapter 9, Robert Minnich focuses on the marginalization perceived by Slovenians and, by extension, other non-Serb or non-Croat ethnic groups in former Yugoslavia via the biography of a middle-class Slovenian woman in a border region. This is a case study in the development of ethnic consciousness and shows how identity is shaped by response to local social conditions, in the context of national and international events.

In a related case study, Hannes Grandits and Christian Promitzer (Chapter 8) describe how originally cooperating communities of Orthodox and Catholic Slavs, settled by the Hapsburgs in the Krajina military border region from the seventeenth to the nineteenth centuries to limit Turkish expansion, ultimately developed antagonistic Serb and Croat identities. In this way they document how the historical relationships of Balkan peoples were shaped by administrative measures and by their relationships to an imperial state. In Chapter 10, Edit Petrović considers the origins and meaning of ethnonationalism throughout former Yugoslavia, which she sees as responsible for generating the recent conflict. She also observes that insider status does not necessarily improve one's analysis or predictive powers, citing her own failure to recognize the factors leading to war in Bosnia. Petrović suggests that the concept of ethnic group, "dormant" in socialist Yugoslavia, was activated as that state collapsed and used by elites to mobilize popular support, a point also made by other authors. She analyzes how the political use of cultural symbols defines ethnic boundaries as state boundaries, invokes nationhood as kinship, and links nationalism to religion and folk traditions.

Part III considers case studies of local social and political processes that affect or have been influenced by the wars in former Yugoslavia. In Chapter 11, Mart Bax analyzes the intraethnic, escalating conflict for control of the Herzegovinian religious pilgrimage center of Medjugorje. He shows how the Western perception of the wars as being waged between discrete groups of self-identified co-ethnics is mistakenly simplified. Instead, he points out that the struggle is really a number of separate conflicts, each with its own particular dynamic and cast of characters, who used a range of local resources and relationships to prosecute their own ends. In Chapter 12, Brian Bennett looks at the war's impact on a Dalmatian village far from the front lines and how its effect on the personal and professional lives of his Croatian ethnological colleagues highlights the unforeseen psychological and emotional consequences of the conflicts and leaves open how such consequences will echo in the future.

Nikolai Botev, a demographer, analyzes, in Chapter 13, marriage across ethnic and national boundaries. Such marriages were long assumed influential in producing a shared Yugoslav identity. Though popular wisdom saw intermarriage increasing in Yugoslavia, Botev instead finds ethnically endogamous marriages the norm. Mixed marriages thus played a negligible role in maintaining state cohesion. Albanians were an especially closed group, but there was also pronounced endogamy among Croats in Bosnia. Serbs and Montenegrins were the least endogamous. Other contributors also consider this question. Thus Simić notes that though Montenegrins have the highest rate of exogamy, this is mainly with Serbs, "in most respects, the same people." In Chapter 14, Julie Mertus considers the international legal framework of nationalism and its historical social implications. She documents continuity in the uncertain application of international law and the difficulty of resolving, through legal specifications, the range of national issues raised by the conflict.

The essays in Part IV depict how expressive behavior both influences and has been influenced by the conflict. Defining an enemy and prosecuting a war involves symbolic violence as well as physical acts. Analyzing art as a reflection of political conflict provides a needed perspective on processes of sociopolitical change. In Chapter 16 Mirjana Laušević's content analysis of war-related rock videos shows music "as the cultural weapon of choice by all warring parties in Bosnia . . . crucial in strengthening morale and maintaining group cohesion as well as in (justifying) war and perpetuating violence." Despite shared patterns of expression, music still served to "create fear and define otherness," in part by a symbolic "cleansing" of prewar music. Complementing this view, Lynn Maners, in Chapter 17, shows how audience responses to folklore performances act as harbingers of social atomization and ethnic strife. He analyzes the "discourse about symbolic national identity" inherent in such performances. To him, these performances were only superficially about romanticizing a predominantly rural past. He sees them as actually the result of extensive "negotiation of identities between the Yugoslav state and its constituent nations and minorities." Responses to these performances were an important barometer of ethnic tension.

In Chapter 15, Goran Jovanović considers conflict-related political cartoons published in former Yugoslavia and Western Europe. As he shows, these cartoons interpret the complex nature of conflict in a manner sometimes crude and stereotypical, other times as succinct and insightful as poetry. The images selected portray the conflict through harsh caricatures and anthropomorphized animals.

They also show quick alternations in perceptions from abroad and the great diversity of participant views in the conflict. Many cartoons offer graphic commentary on other issues in this volume. Botev's discussion of intermarriage, for example, is dramatized by Ota's drawing of a Croatian mother and a Serbian father each tugging on their crying child. These cartoons point out the difficulties of objective analysis, discussed by Hammel and Muršić.

In Chapter 18, Mirjana Prošić-Dvornić examines transitional processes of ethnic-state building among South Slav groups, focusing, in part, on the role of media in these processes. In common with other contributors she highlights the hostilities both within and between the various ethnic groups. Like Hayden, she demonstrates the importance of "Orientalizing" rhetoric, both in and outside of Serbia. She sees such rhetoric functioning to ascribe positive traits to one's group and negative, even demonic ones to the political opposition. Prošić-Dvornić thus shows how the Milošević regime manipulated identities of newly urbanized Serbs by using neo-folk music as part of a televised hybrid mass culture. Thus she and Petrović both offer a perspective different from Simić's, who suggests that Serb ethnic identification has a volitional component. Petrović and Prošić-Dvornić both point to its manipulated and manufactured, i.e., invented, quality (see Hobsbawm and Ranger 1983).

The essays in Part V analyze the interventions in response to the conflict. In Chapter 21. Jonathan Schwartz examines ethnic-based NGOs in Macedonia, considering them a major vehicle by which Macedonia has thus far escaped critical ethnic-based conflicts. Schwartz sees Macedonian identity as practical and responsive to the uncertain circumstances of their nationhood. He is optimistic and suggests that desires for economic and social development may supersede ethnic fractiousness. But Schwartz leaves open the possibility of severe conflict with the resident Albanian population, even though it was avoided in 1999 with great pressure created by the temporary but massive influx of Kosovar refugees. In Chapter 19, Éva Huseby-Darvas examines the culture and living conditions in Hungarian camps housing refugees from Bosnia and elsewhere in former Yugoslavia. She depicts the unhappy result of the lack of external support for Hungarian aid to refugees, as well as the limited attention paid to developing culturally appropriate interventions. Huseby-Darvas portrays lives in the camps and the futures they portend with the infinite waiting and consequent personal decline.

Janet Reineck worked with various international relief efforts in Kosovo prior to the NATO bombing. In Chapter 20, providing detailed ethnographic descriptions of Kosovar society, she focuses on the implications of the repression of Albania life and culture by the Serbian state. Reineck gives a human face to backgrounding the war in Kosovo. Her earlier efforts and those of other outsiders to bridge the divide and, more important, the desire on the part of some Serbs and Kosovo Albanians to resolve the conflict in peaceful ways were negated by Serbian government policies of massive state-sponsored violence. Western efforts to address these concerns were largely palliative and ultimately ineffectual. Even after NATO forces occupied Kosovo, the pent-up angers and frustrations of the returning Kosovar refugees have proved difficult to control and resulted in massive Serbian emigration and the de facto separation of Kosovo from the Serbian state. Her firsthand observations as an NGO representative provide unique insight into how the conflict developed and was maintained in Kosovo, then a formal part of Serbia. This situation contrasts with Bosnia, where the diversity of groups persists despite the consequences of ethnic cleansing and the consolidation of formal and informal national segregation within Bosnia.

By contrast, Stevan Weine, in Chapter 22, deals with the aftermath of the Bosnian conflict. A practicing psychiatrist, he writes of "witnessing" as a psychotherapeutic technique among Bosnian refugees in the United States. He details how the use of an emic Bosnian concept, *merhamet,* a form of compassion and understanding, assists in therapy. Weine's conclusions are equivocal. Though psychiatric intervention is of some help, the costs of the conflict in lives, property, and psychological stability will resonate for decades. His observations are also suggestive of the long-term consequences of the traumas inflicted on other peoples of former Yugoslavia, especially the Kosovars.

The Problematic Origins of the Disintegration of Yugoslavia

These essays look for answers to the question of how to build a foundation for future peace in the Balkans. Some recent writings have rejected attempts to lay bare the historical and structural conditions of these conflicts, preferring instead to see them as expressions of the celebratory aspects of violence and an atavistic response to meaninglessness in the modern world (van de Port 1998). These essays, however, question the complacency and indifference of those overwhelmed by the repetitive horrors of almost a decade of conflict in ex-Yugoslavia.

These conflicts were never simply struggles among discrete, homogeneous ethnic groups or the combat of formal armies. The policies that drive them were frequently not consistent, meticulous, or organized. Rather, proliferating nationalistic militias and local warlords, spurred by greed, cruelty, and vengeance, have sometimes played as large a role in the destruction as that of formal governments and armies implementing planned policies. As Bax shows in Chapter 11, the brutality has often been personalized, sometimes committed by former neighbors and acquaintances of the victims. These actors recall the murder and abuse of civilians in World War II, ironically, by those whose hatred derived from a sense of historical victimization. Though the Serbs as a people claim victim status in both World Wars, individual Serbs have been most frequently indicted by the United Nations War Crimes Tribunal, a fate shared by some Croats and Muslims.

The historical and contemporary fluidity of the conflicts and the changing mix of the parties embroiled in them suggest how these wars and conflicts frame acts of both destruction and creation. Initially in Slovenia, but then principally and sequentially in Croatia, Bosnia, and Kosovo, the conflict brought about the disintegration of multinational Yugoslavia and the destruction of its villages, towns, cities, and cultural monuments. Even Montenegrins are considering secession, threatening to dismantle the last remnant of federal Yugoslavia. Simultaneously, however, new political entities and new identities are being formed. Still, we cannot help but wonder what kinds of political and cultural entities these will be. The proliferation of factions and the dispossession and attempted resettlement of mutually hostile populations foregrounds the complexity and the deep personal level of the hostilities and confounds attempts to bring about lasting reconciliation.

Interethnic complexities can be illustrated by contrasting events in the recent histories of Bosnia's two major cities, Sarajevo and Mostar. The Bosnian Serb siege of Sarajevo is the best known. But the ethnic composition of the city varied extensively; in some instances, almost neighborhood by neighborhood (Gjelten 1995). Bosnian Serbs gunners shelled the city from its surrounding heights, but also lived in other city neighborhoods, which they evacuated only after the 1995 Dayton Accord went into effect. Other Serbs and Croats continued to live in the center of Sarajevo and fight alongside its Muslim defenders, some of whom were not native to the city at all, but who had fled there from the countryside, replacing the many professionals who had left. By contrast, around Mostar an initial multiethnic conflict involving Serbs gave way to one between Bosnian Croat partisans of so-called Hercegbosna with ties to Zagreb and Bosnian Muslims from the other side of the Neretva River. Many Serbs fleeing the wars in Croatia, Bosnia, and subsequently Kosovo found a less-than-warm welcome in Serbia proper; however, thousands of Muslims, including Albanians, have found refuge in Croatia, in Montenegro, and even in Serbia proper.

Action at the international-geopolitical level has also at times served to heighten confusion and prolong conflict. As Mertus comments, NATO intervention succeeded in suppressing large-scale armed conflict in Bosnia but a strong institutional basis for peaceful coexistence has yet to develop. The Dayton Accord, which formally ended conflict in Bosnia did not solve the problem on a regional basis and may have contributed to the expansion of violence in Kosovo. In this connection, Reineck notes, Kosovo Albanians had unrealistic expectations about the ability of the West to ameliorate their plight. By implication, then, when Dayton ignored Albanian claims, the frustrated Kosovars reacted by flocking to the banners of the Kosovo Liberation Army.

Turkey's involvement with Bosnia, Germany's with Croatia, and Britain, France, and Russia's with Serbia echo nineteenth-century imperial interests. Many of the cartoons Jovanović presents depict changing foreign attitudes toward former Yugoslavia. Americans of South Slav descent also have sought to influence U.S. policy. One has only to "surf" the World Wide Web to see their extremes of hatred. A mouse click away one can find unapologetic Serbian

"Chetnik" expansionists, Islamic fundamentalists, and Croatian "*Ustaše*" fascists linked to U.S. Balkan policies. It seems as if World War II and the Holocaust had never happened.

Contested national identities also characterize events at the geographic margins of former Yugoslavia. As Minnich discusses, the economic prospects of Slovenia, always the most prosperous part of Yugoslavia, are now furthered by interregional ethnic ties and links to Austria and Italy. Macedonia's situation seems more equivocal, as Schwartz makes abundantly clear. Macedonia's problematic recognition by neighboring Greece and ambivalent relationship with Bulgaria all suggest uncertainty for the immediate future. These tensions result from the presence of Slavic-speaking Macedonians on both sides of the border with Greece, though their existence is denied. It is appropriate to emphasize that Albanians in Macedonia provide a further point of tension, since here nationality combines with religion and language to further underscore their distinctiveness. As Reineck shows, open hostilities in Kosovo grew from Albanian response to marginalization by the Yugoslav (i.e., Serbian) state. Albania's own conflicted interest in the region and what has been the international community's uncertainty about long-term policies challenges us to think in new ways about how identities are created, preserved, and altered with violent outcomes.

The Past as Prologue: Yugoslavia Doomed by Its History?

Any retrospective on the last eighty years of conflict between the peoples of the former Yugoslavia can obviously be a self-serving rationalization of the present. These essays also consider how both destructive and creative processes of the new polities are affected by differing uses of the Yugoslav past. They also ask to what extent the peoples of the former Yugoslavia ever truly coexisted in peace, particularly after World War II. Furthermore, the historical approach of many of the chapters suggests, sometimes implicitly, the need to evaluate what was destroyed—economically, socioculturally, and psychologically by the violence of the 1990s.

Some of the authors question whether the initial Yugoslav state, crafted from the defeated multinational Hapsburg and Ottoman empires with a Serbian monarchical core, ever had a future. The question now seems particularly appropriate, if not self-evident. Some observers, including Despalatović in this volume, claim that conditions imposed by the victorious Allies at Versailles, and the arbitrary drawing of national borders, started Yugoslavia on its road to ruin. In the Yugoslav case, Woodrow Wilson's plan brought together many disparate groups. There were the previously subject Catholic Croats and Slovenes, and Hungarians on the enlarged Serbian border with truncated Hungary in the north. In the south there were the mainly Muslim Albanians in Serbia adjoining the new Albanian state. At the center of the new state were Slav Muslims in Bosnia, and the most numerous Orthodox Serbs. As Grandits and Promitzer point out, however, the transition to this new state had to be made not only by Slovenes, Croats, and Muslim Slavs but also by Serbs. The choice of Belgrade as capital was the logical consequence of the installation of the Karadjordjevich dynasty to head the new state. In retrospect, however, as several authors note, this set the stage for interwar instability. Reading Mertus, in fact, one can see how the creation of these new states on the ruins of old empires after World War I set the stage for contemporary events. Versailles and Dayton, after all, were both imposed from outside by the external force of the so-called great European powers plus America.

In 1941 after the German invasion ended the monarchy, the partition of Yugoslavia reflected this national and ethnic fractionation. Germany was the chief occupying power but Italy took coastal Dalmatia, Hungary the Vojvodina plain, and Bulgaria "Southern Serbia," as Macedonia was then known. Central Croatia and part of Bosnia formed the Nazi puppet state of Independent Croatia while central Serbia was ruled by the Germans as an occupied province. The ongoing civil war between multinational communists, the fascist Ustasha Croatian state, and royalist Serb Chetniks occurred parallel with the struggle against the German occupiers. Whatever the array of forces, state-authorized slaughter became acceptable policy and, in the end, was never accounted for. Since the communist victory enshrined the multinational ethic in the slogan "brotherhood and unity," multinationalism was consequently linked only to communism and grieving for the opposition dead was selective and proscribed.

Both Despalatović and Simić thus show how these earlier civilian massacres presaged the present. Bette Denich suggests that the communists found the memory of the massacres so threatening, especially those they committed themselves, that after their rise to power they sought to suppress all knowledge of them. Partisan forces thus became the only officially recognized World War II dead and their deeds were memorialized in monuments and published accounts. Thus as "brotherhood and unity" was implemented as part of communist dogma and imposed on the Yugoslav peoples, they were never provided a means to arrive at this concept freely or develop ways to honor it. Ethnic conflicts were evident from the beginning in the continuing assertions of regional, i.e., national, differences in matters such as economic planning, Communist Party decentralization, and in the post-Tito constitutions, as both Denich and Prošić-Dvornić indicate in their chapters.

Still, affirmative links between groups were also built culturally, socially, and in political economy. Intermarriage was viewed by some as one way to facilitate a multinational Yugoslav identity. But as Botev shows, there is considerable disagreement about its extent, distribution, and effects. Other links were developed through the Tito personality cult and related state ritual (Dubinskas 1983; Kideckel 1983), celebration of political nonalignment and self-managed socialism, and above all in military preparedness against potential invasion from the Soviet Union.

Socialism and Yugoslav Integrity: The Views of Social Scientists

To what extent did anthropologists and other social scientists anticipate the Yugoslav conflicts and how do past interpretations shape our understanding of them? In hindsight, of course, there was always a degree of social scientific recognition of the centrifugal possibilities of Yugoslav ethnicity. Still, few researchers anticipated the extent and the intensity of the fragmentation pressures exerted on the Yugoslav state by the rapid demise of communism in East Central Europe and the former Soviet Union. Nor were they able to predict the dimensions of the ensuing disaster in the region. As we (Halpern and Kideckel 1982) and Linda Bennett (1997) suggest, from the 1960s into the early 1980s, both Yugoslav and foreign social science researchers focused primarily on problems associated with economic change, glossed as "modernization." Other related interests concerned social structural changes such as urbanization, internal and international migration, and civic participation. All these forces tended to be interpreted as integrative phenomena working against the fragmentary tendencies of ethnicity. Though in our review of anthropological research in Eastern Europe to the early 1980s we recognized the endurance of certain centrifugal cultural patterns, we assumed economic change and national integration would dampen them.

In contrast, most of our contributors see ethnic identity as never having waned. They speak of the expression of ethnic solidarity in individual identity (Minnich), the selective response to folkloric expressions of either ethnic exclusiveness or shared identities (Maners), or even the use of ethnicity to facilitate organization of nongovernmental organizations in the socialist aftermath (Schwartz). It is a dominant theme in Reineck's chapter on the Albanians of Kosovo and in the discussions of the consequences of appeals to ethnic solidarity in Serbia as presented by Petrović and Prošić-Dvornić.

Still, this is not to say that we as editors or the contributors to this volume accept simplistic views of an end-of-communism explosion of pernicious, but suppressed, ethnicity. Katherine Verdery (1996: 85–87) pretty much destroys that myth for Romania, a case with many parallels with the former Yugoslavia. These include economic downturn, the historical importance of ethnic communities, the vitality of the ethnic idea, the rise of ethnically divisive thinking, and most important, the use of ethnicity by the socialist state for purposes of social control. To be sure, historically based ethnic-national identities became manifest, and to a degree determinant, after the demise of the socialist states of East Central Europe. However, these identities particularly found expression in post-socialist Yugoslavia's struggle for power facilitated by its nationality-based federal structure and weak post-Tito constitution and government. The vital difference between Romania and Yugoslavia and the distinction between murderous ethnic and political riots and proliferating warfare lies in the latter's multinational structure where no group was overwhelmingly dominant.

Of course it is one thing to make such distinctions or even agitate for separate political identities. It is quite another to rape, murder, loot, and burn. As many of the essays note, despite all the problems besetting the post-Tito state and the traumatic history of Yugoslavia, conscious efforts still had to be made to convince, and at times coerce, local citizens to murder their neighbors. In scenes reminiscent of the Holocaust, some individuals resisted these pressures at their own peril. In this regard Bax points out the role of local socioeconomic competition, Bennett suggests the manipulation of sentiments of jealousy, and Laušević considers the uses of rock music videos to whip up ethnic hatred and destructive urges. Once begun, however, the massacres often took on a life of their own. Weine and Huseby-Darvas provide us with a view of the consequences from a victim's perspective. Unfortunately, these hatreds have remained very much alive even after Dayton.

These contributions mark an attempt by anthropologists and other social scientists to confront the sources and the consequences of a disintegrated multinational state. As some essays show, for certain parties to these disintegrative processes, it has been joyful and exhilarating. Others have profited materially by confiscation of property, smuggling, and by consummating extralegal business deals. These new elites, with expensive cars and showy tastes, are visible in Mostar as well as Belgrade. For others, life has had tragic consequences. They have lost their homes and possessions. They have been raped, maimed, or killed. Their communities have been destroyed or occupied. Examples can be found among all groups. Some people, mainly Serbs, have begun to long for their shared past, engaging in what is now termed "Yugo-nostalgia." This is expressed in part by affinity for music and movies of the times and is humorously portrayed in the web site devoted to Tito (Marolt and Srebotnjak 1998).

Even after the conflicts subside the Yugoslav successor states will face new difficulties, not the least of which is creating and maintaining modern states with a limited resource base. In some ways angry thoughts of war provide leaders of these states the means to avoid demanding that their people adapt to a changing global economy. Small as these new states are, they must also contend with increasing demands for local autonomy within their borders set in motion by the form of the wars in the region.

The modern state that was Yugoslavia implied, at least for some, a degree of social stability or at least an absence of struggle. This book documents the failure of not only the communist political economy but also the illusion of modernity as an achievable end in sociocultural development. How will the new states constructed on the ashes of the old endure? The only certainty is that to survive they must evolve new ways to coexist. Hopefully, these chapters will provide new perspectives to reflect on this problem.

Lessons from the Yugoslav Labyrinth

E. A. Hammel

In October 1991, at the beginning of the Yugoslav civil war, I received an anguished letter from an old friend in Belgrade. It brought me face to face with issues of legitimacy and morality that I had until then been able to avoid as a professional ethnographer among my hosts. I responded as best I could, and the outgrowth of that reply was a series of essays, revised as the war unfolded, in response to requests for updated versions, and as my own views about causality and broader meanings developed (Hammel 1993a, 1993b, 1994, 1995). In this rendering I eschew much of the historical detail and personal accounting of previous versions and concentrate on the most general points. My purpose is threefold: first, to give a reliable and objective account of events, as any historian should; second, to allow the voices of contending parties to present their own versions of those events, as any anthropologist must; and finally, to point to similar issues that confront us on our own doorsteps. The personal and professional dilemmas implicit in an analysis of the collapse of Yugoslavia are not new. They confront every anthropologist who has worked in a land torn by strife or burdened by the heritage of colonial influence and raise particular problems in the "postmodernist" social sciences, in which it is often claimed that since objectivity is unattainable, it is not worth seeking.[1]

1. The culture wars are of course nothing new to social science but go back at least to the materialist versus idealist positions of Marx and Weber, emerging again in the various doctrines of cultural relativism. The topic is enormous, but for an informative account, see Gellner 1985.

I disagree with that view. "Objectivity" has two meanings. One refers to events as actually existing in some absolute sense. The other refers to an approach to the data that while possibly contaminated by random error, is not contaminated by bias.

Random error in multiple reports of a single event, such as, for example, in the varying stories informants give about some event they all claim to have witnessed, yields messy information but information that in some sense surrounds and centers on the objective event (if the event does exist in the first sense). Nonrandom error, some persistent kind of difference between the reports and "what really happened" (in the first sense), leads us to believe in the existence of an event that may be quite different from the one that occurred. The middle of the cloud of reportage is not in fact centered on the target. We can demonstrate this by showing that categories of informants have radically different views of an event that they all identify as having occurred, or that some report as having occurred while others deny it. Thus by examining differing reports in a critical way we may approach objectivity in ourselves and manifest its possibility even when our informants have not.

We cannot know whether events are objective in the first sense, that is, whether they really ever happen, but it is folly to use any other working assumption, since if events do not happen, there is nothing to talk about.[2] If we take the reports of events, rather than the events, to be primary, we can compare them to re-create an event that would have been the original objective event, if it had happened, and if the biases of the reports cancel out. It is of course the obligation of an honest analyst to collect a sufficient diversity of reports to increase the chances that their biases will cancel out.

The historian Leopold von Ranke once said that historians just try to tell us what really happened (". . . er will bloß zeigen, wie es eigentlich gewesen ist"). By this he meant that the historian's task was to sift through the statements of observers and commentators, critically examine them, discount their biases, and try to uncover what they had seen. We know enough about the psychology of perception now to understand that the reports of honest eyewitnesses of the same event can differ remarkably, and we have enough practical experience to understand that the reports of involved actors can differ even more (and perhaps not so honestly). Still, it remains the analyst's task to collect and to sift, trying to isolate that now-much-demeaned Grail, objective truth. The truth we actually find is, of course, simply a critically negotiated compromise between reports, but to

---

2. Miracles are a case in point. If the Virgin did not appear at Medjugorje, there is nothing to talk about. If people nevertheless saw the Virgin at Medjugorje, there is the sighting to talk about. If they did not see the Virgin but only thought they did, there is the perception to talk about. Much the same can be said for eclipses. Somewhere, there is an event to talk about, and it is important to decide on the focus of analysis before beginning to talk. Note that even if investigation is restricted to the comparative analysis of reports of events, with no assumption of some real and objective event, objectivity in the analyst is still a necessary foundation.

fail to seek it is an abdication of scholarly responsibility. Ernest Gellner has remarked, "Objectivity is not a misguided aspiration, still less a form of domination, and subjectivism and obscurity are not forms of liberation" (1995: 821).[3] I seek objective truth here, knowing that every day will yield new information that will oblige me to revise my views (Hammel 1996).

I try to lay out the logic of the participants, seen from within, but evaluated from without. It is easy to know when you have told a story that is biased in favor of one set of participants in this Balkan war; that set is pleased, and the others are vituperative (or apathetic). It is also easy to tell when you have told an unbiased story, for then everyone involved is vituperative (or apathetic). The participant audiences in this conflict have a curious mind-set. If a member or a co-ethnic of a group speaks in favor of that group (as a Serb or a Serbian American might speak in favor of Serbia), bias is assumed. If a member or co-ethnic of a group speaks against the politics of his or her identity, treason is assumed.[4] The opinions of an ethnically unrelated commentator give native audiences some pause, because the lack of ethnic relationship suggests either legitimacy (Colson 1966) or ignorance. The more balanced the view the commentator expresses, the more likely the native audience is to assume ignorance.[5]

Background

The idea of a "Yugoslavia," a state composed of the various southern Slavic groups ("yugo" means "southern" in the Slavic languages), goes back to the end

3. I am obliged to Burton Benedict for bringing this quotation to my attention.

4. The tribulations of Anastasia Karakasidou in seeking to publish her account of Macedonia are instructive, even if the extremist accusations against her were more in the minds of her originally intended publishers than demonstrable in fact. See Karakasidou 1996 and the account given at the web site for the Society of the Anthropology of Europe, http: //h-net.msu.edu/~sae/.

5. There are many accounts of this and previous Balkan conflicts in the English literature alone. The old (and pro-Serbian) classic is West's *Black Lamb and Grey Falcon* (1941). Reliable historical analysis of events up to the period just after World War II are provided by Tomasevich 1955 and 1975 and Vucinich 1969a and 1969b. More recent accounts are abundant. Some are by experienced journalists, some by persons with local knowledge advocating a particular cause, some by reflective and objective scholars (Akhavan and Rouse 1995, Almond 1994, Banac 1984 and 1992, Bennett 1995, Cohen 1995, Crnobrnja 1994, Denitch 1994, Djilas 1991, Dragnich 1992, Drakulić 1994, Glenny 1992, Hall 1994, Kaplan 1993, Magas 1993, Mojzes 1994, Mousavizadeh 1996, Pajić 1993, Ramet 1992, 1996, and 1995, Rezun 1995, Samary 1995, Seroka and Pavlović 1992, Silber and Little 1995, Thompson 1992, Udovički and Ridgeway 1995, West 1995, and Woodward 1995). Anthroplogical perspectives are found in a number of accounts (Bakić-Hayden and Hayden 1992; Bringa 1993; Denich 1993 and 1994; Hammel 1993a, 1993b, 1994, and 1995; Hayden 1992, 1993, 1994, and 1995; and Kideckel 1995) and other papers in a special issue of the *Anthropology of East Europe Review* (Kideckel and Halpern 1993). It is just as useful, anthropologically, to read the clearly biased accounts as it is to read the presumably unbiased ones, since the speaker, pronouncing on the object, often says much about the self and thus often about other antagonists of the object. History, like other myths, is as much about the teller as the told.

of the eighteenth century with the emergence of linguistic nationalism in the work of grammarians like Vuk Karadžić in Serbia and Ljudevit Gaj in Croatia, similar to the developments experienced in Bohemia. The growing consciousness of being southern Slavic was specific to particular regions, but the various groups that came to identify themselves this way had one thing in common, they were neither Austrian nor Hungarian nor Turkish, that is to say, they were all relatively powerless members of the polity in which they found themselves. The idea that ethnic identity as defined by language and culture could be a foundation for state formation was borrowed from German romanticism in the works of Herder, Goethe, and the brothers Grimm. Thus the southern Slavs adopted the German definition of themselves as "different," as "not-German," inverted it, and turned it into a vehicle of political expression rather than of political anonymity. Under that peculiar combination of Enlightenment rationalism and French anti-Austrian imperialism that characterized the Napoleonic Wars, in which Dalmatia and much of Croatia were under French dominion, the local identity of not being Austrian or Hungarian became a common identity of being Slavic. Rather grand ideas of a Yugoslav state possibly stretching from the Adriatic to the Black Sea arose, and in the great diplomatic and military chess game played in the Balkans from 1700 to 1914 by Russia, Austria, Turkey, and Britain, the Russians, for obvious reasons, supported Pan-Slavic ideas and movements. Pan-Slavism had a brief life as an ideology, but a Yugoslavia that included Slavic speakers from the Alps to the Bulgarian border was more viable. Its foundation was laid by a linguistic compromise between Serbian and Croatian scholars that established a single literary standard for Serbo-Croatian, and its implementation was effected in 1919 at Versailles. The definition of Yugoslavia was an ethnic one ("being southern Slavic"), but the territory of the southern Slavs was ethnically heterogeneous. It contained a number of southern Slavic groups and also non-Slavic groups (e.g., Albanians). It is also important to observe that the logic of defining a state ethnically does not lead to viable heterogeneous states unless ethnicity is abandoned as the criterion of membership. The oft-quoted journalistic assumption that the population of Yugoslavia is consumed by "age-old ethnic hatreds" is off the mark when external powers themselves have created the ethnic tensions. What was absent in the establishment of an ethnic state of non-Germans was a solution to the problem of how to include ethnic minorities in an ethnic state. What was absent was the idea of citizen as different from subject.

In order to understand the political consequences of ethnicity in Yugoslavia it is necessary to understand the ethnic categories, the perception of them, and the political processes through which they have been expressed. Since its establishment in 1919 as the Kingdom of Serbs, Croats and Slovenes, Yugoslavia has been experiencing the same process of centralization of government and hegemony of cultural symbols that has characterized most European states since the sixteenth century or even earlier in some regions. In the United Kingdom it was the rise to dominance of the English, particularly of the English of southeastern England, over other regional peoples, notably the Celts of Scotland, Ireland, and Wales, and the establishment of the dialect of that region as the national language. In Spain it was the emergence of Castile over other regions, especially Catalonia (not to mention the Basques), and the emergence of Castilian as the standard for Iberian Spanish. In France it was the developing hegemony of the Paris Basin over other regions, especially Brittany, Normandy, Occitania, and Provence and the establishment of Parisian French as the standard. In Germany the developments came late, with Bismarck and the ascendancy of Prussia. In what was the Soviet Union, the expansion of the Russian empire and the ascendancy of Moscow over Kiev and other regions began very early but was perhaps not really solidified until after the Revolution. It had many drastic interruptions, even though it can be seen as a single process, sometimes White, sometimes Red, that still continues. The expansion of Northern industrial hegemony over the agricultural South in the United States is another example of the same process. The commonalities among these historical processes lead us to the conclusion that recent events in the Balkans are not as unusual as they are made out to be. The "age-old ethnic hatreds" of the journalist are all around us, if they are what we choose to see.

Centralization, and the standardization of national languages, began late in the Balkans. If we can identify an original political landscape, it is in the tenth and eleventh centuries with the development of feudal aristocracies in, primarily, Croatia, Serbia, and Bosnia. In the twelfth and thirteenth centuries the Croats came under the Hungarians about the same time that the Nemanjić dynasty of Serbia was attempting to replace the decaying Byzantine Empire. The Serbian empire, along with Bosnia, fell to the Ottomans over a period of a century and a half, beginning with the battle on the Marica in 1371 and the famous defeat at Kosovo in 1389, and ending with the fall of the Serbian Despotate in 1459, and finally the loss of Belgrade in 1521. An important part of this story is that of the *krajina*, a kind of movable border, a no-man's-land that retreated ahead of the Ottoman advance. It was peopled largely by the Vlachs (nomadic shepherds) of the Serbian empire and later by other Christian, usually Orthodox, refugees from the Ottomans (Rothenberg 1960; 1966). Many of these ultimately served as military serfs in the Military Border, which was first a defensive zone, then a customs and sanitation barrier along the Ottoman frontier, until its dissolution in 1871. These refugee streams had two consequences. First, they moved large numbers of Orthodox into areas that had been Catholic. Second, they extended the area of *štokavian* dialects deep into previously *čakavian* regions and of *jekavian* into *ikavian* regions.[6] The northernmost limit of this expansion occurred in the Otto-

6. The dialects of Serbo-Croatian are characterized in two ways. The first depends on the pronunciation of a highly variable vowel that was *jat* in Old Slavonic and is now variously *e*, *ije*, or *i* in *e*kavian, *je*kavian, and *i*kavian, respectively, as in the word for milk: *mleko, mlijeko, mliko*. The second depends on the word for "what," namely, *što, ča, kaj*, in *što*kavian, *ča*kavian, and *kaj*kavian, respectively. (Details are given in Hammel 1993b.)

man occupation of Slavonia after the battle of Mohacs in 1526, in which the Turks defeated the Hungarians and moved on toward Vienna. The direction was reversed after the Turkish defeat at Vienna in 1683 and the reoccupation of Slavonia by Hapsburg armies and their allies by 1691. The Austrian offensive failed deep in Herzegovina and Metohija in 1689, and there was a resumption of the refugee movement northwestward under the Serbian patriarch Arsenije. These movements, and of course the Croatian feudatories' invitation to the Orthodox refugees to serve as military colonists that had already begun by the time of Mohacs, established the tribal map of Yugoslavia up to 1914. Especially after the treaties of Karlovci (1699) and Pozarevac (1718), the movement of Serbs also established eastern *ekavian* as well as *jekavian* areas in Slavonia. Thus the stage was set by the scrambling of ethnicities for a centuries-long contest over the *krajina*, including the Slavonian *krajina*, and other territories.[7]

Mixtures of these tribal groups within and without the *krajina* lived with few exceptions either under the Hapsburgs or the Ottoman empire. The Serbs were partially independent after 1804 and 1815 but not truly so until 1868. The Montenegrins never capitulated entirely, although they were surrounded and largely neutralized. Dubrovnik was similarly independent. The Croatians had some degree of local autonomy in the complex Austro-Hungarian politics after the *Ausgleich* of 1867. The Venetians played an imperial role along the Adriatic, and Dalmatia and some parts of the adjacent *krajina* had a complex history involving foreign domination by Venice, the Hapsburgs, and France. Ethnic mixture at the microlevel reached its peak in Bosnia, as did personal integration, at least among urban professionals and intellectuals; separatism was more the rule in rural areas, with many villages being mono-ethnic even in multiethnic regions.[8]

Being Different

The primary distinguishing characteristics of ethnicity in the Balkans are religion and language. Religion is presumably a discontinuous variable, since people either belong to a congregation or not, but it is not always congruent with ethnicity as recognized by the actors. Albanians, for example, are sometimes Orthodox,

7. In current usage, especially by Serbs in Serbia, Bosnia, and Croatia, *Krajina* (with a capital K) is that region of the historical *krajina* where the Serbian Orthodox were in the majority, namely from the southern border of Lika around the shoulder of Bosnia to Karlovac—the same region as that occupied by the French in the Napoleonic Wars. East of that from Karlovac to Jasenovac is the Banija, a region of the *krajina* with a lower proportion of Serbs and historically controlled directly by the Croats, then east of that the Slavonian *krajina* with a mixed Serb-Croat population, to the borders of Srem, which is politically part of Serbia.

8. Hayden (1996) shows that ethnic mixture in terms of coresidence and intermarriage was substantial before 1990 and was increasing, contesting the conclusions of Botev (Botev 1990; Botev and Wagner 1993). There are important problems of measurement and interpretation of categories involved.

sometimes Catholic, and sometimes Muslim, but they are never judged coethnics by Serbs or Croats, or even Bosnian Muslims. Serbs are usually Orthodox, but there have been Muslim Serbs, and some Serbs in Dubrovnik are Catholic; yet all of these recognize a common ethnicity despite religious differences.[9] There are also degrees of membership and modifications to the discrete quality of ethnic identification. One is that the perceived distance between Muslims and either Orthodox or Catholics is greater on purely religious grounds than that between Orthodox and Catholics, while on other cultural grounds the Orthodox Serbs and Muslims resemble each other more than either resembles the Croats, sharing as they do cultural characteristics ultimately Byzantine, Arabic, and Turkish in origin. Under some circumstances (as currently in Bosnia) the Muslims and Catholics form a political bloc, but that is a marriage of convenience. Another anomaly is that some persons who deny religious affiliation (such as communists) can still classify themselves ethnically. They may do so on the grounds of earlier familial ethnic or religious affiliation, or on grounds of language.

Language is under some circumstances a fairly discontinuous variable, as in the differences between Greeks, Albanians, Turks, and Slavs, although there are many lexical commonalities across these boundaries, and bilingualism is frequent in some linguistic border regions. But in much of the area the issue is mutual intelligibility along a dialect continuum, and at a finer level, whether other people sound like you yourself, on scales of potentially very fine differentiation. Considerable effort has been expended by ethnic politicians to erect symbols of difference through linguistic usage, when speech was otherwise uniform. It is important to note that linguistic similarities are more regional than they are ethnic.[10] It is virtually impossible to distinguish Serbs from Croats from Muslim Slavs by their speech, if they come from the same village or neighborhood, unless they seek to signal their ethnicity by stressing particular linguistic features, some of which may be more characteristic of other regions.[11]

Linguistic and religious definitions of ethnicity have an important overlap, in

9. Some communities that now identify themselves as Croat and are Catholic were once Orthodox. This is certainly true of Uniate communities, which retain the Orthodox rite but acknowledge the pope, and it may be true of some groups in Western Herzegovina who describe the Orthodox as "of the old hand," suggesting Orthodoxy as a prior state in their own history (Andrei Simić, personal communication).

10. The Croatians are perhaps most notable in the construction of "newspeak," inventing neologisms like *brzoglas* (fast-voice) for telephone, by avoiding "Serbian" usages and especially words of Arab or Turkish origin, and constructing an "academic Croatian" that has all the syntactical complexities of academic German. The Montenegrins, especially the political party called the Greens, reject *ekavian* forms and emphasize palatalization to distinguish themselves from the Serbs. A Montenegrin will self-consciously use the form *šnjom* instead of *snjom* ("with her"), but in fact *snjom* is common in the Dalmatian hinterland at least as far as Split.

11. Family names and first names are perhaps the clearest clues to ethnicity. Many baptismal names are particular to Serbs or Croats, and since many Slavic family names are patronymics, so are many last names. Muslims often have distinctive first and last names of Arabic or Turkish origin.

that those groups which were Catholic use the Latin alphabet, while those which were Orthodox use the Cyrillic. The use of a particular writing system is strongly symbolic of ethnic identification. In modern Yugoslavia, persons who are literate in Cyrillic are usually also competent to at least read the Latin alphabet, although they may not write in it. Persons literate in the Latin alphabet are less likely to be competent even to read in Cyrillic, even though all schoolchildren were exposed to both. There have been other alphabets as well. The original script devised by the Saints Cyril and Methodius for the conversion of the Slavs of Moravia in the ninth century was the Glagolitic, and it was widely used in the Balkans but later replaced by Cyrillic. The Glagolitic survived into modern times in Dalmatia and Bosnia in at least two local forms and was an important symbol of regional or ethnic identity. It was used especially during the Protestant Reformation to publish the Scripture for Protestant converts in Slovenia and Dalmatia in a script that could not be identified with either the Catholic or the Orthodox churches. Orthography is still subject to symbolic manipulation. The selection of one or the other of the main alphabets in publishing newspapers or books is a political signal. At least before the war in Bosnia, the newspaper *Oslobodjenje* used to publish alternate pages in the Latin alphabet and Cyrillic as a symbol that could be taken as one of mutual tolerance or of a distinct Bosnian pluralistic identity. Perhaps if the population could still read Glagolitic in its *bosančica* form, they might have tried to publish in that.

Ethnic identification is sometimes entirely divorced from the features listed and is purely political. "Yugoslav" was an admissible category for self-declared ethnicity in Yugoslav censuses. It was used by three categories of persons: those who were committed Yugoslavists, those who were members of the Communist Party and wished to eschew ethnicity, and those who were Muslims and wished to avoid that identification in the same way that Jews often do in the West. Ethnic identification is thus essentially fluid, manipulable, and always has political implications, and the characteristics used in description are rarely necessary and seldom sufficient. The difficulties of classification are even greater in historical context. A classic if unusual example of ethnic manipulation in the region is the reported practice, in some fraternal joint households, of different coresiding brothers professing different religions, so as to be able to present the appropriate ethnic face when necessary.

It is politics and politicians who clarify and emphasize the criteria of ethnic assignment as a way of mobilizing support and allocating both demands and benefits. In the medieval Serbian state, the primary distinction among the common people was between serfs and Vlachs, and intermarriage between them was forbidden. The term "Vlach" is politically loaded (especially in Greece). It originally meant the romanized Celts or other pre-Germanic inhabitants encountered by expanding German tribes and is found in words like Welsh, Wallachia, Walloon, Gaul, Galatia, Galicia, wherever the Germanic tribes roamed. Because such Celtic groups were often pastoral, the term also came to mean shepherd. In some parts of Yugoslavia, "Vlach" is a reference to groups who speak a Romance language; in others it is consistently identified with Orthodox Serbian pastoralists. However, in the medieval Croatian state and its Hungarian and Hapsburg successors after 1102 and 1526 some Vlachs were Orthodox and some were Catholic (Bunjevci). In Bosnia the pre-Ottoman Bogomil heretics may have been originally Catholic or originally Orthodox in Bosnia itself, although the sect was Orthodox when it began in Bulgaria around the tenth century. Many Bosnians escaped the Orthodox-Catholic schism in the eleventh century and later first by adopting Manichaean dualism and then by converting to Islam. It served propertied Bosnians well under the Turks, since Muslims were more privileged than Christians. It is not at all clear (to me at least) how to identify Serbs and Croats in the medieval period except in the core of their areas, yet politicians attempt this in order to justify territorial claims. The modern identification of Croats with Catholicism and Serbs with Orthodoxy only dates back to the eighteenth century and was imposed from without by the Hapsburgs.

Ethnic classification in the Balkans is thus not strictly endogenous but either exogenously imposed or endogenously shaped in response to exogenous pressures. There are continuing political attempts to define the roots of emerging modern states as lying in the territory of others, on the grounds of ancient ethnic identities. Thus the Serbs insist on having all Serbs in a single political entity, which they define as the regions occupied by Serbs both during their fullest dispersion at the height of the Nemanjić expansion and during the diaspora occasioned by the Turks, turning both victory and defeat into territory. The Croats draw their true southern boundary deep in Bosnia and Herzegovina, on the pretext of a medieval presence in the region, which they establish on religious and etymological grounds. Both the Serbs and the Croats are making the politically convenient historical error of extrapolating the idea of the ethnic nation-state back into the Middle Ages, when feudal status was the defining social criterion or into the once Ottoman-held lands, where religion, especially the distinction between Muslims and non-Muslims, was critical.

Ethnopolitics

The story of Yugoslavia's dissolution begins with its establishment, and the major cleavages manifest today were established at Versailles to serve the political purposes of the victors. The Allies were determined to destroy the Prussian and Hapsburg empires for all time. Serbia had been on the Allied side; Croatia, because it had been part of the Hapsburg state, was considered as having been on the German side. Critical to the destruction of these Germanic empires was the creation or reestablishment of independent (especially Slavic) buffer states in the path of the *Drang nach Osten*, specifically Czechoslovakia, Yugoslavia, and Poland. Ironically, the Allies used ethnicity and language as the criteria for nationhood. This was a German idea of the *jus sanguinis* to begin with, an idea that led as already noted to the linguistic reforms and national consciousness that we see in the efforts of linguistic reformers like Karadžić, Gaj, Reljković, and others. The Allies might have located the center of this new country anywhere on its territory, for example in Zagreb, but Zagreb had been in enemy territory, Croatia having been part of the Austro-Hungarian Empire. On the other hand, the Serbs were the largest ethnic group, and Serbia had already been an independent political entity; the Allies accepted a definition of a new state centered on and controlled from Belgrade—the Kingdom of Serbs, Croats, and Slovenes.[12]

The inevitable consequence of locating the center of this new state in Belgrade was that its natural direction was to establish Serbian hegemony and to begin the process of language standardization based on the *ekavian* of the Šumadinci (Šumadija is the core region of Serbia just south of Belgrade). The Serbs were more dispersed throughout Yugoslavia than any other numerous ethnic group, having been displaced farther and for longer by the Ottoman invasions. They could easily identify with Belgrade, no matter how long they had resided in other regions (some as far away as the Slovene-Austrian border). It is not hard to understand why the Serbs of the *krajina* would have welcomed a Serbo-centric constellation, since from the time of Maria Theresa and before they had been under intense Austro-Catholic pressure to abandon Orthodoxy, to abandon Cyrillic, even to abandon Serbian and adopt German as their language. We should also not forget that the uprising in the *krajina* in 1991 is one in a long series going back to the sixteenth century, in which the Orthodox under Austrian or Croatian control rebelled violently and were put down with equal violence. The emerging Serbian hegemony after 1918, was for the Serbs of the *krajina*, a liberation from oppression.

On the other hand, the Croats, especially the Dalmatian Croats, who had a complex history of foreign domination, felt the heavy hand of occupation by a foreign power and a centralist autocracy descend again. That foreign power was Slavic, but it was no more benign than that of the Austrians, Hungarians, or Venetians. At least in the later stages of the Hapsburg empire, after the *Ausgleich* and then the unification of the *krajina* with Civil Croatia in 1881, there had been some feeling of autonomy. The feelings of oppression began to emerge strongly with the dictatorship of King Alexander, the politics of the Croatian Peasant Party, and the events leading to World War II. The growth of Serbian hegemony pushed the Croats back into the German camp despite the basic Croatian desire for independence from both Austrians and Hungarians. They had pursued this

12. That definition was surely advocated by Serbian and Montenegrin advisers to the Paris Peace Conference. There were no similarly credentialed Slovene or Croatian advisers, since their side had lost, and it is said that some who sought a voice were jailed until the Conference was concluded (A. Janos, personal communication, citing Vladko Maček). The newly emergent state actually concluded three separate treaties with three adversaries of the Allies and Serbia—St. Germaine with Austria, Trianon with Hungary, and Ševreš with Bulgaria.

desire even in the nineteenth century by compromising with the Serbs on cultural union, essentially accepting the Karadžić linguistic standard. The Croats were being ground between two millstones, one German, one Serbian, just as for centuries they had been ground between the Austro-Hungarian and the Ottoman. Reflecting a similar dynamic under way in Italy and in Germany itself, the intensity of their desire for independence found political expression in the creation of ethnically defined fascist organizations, such as the Party of Rights, and later the Ustasha, in the late nineteenth and early twentieth centuries. These intense, right wing, political movements were especially effective among Croatian émigrés—in Italy, Australia, and the United States.

Similar irredentist movements were found among Serbs, especially in the infamous *Crna Ruka* (Black Hand), an organization dedicated to the unification of all Serbs, and *Mlada Bosna* (Young Bosnia), the Bosnian Serb group directly responsible for the assassination of Archduke Franz Ferdinand in 1914. In Macedonia the VMRO (*Vnutrašna Makedonska Revolucionarna Organizacija*, or IMRO, International Macedonian Revolutionary Organization) had as its goal the unification of Macedonia out of pieces of Greece, Bulgaria, and Serbia, and was responsible for the assassination of King Alexander of Serbia in Marseilles in 1934, under the direction of the Ustasha.

When Germany attacked Serbia in World War II, the Germans were seen by some Croats as liberators from Serbian oppression. Similar reactions to German invasion or the threat thereof occurred in Ukraine, Ireland, the Channel Islands, and to some extent in Brittany and southern France, and for the same reasons, the prospect of the end of an older tyranny. There were similar inclinations among the Muslims of Yugoslavia, adroitly exploited by the Nazis, who organized a special division of Muslim troops (the Handžar Division). From this situation emerged the puppet Independent State of Croatia and the butchery of which the Ustasha stand rightly accused, despite Franjo Tudjman's attempts to place genocide in historical perspective (1990a) and thereby minimize it.

While politicians have manipulated, their publics have not been blameless. Many, but not all, members of those publics share the blame, for without them the politicians have no discontents to exploit. Such discontents are seldom abstract or impersonal. Indeed, civil wars are often intensely local. While it may be difficult or impossible to identify, say, a Muslim on the streets of Sarajevo by dress or language, it is not at all difficult to identify individuals, families, neighborhoods, by ethnicity if you have grown up with them. While it may be difficult to understand how whole populations can act with such ferocity, it is easier if you remember that anticipatory and preemptive violence can spread like wildfire in the absence of strong central control. It requires only a few acts or rumors of rape, murder, or arson that can be identified, rightly or wrongly as ethnically motivated, to set neighborhoods aflame in a cycle of retaliation. Popular accounts of the war focus on ethnicity and ancient hatreds, but they mislead. The important issues are not ethnicity as a social or personal characteristic, or of a warrior mentality, or about some kind of romantic tribalism; they are about ethnicity with a specific political history and subject to political manipulation in a context of the collapse of civil order. Without an impartial police, there is no defense.

No impartial police were at hand. The Croats and Muslims came to identify centralization with Serbianization in part because Serbs and Montenegrins were increasingly dominating the Yugoslav organs of government, especially the police and the armed forces. In considerable degree this was a matter of ethnic cultural preference; Slovenes and Croats do not pursue glory as much as money, if I may be permitted a scrap of essentialism. We find a similar phenomenon in our own country where the officer corps of the armed forces was long dominated by southern whites. The outcome of this process of Serbianization of the organs of power and control simply pressed home to the Croats and Slovenes their view that they were once again under the control of a foreign occupier.

The economic situation in Yugoslavia worsened through the 1970s and 1980s. This was partly because of failures to achieve economic reform, partly because of debt burden, partly because of a decline in the Western European economies, which diminished opportunities for working abroad. Whatever the causes, the perceived burden for the Slovenes and Croats became not only heavier but symbolically more important. They rebelled against a system of taxation that used their productivity to support underdeveloped regions to the south and east. They had the impending collapse of the communist system before their eyes, not only from internal evidence but from the Soviet Union. If the USSR had been strong, the fear of Russian intervention might once more have solidified Yugoslavia; Tito had used that threat often enough. It seems unlikely that a communist Yugoslavia had any chance of surviving, given the implosion of the economy and the collapse of the world's foremost communist state. The Slovenes and Croats seem to have been unable to mentally disentangle federalism from communism from Serbian hegemony. Unfortunately, the political mechanisms for a smooth transfer of power were not in place. U.S. foreign policy pinned its hopes on a stable federation, not understanding the centrifugal forces, and hoping that the survival of Yugoslavia would provide a beacon for the disintegrating USSR. European policy was no less naive, imagining that a graceful divorce was in the offing, and at least some Germanic actors may have seen no more than the restoration of ancient influence. No one imagined how rapidly the body of the state would collapse when the crutches of raw force and Party domination had splintered under the weight of events, and the War of the Yugoslav Succession began. No one thought to offer the bait of EC membership or special economic concessions on the conditions of stability and civil rights for minorities. Bette Denich (1993) has described the intensification of separatist rhetoric that began within the Party itself, and Robert Hayden (1996) the impossibility of creating or maintaining a multiethnic state when the definition of the polity is ethnospecific.

Other, even more mundane processes played a role. The idea of secession first put forth by the Slovenes and the Croatians, and later adopted by the other republics, was a direct threat to the legitimacy of the Yugoslav government and its army. It was also a direct threat to the positions and pensions of the bureaucrats and professional military. Most of the latter by this time were Serbs and Montenegrins, who were at least nominal communists, and whose support consumed as much as three-quarters of the national budget. They saw looming the breakup of a state whose preservation was their profession and their sustenance, and they acted against that dissolution. The military coup that failed in the Soviet Union almost succeeded in Yugoslavia. It failed as a universalistic military coup because the Serbian agenda within the armed forces had funneled arms to Serbian irregulars, to guerrillas the army found later it could not control. The command structure collapsed; even regular local commanders became locked in isolated local battles, unresponsive to general directives. Finally, the senior hierarchy was purged by radical pro-Serbian junior officers, and the Yugoslav Army became de facto a Serbian one, leaving well-armed remnants outside Serbian territory under the control of co-ethnic bandit warlords whose services could often be enlisted in larger ethnic causes.

In Serbia, Slobodan Milošević emerged from within the Party as the champion of Serbian ethnic rights. His principal competitors for leadership were non-Serbian communists. The system of ethnic rotation of power and privilege that had achieved stability among the *apparatchiki* for over four decades could have continued in a united Yugoslavia. There was no advantage to Milošević to stay in a united Yugoslavia where he would have to share power. As the Slovenes and Croatians began to press for independence, Milošević found himself politically threatened at home by right-wing Serbian nationalists such as Vojislav Šešelj. His position as a crypto-advocate of a Greater Serbia disguised as a communist federation had to give way to a more direct advocacy of Serbian hegemony in order to maintain his political base.

Part of this pressure on Milošević was created by the virtually complete "albanization" of Kosovo, a process that had begun in the fourteenth century under Turkish direction but which certainly accelerated during and after World War II, partly because of the higher Albanian birthrate, partly because of continual Serbian emigration out of Kosovo, and partly because of the politics of the Communist Party and its attempts to reduce Serbian influence and balance ethnicities in a way that left the Party as the real holder of power. The symbolic value of the Kosovo situation was enormous for Serbs; their entire national identity was rooted in their consciousness of Serbian sacrifice on the Field of the Blackbirds in 1389, the presence of major religious monuments in the region (such as the seat of the Patriarchate of Peć), and the associations between Kosovo-Metohija and the medieval Serbian empire. That other Slavs died at Kosovo, that some Serbs were traitors or collaborationists, had no force. The albanization of Kosovo and its continuing status as a semi-autonomous province were seen as a desecration; and Milošević adroitly manipulated this perception to consolidate his hold on power.

The uprising of *krajina* Serbs in Knin was also convenient for central Serbian policy. It allowed the Serbs of Serbia to lay claim to broader territory on ethnic grounds in the same way that the Germans had exploited the presence of *Volksdeutsche* beyond their borders in the years leading up to the Second World War. The local leader in the *krajina*, Milan Babić, was a useful tool, but as soon as he became an embarrassment Milošević discarded him. Indeed, when the Croatian army overwhelmed the *krajina* in 1996, Milošević took no action, and Serbia was obliged to accommodate the refugees.[13] The same fate awaited the leader of the Bosnian Serbs, Radovan Karadžić, as international pressure mounted against Serbian aggression in Bosnia. Milošević, who sees his future as an ultimate power player in the Balkans, will use or discard any Serb, in or out of Serbia, to insure his own continued presence. Sooner or later, Milošević will abandon Karadžić and his military partner, Mladić, for however many pieces of silver the Western powers will give him. He has consolidated his position, abandoned former allies, and removed all but one independent journalistic endeavor (*Vreme*), and is restrained only by the economic isolation of his country, imposed by the West in the hope that the populace will remove him. Economic difficulties and political discontent continue to mount in Serbia, but the codefinitions of ethnicity, loyalty, and citizenship seem to be insurmountable. The West is in fact a prisoner of Milošević's quest for power. He stands in the way of an easy solution to the Balkan problem by his internally necessary advocacy of a Greater Serbia. At the same time, there appear to be no useful alternatives for the West, so that Milošević has been simultaneously the problem and the solution.

In Croatia the old thirst for independence has resurfaced, and Franjo Tudjman has emerged as the leader of the Croatian Democratic Union, strongly supported by a center-right coalition and with particular support from émigrés. He was described in a letter to the editor of the *New York Times* as a moderate, but he is a moderate only in the same sense that Milošević is, namely that there is someone to the right of him (notably Paraga and the Party of Rights). No sensible observer of the Yugoslav scene could have failed to anticipate the reaction of the *krajina* Serbs to the Croat declaration of independence, accompanied as it was by the erosion of Serbian cultural privileges and autonomy and the flagrant display of the same cultural symbols that had been used during Ustasha persecution of the Serbs during World War II. Better diplomacy and symbol management might have prevented the outbreak of vigilante violence that occurred in Knin. By offering immediate concessions and reassurance to the *krajina* Serbs, Tudjman would have lost some political support to the right wing, but guarantees of local autonomy, which would have cost nothing to the left, might have prevented the upris-

---

13. The refugee Serbian populations have not been gracefully accepted in Serbia itself, despite their ethnic identity. Unlike Croatia, which has had to accommodate Croatian and Muslim refugees from Bosnia, as well as Croats expelled from the Krajina and Eastern Slavonia, Serbia receives little or no international assistance in accommodating refugees.

ing at Knin, the bandits on the roads, the killing at Borovo Selo, and what followed as the Serbian-controlled Yugoslav Army swept in to rescue their brethren. Those guarantees have in fact now been made—if not too little, certainly too late. A cynical view is that Tudjman's apparent ineptitude was a deliberate ploy to incite violence and invite invasion, in order to solidify his political position and bring in Western support.

This would not have been the first time that a Balkan people called on surrounding great powers to solve by imposition what should have been arranged by local negotiation in the first place. Austria marched into Bosnia in 1878 for much the same reason that NATO has just over a century later, namely to stabilize a situation that might otherwise lead to conflict between the great powers. It is also not the first time that intellectuals have vanished, to be replaced by patriots. In the sort of political climate currently prevailing in what was once Yugoslavia, politicians must create and maintain a sense of inevitable crisis to narrow the choices available to their constituents to simple, binary ones between loyalty and disloyalty, patriotism or treason, in order to stay in power. Tudjman has created just this kind of political climate, restrained only by the demands of the West that he maintain some semblance of democracy. The disappearance of a free press in Croatia, which blossomed momentarily (*Danas*, *Slobodna Dalmacija*, the *Feral Tribune*), has been notable, and the suppression of information continues.

What Now, and Now What?

At this writing, the economies of the region are in ruins, although even amid disaster, some actors prosper, and the positive economic effects in Croatia of the UN and NATO presence cannot be ignored. The Slovenes may be the first to recover economically, but unless conditions improve in their traditional markets of Croatia, Serbia, and other parts of the former Yugoslavia, they will be dependent on assistance from and access to Western European markets. The situation is worse in Croatia, where goods are so expensive in the local currency that it is often cheaper to buy in the West if hard currencies are available, and even many local transactions must be conducted in German marks. In Serbia, there is a growing confrontation over economic policy, with Milošević committed to a communist system, pitted against technocrats who see Serbia's only hope in privatization and economic reform that will attract international loans and investment. Such international assistance is unlikely to be forthcoming until Serbia renounces the Bosnian Serbs and any claims on territory in Eastern Slavonia or other areas outside its current boundaries. Whether international recognition will hinge on Serbian treatment of the Kosovo Albanians, whether Albania or other states will become involved, is an open question.

No overall solution can be found until the Bosnian situation is solved. At this juncture, there is an unstable Croat-Muslim federation that could collapse easily with the defection of the right-wing Croats of Herzegovina. At this writing and as the Bosnian elections approach, the hardliners of the ministate of Herceg-Bosna still refuse to participate in the joint governance of Mostar. Tudjman has the same problem with them that Milošević had with the *krajina* and still has with the Bosnian Serbs, who persist in seeking full sovereignty. It is easy to imagine Croatia and Serbia simply partitioning Bosnia and leaving the Muslims no independence at all. The Western countries would protest, but how effectively? Both Tudjman and Milošević must balance the hope of Western aid against their own desires for long-term defensible positions and the political pressures from their own right wings. They have striven mightily to suppress dissent, jailing opponents, closing down radio and TV stations and newspapers, but their failure to solve underlying economic problems fuels popular discontent on which their rivals may seize.

What Might Have Been

Could it have been different; were there really choices? It is not clear that the urge to overthrow the Party would have admitted the idea of a confederation of equals, as emerged for example in historical Switzerland after ethnic-religious struggles as bitter as those of Yugoslavia, or in the Netherlands, where Hapsburg hegemony and religious wars also played a role. It is likely that in the actual context of local politics within Croatia and Serbia neither Tudjman nor Milošević had any maneuvering room, even if they had had more confederational goals. An outstanding feature of the catastrophe was the speed with which criminal elements came to play a role, running guns, looting (often with the assistance of the army), and feathering their nests with blackmarket profits. Only history will reveal the intricacy of connections between politicians, military officers, Western participants, and the underworld. This distressing story seems the same whether it happens in Yugoslavia, Poland, Russia, the European colonies in Africa or Asia, or other regions in which rigid control has collapsed.

While a more productive solution from within might not have been expected (even though Ante Marković's policies on the eve of the war might have led in that direction), more decisive action by the Western powers and the United States could have helped. That action would not have been easy. The Western countries had too many conflicting interests not only over foreign policy and the future of Europe but also between foreign and domestic policy. Time was short, but the crisis did not emerge overnight. In the weeks that they had early on, the Western powers might have made it clear that they would intervene militarily if need be, and they could have done so in Gulf War fashion on the plains of Slavonia where their tactical advantage would have been enormous. Even though Yugoslavia had the fourth largest domestic army in Europe, it would have been outgunned by the kind of force assembled to counter Saddam Hussein. Once the fighting had moved into the mountains of Bosnia, the West's opportunity and advantage were much diminished, and the military risks of intervention were higher. Intervention would only have been effective politically if the West had insisted on guarantees to minorities and simultaneously offered economic concessions, including the assurance of market positions in Western Europe. No such efforts were made.

Instead, what happened was a piecemeal approach. Yugoslavia was allowed to fall apart, refugee streams were allowed to mount, enormous economic damage was done, and the inhumanity of ethnic cleansing has reminded the world again that Europe is not immune to the abandonment of civilized behavior. The West was reactive rather than proactive, because of conflicting interests within and between the powers, and because ultimate national interest could not be clearly seen. The potential for broad European conflict to begin in the Balkans has been clear for centuries. The military costs of early and decisive intervention are small, but the political costs are high because the electorates in intervening countries have to be convinced that the risks are worth taking. The military costs of late intervention climb enormously, while the political costs descend, since the need for intervention in one's own national interest finally becomes obvious. Politicians, of course, prefer to minimize their political costs by waiting.

The outcome of this wait-and-see game was a disastrous, expensive, and humiliating action by the UN to keep a peace that none of the participants had been required to want in the first place. The sequel to that debacle was NATO intervention of a kind that should have been initiated in 1991 and the imposition of diplomatic and economic pressures that might bring the combatants and their leaders to heel. Misery is now the only weapon that Western diplomats have. They impose economic sanctions, withhold critical memberships, in an attempt to force compliance with standards of organization and political behavior that are not always honored in their own countries. The leaders of the errant states, notably Serbia and Croatia, are obliged to comply at least minimally to retain their own hold on power. Tudjman may yet be forced to allow a free press, and open criticism may allow the Croatian people to read what they now say behind closed doors. Milošević may yet turn the indicted Karadžić and Mladić over to NATO forces and the war crimes tribunal in The Hague in order to win concessions from the West. Serbia and Croatia may delay for some unknown period the dissection of Bosnia, contrary to their natural instincts to reproduce the ancient boundaries of the Hapsburg and Ottoman empires. The price for all of this will have been paid by the Yugoslavs, hundreds of thousands killed, wounded, raped, vast stretches of productive economy ruined, the resources of the region and of the West now required for rebuilding what never should have been destroyed. In the long run, the price will also be paid by Western taxpayers, hopefully only in treasure, but not in blood, as they will if the conflicting interests and any reemergent nationalism and xenophobia in Germany, Austria, Russia, France, Britain, and the United States again lead to a European war.

Even if the halting progress toward settlement goes on, there are still dangers in the long run and the short, and the ultimate goals of Western policy are not clear. The immediate dangers are an eruption of fighting in Kosovo or Macedonia, especially the latter, in a way that might draw in the Greeks and Turks. The structure of NATO itself would be threatened under those circumstances, and NATO still remains the trump card against resurgent aggressions anywhere. Fundamentalist pressure threatens the stability of the Turkish state, as does the Kurdish insurrection, and the stability of Turkey as a NATO partner is one of the keys to stability in the Middle East. The Yugoslav crisis is intimately connected with the Middle East and with Western policy toward that region.

That connection is not simple. Before the Yugoslav civil war, the Muslims of Bosnia were secular and unattractive as allies to the fundamentalist Muslim movements that have emerged elsewhere. Now, after several years of ethnic persecution, the ground has been tilled for participation by radical religious elements that the Western nations would prefer to keep at a distance. Yet now those same elements have a beachhead on the continent of Europe. The line of demarcation between what is Europe and what is not now stretches from Turkistan to the Atlantic. It is not unthinkable that some of the neglect of Bosnia by the West might have been driven by a desire, in some quarters, to let the Serbs and Croats eliminate the Muslim population and with it the problem. Much the same view may characterize some Western perspectives on Kosovo and Albania. That the problems are not only those of foreign policy is made apparent by the internal political problems in France with Muslims from North Africa and in Germany with those from Turkey.[14]

In the long run, and despite setbacks at the hands of romanticist political extremists, money may talk. Trade may win. It won't solve everything. It will not guarantee civil rights or freedom from exploitation, but it will deny politicians the opportunity to use economic discontent as a vehicle to power. The more

14. As this essay goes to press, NATO has finished eleven weeks of intensive bombing of Serbian positions in Kosovo, Belgrade, and elsewhere in Serbia in an apparently successful attempt to force Serbian military and police to withdraw from Kosovo and an ongoing attempt to topple Milošević. This intervention was in my opinion ill-conceived—too late, in the wrong place, and about the wrong issues. Serbian repression of the Albanian majority in Kosovo was a legally admissible, if morally repugnant, attempt to defeat a separatist and secessionist movement on the internationally recognized territory of Yugoslavia. That movement had gained strength as the proportion of Kosovo that was Albanian increased from about two-thirds after 1945 to about nine-tenths in the 1990s, accelerating after 1960, and radicalized by the Serbian police response to it. NATO intervention triggered a violent Serbian reaction that sought to drive all Albanians from Kosovo in order to deny the separatist guerrillas (the Kosovo Liberation Army) their natural local support. The humanitarian disaster that was always a potential became a reality when NATO struck without acting on its own intelligence sources, which foresaw what would happen. NATO action, undertaken for geopolitical reasons behind a figleaf of humanitarianism, attacked Milošević on his strongest moral ground in the cradle of Serbia, playing the same pro-Albanian role the Germans did in World Wars I and II, and it may yet destabilize broader political relations in the Balkans by encouraging Albanian separatism in Macedonia and Greece, laying the foundation for the same Greater Albania established by the Nazis in 1943. Diplomacy, without a consciousness of history, is always a mistake.

cynical among us may ask whether the ultimate interest of the United States is in a united or a divided Europe. What are the long-term goals of U.S. policy, and can America in fact develop a coherent foreign policy when economic globalization and related issues have such a divisive influence at home? Similar issues were faced in 1919, when the immediate domestic political pressures called for the Allies to punish and contain the Germanic states. By defining their opponents ethnically, they so also defined the buffer states they wished to create. By defining the buffer states ethnically, they planted the seeds of ultimate contradiction. Their error was made more egregious by the fact that the ethnic groups had conflicting but historically deep territorial claims, so that blood and soil were often the same. This same error may be perpetuated, for despite the rise of a new Germany with no obvious territorial aims, some in the West still fear German expansion, and their essentialist logic leads immediately to the conclusion that Serbia must not be weakened overmuch, since in the long run it will be Serbia that will have to stop or delay the Germans again, as she has done twice in this century. This is the same logic that persuades the West not to weaken Iraq too much, lest Iran achieve ascendancy, the same logic that has persuaded the United States to support dictatorial regimes in many places.

Epilogue

There are only three solutions to the inconsistencies created by defining ethnically heterogeneous polities in mono-ethnic terms. The first is to move the borders of states, but that solution works only when heterogeneity is simple. The second is to move the ethnic groups. That solution has been used for centuries all over the world and in the Balkans certainly after the Balkan Wars of 1912–13 and World War I when Slavic, Greek, and Turkish populations were "exchanged," that is forcibly expelled from one country and accepted into another, by agreement between states. It was also employed after World War II, when populations of Volksdeutsche were expelled from the Slavic buffer states like Poland, Czechoslovakia, and Yugoslavia and sent to Germany. (It is also the foundation of admissibility to Israel.) That kind of expulsion or acceptance, although without international sanction, is what has happened in Yugoslavia after 1991, with the flight of Muslims, Croats, and Serbs within and out of Bosnia, of Croats from Slavonia, the Banija and other *krajina* regions to Croatia, and of Serbs from the Serbian *krajina* to Serbia. These are all forms of "ethnic cleansing."[15] Yet another form is extermination, of the kind seen at Jasenovac in World War II, and at Vukovar, Srebrenica, Omarska, and other locations in Bosnia in the civil war. Such exterminations have been local, not achieving the totality

15. Note also the similar approach in wartime internment of ethnic groups, like that of the Japanese in California in World War II.

envisaged by the Nazis in the Holocaust and fail to qualify as genocide only because of their modest scale. All of these are on a continuum of inhumanity in which those who are displaced are seldom asked for their consent or are so confronted by the consequences of remaining that they opt to flee.

The one solution that has seldom been tried is either the renunciation of ethnic definition of the polity or the declaration of the irrelevance of ethnicity to political status, in a word, citizenship. That institution served the Roman Empire well, when free persons of any ethnic or tribal origin could become citizens of Rome if they succeeded in becoming such citizens, by having freedom and acknowledging the divinity of the emperor. Similarly it existed under the Hapsburgs for those who were Catholic and acknowledged the Crown, and under the Ottomans for all who adopted Islam. It was presumably achieved under the communists in the same way, by declaring adherence to a symbolic code that represented a universal church. Thus, while no known state has granted equality of citizenship without demanding some form of symbolic declaration of loyalty, few states have facilitated such organization by adopting purely secular forms of symbolic loyalty. Marxism, although purportedly secular, was in such sharp conflict with preexisting religious forms that by opposition as an alternative to religion, it achieved a quasi-religious status. Only in the parliamentary democracies have we seen the construction of secular loyalties that permit the coexistence of religious affiliation and grant equal citizenship at least in theory to persons of all ethnicities and creeds. It goes without saying that such systems are not perfect, that equality is often honored more in the breach than in the observance, and that the forces of ethnic and religious fundamentalism are continually at odds with secular and rationalistic organization. It should not go without saying that there is a profound difference between political systems in which there is a theory of equality that is only imperfectly realized and those in which there is no presumption of equality at all. That is the difference. That is the solution that the errors of Versailles and their perpetuation have not grasped. That is the infection of Romanticism that even today gnaws at the possibilities exposed when the forces of Enlightenment first overcame millennia of dogmatic oppression. That is the challenge, and it is not only in Yugoslavia.

Unmaking Multiethnicity in Yugoslavia

Media and Metamorphosis

Bette Denich

In late September 1989, the central committee of the Communist League of Yugoslavia held a special meeting to discuss a proposed amendment to the Slovenian constitution that would claim for Slovenia the right to secede from Yugoslavia.[1] The meeting was televised throughout the country and was still going at midnight when I retired for the night in my Belgrade apartment. Tuning in my radio the following morning, I was surprised by the sounds of a roll-call vote, concluding what had been an all-night session. A majority of the central committee voted to request that Slovenia's parliament postpone its vote to allow further discussion of the issues. But later that same morning, the Slovenian parliament voted unanimously in favor of Slovenia's right to secede, ignoring the central committee's request (see Hayden 1992). Upon hearing that news, I spread out a map of Yugoslavia and, scanning it from west to east, quickly perceived that

My research in Yugoslavia during the critical period of 1988–90 was funded by the Wenner-Gren Foundation for Anthropological Research and by IREX (International Research and Exchange Board), whose support is gratefully acknowledged. My work depended upon the hospitality of many friends who shared their lives and thoughts with me, and who were present in my imagination as I wrote this piece. However, they bear no responsibility for the views expressed here.

1. The name "Communist League" was officially adopted in 1952, but the organization continued to be known informally as "the party." This text will use both designations.

Slovenia's secession would lead to the disintegration of the rest of the country. Ethnically homogeneous and linguistically distinct from the rest of Yugoslavia, Slovenia was the only republic in the federation capable of forming a separate nation-state. Yugoslavia's five other republics had mixed ethnic compositions; like Siamese quintuplets sharing vital organs, they were incapable of separation without risking lethal damage. But Slovenia was also integral to the political balance of the federation. The integrity of the whole depended upon the balance among all its parts. In conversations around Belgrade, people were saying: "But Slovenia can't secede, because that would mean civil war." The unthinkable could not happen.

Following the vote in the Slovenian parliament, a satirical troupe from Sarajevo performed a skit on its weekly television show, watched throughout Yugoslavia. In what seemed hilariously farfetched at the time, the comedians imagined the country partitioned into West and East Yugoslavia, with the boundary running through Bosnia so that Sarajevo was bisected by a Sarajevo Wall. (The Berlin Wall was still intact.) The skit enacted an escape from one side of the wall to the other, while guards pelted the escapees with garbage. In April 1992, less than three years later, the civil war that had already ravaged large areas of Croatia reached Sarajevo and inflicted even greater devastation upon what had been the multiethnic republic of Bosnia and Herzegovina. Prior to the wave of postcommunist change that swept through Eastern Europe and Yugoslavia, the three-way ethnic composition of Bosnia and Herzegovina appeared to be yielding a new, Bosnian identity. Bosnia was a testing ground for multiethnicity and also its most vulnerable point. Given Bosnia's previous history, a separation of that population into its Muslim, Serbian, and Croatian components would mean "violence."

Throughout Yugoslavia, a significant proportion of the population rejected nationalist views in favor of maintaining a multiethnic state. But that viewpoint was swiftly overtaken as growing numbers of Yugoslavs of all ethnic backgrounds who had previously supported multiethnic Yugoslavia accepted the arguments and explanations offered by their own nationalist leaders. What accounts for the speed with which interethnic antagonism replaced the multiethnic bonds that had maintained Yugoslavia during the forty-five years of Titoism? If civil war would be required to dismantle Yugoslavia into separate national states, the willingness to wage war was implicit in all nationalist programs. Rival nationalist causes led rapidly to sharpening confrontations, progressing down a "slippery slope" to violence. Once that slide began, why was there nothing to brake it?

Barbara Tuchman's *March of Folly* studies how, throughout history, predictions of disaster have failed to prevent catastrophes from happening. From Troy to Saigon, "rejection of reason [has been] the prime characteristic of folly" (Tuchman 1984: 380). She focuses on leaders who pursue power where reason would instruct otherwise. As a widely predicted outcome, the descent of Yugoslavia into civil war qualifies for Tuchman's definition of tragic "folly." Yugoslavia was torn apart by leaders supported by the near-consensus of ethnic constituencies in crucial elections and referenda. Therefore, the populations at large must share with their leaders the blame for the disaster. Even foreseeing civil war, people cohered into ethnic blocs, supporting leaders who pursued increasingly aggressive policies toward each other. What was the appeal of separating into ethnic nation-states that were incompatible with geography? How could otherwise reasonable people be persuaded to pursue dreams that could not be realized without massive violence and destruction?

In his seminal work *Imagined Communities,* Benedict Anderson (1983) emphasizes that the mass circulation of printed publications, in vernacular languages within particular territorial boundaries, was instrumental to forming a sense of commonality among the residents of incipient nation-states. If printed materials (especially newspapers and popular novels) were the mass media of earlier centuries, the concept must be extended in today's world to include electronic telecommunications. And if mass communication among a population can circulate the concepts from which nationhood is constructed, it follows that it can also circulate the concepts through which an existing nation-state may be dismantled.

Between the summer of 1987 and the fall of 1990, my research in Yugoslavia coincided with the succession of events that replaced the Titoist political consensus with patterns of interethnic opposition. The level of intellectual, artistic, and even athletic output was exhilarating. The public communications media were energized by the release of constraints on what they could write about, speak about, and show to their readers and electronic audiences. Communism was going out in a combustive mixture of exposés of Titoism, ethnic revivals, and the Western democratic ideas then percolating through Eastern Europe.

Recognizing the opportunity to witness a moment of historical change, I improvised an ethnography of transformation as unforeseeable occurrences unfolded from day to day. Emerging from these observations was a case study in interethnic communication and conflict escalation as a prelude to armed violence. While crisis led to crisis, I recognized communication patterns that were polarizing ethnic identities in opposition to each other. In the absence of mitigating factors, such self-reinforcing oppositions were leading rapidly toward schism, reversing the bridging of ethnic boundaries represented by Yugoslavia and turning neighbors into enemies.

Managing Multiethnicity: Constructs in Conflict

To understand Yugoslav debates about ethnicity and statehood, an American must recognize the different meanings assigned to the concept of "nation" and, therefore, to "nation-state." In South Slavic languages, the word *narod* (like the German *Volk*) means both "people" and "nation." Thus the "nation-state" is attached to a specific "nation," or "people," conceived as an ethnic population.[2] The incompatibility between this definition and American concepts is evident in how many Yugoslavs, upon discovering that I was an American, would ask me "What is your nationality?" "American," I would respond. "But American is not a nationality," they inevitably replied, "only a citizenship. You Americans all immigrated from somewhere. Where did your family come from?" The equation between "people" and "nation," contained within the single word *narod*, provides no way to detach nationality from ancestry. Missing is the basic American notion that nationality is derived from citizenship, whether by birth or by personal choice.

A familiar cliché portrays Yugoslavia as an "artificial" creation, wherein "age-old ethnic hatreds" were held in check by the coercive apparatus of the Titoist state. To single out Yugoslavia as "artificial," however, is to presume that other national states are "real." Yet Benedict Anderson and others (e.g., Hobsbawm 1990) make the case that all nations are cultural artifices, "constructed" under specific historical circumstances, not primordial natural phenomena. Since the early nineteenth century, conflicting "natural" foundations for nationhood have been identified in the Balkans. Theorists emphasizing the shared linguistic and putative ancestral origins of all South (*Jugo-*) Slavs have considered "Yugoslavia" to be as natural as any other nation-state. However, other theorists have claimed that the categories Serb, Croat, Slovene, and so on represent unblendable, "essential" identities, and that each merits recognition as a separate nation with a "right" to a state of its own.[3]

The Titoist slogan "brotherhood and unity" was intended to mend the fratricidal divisions between Yugoslavia's ethnically defined "nations" during World War II. But even if these ethnic nations were metaphorical "brothers," brothers are still distinct entities. There was official ambivalence over the definition of "nation" and whether Yugoslavia would evolve toward a common national culture, subsuming the categories of the past. Early policies encouraged mobility and mixing among people of different backgrounds. In major cities and in regions of mixed populations, ethnic background was increasingly regarded as a personal matter. Considering that the definitive ethnic differences among Serbo-Croatian speakers are marked by religion, the urbanized, secular society that grew under Titoism reduced the significance of the religious divisions among the Orthodox Serbs, the Catholic Croats, and Slavic Muslims. Released from the custom of arranged marriage, couples from different backgrounds found few impediments

2. The origins of these concepts in the eighteenth- and nineteenth-century intellectual movements continue to shape the cultural constructions that define the "nation" throughout Central and Eastern Europe (see Dumont 1986, Greenfeld 1992, and Hobsbawm 1990) and specifically in the South Slavic region (see Banac 1984 and Djilas 1991).

3. For articulate presentations of both viewpoints, contrast Djilas's (1991) defense of the Yugoslav concept with Banac's (1984) argument that the preexisting Serbian and Croatian national ideologies doomed Yugoslavia from the outset.

to romantic unions that produced children and extended families of mixed ethnicity. In many ethnically homogeneous regions, there was widespread acceptance of life within the larger Yugoslav state with its regional and cultural diversity.

"Brotherhood" and Rivalry within Titoism

If two postwar generations of Yugoslavs widely accepted Yugoslavia as a multiethnic society, how was that acceptance shattered so swiftly and profoundly?

While ethnic barriers were diminishing in everyday life, communist leaders themselves paradoxically began to reassert national divisions, particularly over regional economic interests. In 1958, the Communist Party program indicated a trend toward "a socialist, Yugoslav consciousness, in the conditions of a social community of peoples" (Shoup 1968: 207). By the early 1960s however, that trend was reversed, as official policy rejected the concept of an overarching Yugoslav nationality (see Bertsch 1976 and Shoup 1968). Instead, for census and other official purposes, citizens were expected to declare their ethnic affiliation. Instead of consulting Marx, the communists were reverting to the theories of national identity and rights that developed during the nineteenth century, and which were anathema to Marx.

During my visits to Yugoslavia in the mid-1960s, conversations over coffee positioned the theme of ethnic identity among the other ironies and absurdities of everyday life under Titoism. To many people in multiethnic settings, it seemed "natural" to identify a person of mixed descent as a Yugoslav. Since declaring themselves Croats, Serbs, and so on meant omitting or denying part of their heritage, why should such persons reject the identity they felt as Yugoslavs, which to them seemed equivalent to French, Italian, and other national designations? Why were official policies moving in the opposite direction?

When communist and intellectual elites started to fracture along national lines during the mid-1960s, the Party banned opinions it considered nationalistic and expelled offending members, including important intellectuals. By 1971, however, the Croatian communist leaders openly advocated the decentralization of federal powers into the republics (Rusinow 1977; Vuković 1989). The major impetus for those demands was the economic conflict between more and less developed regions, but the 1971 "mass movement" also revived the concept of distinctive Croatian nationhood, particularly focusing on language. Rather than welcome the trend that was merging regional dialects into a single Serbo-Croatian language, the nationalists emphasized differences as the basis for a separate Croatian language. The argument over language was incendiary because it implied a return to a nineteenth-century theory of nationalism that declared a distinctive language to be a sufficient basis for an ethnic "nation" to claim the right to a separate state.

The Croatian "mass movement" mobilized anticommunists and reactivated ties to World War II political emigrants. It was the first open challenge to the Titoist order, and Tito himself orchestrated the counteroffensive that was "tantamount to a Titoist coup against the system which the Western world calls 'Titoism' " (Rusinow 1974: 1). To maintain the Party's monopoly over the state, Tito was willing to sacrifice the potential nationhood of Yugoslavia. Although the Croatian party leaders were expelled and the "mass movement" defeated, Tito's "coup" actually co-opted nationalist demands into the new Yugoslav constitution enacted in 1974. In a virtual "pact with the devil" of nationalism, most of the federal government's power was distributed to the republics, which were only loosely connected by federal bodies within which each republic had veto powers. Interwoven among all institutions at all levels, the Communist League held onto its monopoly over public policy and the media, which influenced public opinion. At a practical level, the new Yugoslav constitution of 1974 interrupted Yugoslavia-wide economic and institutional ties (see Horvat 1984).

The Emergence of "National" Republics

Postwar trends through the 1960s had put modernization theories into practice, combining rising levels of urbanization and education with a more universal outlook that encouraged mobility between the Yugoslav republics, intermarriage, and the emergence of a sense of a pan-Yugoslav nationality. Projections of these trends into the future presumed further progress along these lines.

I saw no reason to question the modernization paradigm in 1972, when I left Yugoslavia for what was to be a fifteen-year absence. When I returned in 1987, however, I was taken aback at what I found. Belgrade as I had known it during the 1960s was emphatically the capital of Yugoslavia, an administrative and intellectual center that drew people from the other republics to fill official and professional positions. In its place, I found a Belgrade that was expressly the capital of Serbia. Although still Yugoslavia's official capital, the federal government's reduced functions no longer attracted a mixture of people to the city. Moreover, previously suppressed elements of Serbian national history were visibly resurfacing in downtown Belgrade, where grimy facades were being sandblasted and repainted to reveal the architectural heritage of a Serbia that had existed before 1918, before there was a Yugoslavia. Bookstore windows displayed new works and new editions of classic works on Serbian history, literature, ethnology, and national traditions. It seemed that Belgrade was compensating for its loss of status as the capital of a larger Yugoslavia by more intensely expressing the narrower nationhood and incipient statehood of Serbia.

The trend had also turned in a surprising direction as reflected in the lives of people I knew. Through 1972, I had observed how job and residential mobility took people from villages to towns, from one city to another, and across republic boundaries. Fifteen years later, I found that my friends and acquaintances had returned to their home towns and native regions. Rather than continue to branch outward, families had reoriented toward the villages they had left during the great postwar urbanization process. Among city dwellers, kinship networks had involuted (see Milić 1991) and were being ritualized in new ways that were ethnologically fascinating. But why did young people return home after living and working in other republics, why did students who had gone away for higher education also return home to await employment?

The 1974 constitution had unraveled the fabric of Yugoslavia as a reality in people's lives. There was widespread emigration to work abroad, but not to find work elsewhere in Yugoslavia outside of one's home region. Family networks expanded their scope to span multiple international boundaries. But that global reach represented a turning inward in structural terms, deepening and reinforcing particularistic bonds. That trend occurred in the absence of alternatives to locally based ties and informal "connections," the ubiquitous *veze* that were increasingly the only way to get things done. Many Slovenes crossed into Austria and Italy on a daily basis, while fewer and fewer of them had reasons for traveling eastward toward the rest of Yugoslavia, or even caring what might become of it.

The integrity of Titoist Yugoslavia was further undermined through the 1980s by a systemic economic crisis it proved incapable of resolving, and by increasingly open criticism and public discussion of previously suppressed "taboo themes." Within the communist establishment, republic leaderships blamed each other for failed policies. Since republic delegates to federal institutions voted as blocs, there was little opportunity for individual politicians to make alliances across republic lines. In disputes covered with increasing openness by news media, the communist leaders of each republic were seen as speaking in unison against the communist leaders of the other republics.

News Media and the Ethnic Dramaturgy of Kosovo

As Pierre Bourdieu (1990: 138) has pointed out: "The power of imposing a vision of divisions, that is, the power of making visible and explicit social divisions that are implicit, is the political power par excellence: it is the power to make groups, to manipulate the objective structure of society." The nominal categories of ethnic identity were raw material to be manipulated by those who recognized that social divisions were the vehicle to redefining and obtaining political power. But it is one thing for those with political ambitions to latch onto nationalist ideas, and another to be able to activate implicit social divisions among people who are unconcerned with, or opposed to, ethnic differentiation.

Serbia, Croatia, and Slovenia each had intellectual circles where the "tabooed" ideologies of nationalism were preserved and covertly nourished. However, intellectuals cannot conjure up mass movements alone; they need a way to get their ideas to the public. In Yugoslavia, all public information moved through the mass media, and the mass media were controlled by the government of each republic. Editorial policy was set by the ruling party and reflected by journalists who were themselves involved with the intellectual circles in their own capitals. The journalists selected their material within the parameters controlled by republic political leaders, and as the Titoist "taboos" were lifted, they revealed more and more information that had been concealed in the presumed interest of Yugoslav unity. The same events, reported in different ways, reflected the conflicts between republic political leaders who were themselves absorbing the nationalist ideologies originating in circles of intellectuals.

In 1986, a new factor appeared on the political stage in the form of a delegation of Serbian and Montenegrin peasants from the Kosovo "autonomous province" who arrived in Belgrade to seek a hearing before the federal parliament.[4] An event that posed a minor distraction at the time actually initiated the processes that were to unravel the fragile balances among the republics that had been embedded in the 1974 constitution.

The Kosovo Serbs claimed they had been forced to leave Kosovo by Albanian nationalists as part of a plan for Kosovo to secede from Yugoslavia and merge with Albania. By 1981, steady emigration from Kosovo, combined with the high Albanian birthrate, had reduced the Serbian minority from about 28 percent of the population after World War II to under 15 percent in 1981, falling to around 10 percent by the late 1980s (Petrović and Blagojević 1989: 1). Serbs complained of intimidation and harassment, including physical and sexual assaults, threats, and property damage. Delegations to Belgrade protested they could not obtain justice in Albanian-run courts in the autonomous province. Because the 1974 constitution removed Kosovo from the jurisdiction of Serbia's republic-level courts, they could only appeal directly to the federal government.[5] During 1986, several delegations trekked to Belgrade, and on one occasion the entire population of several villages set out on a demonstrative mass migration that was halted by Kosovo police (see Mišović 1987).

The following year, an event occurred that would change forever the nature of Yugoslav politics. While a Party delegation was visiting Kosovo to investigate, a crowd of Serbian demonstrators was attacked by the police. A communist official named Slobodan Milošević appeared before the crowd, proclaiming: "No

4. For convenience, this presentation uses "Serbian" to also include "Montenegrins." Traditionally, Montenegrins have identified themselves both as Serbs and as a separate "nation," originating in the separate statehood of Montenegro prior to the creation of Yugoslavia. Titoist policy considered Montenegrins a separate "nation," while the Milošević movement built upon their identity as Serbs. "Autonomous provinces" had been created in two areas of Serbia with large non-Slavic populations: Vojvodina in the north, and Kosovo in the south. The 1974 constitution elevated the "autonomous provinces" to all but titular equality with the republics.

5. Although its principal topic is repression against Kosovo Albanians, a report by Helsinki Watch and the International Helsinki Federation for Human Rights also acknowledges "a pattern of failure by Kosovo's criminal justice authorities to protect ethnic minorities in Kosovo, particularly the Serbs, from attacks by ethnic Albanians" (K. Anderson 1990: 24).

one has the right to beat you! No one has the right to beat the people!" That moment transformed Milošević from a Party bureaucrat into a mass leader. He pledged to change the situation in Kosovo, and only four months later, in a televised meeting of the Serbian central committee, he engineered the defeat of the republic leadership in a crucial vote, thereby becoming the effective leader of the Serbian Communist Party.

During the summer of 1988, television sets throughout Yugoslavia were tuned to news programs showing mass rallies in Serbia, organized to support an amendment to Serbia's constitution that would restore Serbia's jurisdiction over its "autonomous provinces" (thereby removing Albanian control over Kosovo). The rallies were led by a traveling cadre of Kosovo Serbs and took on the character of a revitalization movement (see Wallace 1956) emphasizing the mythic significance of Kosovo in the construction of Serbian nationhood. The plight of Kosovo Serbs tapped into a deep vein of national tradition associated with Kosovo since a climactic battle 600 years earlier had marked the subjugation of medieval Serbia to the Ottoman Empire. However, the right of "our people/nation" (*naš narod*) to remain in Kosovo presumed that the Albanian-dominated province should again be subordinated to the Serbian republic, an intransigent stand that was to be matched by equivalent intransigence from the Albanian side. The rallies became protests against the Communist League "chairwarmers," who were seen as resisting constitutional change and as responsible for the economic crisis. Milošević posed as a political and economic reformer, and the rallies became known as both the "anti-bureaucratic revolution" and the "happening of the people."

Instead of maintaining a Titoist unified front throughout Yugoslavia, the media of each republic reported the escalating interrepublic policy conflicts from the viewpoint of its own party leaders.[6] Different publics not only began receiving conflicting information about the same issues but also reacted differently to the same information, depending upon their personal experiences and the collective memories that were invoked by members of the same ethnic constituencies. The dominant media of each republic attacked nationalism elsewhere, while either ignoring or refraining from criticizing nationalism among their own co-ethnics. When people found only "their own" nationalists under attack by media from other republics, they tended to react defensively. Thus the problem was not only in the different information conveyed by different media, but in the responses of different audiences even when they received the same information.

Ressentiment and Schismogenesis

The rapid crystallization of public opinion along ethnic lines can be explained by using Gregory Bateson's (1972) concept of "schismogenesis," a communication

---

6. For a detailed exposition of the media in Serbia, Croatia, and Bosnia and Herzegovina immediately before and during the wars in Croatia and Bosnia and Herzegovina, see Thompson 1994.

pattern of increasing opposition. As both parties assume progressively extreme attitudes, "positive feedback" effects rapidly escalate toward polarization, and polarization into binary opposition. In a modern (or postmodern) society, communications media link mass publics into symbolic interaction processes, within which mutual perceptions and misperceptions constitute systemic relationships and patterns. Unless checked by mitigating and countervailing factors, such progressive opposition leads toward schism.

In the split images I observed in Yugoslavia, each side consistently presented itself as a victim or potential victim, and the Other as a threat or potential threat. No party responded to the Other directly, but only to its own projections of the Other. By reacting to the Other as a threat, each side "as Other" appeared even more threatening.

While making these observations, I puzzled over the relation between the contemporary discourses of victimization I was hearing and the nationalist ideologies that they were being used to resuscitate. Liah Greenfeld's (1992) rediscovery of the concept *ressentiment* in the interpretation of major European nationalist ideologies points to an inherent connection between "resentment" against Others and the historical circumstances under which each ideology originated. By extension, to revive the nineteenth-century concepts of the "nation" that originated in opposition to the rule of foreign empires required new nourishment from contemporary grievances.

During the 1980s, recurrent economic conflicts disrupted Titoist "unity" on a regional basis. Republic leaders used the idiom of victimization to rally public opinion on both sides of the divide between the more developed republics (Slovenia and Croatia) in the northwest and the less developed republics to the south and east. Leaders representing the "richer" republics argued (with justification) that their efficiency was exploited by the federal government to subsidize the inefficiency of the poorer regions. In contrast, leaders from the less developed republics pointed out (also with justification) that their raw materials were being extracted for industrial processing and then sold back to them in the form of profitable finished goods, in the classical colonial pattern. The people on each side of the divide developed a growing sense of victimization at the hands of those on the other. The sense of mutual economic victimization was already well developed when the Kosovo Serbs first appealed for public attention.

The protests of the Kosovo Serbs aroused growing sympathy on the part of the public in Serbia proper, but indifference and even antipathy elsewhere. Public opinion in each republic took shape around its own construction of grievances and threats, so that the Serbian narrative focused on the grievances of the Kosovo Serbs, while the Slovenian-Croatian narrative focused on the threat represented by Milošević and the Serbs themselves. A schismatic communication pattern crystallized along the following lines:

First, in Serbia politicians, news media, and leading intellectuals emphasized the grievances of Kosovo Serbs, as well as the recovery of historical memories that had been either deemphasized or suppressed during the Tito era. As more incidents were reported to the public, Serbs widely identified with their co-ethnics and grew increasingly frustrated over the lack of sympathy that these grievances evoked from non-Serbs. When Milošević presented himself as "savior" before the Serbian public, he articulated a revitalization of Serbian identity that used the Kosovo Serbs as a symbolic focus.

Serbs throughout Yugoslavia saw the Kosovo "drama" as portraying the situation of all Serbs who lived within republics and autonomous provinces dominated by other nationalities. They interpreted the lack of institutional response from Yugoslav authorities as an indication that Serbs elsewhere would also be sacrificed to maintain control by dominant ethnic groups. Their sense of threat was encouraged by media presentations in Belgrade that extended the meaning of "genocide" beyond its literal definition of physical extermination to include the elimination of a *culture* from a territory, should its population be coerced to leave or assimilate. The use of the word "genocide" subliminally linked the current troubles in Kosovo to the mass exterminations of Serbs in the pro-Nazi Independent State of Croatia during World War II.

Second, Party leaders from other republics, particularly Slovenia and Croatia, supported the ethnic Albanian leaders in Kosovo, discounted the claims of Kosovo Serbs as fabrications, and turned Milošević himself into the main issue. For them, the "anti-bureaucratic revolution" threatened to disrupt constitutional stability. The fact that ethnic Serbs far outnumbered any other single ethnic population gave impetus to fears of their renewed domination and was manifested in the widening Serbian versus anti-Serbian split in the Yugoslav party and in media representations to the public.

The Slovenian and Croatian publics were presented with a threat that was very real to them: the specter of domination by a recentralized federal state, controlled by an authoritarian Milošević and the Yugoslav Army, whose officer corps was predominantly Serbian by ethnic background (although not primarily from Serbia itself). The specter of a powerful Serbian leader evoked historical memories of the Serbian royal dynasty, which autocratically ruled Yugoslavia before World War II. The word "Belgrade," employed as a code, exploited the fact that Yugoslavia's capital happened to be in Serbia to link an earlier period of actual Serbian domination with the prospect of its recurrence.

In schismatic communication, each side persists in interpreting new information in terms of its own preconceptions. As Serbian mass rallies proliferated and caused governmental shakeups within Serbia, Serbs were perplexed and distressed over their failure to win support for what seemed to them a just cause. Why, they would ask, do the Slovenes support human rights for everyone except Serbs in Kosovo? The Serbs failed to understand why others did not share their self-perception of victimization. Their disappointment turned to hurt, then to outrage, fueling support for their leaders' attacks against the "northwest republics" (meaning Slovenia and Croatia).[7] Viewed from the other side, the larger and more successful the mass rallies grew, the more they appeared to confirm Slovenian and Croatian fears of Serbian domination. The earlier indifference of Slovenian and Croatian public opinion developed into more active hostility against Serbian views of the situation.

On a personal level, Serbs vacationing or visiting in Croatia and Slovenia experienced hostility and harassment from ordinary citizens, often directed against automobiles bearing license plates with the identifying initials of Serbian cities, particularly Belgrade. Incidents reported in the news were augmented and personalized by firsthand accounts from friends and relatives who experienced harassment. There was no equivalent hostility expressed toward visitors to Serbia, in part of course because the tourist industry is much smaller in Serbia. When Serbs finally boycotted the Adriatic coastal resorts in Croatia in 1990, Croats widely rejected their tales of harassment, preferring to accuse Serbian nationalists of trumping up a pretext that lost revenues for the tourist industry.

What mitigating factors might have counteracted such schismatic perceptions? Attempting to comprehend the opposing viewpoints, I was struck by the absence of what I called "cross-sympathy" between the members of ethnic groups in conflict. In my notes, I commented on the absence in either public or private discourse of efforts to "take the role of the Other." Once an issue was defined in terms of ethnic counterposition, sympathies went to "our" people, without regard for whatever the "other" people were trying to express or how much they were themselves aggrieved. Thus few Serbs were concerned about the ethnic Albanians suffering under the state of emergency imposed to control Albanian protests in Kosovo (see K. Anderson 1990). Interethnic alliances were based on mutual self-interest. Thus Slovenian and Croatian support for Albanian control over Kosovo represented an alliance of convenience in order to maintain the decentralized structure of the 1974 constitution, rather than solidarity with the Albanian cause as such. (Slovenian and Croatian public concern for Kosovo Albanians vanished once the 1990 elections put noncommunist governments in control of those republics.)

From Kosovo to Slovenia

During the fall of 1989, the constitutional crisis provoked by the Slovenian amendment enabling secession was followed by a rehearsal of what it would

7. A major public confrontation between Serbian and Slovenian views of the Kosovo conflict occurred in February 1989, when Slovenian politicians and intellectuals met in Ljubljana to demonstratively support Albanian protesters and denounce the Serbian side. This event, known elliptically as "Cankarjev Dom" for the name of the auditorium in which it occurred, shocked and estranged Serbian television viewers. Documents showing both Slovenian and Serbian views are compiled in Belić and Bilbija 1989.

mean to turn republic boundaries into international borders. In late November, the Kosovo Serbs and their supporters planned a rally in Slovenia's capital to convey the "truth" about Serbian grievances in Kosovo. When Slovenian authorities denied permission for an outdoor gathering, the employees of socialist enterprises in Serbian cities signed up to travel by busload and trainload to Slovenia's capital, Ljubljana. Slovenia's response was to close its border on the designated date. The rally was canceled. Milošević declared a retaliatory economic boycott against Slovenian products and businesses that further escalated Serbian-Slovenian antagonism.

While visiting my dentist in Belgrade at the time, I remarked: "Isn't it understandable that Slovenes fear having so many Serbs arrive at once? How would you react if the same thing happened in reverse, in Belgrade?" The dentist threw up his hands in exasperation: "Let them come! Demonstrators from anywhere in Yugoslavia come here whenever they want!" I had to concede his point, myself having observed convoys and processions of demonstrators in the federal capital. However, the dialogue illustrated that it was not enough for a Belgrade resident to use his own experience to judge the reaction of a Slovene, or vice-versa. On the contrary, for my dentist to imagine himself as a Slovene actually increased his bewilderment and irritation at behavior that was *unlike* what he would do in the Other's place.

In the absence of credible contrary viewpoints, perceptions on all sides grew progressively exaggerated. In the months to follow, the nationalist movements in Serbia, Croatia, and Slovenia held rallies, demonstrations, and marches. The participants rallied behind symbols that represented their own ethnic nation, not simply in its own right, but as opposed to others. As communicated schismatically over mass media, these demonstrations projected the radical reformulations of cultural and mental images that Wallace (1956) associated with "revitalization movements," which mobilize massively around symbols and leaders offering change, often without regard for reality checks or consequences.

Croatia and the Krajina Serbs

During the fall of 1989, the contests for power that had been self-generated within the boundaries of Yugoslavia and among its communist establishment converged with the historical collapse of communism in Eastern Europe. As Soviet bloc regimes fell, so did the wider frame of geopolitical assumptions that had maintained Titoism in Yugoslavia. New organizations and parties quickly formed around a wide spectrum of viewpoints that had been proscribed under Titoism. Most new parties and their programs were not created *ex nihilo*, but were rediscovered as political leaders of the past were rehabilitated and their ideas were retrieved from the historical dustbin. Liberal-democratic and populist programs were revived by intellectuals in the republic capitals, together with movements for pluralism, human rights, and civil society elsewhere in Eastern Europe.

The public politics of nationalism had been contained within the Communist League's embattled republic leaderships. But that situation changed abruptly when the Communist League of Yugoslavia disbanded, in front of TV cameras, at its televised "extraordinary congress" a mere four months after the Slovenian parliament had ignored the Party's command structure to adopt its amendment on secession. Slovenia and Croatia scheduled elections for April and May, and new parties proliferated. In Croatia and Serbia however, the pluralistic celebration was darkened by the appearance of nationalist extremists.

In Croatia, the Croatian Democratic Union (Hrvatska Demokratska Zajednica, known by its initials HDZ) revived ideas and symbols associated with the pro-Nazi Ustasha, who had committed genocide against Serbs, Jews, and Gypsies during World War II. While the "mass movement" twenty years earlier had concealed any connections with Ustasha supporters and apologists, the HDZ refused to disassociate itself from the wartime Independent State of Croatia. Meanwhile, in Serbia and in the Serb-inhabited Krajina region of Croatia, the wartime Serbian nationalist Chetniks were reincarnated in the form of young men flaunting the beards and insignia considered anathema during the Titoist years.[8]

The HDZ electoral campaign featured mass rallies addressed by the party's chief founder and presidential candidate, Franjo Tudjman, while crowds waved flags featuring the same red-and-white "chessboard" (*šahovnica*) emblem used by the wartime fascist state. HDZ supporters defended the emblem as a traditional Croatian symbol of medieval origin. However, survivors of the Ustasha genocide saw the "chessboard" as equivalent to the swastika, symbolizing a concept of Croatian statehood that had attempted to physically eliminate the Serbian population from its territory. The HDZ sought to redefine the republic of Croatia as the national state of ethnic Croats, in which non-Croats would be reduced to a lesser status as "minorities."

At the time of the election, the majority of Croatia's voters supported more moderate parties. However, with 44 percent of the vote, the HDZ took a majority of the seats in parliament and installed Tudjman as president. When I visited Zagreb in early June, souvenir stands on the downtown plazas were filled with items displaying nationalist symbols, but it was not yet clear how much of the HDZ campaign rhetoric the new government planned to implement. Once Tudjman was elected, he might have dropped the most provocative aspects of the program, considering that many Croats as well as Serbs were disturbed by the HDZ's Ustasha associations. Instead, the Tudjman government announced the

8. There is considerable literature in English on the Chetniks, of which Tomasevich 1975 represents the most comprehensive scholarship. Curiously, there is no equivalent body of work on the Ustasha or its wartime Independent State of Croatia. The largest Ustasha death camp at Jasenovac is the subject of Dedijer 1992, while Hilberg 1985: 708–18 summarizes Ustasha conduct of genocide against Jews.

heavily symbolic action of changing the names of public squares and streets to commemorate figures promoted by Croatian nationalism, including wartime Ustasha leaders. Renaming the "Victims of Fascism Square" to honor "great Croats," Tudjman's new government was seen as attempting to erase the memory of the wartime victimization of Croatian antifascists as well as that of the crimes committed against the Serbs, Jews, and Gypsies.

In late July, when the new government officially took power, the event was dramatized by the ostentatious lowering of the flags with red stars and the raising of flags emblazoned with the *šahovnica*. President Tudjman squelched any hope of reconciliation with the Serbs of Croatia in his address to parliament that day. He characterized their protests against the HDZ program with the following remarks: "We are faced with a scenario that wishes to *kosovize* Croatia. [The Serbs] wish to destabilize Croatia and provoke the necessity of armed and military intervention. They wish to overturn the legitimately elected government. . . . Those are the verbatim words of meetings we know about, held several weeks ago, and according to the scenario in which gatherings are also being held by the *allegedly threatened Serbian population in Croatia*" (Tudjman 1990: 10, emphases added).[9] Referring to a rally held by Serbs on the same day, Tudjman asserted "that assembly was not provoked by any of our actions, harmful actions, toward the Serbian population, but has been scripted and stage-managed." The objective of the "scenario" was to "continue with the old hegemonic and other anti-democratic and anti-Croatian politics" (Tudjman 1990: 10).

By invoking Kosovo, Tudjman incorporated the problem of Serbs in Croatia within the schismatic image already imprinted upon Croatian public opinion, in which the grievances of Serbs were *merely* tools of a "scenario" scripted in Belgrade to impose Serbian domination over all of Yugoslavia. The neologism "kosovize" (*kosovizirati*) makes that analogy explicit. That interpretation denied the legitimacy of the grievances of the Krajina Serbs by turning Croatia instead into the victim of Milošević and his allies in Belgrade. By equating "hegemonic" and "anti-Croatian," Tudjman appealed to the *ressentiment* of all Croats faced with a common threat. Belief in their own "victimization" prevented the Croats from feeling any sympathy for the plight of Serbs in a Croatia refashioned along nationalist lines.

The most painful and inflammatory issue among Serbs in Croatia was the real genocide of the Second World War, not the "cultural" and demographic genocide said to be occurring in Kosovo. Extermination sites in Croatia and Bosnia and Herzegovina were potential reminders of the past; and for the sake of postwar interethnic accommodation, the Titoist government had prohibited the excavation of mass graves and reburial of victims according to traditional rites. When some collective grave sites were opened, and the remains of the victims were disinterred for reburial with Orthodox rites, under the eye of the media from Serbia

---

9. The awkward syntax in this passage is in the original Croatian, and is not due to my translation.

the World War II genocide was activated as a focus for Serb/Croat polarization.[10] But it turned out that the Croatian cause had its own graves to excavate, and its own skeletons to display: the remains of Ustasha and other Croatian forces killed in mass executions by the Partisans, which were photographed for a Croatian media campaign representing an ultimate in competitive victimization.

Following Tudjman's parliamentary address and the raising of "chessboard" flags throughout the republic, Croatia's new government enacted the restoration of additional symbols associated with the Ustasha regime. In predominantly Serbian Knin, when policemen were ordered to replace the red stars on their caps with "chessboard" shields, they rebelled instead. When Serbs and Croats armed themselves to guard their villages against each other, they were taking a definitive step in turning from neighbors into enemies.

Conclusion: Nationalist Statehood and "Noble Lies"

Considering the range of possibilities that arose during the "moment" of East European transformation in 1989, why did so many Yugoslavs gravitate toward leaders and slogans that portended a return to violence? Both Serbian and Croatian nationalists claimed overlapping territories, far larger than their respective republics, which could not be annexed peacefully. However, in the rush to reclaim anachronistic ideologies of statehood, people on all sides argued contrary-to-fact propositions as if they were self-evident truths while shutting their ears to information that didn't fit their "own" nationalist versions. In everyday communication, "ordinary people" on all sides stopped listening to each other, either in person or as conveyed by the media. While never voting explicitly for war, majorities followed their nationalist leaders, step by step, into making war against each other.

Narratives of victimization and threat, linking the present with the past and projecting onto the future, had a powerful effect on individuals previously uninvolved with or opposed to nationalist ideas. Only those with intellectual viewpoints outside the ethnic nationalist framework were capable of resisting excessive claims of endangerment to "our people." "Yugoslavs" who resisted nationalist claims on all sides were outnumbered by those who uncritically followed their "own" nationalists to the exponentially increasing degrees of extremism that emerged with the multiparty competition for power during 1990.

While passing through the Dubrovnik airport in August 1990, I chatted with a young ticket agent. He remarked on how well I spoke "Croatian," although I use the standard Serbian variant of the joint Serbo-Croatian language. To create a separate Croatian language for its separate nation-state, the Tudjman govern-

10. For detailed discussions of the symbolic opposition of excavations of Serbs massacred by the Ustashas as well as of Croats massacred by Partisans, see Denich 1994 and Hayden 1993.

ment was introducing vocabulary lists to replace words used in all variants of the shared language. The word lists were largely resurrected from the wartime Ustasha state, whose language reform was considered absurd during the postwar decades by people who assumed it could never happen again. However, my Dubrovnik interlocutor defended the new Croatian language laws, declaring: "Why should non-Croats settle in Dubrovnik and go on speaking just as they did where they came from?" He was nonplussed when I replied that, considering my own relocation to Boston from elsewhere, nobody expected me to speak like a native Bostonian.

Back in Belgrade, friends were aghast at the sight of tough-looking neo-Chetniks peddling magazines and memorabilia on Knez Mihailova street, the city's freshly renovated center of fashion and culture. Among the items for sale was a magazine published by university students in the Serbian city of Kragujevac. My host, a World War II Partisan veteran, protested: "How can these nationalists have their center in Kragujevac, which suffered so much from the Chetniks during the war?" A few months earlier, he had shrugged off my question about the possibility of a Chetnik revival with the hyperbolic declaration: "There isn't a cornfield in Serbia where a throat wasn't cut by Chetniks. Serbia will never want that again." His son-in-law introjected: "How can they print that stuff, when they know it is all lies." Out of my mouth popped: "Maybe they want *their own lies*."

After returning to Boston, I came upon the following explanation: "Myths of foundings, transformations, and redemptions, whether represented in recognizable myths or embedded in accounts of developmental states, correspond to *Plato's noble lie*. . . . Such myths of disjunction are the *foundation points for all states*" (Apter 1987: 303, emphases added).

The Yugoslav Dark Side of Humanity

A View from a Slovene Blind Spot

Rajko Muršič

The more anthropologists write about the United States, the less we believe
what they say about Samoa.
—Bernard DeVoto, cited in Damatta 1994: 124

According to the myths for ordinary people told by the "old regime" in former
Yugoslavia, everything that happened in the country after the collapse of communism was predictable. One such story was a prophecy that Yugoslavia would
disappear in war after Tito's death. The story did not say whether the Russians,
or NATO, or both would occupy Yugoslavia. Even without an attack by an external power, catastrophe seemed inevitable. Tito and other leaders repeatedly
claimed that there was no alternative to a socialist and federative Yugoslavia and
that the reestablishment of bourgeois parties would bring Yugoslavia to civil war.

Immediately after Tito's death in 1980, the government and the people chan-
ted with one voice: "*Po Titu Tito; Posle Tita Tito*" (Tito after Tito). Still, this
magic spell lost its power as early as 1981 when the dissolution of the state began

The author would like to thank Dunja Rihtman-Auguštin, Natalija Vrečer, Joel M. Halpern, and
Božidar Jezernik for comments, suggestions, and corrections on earlier drafts of this paper.

with demonstrations in Kosovo. The prophecy about the future of Yugoslavia became self-fulfilling, and "the Yugoslavs," with the generous help of others, finally destroyed Yugoslavia.

The brutal conflicts in former Yugoslavia, especially in Bosnia and Herzegovina, soon became one of the world's worst problems. The atrocities affected everyone who saw news reports from Vukovar, Dubrovnik, Sarajevo, Srebrenica, Mostar, and elsewhere. It was impossible not to feel compassion for the victims, but the war was also very difficult to understand. When the United Nations and the European Union started their "humanitarian operation," their reactions were unbelievably chaotic. As many journalists, politicians, and intellectuals began to talk and write about the conflict, it became obvious that by and large they did not understand the events they were writing about.

Any analysis of the events in former Yugoslavia that avoids moral issues borders on the hypocritical. The analyses of such conflicts and tragedies are far beyond value-free science. However, since one cannot be a neutral observer, the essential question remains how can individuals transcend opinion (*doxa*) to approach knowledge (*episteme*). In this respect writing about a war is the most difficult of intellectual tasks. Consequently, the most profound essays and reports about the conflict are by authors from the area (e.g., Osmančević 1994). But who reads them? Anthropology as a discipline is also presumably in a position to throw some light on this dark side of "humanity." But can it? Below, then, I discuss the role, potentials, and limits of anthropology in efforts to explain the tragedy of the former Yugoslavia.

Before discussing anthropology's role, I first present some subjective views on what happened in the former Yugoslavia. My writing is neither objective analysis nor moralistic lamentation.[1] I offer what I hope is a rational explanation of why Yugoslavia fell apart. Essentially, as I suggest, it fell apart because it could not be democratized once the "self-managed" economy, its socialist ideology, and the system that ensured the parity of its constitutive federal units collapsed. Nationalism was not a cause but a consequence of the struggle for "Tito's heritage." The wars in former Yugoslavia are not ethnic; they are wars of territorial expansion initiated by Serbia under the cover of the name "Yugoslavia."

The War and the Power of the Self-Fulfilling Prophecy

> Q: "Why did you beat him?" A: "Because he beat me back!"
> —Žarko Petan, cited in Miheljak 1989: 323.

There is nothing as incomprehensible as war. It has its own astonishing logic and is beyond anything that ordinary experience offers. Particular wars may be

---

1. The present work may not be strictly scholarly, for I never did fieldwork in former Yugoslavia outside Slovenia, and my research interests are not oriented toward ethnicity and nationalism. Instead, as a citizen, I was involved vicariously in the dissolution of the state. Here I am only challenging "theories" about former Yugoslavia to better understand how and why the state collapsed.

explained historically. Warfare, in general, may follow the logic of game theory, expected utility theory, or catastrophe and chaos theory (see Casti 1993: 253–322). But these theories can't provide an ultimate explanation for warfare. It challenges our morality. Its victims pressure our conscience. By knowing war, we are part of it. There is no escape.

The wars in former Yugoslavia have been a shuddering combination of the abuse of power to achieve political goals and the exploitation of urban-rural conflict in an aggressive struggle for territory. The crucial reason for deciding to use force was that the goals of the Serbian political regime were compatible with the goals of the Yugoslav Army. The maximum goal was to control all of former Yugoslavia, the lesser goal to control as much territory as possible. A minimum goal was control over Kosovo and Vojvodina, though this was already achieved by amendments to the Serbian Constitution in 1989.

If the new united Serbia did not become the governing part of the Yugoslav Federation, and if other republics tried to "secede," then Serbia planned to annex all territories outside the Republic of Serbia inhabited by Serbs (their "ancient hearths"). That is why the Yugoslav Army and "paramilitaries" destroyed sacred religious monuments and burned non-Serbian villages. In Bosnia and Herzegovina, there were no bursts of passion. This was a planned genocide[2] rarely motivated by ancient hatreds.[3]

Ethnic cleansing, concentration camps, and mass murders are tools of war. Ethnic cleansing[4] is a "political" name for the appropriation of land. There were three states fighting for the same territories: Serbia, Croatia, and Bosnia and Herzegovina. Concentration camps were formed to control potential soldiers.[5] Mass murder became a military operation to neutralize potential enemy forces.

2. However, we must recognize that the Bosnian resistance was a legitimate defense of the state. Furthermore, the army of Bosnia and Herzegovina was not organized on ethnic lines.

3. Contrary to superficial opinion, the Bosnian Muslims were very tolerant. However, the Serbs carried a very old grudge. The medieval Kingdom of Serbia was defeated by the Ottoman Turks in 1389 and militant Serbs still conflate Bosnian Muslims with Turks. Their irrational fear of Bosnia/Turkey motivated their "defense." For Serbian extremists, reality was/is quite a complex mixture of illusion, passion, and fear which Milošević has manipulated very efficiently.

4. In military doctrine, "cleansing" is neutralizing territory from remaining enemy forces (Silber and Little 1995: 188). In Yugoslav discourse, the term "ethnically clean" emerged after 1981 in Kosovo with the accusation, by federal and Serbian authorities, of an alleged plan of Kosovo Albanians to create a Serb-free Kosovo. Serbian media in the 1980s used the term "ethnically clean" extensively. "Ethnic cleansing" as a technique was also not new. In the nineteenth century, after Serbia's emergence from under the Turkish *Pašaluk* of Belgrade, all signs of Islamic culture were demolished (cf. Jezernik 1995) and the remaining "Turks" (including Muslim Albanians) were deported to Turkey (Islami 1989: 50–52).

5. There were few camps for women. Nevertheless, rape became a weapon in Bosnia and Herzegovina. (There were also cases of male sexual abuse.) We also must remember the massive 1980s hysteria when Serbs from Kosovo accused Albanians of raping Serbian women (cf. Jalušič and Kuzmanić 1989). Whatever its truth, it gave Serbian soldiers an opportunity for "revenge" on Muslim women.

We must keep in mind that the so-called Republika Srpska had weapons but not enough men, unlike the legitimate government of Bosnia and Herzegovina, which lacked weapons but had manpower.

Socialist Yugoslavia had been a militaristic state. The army was integrated into civil life and strengthened by the mythology of the victorious National Liberation Struggle during World War II. The "Yugoslavs" were well prepared for war. However, no one believed the army would ever be involved in "internal" conflicts.[6] If the military and political leaders in Belgrade wanted to stop the "irregulars," they could have easily done so before the outbreak of the war. On the contrary, the governing institutions in Belgrade actually engaged the bandits' support of their aims.[7] Besides, the international community also lacked the will to prevent the use of force.

Yugoslavia Between Utopia and Balkanization

> Whoever attacks the equality of nations, the federal set-up, whoever attempts to take away the factories from the workers, or to raise the question of Yugoslavia's independence—we'll break his neck!
> —Edvard Kardelj, cited in Silber and Little 1995: 35

The idea of creating a common South Slav state or of gaining adequate territory within the Hapsburg empire began in the early nineteenth century with the so-called Illyrian movement, also known as Illyrianism or South Slavism (see Rogel 1994: 7) in Croatian and Slovene areas of the empire. It was one of many European nationalist movements at the time. This "awakening of the nations" emerged as a response to Hapsburg Germanization policies that sought to impose German high culture on the educational system and official and government institutions. At the same time, after uprisings at the beginning of the century, Serbia and later Montenegro liberated themselves from Turkish occupation and were internationally recognized in 1878.

A logical consequence of the nineteenth-century programs was the creation of the South Slav state (*Država SHS*) in October 1918. It was not internationally recognized but was soon united with the then sovereign states of Serbia and Montenegro in the Kingdom of Serbs, Croats, and Slovenes on December 1,

6. In former Yugoslavia the armed forces were divided into two parts, the Yugoslav Peoples' Army and the Territorial Defense units. The latter were under the jurisdiction of the federal republics. The former were controlled by the federation with Tito as their commander-in-chief. Republican police forces managed border crossings, while the regular army controlled the borders. Therefore, the attempt of the army and federal police forces to take over Slovenian border crossings in June 1991 was formally illegal.

7. Rebels began to obtain arms in Krajina in 1990. The first barricades in Knin appeared in August 1990. When Croatian police tried to stop this, the Yugoslav Peoples' Army prevented their actions.

1918 (Rogel 1994: 15; Vodopivec 1994: 28–29; *Zgodovina Slovencev* 1979: 597). It was not constituted as a federal republic, as had been planned in Zagreb and Ljubljana, but as a centralized kingdom under the rule of the Serbian king. A constitutional monarchy was established by the "Vidovdan" Constitution on June 28, 1921 (*Zgodovina Slovencev* 1979: 633; Pirjevec 1995: 11; Rogel 1994: 16).

The "First Yugoslavia" was formed at the Versailles Peace Conference as part of the Great Power goal to dismember the Austro-Hungarian Empire. The new political unit was established as the nation-state of the unformed Yugoslav nation. It consisted mainly of Serb, Croat, and Slovene national components, with Serbs as the leading group. Unlike the Croats and Slovenes, the Serbs had fought on the side of the victorious Allied Powers. Croatia, Slovenia, and Bosnia and Herzegovina, as part of the Austro-Hungarian Empire, had been members of the losing alliance of the Central Powers. In a way they were war booty.

Thus the Serbian nation became the hegemonic element in the new Yugoslav nation-state. Formally, in the Kingdom of Serbs, Croats and Slovenes there were political parties operating throughout the whole territory of the kingdom. But in fact, they were mostly formed on a national basis (the *Croat* Peasant Republican Party, the *Slovene* People's Party, the Yugoslav *Muslim* Organization, the Serbian-controlled *Yugoslav* Democratic Party, the *Yugoslav* Radical Union, etc.). This political system was extremely unstable. In ten years there were more than twenty-five governments (Pirjevec 1995: 49).

Democracy was partly suspended in 1920–21 when the Socialist Worker's Party of Yugoslavia, the Communist Party, and other communist organizations were prohibited (*Zgodovina Slovencev* 1979: 632–33). Finally, after the assassination of Croatian political leader Stjepan Radić in 1928 the king proclaimed a royal dictatorship in January 1929 (*Zgodovina Slovencev* 1979: 655–85) and the new name for the kingdom, Yugoslavia, was officially announced on October 3, 1929 (Rogel 1994: 16). The king's policy in the 1930s was "One King, One State, One Nation, One Language" (Pirjevec 1995: 60). Does it sound familiar?

Belgrade's hegemony over the first Yugoslavia generated conflicts between Croats and Serbs that escalated during World War II. The only force prepared to resist the Germans, Italians, and other occupying powers was the Yugoslav Communist Party. In 1941, because it had been illegal for twenty years, it was well organized, though not very large. Tito and the communists succeeded in uniting the peoples of former Yugoslavia via a utopian social compact and proclaimed the idea of a new federal state. During the war, the second Yugoslavia was proclaimed by the communists as a federal state consisting of six federal units (Slovenia, Croatia, Bosnia and Herzegovina, Serbia with the two autonomous provinces Kosovo/Metohija and Vojvodina, Montenegro, and Macedonia) and five sovereign nations (*narodi*) (the Slovenes, Croats, Serbs, Montenegrins, and Macedonians).[8] Regarding the right of self-determination, the founding nations established the nation-states (republics) and simultaneously they united in a federation.

As early as the 1920s, the Yugoslav Marxists had worked on national liberation programs.[9] Tito followed Lenin and Stalin's successful formula of national liberation, combined with instructions from the Third International. The program of national liberation was essential to the success of the communist revolution in the former Yugoslavia.[10] However, after the split with Stalin in 1948, Tito and his comrades were on their own. They tried to impose one of the most "democratic" systems of utopian socialism, anarchism, and Marxism—workers' self-management. The first "Workers' Councils" were established in 1950 in accordance with the declaration of the "Four D's": democratization, decentralization, "debureaucratization," and destalinization (Pirjevec 1995: 208).

The two basic principles for the second Yugoslavia (1943–91) were socialist revolution and the Federal Constitution. Under Tito's leadership, an efficient centralized power maintained the state. Furthermore, the majority of people in former Yugoslavia believed in Tito. They not only assumed his "ideas," but also adopted the authorities' ideas as their own. Many were fanatical believers and were successfully interpellated[11] into the Yugoslav reality. As long as enough ordinary people acted as believers in self-management, one of the bases of support for the second Yugoslavia was affirmed. But when this confidence was lost and a new orientation emerged involving elements of a plural political system and market economy, then questions about the preexisting Federal Constitution inevitably came to the fore.

The first challenge was demonstrations in Prishtina, Kosovo, at the end of March 1981, which ruling Party officials characterized as "counterrevolutionary." This was a typical ideological attempt to cover up the facts. Indeed, if we are to understand the violent dissolution of former Yugoslavia, we must first consider the Kosovo problem[12] that was the contradictory core of the "Yugoslav"

8. Macedonians were for the first time recognized as a nation (*narod*). Later, in the 1960s, a Muslim nation of Slavic origin and Muslim religious affiliation living in Bosnia and Herzegovina, Serbia, and Montenegro was recognized as a nation. Still, the territory of Bosnia and Herzegovina was not constituted as a nation-state.

9. The Slovene national branch of the Yugoslav Communist Party was established in 1920 (Klopčič 1969). The Slovene communists proclaimed their national program, based on the right of self-determination, between 1923 and 1926 (Klopčič 1984: 180).

10. In fact, all genuine communist revolutions (not enforced by foreign intervention) were related to national liberation (Anderson 1983: 12; Szporluk 1991: 345, 360; Connor 1991: 313).

11. In Althusser's concept of interpellation (1980) individuals recognize ideology as their own.

12. The conflict in Kosovo has deep roots. Kosovo is where the medieval Serbian kingdom was defeated by the Turks in 1389. During the Balkan Wars (1912–13), Serbia occupied (or liberated) Kosovo. After World War I, Yugoslavia started to deport Albanians to Turkey. During World War II, Albanians collaborated with the Italian occupiers. After the war, deportations continued and police oppression ceased only after the fall of Aleksandar Ranković in 1966.

problem.[13] It is precisely in Kosovo where post-Tito Yugoslavia especially failed to implement both "brotherhood and unity" and self-management socialism.

The period after Tito's death thus resulted in a struggle for power. Besides events in Kosovo, there was a struggle for changes in the 1974 Federal Constitution (see Ribičič and Tomac 1989 and Miheljak 1995: 53) and growth of a so-called antibureaucratic revolution in Serbia. These developments were additionally complicated by an ongoing economic crisis and the "shock therapy" insisted on by international aid agencies.[14] For the sake of economic efficiency, administrative centralization was encouraged, but this took on authoritarian dimensions. Though, on one hand, centralization was equated to "Serbianization" of the federal state, on the other, a process of liberalization and democratization characterized the communist parties of the republics, especially Slovenia, and autonomous civil society also proliferated, again most effectively in Slovenia (see Mastnak 1992: 54–64, 103–8). The crucial period was after 1986, when Milan Kučan became president of the Slovene League of Communists, and Slobodan Milošević became secretary of the Serbian League of Communists. After these developments the directions of policy development in Slovenia and Serbia diverged. Though Milošević began to mobilize the Serbian masses to attain power, Kučan initiated a process of democratization that sought to lead the Yugoslav state toward Western standards of "consensual democracy" (Kučan 1989: viii; see Rupel 1994). These policies were incompatible. The army and authoritarian federal representatives in Belgrade found Milošević's policy more acceptable.

At the eighth session of the Central Committee of the Serbian League of Communists in 1987 Milošević managed to unseat the president of the Socialist Republic of Serbia, Ivan Stambolić. After that "soft coup" he controlled all power in Serbia and, through his political allies, a great deal of power in the federation. Later he dismissed the "bureaucrats" in the autonomous provinces of Vojvodina and Kosovo and put his men in leading positions among the Serbian populations in Bosnia and Herzegovina and Croatia. For every political move he utilized the support of the anxious and frustrated Serbian masses from Kosovo or *lumpen proletariat* from Belgrade and Serbia. As earlier for Tito, Milošević's picture

13. In political discourse about Kosovo, exaggerated, mobilizing terms were extensive. These included "genocide" (supposedly conducted against Serbs by Albanians via their enormous birthrate), "terror," "ethnically clean province," "rape with nationalistic intentions" (a legal term in Socialist Republic of Serbia's legislation after 1981!) (cf. Gaber and Kuzmanić 1989). These expressions anticipated the subsequent violence in Croatia and Bosnia and Herzegovina. The organizers of Serbian demonstrations demanded the use of police and military forces in Kosovo. In mass meetings after 1987 they shouted: "*Idemo na Kosovo!*" and "*Hoćemo oružje!*" (We are going to Kosovo. We want weapons).

14. Before the breakup of Yugoslavia, inflation raged and the currency's value changed daily. Unemployment varied from less than 3 percent in Slovenia to more than 50 percent in Kosovo (Gaber and Kuzmanić 1989). There were permanent shortages of gasoline, soap powder, coffee, electricity, and so on. Between 1987 and 1990 Yugoslavia had "the highest strike rate in the world" (Kuzmanić 1994b: 164).

became an icon in Serbia. Though enormously popular among Serbs, others in the Federation began to fear and hate him.

In the seventy years of the existence of former Yugoslavia (interrupted in World War II), Slovene politicians played an important role in political and constitutional developments. Jože Pirjevec (1995) claims that the relationship between Belgrade and Ljubljana was crucial for the existence of the common state. Slovenes always understood being Yugoslav as a political status implying a state-based legal category. In the late 1980s, Slovenia's main problem was how to establish an economically efficient system with a level of individual freedom and tolerance in accord with Western standards. In Serbia the problem was how to gain control over federal funds, institutions, and the allocation of capital and the repressive apparatus of the state.

Tito's Yugoslavia came to an end in 1989 with adoption of amendments to the Serbian Constitution that essentially stripped the provinces of Kosovo and Vojvodina of their autonomy. In February 1989 Slovene politicians and civil society movements began to support the Kosovo Albanians after repressive methods to "calm" the "situation in Kosovo" failed and violations of human rights became obvious (see Mastnak 1994: 104). Demands of citizens of Kosovo for their human rights were unacceptable to the Serbian authorities and Slovenian support also shocked the ordinary people in Serbia. There were protests in Slovenia against Serbian hegemony and support for the Kosovars. Serbian authorities answered by imposing an economic blockade on Slovenia. There were Stalinist-style trials in Kosovo and pillaging of the National Bank of Yugoslavia by Serbia and Montenegro (Pusić 1995: 49). At the same time, parallel processes of establishing a market economy, privatization, and political liberalization occurred in Slovenia. When Serbia abolished autonomy for Kosovo and Vojvodina, it withheld their representation in federal institutions. Therefore, Serbia with Montenegro had four representatives in the Presidency, the same number as the rest of Yugoslavia (Silber and Little 1995: 77).[15] Former Yugoslavia had become hostage to Serbia and, after 1989, was at a dead end.

The problem of how to implement democracy in a federal state, constituted of nation-states, republics, seemed to be unsolvable.[16] The basic problem was to

15. Decision making in the *SFRJ* Presidency was not based on principles of parity, since its constitutive function was an operative one. However, as the supreme commander of the army, if the majority of its members supported using force against any republic, it could do so legally. According to the Constitution, only the House of Republics and Provinces in the Federal Parliament needed consensus, and only on issues affecting republican sovereignty. The House of the Federation was a tool for manipulation. If any republic would not agree with its decisions, the republic could raise the problem in the Constitutional Court. The paradox was that the Constitutional Court was also divided on national/republican principles. Its votes were the same as votes in other federal institutions. Naturally, people in former Yugoslavia gradually lost trust in federal institutions.

16. Democracy is, actually, applicable in only limited contexts. There are few possibilities for all nations within multinational states to be satisfied, as the particular interests of the constituent nations vary. There is no universal solution. In all multinational states, there are separatist movements

define the political position of the individual republics within the Federation. Further, what of the status of individuals? How was it possible to combine a plural political system with the sovereignty of national components vested in republics? No structuring of political geography could help. There were only two polar possibilities: to eliminate republics or eliminate the federal state.

On a federal level, Serbian leaders, with support from the Serb majority, argued for a "one person–one vote" system. However, this was not acceptable to the small nations, since they would become "a perpetual minority" (Vodopivec 1994: 42). The other option was to implement a plural political system within particular republics and preserve the parity principle in the function of the federation. This was unacceptable to both Serbs and to the central government, since the requirement for consensus would supposedly lead to a deadlocked federation. There were other possibilities, but none satisfied all particular interests. Furthermore, there were no legal means but consensus for radical constitutional change. All remaining possibilities were illegal and illegitimate.[17]

The nationalities in former Yugoslavia were, besides the Communist Party, the only existing constitutive political subjects and they became dominant with the decline in the Party's power. New parties were inevitably formed on national principles. If it had been possible for a supra-national party to win a federal election, it would have done so. Furthermore, political leaders could not solve the problems involved with the implementation of democracy in the former Yugoslavia. "In its 73 Years, Yugoslavia spent more than 60 in stressful conditions" (Vodopivec 1994: 25). Implementing democracy in Slovenia became tied to its sovereignty.

Slovenia, Slovenes, and the "Balkan Powder Keg"

> Once none had the state, then some had it, and finally all have it.
> —Ernest Gellner 1983: 5

For British and other Western European travelers in the eighteenth and nineteenth centuries, the line between civilization and barbarism started at Trieste (see Carmichael 1995a: 8–9, 1995b), and the Balkans seemed like a world turned upside down (Jezernik 1998). For some Westerners Slovenia still has elements of the exotic (e.g., Silber and Little 1995: 49). The prevalent view of Slovenia in the twentieth century by foreign journalists, and even Yugoslav experts, mostly re-

---

or related tensions. Misconceptions of freedom and democracy were the essential "ideals" in the name of which "ethnic conflicts" in former Yugoslavia began. The purpose of "ethnic cleansing" was to make a "perfect democracy" possible.

17. For example, though the Constitution in its Basic Principles spoke of "the right of self-determination for every nation . . . to secession" (*Ustava* 1974: 9) the method for implementing that right was not defined.

lied on a Belgrade-based perspective.[18] Generally, then, Slovenia is a forgotten part of former Yugoslavia (Benderly and Kraft 1994: ix). From the Slovene point of view, it is very frustrating that the majority of experts on Yugoslavia do not even understand Slovene.

The majority of European nationalities, including the Slovenes, appeared historically in the nineteenth century. The Slovene language was first recorded in the eleventh century (Freising Manuscript). The first book printed in Slovene was Primož Trubar's *Abecednik* (1550), a primer subtitled *Peryatil vseh Slouenzou* (A friend of all the Slovenes). Presumably he had in mind Slavs who would understand his writing. At the end of the eighteenth century, some intellectuals started to write in Slovene, although the official language and the language of the upper class, the aristocracy, and townspeople was German, and Slovene was spoken in the countryside. At the beginning of the nineteenth century, the regional divisions of the population by dialect were replaced by the inclusive category "Slovenes."[19]

In 1848, the first claims for a United Slovenia *(Zedinjena Slovenija)* were made. This program, for the first time, articulated demands for cultural and political autonomy *(Zgodovina Slovencev* 1979: 448–50). After World War I, there was no place for new small states within the frame of the Versailles agreement, not withstanding Wilson's emphasis on national self-determination. At the Rapallo peace negotiations in 1920, following the negative result of the plebiscite in southern Carinthia (Austria) on October 10, 1920, one third of the Slovene population remained in Italy and Austria (see Vodopivec 1994: 31). During World War II, Partisan resistance began in April 1941 when the Liberation Front was established in Ljubljana as a coalition led by the Slovene Communist Party. The first Slovene government was constituted in 1944 in Črnomelj *(Zgodovina Slovencev* 1979: 887).

After initial centralization of post–World War II Yugoslavia, the republics subsequently gained control over their own economies, police, education, and science bureaucracies and their regionally based development programs. The army, foreign policy, currency, and financial policy remained under federal control. Former Yugoslavia had no Ministry of Culture. There were, however, six ministries of culture in the country, one in each republic. Without parity among the constituent nations in collective and individual civil rights, such a state could be neither functional nor meaningful for its citizens.

18. An example is the Mazowiecki report on media in former Yugoslavia. Radio *Studio B* from Belgrade, begun in 1970, is mentioned as the first independent radio station in former Yugoslavia (Mazowiecki 1995: 11). However, *Radio Študent* in Ljubljana began to broadcast a year earlier. Still independent and noncommercial, it was extremely influential in developing 1980s Slovene civil society movements.

19. The Slovene people were divided not only by dialect (there are more than five speech groups and more than twenty-four dialects of Slovenian spoken in Slovenia proper and the surrounding area) but more drastically by old administrative borders. Thus, regional identification prevailed.

Crucial factors in the Slovenian democratization process were the different social and cultural movements, like those concerned with peace, feminism, ecology, lesbians, and gays. There were also movements for human rights and against nuclear power (Benderly and Kraft 1994: xi; cf. Mastnak 1992, 1994). The punk movement at the end of the 1970s offered young Slovenes a way to live, not in opposition or confrontation with the system, but outside it. The new "alternative scene" was not a dissident one; it "understood its own action as *the* production of a social sphere" (Mastnak 1994: 95). Police and legal oppression against punks in 1981 led to the organization of a movement for Slovene civil society (Tomc 1994: 120–21). Equally influential was the oppression of independent intellectuals in Belgrade in 1984. Both actions paved the way for discussions about civil and human rights in all of Yugoslavia (see Mastnak 1994: 98). But only in Slovenia did a powerful civil society develop.

In 1988, in Slovenia, in response to governmental suppression of journalists by military trial, the Committee for the Defense of Human Rights was established. Virtually all civil society activists protested against the military trial. Subsequently from various groups within that Committee, new political parties emerged. The democratization and modernization process in Slovenia was therefore predominately a civil rights movement, not a nationalist one. That was the essential difference with the rest of the former Yugoslavia (Mastnak 1992: 105).

In spite of the importance of civil rights movements, it is not possible to overlook Slovene nationalism. It was not strong, but nevertheless became increasingly powerful during the 1980s. Its basic text, "Contributions to the Slovene National Program," appeared in the journal *Nova revija* in 1987 as a reply to the 1986 *Memorandum of the Serbian Academy of Arts and Sciences*. These theses "made a much greater impact in Yugoslavia than on the democratic movement in Slovenia" (Mastnak 1994: 106). Furthermore, some prominent Slovene politicians were internationalist in outlook (Dimitrij Rupel, cited in Benderly and Kraft 1994: xii) and advocated that Slovenia join the European Union in its own right, instead of via Belgrade.

The choice against Belgrade in December 1990 was rational, though somewhat nationalistic (Carmichael 1995a: 12–13). Nonetheless, the process of democratization and development of an independent civil society naturally led to a desire for increased independence. Independence was essential if Slovenes were to be able to control their own destiny. As citizens of an independent state, they, and not an external power, would ultimately determine the course of their lives (Mastnak 1994: 107). In spring 1991, the majority of Slovenes still felt inclined toward "a confederative arrangement" (Vodopivec 1994: 43). However, the June military intervention unleashed a massive nationalistic response. As a non-nationalistic Slovene columnist put it, paraphrasing Brecht: "In the moment when an unasked and uninvited foreign military starts to demonstrate its primitive force in my home area, I become a nationalist, a rude one" (Miheljak 1995:

121). A similar reaction came from the philosopher Slavoj Žižek, who claimed he had not been a Slovene until the aggression (1991: 29).

Nationalism, Nation and Ethnicity—the Balkan "Mess"

> Who can be confident that Yugoslavia and Albania will not one day come to blows?
> —Anderson 1983: 12

Social-cultural anthropology and other social sciences have problems with definitions of dynamic phenomena. To define a dynamic phenomenon, linear description is not enough. There are obvious circular, auto-poetic, elements functioning in these types of conceptions. What is a nation in a European context? It is, basically, a group of people that recognize themselves as a nation. We may add as many descriptions about the meaning of "being a nation," but we can't exclude the circular one. In spite of the growing discussion about the terms "ethnicity," "nation," and "nationalism," it seems that in public as well as in scholarly discourse there is even more confusion about them than before (see Rizman 1989; Tonkin, McDonald, and Chapman 1989; Alonso 1994; Williams 1994; and Banks 1996). The indistinct concepts "nation" and "ethnicity" have equivocal or at least obscure meanings and are therefore of limited use in analysis.

Ethnic phenomena are ambivalent. There are some primordial elements in the creation of ethnic groups, the so-called cultural stuff. However, recognition of common traits is a sufficient condition for the emergence of an ethnic group. Nation as a concept is historically a recent phenomenon that appeared in a stage of development of industrial society (Gellner 1983) and its accompanying ideology (Williams 1994: 53). The concept of nation has always had political dimensions. Nation is a result of a mixture of objective facts and circumstances based on a subjective political will. In some cases "the state produces nations" (Nagengast 1994: 118), in other cases "nations produce states." In Europe, the difference is both geographic and historical. It may be traced in different "zones," as described by Ernest Gellner (1995).

We have to consider the specific conjunctions of political history, religion, and "local" comprehension of *narod* (folk or people) to understand the mobilization of the masses in the former Yugoslavia after the collapse of the Constitution. As anthropologists trying to understand the situation in the former Yugoslavia, we have to start with the natives' understanding of "ethnicity" and "nation."

In Slavic languages *narod* means people, ethnic group, and nation.[20] However,

20. *Nacija* is a related term. The representative institutions of *narod* (in an ethnic sense) are those providing symbolic identity (myth and the value system). Representative institutions of *nacija* (nation-state) are the state institutions, including its ideological and repressive aspects (e.g., its education system, political institutions, state symbols, and security forces). This terminology, derived from other communist states, notably the Soviet Union, is the result of political and ideological development, and is still changing. Western scholars have never accepted communist period solutions as relevant.

the meaning of the term *narod* in Serbian and Croatian is not equivalent to that term in Slovene, and both are different from the English term "nation" (see Mertus, this volume). When foreigners translate those terms, they may make mistakes. For example, Tone Bringa writes that in the former socialist states in Eastern Europe the term *narod* was supposedly used in the sense of Western "ethnic groups" (Bringa 1993: 85). Is this so? In Russian the term *narod* denotes "people," "folk," "population," "nation," and "ethnicity." Soviet republics were formed on a national basis, so the Russian term *natsija* (nation) denoted *narod* with its nation-state/republic, while *natsional'nost* (nationality) denoted ethnic group, i.e. *narod*, without its nation-state/republic. In the Serbian and Croatian languages the terms *narod* and *nacija* have the same meaning as in Russian. Thus the translation of the term *narod,* either as ethnic group or nation, depends on the context.[21] In the Turkish-occupied Balkans the issue was further complicated by adding the notion of subordinate "people" based on religious affiliation (see Lockwood 1975: 26–27). Under the Ottomans ethnic/religious communities were known as *millets,* which were the starting points for creating historical non-Muslim "imagined communities" (Orthodox, Catholic, or Jewish) during the period of Ottoman rule.

Post–World War II political history additionally "complicated" the situation. While Marx and his later followers may have underestimated national and nationalist problems, Lenin did not make the same mistake (see Lenin 1949). On the contrary, in tsarist Russia his expressed concern for the liberation of oppressed nations was extremely important for the success of the October Revolution. At that time there was significant discussion of the question of internal revolution and the right of self-determination by Lenin and Rosa Luxemburg. After World War I, the right of self-determination became an important issue. Woodrow Wilson and Lenin both offered national liberation. The latter had more than one agenda: class liberation as well as national self-determination within a framework of revolutionary change and unitary leadership. By contrast, Wilsonian self-determination was focused on development of a democratic society with political pluralism.

Solving national problems was crucial for the success of both the October Revolution and the "National Liberation Struggle" in former Yugoslavia. Communism was mostly successful in redirecting the national-chauvinistic energy into the building of a totalitarian communist state. In that process the communists made use of the very powerful revolutionary motivation felt by the deprived masses. After the revolution, this energy was carefully controlled. This is the

---

21. The Latin *natio* is related to *narod*. Both have roots in the giving of birth, being born (*nasci, roditi*). It also refers to a breed, a stock, a kind, a race, a tribe, a people (cf. Just 1989: 73, Rizman 1991: 16, and Citron 1991: 207).

origin of the "widespread myth that the communist or socialist systems collapsed because of the growth of nationalist forces" (Kuzmanić 1994b: 159).

Why was a national identification so powerful, especially if "nationalism does not have any very deep roots in the human psyche" (Gellner 1983: 34)? An individual manifests his or her identity in various ways. Certainly individual characteristics and skills (gender, age, profession, age, etc.) determine a person's life more than national identity (Šmitek and Jezernik 1995: 174). However, national identity still remains a strong value which can lead to extremes of self-sacrifice when its sentiments are fully mobilized, especially reinforced by the emotional effects of "in-" or "we-groups" (see Elwert 1989).

After enculturation, an individual can change his/her national/ethnic identity, switch to another frame of reference (see Elwert 1995: 106), but one can't attain skills without acquiring them in some sort of social context. This implies the adoption of an identity. This identity may be cosmopolitan, it may be constructed from various ethnic/national/cultural backgrounds, but it is unavoidable. An individual may deny any personally felt ethnic or national identity. Such lack of personal manifest identity can't, however, change the fact that this individual was raised, educated, and trained within a particular culture (Gellner 1991: 256–57), with a specific language (van den Berghe 1991: 105), and a particular tradition with an associated ideology, *habitus*, etc. No one is raised in some form of "abstract humankind" (Lévi-Strauss 1994: 17).

Identity is not a matter of ideals but of living practice, performance in a status (Barth 1969: 28). One's identity is a part of everyday life, but is not unchanging. It is continually re-created. Even so, the power of nationalism consists, in part, of an ideal to die for. This ideal "is found in the fusion of the ideological and the sensory, the bodily and the social, accomplished by these tropes and evident in strategies of substantialization by which the obligatory is converted into the desirable" (Alonso 1994: 386). Thus national identification is accompanied by emotions that can diminish individual instincts for survival. We need to understand these emotions and observe how they were manifest in former Yugoslavia.

In times of peace tolerance prevailed between the different nationalities in former Yugoslavia, including Bosnia (Lockwood 1975, Bringa 1993). Also in the 1980s, nationalisms in former Yugoslavia were weak. The exception was the tolerated Serbian nationalism, ultimately used to support Milošević's plans. After 1990, the *ancien régime* intervened in order to survive but the pressure and violence employed by the federal state brought forth nationalistic responses. Latent nationalism, articulated in popular jokes and present among some intellectuals, became a mass movement. After beatings of teenage demonstrators by federal authorities in Kosovo in 1981, Albanian nationalism reemerged there. Some elements of defensive nationalism emerged in Slovenia after a trial against journalists in 1988, but nationalism only became a mass movement in response to military actions by the Yugoslav People's Army (JNA) in 1991. The same response occurred earlier in Croatia,[22] and then in Bosnia and Herzegovina. There was even a similar response in Serbia.

Is every manifestation of nationalism inherently "bad?" I belong to a small European nation and I can't imagine abandoning my particular national identification. Slovene culture is pressed in a vice imposed by its presence between the Germanic and Romance worlds. This country is also on the frontier with other South Slavs. As it is therefore a fragile entity, I can't imagine myself not being anxious about the "survival" of my nation. Am I a nationalist?

I agree with the Croatian ethnologist Dunja Rihtman-Auguštin (1995a: 101), who cites the Italian anthropologist Bernardo Bernardi about the bifurcated nature of ethnocentrism with both its positive and pathological aspects. "Positive ethnocentrism offers identity in the modern and postmodern world . . . (while) pathological ethnocentrism results in ethnic cleansing." Every nationalism has both aspects, the "liberal" and "chauvinistic." At this time in Eastern Europe cultural nationalism prevails. Cultural nationalism can coexist with liberalism but chauvinistic nationalism obviously cannot. To contextualize these matters we need to remember that the small nations of Central and Eastern Europe were dually controlled, first by the domination of continental state-empires and second, subject to a class subordination, initially by the foreign aristocracy and, subsequently, by foreign bourgeoisie. That is why in many cases class liberation was also national liberation.

In the Yugoslav experience, "Yugoslavism" could have been a possible alternative to diverse internal nationalisms. However, it turned out to be a tool of hegemonization exercised by the Serbs, the largest South Slav nation. The Serbs declared themselves the most "Yugoslav." They attempted to define a multinational and multicultural Yugoslavia in their own image. The final truth of "Yugoslavism" may be seen in the burned and looted homes and the remains of the slaughtered inhabitants of former Yugoslavia.

Insider and Outsider Perspectives: Lessons for Anthropology

> The Balkans is just one of the (places) on which (Western) Europe imposed the complexities of peripherialization which constantly pushed (the Balkan peoples) into wars, into mutual hatred, into a deeper, more apocalyptic periphery.
> —Osmančević 1994: 71

The easiest way to understand events in former Yugoslavia is to claim that all those involved in the most recent wars were murderers and that all national poli-

---

22. "The outbreak of the war put an end to the vacillation between aggressive and defensive nationalism in Croatia. The attack of the Yugoslav Peoples' Army, quickly transformed into the Serbian Army, on Croatian territory, shelling of Croatian towns, the destruction of cultural heritage and identity mobilized the second wave of nationalism in Croatia. In an unprecedented way, virtually every citizen was gripped by nationalism" (Pušić 1995: 49).

cies and politicians in former Yugoslavia were equally responsible. Yet it is hard today to consider the majority of Croats, soldiers included, as fascist Ustashas. Though they alone faced attacks by the JNA and by Serbian paramilitaries, the level of violence they directed against Serbian civilians cannot compare to that used by the militant Serbs against the Croat civil population. The same is also true in Bosnia and Herzegovina. In spring 1992 unarmed Muslims demonstrated with old Yugoslav flags in Sarajevo, while militant Serbs loaded their guns in the nearby hills.

Deep frustration was the force that drove militant Serbs into war against non-Serbs in former Yugoslavia. Influenced by their myths, Serbian militants were frustrated because of the defeat in Kosovo in 1389. In Tito's Yugoslavia, Serbian political leaders were frustrated because they were no longer the leading national elite, as was the case with their predecessors. They found an outlet for their frustration by "solving" the Kosovo problem.

An intimation about what was going to happen in the 1990s can be found in Belgrade newspaper and magazine descriptions of events in Kosovo after 1981. A typical commentary was "Albanian nationalists are potent, (and) violent, they threaten, rape, they burn hay, chop down fruit trees, demolish Serbian grave-yards, burn churches and monasteries" (*Politika*, December 11, 1988; cited in Gaber and Kuzmanić 1989: 24). These fabricated "truths" were responded to by violence, first in Croatia and then Bosnia and Herzegovina by forces under control of the same Belgrade elite that produced "the truth" about Kosovo in the first place.[23]

But in spite of the specific situation in Serbia, it wasn't nationalism that destroyed multinational East European communist states. The common denominator of recent disintegrative processes in Eastern Europe (Yugoslavia, the Soviet Union, Czechoslovakia) was the victory of liberalism. The crucial problem for the East and Central European countries after 1989 was implementing democracy (free elections), human rights, sovereignty of nations, and a modern economy. We also must not overlook the motivation of individuals to acquire civil and human rights via self-determination (see Mastnak 1992: 212 n. 57).

Freedom, human rights, and self-determination aren't contradictions. Various "secessionist" and autonomy movements are legitimate and should be supported as long as collective freedom is not a cover for the tyranny of local lords or for the oppression of minorities (see Rizman 1989: 33). Decentralization is not necessarily incompatible with the uniting or associating of states. If the right of self-determination is universal, as declared in the Universal Declaration of Human Rights of the United Nations, then the size of communities demanding

23. Analysis of letters, interviews, commentaries, and essays in Serbian newspapers and journals is a task far beyond the present article. *Politika, Politika ekspres, Večernje novosti, Nin, Intervju, Duga*, etc., offer excellent material for analysis of mass psychosis. Even the monthly popular science journal *Galaksija* published articles about Serbs and their "true" history.

autonomy is actually irrelevant.[24] There are many possible forms of political autonomy and the option of independent state formation is the last, not the first. Furthermore, there is no democracy without freedom. Although developing effective democracy is always a work in progress, a multinational state is as democratic as there is freedom for its smallest nation or for any minority. It is almost impossible to explain this to someone unable to stand in the skin of a member of a small nation that wasn't able to "enter history" in the nineteenth century. Only with complete disingenuousness or ignorance of the causes of the dissolution of former Yugoslavia, can one claim: "Internationally the recognition of the disintegration of Yugoslavia into polities defined by ethnonationalism and thus verging on racism . . . is an ominous sign for those who thought that such political concepts had been discredited for all time" (Hayden 1993: 77).

It is true that warnings of racism can never be overexaggerated. But to reduce the "disassociation" (an official Slovene term) of former Yugoslavia to ethnonationalism and racism is not an analytical approach. Is not denying the right of self-determination to small nations itself "racist?"[25] In fact, assigning responsibility for the disintegration of Yugoslavia to the small nations that rejected "internal colonization" (see Keesing 1981: 454–56), appears a defense of some nineteenth-century thesis about "historical" and "nonhistorical" nations.

The "native" perspective in this mess should not merely be the voice of one crying in the wilderness. "Native" knowledge is not only a cognitive category. It is also derived from individual life experience and inherited from one's "ancestors." It is not only "objective" history that counts in social process. Most important is internalized history, mythical history, for "all peoples, to a certain extent, take myth as reality" (Nagengast 1994: 120). The power that generates a "proper attitude" is hidden behind the curtain of everyday interaction and based on shared experience. Virtually every individual in former Yugoslavia, no matter how opposed to the dominant discourse of national exclusivity, was forced to take sides at the moment of the conflict. That decision was crucial and influenced by the "living history."

Can native ethnology be of use to explain what happened in former Yugoslavia? Certainly, though we must not expect too much of it. In common with foreign anthropological approaches, it has epistemological limits defined by its own disciplinary history. Native ethnographers have some advantages in the field, although foreigners can notice characteristics and appearances not apparent to natives. Still, there is no need to end in *"reductio ad absurdum* of a whole move-

24. It was Hitler who asked what "sovereignty" and "independence" could mean for a country with fewer than six million people (cf. Rizman 1979: 20).

25. Small nations are in fact in danger of disappearing. Over 100,000 Slovenes lived in Austrian Carinthia at the beginning of this century. Today no more than 20,000 would declare themselves as Slovene. Is it important that Slovenes (or any other small nation or ethnic group) exist on the map of Europe? As long as they (we) exist, that question is, of course, an absurd one, but who should decide?

ment of academic anthropology" (Kuper 1994: 545); it is much more productive to stress the merits and demerits of both approaches, native and foreign.

In the late eighteenth century ethnography was defined as a discipline "of nations and peoples (*Völker*)," out of which grew concepts of *Volkskunde* and ethnology (Vermeulen 1995: 47). In the Central and Eastern European traditions of ethnography and ethnology, as well as in Western social/cultural anthropology, the traditions of Enlightenment and romanticism were equally important (see Koepping 1995; Schippers 1995; Kremenšek 1978). In former Yugoslavia, ethnology combined the legacy of *Volkskunde* and *Völkerkunde* into the study of both one's own people and the exotic "Other." It was a historically and ethnographically oriented discipline. Its subjects were predominately traditional culture and folklore, although it was also interested in contemporary and urban phenomena. But ethnology didn't much concern itself with ethnic issues (Rihtman-Auguštin 1995a).

According to Robert M. Hayden (1993: 75), anthropology in former Yugoslavia had limited influence, while national ethnologies were historically close to their nationalisms from the very beginning. While this in essence is true, ethnology still was never able to fulfill "national" goals. Obviously, there are some aspects of national ethnologies that may be described as "scientific euphemisms for nationalism" (Schwartz 1995: 15; see also Šmitek 1995). However, other ethnological studies frequently transcended barriers between nations in searching for both similarities to and differences from other peoples. In this way ethnologists began to comprehend their own cultures as living, changeable, fragile, and "international" in essence. Analyzing their "empirical materials" revealed connections between their own "national treasures" and neighboring cultures (see Rihtman-Auguštin 1994: 80 n. 13). It is difficult to find any genuine cultural element or product that is typical for only one "national" tradition. Analyses of folk songs and music, folk narratives, crafts and arts, architecture, tools, social institutions, have all shown that these are local variants of common regional and European traditions. Artificial "nationalization" of folk traditions became impossible. Consequently, ethnology actually produced a kind of "alienating effect" at the very core of "national" scholarly efforts. In contrast to the above, nationalistic sins in former Yugoslavia are a matter of the "folklorization" and "ethnologizing" of the scholarship in the political sense. This is quite another matter.

In the case of former Yugoslavia, ethnological analysis of events became determined by the war itself. It still provides the basic orientation for our interpretation. To be ethical, we have to be prepared, as scholars, to transcend the existing limits of our knowledge. If we think that we can prevent suffering by telling the truth, then we must do it. And if we find it necessary to criticize, then we also have to do it.

In this regard I compare the anthologies, *War Among the Yugoslavs* (Kideckel and Halpern 1993), *Fear, Death and Resistance* (Čale Feldman, Prica, and Senjković 1993), and *Ethnicity—Nationalism—Geopolitics in the Balkans* (Giordano, Greverus, and Kostova 1995). American anthropologists were trying to understand and explain,[26] European anthropologists were trying to be engaged, while Croatian ethnologists didn't even attempt to generalize—they simply started to collect material and made some analyses of the ongoing events they were unwillingly involved in. The result was a remarkable ethnography of war (e.g., *Narodna umjetnost* 29 [1992], 32(1) [1995]; *Etnološka tribina* 15 [1992]; etc.). In Serbia, Ivan Čolović (1994) has made an excellent ethnological analysis of war "folklore."

There is no doubt that anthropology should study all aspects of life, including war. However, are the methodological tools of anthropology, especially the ethnographic method, actually capable of revealing aspects of fear, death, and destruction "from the native's point of view?" The ethnography of war is by definition beyond the range of participant observation, unless an anthropologist joins one side or another in the conflict as a participant.

That is mostly why, in my view, the attempt of American anthropologists to understand and explain the war among "the Yugoslavs" was not successful. The American anthology was planned from an entirely humanistic perspective. Researchers who worked in some places in the former Yugoslavia were asked to express their views on Yugoslav events with specific "views from the inside." However, even if those researchers were undoubtedly competent, within the limits of their previously stated research goals, the same can't be said about their attempts to explain events in the Balkans.

Even if anthropologists had unlimited access to data, would they be justified in making generalizations based on their particular fieldwork experiences? It seems that "we have to believe in the universality of the human potential behind the relativity of diversity" (Koepping 1995: 89), but today there is not much room for "armchair scholars" to synthesize worldwide ethnographic knowledge. It is important that anthropology now includes the state "as an analytical category" (Alonso 1994: 400). However, I am skeptical about anthropology's power to analyze it. If an anthropologist discusses former Yugoslavia on the basis of fieldwork experience and knowledge, that person can still not understand events at the state level. Such generalizations are more complex.

In the special issue of the *Anthropology of East Europe Review* (Kideckel and Halpern 1993), anthropologists tried to comprehend events in former Yugoslavia in their political-historical context by starting with information and sources from particular areas, not the former Yugoslavia as a whole. Personal, interview, and published information presented the points of view of people from particular

26. When I read *War Among the Yugoslavs* I was upset and wrote comments and criticisms. Parts were published in Slovenia (Muršič 1994), and some are used in the present essay. Croatian colleagues were also dissatisfied with this issue (cf. Rihtman-Auguštin 1995b: 61; Povrzanović 1995: 102).

places. In doing so, they were limited by their language ability, so that these experts on the former Yugoslavia rarely considered the "truths" of Slovenes, Albanians, or Macedonians. It must be noted, however, that the chapters dealing with particular regions were written by people fluent in the specific languages. Nevertheless, few "native" scholars of former Yugoslavia are simultaneously fluent in Slovene, Albanian, Hungarian, and Macedonian as well as variants of the dominant language spoken in Croatia, Bosnia, and Serbia. But if we take language in the metaphoric sense of a symbolic language enclosed in a cultural skin possessed by the insider, then outsiders can never fully reflect or be sensitive to all aspects of an emic view.[27] If anthropologists attempt to engage world problems, as in Schwartz's "peace-keeping anthropology" (1995: 9), they must be careful to not allow themselves too many mistakes. In both of the foreign anthologies we may find factually and conceptually incorrect claims. It is not possible to read them without "passion," because the situation is too serious to be silent.

Bette Denich (1993: 57), for example, writes that nationalistic ideas were imposed on people: "The appeal of 'our people' perceived to be endangered is difficult to resist. It could only be resisted by those with conscious intellectual viewpoints that continually provided reality checks against the claims of grievance." However, "intellectuals" were the main motivators of interethnic conflict in former Yugoslavia! "Ordinary people," especially peasants in ethnically mixed areas, were the last victims of propaganda and paramilitary units, as was the tragic case of the ethnically mixed village depicted in Tone Bringa's documentary, *We Are All Neighbours*.

It is questionable whether anthropology can solve the problem of its limits by challenging "the informants' essentialisms" (Schwartz 1995: 22). When we research phenomena, particular and unique in their essence, we can't avoid the rigorousness and responsibility of the discipline or hide ourselves behind potentially infinite interpretations of the same event/process. The aim of science is to understand and explain both particular phenomena and general principles. In generalizing about particular insights reasonable sophisticated theoretical models of reality can be produced. In historical phenomena there is no single truth and therefore it is necessary to consider all possible "truths." If anthropology as a discipline and a practice arrogantly abstracts "truth" as the basic purpose of its activities, it throws away its moment of critique. Subtle realism, according to Martyn Hammersley (1992), is a possible answer. Or, at least, epistemological criticism (see Roth 1989) within a pluralist epistemological orientation. Generalizations seem nowadays an ever more remote objective for anthropologists than in Malinowski's and Boas's time. The ways in which the powerful dominate the powerless ("ethnic violence" is in fact always the cover for aggression) is not exactly the image that now needs to be generalized, or is it?

27. The editors and I agreed on the importance of this point and I rephrased it after discussions with them.

Our efforts can never be "objective" and "value free." And they should not be if we try to derive any lessons from tragedies such as the "Third Balkan War(s)." "*Wertfrei* (value-free) science" is another name for avoiding responsibility (Kuzmanić 1994a: 106–7). An ethical position always leads us to radical criticisms of our own preconceived knowledge and presuppositions. That means transcending our position. It means, in the words of Alain Badiou (1996), the call of the Radical Immortal, situational Truth: *Continuer!*

Visions and Statements

> It is being realized that not taking a political position, not making a moral commitment, is not neutral; it is making a commitment to the support and continuation of the system of which one is a part and within which one is working anthropologically. . . . Ultimately amorality is immorality.
> —Keesing 1981: 489

In former Yugoslavia there have been four recent wars or conflicts, plus the NATO intervention in Kosovo. First, the repression of Albanians in Kosovo, begun in 1981, has led, after years of nonviolent resistance, to armed conflict in 1998. Second was the brief fighting in Slovenia in 1991. The third conflict, the war against Croatia 1991–92, was characterized by full-scale war. Fourth and finally, the longest lasting and ethnically most diverse war was waged in Bosnia and Herzegovina from 1992 to 1996. The common denominator of these conflicts[28] is Belgrade, not Serbia and Montenegro, and its political and military elite. During these years, Belgrade was never attacked by citizens of former Yugoslavia (only by NATO, and then only certain military and governmental targets). The wars were, however, led by the dominant elite of this city. Their maximal aim has been, since 1987, or even since Tito's death in 1980, a unitary Yugoslavia. The maximal plan was for Federal Yugoslavia to be totally governed from Belgrade with the republics as its "cultural" reservations. The minimal aim was articulated in the slogan: "All Serbs in one country."

National affiliation was obviously an efficient means of mass mobilization to realize the aims of the elite. According to virtually unanimous Serb opinion, the Albanians in Kosovo have had "too many rights," and further, they misused them. The majority of the Serbs outside Serbia simply couldn't imagine being a minority within their area. They were afraid that the new governments in Croatia and Bosnia and Herzegovina would treat them the way the Serbian authorities treated the Albanians in Kosovo. Because Serbian leaders were unwilling to ensure autonomy for Albanians in Serbia and within Yugoslavia, the Serbs outside

---

28. After 1993, the conflict between Croats and Bosnian Muslims emerged, as a consequence of previous conflicts. Given its increased power, after its successful 1995 offensive against the Croatian Serb state, Croatia too will be more responsible for the region's future.

Serbia could not even think about what would happen to them if they became a minority group. They were more than certain that "the others" would treat them the same way as the Serbian government treated "their others," the Albanians in Kosovo and, to some extent, the non-Serbian populations in Vojvodina and elsewhere. That image, with roots in the Kosovo myth, was the driving force for all the tragic events in former Yugoslavia.[29] Nevertheless, the key point remains the way the engine of the state was guided by the men who were sitting at the command console and had the wheel in their hands.—*Je accuse!*

29. Those lines were written in 1994. Unfortunately, events in Kosovo in 1998 have confirmed them.

PART II

ETHNICITY, NATIONALISM, AND CULTURE

Contested Views

The Roots of the War in Croatia

Elinor M. Despalatović

Problems in the Study of Croat and Balkan History

I am an historian who has worked in the field of Croatian and Yugoslav history since the late 1950s. I first studied the Illyrian Movement (1830–48), the beginning phase of modern Croatian nationalism, which was limited to the urban cultural and political elite. By the end of World War I, nationalism had reached the peasants, the vast majority of the population. Throughout the interwar period the most important political party among the Croats was the Croatian Peasant Party, a national populist party. How did nationalism take root among the peasants, when exactly, and why? In the search for background material on the peasants' world at the time the Croatian Peasant Party was founded (1904), I found a wealth of primary sources and little else. What was to be a chapter in a book on the Peasant Party became a work in itself. For the last decade I have worked on a study of peasant life in Croatia-Slavonia before World War I, the period when modernization began to confront traditional peasant culture. My richest sources are village studies done between 1897 and 1918 for the Ethnological Section of the Yugoslav Academy in Zagreb (JAZU/ONŽO, 1897–1918; *Zbornik*: 1898–1927). As a historian of peasant life, my interests clearly overlap with those of anthropologists and ethnologists.

I did not expect the collapse of communist Yugoslavia. Yugoslavia had been through many crises since its founding and managed to survive. The Yugoslavs appeared to have found a way to balance the nationalisms of small, closely related peoples through a federation of national republics. Communism seemed to offer a supra-national identity, and the "Yugoslav Experiment" of workers' self-management and market socialism became an intriguing alternative to Soviet centralized planning. As Tito, Yugoslavia's charismatic leader, skillfully straddled the Eastern and Western blocs, Yugoslavia was, for a while, a leader of the non-aligned movement.

Tito's Yugoslavia seemed to work. In 1945, Yugoslavia was a poor Balkan state devastated by war and civil war, but by the early 1970s its living standards were higher than in most of Eastern Europe. Foreign tourists flooded the Dalmatian coast, and Yugoslav citizens, unlike those in other communist states, could travel and work abroad. By the late 1970s Yugoslavia was officially a "developed" country. Her modernization seemed more humane than the USSR's and its East European satellites, and the Yugoslav government let foreign scholars come and observe the process. Compare the number of books on Yugoslav topics written by American anthropologists, sociologists, political scientists, economists, and historians between 1950 and 1980 with those on Czechoslovakia, Romania, Bulgaria, or even Poland. For decades Yugoslavia's global significance vastly outweighed its size or wealth. Once the cold war was over, however, Yugoslavia lost its strategic importance until it began to disintegrate into war, thus threatening stability in southeastern Europe.

Although I studied Croatian nationalism for forty years, I did not expect Croatia to become an independent nation-state. Perhaps this was because I came from a large country and Croatia seemed so small. For nine and a half centuries Croatia preserved her identity within a larger state structure. Would independence really be better? The depth of national feeling in Croatia was difficult to judge, since nationalism was a forbidden topic. Most Croats I knew were deeply loyal to Croatia, its history, language, and culture. They were angered when the communists associated any nationalist manifestations with the NDH, the Nazi puppet state run by the extremist Ustasha Party in World War II. There was nostalgia for the former Hapsburg empire and an assumption that the term "Balkan" referred to Serbia and points south, not Croatia. Although religion is the most widely accepted marker of Croatian and Serbian identity (Croats are Catholic, Serbs are Orthodox), I rarely knew the religion of acquaintances. Religion was an extremely private affair under the communists and one's Catholic or Orthodox faith did not seem to matter.

Like most American historians who focus on one nationality in Yugoslav research, I worked on Croatian history within the larger context of Yugoslavia, the Balkans, and Central Europe. There are many reasons for this. Yugoslavia had three official languages (Serbo-Croatian, Slovene, and Macedonian), and few researchers have time to master more than one, though we may have reading knowledge of the others. The Southern Slavs straddle two historical regions: (1) Catholic Europe and the Hapsburg Empire, (2) Byzantium and the Ottoman Empire. Study of each region requires knowledge of other languages: Latin, German, Hungarian, and Italian for the former; Greek, Old Church Slavonic, and Turkish for the latter. In addition, each nationality or republic has its own historiographic tradition that helps frame our own work, and few of us have time to become familiar with all of these. Finally, the only way American scholars received permission from Yugoslav authorities for long-term research was through official academic exchanges between Yugoslavia and the United States, and these were usually with a single national republic.

American professional associations also fractured along national lines. We tried to form a Southern Slav Association in the early 1970s, affiliated with the American Association for the Advancement of Slavic Studies (AAASS). It was soon challenged by AAASS affiliated Slovene, Croatian, Serbian, Macedonian, Albanian and Bulgarian associations. We changed the name and focus of the Southern Slav Association and it reemerged as the American Association for Southeast European Studies (AASES), but this organization soon became insignificant. Yugoslavia's breakup divided North American scholars even more. While some became political activists, explaining and defending the actions of the national group they studied, others felt the need for a neutral organization to stand above national divisions. In 1995, AASES was reborn as the South East European Studies Association (SEESA) and is growing steadily.

Once Yugoslavia fell apart, and war began, I found myself called on to explain what had happened and why. This is very uncomfortable for a historian, for we are trained to wait for basic sources, often fifty years after the fact, before making judgment. I have read too many wrong prognostications, too many facile and mistaken contemporary observations about other periods and problems to feel at ease explaining the present and predicting the future. Events are still much too close to be seen clearly. Yet one cannot remain silent when history is misused, as it has been in justifying and reporting on the wars accompanying the disintegration of Yugoslavia. It became obvious in 1991–92, even from the most detailed news coverage, that Croatian history was for the most part unknown and misunderstood in the West. Some flagrant mistakes repeated *ad infinitum* were that the Croatian-Serbian conflict was a "tribal" war, that Serbs and Croats had been bitter enemies for many centuries, that the Serbs of Serbia had been the defenders of Europe against the Turks, that all Croats were "closet" fascists, and that the Serbian minority in Croatia had no rights as a community and faced genocide in 1991 when Croatia declared independence. All these are untrue. History was also used by Croatia to justify its independence, by Serbia to justify her attempts to create a "Greater Serbia," and by the Great Powers to justify inaction. What, then, is important for us to know about the Croats, their history, and desire for independence?

Croatian History and Nationalism

Croatia lies on the northern edge of the historical fault line crossing the Balkans. This line separated the Western Roman Empire from the Eastern, Roman Catholicism from Orthodoxy, and the Hapsburgs from the Ottomans. Rome converted the Croats to Christianity, drawing them into the civilization of Western and Central Europe. The Serbs were converted by the Orthodox Church and their civilization was that of Byzantium and, later, the Ottoman Empire. As a border nation, the Croats have been in precarious positions as borders shifted over the centuries. Croatia has had to fight to survive as a political and cultural entity over and over again.

The war, which accompanied the collapse of Yugoslavia, was not a "tribal" war. The term "tribal" is part of the Western demonization of the Balkans (Todorova 1997). Tribes disappeared from Croatia in the Middle Ages with the introduction of West European feudalism and manorialism. Nor had the Croats and Serbs fought each other for "centuries." Serbs and Croats within the Hapsburg empire (later Austria-Hungary) fought together against common enemies (see Grandits and Promitzer, this volume). The Serbs of Serbia and the Croats did not fight each other until World War I, when the Austro-Hungarian army, which included both Croats and Serbs, invaded the Kingdom of Serbia.

The Croats pride themselves on a history dating back one thousand years, a history which they believe gives them the right to a modern nation-state of their own. The building blocks of this thesis are stated most clearly in the "Historical Foundations" section in the Constitution of the Republic of Croatia:

> Giving expression to the thousand-year-old national identity and statehood of the Croatian nation, confirmed by the continuity of a series of historical events in various political forms and by the maintenance of the state-forming idea of the Croatian nation's historical right to full state sovereignty, which manifested itself: in the formation of Croatian principalities in the seventh century; in the autonomous medieval state of Croatia founded in the ninth century in the Kingdom of Croatia established in the tenth century; in the maintenance of the subjectivity of the Croatian state in the Croatian-Hungarian personal union; in the autonomous and sovereign decision of the Croatian Sabor of 1527 to elect a king from the Habsburg dynasty; in the autonomous and sovereign decision of the Croatian Sabor to sign the Pragmatic Sanction of 1712. (*Ustav* 1991)

The text goes then explains Croatia's traditional rights and constitutional position within the Kingdom of Hungary and the Hapsburg Empire, and the dissolution of this relationship in 1918 by the Croatian Sabor. Croatia's entry into the Kingdom of Yugoslavia is seen as illegal because "the Croatian Sabor never sanctioned the decision of the National Council of the State of Slovenes, Croats, and

Serbs to unify with Serbia and Montenegro in the Kingdom of Serbs, Croats and Slovenes (December 1, 1918), later on (October 3, 1929) proclaimed as the Kingdom of Yugoslavia" (*Ustav* 1991). Croatia reemerged "in the establishment of the Banovina of Croatia in 1939 by which Croatian state identity was restored; in laying the foundation of state sovereignty during the Second World War through decisions of the Antifascist Council of the National Liberation of Croatia (1943), as contrary to the proclamation of the Independent State of Croatia (1941), and subsequently in the Constitution of the People's Republic of Croatia (1947), and later in the Constitution of the Socialist Republic of Croatia (1963–1990)" (*Ustav* 1991). Note the clear separation of lines of legitimacy. Only the *Banovina*, the Partisan-established war government, and Croatia's years as a Socialist Republic within Yugoslavia are seen as further steps in the restoration of the Croatian state. The Ustasha-led Independent State of Croatia is clearly excluded from this list.

Croatia has also been criticized for its red-and-white checkerboard state symbol, because it was used by the Ustasha. In fact the red-and-white checkerboard has been associated with Croatia since the early Middle Ages and has represented Croatian kings, Hungarians, Venetians, Hapsburgs, the Kingdom of Yugoslavia, the Croatian Banovina, and the Socialist Republic of Croatia (Mandić 1970). It is not surprising that the Ustasha reached for the checkerboard in their attempt to legitimize themselves as national leaders. Should the new Republic of Croatia reject the checkerboard because of its misuse during four of Croatia's thousand years of history?

The Croats pride themselves on being the only Southern Slav nationality with a continuous political tradition, which stretches from the early Middle Ages, with only one short break, to the present. The Slovenes and Macedonians did not have states of their own until the early 1990s. The Serbs, Bulgarians, and Bosnians did have medieval states, but lost them to the Ottoman invaders in the fourteenth and fifteenth centuries.

Croatia was an independent kingdom in the early Middle Ages with three core territories: Croatia, Slovenia, and Dalmatia. In 1102 it became a semi-autonomous kingdom within Hungary and, after 1527, the Hapsburg Empire. Within the Hungarian/Hapsburg state, Croatia had its viceroy (the Croatian *Ban*), a parliament (the Croatian *Sabor*), special legal and fiscal privileges (the "Municipal Laws"), county assemblies with a great deal of autonomy, and a native nobility. The final definition of Croatia's special legal position within Hungary, the Croatian-Hungarian *Nagodba* (Agreement) of 1868, gave the Croatian government control over education, justice, and internal affairs. Croatia's special legal status within Hungary and the Hapsburg Empire protected the kingdom from losing its political identity during centuries of foreign rule.

A turning point for the Croats, as for all Balkan peoples, was the arrival of the Ottoman Turks. By the early sixteenth century the Turks had conquered all of Slavonia, part of Croatia, and the Dalmatian hinterlands. Although the Republic of Dubrovnik remained independent, Venice ruled the rest of the Dalmatian coast and islands. A small rump Croatian state, known as the "remnants of the remnants," remained in the north under Hapsburg rule. Croatia now stood at the very edge of Europe. Massive movements of population accompanied the Turkish wars and conquest. Part of the "remnants of the remnants" in the north was made into the Croatian Military Frontier, a strip of land along the Turkish border, which was garrisoned by peasant soldiers, and under Hapsburg Military Command. It was the troops of this Military Frontier, not the Serbs of Ottoman-occupied Serbia, who defended Central Europe against the Turks.

In the next five centuries, piece by piece, the lands of the original Croatian kingdom were returned. Slavonia and the occupied parts of Croatia were recovered from the Turks in the late seventeenth and early eighteenth centuries, but half of the reconquered territory was given to the Austrian military for an expanded Croatian and Slavonian Military Frontier. In 1881, the Croatian and Slavonian Military Frontier was rejoined with the civilian parts of Croatia and Slavonia. Dalmatia, which the Austrians received from Venice in the wars of the French Revolution, remained an Austrian province until the collapse of the Austro-Hungarian Empire in 1918. It was finally reunited with Croatia and Slavonia in 1939.

In 1918, Croatia, Slavonia, and Dalmatia became part of the Kingdom of Serbs, Croats, and Slovenes (after 1929 the Kingdom of Yugoslavia), and in the process the Croats lost the constitutional framework that had protected their territory and institutions. The new state was in many ways an expanded Serbian kingdom. The dynasty was Serbian. Serbs dominated the army, police force, diplomatic corps, and civil service. The new state linked the Croatian core territories to regions and peoples who spoke closely related languages, but with whom they had little else in common. Croatia, Slavonia, and Dalmatia had been among the least economically developed parts of the Austro-Hungarian Empire; now, ironically, Croatia and Slavonia were among the most developed in the new kingdom.

The Croatian Peasant Party soon became the dominant party among the Croats in the new state. Its leader, Stjepan Radić (Livingston 1959; Mužić 1988), was a charismatic and fearless politician and under him the Croatian Peasant Party began to organize and gain followers beyond Croatia and Slavonia. The Croatian Peasant Party was the first modern institution to link Croats throughout Yugoslavia. Stjepan Radić believed Croatia had entered the Kingdom of Serbs, Croats, and Slovenes illegally, without the assent of the historical *Sabor*, and at first tried to win foreign support for an independent Croatia. When this failed, the Croatian Peasant Party entered national political life. Radić even served as minister of education for a short time. In his struggle against Serbian centralism, Radić angered many Serbs. Stjepan Radić was shot during a regular session of the Yugoslav parliament by a Serbian deputy from Montenegro in June of 1928 and died two months later of his wounds. His nephew Pavle Radić and his close party associate Djuro Basariček were killed immediately, and several other Peasant Party Deputies were severely wounded. The assassin Puniša Račić, celebrated as a hero through much of Serbia, was tried and sentenced to sixty years of prison, which was reduced to twenty immediately (Kulundžić 1967: 549–73). Račić spent much of his sentence under house arrest in a comfortable villa with three servants, free to come and go as he wished. In 1941 he simply walked out one day, ending his farcical "confinement."

Stjepan Radić's funeral was a huge national demonstration. The Croatian politicians, shocked and angered, pulled out of national politics once more. A few months after Radić's death, the king declared a dictatorship (Lampe 1996: 160–73). This forced many politicians into exile, the most important being Peasant Party leaders who could represent the party in Europe and America, and members of the right-wing Croatian Party of Rights, who would soon found the extremist Ustasha Party under Italian Fascist protection. Vladko Maček, the new head of the Croatian Peasant Party, remained in Croatia and spent much of the time between 1929 and 1935 under house arrest or in prison (Maček 1957: 119–56).

Political life was reborn in the Kingdom of Yugoslavia in 1935. The Croatian Peasant Party under Maček's leadership developed a mass base even wider than before. It was now a Croatian national movement with an active economic, social, and political program, and Maček soon became the leader of the United Opposition Coalition. Finally, in 1939, on the eve of World War II, Maček negotiated the *Sporazum* with Prime Minister Cvetković that established a semi-autonomous Croatian *Banovina* within the Kingdom of Yugoslavia.

The Croatian *Banovina* (Maček 1957: 192–93; Hoptner 1962: 149–55) was comprised of the Croatian core lands: Croatia, almost all of Slavonia, and Dalmatia from Rijeka to below Dubrovnik; as well as Herzegovina and a bit of Bosnia. The *Banovina* had its own parliament (*Sabor*) and a separate government headed by the *ban*, who was appointed by the king. The *Banovina* was responsible for its own justice, internal affairs, education, social policy, agriculture, forestry and mining, commerce and industry, finance, construction, and health. The Royal Government controlled foreign affairs, foreign trade, defense, transportation, and communications. The *Banovina* gave Croatia even more autonomy than she had received in the *Nagodba* of 1868, the compromise with Hungary. Ivan Subašić, a Peasant Party member became *ban*. Vladko Maček became vice-president of the Cvetković government. The Croatian *Banovina* included 26.44 percent of the territory and 29 percent of the population of the Kingdom of Yugoslavia, and its inhabitants were 75 percent Roman Catholic (Croat), 19.28 percent Orthodox (Serb), and 3.81 percent Muslim (Banska Vlast 1940: 297). The *Sporazum* was supposed to be the first step in the revision of the Yugoslav constitution. The Slovenes and Serbs expected that they would be the next to receive their own national entities. War came before this could happen.

In April 1941, the Kingdom of Yugoslavia fell to German and Italian invaders and shattered into a mosaic of annexed territories and fascist satellite states. The lands of the Croatian *Banovina* plus a much larger slice of Bosnia were incorporated into the "Independent State of Croatia" (NDH). The NDH was split into German and Italian spheres of influence and run by the Ustasha, the extremist nationalist political party which was born and nurtured in exile and had had only a marginal role in Croatian politics up to that moment. Maček decided not to go with the rest of the Royal Government into exile, but stayed in Croatia. When asked by the Germans and the Ustasha to turn over the leadership of the Croats to the Ustasha, he refused, and instead cautioned his followers to accept the inevitable and remain calm (Maček 1957: 227). The Peasant Party organizations and press were shut down by the NDH, and Maček spent most of the war under house arrest, in concentration camp, or in prison. The right wing of the Peasant Party soon joined the Ustasha while the left wing joined the Communist Resistance. The bulk of the Peasant Party supporters remained loyal to Maček and were persecuted first by the Ustasha, later by the Communists (Radelić 1996).

The collapse of Yugoslavia was initially greeted with joy by many Croats, as was the declaration of an independent Croatia, but they discovered quite quickly that the new state was a fascist puppet and that the regime it instituted was a savage one. The Ustasha were never able to mobilize mass support in Croatia (Tanner 1997: 153–57). Many more Croats joined the Partisans. Of the twenty-six Partisan divisions at the end of 1943, eleven were Croatian, five Slovene, two Serbian, and one Montenegrin (Čović 1991: 34).

The population of the territory of NDH was approximately 50 percent Catholic, 30 percent Orthodox, and 20 percent Muslim, Jewish, and other (Tanner 1997: 150). The Ustasha played their part in the Jewish Holocaust by killing or deporting to concentration and extermination camps most of the Jewish population in their territory. They also persecuted the gypsies. These persecutions were standard policy in Nazi-occupied territory and in the Nazi satellites. What was different about the Ustasha regime was its treatment of the Serbian minority. The Ustasha made no secret of the fact that Serbs were unwelcome in their Catholic Croatian state. In the spring and summer of 1941 a wave of mass killing of Serbs spread through villages and towns of the NDH (Tanner 1997: 151), and there was an attempt at mass deportation of Serbs to German-controlled Serbia. The Germans soon stopped the deportation. In addition, some Serbs converted to Catholicism, and many others ended up in detention and concentration camps (Matković 1994: 160–61).

In the 1980s with the revival of nationalism throughout Yugoslavia and growing freedom of the press, details on the Ustasha persecution of Serbs emerged into full light. Stories about massacres with grisly pictures of Ustasha victims appeared on Belgrade TV and in Serbian newspapers and journals. Numbers began to be tossed about on both sides. Some Serbian writers and publicists claimed that between 700,000 and a million people, mostly Serbs, died in the Jasenovac concentration camp alone, and these figures were used to accuse the

Croats of being a genocidal nation (Žerjavić 1992: 15–38). Recent demographic studies indicate that around 500,000 Serbs perished in all of Yugoslavia during World War II, and this includes Serbs in Serbia, Serbs in the NDH, Serbs killed in military operations as Partisans, Chetniks, or Nazi collaborators, and Serbs who died of epidemic disease (Žerjavić 1992: 177). While final figures are still being debated, probably no more than 50,000 Serbs died in Jasenovac. Perhaps 85,000 persons altogether lost their lives in the Ustasha camps. Total Serbian deaths as NDH victims seems to have been around 100,000 (Žerjavić 1993: 29). A reduction in numbers does not make the events any less horrible. Yet attempts to look at the numbers objectively were too often perceived by the Serbs as sacrilege and a way to whitewash Croatian war crimes, while Croats, burdened by the constant harping on the crimes of their "fathers" by the Serb-dominated Party, wanted to set the record straight.

During the 1991–92 war in Croatia, the American media wrote and spoke of the "millions" or "hundreds of thousands" of Serbs who had been killed by the Croatian Ustasha in World War II, drawing their figures from the able Serbian propaganda machine. Once numbers get into the pipeline they are used again and again. The Ustasha past has been thrown against the Croats continually during their fight for independence. Why has France been forgiven Vichy, Germany Nazism, Italy Fascism, Norway Quisling, and Serbia Nedić and Mihailović, while the Croats are still suspected of being "genocidal" fascists (Cushman 1996)?

After World War II, Croatia reemerged as a national republic in a new Yugo-slavia, one that took the form of a socialist federation of national republics. Croa-tia, Slavonia, and Dalmatia were finally reunited in one territorial unit. Serbia still overshadowed the other nationalities. Serbia was the largest republic, Belgrade remained the capital of the new Yugoslavia, and Serbs played a major role in the Communist Party, diplomatic corps, officer corps of the army, police, and secur-ity forces. Communism and Serbian control became linked in the minds of Croats, while the Party and the Serbs considered any manifestation of Croatian nationalism to be dangerous and "fascist."

The Yugoslav communists attempted to control history. This meant, first of all, that historical research and debate in Yugoslavia was limited to "safe" topics. Nationalism was not a "safe" topic, neither were the complex events of World War II in the Yugoslav lands. The communists tried to cover up the deep wounds of World War II with words, declaring that communist Yugoslavia was to be based upon "brotherhood and unity," and stressing that nationalism was out-dated, chauvinistic, and divisive. Thus the peoples of Yugoslavia never had the chance to come to terms with their memories, guilt feelings, or griefs about the war, for they were never presented with a full picture of it. There were the "good guys"—the Partisans, and the "bad guys"—the Ustasha, the *Srpska Garda* (Ser-bian Fascist Militia), the White Guard (Slovene Fascist Militia), *Chetniks*, and other fascist collaborators. Communist brutality during and after the war was hushed up. The Partisan struggle was made into a national myth in which brave

Partisans drawn from all Yugoslav nationalities, young, pure, and loyal to each other, fought a relentless guerrilla war against the evil fascists. Some of the Partisan story was based upon fact, so the Partisan myth struck deep chords in the early years. But heroes who die in battle have a better chance of keeping their mythical status than former heroes who come to power and grow paunchy and privileged. By the 1970s, the myth of the Partisans had begun to lose its effect.

The official version of history was taught in the schools, portrayed in the media, written by "reliable" historians. Unpleasant facts were covered up, just as the graves of the *Domobrani* and *Wehrmacht* soldiers were plowed over after World War II in Mirogoj, the main Zagreb cemetery. Communist Yugoslavia attempted to build a common identity by ignoring the chasms between peoples left by the war. No one could deny that the Jewish and Gypsy populations were victims of the war. The case was less clear for Serbs, Muslims, and Croats. The majority of Serbs, Croats, and Muslims were also victims of the war, yet some members of each of these three nationalities engaged in collaboration with the fascists and or victimization of other nationalities. The Croats, however, had had their own fascist state and one of a particularly nasty kind. As Christopher Cviic observed so aptly:

> It is ironic, in view of their massive wartime participation in the ranks of the victorious partisans, that the Croats should have felt alienated, a "nation on probation" within their own republic of the Yugoslav federation, forever suspected of not being wholehearted in their attachment to the system. One explanation for this was that Croatian Serbs, who still had fresh memories of their attempted extermination under Ante Pavelic's Croat wartime state, were predominant in the party, the police, the influential old partisans' association, and the key managerial and administrative posts in Croatia. (Cviic 1991: 72)

It would have been hard for the Croats, especially the younger generation, to counter the charges made by the Croatian Serbs, for they knew very little about the Ustasha period. There were no detailed histories available, such as we have for the Nazi movement and regime. What was "known" came from the memories of those who had lived through the war, oral tradition, and rumor.

There was one short break in the suppression of Croatian nationalism known as the "Croatian Spring" (Rusinow 1977: 273–318; Ramet 1984: chap. 7; Tanner 1997: chap. 13). It began in 1967 with the "Declaration Concerning the Name and Position of the Croatian Language" by the Croatian Writers' Club and signed by the major Croatian writers and cultural institutions. The "Declaration" demanded equality for the Croatian language and bitterly attacked the predominance of Serbian forms in the official Serbo-Croatian language. Next came a debate within the Croatian Communist Party led by three young reformers: Savka Dabčević-Kučar, Mika Tripalo, and Pero Pirker. They demanded more economic and political autonomy for Croatia and protested the overwhelming number of Serbs in the Party, army, and police. At that time only 12 percent of the population of the Republic of Croatia was Serbian, but Serbs made up 40 percent of the Croatian Party and 60 percent of police personnel (Tanner 1997: 191). By 1970 the debate had spilled into the world of writers, academics, and students, much as it had three years earlier in Czechoslovakia during the "Prague Spring." The venerable Croatian cultural institution Matica Hrvatska took on new life under the leadership of Vlado Gotovac, Marko Veselica, and Šime Djodan. Also active was the retired general Franjo Tudjman, then director of the Institute of the History of the Workers Movement in Zagreb. Matica Hrvatska spearheaded a Croatian cultural and political renaissance and began to function almost as an opposition party, proposing its own revisions of the text of the new constitution, publishing pamphlets, journals and even two newspapers.

Matica encouraged Croats all over the Republic to found new branches, as well as affiliated associations. The mushrooming of Matica Hrvatska gave the reformers a mass audience. Lecturers went out to Matica branches and affiliated associations throughout Croatia to talk about Croatian history, culture, politics, and the realities of Croatia's position within Yugoslavia (Brandt 1996: 86–93). The reform movement soon spread to the University of Zagreb, where students, led by Dražen Budiša, organized the Croatian League of Students, the first non-governmental student union. Finally, in November 1971, the students in Zagreb and the other university branches in Croatia went on strike. The workers stayed quiet.

It was a "spring" because it seemed to end a bleak winter of repression and censorship. The Croats realized that their suspicions about unfair treatment in Tito's Yugoslavia were justified. They began once more to sing patriotic Croatian songs, fly the traditional Croatian flag, and talk freely about Croatian history and culture. The Croatian Spring unleashed a feeling of elation and hope in Croatia and, for the first time since World War II, open pride in being Croatian. The Croatian Spring was ended by a severe crackdown by Tito and the Party, which began in the fall of 1971. Matica Hrvatska was closed and surrounded by police barricades. Liberal communists were expelled from the Party, and leaders in the Matica Hrvatska and student movements were jailed. People spoke cautiously. Continuing prosperity was all that smoothed the edges of frustration. It is not surprising the some of the leaders of the Croatian Spring would emerge once more in the late 1980s, when Croatia moved toward democracy, as leaders of the new political parties (Tudjman, Dabčević-Kučar, Gotovac, Budiša).

During the Croatian Spring the young reformers in the Party had questioned the siphoning off of Croatia's earnings, especially in hard currency, to Belgrade for distribution to the less developed regions. The question was only covered up, not solved, in the two decades that followed. Croatia was still one of the two most developed republics, Slovenia was the other, and a large proportion of the earnings of these northern republics continued to be used for the development of southern Yugoslavia. Hospitals, for example, were built in Kosovo, while Zagreb, whose population had multiplied ten times since 1939, was still served by hospitals built before 1945.

There was also a feeling in Croatia that it was being dragged down by Balkan "sloppiness" and "corruption." Educated Croats identify strongly with Central Europe and the orderliness of the Hapsburg tradition. They wanted to be part of "Europe" again and perhaps even join the prosperous and expanding European community. Once communism fell in the former Soviet satellite states, Croatia began to move away from the tight embrace of Serbia and from a one-party system. The Republic of Croatia held free multiparty elections in May 1990, which brought the right of center HDZ (Croatian National Union) Party and its leader Franjo Tudjman to power.

The new Croatian government did not move immediately to independence. Together with the newly elected Slovene government, it attempted to win support from the other republics for a new kind of Yugoslavia, a democratic confederation with greater autonomy for each state. When Serbia made this impossible, the Croats and the Slovenes decided to secede.

The Croatian Serbs

In 1990, the Serbian minority living in territories of the former Croatian and Slavonian Military Frontier took up arms against the new, democratically elected Croatian government. At that time Serbs represented 12 percent of the population of the Socialist Republic of Croatia (Poulton 1991: 24).

Why was there a large Serbian minority in Croatia? The Ottoman advance up the Balkans from the fourteenth through early sixteenth centuries set in motion a massive movement of peoples: many Croats fled to Austria and Hungary and the parts of Croatia still in Hapsburg hands, while Orthodox Serbs and Vlachs from the south sought refuge in Croatian territory (Miller 1997: 4–7). Large numbers of Orthodox refugees were absorbed into the troops of the Croatian Military Frontier. Other Orthodox Christians were brought in by the Turks to serve as auxiliary troops and workers. Another wave of Orthodox refugees arrived after the Turks were expelled from Croatia and Slavonia in the late seventeenth and early eighteenth centuries.

The Turks left behind depopulated and devastated lands. Slavonia and the parts of Croatia the Turks had occupied were resettled with emigrants who came primarily from Croatia, Dalmatia, Hungary, the Ottoman Empire (particularly Bosnia), Austria, and the German states (Pavičić 1953). About half of the reconquered territory was taken to enlarge the Croatian Military Frontier and to establish a Slavonian Military Frontier. The border with the Ottoman Empire was much longer now. The Austrian Military encouraged large groups of Orthodox

Christians from the Ottoman Empire to settle in the newly established Military Frontier.

The Croatian national awakening of the 1830s and 1840s, also known as the Illyrian Movement, was not a strictly "Croatian" movement. It was designed for a nationality whose historical territory had been fragmented, and which faced the possible loss of its historical rights and its language through magyarization. In 1830, the lands actually under the jurisdiction of the Croatian kingdom were very small. Despite the impressive title "Kingdom of Croatia, Slavonia, and Dalmatia," the kingdom consisted of six small counties: three in Croatia (Civil Croatia) and three in Slavonia (Civil Slavonia). The Croatian and Slavonian Military Frontier, ruled by the Austrian Military, was about the same size as the Civil territories with a slightly smaller population. In 1846 Orthodox Christians made up 8 percent of the population of Civil Croatia, 37 percent of Civil Slavonia, 46 percent of the Croatian and Slavonian Military Frontier, and 19 percent of the Austrian province of Dalmatia (Despalatović 1975: 8–9). It was impossible to ignore the Serbian minority if the Illyrians had any hope of a broad-based national movement. Therefore Ljudevit Gaj decided in 1835 to base the modern Croatian language on the *štokavian* dialect, the dialect that was most widely used in the Croatian core provinces, and not on *kajkavian*, which was the dialect of Zagreb, the political and cultural capital and its environs. If he had chosen *kajkavian* as the basis for modern Croatian, the new language might have alienated the *štokavian* speakers in the Military Frontier, Civil Slavonia, and Dalmatia. The choice of *štokavian* was tied directly to Croatia's goal of reuniting its historical territories, reclaiming the Renaissance literary tradition of Dubrovnik and Dalmatia, and protecting her special position within the Kingdom of Hungary and the Hapsburg Empire (Despalatović 1975: 63–98, 200–201).

Most nationalities have modern languages all their own. The modern language of the Croats does not separate them clearly from the Serbs or the Bosnian Muslims. The *štokavian* dialect chosen by the Illyrians was also dominant in Bosnia and Herzegovina and Serbia and served as the basis of their literary languages as well. Croats use the Latin alphabet, Serbs the Cyrillic, and the Bosnian Muslims use both. Croatian is based on the *ijekvian* variant of *štokavian* and Serbian on the *ekavian*, but until recently the languages were seen, abroad at least, as one and called Serbo-Croatian (or Croato-Serbian). The choice of *štokavian* for modern Croatian deprived the Croats of a key cultural marker. Consider how the "differentness" of the Slovene literary language has buffered its national development. Yet the fact that Croats, Serbs, and Bosnian Muslims have shared a literary language has made it possible for them to escape the cultural parochialism of small nations, and create a significant modern literature for an audience which stretches across the middle of the Balkan peninsula. Today this joint literary language is breaking into three: Croatian, Serbian, and Bosniak (Bošnjački).

Modern Croatian culture has been, for the most part, assimilative. You need only walk through Mirogoj cemetery in Zagreb and read the names of families buried there. There are Croatian, Serbian, Slovene, Hungarian, German, Czech, Polish, Russian, Italian, Turkish, and Bosnian Muslim names, even a few English and French ones. The Hapsburg nobility, army, and civil service were multinational. The towns were for a long time foreign in language and culture: German (Croatia-Slavonia) or Italian (Dalmatia). Assimilation also took place in rural Croatia as serf owners moved peasants from estates in one Hapsburg territory to another and refugees from Turkish territories were absorbed in waves over the centuries. People of many different nationalities were brought together by the recolonization of Slavonia and the Turkish parts of Croatia. Finally, a steady flow of immigrants from other parts of the Hapsburg empire came to Slavonia, where land was good and relatively cheap, in the half century before World War I. Most of these people came in small groups or as individuals and were assimilated in a generation or two.

It was quite another thing when the Serbs of the Military Frontier, a large minority with special rights as a community so long as the Frontier existed (Rothenberg 1966: 8–9,11,13) became part of the semi-autonomous Kingdom of Croatia, Slavonia, and Dalmatia in 1881. At that time half of the Frontier was Orthodox (Valentić 1981: 316). The Civil and Military territories were merged and reorganized into eight counties, four in Croatia, four in Slavonia. After incorporation 26 percent of the population of Croatia-Slavonia was of Orthodox faith (Kr. Zemaljski statistički Ured 1905: 38). The largest concentration of Serbs was found in areas near the border with Bosnia. Smaller minorities made up another 10 percent of the population: Hungarians, Germans, Italians, Czechs, Slovaks, Jews, Gypsies, Ruthenians, Albanians, etc. (ibid., 39).

The Serbs of the Military Frontier became Croatian citizens at a time when the Croatian political parties were increasingly nationalist, and when the growing Serbian polity in the south was finally recognized by the Great Powers as an independent kingdom. The Serbs of the former Military Frontier had to find their feet in this new political world. Should the kingdom and language still be known as Croatian (Roksandić 1991: 145–83)? Should the Serbs be taught in their own national or parochial schools? Should they adopt the Latin alphabet and the standard modern Croatian language? Should their political parties look to Serbia for political direction or focus on improving their position within the Triune Kingdom and Austria-Hungary (Miller 1997)? National tensions in political life were exacerbated by the actions of the pro-Magyar Croatian Ban, Karoly Khuen-Hédérváry (1883–1903), who played the Croatian Serbs off against the Croats. Anti-Serb riots shook Zagreb in 1902, provoked by an extremist article in *Srbobran*, the local Serbian newspaper (Miller 1997: 52–53). Yet the Croatian and Serbian elite still found more common ground than not, and after 1903 Croatian politics were dominated by a coalition of Croatian and Serbian parties.

Nationalism was still of little interest to the vast majority of the inhabitants of the Kingdom of Croatia, Slavonia and Dalmatia before World War I, for they were peasants living in traditional peasant culture. Modern nationalism was only beginning to come to the villages through the public schools, newspapers, and occasional visits by politicians. The village studies made for the Yugoslav Academy at that time (JAZU/ONŽO: 1897–1918, *Zbornik*: 1898–1927) show that while peasants in Croatia identified themselves as Croats or Serbs, peasants in Slavonia still had a regional (Slavonian) identity. The eighty-eight page questionnaire on which the village studies were based (Radić 1897) did not ask specifically about national identity, but the section which begins "Who is our kind of person [*nas čovjek*]?" comes closest (Radić 1897: 67). In Slavonia most of the villages studied answered something like this: "Our kind of person is someone who speaks as we do, dresses as we do, and believes as we do." The first two— speech and dress—were more regional than national. A speaker of *štokavian* could be a Croat or a Serb or even a gypsy. There were mixed villages in Slavonia where Serbs and Croats wore the same folk costume with only subtle differences in color and ornamentation. Religion alone seems to have made a clear distinction between Serbs and Croats. Serbs were Orthodox, Croats Catholic.

Croatian and Serbian peasants acted in unison in the demonstrations that swept Croatian and Slavonia in 1903 protesting the policies of Ban Khuen-Héder-váry. To them the Hungarians were still the enemy, not each other. If there had been deep "hatreds" between rural Serbs and Croats, would there not have been many recorded instances of violence, would they not have turned on each other whenever there was a break in authority?

With the collapse of Austria-Hungary in 1918, the Hungarian "enemy" disappeared. The Croatian Serbs were now ruled by their Serbian "brothers." Lines between rural Serbs and Croats began to be drawn more clearly by specifically Serbian and Croatian political parties and their affiliated newspapers, Serbian or Croatian savings banks, cultural organizations, and cooperative associations. The Serbian Democratic Party, the most important among Croatian Serbs, at first strongly supported the union with Serbia and the centralist constitution. However, by the late 1920s it joined the Croatian Peasant Party in various groupings of the opposition, the most important of which were the Democratic Bloc of 1927–28 and the United Opposition of 1939.

When the Croatian *banovina* was established in 1939, some of the Croatian Serbs were worried. While they knew that the Croatian Peasant Party was not anti-Serb, the Croatian *banovina* was a step toward a Croatian nation-state. Where did the Serbs fit in? Some Croatian Serbs called for the creation of an autonomous Serbian region within the *banovina*. Rade Pribičević, brother of the former Democratic Party leader Svetozar Pribičević, warned against this, saying:

> The Sporazum does not mean the division of our country, but rather the strengthening of it. Therefore it does not make sense to talk about a Serbian Krajina separating itself from Croatia. . . . The Serbian region which these people desire would reach to Karlovac [which is very near the Slovene frontier] and Croatia would only have a narrow band of territory

> linking her to Dalmatia. . . . Secondly, a [Serbian] Krajina would not be
> a viable geographic or economic entity, but would include almost entirely
> poor and economically backward areas. . . . Thirdly [a Serbian Krajina]
> would include a large Croatian minority within its frontiers. . . . Finally,
> the Serbs in the Croatian Banovina do not need to feel themselves threat-
> ened. There are about one million of them. A half million Croats live
> outside the Croatian Banovina. The Serbs have lived centuries with the
> Croats and survived. They [the Serbs] are capable and tough, they can
> fight and create. Should they find themselves compelled to defend their
> nationality, they would fight bravely. (Roksandić 1991: 130)

Pribičević based his predictions about the peaceful coexistence of Serbs and
Croats on his knowledge of the policies of the dominant Croatian Peasant Party.
How could he foresee the coming to power of the Ustasha? He did, however,
clearly anticipate the problems the Serbs would face when they did attempt to
create their own polity within Croatia in the 1990s.

After World War II many Serbs from the poorer areas of Croatia were given
land elsewhere, many resettled on prosperous farms originally belonging to Germans. Industrialization and migration to the cities drew other Serbs to different
parts of Croatia and to other republics. Tito encouraged a Serbian presence in
the League of Communists, the military, the police, and the economy as part of
his balancing act to keep national peace within Yugoslavia. Yet the largest number of Serbs in the Republic of Croatia were still clustered near the border of
Bosnia and Herzegovina. Much of this area was economically passive, a region
of outmigration. There was little industry or even tourism.

In 1989 as Croatia moved toward free elections and began to think about
independence, a wave of fear swept through the Croatian Serb communities. The
recent publication of material on the fate of the Serbs in the NDH had awakened
old memories and anger. The litany of national martyrdom coming from Serbia,
the Memorandum of the Serbian Academy, the speeches of Slobodan Milošević,
all deepened these feelings. By the late 1980s it was quite usual to hear the term
Ustaše used as a synonym for Croat on the Belgrade media. The Croatian Serbs
were told by their own politicians, particularly those in the Serbian Democratic
Party (SDS) and by political leaders in Serbia, that the elections in Croatia would
bring back an Ustasha-type regime, that a Croatian nation-state would have no
place for a Serbian minority (Tanner 1997: 234–40; Silber and Little 1996: chaps.
6–7).

The Constitution of the new Republic of Croatia (January 21, 1990) is quite
clear about minority rights. It says that

> [The Republic] is established as the national state . . . of the Croatian
> nation and the state of members of other nations and minorities who are
> its citizens: Serbs, Moslems, Slovenes, Czechs, Slovaks, Italians, Hungar-

ians, Jews and others, who are guaranteed equality of rights with citizens
of Croatian nationality and with the democratic norms of the United Nations Organizations and the countries of the free world. . . .

. . . The Republic of Croatia guarantees to Serbs in Croatia and to all
national minorities living in its territory respect of all human and civil
rights, particularly freedom of speech and the cultivation of their own
languages and promotion of their cultures, and freedom to form political
organizations. (*Ustav* 1991)

Why then did so many of the Croatian Serbs reject citizenship in the new
Croatian state? The previous constitution had referred to the Socialist Republic
of Croatia as "the national state of the Croatian nation and the state of the Serbian
nation in Croatia" (Tanner 1997: 230). The new constitution spoke of "other
nations and minorities." The Serbs chose to disregard the term "other nations"
in the new constitution, which clearly applied to Serbs, and decided that they had
been reduced to a "minority." As the HDZ began to move its own people into
the governing institutions of Croatia, many Serbian communists lost their jobs,
not because they were Serbs but because they were communists. It was easy,
then, for agitators to play on the insecurities caused by such firings and try to
convince the Serbian community that they represented the beginning of a new
period of persecution.

In January 1991, a large group of Croatian Serbs based in Knin declared
autonomy from the Republic of Croatia and set up a new entity called the Serbian
Autonomous Province of Krajina (SAO Krajina). In 1990 the Yugoslav People's
Army (JNA) disarmed the Croatian Territorial Defense forces and armed the
Croatian Serbs, who were now ready to put those arms to use (Silber and Little
1996: 105–7). The Croatian Serbs were helped in their battle by paramilitary
groups from Serbia and the Serb-dominated JNA. Once Croatia declared independence from Yugoslavia and the conflict spiraled into war, the territory of the
SAO Krajina grew. It soon came to include other territory from Croatia, Western
Slavonia, and the Dalmatian hinterland. In July 1991, another SAO came into
being, "SAO Slavonia," the Serb-occupied sections of Eastern Slavonia and Baranja, and joined the rest. The Serbs of the "Krajina" then expressed their desire
to join "Greater Serbia" and began to call themselves "Republika Srpska Krajina" (RSK). Until August 1995, the RSK comprised about one-third of Croatia,
lying astride the major communications routes between Croatia/Slavonia and
Dalmatia.

The RSK was made up of districts that were predominantly Serbian, mixed
districts, and districts that were predominantly Croatian. In order for the RSK to
be purely Serbian, the non-Serbs had to be removed. Between 1991 and August
1995, despite the presence of UN peacekeepers along the borders, Serbian paramilitary forces and Serbian inhabitants of the RSK killed or expelled the Croats
living there. They are still finding mass graves. In addition, as Rade Pribičević

had warned in 1939, the "Krajina," with the exception of Serbian-occupied Eastern Slavonia and Baranja, proved to be an economic disaster and steadily lost population in its few years of "independence" (Tanner 1997: 283–84).

In the spring and summer of 1995, the Croatian army, now well armed and well trained, recaptured all but Eastern Slavonia and Baranja in a series of brilliant and rapid battles, and the mass exodus of the Serbs from the liberated territories began. Most of the Serbs from the RSK fled with the Krajina army in August of 1995, when Croatian troops swept in to liberate the territory. Eastern Slavonia and Baranja were returned to Croatia in January 1998. Serbs from the former RSK still live as refugees in Eastern Slavonia, the Serbian Republic of Bosnia, Yugoslavia, and abroad, although some are beginning to return to their former homes.

The violence used by some Croats against the remaining Serbian population and Serbian property after the exodus of the Serbs from the RSK should not be used to prove that the Croats in 1990–91 were planning to persecute the Serbs. The violence in 1995 was the end of something not the beginning. It followed the secession of the RSK, a bloody war in Croatia caused by Serbian military aggression, Serbian occupation of one-third of Croatia, ethnic cleansing of Croats from historical Croatian territory, the destruction of Croatian churches, hospitals, factories, bridges, schools, historical monuments, communities, and many Croatian deaths.

In some ways the fate of the Krajina Serbs resembles that of the ten million Germans (*Volksdeutsche*) who lived in Eastern Europe before World War II (Lumans 1993). Of these, the story of the German minority in Czechoslovakia is the most similar. The German minority in Czechoslovakia had little to complain about in terms of minority rights, but they were used to being the dominant nationality in the Austrian half of Austria-Hungary and resented being a national minority in a small Slavic state. The German minority, particularly those in the Sudetenland, gave Hitler a pretext for intervention, helped run the rump Czech state during the German occupation, and were expelled, whether guilty or not, by angry Czechs after the war. Many of the Volksdeutsche in other East European states collaborated with the Nazis, and some were even resettled in newly conquered lands.

Like the Czech Germans, and the other Volksdeutsche, the Croatian Serbs became pawns of a state (in their case Milošević's Yugoslavia) that claimed to act in their interest. Like many of the Volksdeutsche, they violated the trust of the communities in which they had lived. Millions of Germans fled from Eastern Europe at the end of World War II as the Soviet armies approached. Some were Nazi colonists, others were collaborators, others merely feared retribution for German war crimes. Millions more were forcibly deported by the states in which they had lived (de Zayas 1994).

There are, however, some major differences:

1. The Allies looked the other way when the Volksdeutsche fled or were expelled from Eastern Europe, for anti-German sentiment was deep, as was the desire for revenge. The Great Powers today, speaking in highly principled terms, seem much more in sympathy with the Serbian refugees from the "Serbian Krajina" than with the Croatian refugees expelled by the Serbs from the Krajina, Bosnia, and Eastern Slavonia. The Great Powers seem to have forgotten the origins of the war and the realities of Serbian ethnic cleansing, in an attempt to prevent further war and not alienate the man who has now become the peace broker of the Balkans—Slobodan Milošević. They urge the Croats to encourage the Serbian refugees to return, monitor the way the returnees are treated, and indicate that the Croats will be judged harshly if they do not comply.
2. German states, particularly West Germany and Austria, were able to absorb the bulk of the Volksdeutsche refugees. RumpYugoslavia seems neither willing nor able to resettle the refugees from the RSK, except in Kosovo, where few Serbs want to go.
3. In the end, the Volksdeutsche and Croatian Serbs were sacrificed by their fellow nationalists. The Volksdeutsche met their fate because of military defeat, while the Croatian Serbs met theirs by a combination of military defeat and the realpolitik of President Milošević of Serbia.

Bosnia and Herzegovina

Medieval Croatia had also, at times, included parts of Bosnia and Herzegovina and Istria. Croatia's historical claim to these territories is less clear than its claim to the core provinces. Bosnia and Herzegovina remained in Ottoman hands until 1878, when it was occupied, then annexed in 1908, by Austria-Hungary. Those Croats who sought a "Greater Croatia," one that would extend beyond the traditional core, claimed all or part of Bosnia and Herzegovina, as did those Serbs in Serbia who hoped for a "Greater Serbia" (Banac 1984: 70–112, 360–77). Both Croats and Serbs had diaspora in Bosnia and Herzegovina, and both claimed the Muslims to be converted members of their respective nationalities.

Bosnia and Herzegovina became part of the Kingdom of Serbs, Croats, and Slovenes in 1918. Herzegovina and a bit of Bosnia were included in the Croatian Banovina in 1939, and the wartime Independent State of Croatia included more of Bosnia. For Croatia, in addition to historical claims and concern about the Croatian minority, the acquisition of Bosnia and Herzegovina has geopolitical importance, since Croatia is shaped like a crescent and Bosnia and Herzegovina is the "missing" middle part. Croat and Serb claims to Bosnia and Herzegovina were put on the back burner after World War II, when Tito and the Party decided to establish the Republic of Bosnia and Herzegovina. Croatia received most of Istria instead.

The question of Bosnia and Herzegovina was revived once more as communist Yugoslavia headed toward collapse. Once in power, President Franjo Tudjman of Croatia openly stated his belief that Bosnia and Croatia are "a natural geographical and economic unit" (Tanner 1997: 228). In March of 1991, several months before the war began in Croatia, he discussed possible ways of partitioning Bosnia and Herzegovina with President Milošević of Serbia at the secret talks at Karadjordjevo (Silber and Little 1996: 132).

The Croats of Bosnia and Herzegovina have had a very different historical experience than the Croats of Croatia, Slavonia, and Dalmatia. They were located at the meeting place of Catholicism and Orthodoxy, where Catholicism was not well organized in the Middle Ages and conversions back and forth were common. The Franciscan Order was the bulwark of Christianity there, not the parish. The Croats of Bosnia and Herzegovina lived under the Ottomans much longer than the Croats of Croatia and Slavonia, were poorer and more isolated from events in Western Europe. and lived in an area of mixed nationality (Catholic, Orthodox, Muslim) which was to become a powderkeg with the rise of competing nationalisms. Some of the leading Ustasha came from Western Herzegovina. Herzegovinians wield a strong influence today in the Croatian Democratic Union (HDZ), the ruling party in Croatia. Croatia's involvement in Bosnia and Herzegovina has without doubt complicated her first years of independence, and I wonder how many Croats really support President Tudjman's desire for partition.

The Dayton Accord, which halted the tragic war in Bosnia, has attempted to reestablish a multiethnic Bosnia composed of joint central authorities and two ministates: the Serbian Republic (RS), and an imposed and shaky Croatian-Muslim Federation. Unless NATO, the UN, and the Great Powers take a firm stand, really make it possible for refugees to return to areas from which they have been ethnically "cleansed," arrest war criminals, and make the Serbs of the RS cooperate, we will witness a final partition of Bosnia and Herzegovina. This would leave a vocal and angry Muslim population in a tiny state of their own, or as a minority within Croatia, in both cases a canker that could explode into new war.

Conclusion

Living standards steadily rose in Croatia between 1950 and the late 1970s, as Croatia was gradually transformed from an agricultural to an industrial society. Factory complexes, roads, bridges, dams were built. There was a constant need for labor. Modern apartment complexes, schools, hospitals, hotels, stores, and office buildings changed the face of town and city. Daycare centers and maternity leave eased the lives of working mothers. The medical system worked well. Schools and universities educated new generations of skilled workers, technicians, engineers, doctors, specialists of various kinds, and scholars. Television sets, cars, and washing machines were no longer considered luxuries by a growing urban middle class. Good roads and public bus service linked town and country. The potential problem of unemployment was masked by the thousands of Croats, especially from rural areas, who left to become "guest workers" in the factories and cities of Europe. Theater and the arts were lively. Scientists and scholars went regularly to international conferences, were granted fellowships abroad, and had access to foreign books and professional journals. Foreign tourists provided a steady influx of foreign currency. The *dinar* seemed strong. For several decades material progress made up for the lack of democracy and for an ideology in which fewer and fewer believed.

Tito died in 1980. Despite dire predictions of immediate collapse by foreign journalists and experts, Yugoslavia held together. Yet by the mid 1980s life was harder for most people. Tito had left behind an almost unmanageable foreign debt. Inflation was rampant and prices changed from day to day. Unemployment became an admitted fact and an especially serious problem for the young. Stores were packed with all kinds of goods, domestic and imported, but customers bought carefully. There were recurring shortages of meat, oil, coffee, and gasoline. Fuel shortages led to occasional brownouts, which meant cold and dark homes, schools, and empty factories. Old people collected discarded vegetables and fruits from the market to eke out their pensions. Buildings and trams and buses grew shabbier. The health service was overworked and underfunded. A radical educational reform in Croatia wreaked havoc in the schools. When the IMF stepped in to help stabilize the situation, Croatia, as all of Yugoslavia, entered a period of economic austerity, which made things even worse.

There was a grayness to life, and many people turned to alcohol to dull their despair. Everyday conversations overheard in bars and cafes were larded with obscenities. A network of thieves, including respected scholars and booksellers, were caught selling rare books from the National and University Library. Scientists and scholars were cut off from normal professional life as inflation cut their incomes drastically, research and travel funds dried up, and libraries stopped buying foreign books and professional journals. Increasing numbers of young people left to work abroad. Who was responsible for this mess? Nationalism became more and more appealing as a mobilizing force. It drew attention away from the failing economy and replaced empty communist rhetoric with new visions and different enemies.

The communists could no longer argue that their system offered people prosperity. The central government was coming apart as was the League of Communists. There was little holding Yugoslavia together any more, except the Yugoslav Army.

Croatia is better off as an independent state. The "marriage" with Serbia was flawed from the beginning. Neither of the composite nation-states formed after World War I has survived. The division of Czechoslovakia occurred quite peacefully, for the Czechs had little to lose. Slovakia was smaller and poorer than the

Czech Republic. The Czechs had a clear idea of their national identity, while the Slovaks are still defining theirs. Slovakia would probably have acted as a brake on the Czechs' rapid transition to democracy and a market economy. Few Czechs lived in Slovakia. The Croatian-Serbian relationship was much different. Both had well-developed national identities at the time they were joined in a multinational state. Serbia was dominant and bigger; Croatia had a stronger economy and a Serbian minority. Serbia had much more to lose than Croatia in the disintegration of the second Yugoslavia. Now that there has been a bloody and bitter war, the divorce between Serbia and Croatia is irremediable.

Former Yugoslavia has become a collection of ministates. "Brotherhood and Unity" is a pious phrase from the past. Much of what had been built since World War II lies in ruins. Children, women, men, have died. The Yugoslav wars have created millions of refugees, destroyed multiethnic communities, traumatized the population, broken lives. When will it end?

Nationalism as a Folk Ideology

The Case of Former Yugoslavia

Andrei Simić

Underlying Causes of the Tragedy

Probably very few of us who had spent our academic careers studying the Balkans were entirely prepared for the dissolution of Yugoslavia and the ensuing civil war which erupted after more than four decades of relative ethnic quiescence under a Titoist rule that harshly repressed most expressions of nationalism. The ferocity of this conflict and the intensity of the hatreds fueling it have been reflected in the most massive movement of refugees in Europe since the close of World War II, with hundreds of thousands fleeing, or being driven, from regions occupied for centuries by their ancestors. Seeking haven abroad, or in areas dominated by their co-ethnics, they have placed a heavy burden on their hosts, and it now appears all too evident that, in spite of the conditions of the Dayton Accord, most have little prospect of ever returning to their natal homes. For example, Serbian sources estimate that the Federated Republic of Yugoslavia has accepted more refugees than any other country, about 600,000. Of this number 185,000 are from the Bosnian Muslim-Croat Federation, 49,000 from Republika Srpska, and 256,000 from Croatia, and of these all but 43,800 are Serbs (Ministry of Information of the Republic of Serbia 1997: 61–63). If these figures are accurate—and I believe that they are in fact, now larger due to the recent exodus of

Serbs, Roma, Gorani, and others from Kosovo—this should emphatically under-score the fact that so-called ethnic cleansing has been a weapon of war and retri-bution on the part of all the combatants, not simply the Serbs as the Western media have so often implied.

The underlying causes of this tragedy have been attributed variously to a spec-trum of historical, cultural, social, political, economic, and even mythical factors. These speculations are not only numerous, but also at times contradictory. Per-haps the greatest conceptual opposition is between those who perceive the origins of the conflict rooted in "centuries of ethnic hatred" and those who point to years of ostensible harmony between the antagonists. This latter group places the blame on cynical, power-hungry leaders taking advantage of economic decline, ideolog-ical anomie, and the shift in power in Yugoslavia over the last several decades from the federal to the republican level.

Certainly individual political ambitions, decentralization, economic chaos, and the cynical and self-serving meddling of foreign powers must be recognized as among the immediate causes of the Yugoslav wars of succession. However, to minimize the salient role of ethnicity is to ignore what is perhaps the principal energizing force underlying these conflicts.

The Myth of Tolerance and Coexistence in Bosnia

To cite a conspicuous example, Robert Donia and John Fine, in their book *Bosnia and Hercegovina: A Tradition Betrayed* (1994), glossing over a plethora of evi-dence to the contrary, depict the new Bosnian government as a model of multi-ethnic harmony and equality, the inheritors of a venerable tradition of harmonious Bosnian multiculturalism. For instance they note that "the Bosnian cabinet, as of February 12, 1993, contained nine Muslims, six Serbs, and five Croats. . . . In so constituting itself, the Bosnian government has been represent-ing a tradition of tolerance and coexistence that goes back many centuries" (6).

What can be said about this "tradition of tolerance and coexistence that goes back many centuries"? For example, Dušan Bataković (1996: 11) asserts that the ethnic and religious cleavages in Bosnia and Herzegovina date from at least sev-eral centuries ago: "The division between the Christian and Islamic communities, already clearly emerging by the end of the 17th century, was intensified by grow-ing political disorder and social dissent within the empire but especially by the periodic, mostly Serbian revolts. . . . The era of nationalism found Bosnia and Herzegovina in a lamentable socioeconomic state, which was further aggravated by . . . religious-national tensions."

Similarly, in his introduction to Ivo Andrić's classic *The Bridge on the Drina*, William McNeil comments on the tensions between Bosnian Christians and Mus-lims during the waning years of Turkish rule (1977: 2): "As Ottoman power diminished . . . and the might of adjacent Christian empires correspondingly increased, the religious divisions of Bosnian society became potentially explosive."

To cite another of the many sources addressing the long-standing religio-ethnic antagonisms in Bosnia and Herzegovina, H. C. Darby et al. (1968: 66–67) paint the following picture of Muslim-Christian relations during the last century: "During the nineteenth century the main factors important in the fortunes of Bosnia and Herzegovina were the presence of: (1) a conservative landholding Muslim aristocracy more fanatical than the central Ottoman authorities at Constantinople; (2) an oppressed Christian peasantry subject to heavy taxation. . . . The corruption of Turkish officials and the exactions of the tax-farmers continued to make the life of the peasants barely supportable."

Yugoslavia Torn from the Moment of Its Creation by Divisions

In fact, Yugoslavia was torn from the very moment of its creation by internal ethnic and religious divisions and separatist aspirations. The failure of the vision of South Slav unity was to be reaffirmed time and time again during the interwar period. It culminated during World War II with the creation of the pro-Nazi Independent State of Croatia (NDH) which, with its Muslim allies, attempted to kill, "ethnically cleanse," or convert to Catholicism the entire Serbian population of Croatia and Bosnia and Herzegovina. The number of Serbs killed in this genocide have been estimated to be as large as 800,000 to one million (including some tens of thousands of Jews and Gypsies) (see Balen 1952; Martin 1946: 47–67; Paris 1961; Pridonoff 1955: 79, among many others). Such episodes of ethnic hatred and religious fanaticism only serve to underscore the fact that Yugoslavia was largely an artificial creation bringing together over eighteen Slavic and non-Slavic peoples. Even the supposed homogeneity of the South Slavs, based largely on the concept of shared language and distant common "racial" origins, was largely illusory. In fact, the Serbs, Croats, Slav Muslims, Slovenes, and Macedonians were in a variety of ways separated by dialect, religion, historical tradition, worldview, and ties to different civilizations and allies. Moreover, the problem of ethnic divisiveness was further exacerbated by the fact that in Yugoslavia there was no ethnic majority, since the largest single nationality, the Serbs (with the Montenegrins), constituted only slightly over 40 percent of the population. Thus, in spite of the domination of the Serbian Karadjordjevich dynasty during the period between the two World Wars, no single group was able to gain a position of total or lasting ascendancy. Because of this, other smaller ethnic groups, such as the Slovenes, Slav Muslims, Macedonians, and Albanians took whatever advantage they could from the competition and conflict between the two major players, the Serbs and Croats.

While ethnic leaders have clearly played a major role in the manipulation and mobilization of ethnic particularism in the present conflict, this would not have been possible without considerable popular support. For example, William Lockwood (1975: 160) in his study of Muslim villagers in Western Bosnia during the 1970s noted the "relatively strict social separation of ethnic groups." Similarly, it has been my own observation on numerous visits to Bosnia and Herzegovina (spanning the period 1961 to 1988, and including a three-month sojourn in the formerly predominately Muslim town of Zvornik in eastern Bosnia), that there prevailed a deep and obvious separation between the ethnic groups, a separation characterized by both mistrust and apprehension. Thus it seems clear that Donia and Fine have most likely garnered their impressions of ethnic harmony in Bosnia largely on the basis of their association with urban Sarajevan intellectuals and cosmopolitans (see Donia and Fine 1994: 4). With reference to this assumption, it should be noted that the civil war in Bosnia has been portrayed frequently as a conflict of the countryside against the city, and significantly, the majority of Serbs in Bosnia were rural in contrast to the predominantly urban and small-town Muslims.

Ethnically Mixed Marriages and the Census Term "Yugoslav"

Another effort to minimize the ethnic basis of the civil wars in former Yugoslavia has focused on the large number of mixed marriages. V. P. Gagnon (1994) provides such a case in point. However statistics regarding such unions can be quite misleading. For example, the Montenegrins have the highest rate of outmarriage of all South Slav groups. However, the vast majority of these unions are with Serbs with whom they share such close historical and cultural ties as to constitute virtually the same people, although they are listed as a separate nationality in the Yugoslav census data (see Petrović 1985). Also, the demographics do not themselves reveal adequately the underlying social realities. For instance, Gagnon notes that 25 percent of Croatia's population consists of ethnic minorities, and that 16.9 percent of all marriages were mixed. This ignores the fact that 83.1 percent of all unions were ethnically homogeneous, and that marriage in many parts of former Yugoslavia with its strong patrilineal bias simply provided a means for recruiting women into their husbands' kinship groups. Furthermore, the children of such families often assumed the religion and ethnic identity of their fathers (see Petrović and Simić 1990). Also the data on marriage includes the category "Yugoslav" as a nationality, a term frequently employed by Croatian and Bosnia Serbs fearing discrimination and thus serving as a means of masking their true ethnic identity (Simić 1994: 33–34). The entire matter of ethnically mixed marriages brings to mind Fredrik Barth's (1969: 21) classic assertion that "examples of stable and persisting ethnic boundaries that are crossed by a flow of personnel are clearly more common than the ethnographic literature would lead us to believe."

It is particularly significant in respect to the strength of ethnic identity that in the 1971 census (Demographic Research Center 1974: 39), out of approximately 20.5 million respondents, only 273,000 identified themselves as "Yugoslavs." Moreover, while there was a fourfold increase in the number of "Yugoslavs" reported in the census of 1981, this represented only a little over five percent of the total. Even this number is somewhat misleading because the greatest number of those who declared themselves "Yugoslavs" were in urban centers and ethnically mixed regions. Significantly, there were virtually no "Yugoslavs" counted in rural Serbia and less than one percent in Macedonia (Simić 1982: 8–10). It seems evident that in these areas there was no need to hide one's ethnicity.

As noted, none of the preceding observations necessarily negate the salient role of power-hungry native leaders or that of foreign powers anxious to extend their spheres of political and economic influence into Southeastern Europe as immediate catalysts for the recent conflicts in former Yugoslavia. Of the latter, probably the most frequently cited is Germany whose pressure on its Western allies led to the precipitous recognition of Slovenia, Croatia, and Bosnia as sovereign states without any preemptive attempt to solve the convoluted problems of national minorities within these newly created international borders. In the case of Bosnia, its fate was already preordained by the declarations of independence on the part of Slovenia and Croatia. The popular referendum on Bosnian independence (held between February 29 and March 1, 1992) resulted in the overwhelming majority of Croats and Muslim voting in favor. However, it failed to garner the two-thirds majority required by the Bosnian constitution, since it was boycotted by virtually the entire Serbian population. Still, the international community ignored the illegality of the referendum and the legitimacy of former Yugoslavia's international borders, and admitted Bosnia as a sovereign state into the United Nations on April 30, 1992. This set the stage for the inevitable rebellion of the Bosnian and Herzegovinian Serbs, who were unwilling to live under the domination of those they perceived to be their former enemies who had committed genocide against them during World War II. This was essentially a repetition of the same fate that had befallen the Croatian Serbs when Croatia received international recognition in January 1992 (see Bataković 1996: 130–35).

Folk Models of Kinship, Nationalism, and the Nation-State

In contrast to the narrow focus on events of the last few decades, historical explanations of greater depth recognize the significance of Yugoslavia's geographical position straddling a volatile frontier contested for centuries by three great and mutually antagonistic traditions, Roman Catholicism, Eastern Orthodoxy, and Islam. This frontier still constitutes an unstable but strategic link between Europe and the Middle East. In this light, it seems inescapable that regardless of other immediate causes for the violent fragmentation of the most multiethnic state in Europe outside the Soviet Union, the tinder for this conflagration had long been present in the form of a syncretic worldview. On one hand, this derived from a synthesis of nineteenth-century European Romanticism and Nationalism. On the other, it developed from an older and far more pervasive ideological substratum based on folk models of kinship and tribalism extrapolated to the modern nation-state. Here I make reference to the seamless integration of what anthropologist Robert Redfield (1956) labeled the "Great and Little Tradition." Redfield spoke of the contrasting, but symbiotic, relationship between elite and popular culture. An analogous opposition can be hypothesized between contrived, self-consciously held, or propagated ideologies, on the one hand, and those discerned to be intrinsically part of the *natural order* (the term "natural order" is employed here in the *emic* sense, that is, as a reflection of native perceptions). In other words, the latter constitute artifacts of folk culture which tend to be embraced in an uncritical, or even subconscious, manner by ordinary people.

Because of this, such popular belief systems evidence not only greater tenacity and longevity than ideologies deliberately or self-consciously imposed from above by political or intellectual elites, but their assumptions are not nearly as amenable to empirical or experiential validation. Furthermore, they are to a greater extent self-perpetuating. Their tenets are inculcated as an integral part of the socialization process of children and are also reinforced by numerous elements of folk culture integrated into everyday life. Therefore, they do not require the same kind of constant and deliberate reinforcement so typical of newly imposed elite ideologies. In other words, their doctrines are not as privy to cultural entropy (see Hammel 1964). Such a belief system is quite similar in its general outlines to what Carl Jung (1983: 55) has described as "collective symbols" that are perceived to be of "divine origin." and to have been "revealed to man." Moreover, ethnicity (and by extension nationalism) as a folk concept, constitutes an overarching, multistranded ideology locating the individual within a historical, cultural, and kinship context, thus answering one of life's most basic questions— who am I? Few imposed ideologies can lay claim to such an all-encompassing purview or sense of legitimacy. Within this frame of reference, former Yugoslavia provides an optimal setting for the illumination of the very salient role that folk culture may play as a dynamic force in the political process.

The Resurgence of South Slav Nationalism

Sixteen years ago, in June 1981, six children in the remote and impoverished Croatian Catholic village of Medjugorje reported a series of visitations by the Virgin Mary (see Chapter 11). Not only did this result in this backward Herzegovinian community becoming a world pilgrimage site, but also, in spite of the Church hierarchy's failure to legitimize these occurrences as genuine miracles, the phenomenon was quickly coopted by the Franciscans. This Catholic order had been closely associated with, and supportive of, the pro-Nazi Independent

State of Croatia (NDH) during World War II (see Balen 1952). Similarly, at about the same time, construction began in Belgrade on what would become the largest Eastern Orthodox church in the Balkans. Its dedication to St. Sava, the Patron Saint of Serbia, clearly underscored its nationalist implications. Now religion and ethnic affiliation had finally and dramatically emerged into the public arena from their Marxist-imposed semi-obscurity and repression. The significance of this was that religious identification had, at least for several centuries, been the single most defining marker of national identity among the Serbs, Croats, and Slav Muslims.

The Symbolic Self-Definition of the South Slavs

As is elsewhere a common characteristic of ethnicity, the South Slavs define themselves in terms of a limited number of basic symbols, the kind of representations that Jerzy Smolicz (1979: 57–58) has described as "forming the most fundamental components of a group's culture" or "its core values." In former Yugoslavia these basic markers have been phrased as a series of dyadic cross-linkages involving both religion and language. Thus, for the Slovenes, the two most fundamental criteria are Catholicism and the Slovenian language. For the Croats, it is Catholicism and Serbo-Croatian. For the Serbs, it is Eastern Orthodoxy and Serbo-Croatian; for the Slav Muslims, Islam and Serbo-Croatian; and for the Macedonians, Eastern Orthodoxy and Macedonian. (This still holds true in spite of recent efforts by both the Muslims and Croats to introduce linguistic changes into their literary languages to differentiate them as much as possible from Serbian variants.) In addition to these overarching and fundamental determinants of nationhood, there is also a complex of more ambiguous markers largely, though not exclusively, associated with popular culture. Among such symbols are historical myths, regional dialects and folklore, musical genres (Simić 1979: 26–27), ethnic stereotypes, folk rituals and religious practices, family and clan lore, and a plethora of other traits and customs popularly held to be ethnically specific. Curiously, while these ethnic diacritics stress group differences and cultural distance, they also obscure an abundance of similarities shared by the Serbs, Croats, and Muslims alike. Such affinities provided the ideological basis for the nineteenth-century Illyrian movement and the creation of the Kingdom of the Serbs, Croats, and Slovenes following World War I, as well as for what, during the Tito era, was officially lauded in every corner of Yugoslavia as *bratstvo i jedinstvo* (brotherhood and unity).

Unfortunately, this concept of South Slav unity turned out to be an all-too-ephemeral ideal, one regarded during the post–World War II period with increasing skepticism by many, perhaps most, Yugoslavs. Thus, depending on the exigencies of the time, the South Slavs have periodically perceived themselves as variants of a single nation or as implacable antagonists. This suggests that the intensity of ethnic particularism and strife has evidenced a cyclical nature. In this respect, the conditions for the present crisis could not have been more favorable. Among other contributing factors, the Yugoslav Constitution of 1974 had significantly shifted power from the federal to the republican level. Furthermore, with Tito's death in 1980, there followed a period of increasing economic, ethnic, and political chaos (see Denitch 1994: 100–126). What remained after the final collapse of Marxism as a viable and credible ideology was the underlying, deeply entrenched ethos of ethnic particularism ripe to be energized by emergent post-Titoist leaders such as Milošević in Serbia, Karadžić among the Bosnian Serbs, Tudjman in Croatia, and Izetbegović among the Bosnian Muslims.

Paradoxically, some of the formerly most adamantly anticommunist Yugoslavs whom I have known now express a kind of nostalgia for the Titoist period, paying tribute to, among its other ostensible virtues, the role played by the regime in repressing expressions of chauvinism and ethnic rivalry. However, underlying these comments is the implicit recognition of the strength and tenacity of nationalist sentiments and ethnic antagonisms among the masses of South Slavs. As a Belgrade professor of chemistry recently wrote me (June 1997): "I remember that Tito very quickly, and perhaps drastically, brought about order and security for our citizens. Now in this time of hopelessness, I must thank Tito. Whether I desired it or not, Tito placed his stamp on my generation, and I am grateful that under his leadership there was peace, and that no one shot at me or at anyone else. I must say that he kept us from war for half a century. Otherwise, wars in the Balkans are very frequent, and we will return to the old suicidal cycle again, and you can be sure of that" (my translation).

In respect to Tito's role in enforcing a *modus vivendi* by repressing the passionate nationalist aspirations of the country's diverse ethnic groups, Vesna Pešić (1996: 1) notes that "maintaining political balance and diffusing ethnic tensions was the only way Yugoslavia could survive . . . if the Yugoslav state could not maintain these essential functions, the 'separation' of its intertwined national groups in a full-scale war would be the probable result."

The Ethos of Nationalism

Though nationalism is widely regarded as the creation of nineteenth-century European literary and political elites, it also took root among ordinary people as an expression of folk culture. As a popular manifestation, it can be explained as the inevitable result of a long historical process conceptually linking the family, clan, and tribe to the state. Thus ethnic ties can be represented as a kind of ideological charter underwriting social systems grown far too large and vicarious to be validated by the kinds of face-to-face relationships typical of so-called simple societies. In this light, ethnically based loyalties appear to differ little qualitatively or in their affective content from those associated with the family or local community. As such they represent the same ideological basis that has formed the under-pinning of human social organization since at least the Neolithic (see Simić and Custred 1982: 164–66). This view, of course, bears a strong affinity to what has come to be labeled the "primordialist" view of the origins of ethnicity (see Geertz 1963 and Isaacs 1975). Primordalism is usually perceived in opposition to "instrumentalist" and "constructionist" interpretations, which conceive ethnic identity as a modern invention developed by elites to further their economic and political aspirations (Walker and Stern 1993: 1). However, the Yugoslav case amply demonstrates that these contrasting concepts can be operative within the same context and that they need not be mutually exclusive.

One way that the various Yugoslav nationalisms may be conceived is in terms of the imposition by an intellectual and political elite of themes already long present in the indigenous folk cultures (see Sugar 1969). In other words, the general tenets of nineteenth-century European nationalism found fertile ground among the South Slavs who had already defined themselves ethnically both in respect to foreign oppressors such as the Hapsburgs and Ottoman Turks, and to their own South Slav neighbors who differed in religion, custom, and dialect.

Transcending the complexities of the specific South Slav national ideologies, a common underlying belief system can be discerned, one that appears to be shared to a greater or lesser extent by all the belligerents in the current civil war:

1. National identity is held to be the product of common origins, and as such it constitutes a kind of kinship writ large.
2. Regardless of evidence to the contrary, there is a belief that the ethnic group shares a single common culture, and these traditions ultimately define the nation's boundaries.
3. Co-nationals are united not only by shared traditions but also by what are regarded by many as "natural," or quasi-mystical bonds.
4. It thus follows that every nation has a "God-given" or "natural" right to its own territory and sovereignty.
5. Nations are perceived as separate orders of creation and, as such, comprise "objective categories." In this way, a people are not only imbued with a sense of their own innate uniqueness, but also regard themselves consequently in a state of potential opposition, competition, and/or conflict with other nations which comprise entities of a similar order.

Of course, the above-cited general characteristics can be recognized as present to varying degrees in most nationalist ideologies. However, the close congruence of these ideas with traditional South Slav cultural values seems exceptionally manifest. They thus provide a microcosm for observing the process by which the "Great Tradition" integrates and exploits the energies and innate proclivities of the folk culture. In this regard, particular reference will be made to the Serbian case with the understanding that it differs little in its basic characteristics from that of the Croats or Yugoslav Muslims.

The Serbian National Genesis

A detailed account of the emergence of South Slav national consciousness is not necessary in this context, since there are many excellent sources (e.g. Lederer 1969). Only a brief overview is required to place the following discussion in its appropriate perspective.

For the South Slavs it was particularly significant that the rise of nationalism in Central Europe was intimately associated with, and influenced by, the decline of the Hapsburg and Ottoman empires. This was especially true for the Serbs for whom the nineteenth century was a period in some ways analogous to that of the Spanish *reconquista*. It was a time characterized by a national revival marked by an almost fanatical compulsion to eradicate all visible symbols of Islamic rule combined with a desire to become part of Europe and to emulate, at least superficially, its styles. For instance, with the liberation of Belgrade from the Ottomans in 1806, the Serbs began the systematic destruction of the many mosques and other architectural reminders of Turkish domination. Today there remains only one mosque from this period in the city, the Barjakli Džamija (Andrić et al. 1967: 1–60). However, at the same time, there persisted the Turco-Byzantine concept of the inviolable relationship between religion (the Orthodox Church, in this case) and the state. For instance, under the Turkish *millet* system the Orthodox Church wielded both spiritual and secular power as the principal representative of the Serbian people. As a result, religion (and the many folk customs associated with it) became synonymous with ethnic identity. In this context, it seems somewhat paradoxical that Western concepts associated with the Romantic Movement and European Nationalism took root within what was essentially a non-Western tradition. In this way, an alien political philosophy was not simply transplanted in its totality, replacing the indigenous system, but rather was integrated into it, forming a virtually seamless, syncretic whole. In the Serbian lands, as elsewhere in much of Europe, language and folklore became significant markers of national identity. However, in this case, religion together with elements of common law and kinship also became central to the definition of Serbianism (see Bogišić 1974; Halpern and Hammel 1969). No less today than in the past, Serbian identity, as well as the militancy and ferocity evidenced in the current conflict in former Yugoslavia, can be explained to a large part in terms of the interaction of these above-cited values.

Kinship and Serbian Identity

For the Serb, and for most other South Slavs, the conceptual contrast between the "nation" and the "family" is largely one of degree. In contrast the state is viewed as belonging to another order of reality and, as such, associated with nonkinship values. Thus the continuum between the family and the nation is differentiated, for the most part, in terms of scale and level of abstraction. This interconnection was eloquently underscored by Milovan Djilas in his classic family epic, *Land without Justice* (1958: 3): "The story of a family can also portray the soul of the land. This is especially true of Montenegro where the people are divided into clans and tribes to which each family is indissolubly bound. The life of the family reflects the broader community of kin, and through it the entire nation."

Of particular significance for understanding the current Yugoslav civil war, as well as much of the brutal behavior associated with it, is the strong traditional ethos of vengeance among the South Slavs (with the exception of the Slovenes), a value rooted firmly in family and clan corporacy and solidarity. Thus, especially for Serbs living in Montenegro and other areas of the rugged Dinaric highlands of western Yugoslavia (a region where some of the most vicious fighting has occurred during the present conflict), feuding and warfare traditionally took on not only an obligatory nature but also a quasi-sacred one (Boehm 1984: 60). This characteristic is vividly underscored by the venerable folk aphorism, "Only the avenger can be consecrated."

The perceptual coalescence of kinship with ethnicity suggests a process by which the moral boundaries of the family and kinship group are expanded to encompass the entire nation with little alteration in their associated core values (Simić 1975: 48–84). One way that this relationship can be conceptualized is as a series of concentric circles, the innermost of which circumscribes the nuclear or extended family, and the outermost the nation whose circumference defines the final limits of moral obligation (see Allport 1976: 86). Thus the conceptual space bounded by kinship, on the one hand, and the nation, on the other, can be described as constituting a single moral field and those areas outside of it an amoral sphere. In other words, a moral field constitutes an interactional arena where those engaged typically interact with reference to shared ethical considerations phrased in terms of "good" and "evil" (or "right" and "wrong"). Moreover, such imperatives are typically regarded as "God-given" or products of the "natural order." Thus, within a moral field, people are expected to behave with reference to a common set of ethical ideas by which their behavior and that of others is evaluated. In contrast, behavior toward those lying outside its boundaries, in what can be regarded as "one's amoral sphere," may be idiosyncratically benevolent or, inversely, purely exploitative, hostile, or cruel without the threat of the imposition of in-group sanctions (Simić 1991: 27–32).

In fact, aggressive behavior toward outsiders may at times constitute a moral obligation as in the case of the blood feud once so common in the mountains of the western Balkans (Boehm 1984; Karan 1986). Consequently, in terms of this theory, much of the cruelty reported from the recent Yugoslav civil war can be explained by the fact that, in the final analysis, one's neighbors belonging to other ethnic groups fall clearly outside the realm of moral consideration. Even the influence of religion has not significantly mitigated the ethos of revenge and warfare, since Orthodoxy, Catholicism, and Islam in the Balkans have, on the whole, simply reflected and reified the values of the folk society rather than shaping them and imposing a more universalistic ethical system.

The Fiction of a Yugoslav Identity

The demise of former Yugoslavia provides a striking example of the ways that folk concepts of ethnicity have been able to subvert the best efforts of Tito's Marxist regime to create a pan-Yugoslav identity. The all-too-brief period of formal reconciliation on the part of Serbs, Croats, and Slav Muslims following World War II testifies convincingly to the cyclical character of ethnic particularism and nationalist chauvinism. Clearly, the relatively authoritarian Titoist government had made every attempt to create and propagate a dramatic sense of Yugoslav unity. Among other symbols employed to this end were the concept of Yugoslavia as a leader of the so-called nonaligned nations, Tito as the ethnically undifferentiated inheritor of the South Slav heroic tradition, the idea of a unique form of Yugoslav "national communism," the notion of "worker self-management" as a Titoist creation, and of course, the aforementioned slogan "brotherhood and unity."

In contrast to the perception of ethnicity and nationalism as "natural" constructs, for many Yugoslavs Marxism appeared to be an "imposed" or "artificial" ideology. It succeeded in maintaining itself temporarily by means of constant propagation in the schools, workplace, and the mass media, as well as part of a system of punishments and rewards within the context of an elite, authoritarian, and repressive political system. Moreover, in spite of the claims of "scientific Marxism," its moral authority and legitimacy were constantly eroded by the realities of everyday life (see Simić 1993) and the evidence of the privileges enjoyed by Party loyalists in an ostensibly egalitarian society. The final result, one leading inevitably in 1991 to the breakup of Yugoslavia and the ensuing interethnic civil wars, was an ideological and moral vacuum, a vacuum that could only be filled by the more enduring and deeply inculcated ethos of nationalism.

A Personal Epilogue

In midwinter 1904, my father's parents set out on horseback into the Montenegrin mountains from their home near Grahovo. Late that night, my grandmother returned without her husband, reporting to his clan brothers that he had fallen off his horse and perished in a deep ravine. She feared that she would be accused of witchcraft and fled with my four-year-old father, Novak, under the cover of darkness over the border into what was then Austrian-held Herzegovina to her brother, a married but childless Orthodox priest, Sava Simić, who reared the young boy as his own. The Simići are from the village of Žitomislići on the east bank of the Neretva River west of Mostar. Of the sixty-four red-tiled-roofed houses, more than a dozen belonged to the Simić lineage.

During a visit to Žitomislići in 1961, my great-uncle Dragutin warned me not to venture onto the Neretva's west bank into its Muslim and Catholic settlements. He then showed me the store of arms he had hidden in the ancient fortification tower (*kula*) appended to his modest house. This experience belied the bucolic beauty of the setting and the formally polite and superficially friendly encounters I witnessed between Serbs, Muslims, and Croats at the cafe of the local railway station. Then, and on numerous future occasions elsewhere in Bosnia and Herzegovina, I began to perceive the invisible psychological wall separating these ethnic groups. It was all too evident that superficial cordiality, more often than not, masked a deep sense of alienation, suspicion, and fear.

Today, Žitomislići and its fifteenth-century Orthodox monastery lie in ruins, deserted by its Serbian inhabitants, fleeing from the wrath of their former neighbors. It is noteworthy that many responsible for the village's destruction came from Medjugorje, the site of the reputed appearance of the Virgin Mary in June 1981.

The deeper significance of Žitomislići's tragedy is that this very same scenario has been repeated over and over again, victimizing all three of the ethnic groups now embroiled in a seemingly senseless and unresolvable struggle. For centuries these peoples have occupied a marginal and precarious borderland—peoples in many ways very similar to each other, but yet deeply divided and steeped for generations in tales of heroism and imbued with a quasi-religious ethos of revenge and retribution.

Muslims as "Others" in Serbian and Croatian Politics

Robert M. Hayden

The conquest of Constantinople, it has been said, "dealt a wound to European man." Few countries could have taken that blow harder or felt it more deeply than Bosnia.
—Ivo Andrić, preface to his doctoral dissertation, 1924 (1990: xvi)

Bosnia-Herzegovina is a European country, and its people are European people. Even the evil inflicted upon us has not come from Asia, but has a European origin. Fascism . . . and bolshevism . . . are European-made products.
—Alija Izetbegović, speech to the London Conference, August 26, 1992.

In November 1994, newspapers throughout the world carried a terrible picture taken from a broadcast by the Bosnian Serb television station in Banja Luka. Bosnian Serb forces had just carried out a successful counterattack against what had until then been a successful Muslim offensive from Bihac, taking a number of prisoners in the process. In the picture carried by the print media, a laughing Serb soldier was putting a fez on the head of an understandably distraught Muslim prisoner. The mocking triumph of the first and the fearful misery of the second were apparent in their expressions and postures toward each other, the Muslim attempting to shrink from his tormentor.

I find this grim scene revealing of more than the sheer physical dominance of the Serb over his Muslim prisoner. The Serb was forcing a mark of Muslim identity on his victim that the latter had not, in fact, worn himself. Whatever the nature of the prisoner's view of his own identity as a Muslim, the Serb felt compelled to impose one upon him.

This scene from Serb television symbolizes a process of imputation of "Islamic" identity on Bosnian Muslims by their opponents that has been contrary to the personal identity of many of the Muslim people of Bosnia and Herzegovina. This is not to say that Bosnian Muslims deny that they are Muslims; rather, the question goes to the symbolism of the markers of that identity. Whatever many Bosnian Muslims may have thought of their own identity as Muslims, Europeans, or Bosnians, their Serb and Croat antagonists impute to them a cultural essence that dichotomizes Muslim from European. It thus denies the possibility of a Bosnia, since it would be composed of incompatibles: putatively non-European Muslims and "European" Christians.

This paper explores the content of the labels that have been imposed on Bosnian Muslims by their Serb and Croat opponents. This academic exercise has normative implications. In his study of ethnic fratricide and the dismantling of democracy in Sri Lanka, Stanley Tambiah (1986: 5) quotes Voltaire: "If we believe in absurdities, we shall commit atrocities." Certainly, the images of Bosnian Muslims that have been propagated (and propagandized) by their opponents are absurd for most of the Muslims of Bosnia. At the same time, the fact of this absurdity may be irrelevant in practice, for reasons well established in other realms of intellectual endeavor. The first, drawn from structural anthropology, argues that the fact of distinction is more important than the markers of that distinction. Put another way, once units of a system are defined in contrast to each other, the characteristics that supposedly distinguish them may change without changing the basic distinction between the units, or the fact that they remain defined in contrast to each other.

The second reason for pessimism of the intellect, and thus perhaps also of the will, stems from the well-known phenomenon of self-fulfilling prophecy, although in the case of Bosnia, self-fulfilling history might be a more appropriate phrase. The ferocious rejection of a multinational (in European terms) or multiethnic (in American ones) Bosnia and Herzegovina by the leaderships of most Bosnian Serbs and Herzegovinian Croats has reinforced those Bosnian Muslim leaders who would prefer to create a Muslim state rather than a civil society. Just as many Serbs in Croatia did not define themselves primarily as Serbs until the Croatian nationalist regime of Franjo Tudjman defined them outside of the bodies political and social in Croatia,[1] many Bosnian Muslims now see Islam as central

---

1. I am quoting Milorad Pupovac, leader of the moderate Serbs who have remained in Tudjman's Croatia and who are trying to reach an accommodation with the Croatian government. Pupovac refers to himself, but until 1991 the number of Serbs in Croatia who identified themselves as "Yugoslavs" was high.

to their identity, and to that of their country, since other forms of identity, both of state and of nation, are foreclosed. Thus the Serb and Croat insistence on the supposedly Islamic character of the Bosnian Muslims may lead many of the Muslims to become more Islamic.[2]

Orientalist Discourses: Muslim as Non-European

In the political discourses that brought about the dismemberment first of the former Yugoslavia, then of Bosnia and Herzegovina, much of the rhetorical power of some positions has come from a literally Orientalist framework. These assertions are that those peoples to the east (or occasionally, to the south) of the writer's own nation (narod) are not European, thus inferior (Bakić-Hayden and Hayden 1992; Bakić-Hayden 1994 and 1995; cf. Todorova 1994).[3] In this rhetorical framework, the definitive non-European essence is Islam, embodied territorially in the Ottoman Empire. Thus the Balkans, because they were under Ottoman, hence Oriental, rule, are not part of Europe "proper" (Bakić-Hayden 1994). As Maria Todorova is reported to have said at a conference, the Ottoman legacy is "the Balkans."

The political point of Orientalist rhetoric is to exclude the "Other." Within former Yugoslavia, the overall Orientalist framework is appropriated by aspiring leaders of the different Yugoslav peoples to produce a "nesting" set of rhetorics. These distinguish "those parts of the [former] country that had been ruled by Europe 'proper' from parts formerly ruled by Orientals and hence 'improper'; and in those 'improper' parts of Europe, Christians from Orientals 'proper,' European Muslims who further distinguish themselves from the ultimate Orientals, the non-Europeans" (Bakić-Hayden 1994: 6).

The layers of nesting about Bosnia are exemplified in a statement by an official of "Herceg-Bosna," the self-proclaimed Croatian quasi-state within Bosnia and Herzegovina. He warned that it is necessary "to pay attention to the essentially different mental make-up and value system of the creator of the Islamic Declaration (i.e., Alija Izetbegović) and his followers from those of the European-oriented Christians, even if they (Serbs) are on the margins of civilization."[4]

Izetbegović's remarks at the London Conference, quoted at the beginning of

2. The idea that ethnic Muslims (meaning those of Muslim descent, whether or not they are religious) may not be religious or cultural Muslims is not at all contradictory, and is in fact the basis for Alija Izetbegović's call for "the Islamization of Muslims" (Izetbegović 1990).

3. Samuel Huntington describes the current state of the world as a case of "the West versus the rest" (1993). This stance would seem a perfected parody of Orientalist discourse, were it not for the fact that Huntington apparently believes it, as do many "policymakers." Positions such as Huntington's exemplify the "cultural fundamentalism" that seems to be replacing classical racism as a rhetoric of exclusion, particularly in Europe (Stolcke 1995).

4. Slobodan Lovrenovic, in *Danas*, August 11, 1993: 22.

this essay, are a bitter counter to such Orientalist images, both of Bosnian Muslims as "non-European" and of European superiority. Yet hegemony is hard to challenge, particularly when one's opponents are so willing to use the hegemonic arguments. The European-ness of Christianity and the non-European-ness of Islam is an essential contrast in the messages of the dominant political forces of both the Serbs and Croats. Indeed, both Serbs and Croats claim to be defending "Europe" from Islam, the former by preventing the creation of a powerful Muslim state of Bosnia, the latter by using the American idea of a "Croat-Muslim Federation" within Bosnia that is then to be linked in a "confederation" with Croatia as limiting the power of "Islamic Fundamentalists" in Bosnia.[5] Thus a Serbian complement to the Croatian sentiments quoted in the previous paragraph can be seen in the words of Dragos Kalajić, a Serbian painter: "The fact of an Islamic onslaught on Western Europe by peaceful means, by means of mass immigrations, threatening to turn European nations into national minorities within their own states, only accentuates the importance of the Serbian struggle for the overall defense of Europe, European culture and civilization" (*Borba*, August 6–7, 1994: xvii–xix; in Bakić-Hayden 1994: 12–13).

The Strategic Nature of "Othering"

Nationalist evocations of this type ground their arguments in the assumption that cultural essences and national oppositions exist unchanged through centuries. In this case the Muslims (Bosnian and Albanian) now in the former Yugoslavia are in essence the same as the Turks who imposed Muslim rule on the Balkans, while the Christian peoples, now as then, shield the West from the Oriental onslaught. Yet the seeming historicity of these assertions masks the strategic nature of characterizations of the essence of the Other. Serb nationalists throughout the nineteenth century regarded Bosnian Muslims as being lapsed Serbs, who should be reintegrated with their Serb brothers and also, usually, with the supposed faith of their ancestors. At the same time, the dominant Croat ideologies also regarded Bosnian Muslims as the best Croats (Banac 1984: 363–65). Of course, these characterizations of Muslims as "really" being Serbs or Croats coincided with political positions that argued for the incorporation of Bosnia into a greater Ser-

---

5. The putative "Federation" within Bosnia does not, in fact, exist on the ground (see *New York Times*, February 19, 1995, E-6; *Balkan War Report*, February 1995: 7 and December 1994–January 1995; and Hayden 1999: chap. 8). This "Federation" was entered into reluctantly by the Croats, who have worked to ensure that it has and will have no central governmental authority of any kind. For this reason, I have viewed the constitution of this "Federation" as an imaginary constitution for an illusionary federation (Hayden 1994).

bia or a greater Croatia.[6] Even in 1990–91, Serb politicians who sought to induce the Muslim leadership to incorporate Bosnia into a post-Yugoslavian greater Serbia pointed out similarities between the cultures of Slavic Muslims and Serbs (Biljana Plavsić in 1991, quoted in Bakić-Hayden 1994: 19, or Vuk Drasković in 1990). It should be noted that such favorable comparisons between Bosnian Muslims and Serbs distinguished the Slavic Muslims from their Albanian coreligionists, the latter being described, inevitably, as "fundamentalist."

With this point in mind, it is necessary to remember that the recognition that segments of a population are defined by particular differences—of "race" or "ethnicity" in America, "community" in India, "nationality" in Europe—by whatever criteria are locally in use does not have to mean hostility. To the contrary, some political actors may find it advantageous to attempt to minimize the importance of acknowledged differences, often by asserting that the similarities among this particular set of disparate peoples unites them all despite their differences.

The paradigmatic attempt to find such "unity in diversity" may be Nehru's *Discovery of India* (1946). After noting and even exploring the "tremendous" variety of the peoples of India, Nehru discounts the differences among them by declaring that "differences, big or small, can always be noticed even within a national group." He then defined the unity of Indians by comparing them to other national groups, saying in essence that Indians were a nation because "at almost any time in recorded history an Indian would have felt more or less at home in any part of India, and would have felt as a stranger and an alien in any other country" (Nehru 1946: 51). In other words, Nehru defined Indians as a nation, despite their differences, because all of the varieties of Indians are more similar to each other than to peoples outside of India.

Despite assaults on the Nehruvian definition of the Indian nation (see Varshney 1993), it remains dominant within India today, even despite the Hindu nationalist electoral victory in 1997. Yet the India of which Nehru wrote in 1946 stretched from the eastern border of Afghanistan to the western border of Burma, including, in other words, what are now Pakistan and Bangladesh.

Mohammed Ali Jinnah, who wished to form a separate state for India's Muslims, rejected Nehru's category of "Indians" for them, formulating and then implementing the "two-nation theory," which held that India's Muslims were a separate people from its Hindus. Strategically, the assertion of essential difference was as crucial to Jinnah's demands for partition as the assertion of essential unity was for Nehru's demand for a united India. The difference was, of course,

---

6. These parallels were parodied in brilliant fashion by the Croatian satirical weekly *Feral Tribune* in its issue following the announcement of the Croat-Muslim "federation" in Bosnia (March 7, 1994: 1). The front page showed a montage picture of Alija Izetbegović, flanked by Croatian flags and wearing the sash of the president of Croatia, with the caption a Serbian slogan from the time of the founding of Yugoslavia: "Screw the country that doesn't have Bosnia" [Jebeš zemlju koja Bosne nema].

that the assertion of unity presumed cooperation, while that of difference presumed hostility. Empirically, Jinnah was wrong, as Muslims and Hindus have continue to live intermingled within India, as they had for a thousand years before the partition of 1947.[7] Yet Jinnah's success has had the effect of rendering India's remaining Muslim population vulnerable to the charge of being disloyal to India, thus weakening their political position there.

In Yugoslavia, the "unity in diversity" approach was manifested in the Titoist slogan of "brotherhood and unity," which was part of the ideological justification of the joint state of the South Slavs, and expressed in the first section of the introductory part of the Yugoslav Constitution of 1974. Strategically, it was as necessary for those who wished to partition Yugoslavia in 1991 to negate this principle as it had been for Tito to assert it in 1943, when he founded the new Yugoslav state. Ironically, those who posited the incompatibility of the Yugoslav peoples in 1991 were even more wrong empirically than Jinnah had been in pre-partition India in 1947. After forty-five years of life together in the second Yugoslav state, the peoples of Yugoslavia were increasingly commingled, both territorially and in terms of intermarriage. But those who were most intermingled have paid the highest price. The wars have taken place in the most mixed regions of Croatia (Banija, Slavonija, and Baranja) and in the most mixed republic, Bosnia and Herzegovina, precisely because a mixed region is now incompatible with the dominant political ideologies of nation-state.

What is striking about the current strategies of Serb and Croat nationalism, however, is their virtually complete exclusion of Muslims. Even most of those Serbs and Croats who see Bosnian Muslims as descended from lapsed members of their own nations express little wish to see their wayward kindred returned to the flock. This may be a manifestation of the extent to which inherited religious affiliation has now become the one supreme criterion of ethnicity among the speakers of dialects of Serbo-Croatian (see Hammel 1993).

What is important to keep in mind is that the Serb and Croat strategies of "othering" in Bosnia have the same goal as Jinnah's similar effort in India in the 1940s: justifying partition. It is also important to note that the empirical falsity of the Serb and Croat assertions of inevitable and age-old hostility between Muslims and Christians in Bosnia is as irrelevant to the political processes as the similar falsity of Jinnah's picture of Hindu-Muslims relations in 1947. Reality may be socially constructed, but it is reality.

The Vanishing Category of "Bosnians"

One way to counter the Serbo-Croat call for partitioning Bosnia would be to posit the existence of "Bosnians" as an encompassing category for all of Bosnia's

---

7. Note that "living intermingled" does not presume amicability or preclude occasional unrest. It does preclude the kinds of "ethnic cleansing" practiced in Pakistan in 1947 when almost all Hindus were driven from the new Muslim state.

people, just as Nehru posited "Indians" as an encompassing category for the varied peoples of India. Despite the use of the word "Bosnian" in English-language news media and political speech, however, use of this term as one of self-description has nearly vanished in Bosnia itself. Instead, the population of Bosnia and Herzegovina has partitioned itself into Serbs, Croats, Muslims and "others." The closest term linguistically to "Bosnian" (*bosanac*) would be "Bosniac" (*bosnjak*). However, where *bosanac* could refer to anyone from Bosnia, *bosnjak* now is an exclusively Muslim referent, as shown in the Constitution of the Federation of Bosnia and Herzegovina, the Croat-Muslim "Federation" formed at American insistence in March 1994 and now one of the two "entities" comprising Bosnia under the Dayton Accord. There it is used instead of the term "Muslim," and is thus equivalent to Serb and Croat as an ethno-national label.

In the former Yugoslavia, *bosanac* did connote anyone from Bosnia, and had something of a negative connotation; *bosanci* were regarded as unsophisticated, uncultured, "hillbillies" in American terms. Bosnians themselves resented these implications of the term, and the condescending ways in which they were often treated by their colleagues in Zagreb, Belgrade, and Ljubljana.[8] At the same time, many of the people of Bosnia did identify themselves as *bosanci*, Bosnians, religious affiliation unspecified. It is this form of self-description that is now heard less and less often.

The lack of use of the general term "Bosnian" to describe the population of Bosnia and Herzegovina is symptomatic of the absence of a self-defined Bosnian nation that includes all of the peoples living there. Overwhelmingly, the Serbs and Croats classify themselves apart from the Muslims, and from the idea of a Bosnian state, preferring to describe themselves as Serbs and Croats, and to accede to Serbia and Croatia, respectively. Many Serbs and Croats of Bosnia and Herzegovina are as likely now to identify themselves as "Bosnians" as the Muslims of Pakistan are to identify themselves as Indians. The Muslim utilization of "*Bosniac*" to describe themselves stresses their own connection to Bosnia, but thereby implies a Muslim identity for the population of the country. Thus the terminologies of description used since 1991 by the peoples of Bosnia and Herzegovina to describe themselves indicate the lack of a shared concept of a Bosnian nation.

Constructing Differences to Deconstruct the State

The demise of the shared identity of "Bosnians" reflects the success of the politics of partition in the mixed polity, even though the imagery of nationalism would indicate a different dynamic. That is, while nationalists claim that their

8. 1 am grateful to Zoran Pajic, formerly professor of law at Sarajevo University, for reminding me of this point.

nation needs its own state because of the putative differences between that nation and the other peoples with whom its members are at the moment forced to live, it seems more likely that it is the need to establish differences to justify the political goal of partition, rather than the fact of whatever differences do exist, that drives the rhetoric of description. But difference per se is not enough. Separation is called for when the Other can be seen as inferior or degraded. Thus the image to be created of the Other must be a negative one.

In this context, the symbolic geography of "the West versus the rest" (as per Huntington) becomes relevant. The tenets underlying this geography are, first, that "the West" is culturally superior to "the rest," and second, that Islam is not part of Western culture. With these points in mind, it is possible to understand why the Bosnian Serbs and Herzegovinian Croats need to establish that the ethnic Muslims of Bosnia are Islamic in culture. If they are Islamic, they are not European, and if they are not European, they are inferior, thus justifying Serb and Croat demands for separation from them.

The need for the victorious Bosnian Serb in the Bihac region to force a fez onto his captive's head may now be clear. The visible mark of Islamic culture ensured that "Muslim" was more than simply a label of difference, but rather indicated a culture not only apart from, but in the Orientalist rhetorical structure dominant in Europe, including the Balkans, also inferior to that of Europe.

Unfortunately, the dynamics of this exclusionary rhetoric are reinforced by the actions of Muslim leaders who stress the importance of Islam to the identity of Bosnia. This is not to deny the logic, much less legitimacy, of their argument. On the contrary, the Muslim cleric who noted that "it is necessary to preserve the Muslim identity if there is the wish to preserve a multicultural Bosnia-Herzegovina"[9] is perfectly correct. The problem is that it is precisely their Muslim identity that marks the *Bosnjac* as non-European, and hence, in Serb and Croat rhetorics, inferior.

This problem becomes even greater when Bosnian Muslims leaders have looked to Islamic states for political, financial, and military assistance. That the Islamic states have been among the greatest sources of support for the Bosnian government only confirms, to Serbs and Croats, that the Bosnian Muslims are non-European. Rather perversely, the more that the Bosnian government turns for support to the countries most willing to provide it, the more it alienates its own non-Muslim putative citizens.

Bosniacs, Buddhists, Bogomils, or Baptists

The analysis thus far has tied the content of the Serb and Croat rhetorics of exclusion to the Bosnian Muslims' identity as Muslims, and might be seen as

---

9. *Ljiljan*, 8–15 February 1995, p. 7, as quoted and translated by FBIS, 13 February 1995.

implying that these people suffer because of the specifics imputed to that identity, as Michael Sells (1996) has argued. Yet such an assumption is unwarranted. The hostility of the Serbs and Croats to the Muslims is not due to the latter's identity as Muslims, but rather to their refusal to identify themselves as Serbs or Croats. It is the fact of Otherness, not the specifics of the identity of the Other, that provides the potential basis for hostility. Whether such hostility is realized, and the specifics of how it is justified, depend on the circumstances of time in place. In Bosnia in the 1990s, the Serbs and Croats could adopt the general Orientalist framework of Islam as non-European, hence inferior, to justify their own secession from the "*Bosniacs*" and their Bosnia. Yet note that it is the political aim, partition, that requires the rhetorics of denigration.

Indeed, I would argue that the Muslims' identity as Muslims is incidental to their treatment at the hands of the Serbs and Croats. Had the Bosniacs identified themselves as Buddhists, Bogomils, or Baptists, they would probably have faced the same hostility, although the contents of the rhetoric used to justify such treatment would doubtless have varied from that recounted here. After all, the Christian Serbs and Croats have used their own sectarian differences to justify mutual hostility, and treat each other in the same manner that each treats the Muslims where their interests conflict. It is simply because the Bosnian Serbs and Herzegovinian Croats share an interest in ensuring that no effective state of Bosnia and Herzegovina exists that their rhetoric in regard to the Muslims, and their treatment of them, are so closely parallel.

Were the Bosnian Muslims instead Buddhists, the Serb and Croat rhetoric of exclusion used against them would probably reveal the same Orientalism that marks the current depiction of Muslims. Were they Bogomils, a similar rhetoric might be used. After all, the Bogomils would hardly be within any mainstream of European Christianity. Were they Baptists, a different rhetorical stance would of course be taken; but Northern Ireland has shown that such sectarian hostility can easily include Protestants in contemporary Europe.

If the Bosniacs were instead Buddhists, Bogomils, or Baptists, the primary difference that we might see would probably be in regard to their international support. Were they Buddhists, they might attract support from the ASEAN countries instead of from the OIC. Were they Baptists, more support might come from the United States. And of course, were they Bogomils no one would help them at all.

In the end, then, the Islamic identity of the Bosnian Muslims may be seen as the factor that determines the specific content of the rhetoric used to justify Serb and Croat separation from them, and also as the primary determinant of their support from the Islamic countries. It is not, however, the cause of their persecution. The victimization of the Bosnian Muslims is based on the simple fact of their difference from the Serbs and Croats. This now excludes them from the Serb and Croat definitions of their states and has induced the Serbs and Croats to remove themselves from the Bosnian state that they refuse to share with each other, or with any other Other.

"Former Comrades" at War

Historical Perspectives on "Ethnic Cleansing" in Croatia

Hannes Grandits and Christian Promitzer

In 1990 in Croatia, when newly elected political leaders were pressing for national independence from the Yugoslav federation, Croatian Serbs committed the first acts of rebellion that by summer 1991 would eventually develop into an open war when the Yugoslav National Army (JNA) entered the fray on the side of the insurgents. In October 1990 these Serbian insurgents declared the regions under their control autonomous. The following year they then proclaimed the Republic of Serbian Krajina (Republika Srpska Krajina) on the territory of Croatia. In the war of 1991 Krajina-Serb forces expelled several hundred thousand Croats from the region (Amnesty International 1991; Vjesnik 1992: passim; Bilandžić 1991: 14; Rebić 1995: 16; Čirić 1991: 8–11). In 1995 the situation was reversed. The Croatian army conquered the Serbian Krajina. During the Croatian military operations much of the Serbian population fled or, subsequently, was forced to flee. Between 120,000 and 200,000 people left their homes (Human Rights Watch—Helsinki 1995; Puhovski 1995; Mappes-Niedick 1995: 585, 592; Ninčić and Vekić 1995: 8–11). Ten thousand left Croatia earlier because of warfare or political pressure, or simply to escape the miserable economic and social conditions that had prevailed in Krajina since 1991.

The belligerents in the wars in former Yugoslavia have frequently used historically based justifications, complete with hostile stereotypes, to legitimize military
actions. One such image is that of the inhabitants of the former Militärgrenze
(military border) as being, given their history as peasant-soldiers, accustomed to
bearing arms and resorting to them to solve conflicts. Such traditional patterns of
readiness to use violence did not, of course, cause this war, but they do help us
understand some of the roots of present wartime behavior. It is this constellation
of historical traditions related to the use of force that we wish to discuss.

The Historical Background: The Hapsburg Militärgrenze

The similarity of the names "Srpska Krajina" (Serbian Krajina) and "Vojna
Krajina" (Military Border) suggests continuity. But this early 1990s Serb phan-
tom-state had for centuries been populated by Croats as well as Serbs. The existence of a shared territory goes back to the origins of this region within the
Hapsburg empire.

In the sixteenth century, after the Ottoman advance into Central Europe had
come to a standstill, there existed a wide uninhabited and devastated belt of land
dividing the Hapsburg and Ottoman empires. The original inhabitants had fled
these zones. Without serfs to work the land, local feudal relationships collapsed
and the land became worthless. The sole inhabitants were Hapsburg military
personnel. They tried to guard the hinterland with a loose chain of fortifications,
but within several decades this began to change. The border between the Ottoman
and Hapsburg empires became more stable in the second half of the sixteenth
century. Because of this development a growing number of settlers began to
migrate into these uninhabited regions now controlled by the Hapsburg army.
The rulers of the Hapsburg empire encouraged settlement in hopes of being able
to use this manpower to strengthen their defense system. They promised the
immigrants free land and release from feudal obligations in exchange for military
service in the defense of the border. This meant that the settlers became free
people, owing only military service. To avoid tensions, the territory of the privileged border population was administered separately from the feudal heartland.

The border territory was divided into regimental regions, which were in turn
subdivided into company areas that were then localized in particular villages.
This territory was formally designated the "Militärgrenze" (Vojna Krajina / Military Border). In the beginning, in the sixteenth to seventeenth centuries, this
Militärgrenze was still relatively limited in the extent of its territorial administration. During the seventeenth century and, in the beginning of the eighteenth century, this territory expanded due to the victories of Hapsburg armies, especially
after the second siege of Vienna in 1683. New territories were gradually conquered and added to the growing Militärgrenze, so that by the eighteenth century

it was almost as large as Civil Croatia and Slavonia (Adamček 1980; Moačanin 1984: 23, 56; Kaser 1986).

This period of settlement of the Militärgrenze, which began in the sixteenth century, lasted until the end of the eighteenth century. Large population movements occurred in both war and peace. Most of the new settlers were refugees from the Ottoman territories who had been attracted by the promised privileges. The majority of these people were then known as Vlachs. They were Orthodox in religion and spoke a South Slavic dialect. Distinct written traditions did not appear until later but at that time religion was the key differentiating characteristic. They were originally livestock-breeders, mainly of sheep, in their mountainous homeland. At the time they changed to the Hapsburg side of the border, many of them had been transhumant shepherds with permanent villages. These groups of Vlachs, who had originally lived in the Southern and Central Balkans, left their home territories to flee the advancing Ottoman state. They had long lived under Ottoman rule, some not far from the Militärgrenze.

This area had, for a considerable period, been a militarized frontier zone. The Vlachs were the largest group of refugees who migrated into the Militärgrenze. A subgroup consisted of Vlach families of Catholic faith, called Bunjevci. They also came from the Ottoman lands to the "free" Hapsburg areas. But their number was small compared to that of the Orthodox Vlachs. On the other hand, the number of Catholics who moved into the Militärgrenze from the Croatian hinterland, that is, from the estates north of the border territory, was much larger. Their percentage of the border population steadily increased during the centuries of settlement (Kaser 1986: 48–313; 1994: 243–69). This historical background set a frontier pattern for adaptation to recurrent violence. To better understand this pattern we focus on three predominantly rural regions of the former Militärgrenze: These are "Banija," south of Zagreb, the Croatian capital; "Kordun," directly south of the city of Karlovac; and the "Lika," south of the Kordun.

In dealing with traditions of violence in Krajina we intend to try to differentiate between perpetrator and victim. This is not easy to do, since these roles often changed historically. This often rapid alteration in status between victim and aggressor is a familiar development in the most recent history of this region.

A Militarized Society

In the massive eruptions of violence during the recent war in Croatia, the conflict was concentrated primarily in the regions of the former Militärgrenze. This raises a question. To what extent was this war shaped by the specifics of regional history, or differently phrased, did the ways in which historical identities developed in the period before the dissolution of the Militärgrenze play any role in subsequent resort to violent regional conflict?

Dealing with these questions is complex because the societal frameworks changed. These social changes and accompanying economic transformations brought new modes of behavior. But several works on family and kinship concerned with this area of the Balkans show that the changes occurred mostly within the framework of traditional cultural norms.[1] But the processes of adaptation to these new economic, social, and legal circumstances, especially as reflected in family structure and residential patterns, often happened relatively rapidly. At the same time alterations in familial role expectations were more conservative and reflected enduring social attitudes. Bear in mind that we are not suggesting a kind of unilateral cultural determinism; we want only to indicate historical contexts of behavior, which may still have some validity in the present. Here we are not looking at historical experience as a primary causal factor but we are suggesting that the particular historical experience contributes to cultural values and in this way provides for the establishment of parameters of behavior. This militarized culture of the society in the Krajina regions had to be integrated into the complex of historical patterns that structured life in this area, including the ways in which the roles of victim and perpetrator have been reversed. It is not our intention to construct an ideology of blame or guilt, so easily done in the atmosphere of impassioned political rhetoric and violent deeds that has been prominent both today and in the recent past. We begin our considerations here with the middle of the nineteenth century, three decades before the dissolution of the Militärgrenze.

In 1872 compulsory military duty for the men of the Militärgrenze was abolished. This was the single most important step in the process of the dissolution of the whole system. Three years later one of the most comprehensive books about the history of the Grenzer (borderer) society was published in Vienna. The author was František Vaniček, a school director who had served in the Militärgrenze for more than thirty years (Vaniček 1875). Vaniček saw himself as a friend of the Grenzer people and therefore tried to present a "proper appreciation" of their culture. But, inevitably, he found it also necessary to deal with their military tradition and the role of violence in this society:

> Since the middle of the 16th century an armed people was created in this area out of natives and from a few thousand Serbian refugees. Led by captains and vojvods they offered their service to Ferdinand, the king of Croatia, and became settlers. Day and night they shouldered rifles and guarded the border against the traditional enemy of Christianity until 1872. They also tried to keep away the murderous miasmas of the plague [a reference to the function of the border as a cordon sanitaire—H.G/C.P] from our monarchy. Yet, this soldier people effectively, and in a self-

---

1. Such sources include Erlich 1966, Halpern 1967: 109–26, Halpern and Kerewsky-Halpern 1979: 159–72, Hammel 1984: 217–28, Rihtman-Auguštin 1987, Kaser 1995a: 417–71, and Grandits 1996.

sacrificing way, influenced the destiny of our Highest House, the Emperor. . . . Despite these achievements for Christianity and for the Supreme Throne and the Monarchy, it was obtained with much bloodshed. None of the branches of the Austro-Hungarian family of nations is so unknown and so misjudged as this soldier people. Even the higher civic classes . . . judged them solely by the traditional excesses of the embittered Grenzers in the field. (Vaniček 1875: 1/iv)

The name "soldier people" is very appropriate for the everyday life of the men in the Militärgrenze. There was regular military drill, much time spent in guard duty, and recurrent mobilizations. Above all, there was war service, which frequently involved high casualties. In the last decades, before the beginning of the dissolution of the Militärgrenze, for example in August 1849, the Grenzer troops returned as "glorious victors" from the counterrevolutionary wars. These battles took place in 1848–49 within the Austro-Hungarian monarchy. Many Grenzers, however, did not return. Approximately 30,000 to 40,000 of the 120,000 Grenzers mobilized fell in battle or died from infection. But the series of mobilizations did not end with the period of the European-wide 1848 revolutions. In 1850, troops from the Militärgrenze marched against Prussia, and again in 1853, they were employed to stop the Ottoman army advancing toward Montenegro. In 1854, in the Crimean war, Grenzer units were stationed in Transylvania and Galicia. They saw no significant fighting during this mobilization. In 1859, however, they participated in the battle of Solferino, which was a bloodbath. This was the biggest battle in the war the Monarchy waged to prevent the loss of their Italian provinces. Once again, thousands of men from the Krajina were killed or wounded (Wrede 1903: 240; Horsetzky 1913: 377–410).

Rebellions

In the beginning of the 1870s these military duties were terminated in connection with the gradual dismantling of the centuries-old system of a military peasantry. The Ottoman Empire had ceased to be a threat. Thus by 1881 the whole territory was integrated into the rest of the Kingdom of Croatia-Slavonia, which at the time was part of the Hungarian half of the Dual Monarchy of the Hapsburg empire. That meant that Hungarians replaced the military administration of the Viennese government as the new governors of the former frontiersmen. The extensive process of transformation to a civil social order then began. Within a few years the social framework had been changed dramatically (Pavličević 1980: 90–94; Valentić 1981; Grandits and Gruber 1996: 477–98).

This transformation was accompanied by a far-reaching demilitarization. The central administration expected the "peasant-soldiers" of the Krajina to become "normal citizens" and "good taxpayers" as quickly as possible. To abolish the public bearing of arms the authorities imposed, as a first step, a high tax on this practice. Then they began to confiscate firearms. The Grenzer massively opposed these measures, which, they felt, threatened their traditional identity. They had historically defined themselves as "heroes of the emperor" and "free Border-men." It is not surprising then that this perceived loss of status led to conflicts with the authorities (Pavličević 1974: 75–133; Kaser 1995b).

Adding to the feeling of oppression was the development that, as a consequence of the dissolution of the military system and the change to a new social order, the people in the Krajina were also now confronted with an enormously increased tax burden. This change was made more severe by a major agrarian crisis. In Croatia this economic crisis lasted from 1873 to 1895. The former Grenzers found themselves on the edge of a social catastrophe. Indebtedness and forced sales of their properties affected a steadily growing number of families. This precarious situation also triggered a large overseas emigration, especially to North America (Bičanić 1937: 3–5).

The change in the social order and the economic crisis became the determining motives for the development of a widespread rebel movement in the Krajina in 1883. In the Banija region alone, men from seventy-four Serbian and Croatian villages took up arms against the "Hungarian politicians and their assistants," whom they perceived as responsible for the "injustices" that they now had to suffer. This identity crisis of the former Grenzers focused on anti-Hungarian stereotypes. During the uprising they took over official offices, imprisoned civil servants, and burned symbols of Hungarian rule. Finally they fought a series of battles against the troops sent to put down the revolt. Stories began to circulate in the villages at the time of the revolt. These tales illustrate how strongly the former Grenzers were still tied to their historical identities. For example, one tale, which spread through several villages during the weeks of the uprising, claimed that the emperor had lost the Militärgrenze to the Hungarians in a card game. His successor to the throne, a friend of the Grenzer people, was very angry about this. It was he who had called them to arms and ordered them to chase away those who interfered with their lives and to kill all the newly installed mayors, secretaries, and "Madjarones" (persons who voted in the last election for the Hungarian candidate).[2] This appeal to the status quo ante, a past period perceived as secure, became a way to attempt to cope with drastic change. In their millenarian approach they could not conceive of challenging the system, their only hope was to recapture their former status. The emperor could not be wrong, only misguided.

The revolt was suppressed with overwhelming military force. As a consequence of the uprising more than a thousand men were sentenced to prison and

---

2. This is comparable with the stories told by threatened peoples during revitalization movements of an imagined leader who will lead them out of their troubles (cf., for example, Halpern, Kunstädter 1967: 13 and Kaser 1997: 4).

some were executed. The authorities also proceeded with their confiscation of weapons, accelerating the process of demilitarization (Pavličević 1974: 75–133). In 1897 there was another rebellion but one more limited regionally (Mrkalj 1980: 41–44). Their attempts to prevent change in their social system had proved ineffective. They had no coherent program and the authorities reacted to every sign of resistance with intensive prosecutions and severe penalties.

National Differentiation on the Periphery

These examples clearly show that traditional concepts and perceptions from the period of the Militärgrenze were still present at the time of these uprisings. The shared hostile stereotypes of the Hungarians did have the effect of uniting the rebellious former Grenzers, although the process of national differentiation between Croats and Serbs had already begun. This differentiation affected their unity as Grenzers, a status that in earlier times had overshadowed their religious differences. New role and identity patterns came into being and succeeded in replacing the traditional self-definition. This national differentiation, of course, did not have its origin in the border regions themselves but was a proximate consequence of the integration of the predominantly rural border population into the Croatian civil society. Urban influences came in part from officials in Zagreb, the capital of Croatia-Slavonia, but also from politicians of Serbian background, especially from Vojvodina. This area lies just across the Danube and directly north of the capital of what was then the Kingdom of Serbia. It was here that the Serbian national movement in the Hapsburg monarchy had its center (Calić 1993: 120).[3]

The process of national differentiation between Serbs and Croats in the former border area was promoted by the representatives of the Serbian political parties who insisted on the separate national identity of the Serbian people in Croatia. By contrast, the Croatian parties were ready to give the Croatian Serbs freedom on a cultural level but regarded them otherwise as "political Croats." Even for the Croatian supporters of South Slav unity within the Hapsburg empire, it was

3. The process of national differentiation between Serbs and Croats is more complex than summarized here and important aspects of this process require further research. This is particularly true of the prenationalistic phase (see Hobsbawm 1992: 59–96). Since the late eighteenth century the Orthodox Vlachs who immigrated into the Militärgrenze began increasingly to define themselves as Serbs on the basis of religion (Serbian Orthodox). Subsequently, they were more frequently referred to as Serbs by the local authorities (but not in the meaning of a modern nation). A similar situation prevailed with respect to the Catholic Bunjevci in the border area who, in the course of their national development, became a part of the Croatian nation. This situation was also true for many Orthodox Vlachs, who before the nineteenth century had become Catholic, and whose descendants were also integrated into the Croatian nation. These facts clearly show how contradictory ethnocentric national ideologies can be used to define a given nationality as a genetic (even racial) community linked a society of common origin (see also Sundhaussen 1995: 149–87).

clear that the Croats should play the leading role. Until the beginning of the twentieth century the Budapest government was successful in playing off the political representatives of the two nationalities against each other. Both national confrontations as well as alliances, which went across national barriers, were limited to the Croatian Sabor (the regional parliament) in Zagreb, and to the bourgeoisie in a few larger towns. The first clashes between Serbs and Croats on the basis of nationality in the former Militärgrenze occurred as part of this process of national differentiation. These, however, were urban ideas introduced into the rural areas of the Krajina from outside. In July of 1914 the heir to the Hapsburg throne, Archduke Franz Ferdinand, was assassinated in Sarajevo by the Serb Gavrilo Princip. Shortly afterward the members of the "Party of the Pure Right," an extreme Croatian nationalist party, demanded that the Serbian members of the Sabor should be excluded from the parliament. As a consequence, riots against the Serbian population took place in several towns of the Banija and Orthodox churches and graveyards were vandalized (Roksandić 1991a: 117).

The Serbian-Dominated Kingdom of Yugoslavia (1918–1941)

In the late fall of 1918, after the end of Word War I, fierce struggles between Serbs and Croats in the former Militärgrenze took place in a general atmosphere of social unrest. The immediate motivation of the Croats was to protest the uniting of the South Slavs in the Kingdom of Serbs, Croats, and Slovenes in December 1918. The local Croatian population already affected by current revolutionary slogans perceived their hurried incorporation into a state ruled by a Serbian dynasty as both a continuation of the old order and a decline in their social position. Some Croat rioters burned shops in Lika belonging to Serbs who supported the unification. At the same time in Western Slavonia local Serbian leaders burned Croatian flags. The Royal Serbian army, called in by the government in Zagreb, introduced martial law. To a large extent the rural population of Croatia rejected unification, seeing it as a kind of occupation (Banac 1994: 129, 147).

To understand the context of the ferocity of the Serbo-Croatian conflict at this time one must bear in mind that more than a generation had passed since the dissolution of the Militärgrenze. The behavior of the population participating in the demonstrations was no longer motivated by the common experience of frontier troops confronting a common enemy, but by nationalistic goals inspired by urban politics. Also important was the fact that the Serbian politicians in Croatia, mainly born in the area of the former Militärgrenze, were the most determined advocates of a structured South Slavic unification. The hatred of the Croatian population was thus focused on these Serbian politicians as well as on the Serbian population in general.

The subsequent development of the relationships between the Serbian and Croatian populations of this region has been only partly explored. There were two contradictory trends, one drawing the groups together and the other pushing them apart. The first concerns the fact that in 1927 the Independent Democratic Party (Samostalna demokratska stranka), which drew its support from the Serbian population of the former Militärgrenze, entered into an alliance with the Croatian Peasant Party (Hrvatska seljačka stranka). This happened even though each organization had begun with completely different conceptions about the formation of the first South Slavic State. The two parties first formed local coalitions on the district level in the western part of the former Militärgrenze. This was more a result of pragmatic considerations than of ideological harmony. But then they formed an opposition coalition, the Peasant Democratic Coalition (Seljačka demokratska koalicija), in the national assembly. It was aimed at opposing the corruption of the central government, which was dominated by politicians from Serbia (Matković 1972). In 1929 King Alexander prohibited all parties and established his personal dictatorship, but the two parties continued to cooperate underground and later in half-legality. As far as can be ascertained, the alliance did not depend on the historical idea that the Serbian and Croatian populations in the former Militärgrenze had once shared a similar social status and culture.

The second trend was the polarization of the local Croats and Serbs that occurred during King Alexander's dictatorship. Violence was again introduced from outside the area of the former Militärgrenze. In 1932 Ustasha terrorists, who stood for a fascist independent Croatia, attempted, with some local help, an amateurish uprising in Lika. The regime retaliated not against the terrorists themselves but against Croatian peasants who had had no part in the uprising. Hundreds were arrested, and during the search for weapons, their barns were set on fire. These actions greatly increased national antagonisms (Stojkov 1970: 167–80).

These two examples illustrate, apart from the uprising at the end of 1918, that in the regions of Banija, Kordun, and Lika, slogans of hatred and violence were imports from the outside. These events disrupted and, to some extent, destroyed the previous sense of common community. Nevertheless, the Greater Serbian Chetnik movement did not have much support among the Serbian population of the former Militärgrenze. And in 1939, when Croatia was granted autonomy within the Kingdom of Yugoslavia, Serbian nationalists were able to recruit some supporters in Lika, but the Independent Democratic Party prevented their further work (Roksandić 1991a: 132).

Serbs under the Independent State of Croatia

The antecedent for the massive violence from 1991 to 1995 was the actions of the so-called Independent State of Croatia (Nezavisna Država Hrvatska or NDH), which existed from 1941 to 1945. Exactly fifty years later, a few months before fighting broke out in summer 1991, a Zagreb-based NGO representative visited a Serbian village in Banija. National tensions had reached this hitherto peaceful region. An old woman recalled these earlier days and mentioned the earth shelter in which villagers had hidden from marauding Ustasha troops during the Second World War.

The German bombardment of Belgrade on April 6, 1941, brought World War II to Yugoslavia. Within a few days this attack was followed by the total capitulation of the Yugoslav army. The country was divided among German, Italian, Hungarian, and Bulgarian occupiers. The Independent State of Croatia (NDH) was founded a few weeks later as a part of German war policy. NDH-Croatia pretended to act as an independent state but remained, until its collapse, dependent on the Third Reich. Installed by the Germans as a Quisling regime, the fascist Ustasha movement ruled over a territory in which only a little more than half the population was actually Croat. The Independent State of Croatia contained all of the present Republic of Bosnia and Herzegovina but not all of the present Republic of Croatia, since the coastal areas of Istria and much of Dalmatia were under Italian rule. When they came to power, the Ustasha lacked a popular base in Croatia, since even according to their own estimates, they had only a few thousand core supporters. But much of the Croatian population supported the formation of an independent Croatian state.

Soon after the takeover, however, the criminal character of the Ustasha regime became increasingly clear. Following a racist policy they started an intensive war of extermination against their political opponents, as well as the Jews and the Gypsies. They especially focused on the Serbs, who made up about a fourth of the population of the NDH (Sundhaussen 1983). In the months after their assumption of power the Ustasha slaughtered many of the inhabitants of the Serbian villages in Lika, Kordun, and Banija. At the end of April 1941, 250 Serbian peasants in Blagaj in Kordun were shot. Some days later 300 Serbs in Glina in Banija were slaughtered in the town's Orthodox church. Additional hundreds of Serbs were killed there at the end of July 1941. These outrages in Glina cost the lives of about 2,000 Serbs. In addition, many Serbs were transported to concentration camps where they were killed. Those who survived the massacres were transferred to Serbia or had to convert to Catholicism. In the three regions a total of 172 Orthodox churches were closed, plundered, or burned. These horrible events decreased only because Tito's Partisans began to liberate this area. From 1941 to 1945 these persecutions and the "National Liberation War" waged by the Partisans against the Ustasha and the Germans cost the lives of about seventy thousand Serbs and seven thousand Croats just in these three regions (Jelić-Butić 1977: 162–78; Sundhaussen 1995: 181; Roksandić 1991a: 142). In total the massacres cost the lives of hundred of thousands of people in the NDH.

Memories of past mass murders are not only recalled by people when exposed to a threatening situation, they are also stimulated by nationalist regimes and their supporters who use both fears and threats in their propaganda. For example, cassettes of inflammatory songs were distributed among Krajina Serbs in the early 1990s. In one case a popular local poet known as the "Chieftain of the Krajina of Knin" (*Knez Kninske Krajine*) wrote the following in 1991 (Čolović 1993: 78):

> Oj Srbijo, majko naša
> ti pomozi sad Srbinu
> protiv ovih zlih ustaša.
> Daj oružja u Krajinu.
>
> O Serbia, our mother
> Now help the Serb
> against these evil Ustaše.
> Give weapons to Krajina.

This verse refers not only to the Ustasha period, it also outlines the role of the "Serbian Krajina" as the western Serbian frontier dependent on the motherland.

The New Yugoslavia—Living Together after Wartime Massacres

If communist Yugoslavia had, in some sense, come to terms with the past, it would have also had to confront the consequences of Partisan activities during and immediately after World War II. In the final weeks of the war Ustasha soldiers, as well as members and sympathizers of the NDH regime, fled in fear of the advancing Partisans to the British-controlled parts of Southern Austria. There they were handed over to the Partisans by British troops near the small Austrian town of Bleiburg.

One of the leading figures in the Yugoslavian Communist Party in the years during and after World War II, Milovan Djilas, described the fate of these people:

> They were massacred except for the women and those under 18—this was reported to Montenegro and that was what I heard personally from the participants in these acts of revenge evoked by boundless anger and blind fury. How many were they? I think that nobody exactly knows and that nobody will ever know. According to what I heard from high party members who were involved in this act of retribution the number should be higher than 20,000, but did not exceeding 30,000. (Djilas 1977: 570)

Some serious works on this question estimate the number of victims a little higher by some ten thousands of victims (see, for example, Sundhaussen 1993).

Under the postwar ideological slogan of "Brotherhood and Unity" (*Bratstvo i Jedinstvo*) a sort of reconciliation, ideologically based and incomplete, did take place between Serbs and Croats. But there was no sincere and honest discussion about the war and postwar events, and what reconciliation there was not enough to satisfy even the entire communist hierarchy, some of whom later became nationalists. This is best seen in the experience of the former communist Partisan and army general, present Croatian nationalist and current president of Croatia, Franjo Tudjman.*

Thus national prejudices continued to develop in postwar Croatia. These developments increased the inclination to resort to force to realize national aims. Two examples of these prejudices will help us understand the situation. The first concerns the Croatians' criticism of the privileged position of the Serbs in the communist hierarchy of the Socialist Republic of Croatia. This was a result of the fact that the first liberated areas of Croatia were in Banija, Kordun, and Lika, so that the Serbs became overrepresented in Partisan ranks with respect to their proportion in the general population. In contrast to this situation was the contradictory perception by the Serbian population of the Krajina area. The Serbs from this overwhelmingly rural former Militärgrenze area thought of themselves as an increasingly marginalized group when compared to the more industrialized regions of Croatia. This situation caused large-scale Serbian migration to the cities. By 1990 the majority of the Serbs in Croatia no longer lived in the areas of the former Militärgrenze (Roksandić 1991b: 11–21).

Outbreak of the 1990 Conflict

When the conflict in this area began in 1990–91 it originally did not follow the simplified model "Ustasha versus Četnik." The Serbian population interpreted the conflict mainly in stereotypes from the "National Liberation War" waged by Tito, namely, "Partisans versus Ustasha." Later on, however, these stereotypes were supplemented by Greater Serbian ideas. By 1989 "tourists" from Serbia were visiting the Krajina, and they tried to enlist the Serbian population in support of a Greater Serbian state (Cigar 1996: 51–90). But in spring 1990, in the first postwar multiparty elections in what had been socialist Croatia, the Serbian portion of this area voted for the former communists (the results were different in the area of Knin). The former communists, however, went into opposition, and the Party itself then underwent a serious decomposition process that made it unable to play a role as a possible mediator between the two sides.

Increasingly a general national psychosis seized not only the Serbs but also the Croats. These feelings were intensified not only by the reconstituted Yugoslav (Serbian) regime, which followed an openly nationalist policy but also, increasingly, by the new Croatian political leadership. The Serbs in the Krajina were

---

*Franjo Tudjman died in December 1999; a few weeks later his party lost their governmental power in the parliamentary elections.

worried about how the party of President Tudjman would tackle the Serbian question in Croatia. Indeed his party had already eliminated a passage from the constitution. This passage had stated that Croatia was the Republic of both the Croats
and of the Serbs living within its borders. In response to the spreading Greater
Serbian nationalism, fueled by Slobodan Milošević, the president of Serbia, the
Croatian government was preparing to leave the Yugoslav federation. In 1990
some of the Serbs in Croatia had asked the Yugoslav People's Army for weapons.
These were provided, and by 1991 a large part of the Serbian male population
was armed (Livada and Hudelist 1995: 15–25). The Croatian government for its
part initially tried to get weapons by smuggling. The hitherto unimportant and
extreme nationalistic Serbian Democratic Party (SDS), which had its base in the
Dalmatian hinterland, had won only a few parliamentary seats in the first election. But they made use of this increasingly tense situation. In 1990 they built
barricades on the roads around their strongholds, proclaiming them "Serbian
Autonomous Areas." At the same time they extended their influence in the Serbian communities, either winning over former communist adherents or, later,
using violence against those who opposed them (Livada and Hudelist 1995: 15–
25).

The extremist Serbian leaders in the Krajina, supported by the Yugoslav
army and the ruling elite in Serbia proper, began to organize a parallel state and
built up a militia in preparation for an open conflict with the new Croatian state.
After several clashes in different places in the "Serbian Autonomous Areas," the
real war broke out following several hours of shooting in Borovo Selo in Slavonia
in which twelve Croatian policemen were killed in May 1991.[4] The fighting
quickly spread throughout the Krajina. Supported by the Yugoslav army, the
Krajina-Serb militia and Serbian volunteer groups conquered increasing numbers
of villages in the area. Massacres of the Croat civil population accompanied the
fighting. Large numbers of people, mainly of Croatian nationality, were expelled
from their homes and fled the territories. Soon the area become known as the
"Republic of Serbian Krajina" (see Map 2).

The crimes against humanity committed in the course of these events still wait
to be dealt with by the International Criminal Tribunal for the former Yugoslavia
in The Hague.[5] We should add here that "ethnic cleansing" did not take place
exclusively in the newborn state of "Serbian Krajina" but also in the internationally recognized Republic of Croatia. Many Serbs resident in the large cities lost
their jobs and homes and had to leave the country because they were or felt
themselves physically threatened. Those who still continue to live in Croatia try
to hide their Serbian identity.

4. The number of Serbian fighters is unknown.
5. On the problems of verification of war crimes and indictment of war criminals, see Višković
1997: 235–42 and Ivanji 1997: 243–64.

Map 2   The Republic of Serbian Krajina, 1991–95.

Actualizing the Potential for Violence

We want to contextualize these dramatic and sad developments by referring to the contradictory results of a survey conducted by Croatian sociologists in 1989, two years before the war began. This research was based on more than two thousand interviews of Croats and Serbs living in Croatia. One of the authors claimed: "There are no national tensions in Croatia at the end of 1989. They may, however, be anticipated." Results of the survey also indicated that relations between the two main national groups in Croatia had been worsening during the previous years. They found that endogamy had strengthened, while criteria for friendship appeared to be less affected. The interviewees did not feel that the rights of any ethnic groups were endangered, nor did they feel the need for cultural organizations based on nationality (Dugandžija 1991: 113).[6]

How then can one explain the dramatic change in 1990, the subsequent national outrages, and the killing in the war of 1991? A Croatian sociologist interpreted the events of 1990 and 1991 retrospectively: "Nationalism is such a powerful and irrational totality that, if you stimulate it by means of documentation concerning its basis, this may (help) give rise to the phenomenon of blood and soil which annihilates all values of life, and causes people to behave like sheep. The individual ceases to act as an individual, becoming, instead, part of the masses" (Livada and Hudelist 1995: 18).

Here we want to suggest a potentially useful approach. This involves considering symbol systems and their potential for constructing or modifying value systems (Bausinger 1990: 3–7; Erdheim 1992: 201–70). We use symbols here, not in an ahistorical sense, but rather as representing a particular facet of the total of potential meanings in a given historical and cultural situation. One may therefore compare symbolic constructions with the unconscious memory of a culture. In a given set of conditions adverse reactions tend to be triggered.

In the Krajina these conditions were manifested in 1941–45 and 1990–91. In each period the governing authorities lost their monopoly of power and their ability to employ force in the region of Krajina. Both times violence escalated primarily along ethnic lines. The political structure disintegrated in each case because the existing and therefore only legitimate authority was undermined by intense nationalistic propaganda on both sides. This caused an atmosphere of fear and insecurity. In this situation there was recourse to long-standing historically derived values. These values were accentuated through symbols presented to serve as guidelines for behavior in the visibly escalating conflict. The once-valid attitudes toward heroism, virility, and readiness to make sacrifices influenced the existing reality. So one can suggest that in the latest conflict these reactivated historical values were articulated. How they were employed can be

---

6. This study is complex and cannot be easily summarized here, but it is a necessary starting point for further investigation of this matter.

traced back to older values involving the willingness to use force to resolve political conflicts.

The Results of the Croatian Counterattack in 1995

In the beginning of August 1995, four years after its founding, the state of Serbian Krajina, was overrun by the Croatian army. This state, built on "ethnic cleansing," was never internationally recognized. Between August 4 and August 8 almost all of the Serbian population left their homes and fled to the Serbian part of Bosnia, to Serbia, or to Eastern Slavonia. The latter area was not the object of the Croatian attack. Only two to three thousand individuals, mostly old people, remained. Croatian authorities spoke of "ethnic self-cleansing" and tried to hide the crimes committed by elements of the Croatian army. Before the attacks took place, the Croatian army announced its arrival by shelling civilian sites. One can conclude that expulsion was the purpose of the offensive. It appears reasonable to assume that the Croatian government in planning its offensive never had any intention to promote a situation in which Serbs and Croats might again coexist. Publicly, they repeatedly proclaimed the integration of the territory of the "Serbian Krajina" with the rest of Croatia. It also seems to be clear that the army of the "Serbian Krajina" not only organized its own retreat but also the exodus of the population (Mappes-Niedick 1995: 585–92).

But what were the reasons for this exodus? One can say that Serbian civilians feared revenge by the Croats. Possibly they anticipated that they would suffer a repeat of what they with their leaders had done to the Croat population four years before (Mappes-Niedick 1995: 588). But why didn't the values of "struggle and bravery" function any longer as they were purported to in 1990–91? Perhaps a key factor was that a strong Yugoslav army was no longer present on the side of the Serbs. We also have to consider that the uprising of 1990–91 promised benefits to the Serbian population that never materialized. The territory of the "Serbian Krajina" had not only remained on the political and economic periphery but it had suffered from the international sanctions imposed on Serbia proper. It lost all its former trade connections with Croatia. So the values of "struggle and bravery," projected in 1990–91, reflections of a historical reality, had over several years lost their credibility with the Serb population.

From the perspective of the late 1990s there is some hope that a part of the former Serbian population will one day return. In one part of Croatia, in Eastern Slavonia, which was not conquered by the Croatian army in 1995, an international force had managed the reintegration into Croatia under UN auspices. The communities to be integrated held elections in April 1997. Formally, the Croatian Democratic Union (Hrvatska Demokratska Zajednica—HDZ), the party of Franjo Tudjman, and the Serbian Democratic Independent Party (Srpska demokratska samostalna stranka—SDSS), the only local Serbian party, have shared power. There will, however, be difficulties with the return of the former Croatian population. Many Croatian homes were occupied by Serbs, who fled to Eastern Slavonia from parts of the former Serbian Krajina. A large part of the Krajina territory conquered by the Croat army is, however, only partly inhabited. The Croatian population has been slow in returning. In some places the authorities placed Croats who had fled from Serbia and Bosnia in former Serbian houses. The region now is a stronghold of Tudjman's party. Some Serbs have returned but most of the Serbian homes are plundered and empty, appearing much the same as they did after the attack in 1995.

Conclusion

The 1991–95 war in Croatia escalated along national lines. Opposing nationalist organizations supported this conflict. These struggles were the outcome of nation building in this region, which remained a marginal phenomenon until the last third of the past century. We have to constantly keep in mind that the local population did not initially establish these national distinctions. Rather the influence of movements outside the region developed national consciousness in the area. These external influences were successful, especially after World War I, and proved influential in undermining the preexisting cooperative relationships between Catholic and Orthodox frontiersmen, who during the nineteenth century had become Croats and Serbs. The earlier interethnic relationships should, however, not be idealized, since from the time of their initial settlement in the seventeenth and eighteenth centuries these frontiersmen lived mainly in separate peasant villages. As peasants their mutual contact was limited. But the situation was different when they were mobilized, because the military units were recruited from Catholic as well as from Orthodox villagers. Their experience as soldiers was the most important point of interethnic contact. Aside from their religion they did share a common patriarchal mentality. Even with the passing of four generations since the dissolution of the Militärgrenze and exposure of the region to different processes of modernization some continuity in patriarchal attitudes respecting the use of force and the employment of weapons remained.

It is possible to suggest a comparison between the early revolts after the dissolution of the Militärgrenze with the Serbian uprising against the new Croatian state in 1990 and 1991. On the other hand these values were useful in creating two different national identities. Thus the two groups no longer recognized a common tradition. Now differences could be used as a tool to play off one group against the other. This was also due to the fact that the former Militärgrenze had always been under impact of political events and movements from outside. The Krajina served as the object of national aspirations, whether considered as an essential part of Croatia or as the western borderland of Greater Serbia. It has consistently been the case that political motives to inspire violence, be it from the Serbian or from the Croatian side, were primarily induced from outside.

This phenomenon can be fully observed in World War II when the Croatian Ustasha launched massive persecutions against the local Serbian population. Since that time there have been no more appeals to what had once been a common bicultural tradition. Images of the Ustasha persecutions and the fight of Tito's partisans against the Ustasha put a lid on these ideas and formed a new stock for national self-descriptions. But these were not openly manifest in Tito's Yugoslavia. There could be no debate nor discourse on nationality. The communist state did not permit this. Instead there was the official ideology "*Bratstvo i Jedinstvo*" (Brotherhood and Unity). This offered a new and fragile legitimization for living together. When this ideology crumbled with the communist system in the late 1980s, the purveyors of nationalism had an easy job to set free (for their own interests) the underlying national front lines that had been suppressed after World War II. The outcome, the war of 1991–95, was promising to such an extent that it was continued in Bosnia and Herzegovina, where the starting point (three different ethnic groups, not two) was still more complicated, and led into a catastrophe that shocked the whole world.

There were two remnants of the traditional mentality of the prenational situation of the former Militärgrenze. First, when the traditional local perception of the coexisting interethnic relationships was finally abandoned in World War II, it was not replaced by the more ideological than actual regime construction of "Brotherhood and Unity." Second, the values traditionally described as boldness and virility were part of the self-descriptions of both national groups. This worldview was nourished by interethnic clashes and violence that took place after World War I. Studies on the importance of socially based heroic constructions for the self-description of German soldiers in World War II analyze the traditional images of heroism and virility that are activated in wartime (Mersmann 1995). Such images both motivate the soldiers and legitimize the use of violence. This same phenomenon, stimulated by warmongers of both sides, can be observed in the 1991–95 war in Croatia. This situation is reflected in the opposing nationalist declarations of this period even though they do not show a direct connection with the tradition of the former Militärgrenze. It is appropriate to suggest that, based on the historical data presented here, these declarations did unconsciously appeal to the inherited images of heroism in service to a national identity. As the multifold history of the Balkans shows, it is all too easy to take this way in a recurrent situation of violence—at present, after a period of killing and mutual expulsion, it is much more difficult to revive the now-discarded values of bicultural perceptions—if indeed there is still a trace of these attitudes whether from the Partisan ethos of World War II or the earlier interwar cooperation of Serbian and Croatian peasant parties, not to mention the traditions from Hapsburg times. But if there is to be a stable and peaceful future it must be built on mutually acceptable patterns of coexistence that have roots in the past.

Under the Linden Tree

A Slovenian Life on a Contested State Frontier

Robert Gary Minnich

Under floodlights and the welcome gaze of global media Slovenia declared its independence the evening of June 25, 1991. However, raising Slovenia's new tricolor in Ljubljana was both a provocation and the fulfillment of a promise. The promise of Slovene independence inspired residents of Bovec, the small town central to this study, to plant a linden tree, a traditional Slovene way to mark a place of public assembly. But while they toasted the occasion with song and drink, air-raid sirens announced possible attack by the Yugoslav Peoples Army (YPA). Two days earlier, in response to Slovenia's secession, the central military command in Belgrade had ordered the YPA to retake international border crossings into nearby Italy. As it turned out, Bovec was spared any violence during the ensuing Ten Day War. Indeed, Slovenia was only grazed by what came to be

I am greatly indebted to Mrs. Darinka Kravanja-Pirc, who enthusiastically cooperated in the interviews for this essay and consented to the use of her name. Still, I am solely responsible for both the selection and interpretation of the information presented here. This essay is based in part on fieldwork conducted within the framework of the interdisciplinary project (1996–98), *Das österreichisch-italienisch-slovenische Dreiländereck: Ursachen und Folgen der nationalstaatlichen Dreiteilung einer Region*, funded by the Austrian Ministry for Science and Culture.

the violent demise of Yugoslavia.[1] In fact, Slovenia was more profoundly affected by the wars leading to the creation of the South Slav kingdom and to its remaking as a socialist federation.

Depending upon their age, social position, and geographical location, the inhabitants of former Yugoslavia have had profoundly different experiences of the wars that have made, remade, and unmade this tragic land. This essay views such conflicts from the vantage point of an elderly woman and how they affected her life in her community and the multilingual region in which she has lived the better part of her life. Her biography shows how cultural difference was politicized in her native region during the twentieth century and influenced by the concept and experience of citizenship in a contested borderland. I conclude by discussing possibilities for reintegration of this region as a multicultural home for the citizens of three states.

Darinka's Biography: A Slovene Life

Darinka Kravanja-Pirc helped plant the linden tree in the Bovec town square. And since her birth in 1910 in a nearby house she has watched another linden tree prosper in the same place, only to see it cut down. The official name of her town has changed four times in her life. Indeed, without changing residence, she has been a citizen of five different states: the Austro-Hungarian "dual" monarchy, Victor Emanuel III's Italy (in succession a parliamentary democracy and fascist dictatorship), the German Third Reich, the Federated Socialist Republic of Yugoslavia, and the Republic of Slovenia. Moreover, she attended secondary school in Maribor when it was part of the Kingdom of the Serbs, Croats, and Slovenes. Like many of her townspeople, Darinka spent many years away from home pursuing her education and working as an apprentice. Her aspirations as pupil and student, spouse, parent, and provider, as well as her desire to promote her local community's welfare, have been continually confounded by her changing status as a citizen of the various states controlling Bovec. Darinka's life thus parallels the Yugoslav experiment in state making as well as the historical epoch when the authority of the modern territorial state (Sahlins 1989) was consolidated within its most peripheral communities.

Darinka was born into a vast empire where her parents and grandparents moved freely in what might today be called multicultural society. But it was a

1. Although the Ten Day War resulted in fewer fatalities than two months of traffic accidents on the new republic's highways, it was readily seen as a war of national liberation. More appropriately, it might be characterized as the "war of international recognition." Global media, in place because of looming independence, gave Slovenia's newly elected government that exposure necessary to successfully negotiate the subsequent cease-fire. Signed on Brioni, July 7, 1991, this explicitly acknowledged Slovenia's secession from Yugoslavia and facilitated eventual international recognition of Slovenia as a sovereign republic.

dying social order where loyalty to the *Kaiser* prevailed and where the Universal Church, through its local parishes, connected members of peripheral communities and worldly authority. With the dissolution of Austro-Hungary Darinka was confronted as a child by a new reality, the so-called Three Country Region (see Map 3). Here each of three states—Austria, Italy, and Yugoslavia—claimed sovereignty over that remnant of empire her family called home (see Map 4). Here ethnicity was politicized to such an extent that a local historian (Moritsch 1994) characterizes this as the epoch of *integral Nationalismus* (essential nationalism). With the fall of Austria-Hungary new states were to rule the Slovenes for seven decades, largely in the name of other peoples. It was first after the Ten Day War that Darinka fleetingly remarked, "Finally, we can be Slovenes."

Despite the power of this comment, I nonetheless doubt that Darinka would define her life solely by reference to her Slovene identity. This was never questioned. When I asked her how she became aware she was Slovene, she tersely responded: "To ask me if I am Slovene is besides the point! We have always been Slovenes. My parents were Slovenes and their parents as well." The following thus discusses the persistence of this personal conviction in an environment where alternative national identities have been forced on Darinka and her borderland compatriots.

Slovene Self-Determination and the Making and Unmaking of Modern Nation-States

Over the past millennium the southeastern Alps have been a zone of contact between speakers of Germanic, Romance, and Slavic languages. In the wake of the 1848 revolution use of such languages came to signify membership in ethnic nations, each defined essentially as a language community bearing its own literary tradition. In other words, the Three Country Region (TCR) came to be viewed in popular imagination as a historical language frontier and, eventually, as a zone of confrontation between distinctly perceived "peoples." Thus its function and image within an encompassing polity as a multilingual crossroads between east, west, north, and south were lost.[2] At the political level, the dynastic competition for influence and control within this region was superseded early this century by the confrontation of states that politicized cultural difference in pursuit of territo-

---

2. This transition is in part demonstrated by changing patterns in language socialization. Before one's mother tongue became a more or less clear indicator of cultural identity and social position in late Hapsburg society, multilingual enculturation reflected patterns of integration and contact in that society, rather than relative social rank. The politicization of cultural (i.e., language) difference leads to a situation where those whose mother tongue was of a subordinate social group were coerced into learning majority codes while monolingualism among speakers of majority codes rapidly increases. (cf. Fischer 1980, Minnich 1988, and Moser 1982).

Map 3   Slovenia and the tri-county region.

Map 4   International boundaries, 1866 to the present

rial claims. Imagined communities (Anderson 1983) succeeded the deified *Kaiser* as the ultimate reference for citizen loyalty.

Combined with machinations of great power politics, these changing understandings of the political order influenced the partition of the former Hapsburg lands following World War I. As a result, a large segment of "Slovene ethnic territory" remained outside the borders of the newly constituted Kingdom of the Serbs, Croats, and Slovenes. Between 500,000 and 750,000 Slovenes and Croats were incorporated into an internationally recognized "greater" Italy (Singleton 1976; Kacin-Wohinz 1982) while significant populations of Slovene speakers also fell under the jurisdiction of newly constituted Austria and Hungary. From the perspective of Slovene aspirations for national self-determination, this partition was a sad parody of Woodrow Wilson's principled vision for a just resolution of Europe's postwar political map. Bovec's Slovenes were embraced by the *sacro egoismo* (sacred selfishness) of the Italian nation (Singleton 1976).

Following World War I, the majority of Slovenes suffered a different fate. They were incorporated into the first South Slav state. Founded in 1918, it was conceived as a "constitutional, democratic and parliamentary monarchy" under the Serbian Karadjordjevich dynasty (Singleton 1976). However, this constitutional order was never accepted by all the new state's political factions. In particular the Croatian Peasant Party was especially resistant. In an attempt to suppress ethnic and political strife King Alexander took command of the government in 1929 in what was then renamed the Kingdom of Yugoslavia. Eventually, however, a vicious civil war engulfed Yugoslavia. This war was as bloody as the concurrent national war of liberation against the occupying powers of Italy, Germany and their local allies during World War II. Still, despite their claims to the contrary, these first Yugoslav governments failed utterly in their attempts to attain popular support for a constitutionally regulated parliamentary democracy and to construct an ethnically neutral civil administration.

The remakers of Yugoslavia sought legitimacy and attained hegemony via socialism, autocratically yet delicately suppressing and politicizing ethnic difference during the ensuing half century. The remade ethnic environment was expressed rhetorically by the omnipresent slogan "brotherhood and unity." Nonetheless, relative cultural autonomy was constitutionally granted to each of socialist Yugoslavia's "nationally sovereign" (Zagar 1994) republics, as well as to its so-called autonomous regions. The dominant tongue of each republic was adopted as the language of public school instruction and administration within that republic.[3] These rights were also eventually extended to other acknowledged minority languages (e.g., Albanian, Hungarian, and Italian). For protagonists of

---

3. The acknowledged languages of Yugoslavia were nevertheless clearly ranked. While Macedonian and Slovene schools taught Serbo-Croation as a mandatory second language, Macedonian and Slovene were not compulsory in schools of the republics where Serbo-Croation was the dominant tongue.

Slovene nationhood, this was a significant improvement over the interwar situation. The recovery of ethnic territory lost to Italy in 1920 further legitimized the socialist state as guarantor of the Slovene right to self-determination.

By promoting a decentralized political structure the Socialist Federal Republic of Yugoslavia tacitly facilitated eventual Slovene demands for secession (Zagar 1994). Following highly centralized Stalinist rule during the immediate postwar years, economic and political power was increasingly transferred to individual republics through a series of constitutional reforms. Administrative, political, and commercial structures were created that emphasized republican autonomy (Ferfila and Phillips 1994).[4] The Slovene government elected in 1990, following socialist Yugoslavia's first multiparty elections, was led by the DEMOS coalition of parties, which had formed in opposition to but with the support of the Communist Party in the late 1980s. Until the Ten Day War the DEMOS government negotiated with federal authorities for republican autonomy within a South Slav confederation (Brinar and Kuhnle 1994). However, the Serbian-dominated federal government refused to negotiate. Finally, after the YPA was deployed to enforce Serbian hegemony over the fraying federation, the Slovene leadership saw only one realistic alternative: independence and recognition as a sovereign nation-state. Now that recognition has been obtained, the Slovene state remains an imperfect manifestation of Slovene ethnic territory, which still extends into Austria, Italy, and Hungary.

A Citizen in an Ethnically Contested Borderland: The Case of Darinka Kravanja-Pirc

The town of Bovec is located 460 meters above sea level at the convergence of valleys that drain the central ranges of the Julian Alps into the Adriatic Sea via the Soča River. The white limestone peaks of these Alps dramatically punctuate the local horizon of intensely green forested lower ridges enclosing the valley. The relatively low elevation and temperate climate of Bovec (influenced by prevailing winds from the Adriatic) favored its habitation long before its first documented settlement in 1174 (Marušič 1994b). The premodern residents of the Upper Soča Valley experienced hardship common to historical Alpine adaptations. Their economic viability depended on combining animal husbandry, field cropping and horticulture, forestry, and seasonal employment in and commerce with adjoining, more developed regions.

For at least two millennia the Soča Valley functioned as an alternative and more easily defended artery of communication between the Friulian plain and

---

4. Because the Socialist Republic of Slovenia did not include territory contested by Yugoslavia's other ethnic groups, political life within the borders established by the socialist federation essentially enabled ethnic self-determination.

the Carinthian basin and upper Carniola (Podlipnig 1994). This underlies the historical role of Bovec and nearby settlements as way stations for transport over the nearby Predel Pass. Because of its strategic importance, the Valley has long figured in the strategic considerations of great powers interested in the region.[5] In the sixteenth century this competition was waged mainly between the Hapsburgs and Venetians. The subsequent instability of nearby interstate borders influencing the Upper Soča Valley contributed to the region's persisting status as periphery, regardless of which center controlled it (Klemenčič 1974).

Because of its location, the Upper Soča Valley is largely isolated from Ljubljana, the political, administrative, and commercial center of twentieth-century Slovenia. Instead, Soča inhabitants have most consistently gravitated toward Gorizia, which by the sixteenth century, stood out as a commercial and administrative center attracting immigration from the three intermingled language groups of the greater region (Bufon 1995). Cividale, Trieste, and Tarvisio have also been periodically important to the economic viability of the Upper Soča Valley. Between 1866 and World War I, when it was within the Dual Monarchy, Gorizia became a significant center for the Slovene national awakening. It was also the site of the first state-sponsored Slovene "gymnasium" within Slovene ethnic territory (ibid.).

With the rise of Austrian absolutism in the eighteenth century the Bovec elite of innkeepers, artisans, clerics, and traders were supplemented by the presence of state administrative, military, and judicial officials. A century later the local elite were joined by teachers recruited to newly established compulsory primary schools where German and Slovene were the languages of instruction. Bovec became a town, but its role as an administrative center of the region of the Soča headwaters has been confounded by the periodic transfer of these functions to Tolmin, forty kilometers to the south.

Darinka's father was a Bovec innkeeper and merchant and her mother a teacher. Compared to her consociates Darinka had a privileged childhood. Her parents socialized her as a *burgher* capable of participating in and contributing to the institutions of civil society. Through formal education and apprenticeship she acquired the knowledge and skills needed to maintain her family's commercial interests. Her social positioning fostered her unquestioned Slovene self-image, one interwoven with a sense of responsibility for the well-being of her community. If we were to reduce Darinka's biography to the terms of a late modernist "identity project," we might say that it is one of "being a Slovene and becoming a citizen."

Although only four at the outbreak of World War I Darinka has a nuanced and knowledgeable understanding of her grandparents' society. Her paternal grandfather was born in 1829 near Trieste where he attended secondary school and

---

5. Nearby Fort Kluže, first erected in the fifteenth century as a barrier against the Turks, has consistently figured in military strategies to inhibit movement across the Predel Pass.

later learned the baker's trade. He soon met and married a young woman from Soča village, ten kilometers upstream from Bovec, who was working as a maid in Trieste.[6] After marriage they moved to Bovec where he set up a bakery and eventually became a *Armeelieferant*, a supplier of "bread, oats, grass, and firewood" for the Austrian military post at nearby Fort Kluže *(Flitscher Clausen)*. Darinka's paternal grandfather was an able businessman and soon established a local store and inn and traded across the Predel in Tarvisio, which was connected with the empire by railroad (Moritsch 1996b).

Commenting on this period, Darinka mentioned how most Bovec residents were less fortunate than her paternal grandparents and forced to leave Bovec in pursuit of a living. The typical Bovec household had only a small plot of land and a few animals, seldom more than a "cow or two" or a "small flock of sheep and goats." Bovec men found employment in the lead and zinc mines across the Predel Pass at Cave del Predil (Rabelj), and also had rights, instituted under Maria Theresa, as petty traders *(hausierer—krošnjarji)* throughout the empire (see Sedmak 1994).[7] Such men spent the winter trading and working as far away as Bohemia and Vojvodina. According to Darinka this freedom of movement within the vast *Vielvölkerstaat* was necessary for the economic viability of most Bovec residents. Indeed, the relative prosperity of her grandfather's business was dependent on income brought to Bovec by miners, contracts with the state, and commerce north across the Alps and southwest into the Friulian plain. Most significantly, such economic migration was contingent on the universal extension of and standardization of civil rights throughout the monarchy and its constituent Crown Lands. In other words, the subjects of the Dual Monarchy were becoming citizens of a territorial state. Toward the end of the century political rights were even extended to previously disenfranchised rural populations, who thus became potential sources of support during the re-constellation of power within the empire and its regional polities.

Darinka identified her paternal grandparents as Slovenes. It is my impression that their literacy was an essential precondition for their Slovene identity. Attainment of literacy among the Bovec elite obliged burghers to participate in local voluntary organizations that blossomed after 1867.[8] These included voluntary

6. For nearly a century previous to World War II young women from the coastal and western districts of Slovenia supported themselves and their families through employment as maids, wet nurses, and governesses in rapidly expanding Trieste. From there thousands more attained such employment with wealthy families throughout the Middle East, but especially in Alexandria (Širok 1996; Sedmak 1994).

7. According to Sedmak (1994: 84), only two other towns (Kočevje and Ribnica) in the Slovene part of the Monarchy were extended this right.

8. The administrative, legal, and educational reforms undertaken by the Hapsburg state via the December Constitution of 1867 enabled attainment of literacy and the spread of voluntary organizations. Literacy in the lingua-franca of the realm, German, promoted through compulsory primary education, also facilitated literacy in standardized Slovene. Furthermore, Slovene literacy, and hence their constructed heritage as a people, was promoted through rapidly expanding local voluntary organizations (Moritsch and Baumgartner 1992).

fire-brigades, choral societies, reading circles, agricultural cooperatives, and savings associations. In Bovec the local Slovene library (Čitalnica, founded in 1878) and choral society (pevski zbor, founded in 1900) were particularly important for promoting Slovene national awareness and institutionalizing civil society in the local community. Local arenas were created, parallel to those of the modern state, for the exercise of citizenship. But this local right to free association was clearly identified with the authority of the *Kaiser*, affirmed by Darinka's memory that Bovec townspeople planted a linden tree in the town square to celebrate Franz Josef's sixtieth year of rule in 1908.

A literary tradition in one's mother tongue is essential for promoting awareness of imagined associations, the essence of modern nationalism (Anderson 1983; Minnich 1998). Through his support of the Slovene literary standard in Bovec, Darinka's paternal grandfather was among that select group that initiated ethnic self-awareness in the periphery of the Dual Monarchy. During his lifetime the Hapsburg Empire rapidly became the uncomfortable home of many "nations," a transformation that laid the basis for the formation of its ethnic-based successor states.

The Vienna government responded to the ethnic challenge to its authority in a number of ways. First, on the basis of systematic and comprehensive censuses in the second half of the nineteenth century, it categorized its increasingly enfranchised and restive citizenry in terms of specific ethnic groups *(Volksgruppen)*. On the basis of such data, it was then possible, for example, to promote ethnic political parity in multiethnic regions like Görz (Gorizia) by manipulating election districts so that no single ethnic group could dominate the others (Bufon 1995). The Monarchy failed, however, to legitimate itself as a multiethnic social order. Neo-absolutism was buried in the rubble of the "Great War."

During the first decade of this century Darinka's mother attended the Slovene Teachers College (slovensko učiteljišče) in Gorizia and was assigned her first post at the public primary school in Čezsoča, a village across the valley from Bovec, where German and Slovene were the languages of instruction. She too was the daughter of innkeepers who sought to educate their children in a way befitting people of their position. After attending the Slovene gymnasium in Gorizia, Darinka's father, born in 1883, trained there as a confectioner. At this time he met his future spouse. He then returned to Bovec to take over the family businesses after completing, at his father's initiative, an additional apprenticeship as a baker in Klagenfurt (Carinthia).

On May 23, 1915, six years after Darinka's parents were married, Italy declared war on Austria, disrupting the promising future for this young family. A decree read the following morning at mass announced the evacuation of Bovec and surrounding settlements (V. Klavora 1993: 59). Within a few days nearly all 80,000 civilians resident in the Upper Soča Valley had fled to the interior of Austria. Those caught later behind this front were either deported to or sought refuge in the interior of Italy (M. Simić 1996). Darinka fled with her mother across the Predel Pass into Carinthia to the home of her grandmother near Arnold-stein, where they remained for the duration of the war. Her father moved to nearby Mittelbreth (Log pod Mangartom), where he was drafted as the baker for the Fort Kluže (*Flitscher Clausen*). Other refugees from the region ended up in internment camps, but still others used their networks developed through seasonal labor and petty trading to settle in the Austro-Hungarian interior.

The Soča Valley was thus cleared of civilians and over the next two and a half years was occupied by about 1.5 million soldiers (M. Simić 1996), recruited from most of Europe's diverse ethnic nations. The Valley was thus transformed through the construction of barracks, supply depots, medical dispensaries, railways, alpine roads and cable ways, fortifications, and gun positions. Subsequently, it was devastated by eleven major Italian offensives, during which they gained a total of thirty square kilometers (Rauchensteiner 1994). Even today numerous war cemeteries, memorials and museums remind all of the 300,000 soldiers killed in battle on the Soča Front.[9]

Darinka, whose immediate family had survived and was intact following the Great War, returned to a Bovec smashed by shelling and plundered by fleeing soldiers. Reflecting on this she nonetheless stressed, "Each calamity in our history has inspired new enthusiasm to rebuild and get on with life." Such was the case for Bovec's civilians when they were allowed to return.

Darinka had already finished her first year of school in Arnoldstein when her family returned to Bovec. She completed her primary education in the following three years when she became literate in both German and Slovene. At the age of twelve her parents sent her to a boarding school for girls at the Ursolinekloster near Gorizia, where Italian was the language of instruction. It was here in 1922 that she had her initial encounter with Italian fascism when the pupils of her school were ordered to attend a parade of black-shirted young men staged in the center of town. For Darinka this was a frightening sight. After Italy implemented the Gentile educational reforms in 1923, Italian was made the mandatory language of instruction and Fascist ideology was systematically incorporated into the curriculum of public education. Darinka's parents sought an alternative for their children. In 1926 they interrupted her education in Gorizia and sent her to live with an aunt in Maribor, to complete her education at the Ivan Cankar Secondary School. Her brother and sister also attended this school. According to Darinka they were the only Bovec children of her generation who were sent to Yugoslavia for education in their mother tongue.[10] In 1928–29 she was sent to Hotel Europa in Trieste to complete her formal training.

9. Estimates of fatalities on the Soča front vary between 300,000 and 500,000 (cf. Rauchen-steiner 1994, Moritsch 1994, and M. Simić 1996). As large as these numbers are they exclude hundreds of thousands who perished from disease and hunger, from the atrocious conditions in the POW camps.

10. Other Bovec youth who did not have the opportunity to legally enter Yugoslavia also completed their education there after fleeing from Fascist Italy. However, they were unable to return to Bovec until 1947 unless they had joined partisan units fighting in the region.

Like few others of her generation in Bovec, Darinka is not only conversant in the region's three major languages, she was schooled in their literary traditions as well. She admitted once, however, that she finds it difficult to motivate herself to read Italian literature, whereas she is equally attracted to Slovene and German texts. This predisposition can be explained by events in the next two decades of her life.

Although absent from Bovec during much of the late 1920s, Darinka has vivid knowledge of the intensified Fascist campaign there in this period. For example, during this time the headmaster of the local school was deported to the interior of Italy while other local teachers sought refuge in Yugoslavia. They were especially welcome in eastern Slovenia (Lower Styria), where local Slovene leaders were themselves engaged in an "ethnic" campaign to reduce the role of German language instruction in public schools. In Bovec, meanwhile, all the Slovene-speaking teachers were replaced by monolingual Italians. Aside from political pressure, many Bovec residents emigrated for economic reasons. One of Darinka's recollections of the depression years are the tears she shed over the departure of a busload of eligible young Bovec men seeking their fortunes as miners and laborers abroad, especially in Montana and Argentina.

Darinka's memory of this period is one of resistance and opposition to the Fascist campaign against Slovenes. She recalls how her future husband and his schoolmate were temporarily arrested and accused of burning down the Bovec primary school (Sardoč 1983). They were suspects because alone among local youth they had refused to participate in Fascist youth organizations. With a certain glee she recounts how she helped townspeople hide the contents of their Slovene library a few days before it was to be destroyed. Elsewhere in the Julian Province, Slovene and Croatian libraries were systematically incinerated (Zidar 1987). Her memory of this period returns repeatedly to the sign which her parents were forced to post in their inn: "Only Italian is spoken here." And she recalls how, while living in Trieste in 1928, she broke out in tears after reading in a letter from home that Fascist authorities cut down the linden tree in the town square.

On the day before Easter 1943, which was a few months before the *Wehrmacht* took control of Bovec, Darinka saw a truck laden with more than thirty corpses driving through town to the local barracks. The local Italian commander announced that same morning that these were the bodies of young partisans the Italian forces had killed the night before in nearby Golobar and that their families should come and claim them.[11] Darinka recalls that some mothers, out of fear of reprisals, refused to claim their sons. Local memory of this tragedy is perpetuated in the name of the Bovec town square: "Square of the Golobar victims." Ironi-

---

11. Earlier that year in response to Italian military recruitment campaigns within the Soča region, many young men fled and joined the illegal Partisan forces.

cally Darinka recounts how upon visiting her husband[12] in Milan later that same
week, she noticed a poster announcing that a choir from the Slovene town of
Vipava, seventy kilometers south of Bovec, would be presenting an Easter con-
cert of Slovene songs in the Milan Cathedral! Such public performances in Slovene were impossible in her native town. Unknown to her until well after World
War II, Darinka's husband was active in the TIGR resistance.[13]

Once Partisan units were formed in the Soča region to fight in the Yugoslav
War of National Liberation, the local population was exposed to demands for
loyalty and material support from yet another superordinate authority. Since the
Partisans had ready legitimacy by their resisting the injustices of the Fascist
regime, the new "peoples authority" (*ljudska oblast*) was positively received
when it took control of Bovec on September 15, 1947.[14] A local delegation
dressed in folk costumes received representatives of the new authority with bread
and salt, classic Slavic symbols of welcome.

Darinka's husband was appointed the first mayor of Bovec under the socialist
regime. He was of more modest origins than his wife; he had only a middle-
school education and before the war had worked as a miner in nearby Cave de
Predil (Rabelj). His skills as a worker, participation in the resistance, and other
leadership qualities led to his being singled out by the new regime. Still, most of
the Bovec elite of private innkeepers, artisans, and large landholders (including
Darinka's own brother) were treated severely by the new regime. Like its Fascist
and Nazi predecessors, the socialists also nationalized the inn belonging to Darinka's family. But, as Darinka wryly notes, her livelihood after marriage was no
longer dependent on assets from a privately owned family business. And despite
the class-based economic policies and restrictions under socialist rule, Bovec
citizens could openly express Slovene identity. Darinka says that restoring this
freedom was "like the dawning of a new day."

The immediate postwar years were marked by severe economic hardship,
closed state borders, and the ineffective and often unjust policies of revolutionary
government. This situation led to extensive emigration and threatened to deprive
Bovec of its youth. But leaving Bovec for the West at this time was risky, so
most people emigrated to other parts of Slovenia. Two elderly Bovec brothers,
whose assets were nationalized by the "peoples authority," recalled this "dark"

12. Darinka's husband was an Italian conscript during World War II. Along with all other non-
Italians, he was consigned to a so-called special battalion which was not entrusted with the sacred
duty of serving on the front.

13. Fascist campaigns to assert Italian ethnic hegemony within its newly acquired Julian Province led to organized resistance. The first militant antifascist group was formed in the mid-1920s
under the name TIGR (acronym for Trieste, Istria, Gorizia, and Rijeka). And its membership consisted of Slovenes and Croats of diverse ideological persuasions who were united through their mutual experience with the fascist state's brutal repression of its other "peoples" (cf. Zidar 1987 and
Sardoč 1983). Eventually TIGR joined the Yugoslav War of National Liberation during the Second
World War.

14. Bovec fell under Anglo-American military administration between 1945 and 1947.

period in their lives by telling me of associates who were shot by Yugoslav border guards when attempting to flee over the nearby Rombon mountain into Italy. The "Iron Curtain" was sadly real for Bovec residents until the London Memorandum regulating traffic across the Italian-Yugoslav border was signed in 1954. Subsequently, opportunities for interstate commerce opened, and it was once again possible for members of those many Bovec families with kin in nearby Italy to visit one another.[15] During the 1960s Yugoslav political and economic reforms systematically promoted the migration of Yugoslav citizens as guest workers to Western Europe (Minnich 1976). Economic migration, reminiscent of the late Hapsburg period, once again became an option for Bovec residents and contributed to its development hand-in-hand with state policy, eventually creating substantial industry in this isolated Alpine enclave.

Darinka and I did not discuss the communist epoch extensively. It is evident, though, that after the advent of socialist rule she was forced to reorient her life and expectations. Much like her parents during Fascism, Darinka stubbornly promoted the education of her two daughters, both of whom attended university and now pursue careers, one as a research scientist and the other as a secondary school teacher.

For much of the socialist period Darinka was also quite active in secular and church organizations promoting the welfare of her fellow citizens of Bovec. Her Catholic faith is significant for her identity, although during our conversations, I was struck by her lack of emphasis on personal religiosity. Yet she regularly attends the Bovec parish church and avidly participates in community rituals and the rites of passage of her fellow townspeople, activities that clearly manifest local traditions of folk religion. This disparity between Darinka's actions and the "silence" of her Catholicism appears related to her experience during the early Socialist period when verbalization of one's religious convictions was reserved for private conversation. Nonetheless, Darinka's membership in the local parish church has been fundamental to her self-understanding. Throughout her life it has consistently been the chief means through which she could most consistently express her Slovene identity and exercise her responsibilities toward her local community. For her, participation in church activities has been both fulfilling and a refuge from the turmoil of shifting regimes.

The Bovec parish church, like other local Slovene churches, consistently mediated between centrally dictated policy and local norms of public devotion.[16] Even during the height of Fascist repression church activities like the priest's Sunday sermon were the only public occasions in Bovec where Slovene was spoken. This situation even obtained during *Wehrmacht* occupation of Bovec

15. Renewed access to Italy made it Yugoslavia's major trading partner briefly at the end of 1950s (Singleton 1976).

16. That local parish churches accommodated the prevalent local mother tongue in religious services and tolerated local idioms of folk religion relates to Catholicism's claim to universality among an ethnically diverse membership.

between 1943 and 1945.[17] Although participation in church life was not forbidden under socialism, atheism was a precondition for Party membership.[18] Bovec townspeople were quite aware that public expressions of faith limited opportunities for attaining positions of influence and authority in the professional, administrative, and commercial sectors of Yugoslav society. As a result religious expression during this period took many forms, some quite private and hidden, others public and confrontational. The vitality of Catholicism during socialist rule is now apparent. In fact, the Slovene independence movement of the late 1980s was marked by a vibrant revival of folk religion and various political, economic, and cultural organizations that have their wellspring in Roman Catholicism.

In contrast to Darinka's active exercise and recognition of her civic obligations, her experience as a citizen of the states that have dominated her native town is more philosophical and reserved. This reflects the constantly shifting possibilities for local citizens to express their civil and political rights under those diverse state regimes. Darinka was born into an era when political activity was enabled by the voluntary associations that blossomed at the turn of century in this Hapsburg periphery. Largely under the control of an emerging middle class *(Bürgertum),* they substantiated class difference. However, Italian Fascism and National Socialism rejected this social order and radically amputated the political autonomy of the local institutions of civil society. The right of voluntary association and the political franchise were subordinated to centrally dictated ideological concerns that had their wellspring in what Gail Stokes (1993: 4ff.) calls antirational populism. Fascist and Nazi authority sought legitimacy along another avenue, namely, by extending social rights such as guaranteed employment, health care, and various social welfare programs. The classic model of citizenship rights, based on the successive extension of civil, political, and social rights in England, was turned on its head (Marshall 1964; Turner 1993).

Darinka's first encounter with the modern state as the immediate regulator of local affairs grew from her experience of Fascist rule. Citizenship mediated by a centrally imposed ethnic identity was alien to Darinka's upbringing. The locally implanted social and cultural institutions of the Italian Fascist, Nazi, and Yugoslav socialist regimes intervened in the formerly relatively autonomous political arena of her native community into which she had been enculturated in her youth.

17. Recalling this period, Darinka noted that the commanding officer in Bovec imposed a much less severe regimen than his predecessors, tolerating, for example, the public use of Slovene. Significantly, he was a native of Maribor in Lower Styria, spoke Slovene, and his mother was a Slovene. In contrast to his monolingual Italian predecessors he exercised his authority strictly with reference to his obligations as a *Wehrmacht* officer and, according to Darinka, tactfully avoided whenever possible applying the ethno-nationalistic policies of the Nazi regime.

18. In contrast to Poland, for example, party membership in SFR Yugoslavia forbade participation in any of the country's various religious orders.

Until the era of *integral Nationalismus* the initiation, leadership and support of various voluntary organizations had been largely matters of local choice.

The creation of a pluralistic political system in Slovenia, beginning in the 1980s, returned to Bovec residents the freedom for civic action and cultural expression that we identify with Western democracies. The rights to own property, to engage in private commercial transactions, and to hold multiparty elections were fully restored. It remains to be seen, however, to what extent this political transformation will create a legal-administrative structure and national civic culture necessary to promote social equality and accommodate cultural difference. It seems that Darinka also carefully reserves for herself the right to judge whether what she calls "the government in Ljubljana" fulfills her ideals of civic culture as she learned it, through her upbringing in the rationalist spirit of late Hapsburg society.

One thing is certain. The Republic of Slovenia guarantees Darinka and her fellow citizens the right to be a Slovene in a way none of its predecessors could. For the first time in her life Darinka is the citizen of a "sovereign" state where the great majority of citizens perceive Slovene language and culture as their common heritage. As a small country with a population of two million the Republic of Slovenia is economically, militarily, and politically vulnerable to the designs of its more powerful neighbors. Nevertheless, Slovenes have attained new self-confidence by fulfilling that model of ethnic statehood which prevails in the minds of those who yet prevail in the affairs of the territory where the Hapsburgs once ruled.

For Darinka to exclaim following the Ten Day War that *"finally* we can be Slovenes" is both eminently reasonable and patently absurd. In terms of personal conviction she has been a Slovene under the most adverse of political conditions. This of course had more to do with her upbringing and position in local society than with the regime in power. In other words, for Darinka Slovene identity is commensurate with being a citizen; it is based on the right of individuals to assemble under the linden tree, whether located in the town square or church yard. The reconstitution of Slovenia as a "Western" democracy makes it the guarantor of rights that Darinka upholds as fundamental to self-determination. She thus asserts on behalf of her compatriots that now *we* can be Slovenes.

Darinka's Biography as the Representation of a Greater Whole

A dominant yet unsolicited theme of my conversations with Darinka was her participation in various voluntary organizations and public institutions. She consistently described this involvement in terms of her consociates, people in the social universe into which she was born, socialized, and incorporated. (The rules, objectives and structure of these organizations were seldom topics.) Through reference to this group, often by means of vivid anecdotes, she articulates continuity in her life experience. She grounds and expresses her values and sense of obligation toward others in terms of everyday roles such as that of wife, mother, innkeeper, bookstore clerk, *bovčanka* (a Bovec resident). First and foremost Darinka presents her experience of citizenship in terms of this immediate network of social relations rather than with reference to the political rights and evolving institutions of state society which I have used to structure the foregoing biography.

Through deportation, political exile, economic emigration, and marriage, Darinka's network of kith and kin has become dispersed across the globe. She proudly exclaims that when her relatives gather at least five different languages are represented! As such her biography is a paradox. Although Darinka grounds her self-understanding in terms of a small universe of known persons—a small yet dispersed community—she must nonetheless reflect over a larger and more complex social reality. She refers repeatedly to supra-local phenomena that have shaped the lives of her consociates as well as herself. These include the Great War, the Depression, fascism, the German Reich, the National Liberation Front, communism, and most recently "the government in Ljubljana." Through the circumstances of her life Darinka's understanding of the world accounts for the globalization of local lives. And this applies to most older people in Bovec. Hence, any realistic representation of Bovec must transcend the local community in its quest to convey local self-understandings. Darinka 's sense of identity does not correlate in any simple manner to the families, towns, and states to which she has belonged.

Darinka's biography gives us a glimpse into the social structure and cultural character of her native region, but Darinka herself should not be taken as representative of it. Other, differently positioned members of her Bovec cohort are, for example, less involved in civic activity and more focused on immediate family commitments and religion. Furthermore, representatives of other generations who were socialized as children during the fascist and socialist periods have necessarily come to different understandings of their involvement in public life and identity as Slovenes. While her fellow townspeople differ from her in how they view the world, they and she together represent, through the common experience of war, shifting regimes, and economic well-being, voices from which a representation of this borderland community can be gleaned.

The themes of ethnicity and citizenship, nation and state, inevitably inspire normative representations; that is, the construction of categories whereby individuals are assigned to different kinds of group membership. By investigating these phenomena in terms of individual experience we are forced to reconsider how collective identities are constituted and transformed. Darinka's life experience raises a number of significant questions in this regard. Is ethnic identity simply a matter of ascription by those holding the power to name things (Moore 1994), or is it more a matter of self-ascription? Or is it, perhaps, a combination of both that varies across historical time and space? Similarly, is citizenship a condition created simply by the extension of rights by some type of superordinate authority to those within its jurisdiction, or is citizenship more a process shaped by the individual's experience of and actions within everyday life (Shotter 1993)? The foregoing raises these questions without pretending to answer them. However, it does suggest that it may be analytically fruitful to consider the self-reflecting individual (Cohen 1994), rather than the group, as the author of collective identities and the community of one's daily associates as the proper site for understanding the practice of citizenship (Shotter 1994).

The Three Country Region: From Confrontation to Integration

Current trends in the conduct of relations across state borders within the Three Country Region (TCR) optimistically suggest prospects for regional reintegration. The ethnic model for statehood is increasingly challenged by constellations of political and commercial power broader than that of the nation-state that prevailed during the latter part of Darinka's life. A sense of civic awareness is emerging in the TCR that seems able to accommodate those cultural differences which formerly served as the base of ethnic confrontation. But however positive these trends may appear, they are conditioned by the past of massive armed conflict, ethnic violence, and totalitarian government.

The borders of the states in the TCR remain contested to the present day. This is confirmed by unresolved border issues between Slovenia and Croatia, by the persistence of right-wing harassment of Slovene public figures in Carinthia and Friuli-Venezia-Giulia, and by the resistance of the recent Italian center-right coalition government to approve Slovenia's application for association with the European Union.[19]

Contention over borders in the TCR figures in the irredentist agendas of the right wings of *all* the region's states. Italian right-wing radicals living in the multilingual Italian borderland with Slovenia construct their political program around the "collective memory" of exile from their "homeland"—the Julian province, and particularly Istria (Ballinger 1996). The Slovenian right wing gains some of its support from the former Slovene political exile community, formed during the confrontation between fighters loyal to National Liberation Front and those collaborating with the occupying powers during World War II.[20] This latent

19. The May 1996 Italian elections produced a center-left coalition that has been more responsive to demands of Slovene and Friulian minorities for the same political recognition as those gained by the German-speaking minority of Alto Adige (South Tyrol). Though the rights of the Slovene minority in Italy have been established by international and bilateral agreements since 1947 (Bufon 1995), their implementation has been another matter.

20. In Carinthia the situation is different. The radical right wing is not comprised of disgruntled refugees, but of the descendants of German Nazis who in postwar Austria, have never been forced to acknowledge the atrocities perpetrated in the name of the German nation against the Slavic-speaking residents of this borderland.

ethnic nationalism can be traced back to the first systematic round of "ethnic cleansing" in the region and the ideological confrontation perpetrated by the cold war, which had its origins in the initial ideological polarization of clerical and leftist political factions seeking to dominate the politics of late Hapsburg society.

Despite the presence of these radical forces in local public affairs, violent confrontations across the region's borders have been avoided since World War II. Since then a series of treaties and conventions were adopted acknowledging the rights of national minorities and facilitating movement and commercial activity across these borders, particularly for residents of a prescribed border zone. Border adjustments after World War II between Yugoslavia and Italy facilitated this by achieving a more realistic territorial balance (Bufon 1995). Nevertheless, rapprochement along these frontiers depends on economic well-being and rising standards of living in each of these states. Without this relative prosperity it is possible, though unlikely, to imagine a return to state-sponsored ethnic violence in the region. Incorporation of the TCR within the European Union would significantly reduce the potential for interstate conflict. And in June 1996, Slovenia became an associated member of the European Union. This was immediately acclaimed by Slovene minority politicians in Italy as a watershed for formalizing a legal basis to guarantee the integrity of the Slovene nation (*Delo,* June 12, 1996).[21] Slovene ethnic territory now falls entirely within the territorial jurisdiction of states that are either full or associate members of the European Union. But is this traditional program for ethnic self-determination a positive aspect of Europe's integration? Other perspectives seem more promising.

For example, a "working group" has been formed that is dedicated to promoting the idea of the Alpe-Adria, a replication of the southwest corner of the former Dual Monarchy. This group was established in 1978 by common assent of the elected leaders of the provincial legislatures of Carinthia and Styria (in Austria), the Socialist Republic of Slovenia, and the Italian region of Friuli-Venezia-Giulia. The TCR is the axis around which the Alpe-Adria is formed. It is both the historical zone of language contact at the heart of the Alpe-Adria and integrates it as an important hub of communication. The Alpe-Adria idea immediately attracted the attention of adjacent regional polities that perceive themselves as peripheral within their own nation-states. As a result, the Alpe-Adria movement was joined by Bavaria in the north, Istria in the south, the South Tyrol in the west, and western parts of Hungary (Gyor) in the east. Various cultural and commercial activities conceived with reference to the region have since occurred. Moreover, before the incorporation of Austria into the European Union and the association of Hungary and Slovenia, the protagonists of Slovene self-determination gave

21. Regardless of this public optimism it is worth noting that almost every day the Slovene national press discusses some harassment of or violence against Slovenes or Slovene institutions in Carinthia or Friuli-Venezia-Giulia.

high priority to the Alpe-Adria idea as a means of integrating the entire ethnic territory of the Slovenes (see Moritsch 1996a and Klemenčič 1994).

The reality of the TCR was given a further boost in the 1980s when the mayors of the Austrian, Slovenian, and Italian towns of Arnoldstein, Kranjska gora, and Tarvisio jointly proposed the TCR as the host for the 2002 Olympic Winter Games. Support for this initiative then increased. In June 1996 the heads of the provincial governments of Friuli-Venezia-Giulia, Carinthia, and the prime minister of Slovenia initiated a renewed joint application for the 2006 Olympic Winter Games, which was rejected three years later when the IOC selected Turin as the venue for this event. In recent years initiatives such as the foregoing have successfully elicited financial support from EU programs created to promote regional integration and self-determination within the European Union. This, of course, is an explicit strategy for diminishing the prominence of the nation-state in the movement for European unification.

In thinking of these initiatives in relation to Darinka's life, I find it ironic that these tentative steps toward regional integration are facilitated by increased direct contact between local voluntary organizations. These wellsprings of local democratic tradition include choral societies, school boards, sport clubs, alpine tourist associations, and volunteer fire brigades. During the waning decades of Hapsburg society many of the same organizations were instrumental in inculcating ethnic-nationalist sentiments. Today, however, they are transcending ethnic parochialism by cooperating to promote the common commercial and cultural interests of the "borderland region." Thus, on February 10, 1996, an intraregional meeting of mayors was held in Bovec to promote coordination of tourism within the TCR. A common expression heard at that meeting further attested to budding regional integration: "The TCR represents one culture where many languages are spoken."[22]

Furthermore, an annual calendar of "borderland" events has been established whereby TCR residents are invited to join in activities such as hikes, cross-country ski tours, picnics, and pilgrimages to local shrines. All these take place along or across state borders. These meetings build on frequent and spontaneous cross-border encounters of kith and kin who were dispersed in wartime. A growing number of interstate marriages is a likely consequence of this revived contact across borders.

Finally, there has also been a marked revival of public interest in TCR history, especially that concerned with the region's suffering in World War I. Currently, a multilingual reader in the region's history is being written for use in public schools throughout the TCR. And in 1993 the Kobarid Museum organized an exhibition about the region in World War I as a convincing demonstration of the

22. Unfortunately, since many local politicians do not speak their neighbors' languages, this currently fashionable declaration of regional unity is weakened. Some attendees also criticized this informal gathering because professional trilingual translation was not provided!

futility of war. On the strength of this, it was declared Europe's museum of the year. Thus images of destruction and human suffering have been transformed into a metaphor of European unity. The former site of armed confrontation has become a contemporary setting of international cooperation.

More than half a century has passed since ethnic cleansing ravaged the TCR, and in the interim the nation-state has clearly lost its once preeminent position in local politics. But the persistence of collective memories of resistance, exile, and injustice linger. The longevity of ethnically contested borders is contingent not only upon the persistent memory of injustice perpetrated in the name of the ethnic nation but also on the extension of political autonomy to local communities within the framework of an ethnically neutral administration. And importantly, this relative autonomy is conceived in terms of the Western tradition of democratic representation in public affairs. The linden tree must ultimately become a place of public assembly regardless of the "roots" of those gathered there. And as Darinka's life testifies, the human capacity to construct a positive self-understanding under adverse conditions and in the face of injustice makes such public assembly possible. And a sense of moral obligation to participate in the public life of one's perceived community drives it forward. In many ways Darinka's life is a prototype of citizenship in Western European society.

When I last visited the Linden tree in the Bovec town square surrounding benches were occupied by English visitors reflecting over their day's walk along the Soča front. The two elderly brothers (mentioned earlier) and their friends were discussing the Slovene government's policy of compensation for the severe damage to their houses during the great earthquake on Easter Day 1998.

Ethnonationalism and the Dissolution of Yugoslavia

Edit Petrović

> Communism has not abolished the nation-state . . . it may have even strengthened it.
> —Karl Deutch, 1969

For a nationalist, the survival of a nation can become a matter of life and death. The question is why, and under what circumstances, did ethnic or national survival become the crucial matter in the Balkans? Why did the participants come to believe that they had only two options: to win the war and survive, or to lose the war and to be destroyed as an ethnic or national entity? The contemporary Balkan nationalist apparently believes that only a separate nation-state can guarantee national survival. Before the latest wars, Yugoslavia was home to some eighteen diverse ethnic groups, including six constitutive nations. At the end of the conflict, only a few of these groups had achieved statehood. No matter how hard they tried to create nationally homogenized state territories, the fact is that large enclaves of national groups still remain outside the state boundaries. If

Parts of this paper were presented at the colloquium: Ethnonationalism and Identity Politics, Vancouver 1996.

achieving a separate state was the main goal in entering this war, many groups were left shortchanged. They had became dispersed and stateless ethnics.[1]

From 1945 to 1991 Yugoslavia was a multiethnic state, built on a federal principle and held together by the power and political monopoly of one party. The Yugoslav communist elite treated historically complex ethnic disputes in the same way they were treated elsewhere in former communist states: they declared the problem solved. Just as official state atheism presumed that by declaring God dead, God would disappear from the social discourse as if by magic, the communist elite presumed that the same thing would happen to the concept of the nation, which they considered politically spent. Their focus was on the class struggle and the role of the international and domestic proletariat in achieving economic and political power.

Observed more generally, there was an inherent ambiguity in the manner in which communist leaderships treated nationality. While openly rejecting the nation as an organizational principle in society, communist leaders such as Mao Zedong were nevertheless ready to use national rhetoric to mobilize mass support and channel group emotions in order to prepare their people for global social actions (Connor 1992). In Yugoslavia under communist rule, sentiments were manipulated through the inauguration of a pan-Yugoslav national identity.[2] The leadership saw this action as immobilizing all other potentially disruptive national identities: Croat, Slovenian, Serbian, Macedonian, Muslim, and Montenegrin, those formally recognized nations within the federated Yugoslav state. Walker Connor, for example, finds it surprising that despite the philosophical incompatibility between communism and nationalism, Marxist-Leninist leaders turned to nationalistic appeals to gain the support of the masses, especially in times of crisis when the state felt threatened by external enemies. However, if we examine more closely the totalitarian affinities of communism and some forms of nationalism (Deutch 1969), such as German National-Socialism (Stein 1987), the use of nationalist appeals by Marxist-Leninist leaders becomes less surprising. I argue in this chapter that ethnonationalism, which generated the recent Yugoslav conflict, was a dormant concept throughout the period of communist rule (1941–91). It was activated when communism as an ideological and political system was spent and a quest for political changes pressured the existing political elite to find a new way to mobilize mass support.

For almost fifty years, the second Yugoslavia existed as a country of paradoxes and ambiguities. Focusing on the ambiguities, we can try to grasp the genesis of the conflict. The national question in former Yugoslavia was said to

1. There are still diverse ethnic enclaves left in the territories of new, postwar states. In the case of Serbs, Croats, and Muslims, territorial ethnic consolidation within a nation-state is far from being fully accomplished.

2. The genesis of the pan-Yugoslav identity has to be understood in the historical context of Herderian ideas and nineteenth-century pan-Slavism. In the Balkans, ideas of South Slav linguistic and cultural unity were formulated in the Illyrian movement.

have been solved by the imposition of a federal structure that attempted to consolidate its constitutive units by creating a pan-Yugoslav identity embodied in the slogan "brotherhood and unity." The creation of a Yugoslav identity was politically motivated, but in fact, many people declared such identity in the 1960s and 1970s population censuses. However, the government did not recognize the existence of a *Yugoslav* nationality. Paradoxically again, even though the word "nation" was formally out of ideological favor as an inclusive category, the political leadership was so concerned with the so-called processes of ethnogenesis that in the second Yugoslavia (1945–91) three new "nations" were created (Macedonian, Montenegrin and Muslim). This was possibly as an attempt to balance the powers of the three "old" nations (Serbs, Croats, and Slovenes) that constituted the so-called first Yugoslavia (1918–41). The surge of Yugoslav identification was evident in several subsequent surveys (1971–85), indicating the possible basis for ethnic and territorial cohesion at the time when ethnic tensions were increasing (Cohen 1993: 49). However, this trend was not strong enough to prevent ethnic fragmentation of the country.

On an organizational level, federalism was combined with the encouragement of the republican political leaderships to define and defend their own regional interests (Denitch 1990). Although the Communist Party enjoyed a monopoly in ideology and politics, especially after 1970, it did not continue to enjoy a full monopoly of power (White et al. 1987). Through the 1980s, as the state became more and more decentralized, the republics were encouraged to strengthen their national orientation within the federal framework. This also meant that assimilative and integrative processes embodied in the idiom of pan-Yugoslav unification were contrasted with the processes of ethnic/national particularism and distinctiveness. In other words, homogenization achieved on the ideological and normative levels through federalism was contrasted with the ethno-cultural heterogeneity of the country's six republics and two autonomous regions. Each republic, except Bosnia, was considered the home territory of one of the six Yugoslav constitutive nations. This political initiative strengthening national orientation within the republics produced an impact on territorial ethnic structure. The trend of ethnic territorial concentration within republican borders becomes evident when we examine the census data of internal migrations for the period 1971–81 (R. Petrović 1987).

Although the country was officially atheistic, self-identification by religious affiliation remained strong. Complex historical constellations produced a phenomenon of equivalence between religious and ethnic identification in the Balkans. For example, Croat meant Catholic in everyday life, just as Serb meant Eastern Orthodox. These identifications became important during communist rule. After years of enforced socialist internationalism, open ethnic and religious identification increased in importance from the 1970s, leading to the full recognition of religious freedoms at the end of the communist era. As the relationship between state and the church intensified, religious institutions became active partners in political life and a crucial source of populist nationalism. Bogdan Denitch suggests that by eliminating genuine alternatives in political life, the Party may have left traditional national and religious affiliation as the most salient and the most passionately held identification in communist Yugoslavia (1990: 78).

Deeply felt ethnocentrism, often manifested as ethnic or religious hatred and xenophobia, is often explained as a potentially explosive phenomenon inherent in the Balkans. In one of his novels, Ivo Andrić describes the context of ethnic hatred in Sarajevo at the beginning of the century in the following way: "Adherents of the three main faiths hate one another from birth to death, senselessly and profoundly. Often they spent their entire lives without finding an opportunity to express that hatred in all its facets and horror" (Andrić 1961: 77).

Eruption of violent and "savage" conflict in the former Yugoslavia is often linked to the articulation of perceived distinctions. It is explained as the "natural" outcome of cultural and religious differences, and profound hatred among its people. After an elaborate analysis of the complex causes of Yugoslav ethnic antagonism, Sergei Flere concludes that there is a pattern of historical repetition because basically identical processes of ethnic antagonism between the same ethnic groups recur endlessly (1991: 192). However, if hatred were inherent and constant, one would expect that ethnically "clean" territories would have been formed long ago. If coexistence were impossible and all interethnic ties were broken long ago, why did different nationalities continue to live together in potentially hostile territories? The historical record clearly shows us that the Balkans have known both periods of peaceful coexistence and times of violent conflict.

Contrary to those who explain Yugoslav ethnic nationalism as "the thing out there," something inherent to the region, its ethnic history, and ethnopsychology, I argue that ethnonationalism as an ideology and strategy has been created and recreated and instrumentalized by intellectual and political elites. It has been combined with less fully articulated forms of populist nationalism that have always existed in some form among certain segments of the population. However malignant the past, the fact remains that *somehow* the Balkan peoples also found ways to coexist in peace. Statistics of interethnic marriages, for example, show that until 1981 some six million people had become kin-related through intermarriage, indicating possible levels of social integration (Petrović 1988: 88). In her recent book about the life in a Bosnian village with mixed Muslim and Croat populations, Tone Bringa argues that there has been both coexistence and conflict, tolerance and prejudices, suspicion and friendship. When she visited the village in January 1993, during the war, she was told by Croats and Muslims alike: "We always lived together and got along well. What is happening now has been created by something stronger than us" (1995: 4). Interethnic relations deteriorated only when the approaching war forced civilians to declare loyalties and take sides. At that point neighbors turned against neighbors.[3]

The ethnic crisis was mainly generated not by missing factors of social integration as Dušan Janjić (1993: 27) has suggested, but rather by factors of political and social disintegration. Political leaders in the constituent republics failed to reach agreements about the future transformation of the federal state and consciously created the momentum toward war. Feeding the ideas of popular sovereignty ("political legitimacy resides with the people"), a social climate was created prior to the war in which every national group, as well as some ethnic minorities, claimed the right to self-determination, sovereignty, and ultimately, secession. With so many groups involved, including the two most numerically significant national minorities with neighboring states organized by their co-ethnics (the Albanians and the Hungarians), it looked as if the "dilemma of difference" (Minow 1990) was on everyone's mind. All wanted the right to be separate. It became impossible to draw the line and set the criteria of difference. Was there going to be historical and territorial continuity, local control over vital economic resources, a territorial or demographic majority principle? From the other side, previously suppressed freedoms, including expressions of ethnic and religious identity, made nationalism a favored option as formerly suppressed ethnic categories began to reemerge with great force (Eriksen 1993: 118). The conflict in Kosovo carries a potential for further territorial fragmentation, as Albanians there have attempted to articulate their political goals in terms of secession from Serbia.[4]

When communist rule dissolved in Russia and other East European countries, Yugoslavia experienced the phenomenon of (so-called) societies in transition. Ernest Gellner (1983: 1987) describes a global social transition in the context of nationalism emerging from modernization (which follows the transition from agrarian into industrialized society), and the creation of nation-states. In the Yugoslav case, the transitional process from authoritarianism into democracy produced a kind of "ideological chaos" created out of the situation where old values and systems coexisted with the new sets of values and standards that were not yet well defined and established (Bolčić 1993). This situation favored the emergence of different kinds of extremism, including ultra-nationalism. Erik Eriksen (1993) argues that ethnic identities tend to attain greatest importance in situations of flux and resource competition. Political movements based on ethnic or national identities therefore are strongest in transitional societies. Economic and political crises in the former Yugoslavia at the end of the 1980s generated serious doubts about the competence of the existing political elite. In 1990, a program providing

3. The effect of approaching war on neighboring relations is powerfully presented in a documentary by the same author Tone Bringa ("We Are All Neighbors," 1993, an installment in the series *Disappearing World*).

4. Unlike Bosnia, Kosovo, as a part of what was then the republic of Serbia, did not achieve political independence at the time of the dissolution of federal Yugoslavia.

the basis for new economic reforms and democratization through political plural-ism was presented by Prime Minister Ante Marković. Instead of choosing to work together for democracy, the Yugoslav peoples turned inward to their partic-ular national groups as means of protecting their interests.

The introduction of political pluralism and the democratization of the state also catalyzed divisive interethnic animosities in other former communist multi-ethnic states, such as the Soviet Union and later in Russia itself. It appears that democratization and the survival of a multiethnic state cannot be achieved simul-taneously without producing conflict. Whether or not multiethnic states can ac-commodate differences and survive under contemporary conditions is not certain. For example, even Canada as the "consociational state," struggles today to incorporate the legitimate rights of its third constitutive element, Native Cana-dians, into the existing rights of the two Charter groups (the English and the French), without undermining the sovereignty principle defined by the latter (Macklem 1993).

The Praxis of Ethnonationalism

Thus in the former Yugoslavia the ideology of ethnonationalism was fed by a mixture of historical imagining and current discontent, exacerbated by memories of the suppression of religious and ethnic expression under communist rule. Claims were made based on glorious pasts and quasi-kinship ties, linguistic and religious uniqueness, territorial integrity, and the supposed cultural and economic superiority of one group over another. With successive economic crises, each nation could believe that it alone was suffering, that it alone was surrounded by others who were prospering at its expense. If ethnonationalism could be seen as an extreme political expression of cultural identity (Levin 1993), ethnic conflict could be viewed as an extreme expression of ethnonationalism. Though ethnic conflict had not yet emerged at the time of Yugoslavia's deep social and political transition during the 1980s, nationalist rhetoric surfaced in the public discourse.

In Serbia national goals were articulated in an unpublished document pro-duced in 1986 by a group of intellectuals from the Serbian Academy of Sciences. In it they analyze the allegedly unfavorable position of the Serbian nation within Yugoslavia. This document examines the political, economic, and cultural conse-quences of communist rule on the Serbian nation (Cohen 1993). It articulates many implicit feelings of political oppression, and abuse that "Serbs" felt they were subjected to in Tito's Yugoslavia. This document, also known as the "Mem-orandum,"[5] had already deeply influenced public life in Serbia when a year latter, Slobodan Milošević became president of the Serbian Communist League and

5. After the text circulated for some time, it was published in *Naše Teme* (Belgrade, 1989).

gradually started to incorporate many of these ideas into his radical political departure from the Titoist legacy.

A union between some intellectuals and the political elite in Serbia was achieved on the level of a joint nationalistic ideology. It was from this union that the populist movement emerged in 1989–91. This mass movement was promoted in several large political rallies. The most extensive was the celebration of six-hundredth anniversary of the Battle of Kosovo.[6] This battle is considered sacred in Serbian national ideology. It was in that battle on the Field of Blackbirds, six centuries ago, that Serbianhood (*Srpstvo*) was defended against an enemy that wished to eliminate it. It was there in 1989 that Milošević gave a speech that ignited the current phase of Serbian nationalist feelings and set the stage for the political actions that were to follow.

Those who wish to build a nationalistic ideology must focus on the political use of cultural symbols. As Eriksen has pointed out, the use of presumably typical ethnic symbols tends to stimulate reflection of one's own cultural distinctiveness and to generate feelings of nationhood (1993: 100). The main goal of nationalist discourse is therefore to construct *bounded cultural objects* or an illusion that a nation is built up of coherent and solid cultural "material" that as a bounded unit "travels" unaffected through time (Anderson 1983). Thus specific kinds of ethnonational bonds were produced by different groups in the former Yugoslavia which combined several interrelated domains.

Ethnic History and Continuity

Those who wish to evoke the idea of a nation as a bounded group that persists through time must manipulate core *ethical* values such as endurance, rebellion, honesty, and sacrifice as expressions of national identity. This strategy entails the creation of the illusion that the Serbs who fought against the Turks in Kosovo in 1389 are somehow the same as the Serbs fighting for Serbian national survival today. On November 19, 1988, President Milošević made the following declaration at the Brotherhood and Unity rally in Belgrade:[7] "None should be surprised that Serbia raised its head because of Kosovo this summer. Kosovo is the pure center of its history, culture and memory. Every nation has its one love that warms its heart. For Serbia it is Kosovo" (*Naša Borba*, June 14, 1996). A year

6. Kosovo, a part of the republic of Serbia, was the center of the Serbian medieval state. Indeed, many monuments sacred to the Serbs are preserved there today. The battle of Kosovo in 1389 marked the beginning of the Turkish (Ottoman) rule in Serbia. Today Kosovo is mainly inhabited by ethnic Albanians (who constitute more than 90 percent of the province's population).

7. This rally was organized to provide support for the Serbian government in their political and military actions aimed at reestablishing Serbian sovereignty over the territories in Kosovo inhabited by ethnic Albanians. It is somewhat ironic that the slogan "Brotherhood and unity" was borrowed from earlier political discourse referring to a unified Yugoslavia under communist rule.

later, in June 28 1989, at a celebration of the six-hundredth anniversary of the Battle of Kosovo and the first official postwar celebration of the feast of Vidovdan (St. Vitus), he invoked this theme again to generate and articulate national sentiments. He said that by historical coincidence, in 1989 Serbia had regained its state and its dignity and was therefore celebrating a historical event from the remote past that was to have a huge historical and symbolic impact on its future (Naumović 1993: 108). By combining history, memory, and continuity, he set the stage for the subsequent political actions that ultimately led to interethnic conflict.

Ethnic Territories: Nationalism as Patriotism

Taking ethnic boundaries as synonymous with state territory fuses patriotism and nationalism into a powerful emotional catalyst. Political slogans such as "Serbia is everywhere where Serbs live" or " All Serbs in one state," create the illusion of a close relationship between "blood and the earth" or "ancestral land" and the land inhabited by descendants. To defend the nation then comes to mean defending national boundaries that were, or should become state boundaries. This fusion of patriotism, defined as loyalty to the state, and nationhood, defined as loyalty to one's own nation, produced a powerful effect on the process of national imagining.

Nationhood as Metaphoric Kinship

Probably the most important aspect of nationalistic ideology is that based on feelings of belonging to a well-defined and bounded group of people, linked together by ancestral ties and shared descent, "blood." The notions of "common blood," "national family or brotherhood," and "shared loyalties" were introduced into the discourse. Statements such as "Brother Serbs (Croats, Muslims . . .) need our help" functioned to create emotional bonds, to subordinate the individual to a group identity, and to paralyze other political actions that could potentially affect the "image of the nation." The links between national heroes past and present was emphasized. For example, Bosnian Serb leader Radovan Karadžić was shown in a 1992 BBC documentary entitled "The Serbian Epic," playing the single-stringed fiddle (*gusle*) in the house in which Vuk Karadžić, the most famous Serbian nineteenth-century poet was born. This TV segment had a multiple message. First, when a current national leader speaks to the nation from a house in which a prominent (national) ancestor was born, it should symbolize continuity with the past.

There is also the underlying symbolism of having the same last name (Karadžić). In addition, Radovan Karadžić was shown pointing out the facial similarity between himself and the late Vuk Karadžić, whose portrait was exhibited in his home (Čolović 1993). The coincidence of a shared name suggested that the mythical bond to the glorious ancestor was sealed by the bond of "common blood." These examples illuminate what Connor calls the nonrational core of the nation, triggered through the creative use of national symbols. Their power rests on the fact that however precisely we try to explain the metaphoric levels on which symbols endure, they create a bridge to the side of our minds not amenable to rational explanation (1994: 204).

Nation and the Global Village

In 1983 Gellner argued that the nature of the media engenders ideas of nationalism. Media play an important role in creating and maintaining national images, since through them messages to the nation are sent and manipulated. Benedict Anderson is credited for pointing out that a nation is imagined as a community even though there isn't any actual relationship established between its members. As messages are sent through the media producing the global-village effect, the imagined national community is shaped by receiving important lessons from the leadership about the national cause and the responsibilities each member has to fulfill. Members of the imagined national community therefore have more resemblance to baseball fans sitting in front of their TV sets, sharing moments of happiness and sadness and feeling as if they were united by some invisible bond. The following example from Serbia manifests the quasi-kinship quality of the nation created by media "morality." In an extract from an interview, a Serbian writer and declared nationalist comments on some statements given earlier to the French press by a Serbian historian living in exile: "I agree with his criticism, the only problem is that he is criticizing now when he is no longer living in Serbia, *which is wrong. That is an act of cowardice: you should say what you mean at home not go abroad and then throw garbage into your nation's face*" (*Svet*, January 13, 1995, my emphasis).

As I argued elsewhere, it is as if unconditional belonging to the family is synonymous to belonging to the nation; therefore, it is not appropriate to expose internal wrongdoing in front of a stranger (E. Petrović 1995). The ultimate message could be read as: this person is *exposed to the public eyes* as a nonloyal representative of our national family—he doesn't belong with us any more! Expulsion or threats of expulsion were powerful mechanisms by which the traditional societies regulated the behavior of their members. Group conformism and harmony were achieved by the expulsion of "heretics." Media-morality produces the same effect. Many prominent individuals from the former Yugoslavia who dared to speak their minds about national issues were forced to leave the country because of the hate-campaigns orchestrated by the media. Among many others, a life-story of the Yugoslav actress forced to emigrate in 1992 after being stigmatized by the media, was presented in Slavenka Drakulić's book (1994). While heretical views were silenced, consolidated national(istic) strategies emerged.

Ethno-Marketing

The previous section illuminates another important dimension of nationalistic discourse, a dimension we might call ethno-marketing. It refers to the responsibility that individuals have in creating and producing public images of their own nation. In the recent Yugoslav conflict all sides were concerned to present compassionate ethnic images, promoting at the same time negative images of their enemies, so that the world would consequently acknowledge their legitimacy.[8] At home, ethno-marketing served to consolidate mass emotions and send the message that fighting for the national cause was the only right thing to be done at that particular moment. Ethno-marketing promotes the logic that the "Others" are always the evil ones, while "we" suffer and fight for just causes. One example is the way in which the daily press was used in Serbia to promote ethnic hatred and intensify national sentiments during the Bosnian war. A Belgrade daily newspaper, *Vecernje Novosti* (November 19, 1994), printed a photo showing a child mourning at a grave with the following explanation: "The true victims of the war are children. So it happens in this current war in which Serbian people proudly defend their very existence." This photo circled the world. It was taken at the graveyard in Skelani (Bosnia) where the boy, an orphan, laments over his parents' graves. They were killed by the Muslims. In the meantime, it was reported that the boy was adopted by a family from nearby Zvornik and was attending his first year of military school (quotation and photograph reprinted in the magazine *Vreme*, November 28, 1994). This photo was in fact a reproduction of a famous painting by the nineteenth-century artist Uroš Predić. The message sent by this subtle fraud is that "they are killing our people and turning our children into orphans. It is time that we stand up and do something about it."

Nationalism and Religious Symbolism

Nationalism often draws on religion for its symbolic expression. Links between glorious heroes and martyrs of the past and the leaders of the present are often exploited so that the latter benefit from the aura of the former. In Serbia, current nationalism is linked to Orthodox Christianity and the mythology of the past.

---

8. The whole analysis could be based on statements given over time by different foreign ministers from the former Yugoslavia. Whenever a large-scale massacre was committed, ethnic representatives would promptly react trying to convince "the world" that their side was "more civilized" or "played by the international rules" and therefore couldn't possibly have committed such an atrocity.

Thus the Saint Sava cult expressed in national mythology as *svetosavlje,* refers to the particular worldview, ethics, and morality inspired by the life of medieval Serbian duke, Rastko Nemanjić, who was later acknowledged as a saint by the Orthodox Church. In May 1989, a big celebration was held in Belgrade as the arch was installed on the new Saint Sava church, the largest Orthodox Christian monument in the world, which was begun in 1935. The occasion was organized by the political leadership and used to promote the symbolic unity between the state and the church. This ritual symbolizing the unity between the church, the people, and the political leadership under Milošević marked the end of the church's political exile and the beginning of its formal inauguration as one of the main representatives and protectors of the nation (Naumović 1994: 106–7). The symbolism of the Battle of Kosovo with its core religious elements has often also been used as the model of how Serbs should behave in the face of current national tragedy. It is epitomized in King Lazar's decision on the battlefield of Kosovo to choose the heavenly kingdom (death and immortality) instead of the earthly kingdom (life and oblivion). The continuity of these ideas can be seen in a number of statements, such as "Serbs as a mature nation know that the road to the stars leads through thorns. To be born again one has to die first" (interview with the Orthodox priest Amfilohije Radović, *Oslobodjenje,* January 12, 1995). Anotole said, "We pray to the Lord, so that the sun of justice will finally shine on the suffering Serbian nation, and bring a rightful peace, which Serbs as *heavenly* people deserve" (a toast by Radovan Karadžić, *Oslobodjenje,* January 12, 1995, my emphasis). The powerful effect of the Kosovo epic and others in the revival of Serbian ethnic identity, and in the process of national imagining, is key to understanding the conflicts in which the Serbs have been engaged.

National Identity and Language Politics

In articulating national identity politics, three former warring sides are turning to their "cultural baggage." The passion of creating separate identities has flourished especially in the idea of a national language. What has in the past been called Serbo-Croatian is now in the process of becoming the Bosnian, Croatian, and Serbian languages. In this respect, Bosnian Muslims are currently introducing Arabic words and expressions from the Koran into their language. For example, they have replaced the Serbo-Croatian word *junak* (martyr) with the Arabic *shahid.* In Croatia, President Tudjman is inventing uniquely Croatian tennis terminology (*Globe and Mail,* May 16, 1996). In Serbia, a council has been appointed to codify the Serbian language after the division of Yugoslavia, while a new so-called Belgrade-Niksić orthography is in the process of being formally accepted (*Naša Borba,* June 14, 1996). In January 1995, Bosnian Serbs voted to officially recognize both alphabets: Latin, already in use by Bosnian Croats and Muslims, and Cyrillic, the official alphabet in Serbia proper. Along with previously spoken *iekavica* dialect shared before the war by all three Bosnian ethnic groups, *ekavica* dialect, spoken in Serbia proper is also recognized (*Oslobodjenje*, January 12, 1995). Both the Cyrillic alphabet and the *ekavica* dialect are recognized and introduced as symbols of Serbian identity. These examples demonstrate that language is viewed as one of the core elements of ethnic identification. The enforced language transformations that are taking place convey a clear message to the nation: "We are different from them in every respect: we have a unique ethnic territory, religion, and customs, and we also have a unique language that differentiates us."

Conclusion

When we explore ethnonationalistic patterns, we must recognize that the mass appeal of nationalism also produces an oppositional process. While some people are profoundly moved by the language of nationalism to strong emotions and readiness to sacrifice, others remain immune to nationalistic ideas and even challenge them. In the former Yugoslavia mass movements supporting ideas and actions of national governments had a counterpart in pacifist and civic movements. Their main characteristics were an antiwar orientation, concentration in urban centers, and support by more educated segments of the society (Prošić-Dvornić 1994). An illustration is the three-month protest by Belgrade students that took place in 1992. It represented a strong reaction against national and military politics of the Serbian government. Student protests emerged several times in the period 1991–98 (Prošić-Dvornić 1993), the longest from 1996 to 1997. In 1992 student messages ranged from the politically less explicit, such as the badges they wore with the inscription: "It is spring time, and I still live in Serbia," to the more explicit "Sloba—Saddam," alluding to the similarities between the authoritarian rules of Slobodan Milošević and Saddam Hussein.[9] Opposition in the domain of the arts was expressed, for example, by a painting that depicted President Milošević as a personification of the famous medieval fresco "White Angel." Only this white angel has black wings, is holding two pigeons, one black and one white (symbolizing his contradictory political efforts for war and peace), and is sitting on top of a pile of human skulls (reprinted in *Vreme*, November 6, 1995).

Ethnonationalism did not enter into the social discourse as a well-developed and explicit ideology. It was more implicit than explicit, more a fluctuating concept than a fixed one. However, it has had a profound effect on the construction

9. The Iraqi embassy in Belgrade officially protested, which made the symbolic parallel even more significant, since even Saddam Hussein refused to be linked with the "Balkan butcher."

and reconstruction of national identity in former Yugoslavia. It has been and still is the fuel for regional interethnic conflicts. It remains to be seen just how changed, in their own eyes, and the eyes of the outsiders, the "nations" emerge after such conflicts. After the bloodshed, it might well be, that the whole basis for future national imagining will be profoundly changed.

Fig. 1 A fur-hatted Serb and an Albanian Muslim in white skullcap, from Kosovo, sit side by side at the Maglaj (Bosnia) cattle market (1964). Markets were meeting places not only for people from this area but for merchants from all of Yugoslavia. During the Tito era, the slogan "brotherhood and unity" suggested that the various nationalities in Serbia were all truly neighbors. (Photo by Joel M. Halpern)

Fig. 2 A Muslim rope seller and Croat customer at the Maglaj market. At this time, the town had a large paper factory and local craftsmen still prospered. Most of their customers were other peasants from surrounding villages. National differences were no barrier to trade. (Photo by Joel M. Halpern)

Fig. 3 Boy with flute at the Maglaj market, a look toward the future with no overt markers of national identity. (Photo by Joel M. Halpern)

Fig. 4 The large Orthodox Church of the Holy Trinity was constructed in Mostar in 1876, high above the old town on a site said to have been selected by the Ottoman sultan Abdul Hamid himself, with an iconostasis or altar screen given by the Russian Tsar. Early photographs of the city, such as this one illustrating a nineteenth-century travel account, show the prominence of the church on the heights above the city. It was completely reduced to ruins by high explosives in June 1992 by Bosnian Croat extremists, as was the Ottoman bridge (foreground). (Photo courtesy of Documentation Center, Aga Khan Program for Islamic Architecture, Harvard University)

Fig. 5 Serb Orthodox Bishop Vladisav with monk and nuns at the fifteenth-century monastery of the Annunciation at Žitomislići in 1961. This Serbian village was located on the east bank of the Neretva River between Mostar and Capljina. The village and monastery were destroyed by Croat forces and the Serbs were driven out. (Photo by Andrei Simić)

Fig. 6 Serb grandmother and grandchildren in Žitomislići, 1961. (Photo by Andrei Simić)

Fig. 7 One of the characteristics of the preindustrial Bosnian city was the dominance of religious architecture. The Ferhad Pasha Sokolovic mosque was constructed in 1579. Monumental mosques provided the backdrop for the daily, weekly, and monthly gatherings of villagers and their urban customers. Banja Luka marketplace in 1954 provided a setting for different groups to trade and a place where they could interact peacefully. This mosque was blown up on May 6, 1993, by Bosnian Serb army sappers. The destruction of this mosque and the killing and expelling by the Bosnian Serbs of the local Muslim and Croat population has permanently altered this city. (Photo by Joel M. Halpern)

Fig. 8 A mosque courtyard provides a convenient place for Muslim elders to gather on a sunny spring afternoon in Banja Luka in 1954. The white band on the cap of the man at the right signifies his completion of the pilgrimage to Mecca. His cane is a further mark of status. A worker's cap defines another member of the group. (Photo by Joel M. Halpern)

Fig. 9 The Aladja Mosque in Foča, an eastern Bosnian town close to the Serbian border, was built in 1550. After the mosque was blown up by Bosnian Serbs in 1992, the site was completely cleared of ruins, which were trucked away to a secret location for disposal. The photo of the open field where this important monument and its circular ablution fountain (*shadirvan*) once stood was taken by Harvard student Lucas Kello in 1996. (Photo courtesy of Documentation Center, Aga Khan Program for Islamic Architecture, Harvard University)

Fig. 10 Catholic bishop celebrating the Feast of the Assumption in Vareš, 1964. It is reported that the local Bosnian authorities now in control at Vareš, a one-time steel industry town north of Sarajevo, are not permitting the return of Catholics to the area. (Photo by Joel M. Halpern)

Fig. 11 The Roman Catholic Church in Sašina in northern Bosnia was destroyed by Bosnian Serb forces in June 1993. This photo was obtained from the Roman Catholic diocese of Banja Luka. (Photo courtesy of Documentation Center, Aga Khan Program for Islamic Architecture, Harvard University)

Fig. 12 A relatively undamaged apartment building next to destroyed office structures. In the foreground, with shelling and sniping over, a man checks his car. Sarajevo, 1996. (Photo by Joel M. Halpern)

Fig. 13 The *Stari Most* or Old Bridge of Mostar was built in the year 1556 by the order of the Ottoman sultan Süleyman the Magnificent. It succumbed to repeated shelling by Croat gunners in November of 1993. A makeshift suspension bridge now spans the river in its place. Irena Božin-Mirković took this photograph of the temporary bridge in December of 1996. The bridge is now being reconstructed.

Fig. 14 Members of the Morina family building their house in the early 1990s. Their village is located on the main road between Pristina and Djakovica. (Photo by Mark Morina)

Fig. 15 The completed home. (Photo by Mark Morina)

Fig. 16 House destroyed by shelling of Serbian forces in summer 1998. This family found refuge in Austria and as of late 1999 had not yet returned to Kosovo. (Photo by Mark Morina)

Fig. 17 An Albanian and a Serbian woman jointly taking water from a village well in 1997. The village is in the county of Vitia (Albanian), Vitina (Serbian), now located in the U.S. zone in eastern Kosovo. At the time of the photo, these women who had formerly been friendly neighbors had not spoken to each other for seven years. (Photo by Janet Reineck)

PART III

INTERPRETING SOCIAL AND POLITICAL PROCESSES

Barbarization in a Bosnian Pilgrimage Center

Mart Bax

> We do not fully understand . . . the conditions under which a civilizing process
> moves . . . into "reverse gear."
> —Dunning 1988: 243

> Civilized conduct takes a long time to construct but can be destroyed rather
> quickly.
> —Mennell 1989: 248

> If in a society dominant trends can be observed tending in a certain direction,
> we are always well advised to look for countervailing trends as well.
> —Goudsblom 1989a: 84

In early morning on May 27, 1992, Ljerka Šivrić saw something horrible in the
neighboring yard of her father's brother, Djure. Three human bodies, their feet

I want to thank Joel Halpern and David Kideckel for the invitation to contribute to the present
volume. This article is based on documents and field work. Every year from 1983 to 1994, I spent
some time in the research area. Even in 1992, when Bosnia and Herzegovina was formally at war, I
was able to go there. At the end of 1992 I spent some time in Germany with two groups of refugees
from Medjugorje, segments of clans that had been arch-enemies before they fled. The data for the

tied to a pipe and their hands behind their backs, were suspended upside down, immersed to the shoulders in a partially demolished cistern. Djure and his two grown sons, Ante and Djure, had been savagely slain. Two weeks earlier, on May 10, a similar drama had unfolded in Siro Ostojić's yard. Siro's elderly parents were found hanging from a mulberry tree in front of their house, their throats slit and their hands chopped off. These are only two in the long list of atrocities that have dominated life in Medjugorje since autumn 1991. Medjugorje, situated in southwestern Bosnia and Herzegovina, had been a Marian pilgrimage center of international repute since 1981. However, without warning, the villagers there found themselves caught in a vicious spiral of violence. At first they were in danger of losing only their property, but soon it was their lives as well. In early July 1992, when the Croatian army imposed peace on western Herzegovina, local violence came to an end. But Medjugorje's *mali rat* (little war), as the villagers called it, had taken its toll.[1] Of the 3,000 or so villagers, an estimated 140 had been killed, 60 were missing, and approximately 600 had fled. Many of Medjugorje's buildings were also totally or partially destroyed.[2]

Whence this barbarization? How is it possible that after a ten-year reign of the Virgin Mary, referred to locally as the Queen of Peace, villagers began to slaughter each other? Norbert Elias in his magnum opus, *The Civilizing Process*, notes that questions of this kind may be more confusing than helpful. To better understand barbarization, he feels we ought to concentrate on the civilizing process instead (Elias 1989: 226–27).[3] He suggests that because of a wide range of factors, state formation being a major one, in the past thousand years more and

---

following account, in which fictitious names are used, have mainly been gathered in the course of extensive talks with these groups, each of which is aware of the other's whereabouts. I would like to thank my informants in Bosnia and Herzegovina and elsewhere in Europe for their help, protection, and hospitality. For their comments and suggestions, I would also like to express my gratitude to Han Belt, Karin Bijker, Ger Duijzings, Caroline Hanken, Daan Meijers, Leonard Oreć, Erika Revesz, Jan Sjaarda, Fred Spier, Sjef Vissers, F. G. Bailey, Johan Goudsblom, and M. Estellie Smith. Of course I alone am responsible for the contents of the article.

1. *Mali rat* (small war) is the regional term for small, often local violent operations of the kind traditionally endemic to the area. These include complicated blood revenge, where whole families were occasionally killed or driven away. It also included surprise attacks or pillaging raids on neighboring villages by roaming gangs of armed men or other small, informal violent groups. According to informants, *mali rat* can be a side effect of organized warfare, though not equivalent to it. The Second World War and the recent hostilities in Croatia between sections of the former federal army gave rise to numerous eruptions of local violence in Bosnia and Herzegovina. When the "large" war broke out between the "real" armies at Sarajevo and elsewhere in April 1992, it reactivated these local feuds. The small-scale local wars are closely interwoven with the larger ones. *Mali rat* is related to a stage of state formation that is characteristic of this part of former Yugoslavia, where the state has not yet fully established a monopoly on the means of organized violence.

2. I can only provide rough estimates. Registration records in Ćitluk were destroyed, which seems part of a war strategy to void the territorial claims of certain segments of the population. The parish of Medjugorje has its own records, but they were destroyed as well.

3. Jonathan Haas develops a similar premise in his book *The Anthropology of War* (1990).

more people in Western Europe have become ever more dependent on each other in even more respects. As a result, they were forced to take each other into consideration and keep their own emotions, such as rage or tendencies toward violence, under control. These external or social constraints are, furthermore, expressed in all kinds of prohibitions pertaining to the use of violence and aggression.[4] For a better understanding of barbarization Elias's maxim seems a useful point of departure. From this perspective, the *conditions* for barbarization processes can be clarified. But it is also a limited point of departure, for it does not give us the instruments we need to elucidate the structure and dynamics of these processes. Elias seems to focus on the civilizing process and to view barbarization as little more than a temporary deviation from what is "normal." Here he resembles the structural functionalists he repeatedly reproaches for their one-sided preoccupation with structure while overlooking "change." This article explores barbarization as a relatively autonomous process that, in an academic sense, is of the same ilk as the civilizing process and should be studied in conjunction with it. More specifically, it gives a systematic description of a local episode in the war in the heart of former Yugoslavia that has often been termed "bizarre" and "pointless."

Civilization: A Crippled Process

"Here the knife does not go blunt and the (rifle) barrel does not rust," or so a seventy-eight-year-old local informant of mine concluded his description of the history of the region. The recent violence did not surprise him, for it was part of an old tradition of warfare and revenge.

To a certain extent, this long tradition of violence has to do with geopolitical circumstances. Until recently, large parts of former Yugoslavia were border regions disputed by powerful kingdoms and other political power blocs.[5] For almost five hundred years, from the fifteen century to far into the nineteenth, the whole area was a pawn in the power game between the Austrians and Hungarians to the northwest and the Ottomans to the southeast. Then it was torn between the Italians and Germans on the Axis side and the Russians and the Allies on the other. And after World War II, up until the end of the cold war, the capitalist West and the communist East drove a deep wedge into Yugoslav society (Alexander 1979 and Jelavich 1990). These powers not only severely impeded the development of a stable state with an effective central control over the means of physical violence, they also created the conditions for the growth of nationalism and ethnic

4. A very stimulating introduction and discussion of Elias's work is found in Mennell 1989.

5. As to the relation between the shifting spheres of influence on the peripheries of polities and the occurrence of self-help and local formations of violence, see Boehm 1985. Cf. also Seers et al. 1979.

antagonism (Banac 1984; Cole 1981; A. Djilas 1985; 1991; Ramet 1985; Simić 1991; Talcum 1994).

In what was formerly the republic of Bosnia and Herzegovina in the central part of former Yugoslavia, these developments can be traced with the greatest clarity. More than four hundred years of warfare between the Ottoman and the Hapsburg empires made the region an ethnic hodgepodge. Large groups of Serbs from the southeast fled to the Bosnian countryside, settling mainly in the less fertile parts (Krajina). Population pressure and a sense of adventure led Croats, mainly from the bleak Dalmatian Mountains, to move southeastward. Large numbers of people eager to take advantage of any opportunity to "get ahead" converted to Islam, thus laying the foundation for the third ethnic group, the Muslims (Koljević 1980; A. Djilas 1991).[6] During this same period, and in part as a reaction to the frequently harsh Ottoman regime, a tradition of small-scale violent resistance developed in Herzegovina: guerrilla bands of hajduks, ustashas, and chetniks.[7] Clusters of these resistance groups made it difficult to pacify the area permanently, and their rivalry promoted acts of revenge and retaliation within and among the various villages (Jelavich 1990; Koljević 1980; Dedijer 1974; Soldo 1964; Vego 1981). Owing to their strategic position vis-à-vis the population, only Roman Catholic clergymen could curb the violence even temporarily (Bax 1995).

The fall of the Ottoman and Hapsburg empires in 1912 and 1918 did not put an end to these forms of small-scale violence or stop people from taking the law into their own hands. On the contrary, ever since the Kingdom of Serbs, Croats, and Slovenes (renamed the Kingdom of Yugoslavia in 1929) was founded in 1918, these forms of violence constituted an integral component—overtly or covertly—of the interaction between the most important groups, the Serbs and the Croats (Banac 1984; Ramet 1985).

The prevalent opinion is that Serb and Croat national consciousness goes back to the Middle Ages. At the time, each of the groups was a separate kingdom, parts of which are now disputed territory (Simić 1991). Foreign rule put an end to their political independence, but their religious beliefs (the Serbian Orthodox Church for the Serbians and Catholicism for the Croats) have always remained important to their identities (Ramet 1984; Rathfelder 1992; Rusinow 1982).

When the Serbs and Croats united to form one independent kingdom, these old distinctions were transformed into ethnic differences that soon escalated to dominate virtually the entire political arena. Each of the parties was convinced that the other was after hegemonic control. Certainly at the beginning, the Croats had the most grounds for apprehension. The king was a Serb, the Serbs were by far the largest single ethnic group, and Serbs held almost all the important posi-

6. The Muslims do not play a role in the story to be told here.

7. Aleksa Djilas (1991) noted that these terms refer to small paramilitary groups that were first observed in the early days of Turkish rule.

tions in the government, the bureaucracy, the army, and the police force, and whenever they could, they gave their fellow Serbs preferential treatment (A. Djilas 1991; Soldo n.d.). This intensified nationalist feelings, and particularly in the ethnically mixed areas, with Bosnia and Herzegovina at the top of the list, tension ran high. The Serb domination there was characterized by brutal injustice to the Croats, whose political leaders and their local representatives were removed from office and imprisoned. The Croats in turn organized armed gangs called *ustaši,* who kidnaped Serb leaders and were not unlikely to murder them as well. Neither of the parties had much patience with traitors (Banac 1984; Jelić-Butić 1983; A. Djilas 1991; Čopić 1963; Krizman 1980, 1983; Starčević 1941). Soon this ethnically mixed area, with borders sometimes running through the middle of villages, turned into a "complex of snake pits joint together by murder, manslaughter, destruction and betrayal" (Soldo 1964).

When the tension spread to other regions and the country became ungovernable, the king disbanded the parliament and instigated a veritable reign of terror. Every trace of opposition was harshly suppressed by gangs of Chetnik national police, consisting of Serbs who roamed through the Croat areas, robbing and plundering along the way. Their horrendous conduct, which I described elsewhere (Bax 1993), provoked similar behavior on the part of the Croats, particularly the Croats of southern and western Herzegovina. In this inhospitable region with its coarse and truculent inhabitants, the ustasha groups burgeoned.[8] In tiny guerrilla units, they terrorized the Serb communities (Krizman 1980; Jelić-Butić 1986; Tomasevich 1975).

The Second World War deepened the chasm of hatred and magnified the violence to almost unprecedented proportions. With the backing of the Axis powers, the Independent State of Croatia was founded, and Bosnia and Herzegovina was part of it. With the help of the extremely vicious and pugnacious Ustaša organization, the new state made every effort to cleanse Croatia and Bosnia and Herzegovina of all the Serb elements. The Serbs in these regions sought the help and support of the Chetniks, who had gone underground *en masse* after the German demobilization of the Yugoslav army. Bosnia and Herzegovina turned into one huge battlefield, where guerrillas attacked not only each other but also each other's towns and the civilians residing there, enormous numbers of whom they assaulted, mutilated, and murdered in the most atrocious ways (Čopić 1963; *Hercegovina* 1986; Jelić 1978; A. Djilas 1991; M. Djilas 1980).

During this period, the Ustasha stronghold Medjugorje lost almost half its population. The village also suffered huge material damage, for almost all the cattle were slaughtered or stolen and many of the homes were destroyed, as were the crops in the fields (Bax 1991).

A third, perhaps even crueler party soon joined the war, the Partisans led by

8. "Mars must be more hospitable than western Hercegovina and it is hard to imagine anybody wanting to conquer it" (Glenny 1992: 155).

Tito. With his dreaded and later renowned guerrilla troops, this communist leader was soon victorious, thanks in part to his incorporation of the Chetniks, who were being defeated at the time. In 1943, aided by the Allies and the Russians, he founded a new Yugoslav state on Bosnian territory (Parin 1991; M. Djilas 1980, 1983).

Tito established a modern political system and put a formal end to the ethnic violence and personal feuds. The goal of his new order, whose motto was "Brotherhood and Unity," was the total economic and social modernization of Yugoslavia along socialist lines. For years, an extremely effective system of repression enabled the authorities to present this fiction to the outside world as reality. Although there was a decline in open hostilities, behind the communist front the old enmities and antagonisms lived on undiminished.

Southwestern Herzegovina, the regional focus of this essay, may have been cleansed of its numerous ustashas, but their relatives were still treated as second-class citizens. They were barred from the ruling Communist Party and thus could not obtain state benefits and civil service jobs. In all the public sectors, the Serbs in the region were in control. As former partisans or their offspring, they dominated the Party, the public administration, the police, the army, the bureaucracy, and the numerous modern government enterprises (Vego 1981; A. Djilas 1991). Since the methods the Serbs in the region were using to achieve their aims were legal, the Croats had little choice but to resort to the old forms of self-help. In formal, legal, and political discourse, there were no Croats, there were only "criminals," "subversive elements," and "reactionary forces." In the hidden discourse of the dominated Croats, however, the opponents were referred to as *Srbi* or *Četnići*. Thus formal rules covertly contributed to the systematic exclusion of the Croat opponent—an ethnic cleansing avant la lettre (M. Djilas 1977, 1983).[9] The veneer of the "new order" gradually began to wear thin. Driven by circumstances, in the early 1970s groups of armed young men who called themselves *ustaši* began to gather in Bosnia and Herzegovina. Their targets were government institutions, the region's numerous arms depots, Party officials, and villages dominated by Serbs (Hofwiler 1992; Gelhard 1992; Soldo n.d.).[10]

9. It was not until the late 1980s, after the decline of communism in Yugoslavia, that hesitant steps were made toward a certain extent of openness about the reign of the Partisans and the communists. It is only with the greatest reluctance that Aleksa Djilas (1991) cited the names of a few writers. Nowadays there are no longer any traces of candor among the authors in former Yugoslavia.

10. Until recently, Bosnia and Herzegovina was known as the republic with the greatest firearms density and the largest military arsenal of all of Yugoslavia. In addition to numerous arms and munitions plants, there were factories for tanks, various armored vehicles, cannons, military aircraft and missiles, and there was hardly a village or town without its own arms and munitions depot (Wiener 1986). There were various reasons for this high concentration of ordnance. After the Second World War, the Tito administration decided to transfer the military industries along the borders of Yugoslavia to safer sites further inland. With its dense forests and relatively inaccessible mountain valleys, the republic of Bosnia and Herzegovina was viewed as the appropriate spot for the federal

In Medjugorje as well, an ustasha cell assembled that, according to my informants, was incorporated in the late 1970s into a regional network consisting of several thousand men. In essence this "organized crime that has spread from the capitalist West," as the regional authorities referred to it, was a reaction to the fact that the Croats had no rights. The response was not long in coming. Particularly in the smaller towns and villages, where the presence of the official authorities was not so keenly felt, vigilantes gathered, which their opponents referred to as Četnići. Groups of ustashas seemed to be playing a cat-and-mouse game with these Chetniks, who were sometimes assisted by the official authorities (Soldo n.d.).

Once again a wave of violence began to gather in the region, but this time there was a countervailing trend of a totally different kind. Its locus was Medjugorje, a humble peasant village in a part of Herzegovina so bleak that only snakes, stones, and ustashas could thrive there, or so the saying goes.[11] In 1981, that tiny village became the center of a Marian devotional movement focused on peace that rapidly assumed international proportions (Bax 1989, 1990, 1995).

The civilizing influence this pilgrimage center exerted for almost a decade can be briefly summarized as follows.[12] The mass influx of more than seventeen million pilgrims from all over the world imposed peace-oriented standards of conduct upon the people of the village and the entire vicinity. During this period there was a spectacular decline throughout the region in the number of registered crimes, feuds, and other forms of violence.[13] The inhabitants of Medjugorje, the entire region, and indeed the regional authorities benefited from the economic boom resulting from the religious tourism.[14]

---

state's military arsenal. The fact that the area was rich in coal and mineral deposits promoted the further expansion of the military industry. In response to the Russian intervention in Czechoslovakia in 1968, Tito decided in 1969 to organize people's militias, making it feasible to mobilize the entire population in wartime. The Teritorialna Odbrana or T.O. (Territorial Defense) was set up, which not only served to support the regular army, but could also operate completely independently. For this purpose, in almost all the towns and villages arms and munitions depots were built, which were under the supervision of local militia and where all the adults, women as well as men, played a role. Each local community could thus function as a relatively autonomous paramilitary unit. Although designed to create a unified Yugoslav military powerhouse, the system contained the seeds for a highly complex internal "total war" like the one that engulfed Bosnia and part of Croatia. More information about the Territorial Defense and its problematic relation to the regular federal army can be found in Mladenović 1970, Ramet 1985, Hofwiler 1992, Wiener 1986, Remington 1979, Ross Johnson 1973, and Rusinow 1971.

11. Snakes feature in many of the sayings and proverbs of the region, symbolizing unreliability and unpredictability. Relations in Herzegovina were often described to me by way of the saying "Ne vjeruj zmiji ni kad bi imala sobje strane rep" (Never trust a snake, not even if it has two tails).

12. I described these changes at great length from various angles in other publications (cf. Bax 1989, 1990, 1991, 1993, 1995).

13. See Bax 1991.

14. In 1990 Zagreb Turist reported that 19 percent of the total turnover in the country's tourist sector was from the devotional center in Medjugorje.

Barbarization: The Logic of a Development

Almost all the villagers renovated their homes to be better able to accommodate more pilgrims, enlarging their capital and taking out new loans all the while. Times were good for all of them, although of course they were better for some than for others.

The Ostojići fared by far the best, everyone agreed about that. It had once been a poor clan with very little land, most of which was barren because of its location at the foot of the Mountain of the Cross. This was why so many of the Ostojići had regularly lived and worked abroad, mainly in Germany, the United States, and Canada. According to the local population, this had made them a bit *stran* (different, strange).

The more signs Medjugorje showed of turning into a flourishing pilgrimage center, the more Ostojići returned to their native village. With the capital they earned, they soon rose to occupy a dominant position in the religious tourist industry. They built the only two "real" hotels in the village, and in a neighboring hamlet a large bungalow complex for pilgrims, complete with a small chapel. Most of the taxi licenses were registered in their name, and at the foot of the Mountain of the Cross, the holiest shrine of all and frequented by virtually all the pilgrims, they set up a number of restaurants, outdoor cafés, and souvenir shops. They had a monopoly on almost all the bread and alcohol supplied to the village and ran the most important local branches of national travel agencies. Their influence was not limited to the immediate vicinity. At the most important arrival sites, the airports at Mostar, Split, Dubrovnik, and Zagreb, Ostojići agents picked up the pilgrims in Ostojići coaches and brought them to accommodations owned by . . . the Ostojići clan. None of these facilities would have been feasible without an extensive network of connections in the bureaucracies of the district and republic governments.

Of course this super-entrepreneurism gave rise to jealousy. The Jerkovići and Šivrići, the oldest and most respected clans, felt particularly humiliated by those "stone eaters," as they called the Ostojići, whose land was indeed strewn with stones. They themselves had the best land, and there they grew grapes and tobacco. From Vienna to Istanbul, their produce had been renowned for centuries. They looked down on the Ostojići because they were so dependent on *biro čet-nići*, as they called the Serb government officials. A good Croat—and the population of Medjugorje, including the nearby hamlets, consisted of Croats—was independent and took care of business without needing any help. That was the rule they lived by, though they did on occasion have to pay a bribe or two themselves (cf. Bax 1993).

As long as everyone was able to profit from the expanding pilgrimage economy, the outbursts of jealousy remained small. But when the impending violence of war gradually cut off this lifeline, matters clearly changed. It started in the latter part of the summer of 1990. Serbian and Montenegrin terrorists had made the southern coastal regions of Croatia unsafe and difficult to reach, which meant a sharp fall in the number of pilgrims. Croatia's declaration of independence in December of that year only served to intensify this trend. And by early spring of 1991, when Croatia and the federal troops were engaged in open warfare, most of the boarding houses in Medjugorje were standing empty much of the time. Thanks to bribes and good connections, the ones owned by the Ostojići were, however, still partly occupied. Virtually all the villagers had gone deeply into debt, and when they were hit by hard times, they could no longer tolerate the "inequality" of this situation. Leaders of other clans began to negotiate with the Ostojići about dividing "what little there was." The negotiations, it is said, did not proceed smoothly. On the contrary, a lot of old resentment surfaced, and in the end the Ostojići refused to share their position in the tourist industry with anyone. The story goes that the parties did not part in friendship; in fact Medjugorje's little war was already looming.

On August 15, 1991, the Feast of the Assumption of the Holy Virgin, two groups faced each other at the access road to the Mountain of the Cross. A few dozen armed and masked men kept a good three hundred pilgrims, guests of the Ostojići, from carrying out their plan to climb the Mountain of the Cross in prayer. The pilgrims were ordered to leave, which they did after several warning shots were fired in the air. Later that day, accompanied by several Ostojići and a local clergyman, they made a second effort. Again it was in vain. Following the advice of the priest, the pilgrims abandoned their efforts. But this was not the end of it for the Ostojići. They felt they had been humiliated and their rights had been violated, for the mountain was free territory open to everyone. Behind the masks, they had recognized the faces of a number of villagers, whom they then reported to the police at the district capital of Čitluk. In a police raid a few days later, several men were taken from their beds, all of them members of the Jerković clan.

The Jerkovići were quick to express their great indignation and their contempt. In Croat communities in this part of Herzegovina, it was considered cowardly to solve a conflict by summoning the police. Up to the war, the police department was an alien power apparatus, and what is more it was staffed by Serbs, the sworn enemies of the Croats (Soldo n.d.). By calling in the police, the Ostojići had proved to be friends of the enemy, "little Serbs" as one informant put it.

A few days later, two policemen were attacked and beaten in their homes in Čitluk.[15] And in the following week, in one night all thirty-two of the Ostojići's taxis were wrecked. The Čitluk police, summoned once again, did not arrive in time to catch the perpetrators; approximately forty men of the Jerković and Šivrić clans had disappeared from the village.

By now the war in Croatia had expanded drastically, and its repercussions were being felt in Bosnia and Herzegovina more and more. Serbia supplied arms

---

15. *Mostarski list*, August 28, 1992.

to the Serb communities so they could defend themselves against "the fascist aggression of the *Ustaša*," as it was called (Glenny 1992). In response, the Croat inhabitants of Bosnia and Herzegovina felt threatened, and large numbers of them broke into the numerous local munitions and arms depots of the Territorial Defense, which was soon dismantled as a result. In no time, all of Bosnia and Herzegovina had turned into one vast constellation of heavily armed settlements (Rathfelder 1992). Side by side with these local vigilantes, small mobile armed units of Serbs and Croats, roamed the countryside independently or in larger groups, causing trouble wherever they went and burglarizing the army's numerous munitions depots. These units, often referred to as *režervisti*, consisted of deserters from the Croatian front, men evading mobilization, members of secret paramilitary organizations of either Croats (*ustaši*) or Serbs (*četnići*), villagers who lost their jobs in the now defunct tourist industry and were on the lookout for loot, and lastly, as in Medjugorje, people running away from the police (Hofwiler 1992). In addition, the various sections of the former Yugoslav army, now divided along ethnic lines, also belonged to this extremely dynamic and complex configuration of attack and defense units, sometimes collaborating with each other and sometimes fiercely battling. "Armies" of Serbs, Croats or Muslims, who barely differed in any way from the *režervisti* described above, operated in the various regions of Bosnia and Herzegovina. Each group tried to gain control over its own patch of the ethnic quilt.

In Medjugorje, the Ostojići feared the rapid disintegration of official authority. These people, whose conduct, ideas, and conceptions were so deviant in the region, were regularly identified with the Serb archenemy, and were in danger of becoming the victims of a "cleansing" (*raščistiti teren*). In this predominantly Croat area, it was not easy to defend oneself against this kind of campaign with the help of one's "own" *režervisti*; self-defense and the help of the police were what was needed.

In the course of September 1991, the Šivrići claimed to have observed some changes in the Ostojići hamlet at the foot of the Mountain of the Cross. Every day a small police patrol from Ćitluk would come by. The police officers would inspect the streets and fields of the hamlet and then withdraw to the dining room of one of the boarding houses. The men of the Ostojići clan were rarely observed outdoors, and it seemed as if the community solely consisted of women and children. But in the darkness of the homes and late at night on the edge of the Mountain of the Cross, behind bushes and trees, attentive observers regularly noticed men with guns. Judging from their numbers, they were not just Ostojići men, and further probing revealed that some of them were men no one in the district had ever seen before. It was later concluded from the license plates on their cars that they were Ostojići in-laws from a non-Croat town on the other side of the Neretva River.

The wary Šivrići observed these developments with suspicion. It was becoming clearer and clearer that the Ostojići maintained ties with the chetniks and thus belonged to the enemy camp. Tension rose to a peak when one of their boys, said to have been working on a chimney, was shot twice from the direction of the Ostojići. It gave him such a scare that he lost his balance, fell off the roof, and broke his arm.

The next night explosions were heard from the direction of the churchyard, and on the following morning the Čitluk police found all the Ostojići graves blown up. The meaning of this act was immediately apparent to everyone: a denial of the rights of the Ostojići in the community and the destruction of their historical roots. In the past year, this age-old custom had been regularly revived on a large scale by Serbs and Croats in the neighboring extremely militant Krajina region, and it always marked the start of a "cleansing" (Reissmüller 1992, Rathfelder 1992).

After this act of open aggression, things quieted down. But it was a menacing kind of silence, and the Jerkovići and Šivrići were waiting with bated breath to see how their opponent would respond.

Together with men who had left and were now returning, equipped with ample arms, munitions, and explosives from the depot in Čapljina, the Šivrići and Jerkovići prepared to "settle matters once and for all" with the enemy. They made good use of know-how acquired in the army and the Territorial Defense. In Čapljina, some of them had joined the notorious Croatian HOS militia.[16] Stepan Jerković, a former army officer, became their leader and the troops were called Stepanovći (Stepan's men). Stepan, usually called Stjipe, was backed by six subgroup leaders (*časnići*), each of whom had a number of soldiers (*vojnići*) under their command.

The first thing they did was barricade the access road at the mountain pass to the plateau where Medjugorje is situated. Day and night, they would hide there and guard the road. This made it impossible for the enemy to receive sizable reinforcements. Limited help could only arrive via the mountain paths, but regular patrols were on duty there, too.

Medjugorje began to resemble a stronghold, not only outwardly but inwardly as well. All the windows in the homes of both the clans were blacked out, and wherever possible the lanes were hidden from sight by lines hung with tobacco leaves, branches or straw mats. Under this cover, they could reach each other's property and gather in groups inside the walled courtyards without being detected by Ostojići.

The Ostojići were taken completely unaware by the swift transformation of their enemies' homes into fortresses. And when they too wanted to make a safe place for themselves, they found themselves in the line of fire, though none of

16. The HOS (*Hrvatske Obrambene Snage*) is the paramilitary wing of the extremely militant and violence-oriented nationalist Party of the Right (*Hrvatska Stranka Prava*) formerly led by Dobroslav Paraga. In its aims and methods, this party is similar to the Ustasha movement in the days of World War II. In the past, the men of the Šivrići and Jerkovići clans had been members of a gang that covered the entire Brotnjo area and regularly attacked the (Serbian) government.

the shots hit the mark. Some of the women and children fled to the Mountain of the Cross, where they were guarded by clansmen hidden from sight. It was only at night, protected by darkness, that they sometimes ventured to return home for their clothes and something to eat or drink. But the enemy was on guard and responded to their every move with gunfire.

In November 1991, the Stepanovći launched their offensive. Their aim was to destroy the cisterns at the homes of the Ostojići. In only a few nights, they managed to blow up 30 of the almost 170 cisterns, or at any rate render them useless. Thirty families and their livestock had to fetch water elsewhere. From their hiding places, almost every day the Stepanovći managed to shoot a few head of cattle on the paths.

Fear was growing in the Ostojići camp, for it was evident that their superior opponent had begun a "cleansing." One night early in December, there was a skirmish between several of the guards and a Ostojići. After a fracas, the men managed to break away. It was clear to the Stepanovći that they had gone to fetch reinforcements, and they intensified their guarding patrols.

To this very day, Stepan's men still do not know how their opponent managed to bring in forty men (the size of two paramilitary units) without their noticing anything. They were soon confronted with these reinforcements—relatives of the Ostojići from a village to the south that had been "cleansed" by Serb militiamen. It was a ferocious confrontation. Firing their rifles as a diversionary measure, the Ostojići succeeded in destroying twelve of the Šivrići's cisterns. This made a large segment of the Šivrić clan vulnerable and dependent upon others.

By Christmas 1991, Medjugorje's little war took a virtually inevitable turn. On the name day of his deceased wife, Mate Jerković, one of the Jerković clan elders, went to her grave to honor her with dried flowers and wild fruit.[17] Mate had trouble walking, which was why he went by mule. As he was passing the ravaged graves of the Ostojići, a bullet hit him in the thigh. The bullet was aimed at the mule and not at a person, or so the Ostojići later informed me when I spoke to them in their hiding place. But the flow of human blood had awakened the spirit of revenge.

Blood revenge as a form of self-help is an old and still fairly widespread institution in this corner of former Yugoslavia (Bax 1995; A. Djilas 1991; Vego 1981). In addition to the state, it was mainly the clergy who—by way of reconciliation rituals—made every effort to attenuate this way of eliminating one's opponents. In the course of 1991, however, state power crumbled and the clergymen of Medjugorje were "summoned back" to their monasteries in Humac and Mostar. This left the parties to their own devices, abandoned to the dynamics of the devastating process they formed with each other. Once it had been set in motion, the process tended to escalate, driven as it was by the principle of retribution.

17. More information on this custom can be found in Bax 1991.

Shortly after the start of the new year, this was demonstrated for all to see. Mate's eldest son, the avenger, had shot one of the Ostojići clan elders in the thigh. But when Mate fell ill and died of his wound, his own clan's elders all agreed the retribution had to be taken one step further; then Jure Ostojić, a brother of the clan elder shot in the thigh, was shot in the lower back and paralyzed for life. His clan refused to accept this and took double revenge: two young Šivrić men were shot in the back and died on the day of the Feast of the Epiphany (January 6). Obviously this bloodshed put the parties on guard, for since then neither of the clans, at any rate their male members, have dared to show their faces much on the streets in the daytime.

Together with a good two hundred other men, most of whom were from the Jerković and Šivrić clans, the Stepanovći kept the area closed off. This put the Ostojići and their relatives from outside the area, more than a hundred men in all, in a perilous position. Their ammunition and food were running out, but if they made a mass break for it, it would probably mean a massacre of their own people. Waiting longer, however, would only force them to surrender in the end and leave Medjugorje forever.

For a couple of weeks, nothing special happened; everyone seemed to be waiting for an explosion of violence. It came from an unexpected quarter. Late one afternoon at the end of January 1991, a few military airplanes from the base in Mostar flew low over Medjugorje. It later turned out that they were looking for a group of Montenegrin soldiers who had deserted in East Slavonia and were now headed home, plundering as they went (*Mostarski list,* January 25, 1992). Above Medjugorje, the planes (with Serb pilots) began to shoot at the church steeples. They missed, but they did hit a few of the homes of the Šivrići. The incident distracted the attention of the dominant clans, and the Ostojići were quick to take advantage. Together with some women and children, a group of men managed to reach the pass. Once they got there, however, they ran into the guards. Fierce fighting broke out, and the unprotected Ostojići were clearly at a disadvantage. Quite a few men, women, and children were killed, others managed to escape. Some guards also perished in the fighting. In the next few days, each of the parties saw to its dead.

Things were quiet again in Medjugorje, so quiet that a group of unsuspecting pilgrims moved about freely for several days in the Marian Peace Centre.[18] At

---

18. Inquiries among the refugees from Medjugorje in Germany revealed that the clan sections were not in agreement. One section claimed the relative tranquillity was promoted by the arrival of a group of pilgrims. The other party maintained that a group of pilgrims took advantage of the relative tranquillity in Medjugorje at the time. Further investigation made it clear that up to the end of February, a group of pilgrims from Canada led by two of their own priests was in Medjugorje for more than ten days. When I questioned him over the telephone, one of the priests informed me that they had not noticed any traces of warfare in Medjugorje. They found it quite understandable that there were no priests in the village, and that uniformed men had blocked their way to the Mountain of the Cross "because of hostilities." This information reveals something of the difference in perception between the villagers and the pilgrims.

regular intervals they saw groups of people, mainly women and children, leave the village with their luggage. When the pilgrims asked them what they were doing, they said they were fleeing "the war." The pilgrims did not see the armed men entering the village in the dead of night and spreading out over the houses. They were the relatives of the battling clans who had come to the village from "liberated" areas, men who were no longer needed at home because their villages had been cleansed, and who had sworn to avenge all their dead kin.[19]

The exodus continued until the end of March. Growing numbers of women and children left, and Medjugorje increasingly became a stronghold of armed men.[20] A small incident sparked off enormous repercussions. At a courtyard of the Ostojići, a few intoxicated men were showing off their skills as marksmen by shooting tins and bottles off a wall with their little Scorpio rifles. One of them recklessly tried it with a grenade launcher. The grenade exploded and blew a big hole in the wall of Ante Šivrić's stable a bit further down the street. The shot was immediately answered in kind, and mortar shells soon set two homes ablaze, killing the elderly tenants.

Hardly a day went by without each side doing some damage to the other's property, especially their livestock, supply sheds, and cisterns. But it was the sharply rising number of avengers inside the gates of Medjugorje that gave "the war" another turn: personal retribution in the dead of night or at dawn with a knife and a rope. An estimated eighty people, almost sixty of whom were locals, lost their lives this way, their mutilated bodies, usually hanging from a tree or ceiling beam, bearing witness to the atrocious acts.[21]

The complicated process of retribution went on until the end of May, when the denouement came just as suddenly as the start. It was linked to military developments in Bosnia and Herzegovina at large. Flanked by irregular militia, a unit of the Croatian army was on its way from Čapljina Listica. There a Serb military unit that wanted to force a passageway through to the west was being obstructed by armed groups of *ustaši* from the region. The Croatian troops stopped near Medjugorje for the night. When patrols found out about what was going on there, a HOS unit from Čapljina decided to go off and rescue their "Croat friends." It was a short surprise attack that resulted, as informants later related, in a complete "cleansing" of the Ostojići hamlet. About a hundred peo-

19. They were mainly men from Croatian villages that had been "purged" of Serbs. There were also a few relatives from East Slavonia, the children or grandchildren of former Ustasha members who had emigrated from the region. The vengeful mentality of these emigrants in their battle against Serbs in East Slavonia—who also come from Herzegovina—has been disconcertingly described by Glenny (1992).

20. It was mainly during this period that the exodus to Germany took place (see the note at the foot of the first page of this chapter).

21. The mutilations followed a fixed pattern, with more and more parts of the bodies being removed. The symbolic dynamics would undoubtedly be an informative field for further research.

ple, mostly men, were captured and taken off to a ravine in the vicinity, or so the story goes, where they were shot and killed.[22]

At the end of June 1992, I was able to see for myself that Medjugorje was once again accessible to pilgrims. From the coast up to approximately thirty kilometers past the pilgrimage center, the area had been "purged" of the "Serb aggressor." The area had "the protection of the Croatian army and its allies," as pamphlets at the Customs Office announced. The hustle and bustle had returned to the devotion center. Several hundred pilgrims from Italy, Canada ,and the United States were being catered to by villagers, who apologized for the inconvenience and the disarray "the war" had caused. The pilgrims were very understanding, and they were glad that "these people could live in freedom again" and that "the Message of Peace had triumphed." Once again houses were being built and repaired throughout the vicinity, but it did not seem out of the ordinary, since construction work had been a familiar sight for years. Singing resounded from the Mountain of the Cross: groups of pilgrims were praying the stations. Work was also being done on the private homes in the Ostojići hamlet—by Jerkovići and Šivrići and their relatives who had come to join them. At the cemetery of Medjugorje, concealed behind bushes and trees, part of the ground was left fallow. Only a year earlier, this had been consecrated earth, the last resting place of a clan that was part of this district. Now not a single trace of their existence was left. But somewhere out there, the people of Medjugorje knew, a hatred smoldered that would one day be sparked into flame again.

Discussion

A discontinuous state monopoly on organized violence, a limited pacification of state territory, and a long tradition of feuding and other forms of self-help might indeed have been the major preconditions for the barbarization process in Medjugorje, but they do not explain the dynamics of the process itself. Elias felt the dynamics of what he called cycles of violence had to do with "double-bind processes . . . which trap [the constituent] groups in a position of mutual fear and distrust, each group assuming as a matter of course that its members might be harmed or even killed by another group if the latter had the opportunity and the means to do it." He went on to note that a social configuration of this kind is usually characterized by a "strong self-escalating impetus" (Elias, in Elias and Dunning 1986: 26). This definition does not seem to be all that applicable to the events in Medjugorje. Perhaps a better explanation can be sought in the principle

---

22. It is said to be the same ravine as where a similarly horrendous mass grave was dug toward the end of World War II. It is one of the many historical sites where hatred lives on for the suffering that has been afflicted (Bax 1993, 1995).

formulated by Johan Goudsblom, although in a different context, of "paired increases in control and dependency" (Goudsblom 1989b: 21ff.). It can be phrased as follows: the parties strive to dominate each other, but as a consequence they unintentionally become increasingly dependent on each other. The Šivrići and Ostojići each tried to reinforce their position and made every effort to recruit outside help to do so. As a result, the violence formation they created together expanded, and the escalation potential increased. Nonetheless, the duration of the actual escalations was short, and they were more like (external) incidents that were quickly hushed up (see also Collins 1990). The course of the process described here has something paradoxical about it: more and more of the actual acts were increasingly "barbaric" and cruel, but at the same time there was less and less "spontaneity" and a relatively greater "control" or "regulation" of the conduct toward each other. This would also seem to be in keeping with the principle of "paired increases in control and dependency" referred to above. More and more people imposed more and more pressure upon each other and upon themselves to engage in harsh forms of revenge, but the menacing effect of this also had a deterrent effect and served to inhibit a spontaneous implementation—a striking similarity to the cold war, a theme Elias (1987) wrote about at great length, though according to Benthem van den Bergh (1989) in a rather one-sided manner.

A question now arises that might in the first instance seem quite absurd: Can the process described here indeed be characterized as barbarization? Speaking colloquially, of course it can. But in terms of Elias's civilizing process, in which increasing control and regulation of behavior are important features of "civilization," it seems far more difficult to give a simple answer to this question. A certain extent of ambiguity has been noted in this theory by other authors (e.g. Dunning 1988, Mennell 1989, Goudsblom 1989b, and Spier 1993), but the proposed alterations mainly illustrate the complexity of the academic question. Civilizing and barbarizing seem to be such closely linked or interwoven aspects of processes that it is difficult to stipulate where one stops and the other starts. If we are to adequately describe and explain this interrelatedness, a theory is required that focuses on these close links.

Consequences of the War in Croatia at the Village and Urban Professional Levels

Brian C. Bennett

"We will take back the Krajina,"[1] my friends in Sutivan, a village on a Dalmatian island belonging to Croatia told me repeatedly in the summers of 1991 through 1995 when I spoke with them about the war. People gathered every evening around the quay speaking with friends about their businesses, village affairs, and the larger political situation. As we talked one evening in June 1991, one man expressed his outrage at the Knin Serbs' seizure of the highway and rail system connecting Dalmatia with the rest of Croatia and Yugoslavia the previous summer. This was a year before Croatia declared independence and the subsequent Serb-dominated Yugoslav National Army (JNA) assault on Croatia in July of 1991. By closing the transport system the Knin Serbs had also cut off Dalmatia from European tourists; an action that devastated the local economy. As my friend put it, "We gave Serbian families refuge in the Krajina (Banija) three hundred—four hundred years ago when the Ottomans advanced into Bosnia and Serbia. Now the descendants of these families declared their independence in a 'Republika Srpska Krajina.' "

1. Krajina, or "frontier," refers to that ill-defined swatch of land on the borders between Croatia and Bosnia. See Hammel and Grandits and Promitzer, Chapter 8, for a good discussion on the origins of Krajina settlement.

With such statements, Sutivan villagers interpreted a reality forced on them by events beyond their control. Such interpretations existentially echo Sartre's "No Exit." Villagers too have been led into a room filled with people (and events) with whom they must contend and from whom they cannot remove themselves. The political processes that shaped Croatian reality over the past six years have had direct personal consequences, from the terrible killing and "cleansing" in Vukovar to the collapsed economy and strained political transformations with which all must contend. Still, villagers like those in Sutivan are almost passively out of the political processes. They are victims of both the Serb drive for hegemony in zones of mixed populations and the self-serving politics of the Croatian Democratic Union (HZD) hierarchy and the Sabor (parliament) in Zagreb. They are also victims of HZD responses to the politics in Belgrade, as well as the politics in the larger context of Europe. As one villager said to me: "I am a businessman. I don't understand these politics."

The Serbian-dominated Yugoslav National Army (JNA) invaded Croatia in 1991. The villagers mobilized when the JNA established a naval blockade of the islands. Fortunately, the only damage suffered directly by the island communities, and their industries and commerce, was the Serb destruction of the Peruca Dam near Split and the consequent disruption of electrical service. The continuing war in Bosnia did bring an influx of refugees into the village, which only added to local economic difficulties. The villagers saw all these local events, then, in relation to developments in former Yugoslavia. In a larger context, however, they also felt that the European Union and the UN's often deliberate ineptness reflected a pro-Serb bias in the war in Croatia and Bosnia. Similarly, colleagues in Zagreb also spoke of the causal role of "larger forces" in European and U.S. politics in the war. Constant mention was made of then-U.S. secretary of state James Baker's May 1991 statement supporting federalism in Yugoslavia. My friends interpreted Baker's statement as pro-Serb and a go-ahead for Milošević to create a Greater Serbia under the guise of that federalism.

Such conversations in the village and in Zagreb essentially reinforce my own view that the war in the former Yugoslavia very much resulted from deliberate, often inept and sometimes pathological, nationalistic decisions by self-serving political leaders in Serbia, Croatia, and Bosnia. Furthermore, geopolitical processes related to the end of the cold war and resulting intrigues between England, France, Germany, and Russia also contributed. Such intrigues sought the extension of political influence into the Balkans once again, and indeed, Western and Russian political leadership continues to play a very involved role, whether in the UN Security Council, attempts at direct negotiations, or the implementation or nonimplementation of the "Dayton Accord." My friends in Sutivan and other villages and my professional colleagues in Zagreb are victims of these political processes; however, they have been denied any influence on them or participation in them at a meaningful level.

Thus the war and related events affect not only people's economic well-being but also their ability to understand objectively the situation that has befallen them. I, too, am at a loss for objective explanation. Even writing an essay such as this about the lives of real people on the edge of the conflict gives me ethical pause. I am interpreting their suffering from the perspective of an outsider comfortable in a home thousands of miles removed. Such vantage points have often resulted in misinterpretation, especially in journalistic reporting. Yet if there is some meaning and significance in the villager's or in my colleagues' observations and interpretations, then it is my obligation to present to the reader their attempts at objectivity. Ironically, this raises a further issue that both I and my Croatian colleagues have attempted to deal with in writing about the war; the readers' interpretation of what we write. In today's postmodern moment the very act of accusing the anthropologist of subjectivity often masks the problem that it may be the reader who is guilty of ignorance, of bias, of subjectivity. This is especially the case with the so-called Yugoslav situation.

What follows, then, is my attempt to interpret this war and its effect upon people in Croatia who are known to me personally. My discussion will range from my most recent relationship with anthropologists and ethnologists in Croatia growing from my 1994–95 Fulbright lectureship with the Institute for Anthropological Research in Zagreb, to my continuing interaction with friends in Sutivan. I shall consider how my anthropological colleagues in Zagreb attempted to maintain some sort of objectivity to the war in their research and publication and how the villagers of Sutivan have tried to deal with the consequences of war by trying to maintain their standard of living and remain tolerant of others in this political and economic disaster.

Sutivan, September 1994

That summer, like the year before, the plane flew out to the Adriatic Sea, to the island of Krk, and then down the coast to avoid the UNPROFOR "protected" areas of Croatia. The UN's failure to maintain the cease-fire in the Knin-Zadar areas of Croatia and the continuing conflict in the Bihac area of Bosnia made it too dangerous to fly the former air routes from Zagreb to Split. Once again, the Croatian government was threatening not to renew the UN mandate to maintain the cease-fire in the self-proclaimed Republika Srpska Krajina.[2]

The flight down the Adriatic coast revealed the beauty of the islands, a view from 10,000 feet unavailable to me twenty-four years before when I first drove the new tourist highway from Rijeka to Split. Then, what unfolded before my eyes was a harsh landscape and a road with hairpin turns and buses and trucks

2. This zone was also known as the Croatian Banija of the former Austrian Empire. Here the Ottoman attempt to conquer Vienna and Central Europe was held at bay with the help of Serbian troops.

pushing us to the edge of the precipice and its 700- to 1,000-foot drops to the sea below. Today, from the air, in a setting of waves sparkling in the constant sunshine that tourists had come for, the islands did not seem quite real. The present political situation also seemed unreal and distant, although when I was in the United States I had followed it on the news and stayed in contract with my colleagues here via e-mail. Now, I wanted to be on the ground once again. I wanted to talk with my friends of a quarter-century, to renew my understanding of their lives and discover how they had changed under the pressure of recent events.

That morning, as I waited for my flight in Zagreb, Croatian MIG fighters made passes down the runway in an open display of air power; maybe related to the planned visit of the pope to Zagreb scheduled for September. As the MIGs blasted by a few feet over the tarmac, a man across from me in the airport waiting room picked his teeth, oblivious to this display of Croatian state power. It contrasted so with my visit a year earlier when I had caught sight of one MIG hidden in the woods beside the runway.

Croatia was different in 1993. Now it is more confident in its identity as an independent state. Its military strength rests behind the consolidation of its earlier tentative political steps. Patience wears thin over such things as the controversy about the symbolism in the Croatian coat of arms (*sahovnica* or *grb*) in their flag's design, or in naming its new currency, the *kuna*, as it was previously in the Croatian state in World War II. Serbs see these as indicating the current Croatian government's relationship to the former Ustasha government's wartime human rights abuses against the Serbs. However, Croatians identify the *grb* and *kuna* with the medieval Croatian nation, not with the Ustasha state. Colleagues in Zagreb are very sensitive and defensive about any suggestion of an association of the current state with the events of World War II. Belgrade forgets the Pavelić regime was imposed on the Croats by the Italian and German occupying forces in 1941. Belgrade also forgets there were crimes committed on both sides and that many today are a generation or two removed from those events. Furthermore, many Croats have intermarried with Serbs and many urban Croats find their identity in their professional careers and not in their ethnicity.

From the air, I could see one abandoned vineyard or olive grove after another. The islands seemed dry, some almost desert-like. We flew over the coast of Brac, then turned toward its interior. We flew over Sutivan, then Supetar and Postira before turning to land at the new airport near Vidova gora, the highest peak on the coastal Adriatic islands.

How different this experience was from that of twenty-four years earlier when I drove down the coast to the unfolding adventure of my initial fieldwork in the former Yugoslavia and my attempt to understand Marxist political economy as lived at the local community level. Still there was one constant through the centuries, regardless of the overlying political system. That was the harsh dryness and endless stone terraces; the walls and piles of stones that peasants had built while clearing the fragile soil for a few hectares of vineyards and olive groves, in many cases just a few square meters of arable land. Much of this land had been abandoned early in the twentieth century when viticulture collapsed spurring extensive emigration abroad. Only recently had a new generation developed a living from tourism. Ironically today, because of the war, people have returned to a dependency on those vineyards, with their fragile soils and uncertain summer rains. Like them, I too was returning, though now to a village that a young man described to me over the phone: "Sutivan looks like it did a hundred years ago."

As the plane banked over Brac, I could see some changes. Limestone walls had been leveled to build the asphalt runway for the airport. In sharp contrast, the bus ride down from the airport is on the original unpaved donkey paths of past centuries. According to friends, money is unavailable to improve the road because of the war. In fact, it is remarkable that the airport was even built, though maybe military considerations in these strategic islands had a part in that.

Later, in February 1995, the CIA used the Brac airport to send drone planes over Bosnia to map the terrain and identify military targets for the NATO air strikes that followed in August and September. I find the CIA's presence on Brac ironic. In 1970–71, when I was first in the field, the people of Sutivan constantly accused me of working for the CIA. In 1970, the JNA officer in charge of soldiers in the village working on a water pipeline tried to get me drunk one day so he could find out "who paid me." One state official did come into the village to ask questions about me and while he was there several rolls of my undeveloped film mysteriously disappeared. Today, we can laugh about those accusations that I was CIA or an advance agent for President Nixon's 1970 visit to Yugoslavia or, at the very least, an industrial spy trying to learn the secrets of Brac Plastika.

Still, I can understand why the villagers found my presence confusing. The cold war was a time that lent itself to paranoia. Though I was a 1960s American ideological idealist, politically to the left, I was asking political and economic questions that made many in the village uncomfortable. Issues of subjectivity have thus been with me throughout all my time in Sutivan. However, today people are more accepting of me than they were through the 1970s. They clearly want others to understand the events of the war and life in the new Croatian state from their perspective. Perhaps they see me as a vehicle for this. But, maybe more important, my return confirms I hadn't forgotten them.

The war was still disrupting tourism in 1994. Though Istria and the northern Adriatic islands had had a good season and the Croatian government claimed a 1.5 billion kuna balance of payments surplus, tourism had not recovered in central Dalmatia. Travel down the coastal highway remained precarious and the rail lines remained blocked in Knin. The Brac communities of Supetar and Bol did have a few organized tour groups in their hotels and the July and August flights to Brac brought ten thousand people for holidays. Still, on my flight the plane was only half full and most of these passengers went to Bol. Only three of us went to Sutivan. Throughout July 1994 there were perhaps five hundred tourists in Sutivan, mostly Croatian weekenders with summer homes. Normally, there would have been five thousand, including weekenders. Many summer homes are owned by Serbs who cannot holiday here because of the unsettled political conditions. In fact, it is questionable if they will be able to reclaim their summer homes at all, though formally the Croatian government allows this practice.

Walking through village streets in 1994 I noticed the lack of Croatian flags. How different this was from the spring of 1991 when people were apparently caught up in nationalistic fervor and the June 25 declaration of Croatian independence from Yugoslavia. Then, flags were flying everywhere, on the church and the town hall, from windows and balconies, and from the masts of the boats in the harbor. In Supetar the priest scheduled first communion to coincide with the first anniversary of Croatian statehood, to emphasize the association of the church with Croatian national identity. As the communion processional made its way along the quay, an auto with Austrian license plates, no doubt occupied by a Croatian émigré, drove by with a huge Croatian flag fluttering on a pole stuck out the window.

In 1994 there was only an occasional flag. Sundays one flew in the church yard and miniature ones occasionally hung from automobile rear view mirrors. The flag on the community pole at the harbor was worn and tattered, and some people commented that they needed to take up a collection to replace it. Perhaps the tattered flag symbolized their feelings about the political situation. However, the Croatian coat of arms, the *grb* or *sahovnica*, has replaced Tito's picture in the few buffets that are open. So much had happened since the summer of 1991: the war in Croatia as Serbia and the JNA tried to block Croatian independence; the years of UNPROFOR "peace keeping" in the Krajina and Slavonia resulting in the consolidation of Serb control of over 30 percent of Croatian territory; Croat resistance to *de facto* UN recognition of "the Serbian Republic of Krajina"; and three years of horrifying war in Bosnia. All this, along with ethnic cleansing, refugees, and a collapsed economy, had taken a terrible toll in lives. In 1994, the tourist economy in Sutivan was gone, and at times there were more refugees in the expropriated Serbian hotel complex outside the village than residents in the village. Enthusiasm for nationalism and the war was muted as people were forced to focus on their immediate financial problems.

It was another year of a "return" to agriculture and fishing to survive. Always, behind the dominant summer tourism businesses, there had remained a sustainable traditional agricultural core to the village economy. Most villagers kept vineyards and olive groves and some experimented with mandarin oranges and kiwis. Two households successful in the tourist business had also planted large numbers of mandarin orange trees in the 1970s and 1980s and maintained vineyards and olive groves. Alongside these agricultural practices were kitchen gardens, sheep and cheese production, chickens, and the like.

Many people also fished commercially for the village market and sold occasionally to commercial fisheries in Milna and Postira. In September 1994, my friend Tomo was expanding his commercial fishing with a second trawler. He showed me his new boat, purchased used in Italy, and discussed this new business enterprise. The trawler was being completely overhauled, an investment of $200,000, and would be added to their other trawler fishing the waters beyond Hvar and Vis. The catches were iced and transported to Italian markets in refrigerated trucks. These trawlers provided a business alternative to tourist restaurants that two of the investors have had to close (Bennett 1998). Over all, then, I was impressed. The people of Sutivan had demonstrated a practicality and an ability to adapt that had allowed them to survive the war and the collapse of tourism. But it was an adaptability built on a traditional economic core wisely preserved throughout the tourist economy of the 1960s–80s.

Sutivan: June 1995

Whenever I passed by the gate to "Teta Zoe's" home throughout the summers of 1993 and 1994, I wondered how the house had fared since 1970. I could still see my son Langdon standing on the terrace; I would turn in the road to see where we had swum together in the sea in front of her house. However, I never went up to take a look.

I had made some inquiries about the building itself: Did the Serbian doctor from Belgrade have it on the market? I was told in 1993 that he did and that the price was $800,000! Supposedly a Croatian businessman was interested in it at around $500,000. Frankly, I thought that $80,000 was a more realistic price. In 1994 I picked up a hint from a friend that things might not be right with it. Serbian-owned summer homes had not been vandalized, though many had been spray-painted with the Croatian coat of arms and apparently some appliances had been stolen from a few of them. In 1993 I had observed anti-Serb graffiti painted on a public pump house; graffiti that was later removed. I wasn't prepared for what my wife and I encountered at Teta Zoe's.

From the road we could see that one of the upstairs windows was open. As we walked up the path I could also see that the doorway leading to the downstairs servant's quarters, which I rented in 1970, was also open. The lower terrace was where Kristine and I had shared the hospitality of the Serb doctor and his wife in 1991. As we approached I realized that the door had been ripped from its hinges. Inside, the remodeled kitchen that the doctor and his wife had so proudly shown us was totally destroyed, the cabinets ripped from the walls, appliances gone, feces smeared on the wall, and debris covering the floor. Upstairs was even worse. Every electrical socket and switch had been dug out of the walls. Every bathroom fixture had been removed. Chairs had been smashed and mattresses slashed, their fillings littering the floor. Plaster had been knocked from the ceiling. Every pane of glass had been deliberately smashed. Kristine was in tears, and I was in shock.

When we lived there in 1970, we—Marietta (my former wife), Langdon, and I—had started out in the downstairs servants' quarters, but Teta Zoe had had us move upstairs. She gave us her bedroom and moved into a sitting room. Everything in these rooms was destroyed. Langdon's little bedroom (that was also my study) was in shambles. Closet doors had been ripped off and a hole punched in the closet ceiling as the vandals tried to get up under the roof. The window was broken. The shutters of windows through which I had looked while writing up dissertation notes and through which I had listened to the drone of cicadas and smelled the fragrance of the pines was swinging in the breeze.

In 1970 this room had been where many of my thoughts about Sutivan had started to take shape. They were benevolent thoughts; positive interpretations about a country that had received so much negative analysis in the cold war. Now the shocking vandalism came crashing up against those positive memories; the vandalism was one more expression of the chaos that had ruled this sad country for the past four years.

How was I to interpret this? Kristine and I wandered in Zoe's yard, fingering the bay leaves. I remembered the complexity and intelligence of Teta Zoe. One person in the village referred to her as "our Queen Elizabeth." She spoke nine languages fluently. One afternoon in the "salon" of her living room, I listened as she conversed with friends, first in Czech to a friend from Prague, then in German and then in Serbo-Croatian, with two others, then finally in English with me. Kristine remembered the cordiality of the elderly Serbian couple. How could I sort this out?

"Teta Zoe" is also the title of a short novel that I've only thought of writing. Maybe it will be written now. Her home has ended up vandalized, as I thought it might twenty-five years ago in my anticipated novel, though the circumstances of the destruction were unanticipated. I had imagined someone in the village might well do this, but I didn't know that a Belgrade doctor and his wife would figure in the story. And I really didn't believe that this war, which Teta Zoe had predicted in 1970, would actually occur. But she knew more than I was willing to accept with my young American optimism and naïveté.

Teta Zoe might have been a character out of Kazantzakis's *Zorba the Greek*. Not exactly Madame Hortense, but an outsider in the same deep sense. She was born in Poland, educated in England, and married in tsarist Russia. She spoke with me time and again about her fears for her home. Her stepdaughters from the marriage in Russia lived in the United States, so they couldn't inherit. She knew the village priest and nuns were interested in her property as a nursing home, and she feared the acquisitive anticipation of the village registrar. But she was determined that no priest or village communist was to have her home. The sad irony, given the war and the present political events, was that a Serb doctor acquired her home, supposedly in exchange for taking care of her at a nursing home in Belgrade before her death.

The wrath of vandalism had come down on Teta Zoe's home in a complex way; its intent is difficult to sort out. It was directed both at the memory of her as an outsider, and at the Serb who had taken over that home from the outsider. More likely, it was also directed at the events of the present. There was no anti-Serb graffiti in the home, but I knew that many people in Sutivan had not been pleased to see people from Belgrade living in it.

The full meaning of this vandalism must be understood subjectively; it must be made the focus of a narrative. The vandalism might have been partially opportunistic, since the house was abandoned and isolated in the woods beyond the village. It may have been directed only at the doctor and his wife from Belgrade. Ill-will toward Teta Zoe could have played a role; she always remained an outsider and some spoke of her derisively. Still, many others spoke well of her. My friend in the village, with whom I stay, seemed embarrassed that some person or persons had done this, so we didn't really talk about it. The vandalism may also speak about the ethnic conflict and how some people in the village have responded to it, but it is ultimately a symbol of the stark reality that has been repeated with far more tragic, indeed far deadlier, consequences elsewhere in Croatia and Bosnia.

Telling this story here in a way violates a trust because it allows the reader to do with this information as they subjectively wish. I have not told you the story of Teta Zoe's house to reify any pernicious ethnic hatred endemic to the village. Sutivan really is a relatively benign place and, as I indicated in the introduction, a place "off to one side" of the political processes redefining this country. Lest anyone decide that Sutivan has become a violent place, I can offer a corrective note from a medical doctor friend from the island who indicates that, apart from events during World War II, he was aware of only one homicide on the island in the twentieth century.

Professional Objectivity: Zagreb, 1995

My attempt to explain and interpret the consequences of the war at the local level corresponds to the dilemma faced by my colleagues in Zagreb at the Institute for Anthropological Research. To their credit, they have maintained the continuity of their research in population genetics, linguistics, and cultural anthropology throughout the war. At the same time, they have also tried to respond to the particularities of the war by researching the circumstances and needs of refugees and displaced persons in camps on the island of Hvar (Gilliland, Špoljar-Vržina, Martić-Biočina).[3] The ethnologists at the Institute of Ethnology and Folklore have

3. Sanja Martić-Biočina (1996) has also interviewed refugees from the war in camps in the Netherlands. In 1997 Sanja Špoljar-Vržina organized an international conference in Hvar, Croatia, entitled "The Study of Forced Migration—Psychological, Legal, Humanitarian and Anthropological Interventions."

also responded to the war by research focused on daily life in the war and by the publication of a self-conscious collection of essays by young Institute ethnologists titled *Fear, Death and Resistance: A Ethnography of War: Croatia 1991– 1992* (Feldman, Prica, and Senjković 1993).

This collection examines the professional dilemmas and basic questions of objectivity in research and writing that ethnologists in wartime confront in all phases of their work. In my review of the collection I stressed that the war produces ethnologists with a "new self-awareness of writing [that] comes from both the self-conscious, reflexive situation the authors experience in Croatia today and from the reflection that is currently taking place in anthropology, i.e the postmodern analysis of text" (Bennett 1995a: 257). I find their research to be a creative response to what they refer to as a Croatian ethnography of war. The essays cover a range of topics. Lada Čale Feldman's essay, "The Theatralization of Reality: Political Rituals," analyzes the symbolism of Croatian political rituals to reveal the hegemonic processes in ethnic discourse. Ines Prica's "People Displaced" enables the victims of the war in Croatia to speak for themselves about their personal experiences. Their recorded voices bring us one step closer to the objective experience of the war. The collection also considers the dilemma of objectivity faced by these ethnographers. How do ethnographers deal with the reflexive "bifocality" problem when they are immersed within the objects of their inquiry? Renata Jambrešić's essay, "Banija: An Analysis of Ethnonymic Polarization," reminds us of Michael Fisher's observation that "ethnic research is a mirror of the bifocality . . . seeing others against a background of ourselves, and ourselves against a background of others" (Jambrešić 1993: 111).

In 1995, in a collection of essays I edited in *Collegium Antropologicum*, I asked these scholars to continue their discourse on war and ethnicity. In her essay, "People Displaced," Ines Prica anticipates the critique from abroad on the basis of "global objectivity." She cautions the outside world against dismissing an ethnographer's work as "nationalistically" biased simply because he or she resides in a warring state. I concur that this would be entirely too easy and self-serving a judgment. As I noted in my introduction to the Collegium volume, our (the West's) alleged "global objectivity" played a large role in creating the Lewis Carroll world they inhabit. As I suggested there, "We must not become so immersed in the subjectivity/objectivity . . . debate that we reject these efforts to understand and explain a world where . . . modernist ideology has been turned on its head and from its pockets have fallen, for our discourse, the Postmodern fragments of ethnic identity" (Bennett 1995b: 6).

The Zagreb ethnologists writing in *Fear, Death and Resistance* organized an international conference in Zagreb, in March/April 1995, entitled "War, Exile, Everyday Life," for which I wrote some preliminary comments. There I expressed how impressed I was that this conference was bringing together people to discuss the psychosocial problems war refugees and the displaced from Croatia and Bosnia must deal with daily. In discussions concluding the conference several people spoke of the difficulty of maintaining a balanced perspective. This is particularly the case in present-day Croatia where the relationship between the citizen and the state tends to be defined in terms of ethnicity.

The conferees asked whether Croatia could resist this ultranationalist trend to define citizenship in terms of ethnicity. Such resistance was weakened by the problem of the war and a collapsed economy, which has prevented political normalization and development of a civil society. Many asked, more than once, how ethnographers can and whether they should remain objective, given the current situation in the region. Paul Stubbs and Renata Jambrešić Kirin speak to this issue in their papers as well.

Before the conference some of the foreign participants had stereotyped contemporary Croatian ethnography and ethnographers as rightist and ethnic nationalist. The conference discussions brought out the complexity of the political situation with which the Croatians are dealing. They highlighted the implications of such accusations of bias, including inaction. The important thing was that the ethnographers continued their research, collecting testimonies of exile and everyday life, and organizing the conference. They and the psychosocial workers at the conference who work with refugees from the war throughout Europe saw ethnography as a legitimate tool in research and assessment of refugee needs. Standard approaches to handling refugees, the shelter-food-clothing model, are clearly insufficient in this war.

Ethnography is thus especially critical in recognizing the psychosocial needs and contributing to rebuilding the psychological health and social relationships of the refugees in this war. The conference offered many examples of the uses of ethnography for work with refugees, such as dance and music therapy, which draws on ethnomusicology in its programs. Anne-Marie Miorner Wagner reported on the psychotherapeutic benefits of music, folk dancing, and music theater workshops with refugee children in Graz, Austria (1996: 265–71). Albinca Pesek's project placed music education students in three refugee centers to develop music therapy programs to ease psychosocial tensions between children and their mothers (1996: 257–63). Lada Čale Feldman presented an analysis and description of the use of theater as a therapeutic activity with children in the camps: "The theatrically induced possible worlds that they fictionally experienced served . . . as a chance to re-live suppressed emotions, confront them, accept them, search for positive solutions and survive, having realized that the strength to succeed in fighting one's torments lies also in one's own spiritual and creative potentials" (1996: 224).

Other scholars see things differently. For example, Ina-Maria Greverus questions the efficacy of the ethnography actually being done in the refugee community. In her opinion, the closer the personal history of the refugees comes to that of the ethnologist, the more likely the latter is to attempt to document his or her experience of the war through the testimonies of its victims. This raises the prospect that these people, the refugees, might be made into "professional victims"

by the new gatekeepers of ethnic nationalism for ideological or political purposes. Thus she warns us that refugees and displaced persons defined as professional victims with fixed ethnic identities might find that their status as such has
been made permanent so that the "nation" can use them to present itself to the
outside world as a victim. And these gatekeepers—whether they are journalists,
historians, linguists, teachers, or anthropologists—are experts in the management
of ethnic identity (Greverus, 1996: 283). I make a similar point in my review
of *Fear, Death and Resistance*. There I warn that, despite the efforts Croatian
ethnologists have made to remain objective, their work could be appropriated and
put in service to a Croatian ethnic and national narrative.

Renata Jambrešić Kirin, in "Narrating War and Exile Experiences," reminds
us of elusiveness of objectivity. She cites James Clifford's observation that "ethnographic texts are orchestrations of multivocal exchanges . . . in politically
charged situations. The subjectivities (of) these often unequal exchanges—
whether of 'natives' or visiting participant-observers—are constructed domains
of truth, serious fictions" (Clifford 1988: 10, quoted in Jambrešić Kirin 1996:
63). Jambrešić Kirin notes Maja Povrzanović's observation that Croatian ethnographers "have neither been ordered nor recommended (by the ministries financ-
ing them) to produce texts on the war (64). Rather, the war ethnography, dealing
with physical and emotional displacement, is grounded in an ethnographic tradition of research about people in transition: rural/urban, tradition/modernity. Their
new ethnography, in coping with the postmodern condition, is expanding the
genre by seeking "appropriate concepts of identity, ethnicity, locale, and value"
(ibid., 64). Thus the Croatian ethnographers are keenly aware of the problems in
providing "proper scholarly response" to the war, its aftermath, and the refugee
situation.

Hermann Bausinger, in his "Concluding Remarks," indicates "the necessity
of practice" by the ethnographers responding to the war and the refugee situation
and compliments their soft-participant methods of bringing therapeutic music,
dance, and theater to the refugees. He goes on to note that it was "not the music
per se that guarantees cooperation and leads to peace. . . . It is your concepts,
your creativity and your control of the ideological implications which make these
efforts an important contribution to humanity and peace" (1996: 291).

The ability of the Croatian ethnographers to confront and control the political
and ideological implications of their work derives, I think, from the methodological self-awareness that permeates their writing. This itself derives from a familiarity with the postmodern critique of anthropology developed by James Clifford,
George Marcus, Michael Fischer, Clifford Geertz, and others. The Croatian ethnographers understand very well their dilemma with their audience; they know
that we are reading over their shoulders, deconstructing them and their texts,
questioning their intentions, looking for self-serving apologias. They can see the
shadow we cast over their texts. But they are also aware of their own shadows.

Familiar with Crapazanno's discussion in "Hermes' Dilemma" (1986: 51–76), they are aware that they are telling only part of the truth. Feldman acknowledges that their war ethnographies are to some extent auto-biographical; however, she provides a rationale for such a treatment of refugee testimonies: "Let us hope that their voices, which are now suffocating in collective oblivion, will resurrect through ours, thus saving us both from the horrible, yet growing political and intellectual indifference towards the only apparently unreachable reality of moral issues" (Čale Feldman 1995: 88).

This statement was made to an audience representing the American Council of Learned Societies responding to questions of why Croatian ethnographers had not made a public, and collective critique of the political situation in Croatia. Feldman's statement is poignant. There needs to be a sensitivity to the realities of the political system and oppression that they have dealt with in the past and the difficulties and disappointments they now face with not only political indifference and growing oppression at home but the inexcusable intellectual and political indifference abroad.

Croatian ethnographic self-awareness also developed in response to foreign reactions to the war ethnographies. Thus Maja Povrzanović spoke of how she and her colleagues encountered "irritation" and "disbelief" when they were unable to conceal their emotions when speaking about victims' testimonies. Some accused them of "proliferating Croatian propaganda." Others simply dismissed what they had to say because they were "Croat" and therefore neofascist. Still, their work is appreciated in other circles: "The cultural critique implied in some Croatian war ethnographies, as well as the mere readiness of their authors to try to deal with the immediate reality turned upside down, have been regarded as courageous—among intellectuals at home and abroad" (Povrzanović 1995: 100).

I am struck by their self-awareness when I try to explain what is happening in their society. Even though I am an outsider, I participate in the same anthropological traditions including familiarity with postmodernist reflexivity. Long discussions with my Croatian "insider" colleagues have made me aware of their struggle with objectivity, their need to be attuned to their bifocality and to support a wide range of diverse voices describing the consequences of the war. So, by reflecting on their struggle, I can better express my own circumstances and recognize how I am pulled in various directions.

When I consider my own bifocality—how I am both an outside observer and a friend and colleague of villagers and professionals alike—I wonder whether I should have written about the vandalism of Teta Zoe's home. Several friends in Sutivan who are embarrassed about this vandalism asked me not to, and I have violated their trust. Indeed, they did not want me to find out about it, since they knew it would upset me, since I was very close to Teta Zoe. They know as well as I do how negative data can be used against them. I am sensitive to this issue and could have simply described the economic consequences of the war and how the village had returned to sustainable agricultural and fishing. But there are strong feelings about the consequences of this war. Maybe Teta Zoe's home was simply vandalized and that is that. However it is more likely that the vandalism reflects some of those same feelings expressed in graffiti sprayed on village walls denouncing the Serbs. Maybe all Serb property will be confiscated but even if it isn't, it will be a long time before Serbian tourism is revived.[4]

Relations with the Serbs are complicated by the multiple conflicts and between Bosnian Muslims and Bosnian Croats. The federation between Bosnian Muslims and Bosnian Croats today is tenuous at best. In 1993 there were 800 refugees in Sutivan, some of them Muslim, many from the same community in Bosnia. One of them sought me out. She was their school teacher and a Serb. She indicated there was tension between the Croatian and Muslim refugees in the camp, a tension that intensified in 1993 when Croatia and Bosnia openly fought each other and many Croatian refugees from Travnik were forced by Bosnian Muslims to flee to Split. Villagers were not happy with this turn of events.

Still, I felt that the villagers were tremendously patient with the Muslim refugees. Of course, I must note that Alija Izetbegović's daughter has a summer home in Sutivan, and he himself has been a visitor to the village. In 1993, my friend Jure and I talked over coffee as several Muslim girls, refugees from Bosnia, walked by us on the quay. One was with a village girl, and Jure noted to me that they were friends. I replied, "It is necessary." Today, I feel the same but recognize that such reconciliation, though necessary and correct, is nigh impossible. It will take strong leadership and wise diplomacy by the UN and NATO to help bring this about. However, when Croat, Muslim, and Serb end up in the same refugee camp in a quite cosmopolitan village whose tourist economy reflected the multiculturalism that Yugoslavia had once had, the wounds of this war may begin to heal themselves.

My Croatian friends, both in the village and in Zagreb, have a right to be upset about the war. For the past six years I have read and sorted through the information and (too often) misinformation about events in the former Yugoslavia. It would be easy for me to agree with Misha Glenny's observation that "the only truth in the Yugoslav war is the lie" (Glenny 1993: 21). My village friends and professional colleagues are not participants in a truth that is a lie. This is reflected in the efforts of the villagers to survive economically while remaining relatively tolerant. It is reflected in the attempt by my urban colleagues to retain some sort of objectivity in their production of war ethnography and efforts at providing psychosocial aid to the refugees.

No matter what the outside world may say, my colleagues in Zagreb are striving for truth. It would be easy to be critical and negative (as is currently fashionable in American academe, especially in this postmodern moment). It would also be easy to accept the "global objectivity" line about what is happening in Croa-

---

4. Even twenty-five years ago there were strong feelings in the village against Serbian control of the military and influence in national politics.

tia; that it is hopelessly subjective, and following Glenny's observation, that everything reported about it is a lie. But these villagers are my friends and the
anthropologists in Zagreb are my colleagues and they have to deal with what has
happened. They certainly didn't want this war. Yet Teta Zoe predicted it twenty-
five years ago, as did a linguist colleague in Split. I didn't want to believe them,
but it has come to pass and I have also had to deal with it. There is no exit and
though it is difficult to write about a situation this complex and subjective, I
must. In doing so maybe I can make a small contribution to objectivity. That
certainly is what the Croatian ethnologists/ anthropologists have had to do. For
them it is a continuing dilemma.

The next phase in their writing will have to deal with the expropriation by
others of their labor and its effects in the past war effort and with their current
circumstances. Those individuals who sacrificed their lives, their families, the
displaced persons and refugees, and even the minutiae of everyday life has been
and is being claimed by the HZD and its nationalist Croatian Herzegovinian right
wing. Social scientists, anthropologists, ethnographers, are in a terrible quandary.
I have argued that they have struggled to situate themselves as fairly objective
observers, perhaps as objective as insiders could be in a war experience. Now
Croatian society based on a civil contract between citizen and state is threatened
by the demagoguery of the Tudjman government as it closes opposition presses
and radio stations and appropriates the media for the HZD's "politically correct"
purposes. Though the war victims' testimonies cry out against this turn of events,
ethnographers and anthropologists must struggle to sort out how they might respond in writing so as to maintain the credibility of their profession within Croatia and the international community. I face the same quandary.

Postscript

Boris has just written to tell me that the olive harvest this winter in Sutivan has
been one of the best in years. With this abundant oil many households will have
the aid of another traditional agricultural activity to get them through the economic hardship brought on by the war. I remember how much Boris's father
hated picking olives in the 1970s when he helped his brother build their tourist
home and restaurant.

The Croatian army has now taken back the Krajina (Banija), and a cease-fire
and the unsteady peace of the Dayton Accord are in effect. President Tudjman
made the opening of the rail system through Knin to Split a political event confirming "his" Croatian army's successful retaking of the Krajina. I write "his"
because I watched hundreds of thousands of Zagreb citizens in April 1995 as
they cheered the new army and its equipment, tanks, rockets, and fighter planes,
which Tudjman "presented" to them.

When tourism is revived, it will be Boris and his cousin, both educated in

Opatija's tourist school, who will expand the family tourist business. His father was constructing a disco restaurant above the village in anticipation of the future tourist business as Croatians and Europeans return to central Dalmatia. Interestingly, the Ilic home, which is part of the historical heart of the village on the quay, was on the market. This family's descendants, now resident in the United States, apparently prefer Dubrovnik for their vacations. Only a commercial transformation of this estate into a tourist hotel will provide the cash flow, since the Ilic family is asking a million dollars for the property. Possibly a foreign investment interest will be part of this transformation?

Still, the return to "business as usual" will be much easier in the small private family tourist restaurants and homes in this Dalmatian tourist community than in the traumatized communities in Croatia and Bosnia, which felt the destruction of war and ethnic cleansing directly. In those communities, normalcy, objectivity, and forgiveness may never come. It seems that NATO's unwillingness to enforce the indictments of the Hague war crimes tribunal and to protect refugees returning home in both Croatian and Serbian-controlled parts of Bosnia will ensure that the perpetrators of the violence will remain unaccountable and the victims uncompensated, as if compensation could ever be possible.

A return to normalcy in Sutivan will require some sort of resolution of the issue of Serbian summer homes in the community. The destruction at Teta Zoe's home cannot be undone. But I'm sure that many Serbian summer homes are owned by people who were not part of or were even in opposition to the recent political processes in Belgrade that contributed to this terrible chaos. The demonstrations against the Milošević government in Belgrade attest to this fact, though whether or not the more liberal and reasonable demonstrators will have their say in Zajedno over the radical nationalists remains to be seen. Maybe it is again my American naïveté, but I hope that some may return to their summer homes when vacations in Dalmatia become possible again. I still retain some idealism and hope for reconciliation when interpreting events in this sad country. That is the only kind of perspective I can have. It is part of a complex bifocality of which my colleagues at the Institute for Anthropological Research and the Institute of Ethnology and Folklore constantly reminded me; that they were and remain multicultural in their collegiality.

13

Seeing Past the Barricades

Ethnic Intermarriage in Former Yugoslavia, 1962–1989

Nikolai Botev

It is popularly believed that ethnic intermarriage in the former Yugoslavia increased after World War II and that mixed marriages there were common at the time of its breakup. Media accounts have supported this view, painting pictures of pervasive exogamy—see, for example, the articles in the *Los Angeles Times* ("Thousands of Mixed Families Caught in Yugoslavia's Bitter Ethnic Divide," July 21, 1991: A4) and the *Washington Post* ("War Takes Toll on Serbo-Croatian Couples," August 4, 1991: A33). Several studies of ethnic exogamy in Yugoslavia have also indicated that intermarriage has been on the rise. For example, the Soviet ethnographers Yu. V. Bromlei and M. S. Kashuba (1982) maintain that ethnic exogamy grew steadily between 1953 and 1974. They report the percent-

This is an abridged and adapted version of a paper published in *American Sociological Review* 59, no. 3 (1994), written while the author was affiliated with the University of Pennsylvania's Population Studies Center. The author thanks Susan Watkins, S. Philip Morgan, Herbert Smith, and Samuel Preston for their suggestions, encouragement, and criticism at all stages of this research. This paper also benefited from the comments of Joel Halpern, Jane Menken, Adrejs Plakans, Eugene Hammel, Robert McCaa, Richard Wagner, Richard Alba, and Gerald Marwell. The views expressed in this article are those of the author and do not necessarily reflect the views of the organization in which he is employed.

ages of ethnically mixed marriages in 1956, 1963, 1971, and 1974 as 9.3 percent, 12.4 percent, 13.5 percent, and 13.5 percent (Bromlei and Kashuba 1982: 61). The Yugoslav demographer Ruža Petrović ([1966] 1970; 1986a; 1991), concurs, concluding that ethnic exogamy in Yugoslavia is "very high and it is permanently growing" (1986a: 239). A number of other authors assume, either explicitly or implicitly, that ethnic exogamy in Yugoslavia has been increasing (e.g., Flere 1988).

If we consider, however, Yugoslavia's disintegration, the picture of increasing intermarriage seems perplexing. Ethnic intermarriage has always been viewed as both a primary cause and an indicator of social and cultural integration (Merton [1941] 1972; Blau, Blum, and Schwartz 1982; Pagnini and Morgan 1990). This reasoning assumes that intermarriage is not likely to take place when social and cultural boundaries are rigid. When exogamy does occur, however, it erodes these boundaries faster than any other social process. The question that emerges is that if intermarriage had increased and if exogamy is an indicator of social integration, why did the former Yugoslavia disintegrate so convulsively?

There are reasons to doubt the accuracy of the picture of increasing intermarriage. For example, percentages presented by Bromlei and Kashuba (1982) are single-year figures that may not adequately represent the overall trends. Most authors do not consider the effects of changes in the definitions of various ethnic groups over time. More important, they pay little or no attention to the effects of group size and sex ratios, factors that may strongly affect the levels and trends of exogamy (e.g., Gray 1987; McCaa 1989; Jones 1991). This study aims at applying more sophisticated analytical techniques to the question in order to come up with a better picture of the patterns and trends in ethnic intermarriage in the former Yugoslavia.

Data and Its Limitations

The analysis is based on vital registration data on the ethnicity of newly married spouses published by Yugoslavia's Federal Statistical Office (Savezni Zavod Statistiki 1962a–1989a). Vital statistics are generally considered to have a major advantage over census returns for the study of intermarriage, since they are less affected by changes in ethnic self-identification. Several characteristics of these data, however, limit the scope of the analysis.

First, these data are limited to cross-classifications of the marriages by ethnicity of the spouses. Ethnicity is not the only dimension of assortative mating, since educational and age homogamy are also prevalent and might potentially reinforce or diminish certain ethnic preferences. There were substantial gender differences in education and literacy in Yugoslavia. For example, according to the 1981 census data the percentages of Slovene males and females over fifteen who were illiterate were 0.6 and 0.8 percent. For the Montenegrins these figures were 2.0 and 14.2 percent; for Macedonians, 5.0 and 12.7 percent; for Serbs, 4.6 and 19.8 percent; and for Albanians, 12.1 and 33.9 percent (see Šijaković-Blagojević 1986). Unfortunately, with the available data it is not possible to consider the interaction of ethnicity with education or other characteristics that might influence ethnic exogamy.

A second limitation of the data is that they refer only to officially registered marriages and exclude cohabitation. If cohabitation has been on the rise during the period under study, and if couples who cohabit are more (or less) likely to be ethnically mixed than couples who marry, then the results will be biased. Common-law marriages have existed, especially among the rural Orthodox population, since as early as the end of nineteenth century. Ethnographic evidence, however, suggests that these have been limited largely to cases in which the bride or groom are under the legal age limit, or are too poor to afford a legal marriage, or other such special conditions (Čulinović-Constantinović 1976). More recently there has been evidence of premarital cohabitation in Yugoslavia. However, as in other East European countries, with the possible exception of the former East Germany, it was never considered a viable alternative to marriage (Sardon 1991) and thus never reached levels that might affect the results of this study.

Another limitation is that the data do not distinguish between first and subsequent marriages. One source of change in intermarriage rates may be changes in the levels of divorce and remarriage, rather than changes in marital preferences. In most republics of the former Yugoslavia, divorce was uncommon prior to World War II, but has subsequently increased rapidly. If those who have divorced are considered "innovators," they may be more likely to innovate by choosing a spouse with a different ethnic background the second or third time around. In addition, since those who remarry are typically older, they may be more geographically mobile, have a wider circle of acquaintances, and hence, be more likely to marry exogamously. If an order-of-marriage effect exists in the case of Yugoslavia, it should be counterbalanced by the fact that heterogamous marriages tend to have higher rates of dissolution, as suggested by existing research (Bentler and Newcomb 1978; Johnson 1980; Schwertfeger 1982).

Finally, the most serious limitation of the data is that the definitions of some ethnic groups have varied over time. Differences in ethnic definitions create fluctuations in the sizes of the groups and thus distort the levels and trends in the rates of exogamy. The existence of such differences in Yugoslavia is well documented (Petrović 1973; Hoffman 1977). In the early postwar censuses (1948 and 1953) members of many smaller ethnic groups (Albanians, Hungarians, Gypsies, Germans, etc.) reported themselves as belonging to the larger ethnic groups among which they lived. This was due both to pressure from the authorities for ethnic assimilation and to other specific circumstances. For example, during the 1953 census many Albanians and Macedonian Muslims chose to declare themselves as Turks, trying to benefit from the permission given to the Turkish population to emigrate to Turkey.

Ethnic Muslims[1] pose an especially difficult problem in terms of accuracy of registration in censuses (see Dyker 1972). In the first postwar census in 1948, as in the previous Yugoslav censuses, "Muslim" was considered a religious rather than an ethnic category. Thus those who declared themselves as Muslims had to also identify themselves as belonging to one of the large nationalities and were thus registered as "Serb-Muslim" or "Croat-Muslim." Only a small number were classified in the category "Muslim—undeclared." In the 1953 census the "Muslim" category was abolished, and Muslims of Yugoslav ethnic origin were classified as "Yugoslav—undeclared," a group that also included people of other nationalities who chose not to declare their actual ethnic background. The 1961 census was the first to include the category "ethnic Muslim." It also allowed freer declaration of national identity. This spirit and methodology was preserved, with some slight modifications (affecting mainly the smaller ethnic groups), in the subsequent period.

My analysis begins with 1962, since this is when data become consistent enough to allow a comparative study of intermarriage. I looked at four periods of three years each (1962–1964, 1970–1972, 1980–1982, and 1987–1989). Three-year periods are long enough to reduce random fluctuations, but also short enough not to dilute any possible trends. I limit the analysis to these four periods to keep the models manageable and to avoid the gap between 1966 and 1969 when data on marriages by ethnicity were not published. I also consider only the eight largest ethnic groups—Albanians, Croats, Hungarians, Macedonians, Montenegrins, Muslims, Serbs, and Slovenes—to avoid the inconsistencies in the registration of the smaller ethnic groups and complications stemming from small group sizes. In addition, I do not consider the category "Yugoslavs-undeclared," although many authors interpret this category as an indicator of political integration (Burg and Berbaum 1989). It includes those who have chosen not to declare an actual ethnic background. Some people in this category have mixed ancestry, but others have a clearly defined ethnic background and are usually well-educated urban residents. "Yugoslavs" were overrepresented in the Communist Party: 19.5 percent of the members of the federal party organization identified themselves in 1981 as "Yugoslavs-undeclared" (Cvjeticanin as cited in Burg and Berbaum 1989: 539).[2]

All these factors make the category "Yugoslav-undeclared" fluid and heterogeneous. This is particularly well illustrated by fluctuating proportions of brides and grooms identified as "Yugoslavs-undeclared" in the marriage statistics. Thus there were 2.0 percent in 1962 (the first year the vital statistics used the "Ethnic Muslims" and "Yugoslavs-undeclared" categories), 1.1 percent in 1972, 4.4 per-

1. "Muslims by ethnic identity" or "ethnic Muslims" include mostly people of Slavic background who were converted to Islam during the Ottoman domination of the Balkans, and who gradually developed a distinct ethnic consciousness (Dyker 1972).

2. See Sekulić, Massey, and Hodson 1994, Burg and Berbaum 1989, and Flere 1988 for a discussion of the changes in the political connotation of the Yugoslav identity.

cent in 1986, 3.7 percent in 1987, and 5.3 percent in 1989 (see Savezni Zavod Statistiki 1961a–1989a). The proportion of the total population that selected "Yugoslav-undeclared" according to the last three censuses was 1.7 percent in 1961, 1.3 percent in 1971, and 5.4 percent in 1981 (see Table 13.1). These fluctuations make estimates of intermarriage between this and other groups unstable across time and republics.

A related problem is that two of the ethnic categories included in this analysis are culturally ambiguous. Neither the Macedonians nor the "Ethnic Muslims" articulated a clear ethnic identity until the early twentieth century (some might argue that the same is true for the Montenegrins). Even in recent years, there have been cases where close relatives identify with different nationalities. For example, of five brothers living in Macedonia, two identify as Macedonians, two as Bulgarians, and one identifies either as Serbian or Yugoslav.[3] Clearly, if these brothers marry women from the same social and cultural environment as themselves but who all identify as Macedonians, we will observe three exogamous marriages and two endogamous ones, although all five marriages involve people from more or less the same background. The available data make it impossible to avoid such biases. Ethnographic evidence, however, suggests that the numbers of cases like this are limited, and their net effect is not significant.

Mixed Marriages by Republics—Results and Significance

I begin by briefly considering the proportions of exogamous marriages in the republics and autonomous provinces of the former Yugoslavia (Table 13.2). The data indicate no clear upward trend in the proportion of mixed marriages. According to marriage registration data between 12 and 13 percent of marriages in Yugoslavia as a whole are mixed, with little variation over time. The 1981 census returns indicate that only 8.6 percent of the intact families (married couples with or without children) involved spouses that have declared different ethnic backgrounds (Petrović 1991: 65). These figures are modest compared to many other ethnically mixed societies. For example, according to the 1980 census, in the United States among American-born couples where women are in their first marriage, the proportion of ethnically mixed marriages was over 20 percent. This includes about 30 percent for whites/Caucasians (Lieberson and Waters 1985: 51). In Canada in the early 1970s, the proportion of exogamous marriages was over 30 percent (Richard 1991: 108–11). In the former Soviet Union according to 1979 census data, 14.9 percent of families involved spouses of different nationalities (Volkov 1989: 12). There is, however, considerable regional variation in Yugoslavia. In Kosovo the proportion of exogamous marriages declined from 9.4 in 1962–64 to only 4.7 percent in 1987–89; during the same period the percent-

---

3. This specific case was brought to my attention by Joel Halpern.

Table 13.1 Ethnic composition as percentages of the population in Yugoslavia, by republics and autonomous provinces, 1961 and 1981 censuses

Year/Ethnic Group	Yugoslavia (Total)	BiH	Croatia	Macedonia	Montenegro	Slovenia	Total	Proper
1961								
Total population (in 1,000s)	18,549	3,278	4,160	1,406	472	1,592	7,642	4,823
Ethnic group (percent)								
Slovenes	8.0	0.1	0.9	0.0	0.2	95.8	0.2	0.0
Croats	23.2	21.6	80.6	0.3	2.2	2.0	2.6	0.9
Hungarians	2.6	0.1	1.0	0.0	0.0	0.7	5.0	0.0
Serbs	43.5	43.1	15.0	3.1	2.9	0.8	75.9	93.1
Montenegrins	2.8	0.3	0.2	0.2	81.6	0.0	1.3	0.6
Macedonians	5.5	0.0	0.1	71.3	0.1	0.0	0.4	0.4
Muslims	5.2	25.6	0.0	0.2	6.4	0.0	1.2	1.7
Albanians	4.9	0.1	0.0	13.0	5.4	0.0	9.1	1.0
Yugoslavs–undeclared	1.7	8.4	0.4	0.1	0.3	0.2	0.3	0.2
Others	3.6	0.5	1.8	10.9	0.7	0.5	4.0	2.1
Total	101.0	99.8	100.0	99.1	99.8	100.0	100.0	100.0
1981								
Total population (in 1,000s)	22,425	4,124	4,601	1,909	584	1,892	9,314	5,694
Ethnic group (percent)								
Slovenes	7.8	0.1	0.5	0.0	0.1	90.5	0.1	0.1
Croats	9.7	18.4	75.1	0.2	1.2	2.9	1.6	0.6
Hungarians	1.9	0.0	0.6	0.0	0.0	0.5	4.2	0.1
Serbs	6.3	32.0	11.6	2.3	3.3	2.2	66.4	85.4
Montenegrins	2.6	0.3	0.2	0.2	68.5	0.2	1.6	1.4
Macedonians	6.0	0.0	0.1	67.0	0.1	0.2	0.5	0.5
Muslims	8.9	39.5	0.5	2.1	13.4	0.7	2.3	2.7
Albanians	7.7	0.1	0.1	19.8	6.5	0.1	14.0	1.3
Yugoslavs–undeclared	5.4	7.9	8.2	0.8	5.4	1.4	4.7	4.8
Others	3.6	1.6	3.1	7.6	1.4	1.3	4.6	3.2
Total	99.9	99.9	100.0	100.0	99.9	100.0	100.0	100.1

SOURCE: Savezni Zavod Statisiki (1965b:6–25; 1986c:451).

NOTE: Totals may not add to 100 percent because of rounding errors.

age of mixed marriages in Vojvodina increased from 22.5 to 28.4 (see Table 13.2).

These data should be interpreted with caution, since as I have already noted, the conventional indices of intermarriage are strongly affected by structural factors. It is widely recognized that small groups and groups with skewed sex ratios are more likely to intermarry because of the limited in-group marriage markets they face.[4]

The analysis described below controls for these factors, allowing for a better assessment of the intermarriage propensities. It uses general log-linear models, which distinguish the effects of changes in the marginal distribution of spouses' traits from patterns that reflect the association between these traits. This technique offers several advantages over most other techniques for analyzing categorical data. For example, instead of distinguishing between dependent and independent variables, as in the case of logit models, log-linear analysis examines patterns of deviation from baseline assumptions about the associations in a contingency table, a natural way to present the association between the ethnicity of spouses. A potential drawback of this approach is that it considers only actual marriages rather than the marriage market as a whole, so the information on who decides not to marry, given the current marriage market conditions, is lost. This may lead to biases in situations of aberrant marriage patterns (very late marriages or high levels of celibacy), but should not be a major concern here.[5]

I analyze intermarriage in the former Yugoslavia along two dimensions. The

Table 13.2 Percentages of exogamous marriages in Yugoslavia, by republics and autonomous provinces, 1962 to 1989

Republic/Province	1962–64	1970–72	1980–82	1987–89
Yugoslavia	12.7	11.7	13.1	13.0
Bosnia-Hercegovina	11.4	9.5	12.2	11.9
Montenegro	17.9	14.6	13.4	13.1
Croatia	15.8	15.4	17.1	17.4
Macedonia	13.5	9.9	8.2	7.8
Slovenia	7.7	7.8	11.0	13.0
Serbia (total)	12.3	11.9	13.1	12.9
Proper	8.5	7.8	9.9	10.4
Vojvodina	22.5	25.3	27.6	28.4
Kosovo	9.4	7.7	6.1	4.7

SOURCE: Savezni Zavod Statistiki (1961a–1989a).

4. Peter Blau has formulated this as a theorem within his theory of social structure, stating that "for any dichotomy of a society, the proportion of group members intermarried is an inverse function of group size" (Blau 1977: 42).

5. The marriage patterns in the republics and autonomous provinces of the former Yugoslavia range from early and universal to moderately late, but nowhere does the proportion of people never married by age fifty reach levels that can be termed aberrant.

first is the association between the ethnic backgrounds of the spouses. The second is the variation of this association across republics (or autonomous provinces) and over time. The first dimension is operationalized in five models.[6] The "independence model" includes only the marginal effects and assumes random mating (i.e., marital choices reflect only the relative supply of potential husbands and wives and are not affected differentially by ethnic background) and is used as a baseline representing the opportunity structure. It fits the data very poorly. The other models include parameters that reflect the preference for endogamy. They present mate selection as an outcome of two distinct tendencies: an endogamy tendency, which reflects the preference for marrying endogamously, and an exogamy tendency, where those who do not marry within their own group choose mates according to specific rules. Two of the models are based on the assumption that once people cross the boundaries of their own ethnic group, they face a random mating situation. The "uniform endogamy" model assumes that all ethnic groups have the same degree of preference for ethnic endogamy, while in the "variable endogamy" model ethnic groups vary in the degree of preference for members of their own group. Both the uniform endogamy and the variable endogamy models fit the data much better than the independence model does. This finding underscores a strong tendency toward endogamy in the former Yugoslavia, while the fact that the fit of the variable endogamy is better than the uniform endogamy model, indicates that the different ethnic groups vary in their degree of preference for endogamy.

Before presenting the remaining two models of the association between the ethnic backgrounds of the spouses, I turn to the second dimension of the analysis. Six sets of models were used to operationalize different assumptions about the variation of mating preferences across republics and over time. The "republic and time–invariant models" assume that the same mating preferences characterize all regions at every period. Two sets of models include interactions of mating preferences and period, so the mating preferences remain the same across republics, but vary over time. I use two specifications of these interactions: one where mating preferences are assumed to change linearly and another where no constraints are placed on these changes. Alternatively, the fourth set (time-invariant models) includes interactions of mating preferences with republic (province), but not with time period (i.e., mating preferences remain the same over time but vary across republics), thus allowing for analysis of the regional differences in intermarriage without considering the trends in endogamy. In the fifth set of models (unconstrained models), mating preferences vary both over time and across regions and provide a test for both regional differences and time-trends in endogamy. The last set of models combines the previous two sets—it constrains

---

6. Because space is limited, the models are described here very briefly. In addition I present neither the statistics of fit nor the parameter estimates. The reader interested in methodological details is referred to the original paper (Botev 1994).

certain mating preference parameters to be time-invariant and leaves others unconstrained.

Table 13.2 shows no clear trend in the proportion of ethnically mixed marriages over time in Yugoslavia as a whole, but also reveals that this proportion varies substantially across republics. Log-linear analysis permits us to validate these findings and perform tests for statistical significance. It confirms that there is no significant trend in the levels of endogamy, while the differences among the individual republics and autonomous provinces are substantial (Botev 1994).

The models also suggest the existence of "zones of attraction" corresponding to the three cultural traditions cross-cutting the ethnic map in this region. Thus there is a "Western" tradition among Slovenes and Croats, who have been under Austro-Hungarian rule and are predominantly Catholic. There is an endemic "Balkan" cultural tradition among Serbs, Montenegrins, and Macedonians, who have been part of the Ottoman Empire and are predominantly Eastern Orthodox; and a "Middle Eastern" cultural influence among most of the Islamic populations in the former Yugoslavia (Albanians, Turks).[7] It appears that those who marry outside their own ethnic group prefer partners from their own cultural tradition.

These observations are formalized in a model, which I refer to as a "crossings model." As in the variable endogamy model, the ethnic groups vary in their degree of preference for ethnic endogamy, but those who marry exogamously no longer choose randomly. Rather, they prefer mates who come from their own cultural traditions, and as long as this preference is met, the choice is random with respect to ethnicity. "Crossings models" presuppose ordinal data (e.g., socioeconomic status, educational level, etc.). Although ethnicity is a nominal variable, ordinal properties can be assigned to it based on the place of a specific ethnic group in a "cultural continuum." In the case of Yugoslavia, I assume that the "Balkan" cultural tradition occupies the midpoint, while the "Western" and "Middle Eastern" traditions occupy two divergent poles. The cultural traditions are assumed to be separated by boundaries that must be crossed sequentially: a member of the "Western" tradition who marries outside that tradition is assumed to be more likely to marry someone from the "Balkan" than from the "Middle Eastern" tradition. Within each cultural tradition, ethnicity is irrelevant. Thus a member of the "Western" tradition who marries someone from the "Balkan" tradition is presumed to prefer a Macedonian, a Montenegrin, or a Serb equally as a marriage partner. To account for these patterns I add "barrier parameters" to the model, which measure the permeability of the boundaries between the three cultural traditions and provide a way to estimate the social distances among them.

The "crossings models" represent the data better than any of the previous models. Again, the time-invariant crossings model is preferable in terms of the

---

7. The terms "Western," "Balkan," and "Middle Eastern" are ambiguous, but are employed here for lack of better alternatives. Using the religious affiliation as an identifier is even more misleading.

trade-off between fit and parsimony than the unconstrained crossings model. This reconfirms the finding of no significant trend in the levels of endogamy and of substantial differences among the individual republics and autonomous provinces. Rather unexpectedly, however, the extent to which exogamous marriages occur within the same cultural tradition does vary over time. As demonstrated in the original article (Botev 1994), these variations over time are up-and-down movements and do not amount to a clear trend in the degree to which cultural traditions constrain exogamy.

There is an important assumption embedded in the models thus far presented—that exogamous marriages are quasi-symmetrical; that is, males and females of a given ethnic group are equally likely to marry persons from the other ethnic groups. The modeling process indicated that relaxing this assumption could further improve the fit of the models. This observation was formalized in an extension of the time-invariant crossings model with added asymmetry and special affinity parameters. The asymmetry parameters capture sex differentials in assortative mating, which may be due to sex differences in the conscious selection of a marital partner (e.g., some form of hypergamy or hypogamy). The special affinity parameters account for marital preferences beyond those implied by the framework underlying the crossings models and allow the identification of pockets of ethnic affinities, or conversely, dislikes. Whereas the parametrization of the models so far was theoretically driven (there were a priori reasons to believe that ethnicity, republic, time, and cultural tradition mattered), the addition of asymmetry and special affinity parameters was an empirical "fix," and further improved the fit and produced the model on which the further analysis is based.

Contrasting Intermarriage Possibilities by Nationality

The estimates of the intermarriage parameters, which show the relative chances that members of different ethnic groups have to marry within or outside their own ethnic group, demonstrate that the Albanians are an especially closed group: They are 60 (in Montenegro) to 269 (in Serbia proper) times more likely to marry other Albanians than random mating would imply (after controlling for cultural background, asymmetry, and special affinity effects). This finding is especially important, given the conflict in Kosovo and the long history of attempts by Albanians there to achieve independence. In some cases endogamy is even more pronounced than among the Albanians. Thus Croats in Kosovo, after controlling for cultural background, asymmetry, and special affinity effects, are over 560 times more likely to marry within their own ethnic group than the level implied by random mating. This result is not unexpected, given the fact that the small Kosovo Croatian minority lives amidst ethnic groups belonging to the "Middle Eastern" cultural tradition and other groups belonging to the "Balkan" tradition. The former include Albanians, who in 1981 constituted over three-fourths of the population in Kosovo, as well as some ethnic Muslims. The latter includes Serbs, who in 1981 accounted for 13 percent of the population, and some Montenegrins. This finding further underscores the importance of the cultural traditions in the choice of marital partners, and conceivably in the broader social life.

The least endogamous group is the Serbs. They are only between 2 and 8.5 times more likely to marry within their ethnic group than implied by random mating. This probably reflects their position as the dominant group in the Yugoslav society. Further, it is generally in accord with the arguments of minority group effects theory, which postulates that a group's social behavior (including mate selection) depends upon its relative size in a given population (Blalock 1967; Goldscheider and Uhlenberg 1969). The attempts to account for such effects by including parameters that distinguish majority and minority groups in the log-linear analysis did not yield significant improvement in the fit of the models.

How open have the Croat, Muslim, and Serb communities in Bosnia and Herzegovina been compared to their behavior in the other republics where conflict has been less prevalent historically? It is significant that both the Croats and the Serbs in Bosnia and Herzegovina are more endogamous than they are in the other republics. As noted earlier, the Serbs have lower levels of endogamy than do members of other ethnicities; in Bosnia and Herzegovina, however, their levels of endogamy are higher than in any other republic except in Croatia (the difference between the estimates for Bosnia and Herzegovina, and for Croatia is not statistically significant). Similarly, the Croats are less likely to marry exogamously in Bosnia and Herzegovina than they are in most other republics—only in Kosovo are the Croats significantly more endogamous. For Macedonia and Montenegro the estimates are not significantly different from those for Bosnia and Herzegovina, while for the rest of the republics and provinces they are lower.

By contrast, the Muslims, who generally tend to be a closed group, are more likely to marry exogamously in Bosnia and Herzegovina than they are in the other republics—the endogamy parameters for the Muslims are significantly higher everywhere else in former Yugoslavia except in Slovenia and Vojvodina. Nonetheless, levels of endogamy among the Muslims in Bosnia and Herzegovina are still relatively high. Indeed, the difference between the endogamy parameters for the Muslims and the Serbs in Bosnia and Herzegovina is not statistically significant; the Croats are significantly more endogamous than the other two groups. Thus the three communities have remained very much closed (endogamous) during the period under study. There are indications that in the large urban centers (especially Sarajevo) the intermarriage among these three groups has been more prevalent; however, the data used in this study do not allow this to be verified.

Another interesting case is the autonomous province of Vojvodina. In contrast to Bosnia and Herzegovina, the proportion of mixed marriages there is high, and ethnic conflict has been low. But does the high proportion of mixed marriages reflect social integration? Or does it simply reflect the fact that, as Table 13.1 showed, Vojvodina is inhabited by a dozen or more small groups, all of which face a limited marriage market (the total population of the province is only 5.5 million)? The analysis demonstrated that the various ethnic groups there have the same propensities to intermarry as they do elsewhere. Only the Serbs, who are the majority in Vojvodina and constituted almost 55 percent of the population in 1981, tend to be less endogamous in Vojvodina than elsewhere. (The difference of the estimates for Vojvodina and Serbia proper are not statistically significant; the estimates of the endogamy parameters are significantly higher for the rest of the republics and autonomous provinces.) This suggests that the higher proportion of intermarriage in Vojvodina than in other provinces is due to structural factors. We can, however, speculate that the maintenance of peace in this province, at least so far, may be in part a consequence of the high proportion of ethnically mixed marriages.

Barriers to Intermarriage and Cultural Traditions

As already noted, the influence of cultural tradition on mating preferences was quantified in the barrier parameters. These parameters are interpreted as presenting the relative chances that someone will marry a person from another cultural tradition. The estimates indicate that the barrier between the "Western" and "Balkan" cultural traditions tends to be more permeable than the barrier between the "Balkan" and "Middle Eastern" cultural traditions. Intermarriage between people from "Western" and "Balkan" cultural backgrounds are about half as likely to occur as implied by random mating (after controlling for ethnic endogamy, asymmetry, and special affinity effects), whereas intermarriages between people from "Balkan" and "Middle Eastern" cultural background are up to 12.5 times less likely to occur than the level implied by random mating (after controlling for ethnic endogamy, asymmetry, and special affinity effects).

Where are barriers to intermarriage the highest, and where are they the lowest? Interestingly, the barriers between "Western" and "Balkan" cultural traditions are particularly weak in Bosnia and Herzegovina and in Kosovo. Both of these regions have relatively large Islamic populations. This indicates that in these regions the two cultural traditions based on Christianity (the "Western" and the "Balkan") tend to stick together. Conversely, this barrier is least permeable in Slovenia, the most westernized republic in Yugoslavia. Its values are also low in Vojvodina, where a sizable Hungarian minority (which belongs to the "Western" tradition) lives among the Serbian majority.

The barrier between the "Middle Eastern" and "Balkan" cultural traditions is least permeable in Macedonia, where there is a long history of tension between the Macedonian majority and the Albanian minority. The barrier is most permeable in the most westernized republic, Slovenia, where it is coupled with high absolute values of the barriers between "Western" and "Balkan" cultural traditions. This may indicate that the people belonging to the "Western" tradition in Slovenia tend to distance themselves from the rest, thus forcing population groups belonging to other cultural traditions to stick together. A similar but weaker effect is observed in Croatia and Vojvodina.

The barrier separating the "Western" and "Balkan" traditions has remained rather stable over time, while the estimates of the permeability of the barrier between the "Balkan" and "Middle Eastern" traditions increase and decrease, but with a few exceptions, there is no discernible trend. Among the exceptions is a gradual increase in the permeability of the barrier between the "Balkan" and "Middle Eastern" traditions in Serbia proper. In Bosnia and Herzegovina the permeability of this barrier increases until the early 1980s, and then decreases, while in Macedonia it has been decreasing since the early 1970s.

These findings once again emphasize the importance of the differences in the cultural traditions within Yugoslav society and underscore the inherent fragility of the former Yugoslavia as a federal state. On the other hand, they suggest that what remains of the former Yugoslavia, a union of Serbia and Montenegro, may have better prospects for survival, because it unites populations with similar cultural backgrounds (Kosovo is a notable exception).

The asymmetry and special affinity parameters reflect mainly empirical particularities, so in general they are hard to interpret. An interesting finding is that the Croats are more likely than other ethnic groups belonging to the "Western" tradition to cross cultural barriers to marry people belonging to different traditions. In Croatia, for example, Croats are more likely to marry Serbs than is implied by the framework underlying the crossings model; in Kosovo they are more likely to marry Albanians. The asymmetry parameters also provide interesting insights on the residence patterns in Yugoslavia. Most ethnic groups there are known to have been patrilocal (e.g., Bromlei and Kashuba 1982). If this is still the case, and if we assume that a substantial part of the intermarriages involve not simply people from different ethnic groups but also people from different parts of Yugoslavia, we might expect to find positive values on asymmetry parameters corresponding to grooms from the ethnic group constituting the majority in a given region. This is not the case, which may be interpreted as confirming the findings of anthropologists that residence patterns in Yugoslavia have shifted toward neolocality.

Conclusions

The theoretical basis of this study is drawn from the theories of social distance and social structure. These theories share the assumption that intermarriage is both the main indicator and a cause of social integration. I have examined whether the popular notion, that ethnic intermarriage was widespread in the former Yugoslavia, is true. On the basis of marriage registration data, and using log-linear models to characterize associations and differential change, I have found this notion to be an exaggeration. Rather, ethnic endogamy has been the norm in Yugoslavia, and over the years studied (1962 to 1989) no clear trend emerged, either in terms of increasing rates of intermarriage or decreasing social distance between the various ethnic groups and cultural traditions.

These findings are supported indirectly by the persisting differences in the timing and prevalence of marriage. Three broadly defined marriage patterns co-existed in the former Yugoslavia.[8] The "European" pattern was characterized by late marriage and high celibacy (observed in a moderate form in Slovenia, where in the beginning of the period under study the mean age at first marriage for women was 24.3 years, and 17 percent of women above age 50 were single).[9] The "Mediterranean" pattern was characterized by early marriage for females and late marriage for males, resulting in wide age gaps between spouses (observed in a moderate form in Kosovo and Montenegro, where the mean age at first marriage is 28 years for the men and only around 22 years for women). Finally, there was the "Traditional" pattern, with early and nearly universal marriage (characteristic for the rest of the former Yugoslavia, where the mean age at first marriage for men is between 24.5 and 25.5 years and for women is between 21.5 and 22 years, while the percent never-married varies between 1.5 and 6).

The timing of marriage may have potential implications for the choice of a marital partner and the patterns of intermarriage through two separate mechanisms. The first mechanism implies that men from early marrying populations should be less likely to intermarry with women from late-marrying populations if the social norm is that men should marry women younger then they are. Thus, for example, Slovenian women should be less likely to marry men from early marrying populations. Part of this effect should be reflected in the asymmetry parameters, but no such effect is observed. Adding an explicit parameter to account for this effect did not significantly improve the fit of the model. The second mechanism implies that late-marrying persons should be more likely to intermarry, because they have been longer on the marriage market and are more likely to meet partners from outside their immediate surroundings. Again no significant net effects could be detected with the data and methods employed here.

8. These three marriage patterns differ from the three cultural traditions introduced earlier. The idea that there are two marriage patterns in Europe—the "European" and the "Traditional"—was introduced by Hajnal (1965), who drew the approximate dividing line between the two from Trieste to St. Petersburg. Later, other authors suggested the existence of a third pattern, the "Mediterranean" (Smith 1981; Laslett 1983).

9. According to Hajnal (1965), what distinguishes the European pattern are late marriages and high celibacy among women—the mean age at first marriage is above 23 years, and more than 10 percent of the women in the 45 to 49 age group remain single. As in most countries exhibiting the European pattern, during the 1960s and 1970s a tendency toward earlier and more universal marriages was observed in Slovenia—by the mid-1980s, the mean age at first marriage there had dropped to 22 years, and according to the 1981 census the proportion never married at age 50 was 12 percent.

More important from the point of view of this study is that intermarriage may affect nuptiality by producing behavioral assimilation in the form of converging marriage patterns. This is noted by Anderton (1986), who suggests that with exogamy there is a tendency for marriage behavior, and specifically the age at marriage, to be more similar for the out-group than for within-group marriages (Anderton 1986: 343). So whether nuptiality patterns in the individual republics and autonomous provinces are converging or not might serve as a basis for confirming or questioning our findings on the levels and trends of ethnic exogamy. The nuptiality differentials in Yugoslavia, though, persisted during the years studied (Petrović 1986b), and the small convergence that has occurred does not go beyond the general trend observed in most modern societies (e.g., Hajnal 1965; Dixon 1971; Watkins 1981).

Recent events in Yugoslavia challenge the conventional wisdom that in modern industrial societies ethnic divisions and conflicts will eventually disappear.[10] Despite decades of industrialization and modernization, ethnic divisions in Yugoslavia obviously remained strong enough to lead to war. The conventional sociological wisdom that intermarriage is an indicator of social integration remains intact, however, at least in this case. Judging from the levels of ethnic endogamy, Yugoslavia has never been fully integrated. Thus there is no mystery in that country's disintegration, although the violence accompanying the disintegration remains profoundly disturbing. Rudyard Kipling is also proven right: Although geopolitically the East and the West met in what used to be Yugoslavia, those meetings rarely took place in front of the marriage altar.

---

10. The intellectual roots of these theories were laid by Marx, Tonnies, and Durkheim. A modern proponent of such a theory, especially regarding Yugoslavia, is Bertsch (1971, 1976).

National Minorities under the Dayton Accord

Lessons from History

Julie Mertus

After the First World War, the victorious allies used international law to rearrange the European landscape, parceling out the losses of Germany, the Ottoman Empire, Bulgaria, and the successor states of the Hapsburg empire, Austria and Hungary. "The principle 'one nation, one state' was not realized to the full extent permitted by the ethnographic configuration of Europe, but it was approximated more closely than ever before" (Claude 1955: 12). Protections for religious, cultural, linguistic, and ethno-national minorities[1] within the newly created nation-states were designed as a compensation for national self-determination for the millions of people left out of "their" nation-states. Under the interwar agreements, "the victors took the spoils, but with the stipulations often clothed in the idealistic language of national self-determination and justice" (Jelavich 1983: 122).

Research for this chapter was made possible by the support of the Stable Foundation and the Human Rights Program at Harvard Law School. The author wishes to thank Henry Steiner, Barnett Rubin, Nathaniel Berman, Paul Hunt, Steven Wheatley, and Peter Cumper for their comments and suggestions. An expanded version of this work is published in *Brooklyn Journal of International Law* 23(3) / 793 (see Mertus 1998).

1. The terms "ethno-national" minorities and members of "national" minority groups to refer to groups united not necessarily by geography, but by a sense of identity based on their common history, language, and tradition.

More than half a century later, the peace settlement negotiated for the former Yugoslavia at Dayton, Ohio, made a similar compromise: the territorial victors were rewarded in a peace process that trumpeted self-determination and justice. Through formal affirmation of the legal integrity of the internationally recognized state of Bosnia and Herzegovina,[2] the Dayton Accord claimed to respect that state's earlier act of self-determination. Yet the peace settlement also took steps to eviscerate that act. It divided Bosnia and Herzegovina roughly in two, giving the Serbs what they had wanted all along, a semi-autonomous state, and paving the way for what the Croats had long desired, the securing of their borders and political and military inroads into Herzegovina.

Under the Dayton Accord, post–World War II international human rights provisions constitute a corollary and corrective to well-worn attempts to address the tensions between states, ethno-national groups, and nationalisms. Nevertheless, despite changes in international law and policy, the grand scheme to protect ethno-national groups embodied in the Dayton Accord is remarkably similar to the guarantees for minority rights created after the First World War. The "minorities treaties"[3] concluded under the auspices of the League of Nations and other interwar minority rights measures failed both to protect the rights of ethnic, religious, and linguistic minorities and to create lasting peace. The Dayton Accord appears predestined to similar failure. Dayton not only repeats the international peace techniques of earlier times but also jettisons the language through which the people of the former Yugoslavia had become accustomed to define themselves—that is as a nation (*narod*) or a national minority (*narodnost*). On top of all of its heavy human rights machinery, the Dayton Accord creates a government that imposes a slightly different set of ethno-national divides. What vision of society does Dayton impose? Is it likely that the people of the former Yugoslavia will accept this vision? Will Dayton be any more successful than the interwar plans were at fostering rights and securing peace?

Examination of the historical underpinnings of the Dayton Accord has been missing from policy discussions on protections for members of ethno-national minority groups in Bosnia and Herzegovina, Croatia, and other troubled parts of Central and Eastern Europe. Yet Dayton was not concluded in a policy vacuum; it was influenced by earlier international and regional responses to crumbling states, nationalisms, and the need to protect the rights of members of minority groups. Understanding the stumbling blocks to Dayton's effective enforcement requires an inquiry into earlier international frameworks designed for constructing peace.

---

2. See Article 1 of the Constitution for the Federation of Bosnia and Herzegovina: "The Republic of Bosnia and Herzegovina . . . shall continue its legal existence under international law as a state, with its internal structure modified as provided herein."

3. "Minorities treaties" were included in the Treaties of St. Germain, Triano, Neuilly, and Lausanne and in the Albanian and Lithuanian Declarations. They empowered the League of Nations to receive petitions, conduct fact-finding investigations, and issue directives to those nations in violation of the treaties. See League of Nations Publication 1927, Azcarate y Florez 1945, and Capotorti 1979.

Additionally, Dayton's attempt to address the question of "national minorities" runs headlong into previous Yugoslav efforts to manage and construct ethno-national identities. Thus an assessment of Dayton also requires that we analyze how Dayton projects identity constructs onto an already laden identity field in which deep-rooted cultural and legal identity tags have already been deployed.

This chapter explores the Dayton Accord through two historical inquiries. First, it analyzes how Dayton responds to the question of national identity as framed by earlier notions of group identity. Second, it examines Dayton in light of the minorities rights agreements of the interwar years, beginning with a brief outline of the interwar system and proceeding with a comparison of that system with Dayton. My thesis is twofold. I suggest that while the similarities between Dayton and the treaties of the interwar period could spell disaster for minority groups in the Balkans, and perhaps elsewhere as well if the international community continues to repeat its mistakes, the differences between Dayton and the interwar agreements could be sufficient to avert that disaster.

Addressing the Problem of Ethno-National Identity

Given the regime's attempts to enforce Yugoslav national identity over all other senses of belonging, the matter of national identity became increasingly important in the former Yugoslavia. Although ethno-national identity issues did not cause the wars in Croatia and Bosnia and Herzegovina, they provided the soil in which the elites' struggle for power could take root. In turn, this soil was fertilized by a combination of ingredients. These include the actions and inactions of international financial institutions that led Yugoslavia to the brink of disaster. In addition there was tremendous fear and uncertainty among the general populace, heavy state and Party control over the broadcast media, a "heritage of authoritarianism" (Janjić 1995: 33), and a lack of a civil society that could challenge government and support a diversity of opinions. Although commentators have recognized the role of nationalism in fanning the flames of war in the Balkans, few have analyzed how the Dayton Accord responds to national identity constructs hardened by years of war. To be viewed as legitimate by the people of the region, the Dayton Accord must, at the very least, address the past ways of naming identities; in order to promote long-term peace, it must somehow take steps to break down the virulent national divides that have become a reality in Bosnia and Herzegovina. Dayton accomplishes neither of these tasks.

This section will examine the development of national identity in the former Yugoslavia over three periods: (1) the formal naming of groups in the constitutional developments between 1946 and 1974; (2) the impact of the collapse of Yugoslavia; and (3) the impact of war (1992–95). Against this backdrop, the section then outlines the response of the drafters at Dayton.

Development of National Identity in Yugoslavia

Constitutional Development

Yugoslavia had three main constitutions between 1945 and its collapse:[4] 1946, 1963, and 1974. By arranging the legal and social terms with which people were to operate, each of these constitutions had an impact on shaping national identity.[5] Officially, everyone enjoyed Yugoslav nationality; however, by time of the 1946 constitution, the people of Yugoslavia were *de facto* divided into two categories—in Zoran Pajić's terms, the "hosts and the historical guests" (Pajić 1995: 162). The hosts, or nations (*narodi*), were Serbs, Croats, Slovenes, Macedonians, and Montenegrins. The guests were called national minorities.

In the 1963 constitution, the term "national minority" was replaced by the term "nationality" (*narodnost*). The word "minority" was perceived to be demeaning. The term *narodnost* was understood to include all those with national homelands elsewhere: Albanians, Hungarians, Italians, Bulgarians, Turks, Slovaks, Czechs, and Russians. Those without homelands elsewhere, such as the Romany and Vlachs, seem to have been ignored by the constitution. Perhaps the most significant development in the 1963 constitution was the elevation of the Muslims from a nationality to a nation.

In the 1974 constitution national difference became "constitutionally enshrined" (Verdery 1993: 179–203; Kaldor 1996: 42–58). Article 1 of the 1974 constitution defines Yugoslavia as "a federal state having the form of a state community of voluntarily united nations and their Socialist Republics" (Durović 1974). The possessive construction of this provision is important: the republics belonged to the nations. But many people lived outside their national homelands; the fit between homeland and nation was not perfect. Unlike earlier constitutions, under the 1974 constitution, sovereignty did not rest with the people but in the "sovereign rights" that the "nations and nationalities . . . shall exercise in the socialist republics, and in the socialist autonomous provinces . . . and in the SFRY[6] when in their common interests" (ibid.).

In a manner that lent more importance to national identity, power under the 1974 constitution was decentralized from the federal level to the republican. Each of Yugoslavia's six republics and two provinces had its own central bank and separate police, educational, and judicial systems. These units, with the exception

4. The exact date of the collapse is open to dispute. Some would set the beginning of the collapse before Tito's death in May 1980. Others would point to eruptions in Kosovo in March 1989, after the Serbian parliament had stripped Kosovo and Vojvodina of their autonomous status. Still others point to January 1991, when the Assembly of the Republic of Slovenia adopted the Charter announcing that it would initiate the procedure of disassociation from Yugoslavia. Still other dates can be found. See Silber and Little 1995.

5. This does not of course settle the question of which came first, the identity or the constitution.

6. SFRY stands for the Socialist Federal Republic of Yugoslavia.

of Bosnia and Herzegovina, were *de facto* organized largely around national identity, based on the majority nation of that region. Thus benefits from the state were in fact made based on national status. Through such arrangements, national status, "which had seemingly been buried by the 1971 intervention (Tito's squelching of nationalist movements in Croatia), returned by the back door" (Schopflin 1993: 190).

The "nationality key" system was another institutional arrangement that pushed national identity into the forefront. A scheme to ensure proportional representation of all nationalities within a republic, the "key" system became a means for many incompetent and/or corrupt Party members to achieve positions of importance simply because they were of the right minority national status. Within each republic or province, members of the majority nation complained of the incompetence of the members of the minority nation who had been promoted to high positions of power; widespread backlash against the "key" system widened national divides.[7]

Even after the 1974 constitution, Yugoslavia operated politically as a unitary state governed by a centralized communist party. The greatest flaw of the 1974 constitution was that it set up a "consensus" system that officially "prevented any decisions from being adopted if opposed by any single federal unit (including the autonomous provinces)" (Dimitrijević 1995: 60). This further weakened the federation "by paralyzing the decision-making process and removing real authority of federal decisions" (71), placing it back in the hands of the Party. With everything in the control of the Party, individuals had little incentive to become involved in politics, and under these circumstances, the concept of civil society among the population was nearly nonexistent.

The Collapse

During the years after Tito's death, the population of Yugoslavia was increasingly forced to choose sides according to national identity. Many politicians used the notion of "sovereignty" as a rhetorical device, claiming that another group was violating their own group's "sovereignty." Similarly, national status was used as a rhetorical device, with each side, beginning with the Serbs, pitting themselves against the evil Other.

In the first democratic elections, nationalism became the mechanism for political differentiation. The electorate had almost no other way to distinguish the candidates; the previous authoritarian regime had not encouraged the development of a civil society in which more sophisticated distinctions could have

---

7. Other key attributes of the Yugoslav constitutional system pertaining to national minorities included poly-ethnic rights, such as the right to use one's own language in public and to primary education in one's own language. These were counterbalanced by constitutional prohibitions *against* propagating or practicing national inequality and incitement of national, racial, or religious hatred and intolerance.

emerged. Political and economic structures swayed under the weight of internal bickering as new leaders struggled for power and international financial institutions pressed Yugoslavia to restructure its economy.[8] This situation fostered intense nationalist bureaucratic competition, and often corruption, usually along national lines (Woodward 1995: 47–81). Certainly, nationalism was not the only force pushing Yugoslavia toward collapse, but once it was co-opted by the politicians, it became one of the most important.

The Impact of War

The war affected national identity in three ways. First, it accomplished the complete demonization of other nations and national groups. State-controlled propaganda machines initiated the process by broadcasting stories of the Other's inhumanity. Over time, many of the witnesses and victims of acts of great cruelty began to tell their stories as well—and their neighbors listened. The diaspora often played an important role in this demonization process. Far away from the home region, living in nationally homogeneous marriages (at least at a rate much higher than their kin back home), the diaspora had an easier time painting the Other as evil.[9]

Second, the war precipitated the physical segregation of the population by nationality. People who had been forced to leave their villages and cities because of their national background now crowded into new cities, creating new enclaves of "their own people" (Helsinki Watch 1993, 1994). This segregation exploited and reinforced otherness.

Finally, the war closed the ranks within each nation. People throughout the former Yugoslavia were forced to decide who they were among three narrow choices: Serb, Croat or Muslim. This left four categories of people without any identity: those of mixed parentage or marriage; those of another national identity, such as Albanian or Hungarian; those who wanted to identify themselves as something else, either above the nation, such as European, or below the nation, such as a member of a particular neighborhood or organization; and those who wanted out of the labeling process altogether. Those who failed to make a choice usually left the country (if they could) or fell silent; a few stubbornly fought back, despite the extreme backlash by co-nationals against anything different and potentially challenging to the Nation (Milić 1996: 169–83).

Dayton's Response: Cementing the Ethno-National Divides

The Dayton Accord jettisons the terminology of the most recent Yugoslav constitutions—nation (*narod*) and nationality (*narodnost*). The agreement does not

8. For one review of the economic situation, see Cohen 1995: 45.

9. Those who experienced wartime atrocities tend to be much less likely to seek revenge against an entire group of people, although they may want to avenge the death or torture of a particular family member (Mertus 1997, 1999).

even mention the words "nations" and "nationalities," except in referring to international documents by name and in a section on the rights of refugees to return. Instead, Dayton and the Preamble to the Constitution of the Republic of Bosnia and Herzegovina (an annex to Dayton) refer primarily to three groups: Bosniacs,[10] Croats, and Serbs as "constituent peoples . . . (along with others)." Those who did not fall into this "group of three" saw their status reduced from nation (*narod*) or national minority (*narodnosti*) to complete invisibility. The Constitution of the Federation of Bosnia and Herzegovina (the smaller entity) makes clear that there are only two constituent nations, Muslims and Croats—thereby devaluing the status of Serbs to that of the invisible. The omission of the words *narod* and *narodnost* from the Dayton Accord did not make the problem of group identity go away; rather, it created a new basis for conflict.

Dayton, it may be argued, actually cements the national divide by creating a system of nation-based governance. Under its provisions, two smaller sub-entities are drawn according to battlelines, which in turn reflect national identity: Republika Srpska (Bosnian Serb) and the Federation of Bosnia and Herzegovina (Croat and Muslim/Bosniac). These two entities are held together by a "thin roof,"[11] a central government with so little power that it "makes the American Articles of Confederation of two centuries ago look like a centralized, unitary form of government" (Morrison 1996: 145). The central government, the "Republic of Bosnia and Herzegovina," is responsible for foreign policy; foreign trade and customs; monetary policies; immigration, refugee, and asylum policy and regulation; international and inter-entity criminal law enforcement; establishing international communication facilities; regulation of inter-entity transportation; air traffic control; enacting legislation to carry out the decisions of the presidency or responsibilities of the federal assembly; and funding and budgeting for federal institutions (Constitution for the Federation of Bosnia and Herzegovina [hereafter Constitution], Art. 3, sec. 1, and Art. 4, sec. 4). The remaining responsibilities of government, including promulgating and enforcing local civil and criminal laws and control over courts (except for the joint Constitutional Court, the only federal court) is given to the entities.

The entire federal government is divided into three parts, according to the same limited choice of ethno-national identity—Serb, Croat, or Muslim ("Bosniac"). The executive arm of the government has three presidents, one from each group. Even the armed forces is decentralized in threes: "Each member of the Presidency shall, by virtue of the office, have civilian command authority over armed forces" (Constitution, Art. 5, sec. 5[a]). Given that each ethno-national group has at least one army, this provision effectively creates three armies di-

10. According to some observers and participants in the peace process, the term "Bosniac" has become "a euphemism for Muslim" (Szasz 1996). However, "Bosniac" could also mean all persons who do not identify themselves as Serb or Croat.

11. This term was used by Muhamed Sacirbey and others involved in the Dayton negotiations (see Sacirbey 1996).

vided along ethno-national lines. Similarly the bicameral legislature is proportioned equally into the three national categories. The upper house (House of Peoples) has five representatives from each group; the lower house (House of Representatives) has fourteen from each (Article 4, secs. 1, 2, 3[b]).

Dayton consequently perpetuates the rule of consensus that previously worked so well to block any chance of democratic decision-making and promote national splintering. In either house of parliament, block voting by any one national group, and in some cases the simple failure of a group to show up for a vote, can defeat a legislative proposal. In the upper house, for example, any action can fail if opposed by two-thirds of a national group. These complex consensus provisions were adopted at Dayton, not because they will work, but because Serbian president Milošević refused to sign the agreement without them (Silber 1995: 308). Milošević was well aware that if the government had been permitted to operate through some form of majority vote, a coalition of Muslims and Croats representatives could have always outvoted the Serbs. On the other hand, the present compromise grants any national group the power to make the central government unworkable; a *de facto* delegation of all state power to the entities.

"Kin-states"—that is, states composed primarily of the same national group as another entity—are recognized as having special status under the plan. Unlike most federal constitutions, which forbid their subnational units to enter into treaties or other agreements with foreign governments, the Constitution for the Federation of Bosnia and Herzegovina explicitly permits each entity to "establish special parallel relationships with neighboring states consistent with the sovereignty and territorial integrity of Bosnia and Herzegovina" (Art. 3, sec. 2[a]). Among the foreseeable arrangements, this provision will likely permit Republika Srpska to enter into agreements with "Yugoslavia" (also predominately ethnic Serb), thus effectively achieving the Serb nationalists' goal of creating a "Greater Serbia."

On what appears to be a more positive note for ethno-national minorities, outsiders play a creative and essential role in the new government, particularly with respect to decision-making bodies considering questions of human rights and related issues. The people of the former Yugoslavia tend to view the intervention of outsiders in tie-breaking and supervisory positions as legitimate and potentially helpful. The Constitutional Court is made up of nine members, two from each national group and three foreign "neutrals," appointed by the European Court of Human Rights (Constitution, Art. 6, sec. 1). The European Court of Human Rights also appoints three outsiders to join the six local members (again two from each group) of the commission that considers the claims of refugees (Dayton Accord, Annex 7, Art. 9, sec. 1). The Organization for Security and Cooperation in Europe (OSCE) appoints the Human Rights Ombudsman, an individual who in the beginning will be a citizen of another state, to investigate and make reports on the existing human rights violations (not those committed during war) (ibid., Annex 6, Art. 5). The Committee of Ministers of the Council of Europe appoints eight outside members to complement the six local members (again, two from each group) to a Human Rights Chamber, a body that reviews complaints filed by individuals or by the Human Rights Ombudsman (ibid., Annex 6, Art. 5, sec. 7). Similarly, UNESCO appoints two outside members to a five member "Commission to Preserve National Monuments" (ibid., Annex 8, Art. 2).

The Dayton Accord further establishes an extensive structure for human rights protection: "Bosnia and Herzegovina and both Entities shall ensure the highest level of internationally recognized human rights and fundamental freedoms" (Constitution, Art. 2, sec. 1). To accomplish this goal, Dayton both creates new mechanisms, such as the Human Rights Chamber and the Refugee Commission, and builds in an array of existing international and regional human rights systems and mechanisms; it both lists a series of rights and incorporates a list of international and regional instruments. Of these instruments, the European Convention on Human Rights (United Nations Treaty Series 1950: 222) is supreme. The constitution specifies that this convention and its protocols "shall apply directly in Bosnia and Herzegovina" and that these "shall have priority over all other law" (Art. 2, sec. 2).

Dayton includes numerous protections for people of minority nations, albeit for the most part of an individualistic and not of a collective nature. At the same time, the Constitution of Bosnia and Herzegovina grants citizenship regardless of "association with a national minority" (Art. 1, sec. 7[b]). Also the Annexed Agreement on Refugees and Displaced Persons calls for the prosecution of persons in the military, paramilitary, and police forces who are "responsible for serious violations of the basic rights of persons belonging to ethnic or minority groups" (Dayton Accord, Annex 7, Art. 1, sec. 3[e]). In addition, many of the regional and international guarantees referenced to in the document safeguard the rights of minorities.[12] Also, the Dayton Accord contains extensive provisions requiring cooperation with international human rights organizations (Annex 6, Art. 13). These include the UN Commission on Human Rights, the UN High Commissioner on Human Rights, the OSCE, the supervisory bodies of human rights treaties and the International War Crimes Tribunal for the Former Yugoslavia and Rwanda.

To be effective, these human rights guarantees must be enforced. Without enforcement, the operation of the Dayton Accord may well serve to legitimize nationalist interests under the guise of protecting minority rights and securing peace. Will the positive measures undertaken to promote human rights be sufficient to offset the seemingly inoperable system of government created by Dayton and its demeaning of peoples who do not or will not fit into the "group of three?" As we shall see, the legal approach to minority protection adopted at Dayton has much in common with that adopted in the interwar period, which, as history attests, proved insufficient to protect religious, national, and linguistic minorities.

---

12. Two of the regional instruments provide particularly extensive guarantees for national minorities. See *European Charter* 1992 and "Framework Convention" 1994.

The Interwar Plans: Dayton's Ghost

After World War I, despite the radical rearrangement of European boundaries to conform to a principle of nationality and despite wide-scale movements to conform with the goal of "one nation, one state," it proved impossible to avoid creating religious, ethno-national, and linguistic minorities. The twenty to twenty-five million people who remained "outside of their nation-states" were placed under the protection of the League of Nations. This was to enable them to "live side by side in one and the same state, without succumbing to the temptation of each trying to force his own nationality on the other" (Robinson 1943: 35).

Scope of Protections

By design, the League of Nations system for the international protection of minority groups was exceptional: it applied to a limited set of states a limited set of rights. "It purported not to establish a general jurisprudence applicable wherever racial, linguistic, or religious minorities existed, but to facilitate the solution of problems of minority groups in countries where 'owing to special circumstances,' these problems might present particular difficulties" (Claude 1955: 17). Moreover, states subject to the provisions—the so-called "minorities states"— felt unjustly discriminated against, since the obligations imposed on them by the great powers differed from those required of other states. The selective nature of the system eroded its legitimacy and hindered adherence to its terms.

In general, the system consisted of three types of obligations: multipartite minorities treaties and the special chapters of peace treaties dealing with minority groups; declarations made by certain states before the Council of the League of Nations; and regional, bi-partite agreements—notably the Germano-Polish Convention of May 15, 1922, relating to Upper Silesia (Stone 1933).

The terms of obligation varied according to the status of the state (Claude 1955: 16). Defeated states—Austria, Hungary, Bulgaria, and Turkey—were bound by minority provisions inserted into the various peace treaties. New or enlarged states—Poland, Czechoslovakia, Yugoslavia, Romania, and Greece— concluded special minorities treaties with the Principal Allies and the Associated Powers (France, Japan, the United Kingdom, and the United States). Some states that fell within or between these two categories made declarations to the Council of the League of Nations, including Albania, Lithuania, Latvia, Estonia, Finland (concerning the Åland Islands), and Iraq. As a great power, Germany was treated somewhat differently. Instead of agreeing to general minority clauses for all of its territories and populations, Germany signed a bilateral treaty with Poland, which created a special minority regime for Upper Silesia.

The instruments purported to safeguard certain rights of "racial, religious or linguistic minorities," but the framers of the system made it clear that they regarded this terminology as synonymous with "national minorities." The obligations contained in the minorities treaties and declarations fall into four general categories: (1) nationality provisions; (2) negative rights; (3) positive rights and; and (4) specific minority provisions. With the exception of the last category, the exact wording of the articles varied little from treaty to treaty. These obligations shall be considered in turn.

Nationality Provisions. The nationality provisions concerned the acquisition of nationality by persons belonging to minority groups. For example, the Treaty Between the Principal Allied and Associated Powers and the Serb-Croat-Slovene State declared "to be Serb-Croat-Slovene nationals *ipso facto* and without the requirement of any formality, Austrian, Hungarian or Bulgarian nationals habitually resident or possessing the rights of citizenship" (*Treaty* 1919: chap. 1, art. 4) or "born in the said territory of parents habitually resident or possessing the right of citizenship" (ibid.). Furthermore, the treaty provided that "persons referred to above who are over eighteen years of age will be entitled under the conditions contained in said treaties to opt for any other nationality which may be open to them" (ibid., chap. 1, art. 3)

Negative Rights. Individuals belonging to minority groups were granted non-discrimination and negative equality rights, unimpaired by their membership in the minority group. The treaties demanded, with only minor variations: the right to life and liberty (chap. 1, art. 2); freedom of religion (chap. 1, art. 2); equality before the law and enjoyment of the same civil and political rights "without distinction as to race, language or religion" (chap. 1, art. 7); and freedom from interference with the "enjoyment of civil and political rights, as for instance admission to public employment, functions and honors, or the exercise of professions and industries" because of "differences of religion, creed or confession" (chap. 1, art. 7).

Positive Rights. The treaties also included provisions that promoted "positive equality," to enable minority groups to "preserve and develop their national culture and consciousness" (Azcarate 1945: 82). These included the right to the use of their own language in private relations; the use of their own language before the courts; adequate facilities for a public education in primary schools in their own language, whenever there was a "considerable proportion" of minority students; the establishment of religious and welfare institutions, schools, and other educational facilities under their own control and with their own language; and the right to an equitable proportion of state and communal expenditures for educational, religious, and welfare purposes.

Specific Minorities Provisions. For the most part, the provisions applied equally to members of all minority groups within the jurisdiction of a particular treaty. However, Muslims received special protections in the treaty with the Kingdom of Serbs, Croats, and Slovenes as did the Jewish minority population in treaties between the Allied Powers and Greece, Poland, and Romania, as well as in the Lithuania declaration (Macartney 1934: 230–52); stipulations for the Magyar and Saxon communities in Transylvania were included in the treaty with

Romania; Czechoslovakia provided for an autonomous territory for Ruthenians; and Greece accepted special obligations for the Vlachs of the Pindus region and for the non-Greek communities of Mount Athos (ibid.).

As worded, most minority clauses provided protection for the rights of individual members of minorities and not the minority groups as collective entities (Claude 1955: 19; Robinson 1943: 71). This was intentional; the drafters deliberately avoided most terminology that would have clearly given minorities status as corporate units, except for the purpose of allocation of an equitable share of public funds for schools and the like (Temperley 1920: 137). To recognize minorities per se, the drafters feared, would be to recognize "states within states," a concept at odds with then prevalent absolute notions of state sovereignty. Thus even the positive rights were framed in individual terms, as arising out of membership in a minority and facilitating the maintenance and development of group life (Chaszar 1988: 3). At the same time, however, the minorities treaties included references to group-based rights, such as stipulations concerning proportional representation and political and cultural autonomy.

Innovations over Earlier Times

Three interrelated elements differentiated the minorities clauses from the previous systems: who established and guaranteed the provisions of this system; the methods by which it was to maintain peace and protect the rights of ethno-national minority groups; and the assumptions upon which it rested.

For the first time, enforcement was not left merely to the signatories or to the prerogative of an interested state, usually a "kin-state"; instead the League of Nations guaranteed the agreement, thus intending to give a "more disinterested character to the performance of international obligations toward minorities" (Robinson 1943: 40). Unlike previous attempts to guarantee minority protection, an independent judicial institution, the Permanent Court of International Justice, was to settle disputes and not the state that had the most political power (or the highest degree of self-interest) (Capotorti 1979: 24–25). Outside "neutrals" played a special role in other aspects of minority protections as well. The plan for Upper Silesia, for example, envisioned the establishment of a Mixed Commission (presided over by neutrals) to which members of minority groups could address complaints, and an Arbitral Tribunal (also presided over by neutrals) (Kaeckenbeeck 1942).

Not only were "neutrals" brought in to guarantee minority rights, but also the methods at their disposal were revolutionary in admitting the right of individual minority groups—who were not then recognized as subjects of international law—to appeal directly to an international body. Although individual complaints were not provided for in the treaties, through a series of interpretive documents members of minority groups, other states, and other entities gained the right to petition for redress of discrimination.

The assumptions on which the minorities treaties were grounded also demonstrated a dramatic change in the use of international policy proposals. In contrast with the earlier ad hoc system of opposing alliances, collective security was viewed as essential for maintaining the peace.[13] The treaties also rested on the belief that people of different nationalities could live in peace, side by side, in the same state; political democracy and economic liberalism were values to be promoted. Moreover, the system recognized a need for both external and internal guarantees for national minority protection. As Inis Claude explains: "The operation of the treaties and declarations depended heavily upon the compliance of minority states with the obligation to treat the stipulations as fundamental laws and to implement them by internal legislation. However, it was deemed essential to supplement internal provisions by an external guarantee, based on the premise that the treatment of minorities in the treaty-bound states was a problem of international concern" (Claude 1955: 20).

By implicitly and explicitly providing for both external and internal guarantees, the interwar plans posed a challenge to the then accepted notion of sovereignty. The "intervention of an external agency in the relationship between a state and its own nationals was clearly incompatible with the concept of absolute sovereignty" (21), the invalidation of which the interwar plans demanded: "In the Versailles peace system, the minorities provisions constituted a corollary and corrective to the principle of national self-determination. They became possible only through the restriction of absolute state sovereignty. Insofar as the disturbance of external peace was caused by internal discord, the minorities provisions, as a means of regulating the relations between national groups were a part of the general peace structure" (Robinson 1943: 41).

Indeed, the Kingdom of Serbs, Croats, and Slovenes, Romania, and Poland fought against the minorities treaties largely on these grounds (Robinson 1943: 154–55). Despite these innovations, the minorities treaties proved insufficient to protect the rights of minority groups and preserve peace. The explanation may lie in the lack of political will on the part of the international community to stand behind the League of Nations and enforce the provisions, and the lack of the will of the "Minorities States" to stand by their agreements. However, weaknesses within the system encouraged and exacerbated the lack of political will, and the system was crippled at the outset by the impression that it was of a temporary nature. Enforcement mechanisms were weak: the treaties were not enforceable in domestic courts, and the Council of the League of Nations established no effective rules of enforcement. At the same time, "Minorities States" frequently did everything within their power to block enforcement[14] and would forestall peti-

---

13. For historical background, see Grenville 1987.

14. States could enact provisions to undermine the intention of the treaties. For example, although minority groups are allowed schools in their own language, a state could deprive private schools of the right to issue diplomas. In addition, economic measures that would have a particular impact on a national minority could be enacted as long as the provisions did not single out the minority explicitly.

tions by imposing obstacles intended to intimidate and discourage complainants. While individual minorities filed few complaints, self-interested kin-states that were members of the Council of the League of Nations tended to take the initiative in implementing League guarantees. The provisions within the treaties were vague and sketchy; they failed both to account for differing needs for and claims to education and autonomous institutions among minority groups and to settle major, explosive issues such as language rights. Finally, the minorities provisions applied only to a select number of states. Ultimately, these drawbacks outweighed the treaties' innovations, and the agreements failed to safeguard the rights of members of minority groups.

Looking Forward: Foreboding and Hope

The Dayton Accord displays a persistent faith in some of the underlying assumptions and practices of the interwar international legal policy proposals. At the same time it shows a pragmatic shift to address today's conflicts between members of different ethno-national groups in the context of postwar regional and international human rights systems and mechanisms. This section examines the similarities and differences between the Dayton Accord and the interwar minorities treaties and asks whether members of minority groups will fare better under Dayton.

Similarities with Interwar Schemes

The discredited schemes, designed to protect minority rights in the interwar period, evinced a "paradoxical 'alliance' between turbulent nationalist passion and a newly autonomous international law" (Berman 1993: 1798). In contrast, today's international law, grounded in a host of post–World War II agreements and practices, can no longer be considered newly autonomous. The place of law in the regional and international spheres has taken hold; and in the words of the Vienna Declaration from the 1993 World Conference on Human Rights (United Nations Department of Public Information 1993: 20M), human rights can now be said to be "universal, indivisible and interdependent and interrelated." Regional and international systems and mechanisms designed to protect human rights are now in place. Still, given its own paradoxical alliance with nationalism, the Dayton Accord has much in common with the minority protections spawned by the Treaty of Versailles. Some of these similarities are beneficial for members of minority groups; many are foreboding. I consider only the foreboding ones here.

First, the Dayton Accord, just like the minority rights protections of the interwar period, approaches nationalism with a "mixture of desire and terror" (Berman 1993: 1805). The carving up of the newly recognized state of Bosnia and Herzegovina along ethno-national lines reinforced the concept of the "nation," an imaginary community defined in opposition to the "Other" by reference to real and imagined differences in history, culture, language, and tradition. The national purification of Croatia, and the establishment of a "blood" principle for Croatian voters (whereby "Croats" living anywhere could vote in Croatian elections), further entrenched Balkan nationalism as a defining social, political, and legal principle. Granted, Dayton did not create the nationalisms or draw the battle lines; it only recognized territories already controlled by the parties, a situation that no state had the will to reverse. Nevertheless, in doing so, ethno-nationalism was not only tolerated by the Dayton Accord, but once again in European history, the nation became part of a "solution" for peace.

Second, international diplomacy in the former Yugoslavia may have begun with a call for human rights, but it culminated in the same legal pragmatism of the interwar period: those with power to act as the state *were* the state. Whether and how the powerful gained their power became less and less relevant. U.S. Assistant Secretary of State Richard Holbrook's guiding principle for diplomacy was simple: negotiate with those who have power over people at any given time—stop the war at all cost. This strategy brought accused Bosnian Serb war criminals Karadžić and Mladić to the bargaining table and then, ultimately, Serbian president, Slobodan Milošević, as the negotiator for Bosnian and Croatian Serbs, populations that never elected Milošević as their leader. Croatian president, Franjo Tudjman, became the negotiator for Bosnian Croats, a group from which he enjoyed no formal legal mandate.

Holbrook and the other diplomats cannot be blamed for adopting a strategy that merely reflected political and military realities. Indeed, Holbrook's negotiations only became potent when power shifted, in particular when Croatia destroyed the Krajina Serbs and threatened to drive the Bosnian Serbs out of Banja Luka, and when, after Srebrenica, NATO finally became involved in the conflict. The fact that negotiations divided the peoples by nationalist groupings was of little concern to Holbrook and his team. That the success of the agreement depended on Milošević gaining and retaining power over Bosnian Serbs and Tudjman doing the same for Bosnian Croats could not stand in the way of negotiations. The success of the Dayton Accord, like the interwar agreements, *required* the support and cooperation of nationalist leaders.

Third, many of the fundamental assumptions underlying both Dayton and the interwar minorities schemes were the same. Both saw a need for collective security, the promotion of political democracy and economic liberalism, external and internal guarantees for minority rights, and the limited right of external bodies to interfere in the relationship between a state and its own nationals.

More troubling for members of minority groups, just as in the interwar years, in the former Yugoslavia "the problem of nationalism came to be perceived as a primal 'clamoring' to which one should respond with a sophisticated and hetero-geneously composed 'Plan' " (Berman 1993: 1800). Nationalisms, supported by myth and history, are firmly rooted in the culture of the Balkans. Economic crisis and political and social insecurity laid the foundations for chauvinist ideologies in the then Yugoslavia. Far from a primal clamoring, however, nationalism in the former Yugoslavia spread as the direct result of a deliberate political plan crafted by political and academic elites at the top. The emergence of nationalist ideologies was far from inevitable; in a calculated series of maneuvers, political and academic elites tapped nationalist undercurrents, squelching alternative voices and pitting national groups against each other. It is of some concern, therefore, that the Dayton Accord does nothing to challenge those in positions of power, but instead further entrenches their grasp. At the time of this writing, Serbian president Slobodan Milošević and Croatian president Franjo Tudjman continue to direct, or at least condone—human rights violations with impunity, as the foreign media continue to read the conflict as primal, overlooking the hand of political elites in shaking the nationalist tree.

Fourth, during the interwar years and under Dayton, relationships with neighboring kin-states and subsequent bilateral treaties were permitted and even encouraged. In the interwar years, bilateral treaties with kin-states, although initially bolstering the minorities agreements, eventually led to their demise (Robinson 1943: 50). There is every reason to believe that unless preventive steps are taken, the same problem with bilateral agreements will reoccur in the Balkans.

Fifth, the Dayton Accord contains many of the specific attributes of the interwar plans; in particular it is reminiscent of the plans designed to resolve the disputes over the Saar, Danzig, and Upper Silesia. Similarities include (1) minority guarantees, including nationality provisions, nondiscrimination provisions and the guarantee of negative rights, and even some positive rights; (2) provisions for emigration and restitution of property; (3) provisions for self-determination of the peoples, including popular elections; (4) limited supranational integration, including a joint presidency, parliamentary assembly, constitutional court, and institutions pertaining to arbitration, human rights, refugees and displaced persons, preservation of national monuments, and public corporations; and (5) internationalization, such as agreement to a short-term international military presence and an international police task force, and to neutral regional and international organizations and individuals playing a critical role in the structure and operations of the new federal government.

The core similarities between the Dayton Accord and the interwar schemes are foreboding. The possibility that the rights of minority groups will be better safeguarded under the Dayton Accord than in interwar times is guided not by technical innovations, as there are very few such innovations, but rather by something else: shifts in international law and diplomacy.

Shifts in International Law and Diplomacy

The interwar minorities treaties and the Dayton Accord were both reached during a time of complex changes in international law and diplomacy. In both periods, lawyers and diplomats struggled to reconcile international law with nationalisms.

The interwar lawyers bypassed "the dichotomy between statist positivism and liberal nationalism in favor of a simultaneous affirmation of the autonomy of international law and an openness to the vital forces of nationalism" (Berman 1993: 1803). This meant reshaping nationalism by endowing it with legal form. At the same time, "the constraints of the stable legal order grounded in sovereignty were rejected in favor of an autonomous, 'experimental' exploration of specifically legal international techniques, doctrines and institutions" (1805). Similarly, the Dayton lawyers endowed the nationalisms of the former Yugoslavia with legal form, setting up a system under which today's international human rights techniques, doctrines, and institutions would check nationalisms. The main difference between the two periods is that the global legal environment has changed, shifting further away from states to regional and international systems and mechanisms. While this shift may be seen as cause for alarm, as states may be presupposed as necessary enforcers of rights (Ghai 1996), it may also provide an opening in which we can locate hope.

On its face, the Dayton Accord acts as if it supports statist positivism. On the one hand, it trumpets the legal fiction of an independent, functioning state of Bosnia and Herzegovina. It creates entities formed through battle and takes steps to encourage the development of a government within the resulting structure. In doing so, the Dayton Accord bows to the kind of statist thinking that is a core tenet of many of the leaders of Croats, Serbs, Muslim Slavs, and Albanians of the former Yugoslavia. According to these leaders, every nation must have a state and every state must include all members of the nation, although the collective identity may indeed transcend state boundaries. The provisions of Dayton protecting human rights and the expression of minority viewpoints can be an attempt to open space for the development of civil society within the resulting weak federal state.

On the other hand, however, the state created by the Dayton Accord is at odds with the statist paradigm. Each of the two internal entities of the state of Bosnia and Herzegovina have more power than the federal unit, and as a result of formal and informal agreements with kin-states, the boundaries of the state are de facto porous. Moreover, and also contrary to the traditional statist paradigm, the international community is invited to make decisions and take actions normally within the sovereignty of a state, from international policing to choosing members of the Constitutional Court of Bosnia and Herzegovina. In addition, to the extent that self-determination is viewed as an element of a state, the Dayton Accord's recognition of a Bosnia created by battle runs squarely against this principle. The Bosnia that the local population had voted for prior to the war and that the international community had originally recognized no longer effectively exists; the boundaries, character, and composition of the state have changed dramatically. In reality, today's Bosnia and Herzegovina does not operate like a state, but rather more akin to an interim arrangement, enforced from above by the international community.

In moving away from the statist paradigm, the Dayton Accord is influenced most by the environment in which it finds itself: a world marked by rapid globalization in markets, information, and security arrangements. "The past role of the nation-state," Lung-Chu Chen writes, "cannot be taken for granted without a critical reappraisal in light of the changing demands, expectations and conditions of the present" (Chen 1989: 26). These developments chip away at state boundaries. According to Richard Falk, "The essence of the new order is the globalization of capital and the power of market forces, bypassing even the strongest states. States are now unable really to control interest rates or the value of their own currencies, the most elemental aspects of traditional notions of territorial sovereignty" (Falk 1993: 398). Residents of Europe, especially in areas of conflict, look to regional and international legal institutions for protection, jobs, and goods. Their leaders look to international bodies for markets, military support, and other assistance.

Where the interwar period witnessed a shift in international law from states to nations (and to individuals as well), Dayton demonstrates a double shift. Global power and the reach of international law have moved simultaneously out to international and regional actors (such as financial institutions, security arrangements, and mechanisms and institutions to protect human rights) and down to transnational social forces. Transnational social forces, from environmental and human rights NGOs to communal groups that spread over nation-state lines, are "gradually shaping a very weak but still real global civil society that represents a form of globalization from below" (Falk 1993: 399). Leaders of nation-states today have lost power, as they must answer to both of these levels if they are to survive. At the same time, with the decline of the nation-state, responsibility for rights enforcement has shifted increasingly from the state to regional and international entities. Both today's problems and tomorrow's solutions must recognize a new concept of state sovereignty.

Conclusion

The main failing of the Dayton Accord lies in its attempt to impose a firm set of ethno-national categories on the people of Bosnia and Herzegovina. On one hand, these categories jettison the identity constructs of the past, and on the other, they perpetuate much of what went wrong in the old Yugoslav government, in particular the charade that an ethno-nationally divided government could function on "consensus." The Dayton Accord offers few technical innovations over the schemes to protect minorities of the interwar years. However, the legal, economic, and political landscape has changed greatly since the interwar minorities treaties. Today's international policy proposals for dealing with the tensions between states, ethno-national groups, and nationalisms are framed within the context of increased global interdependence, accelerated regionalization, and marked development in international legal systems and mechanisms. It is within these changes that we may find salvation.

The Dayton Accord also reflects the understanding that in today's Europe nation-state boundaries have become more fluid and less relevant for the purpose of fashioning guarantees for regional and international security and minority rights. International and local elites create regional and international law and policy on treatment of minority groups; international treaties and customary law on human rights can serve to set their boundaries. This process in turn influences the identity of national groups and the range of acceptable solutions to their problems. Ultimately, as in the interwar period, enforcement of the Dayton Accord will depend not only on legal technique but also on political will. Given the shifts in the global landscape, it will be actors above and below the state who are called upon to act.

Map 5   Post-Dayton Bosnia and Herzegovina

PART IV

EXPRESSIVE CULTURE AS INSTRUMENT AND OUTCOME OF WAR

The Yugoslav War Through Cartoons

Goran Jovanović

A political cartoonist is a social satirist of his time. He looks for the contradictions in social phenomena normally seen as rigid and serious. In fact, the cartoon induces the newspaper reader to apprehend the core values of his social environment, the shared concerns and emotions of his time. The cartoon represents and reproduces social reality as a fiction that through pictorial representation, becomes the reality. While remaining a product of mass media, the political cartoon constitutes an authentic document of the time.

Besides graphics, a political cartoon often contains text. To achieve the narrative purpose of the composition, the author speaks to the newspaper reader through the persons, symbols, or icons depicted in the cartoon. Playing with pictures and words to make a joke, he may emphasize any of these elements. The visualization of the joke is the essential feature of the cartoon and distinguishes it from both the newspaper article and the illustration.

The author wishes to thank all the cartoonists whose work appears in this essay, who, without exception, agreed to the publication of their drawings without charges or royalties. The cartoons in this chapter first appeared in the Yugoslavian, German, Swiss, Austrian, and Turkish press. The paper received the "Thomas Inge Award 1998" in comics scholarship by Popular Culture Association at the national conference in Orlando, Florida. This article is part of a larger project that includes about seven thousand cartoons on the Yugoslav crisis originating from all former republics and the international press and over a hundred interviews with cartoonist worldwide. The conclusion refers, therefore, also to a series of drawings and interviews that constitute part of the author's archives.

Within the field of political action, the cartoonist challenges common views on political issues. His sources of information include the mass media, TV news and documentaries, and conversations with ordinary people about their daily concerns on political affairs. Observing the political scene and following major news, the cartoonist pictorially represents events and the decisions and declarations of political leaders. He not only integrates and condenses opinions and debates from the public sphere but also goes one step further. By evaluating his surroundings, he expresses his subversive desire for improvement.

As a medium of mass communication, the cartoon provides a framework within which one may recognize, announce, and dissect controversial social issues that affect the lives of ordinary people. Of course, the political cartoon is a medium of contemporary political and cultural criticism. Through paradox, absurdity, and black humor, the cartoonist draws public attention to political events. Thus the cartoon may anticipate what could happen in the society if current political trends persist. Democratic, grotesque, and appealing, the political cartoon encourages the participation of ordinary people in public affairs. Thus, while subtly analyzing the political environment of the day, the cartoonist actively participates in the social history of his time (Jovanović 1997).

The media events and decision makers most involved in the war in former Yugoslavia are prime source material for political cartoons. By commenting on the political attitudes of decision makers, political cartoons become an important means for understanding the public perception of the Yugoslav crisis. In addition, when it reflects the mutual images of the warring parties, including those held by outside observers, the political cartoon becomes a powerful instrument of war propaganda. Yet it may also convey antiwar views and critique the war. In fact, social and political satire is often only a step away from political and war propaganda.

Cartoon Art as the Anticipation of War

Invisible during times of peace, the increased importance of group identities may radically transform the self-perception of ordinary people and put ethnic and religious identity at the service of the politics of the day. As a result, belief in interethnic coexistence and religious tolerance—a cornerstone of multiethnic and multiconfessional societies—is called into question. Notions of partnership and union within diversity are replaced by mistrust and a rejection of that which appears strange and foreign.

At the end of the 1980s, the Yugoslav Federation was under enormous pressure from both domestic and international sources. The emergence of centrifugal forces from within the Federation, coinciding with the end of the cold war, accelerated the implosion of the Federation that led to the Slovenian and Croatian declarations of independence in June 1991. Thus the Yugoslav puzzle broke into its basic ethnic and confessional elements (Koch and Jovanović 1997: 493–97).

For almost a decade before the war, Yugoslav cartoonists were producing drawings that anticipated the events of the 1990s.[1] Through the language of humor and satire, they were already expressing their views about the social and political changes of the time and the impending disintegration of societal structures (Dragojević 1993; Jovanović 1996). One cartoonist, a Serb from Belgrade named Predrag Koraksić ("Corax"), published a cartoon one year before the war began showing a person watching live television coverage of a bomb falling on his own house (below).[2] The house stands for the Yugoslav state; the man inside, for the ordinary people of Yugoslavia. The use of white on black for the exterior, rather than black on white, increases the dramatic effect. The drawing depicts a

1. For a cartoonist's view of the changes in Yugoslav society in the 1980s, see the catalogs—especially the prize-winning cartoons—of the annual *Yugoslav Cartoon Competition "Pjer"* (Beograd: Večernje Novosti). Also see the monographs of the cartoonists listed in the references.

2. Predrag Koraksić ("Corax"), *Demokratija Danas* (Belgrade), June 1990.

quiet night scene: chimney smoke, a sky full of stars, a quarter moon in the background, a garden with a small tree and a wooden fence behind the house. The bomb is about to shatter the quiet of the scene as well and kill the man inside the house.

The scene reveals the tension between the falling bomb and the motionlessness of the person looking at his house on TV. Corax: "I had no specific event in mind, just the general mood leading toward the fatal events that were to follow."[3] The expression "general mood" reflects the force of unspoken, shared sentiments, but ones not expressed in terms of collective action. The people feel but do not act. The paradox is made up of two apparent contradictions. The falling bomb is dynamic, the man is static. Nothing can stop the bomb from reaching its target; nothing can prevent the destruction of the house representing the common Yugoslav state and the death of the man representing the shared Yugoslav identity.

The inescapable nature of fate is thus emphasized. Apparently, the only option is to do nothing and wait for events to unfold. Although Corax's drawing illustrates the last image before the end, he allows the newspaper reader to look at an image of a catastrophe that already happened. Living under conditions of the prevailing political instability, the cartoon illustrates concerns felt by ordinary people about the fatal consequences that the political change may have for their everyday life.

In the prewar press of the different Yugoslav republics there was already significant cartoon art. The international press was attracted to the conflict only when it became an international event. The declarations of independence of Slovenia and Croatia from the Yugoslav Federation put the crisis at the top of world news and on the agenda of international decision makers. It is, however, interesting that Turkish, Austrian, and German cartoonists were among the first to portray the conflict. Public opinion in these states was generally more sensitive to the Balkan conflict than that in France, Britain, or the United States. This seems due to geographical proximity, historical ties to the Ottoman and Austrian empires, and the military involvement of the Second and the Third German Reichs in the Balkans during two world wars.[4]

Self-Destruction, Collective Suicide, Disintegration

The first international cartoons published in spring and early summer 1991 perceived the conflict as a civil war. The most common interpretation was to represent the disintegration of the Yugoslav Federation into its ethnic components or

---

3. Corax, letter to the author, Belgrade, June 3, 1997.
4. Soviet/Russian cartoonist did drawings on the crisis, but I did not have copies of them in my collection.

distinct republics. German cartoonist, Rainer Hachfeld from Berlin and Austrian cartoonist Gustav Peichl ("Ironimus") from Vienna both used the metaphors of self-destruction and collective suicide in commenting on the Yugoslav conflict.

Rainer Hachfeld uses the image of a human body whose arms and legs are fighting against each other (below).[5] The body carries the Yugoslav communist flag with the red star in the middle representing the Yugoslav Federation as a common state. While three limbs are missing (both legs and the left arm), the body still retains its head and right arm. In the scene, blood splashes from the limbs and body, thus depicting imminent violence and self-destruction. Working from the German viewpoint, in 1997 Hachfeld summarized his views on the Yugoslav crisis as observed in 1991: "I suppose that a lot of cartoonists at the beginning of the civil war in Yugoslavia looked upon the country as an unit, so that the image of a person tearing one's self apart [Selbstzerfleischung] seemed appropriate. It was only later that distinctions were made between particular ethnic and political groups."[6]

Austrian cartoonist Gustav Peichl ("Ironimus") works with ideas of self-destruction and collective suicide, like those of Hachfeld, but uses yet another

5. Rainer Hachfeld, *Neues Deutschland* (Berlin), 1991.
6. Rainer Hachfeld, letter to the author, Berlin, May 13, 1997.

iconographical language (below).[7] He distinguishes between the two major national groups, Croats and Serbs, on whose mutual consensus the Yugoslav communist state (1943–91) was based. Ironimus represents a Yugoslav man as a Balkan cliché seen from the Austrian viewpoint. The man has a mustache, a wide nose, and military hat with red star that reminds one of the partisan fighters of World War II. In his mid-forties, he represents the generation born immediately after 1945. He is wearing officers' epaulets, the one on the right labeled "Croatia," the one on the left, "Serbia." He holds a revolver to each side of his head. No doubt, he is committing suicide. He has not killed himself yet, though death seems imminent.

Croatia and Serbia are regarded as major powers within the multiethnic Yugoslav Federation. Their unity under the communist power structure was seen as constituting the cornerstone of the common state. Subsequently, both are seen as equally to blame for the disruption of that unity. Their rivalry makes them equally responsible for the act of self-destruction and collective suicide.

However, ethnic conflict also produces social conflicts. Nikola Otaš, a Serb cartoonist from Belgrade who lived in the Croatian town of Split until 1991, points out these changes. By considering the breakup of interethnic marriages, he looks at changing social cohesion in everyday life (page 261).[8] A retired officer of the Yugoslav People's Army (JNA) and married to a Croatian woman, Otaš experienced the changing social attitudes toward interethnic marriages. His cartoon depicts a Serbo-Croatian couple (Serb man and Croat woman) with their son in the middle. Each of the parents carries the national symbol of his or her

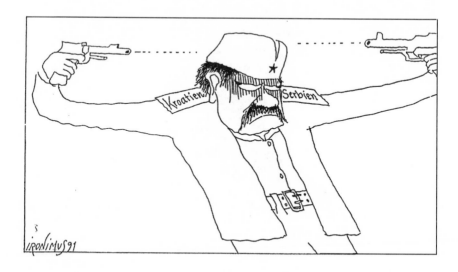

7. Gustav Peichl ("Ironimus"), *Die Presse* (Vienna), May 8, 1991.
8. Nikola Otaš, *Ilustrovana Politika* (Belgrade), February 3, 1992.

respective ethnic group: their son in the middle carries half of each emblem on his clothing.

The parents confront each other head on shouting at the same time. Their wide open mouths indicating the loudness of their voices and the uneven position of their bodies, their waving hands and pointing fingers and their eyes springing from their heads depict their opposition. In between, their son is not looking at either of his parents as they each attempt to. Caught in the middle, he is subjected to their arguments. The son faces an impossible choice. Is there a place he may still call home? In response, he cries. Nikola Otaš raises questions concerning the social disintegration that mixed marriages revealed on the eve of war (or, if viewed from another, "global," perspective, the disintegration of the "mixed marriage" of Serbia and Croatia, as they fight over the "child," the Yugoslav federation itself).

Comparing International Events

Drawing cartoons also involves reconstructing political affairs by looking for their possible linkages. The comparison of two distinct events may reinforce the message of the newspaper where the cartoon is published and thus the political views of the editorial board. As an example, we may look to the cartoons drawn by Swiss cartoonist Patrick Chappatte from Geneva (below) and German cartoonist Pepsch Gottscheber from Munich (page 263).[9]

Although Chappatte and Gottscheber convey different political attitudes toward distinct international events, their drawings are similar in several respects.

9. Patrick Chappatte, *La Suisse* (Geneva), September 19, 1991; Pepsch Gottscheber, private collection (Munich), July 31, 1995.

Both examine Swiss and German public opinion on the war in Croatia and Bosnia and Herzegovina; both use ordinary people and their everyday activities to convey the message on war. While Chappatte compares the attitudes of the Swiss public opinion toward the Gulf War and the Balkan War, Gottscheber illustrates the situation at the German border where the flow of Bosnian refugees is blocked by Germans going abroad for their summer vacations. Chappatte and Gottscheber thus point out the lack of interest in the Yugoslav war in Switzerland and Germany, whose borders are nonetheless only a few hundred kilometers from the battlefields. The two cartoons, produced in September 1991 (Chappatte) and July 1995 (Gottscheber), also testify to the persistence of indifference in Western Europe for over four years to the warfare in former Yugoslavia.

Patrick Chappatte's cartoon consists of two separate drawings that form a single composition. The first is titled "Gulf War" ("Swiss view"), and the second "Balkan War" ("Swiss view"). He portrays the interior of an ordinary supermarket in Switzerland with the shelves labeled in both drawings with the same inscriptions, "Pasta," "Cooking Oil," "Butter," etc. In the first drawing, "Gulf War," Swiss people are portrayed as a mob emptying the shelves in panic. In the right-hand corner, one person reads a newspaper with the title "Ground Attack Being Readied," which further increases the tension in the scene. However, it could also be interpreted as the customers attacking the stores and shelves in the supermarket. In the second drawing, "Balkan War," there are only two customers, one child, and two cashiers. Nothing exceptional is happening. The food shelves are full. Pasta is on sale. The two customers are only looking at the items, but not buying anything. The cashier in the background is saying, "There is something that I do not understand!"

Commenting on the public opinion in Switzerland toward the Gulf War and Balkan War in 1991, Chappatte stated:

> It was a way of comparing the manner in which we behaved in Switzerland regarding the Balkan War, which seemed very far away. And some months ago, there was the Gulf War. There was some kind of mood in Europe, absolutely amazing, where people were buying pasta and oil as if we would have a conflict in Europe. This was reflected in the completely crazy attitudes of the mass media. If there was a war that could potentially threaten Europe, this was the Balkan War and yet people did not react at all! I therefore found it appropriate to contrast these two situations.[10]

Like Chappatte, Gottscheber uses contrasting situations from the German viewpoint. Since his cartoon was published in July, he used the images of summer time—leisure and mass vacations. The drawing is titled "On the road in Europe"—an expression that suggests several interpretations, literary but also symbolic. Gottscheber is confronting the stream of refugees coming from Bosnia and Herzegovina to Germany: the man in front is carrying a sack labeled "Bosnia." The other stream consists of Germans leaving for their vacations abroad. The distinction rests on opposite notions—they and we—as a categories of space, but also of social distance. Arriving from far away, the refugees from Bosnia and Herzegovina stand in the background. Their stream is endless. The German tourists, on the other hand, appear in the front of the drawing. Although they are leaving Germany, they are closer—geographically, culturally, historically,—to the German newspaper reader than are the refugees from Bosnia and Herzegovina. The meeting point of Bosnian refugees and German tourists is the German border. The German emblem (a black eagle with outstretched wings) and below it the sign "Customs" indicates the physical point of their meeting, but also the line of their separation.

From the German point of view "On the road in Europe" thus becomes an image of contradictions. On one hand there is depicted the misery of the Bosnian refugees who left their homes involuntarily with no certainty of returning, and on the other hand one sees leisurely Germans going abroad for fun, to return home in a week or two. They go in opposite directions. The first left the south and are on their way north, the latter group is leaving the north and going south. While the Bosnians are walking with their provisions on their back or without

10. Patrick Chappatte, interview by the author, Geneva, May 12, 1995.

anything at all, the German tourists are driving cars with boats, windsurf boards, and other vacation gear. Because of the line of German cars, the refugees from Bosnia and Herzegovina cannot cross the border and enter Germany. Thus the refugees stay where they are. Those who are sitting appear to have been waiting for some time. The German drivers appear indifferent. Patrick Chappatte and Pepsch Gottscheber are each expressing irony and paradox in their respective societies. The ordinary Swiss or German does not seem to care; not even if they represent their neighbors. The Swiss and German public opinion are thus targets of both cartoonists.

Changing Attitudes over Time

As with the journalist, so too the cartoonist may change his attitudes toward the same political event. This is especially true when the event is an international crisis that extends over time.

In a cartoon mentioned earlier (see page 260), Austrian cartoonist Ironimus made the Croats and Serbs equally responsible for the destruction of the multiethnic, communist-run Yugoslav Federation. Several months later, in 1991, he published another cartoon in which he depicted Serbia as an alligator eating Croatia (below).[11] In order to describe the evil element of warfare, Ironimus introduces a dehumanization model—"alligator Serbia"—that will reappear in modified forms in the later stages of the war. "Alligator Serbia," however, does not look very cruel, and could also be seen as an image from a book of children's fairy tales. It wears a communist hat, a cliché that reminds one of the Partisan soldiers of World War II. The same cap was used for fifty years by the soldiers of the JNA. Serbia and the Serbs are identified on two levels; in ideological terms as communist, and in military terms as the federal army. The dehumanization model

11. Gustav Peichl ("Ironimus"), *Die Presse* (Vienna), September 14, 1991.

functions as an enemy image representing both, the ideological opponent and the military power of destruction, evoking iconographically a feature of the cold war.

In the cartoon published in 1992 (below),[12] the dehumanized image of Serbia evolved further. Instead of an alligator, Ironimus represents Serbia as a dragon. "Dragon Serbia" has two horns, claws, a tail, and spines. Its mouth is open, its eyes are fixed, and its body is poised to spring forward and attack the UN soldier. The UN peacekeeper is armed only with a lasso that he is about to throw at the dragon. He is trying desperately to subdue the cruel animal. Having already been pierced by three arrows on the left side of his body, the "dragon Serbia" is bleeding from its wounds. But it has become even more aggressive, and the UN soldier is almost at his mercy.

Three years later, in 1995, Ironimus drew a scene titled in capital letters "Battle of the Monsters" (page 267).[13] There he portrayed the Croats and Serbs as equally cruel "alligators" fighting each other while the UN soldier observes them from distance. The fights rages not only at the border between (Greater) Serbia and Croatia (signs in the background), but also deep in the hinterland. There are dying and dead alligators on both sides. The central image is a duel between the Serb and the Croat alligators in the process of biting each other. Thus there is no

12. Ibid., May 30, 1992.
13. Gustav Peichl ("Ironimus"), *Süddeutsche Zeitung* (Munich), August 7, 1995.

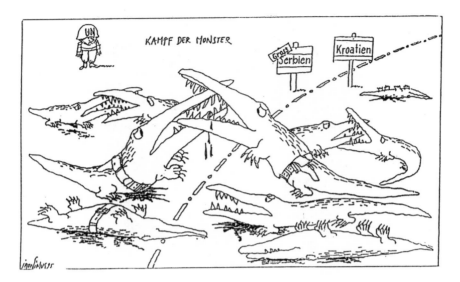

longer any difference between the alligators. "Monsters," whether Serbs or Croats, are equally bad.

Over the four-year period, Ironimus changed his attitude toward the war in former Yugoslavia. In May 1991, he represented the war as a case of "evil against evil" (see page 260). In September 1991, he characterized Serbia as an alligator without making any value judgment of Croatia (see page 265). In May 1992, he dehumanized Serbia still further; "alligator Serbia" became "dragon Serbia" (see page 266). Finally, in August 1995, he depicted Croatia and Serbia as equally bad. They have both become "monsters" (above), thus completing the cycle and returning—although through other iconographical means—to his 1991 model of "evil against evil."

How Serb Cartoonists Depicted General Mladić

The perception of political events and top decision makers can be very different, in some aspects radically so, within the same warring party. In fact, the social production of political images during the war reveals the existence of competing political views and strategic interests.

A few months after the beginning of the war in Bosnia and Herzegovina, Serb cartoonist Corax from Belgrade published a cartoon in mid-June 1992, showing Bosnian Serb general Ratko Mladić in the act of destroying Sarajevo (page 268).[14] Corax: "You see on the drawing General Mladić, who—like a 'King

14. Predrag Koraksić ("Corax"), *Vreme* (Belgrade), June 15, 1992.

Kong' or 'Godzilla monster'—destroys and demolishes Sarajevo."[15] Thus the
destruction of Sarajevo became personalized and represented iconographically
through the image of General Mladić.[16] His later indictment by the International
Tribunal in The Hague for war crimes is foreshadowed in this cartoon.

What does Corax show in this cartoon? Against a night sky, Mladić is wearing
the uniform of a high-ranking Serb officer and the cap (*šajkača*) that traditionally
has dual iconographical use: during the peace it is worn by peasants, while in
wartime it becomes part of the military uniform. Perched atop the highest building in the city, he seems to be looking directly at the reader. In the background
are burning buildings. The seriousness of the destruction is reflected in the expression on his face. No sign of life remains around him.

Using similar metaphorical language, Bosnian Serb cartoonist Darko Samard-
žić-Kodar, from Banja Luka (*Republika Srpska*), expressed in 1994 a completely
different view of General Mladić. He glorified the general as the protector of the
Bosnian Serbs (page 269).[17] His enemies are a NATO plane; a UN plane carrying
then-secretary general Boutros-Boutros Ghali; a United Nations tree protecting

15. Corax, letter to the author, Belgrade, June 3, 1997.
16. In the Western media, General Ratko Mladić is known as the commander of the Bosnian
Serb forces. Further, some identified the Bosnian (and Croatian) Serbs with Serbs from Serbia, in
fact with all Serbs. It should be noted, however, that Corax did not intend that General Mladić
represent the Serb people. He considers social actors as individually responsible for their acts (Corax,
interview).
17. Darko Samardzić ("Kodar"), *Zapadna Srbija* (Banja Luka), April/May 1994.

Bosnian Muslims with the sign "Muslim Fundamentalists"; and Bosnian Muslims represented as Indians doing a war dance at the base of the ladder on which he is standing. In the center of the composition, General Mladić is wearing a uniform but not a *šajkača*, which gives him a rather informal look. While all other characters orient their action toward him, he dominates the composition. Note finally the physical disparity between him and the Bosnian Serb soldier, the only one not represented as an enemy, with whom the general is speaking. General Mladić asks: "Do you know, my son, why the dinosaurs died out?" Soldier: "No Mr. General!" General Mladić: "Because they attacked unarmed Serb people." Kodar says about the cartoon:

> We were in a situation of complete isolation and the world wanted us to eat each other like dogs. Sometimes they succeeded, sometimes they did not. This cartoon was inspired by my revulsion against the NATO aircraft that were shooting at everything that was Serb. Goražde[18] was in fact a media event as was Sarajevo. It was necessary to create an image of people being in a kind of "Indian reservation," slowly dying because of somebody outside. This is their mirror image of the "Indians," because they annihilated them. Now, to assuage their guilty consciousness, they have transformed the [Bosnian] Muslims into "Indians" and accused us [Serbs] of having done [to Bosnian Muslims] what they did [to the "American Indians"].[19]

18. Town under (Bosnian) Muslim control surrounded by (Bosnian) Serb forces.
19. Darko Samardzić-Kodar, interview, Banja Luka, May 24, 1996.

Looking out from within "Republika Srpska," Kodar praises General Mladić as a Serb national hero and ascribes to him supernatural powers. Like King Kong, General Mladić can also fight planes with his bare hands. That is how he is able simply to catch and stop the NATO plane with his left hand, while protecting his soldier from the UN plane flown by Boutros-Boutros Ghali with his right. Commenting on General Mladić, Kodar said: "He is the most appreciated person. I think that Serbs respect and honor their rulers. Sometimes they wait until they fall, and then trample or spit on them. . . . I think that this man will never be [in that position]."[20]

These cartoons depicting General Mladić as King Kong, one by a Serb cartoonist from Belgrade and the other by a Bosnian Serb cartoonist from Banja Luka, demonstrate the existence of two contrasting images within Serb public opinion on the war in Bosnia and Herzegovina. In some respects, by wielding unlimited power, Corax's and Kodar's General Mladić are very similar. The interpretations differ, however, concerning the way in which General Mladić used his power, whether destructive (Corax) or defensive and protective (Kodar). Nonetheless, both interpretations, one liberal (Corax) and the other nationalist (Kodar), share a common debt to American popular culture, a country whose use of superior military power played a crucial role in ending the military conflict in Bosnia and Herzegovina.

Geopolitical Concerns and People's Interests

In 1992 Bosnian cartoonist Zoran Tovirac from Novi Travnik produced a cartoon where he represented an American and a Russian talking to each other. In fact, the articulation of their toothy mouths represents the map of Bosnia and Herzegovina (page 271).[21] Except for their hats, there is no important iconographical difference between the two men. Both are dressed in Western style coats, and wear white shirts with ties. Also, their faces have the same features: ears, haircut, nose, eyes, eyebrows. They look just the same. The American cowboy and the Russian peasant are discussing international affairs, Bosnia and Herzegovina in particular. They are arguing about war and peace in the region without asking the people concerned for their opinion, too. Tovirac: "The Latins from the West and the Orthodox from the East are discussing Bosnia. Only, the people inside do not exist. Nobody asks them for anything."[22]

The message is that "speaking-discussing-arguing" about war and peace in Bosnia and Herzegovina over the heads of its people solves nothing. Rather, it

---

20. Ibid.
21. Zoran Tovirac, private collection (Novi Travnik), 1992.
22. Zoran Tovirac, interview, Belgrade, May 25, 1996.

creates additional problems. The hole or emptiness in the space between the American cowboy and the Russian peasant indicates that the Bosnian people have no power over their fate.

Intervention Debate

Since the beginning of the war in Croatia (1991) and Bosnia and Herzegovina (1992) the central question debated by the Western media and political leaders has concerned whether to end the conflict by intervening militarily on behalf of the weaker party or through negotiations. From the standpoint of Western public opinion, it made no difference whether the conflict in question was the war in Croatia or the war in Bosnia and Herzegovina, since the "aggressor" was the same—the Serbs.

Since 1991, many cartoons have been produced in Western Europe concerning this intervention debate. Take, for example, Patrick Chappatte's 1994 cartoon, "Stop immediately, or we negotiate!" (page 272).[23] Chappatte illustrates the situation of a United Nations ultimatum. He presents the three actors of the ethnic conflict in Bosnia and Herzegovina: the Bosnian Muslim as "victim," the Bosnian Serb as "aggressor," and the UN as "protector-prosecutor." The victims (the Bosnian Muslims) are represented as a woman lying with her back on the ground; the aggressors (the Bosnian Serbs), as a soldier crouching over her with

23. Patrick Chappatte, *Tribune de Genève* (Geneva), September 28, 1994.

his hands around her throat. The United Nations is represented as a civilian standing on a military vehicle and shouting at the "aggressor" through a loudspeaker.

The cartoon makes its point through a series of visual and verbal contradictions: first, between the soldier and his victim, then between the soldier and the
civilian. Between the soldier and his victim, there are other elements that demonstrate the power of the man and the fragility of the woman, besides the act of
strangling. Although the man has a machine-gun on his right shoulder and a
dagger on his left hip, he has decided to kill the woman with his bare hands rather
than with one of his weapons. Literally "un-armed," the woman is completely at
his mercy. The man's enormous body, shoulders, and hands, contrasted with his
abnormally small head, represent his physical force and intellectual impairment.
Is it a genetic error? The death skull symbol he is wearing on his left arm identifies him as bringing death. With his military equipment and heavy boots, he
represents the brutality of the Bosnian Serb army. Barefoot, with open mouth and
eyes, the woman represents the defenseless Bosnian Muslim civilian population.

The visual and verbal contradictions are expressed by the attitude of the
United Nations representative warning the Bosnian Serb soldier. The ultimatum
he issues from the military vehicle is not real, since the UN is not ready to
intervene. The verbal intimidation is formulated in a way that the soldier under-
stands it as not valid at all. Chappatte: "This shows a complete repeal of intimidation. The ultimatum would be: 'Stop or we intervene'—while the ultimatum here

is 'stop or we discuss.'"[24] In fact, as Chappatte supposes, the Bosnian Serb fighters know that there is no serious threat behind the United Nations ultimatum. They can continue their acts of violence.

Yet Patrick Chappatte's cartoon also reveals distinct features from the collective unconscious of Western newspaper readers. Besides the text in the balloon, there are only two labels in this drawing: "Bosnia" for the victim and "UN" for the protector-prosecutor. Why is there no label for the aggressor, whose huge body occupies the central space, and whose act of violence is main action in the composition? After more than three years of warfare, the average newspaper reader in the West knows that the "bad guys" in the ethnic conflict in Croatia and Bosnia and Herzegovina are the Serbs. Yet by abbreviating the name "Bosnia and Herzegovina" as "Bosnia" and using the latter as an unspoken synonym for the Bosnian Muslims, one labels Bosnian Croats and Bosnian Serbs as simply "Croats" or "Serbs." The latter two, apparently considered as "foreigners" in Bosnia and Herzegovina, may eventually be considered as "aggressors," too.

Of course, the processes of abbreviation and reduction are common in the field of journalism. In cartoon art, the simplification represents the means to convey a message and thus improve the immediate understanding of a news story. Nevertheless, by using simplification here—the sparest possible, verbal or iconographical—represents a danger that the complexity of social and political issues will be lost. As a consequence, the processes of abbreviation and reduction may lead, even unintentionally, to the falsification of information. The abbreviation, reduction, and simplification serve in the construction of the collective unconscious. They help to produce social values and thus convictions that reveal political views that exist in society.

As Patrick Chappatte shows, the triangle "victim-aggressor-protector" is unstable, since a change of roles is inherent in the system of inter-party relations. The United Nations attitude portrayed is one of hesitation toward intervening against the Bosnian Serbs. In the interests of "justice," eventually the "protector" is tempted to become a "prosecutor." By attacking the "aggressor," the "prosecutor" defends the "victim." If, however, the United Nations attacks the Bosnian Serbs in order to defend the Bosnian Muslims, the United Nations acts as an "aggressor" to the Bosnian Serbs who then become their "victims." The Bosnian Muslims, whose rescue was the purpose of the initial intervention, are out of game. The debate in Western public opinion and mass media oscillates between contradictory visions, intervention and nonintervention, interference or hesitation. Political cartoons express contemporary attitudes and changing sentiments in the public sphere and contribute to the controversy over that issue.

In 1993, Serb cartoonist Miro Stefanović from Indjija (Vojvodina, Serbia) made a cartoon in which he represented a Serb, a Bosnian Muslim, and a Croat

24. Patrick Chappatte, interview, Geneva, May 12, 1995.

playing dice and gambling with people's heads (below).[25] Each player wears a hood concealing his head perhaps? The three small flags on the table indicate, from left to right, the Serb, Bosnian Muslim, and Croat parties. The other flags in front represent the European Union, the United States of America, and the United Nations. There are three heads on the table, indicating the players' winnings. The Serb player already has two heads, the Bosnian Muslim player has one, while the Croat, who does yet not have one, is taking his turn to compete for a head as well. On the ground, next to the Serbian and Croatian players are two baskets full of heads—for later use?

Gambling with people's heads under the supervision of the European Union, the United States, and the United Nations is a macabre and surrealistic representation of the Yugoslav war. Except for the flags at their sides, there is no difference between the players. Since they are playing the game together, they have at least one feature in common: a passion for gambling with people's heads, i.e. wielding power over peoples' lives. The ethnic elites are playing their game with the heads of their people; without specific ethnic reference, the heads are all the same. As Stefanović says: "I wanted to show the whole horror and the ease with which the people in power in this country did what they did and are doing what they do. That means they are gambling with people's heads. Obviously, here are

25. Miro Stefanović ("Indjija"), *Mislio sam . . .* (Novi Sad), 1995.

also the flags of international actors which means that, under certain conditions, everything is happening under the sponsorship of these actors."[26]

Another iconographical symbol: hoods and gloves. Stefanović: "When a person wears a white hood, like a Ku Klux Klan member, it means that besides the fact that he is a criminal, he is also a racist; he does not tolerate other ethnic groups or religions. When I use the hood, it means that this does not rest on only one person, but on a wider group of people that is ruling in a country. This is a more general symbol."[27]

Thus playing dice is playing with the lives of their ethnic brethren. Although the killing occurs among ordinary people, the real conflict does not take place among Croats, Bosnian Muslims, and Serbs. Instead, it takes place much higher on the social ladder, between the ethnic elites united in their struggle against the people of their distinct communities. The power exercised by the ethnic elites is seen to be destructive for society as a whole. Thus to destroy the other side, one should first, at least symbolically, destroy oneself. This mutual destruction perpetuated through time and space brings about a collective suicide. How to break the causal chain?

Fighting the Present with Memories of the Past

Memories of events that occurred fifty to eighty years ago are still alive. In the following three cartoons, World War II serves as a historical reference for the views expressed by Serb cartoonists Ranko Guzina and Corax from Belgrade and German cartoonist Barbara Henniger from Berlin.

The war in Croatia and Bosnia and Herzegovina is often seen by insiders ("Yugoslavs") and outsiders (foreigners) as a repetition of the events of World War II, with the present decision makers seen in relation to those from half a century ago. Insiders and outsiders tend to favor historical analogies when making their observations on the present. The iconographical representation of Adolf Hitler and the phenomenon of national socialism often serve as a metaphor for the enemy side. There are no exceptions. The three parties in conflict—Croats, Bosnian Muslims, and Serbs—all use the iconography of the Third Reich. Their aim is to recall the past and, by labeling the other side symbolically, "to demonize" the enemy (Reljić 1994; Roth 1995).

In 1991, Serb cartoonist Ranko Guzina from Belgrade (originally from Croatia) drew a cartoon in which he compared Adolf Hitler, Ante Pavelić, and Franjo Tudjman (page 276).[28] The three characters are standing in single file. Each has his right arm raised in the Nazi salute. Hitler's hand is just behind Pavelić's head,

26. Miro Stefanović, interview, Belgrade, May 22, 1996.
27. Ibid.
28. Ranko Guzina, *Večernje Novosti* (Belgrade), 1991.

Pavelić's hand is just behind Tudjman's head. Hitler is the largest figure. Pavelić is smaller than Hitler but a bit larger than Tudjman, while Tudjman is the smallest figure in the composition.

Guzina's cartoon constructs as many analogies and parallels as possible, both in relation to the characters represented and the states each of them symbolizes. The similarities in their bodies suggest their identity. The equation would be: since Hitler = Pavelić = Tudjman, therefore Third Reich (1933–45) = Independent State of Croatia (NDH, 1941–45) = Republic of Croatia (1991–today).

The comparative use of iconographical tools and their repetition in each character with historical references conveys the message. The reading from left to right gives a needed spontaneity to the composition. The absence of any backdrop helps the reader to focus easily and rapidly on the three characters and grasp their significance. Hence, there is no longer any difference between the past, present, and future. Everything becomes one and happens simultaneously in space and time. Within the same geographical space, the past repeats itself in the present.

Historical references and analogies may also be used in successive stages through time. The image of an event from the past can be filled out with the features of the present to anticipate events in the future. Under certain conditions—through appropriate iconography and vocabulary—or so this cartoon implies, the past will repeat itself in the future in the "same" yet "another" way. Serb cartoonist Corax from Belgrade represents the Nuremberg War Crimes Trial (1945–46). Corax applies the iconography of the well-known historical photo and makes a cartoon where he puts on the same bench—beside high-ranking Nazi officers accused of crimes against humanity and all condemned on death[29]—

29. Frank, Frick, Goering, Jodl, Kaltenbrunner, Keitel, Ribbentrop, Rosenberg, Sauckel, Seyss-Inquart, and Streicher, all Nazis on trial in Nuremberg.

the president of Serbia, Slobodan Milošević (middle left), and the president of Croatia, Franjo Tudjman (middle right) (below).[30] In Corax's cartoon, presidents Milošević and Tudjman are under arrest and investigation.

While the background is represented realistically, Milošević and Tudjman are caricatured. Drawn in a similar style, this could indicate the equality or reciprocity of their images. Their bodies and especially their heads are bigger than those of their Nazi counterparts. Both are sitting on the same bench with arms crossed in the same manner. Although their eyes are not represented, they are looking in the same direction, straight at the judges. Corax: "This is my comment on the fact that these two, Milošević and Tudjman, are the men most responsible for the war and ethnic cleansing on the territory of Yugoslavia. I still do believe that the whole thing will end in this way. There will be other [people], too."[31] Published in December 1991, this cartoon anticipated the public debate, especially in the West, that has focused on war crimes. It has also anticipated the establishment of the international criminal tribunal for the former Yugoslavia (ICTY) in the Hague. Public and journalistic debate on these issues began only in 1992–93.

The prescience of Corax's cartoon summarizes the views and emotions related

30. Predrag Koraksić ("Corax"), *Vreme* (Belgrade), December 23, 1991.
31. Corax, interview, Belgrade, February 10, 1995.

to the aftermath of World War II. By translating current events and characters
into the iconography of the past, the composition extrapolates the past into the
future. The caricatured features of Milošević and Tudjman become an iconographical framework for the phenomenon of the war crime and the crime against
humanity. Structural analogy and historical reference lead to grasp the particular-
ity of an event in history and evaluate its repetition.

Historical reference, analogy with the past and comparison with present events
influence public opinion and thus decision makers too. German cartoonist Barbara Henniger from Berlin comments on the public debate in Germany surrounding the issue of whether German soldiers should participate in United Nations or
NATO operations in the former Yugoslavia (below).[32] She introduces us to a
middle-class German family. The intimacy and privacy of the home and family
are enhanced with two family photos, nostalgic souvenirs, that represent the past.
On the left, a remembrance of World War II—a photo of a German officer in
uniform with ruins in the background. The script below reads: "Greetings from
Yugoslavia! Dad!" The black ribbon at the right corner of the frame indicates
that the father is deceased. In the middle, is a vacation souvenir. A middle-aged
man stands in water on the beach suit, sun glasses, and fake smile for the camera.
In the background, sun umbrellas indicate summer weather, leisure, and vacation.
The script reads: "Greetings from Yugoslavia! Husband!" On the right, a mother

32. Barbara Henniger, *Tagesspeigel* (Berlin), July 1, 1995.

dressed as a housewife holds the hand of her son, dressed in the uniform of the Bundeswehr and now leaving for Yugoslavia. The script in the balloon reads: "Please write me."

Looking at the Yugoslav conflict from the German point of view, Henniger compares three historical periods and the involvement of the Germans in Balkan affairs over the last half century. First, the war of the 1940s, then the summer vacations of the 1960s, 1970s, and 1980s, and finally, the war of the 1990s. The three periods represent three different stages, giving historical references and portraying the everyday experience of Germans from three generations. Henniger: "They were in the war there, afterwards they were there as tourists, and now the son leaves too. So there is a continuity between the generations."[33]

The cartoonist portrays a single family where each male member leaves once for Yugoslavia, emphasizing thus the female point of view. Once a daughter, then a spouse, and now a mother, the woman remains at home while the male members of the family leave for Yugoslavia. For the German public the dilemma in 1995 was whether German soldiers should participate in the Balkans (as a part of UN or NATO forces). The cartoon represents that controversy. Thus, considering the *Vergangenheitsbewältigung* (the overcoming of the past) of the Germans, Henniger leads the reader to form an opinion on that issue.

Media and War

In 1992, Turkish cartoonist Tan Oral from Istanbul represented the process of routinization in the Yugoslav conflict (page 280).[34] "The News of War" cartoon illustrates the changing public opinion toward the war with a single person reading a newspaper. Oral describes the collective mood by placing the newspaper reader in five sequential situations, each corresponding to successive time periods.

The first drawing is of the man sitting in his armchair quietly reading his newspaper. The second pictures him startled by an explosion. He jumps out of his armchair while the paper falls from his hands. Then, he hears two explosion. He still drops his newspaper, but he does not jump up. Instead, he turns to see what is happening. The third drawing continues the action from the previous frames and maintains the tension, but the man has resumed his seat. The fourth drawing shows the reader again sitting in his armchair. He is holding his newspaper with his right hand, but not reading it. There are several explosions, but he remains seated. He shows no inclination, as he previously did, to see what is going on. He even seems irritated, or perhaps bored. In the fifth drawing he is

33. Barbara Henniger, interview, Berlin, February 16, 1995.
34. Tan Oral, *Cumhuriyet* (Istanbul), October 31, 1992.

THE NEWS OF WAR

completely indifferent to the explosions. He is sitting securely in his armchair and quietly reading his newspaper exactly as he was doing in the first drawing.

The explosion balloons in Oral's cartoon announce the approach of the war; with each sequence, the explosions are closer and increasingly violent. At each stage, the danger for his personal security becomes greater. However, as the fifth drawing shows, he does not have any consciousness of this. On the contrary, he behaves as if nothing is happening, an absurdity that illustrates the joke.

This cartoon is a representation of Turkish public opinion. Oral is criticizing the apathy of ordinary people and the routinization of information. It is also a subtle analysis both of how the public attends only to news that is sensational, and of how news is sensational only when it is new. News that has become a part of everyday life does not attract the same level of attention. Thus metaphorically, public opinion and society as a whole are no longer interested in it. They are only "curious" to see and follow what is happening. "The news of war" becomes a paradox that runs as a TV story in episodes on a daily basis.

In a country at war the information becomes distorted, deformed, hidden between the lines, partially expressed, confused with other sources, or entirely falsified. The question remains how to read the newspaper, how to look at the TV news, how to listen to comments on the radio (Bonnafous 1996; Charaudeau, Lochard, and Soulages 1996; Leblanc 1996).

Serb cartoonist Dušan Ludwig from Belgrade drew a cartoon in which he describes the process by which public opinion becomes manipulated by mass media through the daily consumption of information (below).[35] Like Oral, Ludwig also draws a man reading a newspaper. The reader wears glasses and the open newspaper is in his hands. There are, however, two unusual elements that introduce a contradiction in the drawing. First, while the right pages of the newspaper are white with printed columns, lines and words, the left pages are black and do not contain any words at all. Second, the glasses the man wears reproduce the same phenomenon. While the left lens is ordinary, the right lens is black. The man can see with his left eye the black pages of the left, but cannot see the pages on the right because of the black lens. Thus what he "reads" is not written (and what is written, he does not read).

Ludwig's cartoon illustrates a paradox. Although the newspaper reader "reads" with full attention, he cannot read the newspaper. What matters (the white pages on the right) he does not see, and what he does see (the black pages

35. Dušan Ludwig, *Pjer* (Belgrade), 1993.

on the left) does not matter. The visual contradiction—black and white (for the pages), and black and transparent (for the lenses of his glasses)—culminates in a paradox. During the war, ordinary people cannot read what they should (to know what is happening), but read what they do not need (and become disinformed). The newspaper reader does not see what is going on in the society; what he does not see does not exist for him.

Although Ludwig's cartoon focuses on war reporting in Serbia, his drawing has a broader meaning. It could also illustrate the media and the public opinion in Croatia and Bosnia and Herzegovina, and the war reporting in the West (Woodger 1996). At the end of twentieth century, no one can escape the process of the industrial production of information and the lure of the dominant view. However, the dominant ideas of the time are ideas where social power is concentrated. Under certain social circumstances of high tension—such as war—the use of institutional violence may determine what ordinary people should know, think, and feel. In mass society, information is an industrial product like any other good or service. It is fabricated with a commercial purpose and political use.

Ending the War

Officially, the war in Croatia and Bosnia and Herzegovina ended with the agreements initiated at Wright-Patterson Air Force Base near Dayton, Ohio, in November 1995, and signed in Paris in December 1995. In one view, the war stopped as suddenly as it had begun. There were many cartoons representing the Dayton process. Yet they were less than optimistic about their prospects. After four and a half years of warfare, a series of failed peace talks, and numerous international negotiations, public opinion in former Yugoslavia and in the West was not convinced that the war was over. The general impression of that time was that none of the three warring parties was satisfied with the deal reached in Dayton.

In his cartoon of the Dayton Accord, the German cartoonist Gerhard Mester from Wiesbaden uses the metaphor of a boat named "Bosnia" in which he draws the three warring parties together (page 283).[36] The cartoon is entitled: "Croats, Serbs, Muslims—all in one boat." Iconographically—"Muslims," "Serbs," and "Croats" have the script on their hats and are represented in the same manner: impersonally and thus equally. They have the same uniform and hats, and they look at their saws as they saw the sides of the boat in which they are sitting together. Mester: "Incomprehension. They must be really crazy: by damaging the other, they damage themselves."[37] The official document with the script "Dayton Accord" has just been sawn in two pieces. It is still floating on the surface of the

36. Gerhard Mester, private collection (Wiesbaden), November 1995.
37. Gerhard Mester, questionnaire, Wiesbaden, May 13, 1997.

Kroaten, Serben, Moslems — alle in einem Boot

water, while the three men continue to saw away at the boat. The look on their faces conveys the seriousness and thus the decisiveness of their action of mutual destruction. Shortly the boat should sink.

In portraying the three warring parties as equal—in their iconography and their collective action—Mester considers them as equally responsible for their destiny. They are represented through the metaphor of the common boat, and the their common state, in the "Bosnia," as written on the boat. From the German perspective, the insiders—Bosnian Muslims, Croats, and Serbs—have the last word on whether they will live together.

Use of History

History functions in the Balkans as an invisible hand and puts constant pressure on the collective unconscious. Bosnian Serb cartoonist Vojin Stanković from Banja Luka made a drawing just before the breakup of the Yugoslav Federation in spring 1991 (page 284).[38] There, he summarized his views of what had happened in the past, what was happening in the present, and what was likely to take place in the future. Observing political events that succeeded each other on a daily basis, he expressed what he saw as the mood of his time. Stanković: "The

38. Vojin Stanković, *Borba* (Belgrade), 1991.

symbolism of that drawing rests on a projection of real events before and apropos the breakup of the former Yugoslavia."[39] Thus there is no recognizable event in that composition, nor decision maker, nor are there any recognizable people in action. It is rather an illustration, an analysis of a historical process. The cartoon also expresses the current direction of social change and transformation. Society is a set of cumulative structures. Present events and social actors are part of a broader historical process extending through time and space.

The cartoon illustrates a book with the title "History." On the cover is the map of Yugoslavia within its post-1945 borders. The cover and the pages inside have been cut from all sides. Around the scissors, previously used in cutting the book and pages, are wreaths, which symbolically commemorate the act of cutting as an act of killing. Stanković:

> The history of that state suddenly became an unprotected oasis (meadow) where everybody mowed—what he needed and how much he needed. In other words, history was excised following the needs and interests of political leaders from the former republics, as well as their mentors (assistants) from the outside world. With each part of the history that was cut, an era of common life was sacrificed—part of constitutionality and

39. Vojin Stanković, letter to the author, Banja Luka, June 2, 1997.

culture—and, obviously, the truth has been dissolved. Everything was happening so recklessly and open, that I have represented it sarcastically like traffic accidents, where at the site of the tragedy people put small wreaths. Thus, history is on a moving tape, an eternal path. . . . The scissors represent figuratively the actors (killers) of these events that this history fatally punishes. In fact, some are abandoned immediately on the battlefield of events, while others will follow them.[40]

The past of the Southern Slavs ("Yugoslavs") has been "officially" revised at least three times in the twentieth century. Following major events—the two world wars and the breakup of the Yugoslav Federation in 1991—their "common history" has each time been rewritten from the standpoint of that time and the most recent events. On each occasion, some facts are played down or overlooked entirely, while others repeated and celebrated. These historical interpretations are likely to express current views of the past emerging from society and its dominant public opinion. This facilitates the apparent ease with which the "Yugoslav" people switched from one historical interpretation to another. Symbolically, to cut and to kill becomes suddenly easy, too easy, since it is justified by the pieces of History that were cut for daily use, and thus for misuse and abuse.

Conclusion

Cartoon art anticipated the ethnic conflict, the disintegration of the Yugoslav Federation and the war (see page 257). Portraying images arising from the viewpoint of ordinary people, they transmitted messages that help us better understand the effects of actual policymaking on everyday life. In 1991, the first reactions to the disintegration of the Yugoslav Federation are self-destruction (page 259), collective suicide (page 260), and family disintegration (page 261). Following several months of warfare, firmer attitudes appear in the domestic and international press. By the end of 1991, the mass production of enemy images is a dominant feature. Now an international crisis, the war in Croatia and Bosnia and Herzegovina is compared with other armed conflicts, such as the Gulf War (page 262), the Israeli-Palestine conflict, the Rwanda crisis, and so on; or with their humanitarian effects, like the issue of refugees (page 263). The disintegration of the Yugoslav Federation is also contrasted with the process of the European integration.

The cartoon art of the Yugoslav crisis is not homogeneous. Part of cultural production, it contains major and minor currents with mutually opposing views. Thus the political attitudes of the cartoonist and the newspaper where the drawings are published may evolve over time (pages 260, 265, 266, and 267). Even

---

40. Ibid.

within one warring party, cartoon art reproduces contrasting views about their respective political and military leaders; for example, the contrasting views of Bosnian Serb general Ratko Mladić from Belgrade and from Banja Luka (pages 268 and 269).

There are various ways in which cartoonists may have influenced national and international decision makers. They may have reinforced, through their drawings, stereotypical views of the different warring parties and external players, the United Nations, and the great powers. In the successive stages of the warfare, their work has called into question the credibility of the international community, the United Nations, and NATO (pages 272 and 274).

Promoting grassroots consideration of high politics, cartoon art expresses attitudes of ordinary people. From their viewpoint, the geopolitical concerns of great powers ignoring the interest of Bosnian people cannot be legitimate (page 271). Thus cartoonists sensitized public opinion and decision makers, including those playing roles in the context of the United Nations system and the great powers.

The major trend in cartoon art production is the identification of the producer with their warring party. Thus the Bosnian Muslim, Croat, and Serb cartoonists expressed the political views of their respective ethnic communities. By drawing their ethnic views in affirmative terms, they were promoting the "national interests" of their group and, above all, the war aims of their ethnic leaders. Representing more independent views from the official policy, some Serb authors published series of cartoons where they have criticized Serb and Bosnian Serb decision makers (Milošević, Karadžić, Mladić).

The mainstream among Western authors shows a tendency to identify with the militarily weaker party. While in the Serbo-Croatian war in Croatia, the dominant pattern was anti-Serb and pro-Croatian, in the war in Bosnia and Herzegovina, the dominant pattern remained anti-Serb, sometimes anti-Croatian, and always pro-Muslim. Considering all three parties equally "bad," the minor stream among Western cartoonists rejects identification with any of protagonists. The mainstream, which favors the militarily weaker party, acts as interventionist; equally condemning all three parties, the minor stream acts as isolationist. Cartoonists working in the mainstream are not likely to make drawings in the minor stream. However, the minor stream cartoonists also produce drawings following the major stream. Since the Serb party was considered as militarily stronger, there were no pro-Serb Western cartoons; the Serbs are never "martyrs." Within the Serb cartoon art production the main stream draws Serbs as "victims." However, they do not see themselves "victims" of the Croats and Bosnian Muslims, whom they consider as militarily inferior. The Serbs see themselves a "victims" of the United Nations and the NATO, as well as of the Western powers, considered militarily superior.

Cartoon art production also reveals a continuation of the Yugoslav conflict from the past as generated by World War II; to some extent by World War I and the presence of the Austrian and Ottoman empires in the Balkans since the Middle Ages. Thus the dramatic Serb experience of World War II considers Croatian secession and independence from the Yugoslav Federation in the 1990s as a renaissance of Hitlerism from the 1930s and 1940s in the Balkans (page 276). The nazification of the "Other" is not the only consideration among Serb cartoonists. The reference to the Nuremberg War Crimes Trial defines an evil in ethnic terms (Serbs and Croats) and class terms (political elite). However, it also serves to publicly condemn some individual actors—Milošević and Tudjman—considered as most responsible for the war and the associated atrocities (page 277). From the German prospective, the participation of German soldiers in United Nations and NATO operations on the Balkans is also overshadowed by memories of World War II. Thus the hesitation within the German public opinion concerning whether to participate in "peace-making" military operations in Croatia and Bosnia and Herzegovina (page 278).

The role of the media in an ethnic conflict is another passionate field of cartoon art production. Accused by insiders and outsiders for broadcasting war messages, hate, and xenophobia, the mass media and public opinion in former Yugoslavia and in the West represent a target for political and cultural criticism. The routinization of war news leads to frequent repetition and broadcasting of violence. Thus the banalization of war-reporting reproduces inertia and indifference publicly (page 280). The mass media systematically turns aside critical observations. The more one consumes mass information on the war, the more likely one becomes manipulated (page 281).

After four and half years of warfare in Croatia and Bosnia-Herzegovina, the cartoon art production did not consider the signing of the peace treaties in November 1995 as the definitive end of hostilities. According to the mainstream, each warring party—Bosnian Muslims, Croats, and Serbs—would continue pursuing their interests and destroy the fragile peace agreement that the three parties signed apparently against their will (page 283).

Ending the war over Yugoslav succession does not end the history of the Southern Slavs. Certainly, it is the end of an era and the beginning of an other. As a pattern of mutual destruction, the steady historicization of the present leads to periodic destruction of the "Self" and thus to sequential historical discontinuity. The common use of History in the Balkans is also a history of its misuse (page 284).

Even though the cartoonists are not the creators of ethnic clichés—which already exists in the collective unconscious—they are responsible, via the press, for their reinforcement in the public space. A medium of war propaganda, the cartoon may considerably enhance negative images. By identifying with some and opposing others, cartoon art produces fiction of warfare, and thus the image of the enemy.

The war cartoons of the ethnic conflict in the former Yugoslavia illustrate the fear of common people as they are experiencing, directly or indirectly, the consequences of the war. As a means of social conversation and gossiping about political leaders and events of the day, political cartoons always address the common people. And, not least, cartoon art production offers the newspaper reader, momentarily, a way of escaping the hardships of everyday life. Through satire and humor, the cartoon provides a place to reconsider one's conviction that may provoke a smile in the moment that is already gone.

Some Aspects of Music and Politics in Bosnia

Mirjana Laušević

The war in Bosnia and Herzegovina has usually been portrayed as an awakening of Balkan ghosts; a dissonance that is genetically engraved into Balkan blood. The conflict is presented as timeless, thus ahistorical, inherited, beyond control. It is also considered locally specific, thus alienated from larger political and economic turmoil in the world. Seeing tangled and extremely nuanced conflict as a series of easy-to-grasp, black-and-white slides does not help us understand it. The task of scholarship is to deal with complexities of world conflicts, to de-essentialize and destabilize stereotypes and to avoid empty assumptions. By analyzing particular aspects of Bosnian musical reality I want to re-channel the discourse from an oversimplified, apocalyptic view of a human culture to down-to-earth daily fabrications of meaning.

In this essay I will address particular processes of cultural politics and musical production in Bosnia, and to some extent in Serbia and Croatia as well. The

I am grateful to the friends and family members who helped obtain material for this work. I am also indebted to Mark Slobin and Tim Eriksen for insights on earlier drafts of this essay. Part of this essay was presented at the 1994 Annual Meeting of the Society for Ethnomusicology, Colgate University and Central Connecticut State University. Discussions following these presentations, as well as suggestions from Dane Kusić, Jane Sugarman, and many others helped improve this work. However, the views presented here are mine and I take the full responsibility for them.

limited number of examples that will be discussed here should certainly not be perceived as exhaustive of the subject. Each of the examples is carefully chosen, not to represent or evaluate the activities and decisions of a particular warring party, but to address and illustrate the specific issues relating to the state of music during the war. My goal is to emphasize strategic, conscious moves of individuals and groups involved in conflict.

Music was used not only as the cultural weapon of choice by all warring parties in Bosnia but also as a fuel for the war machine. It was crucial in strengthening morale and maintaining group cohesion as well as in providing justification for war and perpetuating violence. No other symbolic expression is more powerful when it comes to creating fear and defining otherness. As a journalist of a Serbian magazine *Vreme* (November 30, 1992) puts it, listeners are forced to "rejoice in their own destruction while listening to "patriotic" songs which . . . cut with a sonic guillotine the little tolerance that was left." Snare drums, trumpets, and bagpipes are replaced by cassettes and music videos, radio and TV waves.

During the war in Bosnia it was a common practice to blast music through loudspeakers turned toward the enemy. One can say that using music to claim territory and threaten the enemy is an ancient practice. The expression of power through the use of amplified sound is not exactly a novelty either. But the reader needs to bear in mind that whether one wants to hear them or not, these "patriotic" songs are all pervasive, sneaking deeply under the skin. A Muslim refugee from Mostar told me, for example, that she was so haunted by the Croatian "patriotic" tune, "HVO te brani, HVO te hrani" (The Croatian Military Defense defends you, the Croatian Military Defense feeds you), she found herself humming it, even though that same Croatian Military Defense had imprisoned her husband, stolen her livestock, and destroyed her house. Music has the power to subconsciously enter a mind against its will. Many more tunes generated by the warring parties created many more "music victims" on all sides in the Bosnian conflict.

Ethnic Labeling of Existing Musical Repertoires

The "cleansing" of prewar music not only dominated the cultural politics of the warring parties but preceded the actual realization of this ideology on the battle field. The carving away of whole sections of the musical repertoire was sometimes culturally and historically grounded, as in the case of traditional genres which were already associated with a particular ethnic group, but at other times it was done randomly, as in the case of various genres of popular and Western classical music. Who decided, and on what grounds, which part of this body of music was Serbian, or Croatian, or Muslim?

Radio and TV stations were the main institutional centers where the cleansing and ethnic labeling of all preexisting music took place during the war. However, to the best of my knowledge, there was no particular decree issued by any political leader that instructed music directors at these institutions to identify particular pieces of music, or even particular performances, as Muslim, Serbian, or Croatian. At first, this process was regulated by fear and self-censorship rather than defined cultural policy. It did not take long for individuals in public positions to realize that they needed to prove their political correctness at every moment and that the choice of which music to air carried a highly loaded political message. For example, Tchaikowsky's Symphony in B-minor became Serbian if performed by the Belgrade Philharmonic Orchestra and as such could not be aired on Sarajevo Television without getting the music director of the TV program into trouble.[1] Obviously, the ethnicity of a performer became a crucial determinant for assigning new "ownership" to a musical piece. However, things were not quite so simple. A music director of the Bosnian Serb TV station at Pale got into trouble for airing the music of an all-Serbian rock band based in Serbia.[2] As the material broadcast happened to be a remake of a song once made popular by a Croatian band, the song was denounced as Croatian. The denunciation was made by an individual who tried to prove his "political correctness" and nationalistic awareness, and by so doing to ensure his security and upward mobility. Incidentally, both the accuser and the accused in this story were Bosnian Serbs.

Furthermore, it was not enough to know the ethnicity of the performer to safely broadcast a piece. The performer also had to have appropriate political affiliations. Music directors needed to know where the performer was at the moment, on whose side, in the country or in emigration, and also had to be on top of all the gossip in the "patriotic," yellow press regarding music stars. In any case "swimming" in the very muddy waters of the undetermined but dangerous business of assigning potential ethnic ownership of a musical piece demanded a lot of skill and cultural knowledge for the individuals in charge. To avoid mistakes music directors at public institutions avoided airing any "questionable" kind of music. Radio and TV archives were "cleansed" of virtually all material that could not safely be claimed by a warring party as their own.

1. The Muslim-led Bosnian government "inherited" the building, equipment, and most of the personnel of Sarajevo Radio and Television. The majority of employees that remained in Sarajevo during the war kept their positions at the television station. It is also important to note that Sarajevo Television personnel were and still are ethnically mixed. However, since the institution is controlled by the Muslim government, it naturally represents its interests. Another TV station in Sarajevo, the "Hayatt," has exclusively Muslim personnel and is aimed at Muslim audiences.

2. The Pale station was established by Bosnian Serbs after the war began. All its employees are Serbs. It is important to note that the speakers on this TV station were, at one point, forced to use the *ekavian* dialect spoken by Serbian Serbs, instead of the *ijekavian* dialect of Bosnian Serbs. This was an attempt to distance the Bosnian Serbs from the Muslims and Bosnian Croats and make them closer to the Serbians. In a similar manner, Sarajevo Television introduced in its official vocabulary many borrowings from Turkish and Arabic to replace Serbo-Croatian expressions. The "purification" of "Croatian" has long preceded the described attempts made by both Muslims and Bosnian Serbs.

I will provide an example of this kind of self-censorship. In the summer of 1993 I was trying to dub some of the prewar recordings of the most popular pop, rock, and folk-pop singers from all over former Yugoslavia in a local radio station in Serbia. With a certain amount of wonder and disapproval, the music director showed me densely stacked records on the floor of the otherwise half empty music archive, saying: "*Those* records are over there, if you really want to listen to *them,* but *we* do not air them anymore." "Did somebody tell you not to air these records?" I asked. "No," he responded, "but I will not put my head on the block." This spatial division of "polluted" music—it could not even be put on a bottom shelf, but rather on the floor—illustrates the impact of politics on musical choice. I must remind the reader that the above story comes from a town in Serbia, thus outside the war zone. While this music director was only figuratively putting his head on the block, a wrong decision made by a music director in Bosnia could have literally done so.

It is interesting that the overall sound of the song and musical content did not play a crucial role in determining the ethnic labeling of a particular prewar musical piece. This is probably so because popular music genres were not created for specific ethnic audiences. It is perhaps paradoxical that the "Islamic" sounding Newly Composed Folk Music style dominated the Bosnian Serb radio and TV, while music in an "ethnically neutral" rock idiom could not be aired unless the band members were Serbs. Many similar examples can point to the inevitability of "flows" and arbitrariness involved in the attempts to cut a diverse, intertwined culture into three clear pieces.

Recontextualization of Past Musical Resources

The recontextualization of past resources, manipulated both musically and textually, is directed inward toward the cohesion of a warring party, toward defining the boundaries from which others are excluded. I have noted elsewhere (Laušević 1996: 134) that "the rhetoric of nationalism on all sides depends on presenting three rigidly circumscribed groups, each having clear and inherent national interests. This rhetoric has been largely accepted and perpetuated in the West as well." The complex and diverse Bosnian society is usually reduced to three clearly defined and unified ethnic groups labeled "the Muslims," "the Serbs," and "the Croats." This reductionism obscures the segmentation within each group as well as similarities and connections between members of different groups. Personal identities of Bosnians (Muslims, Serbs, and Croats) are based not only on ethnicity but also on categories such as age, gender, regional belonging, education, urban versus rural lifestyle, and so on. Traditional as well as popular musical styles are not distributed solely along ethnic lines. On the contrary, traditional rural Bosnian music has a highly local character. Members of different ethnic groups within the same geographic region share much of their repertoire and have more in common with each other than with members of their respective ethnic groups who live further away. Similarly age, education, and urban or rural origins were more crucial than ethnicity in determining which popular music genre, if any, people listened to.

"Exploitation" of traditional musical genres as well as traditional instruments creates and reinforces difference among various ethnic groups. To a certain extent it parallels the current cultural policy of revising the language into three separate languages, Croatian, Bosnian, and Serbian, in an attempt to deny commonality among the ethnic groups. The musical genres that do have strong ethnic connotations and are traditionally associated with a particular ethnic group appear in current musical productions both in their traditional form, namely, as renditions of traditional songs, or as new creations in the spirit of their respective genres. Most of this music is broadcast over radio or television and performed at live concerts and festivals. *Sevdalinkas*,[3] preferably accompanied by *saz*,[4] for Muslims, epic songs accompanied by *gusle*,[5] for Serbs, or cheerful *poskočicas*,[6] preferably accompanied by *tamburica*[7] orchestras, for Croats, are used as symbols of ethnic identity as well as means toward redefining history by bringing ethnic difference into the foreground.

It is far beyond the scope of this essay to discuss how and why particular traditional music genres were chosen as symbols of national identity of "the Muslims," "the Serbs," and "the Croats." What is pertinent to this discussion is to note that these choices were not random, nor were they necessarily a "natural" outcome of a culturally, historically, and ethnically contrived musical practice. Even the *ilahija,* a Muslim religious hymn, that was by its religious nature exclusively Muslim, had to be constructed into a symbol of Muslim national identity through conversion from a private religious form into a mediated mass music.[8] In the case of *tamburica* as a Croatian national symbol, epic poetry with *gusle* accompaniment as a Serbian national symbol, or *sevdalinka* as a symbol of a secular, Bosnian national identity, the situation is much more blurred. "The Muslims," "the Serbs," and "the Croats" needed to recognize a particular sound, or a particular musical genre, as their own in order to identify with it. This is true not only for traditional music genres, but also for current musical production in which a particular sound is qualified and preferred as Muslim, Serbian, or Croatian. However, a particular sound is defined as such, not by the fact that it is the

---

3. A *sevdalinka* is a type of love song associated with the urban Muslim population of Bosnia. Its name derives from the Turkish *sevda,* "love" or "desire."

4. A *saz* is a long-necked lute that was introduced to Bosnia during the Turkish rule in the region. It is used either as a solo instrument, or to accompany *sevdalinka.*

5. Epic singers accompany themselves on a single string, short-necked, bowed lute called the *gusle.*

6. *Poskočica* is a song and dance genre of a lively character, often with humorous lyrics.

7. *Tamburica* orchestras are comprised of plucked lutes of various sizes.

8. See Laušević 1996, "The Ilahiya as a Symbol of Bosnian Muslim National Identity."

only musical style used by the particular group, but rather by the fact that other groups do not use it as their national symbol and will not mistake it for their own. While it is easy for an insider to recognize a Muslim, Serbian, or Croatian sound upon hearing it, it is almost impossible to briefly describe the specific musical characteristics of these sounds to outsiders. What enables this "recognition" is the fact that these "typical" sounds evoke certain cultural and historical ties that enable the listener to place the sound in one of the three categories. However, these cultural and historical ties are as much evoked as they are provoked and established through specific practice and national rhetoric.

For example, singing epic poetry with *gusle* accompaniment became established as a symbol of Serbian national identity. However, this musical practice is a part of the cultural heritage of many Bosnian Muslims and Croats as well. Even recently an epic poem was sung to glorify a contemporary Croatian hero, President Franjo Tudjman. In a recent article Čale Feldman (1995: 45) provides us with a brief description of an "epic song sung by a popular author, Željko Simić, accompanied by *gusle,* which worships Tudjman's figure, biography, and role in recent Croatian political history." According to Feldman "this song is both within the style and metrics of oral rhetoric and within the framework of traditional values, as well as presenting a myth-like vision of the current events." Thus the same musical genre, in this case epic poetry accompanied with *gusle*, can be used by two different groups. While for one it might provide means for glorification of a national leader and a way of mythologizing the present, for another it will serve as a symbol of national identity. This enables us to conclude that the power of music as a national symbol does not lie in the music itself but in the meaning assigned to it and shared by a particular group of people.

Similarly, both Croats and Serbs could have established strong cultural and historical ties to *tamburica* music. However, only through particular national discourse and the complex processes of assigning national meaning to this musical practice could *tamburica* become a symbol of Croatian national identity.[9] In an article on *tamburica* as a political and cultural phenomenon in Croatia, Ruža Bonifačić (1995: 65–77), a Croatian ethnomusicologist, questions statements that declare *tamburica* the "Croatian national instrument." On one hand she sees the "oriental origin of the *tambura/tamburica*" and "its nurture among the various communities (Muslims, Croats, Serbs, Gypsies, Czechs, Slovenes, etc.)" as a

9. In an oversimplified and nationalistically biased analysis of Serb and Croat musical choices, Croatian ethnomusicologist Naila Ceribašić has suggested that "[the contrast between] the 'masculine,' war-like option of Serbia and the 'feminine,' peaceful option of Croatia is best symbolized by the contrast between the two musical instruments—the *gusle*, the Serbian national symbol, and the *tamburitza*, the Croatian national symbol" (Ceribašić 1995: 51–103). Through further black-and-white juxtapositions between Serbs and Croats she concludes that "the *gusle* symbolizes the 'tribal' and patriarchal world of the Balkan warrior-hero and the *tamburitza* evokes the world of the 'member of the cooperative,' a farmer, a conscientious and peaceful labourer, good, honest and hospitable people."

possible argument for perceiving this Croatian national instrumental tradition as an invented one. At the same time, she argues that "there are both historical and present-day grounds for ascribing *tamburica* the attribute and then also the meaning Croatian." Even though Bonifačić does not discuss the process of construction of *tamburica* as a Croatian national symbol, she acknowledges that "the long way from the concept of a Croatian *folk* instrument to *the* Croatian *national* instrument will once again be left to the concept of invented tradition, as well as multiple meaning, perception and interpretation of symbols."

Whether particular national musical traditions are invented or not, they need to be reinforced through practice. Just as the coat of arms, whether based on preexisting national imagery or newly created, needs to be visible and displayed to the nation in an appropriate context for it to become a meaningful symbol, music also needs a specific space in media and daily life to be an effective national symbol. Thus we can easily glimpse how certain musical genres came to be recognized as national symbols. For example, there were more than 240 performances of *sevdah* given for Bosnian Army soldiers (BiH Ekskluziv, March 18, 1994). Not to be outdone, Croatian Television constantly aired *tamburica* arrangements of patriotic and other tunes. And former Bosnian Serb leader, Radovan Karadžić, played *gusle* himself in televised appearances.

The knowledge and appreciation of traditional musical genres identified as "national" have also become expressions of the "national propriety" of an individual. A good Croat should appreciate *tamburica* music, a good Muslim should know *ilahija*s, a good Serb should love the epics. For example, it is assumed that the Serb who plays *gusle* knows more about "Serbianess" than other Serbs. He is, furthermore, an embodiment of cultural and historical ties with the nation's past; he knows what being a Serb is about. For that reason Radovan Karadžić, the former leader of Bosnian Serbs, claims his propriety, traditionalism, and Serbianess through playing *gusle* and singing epic poetry himself. It is important to note that in a traditional context, Karadžić would be considered an exceptionally bad epic singer and would not be able to capture or keep his listeners' attention. Unlike other epic singers who sing in their high register, where the voice is strong and piercing, Karadžić sings in a low register, in an intimidated and insecure way. This is contrary to the traditional manner of singing epic poetry. However, in spite of the low quality of his performance, he presents himself as someone who knows his national past and tradition and hence deserves to be national leader. Through playing *gusle* he is trying to establish himself as a defender of Serbian cultural heritage.[10] Similarly, other national leaders, though not person-

---

10. In a documentary film "Serbian Epics" produced by the BBC, Karadžić was filmed singing an epic poem with *gusle* accompaniment in the house of Vuk Stefanović Karadžić, a highly respected early nineteenth-century linguist and ethnologist who reformed the Serbo-Croatian language, collected, translated, and published numerous folk songs, tales, and customs. In this documentary Radovan Karadžić claimed his authority as the leader of Bosnian Serbs not only through his knowledge of Serbian tradition but also through an implied genetic link between himself and Vuk Karadžić.

ally involved in music production, chose the respective traditional music genres as accompaniments to their public appearances.

Concerts of traditional music were organized throughout the war for both soldiers and civilians. An interesting aspect of the war music business were live performances obviously catering to war profiteers, since they were the only ones who could afford to pay 30 DM to attend a show. The following excerpt from an article in the Sarajevo paper, *Večernje Novine*, quite clearly reveals how, in some cases, the financial interests of the organizers superseded patriotism: "The festival of folk music 'Bosnia sings to freedom' was held, with performance of 29 songs, in Lukavac (the songs are identified as 'patriotic songs in the form of *sevdah*'), but the organizers (unspecified) forbade television coverage. The reason is simple: to keep a monopoly of the market (in cassettes). Already tomorrow these cassettes will be sold on the black market in Germany, Austria, etc. That is the hard currency business of our *sevdah*."

Cassettes and music videos of patriotic, nationalistic songs circulate among refugees and emigrants throughout Europe, America, and Australia. Some of the nationalistic songs are even aimed at these audiences. Young men who fled the country are invited to come back and join the "common" cause. Of course, within the war zone this type of song provides a model of "proper" manhood for the soldiers, reinforcing the "family" bond between the mother country and her brave sons, and reaffirming the position of the soldiers as proper sons of the homeland.

New Music Production

It is not accidental that all three warring parties have resorted to traditional music genres to spur nationalistic feelings and create new typical national sounds while, at the same time, using popular music idioms to boost the morale and image of the young soldiers. After all, a large percentage of Bosnian youth does not appreciate traditional musical genres and can relate, and thus react, much better to patriotic or nationalistic songs in popular musical styles. The traditional musical genres were recontextualized in order to establish the ties of a group to its cultural history, emphasize ethnic difference, and provide historical justification for the fighting. The soldiers, however, did not generally see themselves as ghosts from the past, but rather as trendy action heroes. More than anything else, popular music, particularly in the form of music videos, was designed to contemporize the conflict and to direct the gaze of the fighting youth toward the future.

Music video production on all three sides uses the same image of hip-looking young fighters, who smoke Marlboros, wear Ray-Ban sun glasses, and know how

---

Whether true or not, he is implying a parallel between Vuk's contribution to Serbian culture and his own role as a "defender" of Serbianess.

to handle arms. The aim of music videos is to boost the morale of the soldiers and offer them a "movie-like" and thus prestigious and desirable image of themselves. Music video is a medium that can visually glorify soldiers and fighting, while verbally dismissing war as an option. It was enthusiastically adopted by the various warlords of all the warring parties as a medium through which they could express and assert their individual power.

There is a story about the gangs of two warlords nominally on the same side in the conflict, but literally fighting for primacy, not on the battle field, but at the TV station that aired their music videos. This story does not tell us anything about the ethnicity of the actors but rather about the drive for power that music videos embody and the importance given to music video production by warring parties. The music video scene was either dominated by the warlords whose war profits and military power enabled them to assert themselves as "music stars," or by TV stations which manipulated this genre with different goals in mind (although the TV stations are often controlled directly or indirectly by the warlords). It is not only that certain songs are devoted to particular warlords, but they either star in the video, or hire musicians to lip-synch for them or sing songs themselves.

Common to most war music production is the glorification of soldiers, a certain kind of fascination with weapons and stereotyped images of manhood. The suggested images of manhood stem from sources as different as local patriarchy, European fashion magazines, westerns, and the latest American action films. In August 1992 Sarajevo Television released a music video titled *Vojnik Sreće* (The Soldier of Fortune). The stars in this video are members of special troops of the Bosnian Army. Since this video was done by Sarajevo Television itself, rather than foreign media, through its analysis we can address some issues of self-representation of this warring party.

Broadly speaking, the video is organized in three sections, scaling from narrow to large. The opening of the video is focused on an individual, the middle section on the military unit itself and its strength, ability, and military preparedness, and the final one where the soldiers are presented as warm human beings that smile, play, love, and care for each other and their hometown.

The video starts with a shot of a muscular, bare male back superimposed over a background of green trees, toward which the man is looking. (There are multiple possible interpretations of this image, some of which might be that the male body is compared to the green tree in its beauty, its strength, and its youth. The bareness of the man suggests his innocence, and again emphasizes his youth.) Then he turns around. We see a close-up of his slightly worried, but calm and controlled face. The next cut shows us his gun and ammunition, a pack of Marlboro cigarettes, and a lighter. He then puts on a shirt and buckles his belt and then we see another close-up of his face. This time he blinks, as if to show that he is closing his eyes in front of his reality, to show that he is a soldier because he has to be one. Then he fastens the ammunition around his waist and puts a gun in his belt. He ties a bandanna around his neck and zips up his bulletproof vest. Now we see that the man is standing in front of a green flag with a yellow circle in the middle and a dark-skinned male arm holding a lit torch.[11] Then he picks up his Ray-Ban sun glasses and puts them on.[12] We get several shots from different angles and a close-up of the glasses with rays of light reflecting from its metal edges and from the lenses themselves. The man now disappears behind the glasses, as if the glasses provide a shield to his individuality and depersonalize him. This is the last time we see him in the video.

We get even further removed from the man in the next cut. Now we see only his shadow superimposed over a lit circle (either suggesting some kind of a spotlight, or maybe paralleling the circle on the flag, in which case the man's shadow has replaced the arm with the torch). In any case, the man whose shadow we are watching takes a puff on his cigarette. He then replaces the cigarette in his hand with a gun, brings it up to his face, props it, and then leans it on his shoulder (end of the introduction). During this section of the video we hear drums and male voices singing heya-heya-hey.

To briefly sum up, the above video imagery shows us a macho man like that from European perfume commercials. He is a determined fighter and a defender of his country/town/ family. As a real man he smokes (Marlboros, no less). That he wears Ray Ban sunglasses also suggests that he is trendy and hip.[13]

In the rest of the video we see other images of manhood. Able, strong, brave, fast men are first portrayed, then they begin to "melt." Under all their strength and heroism warm hearts hide and wait for an opportunity to express love, humor, and gentleness. Then, in the next section we see a number of young men in action displaying their military skills. They are dressed in the same uniforms as they zig-zag through a street shooting. They climb into an abandoned shelled building and also drive tanks through the streets of Sarajevo. In the background a song plays. It has the following lyrics:

> If the evil happens, if it hits me tonight
> I will not die of death, I will die of love.
> Because I am a soldier of fortune, the bullet does not want me.
> You can kill my summer, but the Spring will live.

11. The flag, in fact, is that of Zaire. I cannot suggest any interpretations of the choice of the Zairian flag as background.

12. Senjković (1995: 59) has noted the appeal of Ray-Ban glasses to the young men in the Croatian military forces. He believes that "the obvious popularity of Ray-Ban glasses and the mask uniform probably came from the image of an American soldier as represented in the 'Desert Storm' operation or in numerous films such as *An Officer and Gentlemen*, *Top Gun* and others." Ray-Ban glasses were worn by Serbian soldiers as well and also used as an accessory in music videos (also see Luković in *Vreme*, 1992).

13. Both Marlboros and Ray-Bans are status symbols. They represent top quality, desired goods that are hard to get. The video's message might be that as a soldier you get to have the things other people cannot afford. Any kind of cigarettes, but particularly Marlboros, were in high demand in Sarajevo during the war.

If the evil happens, if it hits me tonight
don't cry, put a smile on your face
it is not a sin to die for this city.

Shoot! You can't do anything to me
I am as big as the universe.
Shoot from three hundred cannons,
this heart is steel.

While music videos are costly to produce in terms of necessary material, time, personnel, and money, audio production was widely accessible. Local radio stations and cheap private cassette production enterprises have flourished during the war. The soldiers were allowed to take time off from the front lines in order to produce recordings. Some of these recordings were very locally specific, since their distribution was often extremely limited. The lyrics would often target a specific military unit, describing the most recent events, celebrating small victories, glorifying the military commanders, mourning the losses, encouraging rage against the enemy. The battlefield was virtually bombarded by these cassettes, which seemed to be the main morale booster for young fighters. In the Serbian paper *Naše ideje* (1993: 71), Dragoslav Bokan reviews a Serbian nationalist cassette by Baja-Little Kninja in the following words:

> Get rid of your collection of classical music, stand against the potential disdain of your friends, prove your fearlessness and buy the cassette "Stop pashas and ustashas." If this cassette were not there, I am sure (and convinced from my own experience and that of my fellow fighters) that the results of our fighting would be maybe even 30 percent worse, and again I am convinced by experience that nothing would change with all the speeches of our academics, string quartets, Serbian parties and movements and all our "culture." These simple melodies, despised by the cynicism of godless intellectuals without soul, are winning this war.

This statement is so blatant that it almost does not need comment. However unpleasant the thought might be, we have good reason to believe that nationalistic songs have a tremendous impact on soldiers. What do these "simple melodies" talk about? There are several distinguishable categories according to the target audience and the general content of the lyrics. General topics could be summarized as follows: to justify the war, to threaten others, to offend others,[14] to encourage one's own military morale, to encourage hatred, to reiterate groups victim status, to plead for help and recognition of others. Various groups deal

---

14. In many cases the songs have extremely offensive and vulgar lyrics. I have chosen not to discuss these examples.

with these issues in different ways, but in general all of the war songs carry the dangerous message that one group's prosperity and future is independent of other groups' actions. Songs with the theme "You can't do anything to us" are the most common next to those which suggests "We are the winners of this war." The gap between them and us is presented as unbridgeable in terms "They will never know" or "They cannot understand," or in a threatening version such as "We will teach (show) you." In any case, whether it is because of crying babies, mourning mothers, burnt homes, or departed friends, the war is always "worth it." In most of the songs it is not only worth dying for this city, country, army, or nation but it is also an honor to do so.

Postlude

There was a real musical war in Bosnia: a war against the Other, whether defined as Muslim, Serb, Croat, communist, or simply intellectual. One of the first victims of this war was an appreciation of Bosnian cultural diversity and the interconnectedness of Bosnians of various ethnic backgrounds.[15] This war was constructed and perpetuated on a daily basis by conscious decisions of social agents. These are individuals or groups governed by their sense of justice, their drive for power, the fear from the same agents who acted in the midst of culturally, historically, politically, and economically specific circumstances. With the change of these circumstances there is hope for a collective musical healing.

Once the actual fighting stopped, the market economy and the nostalgic demands of the people for the music that they had listened to before the war made possible the return to Bosnian markets of music from all over former Yugoslavia. Only television and some radio stations, as strongholds of governmental ideologies, are still trying to keep their musical programs divided along ethnic lines. Currently one can find not only the cassettes and CDs of the most popular prewar singers and bands on the tables of street vendors in Sarajevo, but also those recently produced in Croatia and Serbia, as well as in the West. One might find it hard to believe that in Sarajevo one can buy even the tapes of Serbian Newly Composed Folk music star Ceca (Svetlana Veličković), who during the war married Arkan, the leader of a Serbian paramilitary formation known as the *Tigers* and alleged war criminal. This is certainly an indication that historical, cultural, political, and economic circumstances in Bosnia have changed dramatically and that, hopefully, the musical war is over. It is also an indication of the capricious

---

15. With the rise of national ideologies ethnicity became the main Bosnian marker of personal identity. Before the resurgence of nationalism various ethnic groups within Bosnia were more interconnected with each other than tolerant of each other. The difference I see between the concept of ethnic tolerance and interconnectedness is that the former relies on difference as precept for mutual interaction, while the latter relies on commonality and an overarching, inclusive identity as the dominant one.

and often random nature of the relationship between music and politics. In one set of circumstances, music as unrelated to the conflict as Tchaikowsky's Symphony in B-minor can take on nationalist meaning and be perceived as threatening. Just as quickly, under new circumstances, music by the wife of a nationalist paramilitary leader can be stripped of its extra-musical meaning and be accepted as just another song to dance to.

17

Clapping for Serbs

Nationalism and Performance in Bosnia and Herzegovina

Lynn D. Maners

This essay examines the role of the amateur folk ensemble in the political, moral, and symbolic economy of Bosnia and Herzegovina in the Yugoslav era, roughly 1942–92. A postscript updates the situation of these folklore ensembles during the Serbian war of aggression against Bosnia and Herzegovina and the current uneasy peace in the post–Dayton Accord environment. The folklore performances considered in this work, at first glance epiphenomenal, are in fact integral to ideological considerations, and as such, subject to transformation and reinterpretation.

Amateur Folklore and the Idea of Yugoslavia

Originally intended as living examples of the unity of all the Yugoslav peoples, in the late 1980s both amateur and professional folklore ensembles became sites of contested meanings as the Yugoslav national model began to wane and ethno-nationalism to wax, especially in Serbia and Croatia. Bosnia and Herzegovina, the only republic of now former Yugoslavia without an eponymous ethnic majority, became a critical cultural and, later, actual, battleground for aggressive ethno-nationalism.

In the decade following the death of Tito, cracks began to appear in the elaborate structure of cultural symbols (Hammel 1993: 36) of "Yugoslav" nationality. These had been developed by the Yugoslav state both during and after World War II. An important feature of this endeavor to create a Yugoslav national identity, composed of approved diverse identities, was to find expression through folklore ensembles, professional, semi-professional/seasonal, and amateur. Modeled on Soviet institutions and formally sponsored by state institutions such as universities and workers organizations, the cultural art society (*kulturno umjetnicko drustvo,* or KUD) functioned in all the republics and autonomous provinces of the country. KUDs were established in both urban and rural areas, and few villages were too small to have a KUD. Those that were too small or (at least in Bosnia) too mono-ethnic had village folk ensembles, which lacked state support. In the KUDs, traditional dances, instrumental pieces, and songs were arranged into suites and adapted for presentation on stage at numerous public events as part of the transformation and recontextualization of traditional music and dance within the new socialist order. In some cases this created a very odd performance. In his dissertation on folklore performance in Slavonia, Frank Dubinskas (1983) notes the incongruity of older KUD members, dressed as youths and performing ritually associated folklore from the period of their young adulthood.

As contrasted with the re-creation of youthful experience, one of the goals of the KUD was to literally create for its performers and audiences the symbolic experience of being a "new" Yugoslav. KUD members performed folklore from all parts of the reconstituted Yugoslavia regardless of the members' individual ethnic backgrounds. This was considered to be an especially important goal in multiethnic BiH (as Bosnia and Herzegovina is frequently abbreviated). As one "veteran" of the *Pokret* KUD in the late 1940s and early 1950s told me: "KUDs were intended to inoculate us [literally *peljovan od*] against nationalism." Pre–Second World War ethno-nationalism was thus analogized as a virus whose harmful effects could be prevented by socialist progress.

KUDs were fully incorporated into the political economy of Tito's Yugoslavia. Until 1966 and the extension of worker self-management to cultural activities, control came from the federal center. After 1966 it devolved to the republics. In Bosnia, this meant that the Savez KUD BiH (KUD Committee of Bosnia and Herzegovina) was responsible for administering and distributing funding to the more than four hundred KUDs in the republic. A *gradski savez KUD* (city KUD committee) supported the KUDs in a particular area and its suburbs. For example, some three dozen city and suburban KUDs came under the purview of the Gradski Savez-Sarajevo. The *gradski savez* was also tasked with ranking KUD performances for budgetary purposes, sponsoring some performances, and storing costumes and archives, especially for KUDs too small or new to have their own dedicated institutional space. Individual KUDs were administered by a committee made up of representatives of the sponsoring institution, the groups' choreographer / artistic director, its orchestral/musical director, and interested volunteers. It should be mentioned that unlike Serbia, Croatia, and Macedonia, Bosnia never had a professional folklore ensemble; thus the highest-ranked KUD in Sarajevo was generally regarded as the functional equivalent of a professional ensemble.

KUDs were categorized as either *izvorni* (traditional) or *stilizatsia* (stage-oriented, and the vast majority). *Stilizatsia* KUDs were organized internally into A, B, C, and *pioniri* (children's) sections and ranked among other KUDs by whether and how well they could present a complete evening program (or *komplet*) of Yugoslav folklore, that is to say, a satisfactory performance of at least one suite from each of the Yugoslav republics and autonomous provinces, although this political requirement was disguised as a requirement to represent all of Yugoslavia's ethnographic zones. This material was conveyed to aspiring choreographers at a three-summer-long course, the Ljetna Škola Folklora (the Summer Folklore School), administered by an institute in Zagreb, Croatia.

The *komplet* suite was the dominant model and was even found outside the country among, for example, folk ensembles of Yugoslav emigrant groups in Sweden (Ronstrom 1991). In the United States, a *komplet* performance was generally seen only in the performances of university-sponsored folklore ensembles such as those of the Duquesne University Tamburitzans. They perform not just a pan-Yugoslav program, like a first-class *stilizatsia* KUD, but add the music and dance folklore of other Balkan countries into their performances. Ethnically oriented community folklore ensembles from Serbian and Croatian communities in the United States tended to perform only the folklore of their home republics. To the best of my knowledge, before the dissolution of Tito's Yugoslavia there were no specifically Bosnian community folklore ensembles in the United States, though a number have now appeared in Bosnian refugee communities.

The raw material for *stilizatsia* KUDs and professional ensembles alike was traditional folk performance, recorded ethnographically, and then transformed and recontextualized to fit the stage. (Bosnia in particular was considered to be a "treasure chest of folklore.") Both *stilizatsia* KUDs and professional ensembles were expected to specialize in a wide range of folklore from their own republic, while competently presenting the material of the other republics and autonomous provinces. This rapidly resulted in some suites becoming iconic for their republic/province, namely, a Šumadija suite for Serbia, a Posavina suite for Croatia, a wedding suite for Kosovo. The village folklore ensembles, the source of much of this material, where villagers actually performed their own local folkloric repertoire, were excluded from the KUD system. They could not perform a pan-Yugoslav program, and, of even greater concern from an ideological point of view, might have represented only a single ethnic group. These village ensembles were generally only seen in events known as *smotra folklora* (folklore reviews), where the emphasis was on traditional authenticity of performance. The first Smotra

Folklora BiH in 1985 featured just such performances by village ensembles and KUDs. However, by the next year, KUDs dominated the event.

Before the socialist era, and even before World War I during Austrian rule in Bosnia (1878–1914), cultural performances tended to be mono-ethnic in nature. In that era many festivals were sponsored by nationalist organizations, causing the Austrian administration to monitor them closely (Besarović 1968). In the post–World War II era of socialist Yugoslavia, folklore performances became not so much celebrations of ethnic identity as celebrations highlighting the cultural diversity within the unity of the new Yugoslav nation. A major symbol of this new ideological emphasis appeared in June 1950 when the first national folklore festival (Smotra Jugoslavije) was held in Belgrade. Through amateur performance, this event celebrated the many regions and republics of the new Yugoslavia. Folklore groups from Bosnia and Herzegovina performed multiple couple dances such as the Staro Bosansko Kolo (see Dunin 1966) and the Lindjo, soon be elevated to the level of icon for the republic. Nationwide, these state-sponsored performance ensembles came to represent an important aesthetic locus in Yugoslav culture.

The transformations and recontextualizations of folklore for national purposes were ideological in nature and ultimately based on Gorky's maxim that folklore was the creative activity of the working class. The raw stuff of quotidian folk practice was transformed into a superstructural commodity in service to the state. In part this was achieved by shifting the audience for these performances from a traditional intimate one experienced directly by participants, to a mass approach in which the majority of the audience watched but did not participate. Unlike village performance where audiences produced the performance through their participation, the new national folklore alienated the audience from folklore production and turned participants into consumers. This certainly marked an odd inversion of the traditional Marxist proletariat-production relationship under socialism. Though the majority of people, as audience members, were divorced from folklore production, we shall see that they were not necessarily passive or neutral.

As noted earlier, most KUDs were deliberately multiethnic in their membership and multiregional in their repertoire. The few examples of mono-ethnic KUDs in Bosnia were generally composed of an ethnic minority (*narodnost*) such as the Ukrainian KUD *Taras Ševčenko* or an alleged Rom KUD in Banja Luka. This system attempted to build, brick by brick, a Yugoslav identity that embraced a pan-Yugoslav vision of *narod* (nation) and *narodnosti* in happy coexistence and rejected the radical ethno-nationalisms of the pre–World War II era. KUDs, along with other institutions, contributed to the creation of a multiethnic whole. The amateur folklore organizations were deliberately created to foster just this sense of ethnic integration and, in this way, were considered as important as economic development. One of my *prava raja* (slang for a real Sarajevo native) friends remembers a meeting held right after the war in which a Communist

Party cadre "practically foamed at the mouth while insisting that having a first-class KUD was as important as having a factory!"

However, just as *bricolage* can build something out of individual pieces, cementing them into a perceived coherent whole through experience and interpretation, so too can the pieces be disassembled through *demontaza* and reinterpretation. In the post-Tito era after 1980, this latter process began to take hold. Furthermore, the process of disassembly only accelerated after communism lost its credibility as a viable ideology through which to balance the centrifugal and centripetal forces of then-Yugoslavia. This conflict was played out on stages both large and small, in both the literal and figurative sense.

In the course of the 1980s, as stresses accumulated in the system, some of the consumers of the various cultural performances began to deconstruct them. They removed themselves from the experience the state had designed for them as Yugoslavs and reinterpreted their experience of these performances as ethno-nationalistic. For example, friends told me of audiences in Zagreb walking out of performances of the Wedding Dance Suite from Kosovo in protest against the Serbian repression in that province.[1]

In Tone Bringa's remarkable documentary film on the advent of hell in a very small place, *We Are All Neighbours* (1993), there is a scene which aptly illustrates the moral confusion put into motion by the start of this deconstruction. Set in the town of Kiseljak near Sarajevo, the film depicts events both before and after the ethnic cleansing of Muslim families through systematic terror and intimidation by Croatian militias. One scene in particular emphasizes the seemingly unstoppable creep of radical nationalism that resulted in the first so-called white stage of ethnic cleansing. The camera focuses on two young women involved in the typical Bosnian hospitality ritual of coffee grinding. Their comments concern the irrationality of it all. The same people who are their enemies now were their friends together in the town folklore group. In those days, no one in the group formally seemed to know or care what another's ethnicity was. The unspoken question is how this could have happened to friends who previously had no concern about one another's pedigree. Poignantly, what had happened to brotherhood and unity?

"Bosna Moja": The Multiethnic Heart of a Multiethnic State

It is not possible to emphasize enough the importance of both the symbolic and actual role of Bosnia and Herzegovina within the post–World War II Yugoslav state. After the war of Yugoslav dissolution engulfed Bosnia, I was reminded by

---

1. The Wedding Dance Suite had become so iconic of Kosovo that, according to Reineck (1986), parts of its choreography began to appear at Kosovo Albanian wedding celebrations as a "traditional" folk dance.

Bosnian friends that Sarajevo, then under Serb bombardment, had been proposed in the immediate post-Liberation era as the capital of the new state. Yet at the same time, BiH held an anomalous position as the one republic of post–World War II Yugoslavia in which no ethnic group was dominant. Serbs were the majority in Serbia, Croats in Croatia, Slovenes in Slovenia, Macedonians in Macedonia, and Montenegrins in Montenegro. In the Republic of Bosnia and Herzegovina in socialist Yugoslavia, however, no ethnic group was in a majority, though the Muslim population held a plurality of 43 percent in the 1981 census. While Serbian (and later Croatian) war propaganda attempted to rewrite the ethnicity and nationality of Bosnia's Muslim population as "Turks," it should be remembered that Bosnian Muslims are of Slavic ancestry and the descendants of those who accepted Islam as a result of the Ottoman conquest.

First mentioned in Constantine VII Porphyrogenitos's *De Administrando Imperio* in the tenth century, Bosnia lies on the periphery of Europe. First home to the Illyrian peoples, then colonized by the Roman Empire, and later settled by the great movement of Slavic peoples in the sixth and seventh centuries, Bosnia began to take on its qualities as a contact zone between East and West. Its isolation on the periphery is seen in the development of Bogomilism, a set of Christian religious practices divergent from Catholicism and Orthodoxy and condemned as heretical. Emerging from the Middle Ages as a classic feudal state, Bosnian and Serbian nobility alike fell to the advancing Ottoman Turks at the battle of Kosovo on Vidovdan, June 28, 1389. Within the next century, the native Serbs and Croats of BiH found themselves under Turkish domination. Incorporated into the Turkish *millet* system of self-administering confessional communities, many Bosnian Christians found it to their advantage to convert to Islam. These conversions thus mark the beginning of the modern Bosnian Muslim population.

The next four centuries comprise the period of Turkish Bosnia, an outpost standing against a Europe looking down on the newly Turkish lands from across the Sava. In Bosnia itself, as Turkey went from threatening the walls of Vienna to being the sick man of Europe, conditions gradually worsened, especially for Christian peasants. Tax farming elites reduced useful production and by the middle of the nineteenth century peasant revolts were common.

In 1878, at the Congress of Berlin, the Ottoman Empire ceded control over Bosnia to Hapsburg Austro-Hungary. Acting as the colonial power, Austria set out to make Bosnia into an ideal, though primarily self-sufficient, colony. The Austrian period, 1878 to 1917, saw attempts to rationalize agriculture, develop industry, and create a modern administrative infrastructure. At the same time, under Baron Kallay's administration, an attempt was made to promote the development of a uniquely Bosnian interconfessional identity, the so-called Bosniak. Austro-Hungary hoped this would act as a counterweight to perceived ethnic agitation from Serb and Croatian sources.

Much of this ethnic and nationalist agitation took folkloric forms. This emphasis on performance and ethnicity was especially apparent in various ethnic-based cultural, educational, and benevolent organizations that, banned from direct political expression, sponsored a range of other activities. The first specifically Muslim festival in Bosnia was held in Tešanj in 1895 and included lectures, plays, and dramatic presentations (Kemura 1986: 135). Gajret, an organization for "Serb Muslims," was also an active sponsor of cultural events, beginning in 1905. Croatian performance groups, such as *tamburitza* orchestras and choruses, appeared in this period as did Serbian (Ekmečić n.d) and Croatian (Alilović 1980) elementary schools.

The armistice of World War I brought the end of Hapsburg Bosnia. The region was incorporated into the new Kingdom of Serbs, Croats, and Slovenes. Although ethnic agitation was particularly rancorous in much of the new kingdom, Bosnia remained a predominantly rural backwater. Even so, in a state-wide attempt at dealing with ethno-nationalism, the entire country was divided up into *banovine*, or regional governorships, which deliberately cut across traditional ethnic borders.

The beginning of World War II triggered a reign of terror in much of what is now former Yugoslavia. The war had an especially strong impact in Bosnia, since its mountainous terrain was especially amenable to small-unit, guerrilla-type tactics. Bosnia thus took on a central role in the communist-named national liberation struggle (NOB). Bosnia was in fact so central to Yugoslav identity that it was from the Bosnian town of Jajce in 1942 that the country's new existence was proclaimed in a meeting of the Anti-Fascist Council for the Liberation of Yugoslavia, or AVNOJ. Despite its centrality to the Yugoslav concept, Bosnia's unique multiethnic composition allowed for the continued creation and exploitation of grievances, both perceived and actual. Thus much of the slaughter in Bosnia took on an intercommunal aspect. Pedro Ramet (1992: 255) notes, for example, that approximately 328,000 people lost their lives in Bosnia in the NOB. This intercommunal violence has come back to haunt Bosnia in the recent war. Grievances dating back to the war are still fresh enough in memory to be exploited for ethno-nationalist purposes.

The National Liberation Struggle also marked the beginning of the use of cultural performances by the socialist Yugoslav proto-state as an aid in nation building. The 1942 statutes of the Proletarian National Liberation Brigades required every Partisan unit to have a culture team (Dedić 1981: 123). Along with "agitprop" theater, members of these culture teams were responsible for the creation of an invented tradition of "Partisan *kolos*." These circle dances were either choreographed *de novo* or transformed from an existing ethnic-associated dance into non- or multiethnic "Yugoslav" forms of folk dance. Until the breakup of modern Yugoslavia, festivals where these wartime Partisan dances and their postwar descendants were performed were a regular feature of the choreographer's calendar. At the same time that Partisan kolos were being created as a step to defuse ethnic differences, the choreographed "folk" dances of the urban bourgeois, known as "ballroom *kolos*" (*Radikal, Salonsko Kolo, Trgovačko Kolo,* etc.), popular in the interwar period, disappeared from the repertoire of both quotidian and symbolic performance. This resulted from a coordinated state campaign to erase class distinctions.

In the postwar era, national unity as represented in performance by the creation of a pan-Yugoslav standard repertoire became an important goal. After 1948 and Tito's break with Stalin, Yugoslavia began to develop an independent third way between East and West.[2] The Muslim population in Tito's Yugoslavia, especially the relatively well educated one of urbanizing Bosnia, was thus seen as an asset, especially in facilitating relations with Muslim countries. After the first "oil shock" of the 1970s, and continuing into the 1980s, many a nominally Muslim Bosnian engineer was found working on projects in Iraq or Saudi Arabia. Foreign projects with large numbers of Yugoslav workers had culture workers, such as folk dance choreographers, assigned to them, as indeed happened to a Sarajevo KUD director of my acquaintance. Showing off a suite of Muslim dances from Sarajevo was a useful propaganda tool when performed for visiting foreign dignitaries from countries hosting Yugoslav guest workers.

However, this recognition of Muslim ethnicity was fairly late in coming and the result of some negotiation at the national level. The position of the Muslims of Bosnia and Herzegovina was an anomalous one in the early years of Tito's Yugoslavia; in fact, the original 1948 census allowed for categories of "Serb-Muslim," "Croatian-Muslim," and "Undefined Muslim" (Velat 1988: 139), while the 1953 census only allowed for a category of "Yugoslav unidentified." Following that experiment, a new category emerged, that of *Muslimani (etnički pripadnost)*—"Muslim by ethnic belonging," which eventually led to the descriptor, *Muslimani u smislu narodnosti*—"Muslim in the sense of a national ethnic group." Bosnian Muslims, though, in no way resembled a unified group. Individuals of my acquaintance ranged in their self-descriptions from *mahala* Muslim (highly devout, living in an Old Town *komšiluk*, or neighborhood), to "suburban" Muslim (nonreligious intellectual of Muslim family), to "communist" Muslim (officially atheist, from a strong Party family).

As might be expected in a multiethnic environment, where mobility between groups was allowed, intermarriage was not uncommon. These intermarriages also created the all-important *veze*, or connections, across ethnic lines. As in many socialist/communist states, individuals perceived and often expressed to me that in their experience, connections were often far more important than any other factor in obtaining access to scarce resources. Urban folklore ensembles, such as KUD *Slobodan Princip-Seljo* of Sarajevo, were one of the venues of interethnic structural integration in Bosnia; many of the members of the *Veterani* section had met their future other-ethnic spouses at a rehearsal. Crossing all ethnic lines,

---

2. Tito, of course, along with Nehru of India, Nasser of Egypt, and Sukarno of Indonesia, spearheaded the development of the nonaligned movement, given life at the conference at Bandung (Indonesia) in 1955.

many young KUD members told me that they had chosen "Yugoslav" as a descriptor in the most recent census.

The republic itself was also in an anomalous position vis-à-vis the federal state. Bosnia was neither of the rich north (Slovenia, Croatia, Serbian Vojvodina), nor was it an obvious part of the poor south (Macedonia, Montenegro, parts of Serbia, and Kosovo). As tax monies flowed from the richer north to the LDRs (less developed regions), Bosnia found itself betwixt and between. According to Plestina (1987: 200) Bosnia was considered an LDR in the first five-year plan, only to be dropped from that status in the second and then subsequently reinstated. Traditionally rich in natural resources, its uneven development contributed to its being seen from the federal center as neither one nor the other. Thus, in some calculations, Bosnia was part of the north, in others part of the south. As an example of its "Northern," developed status, in interviews with Bosnian KUD members in their early twenties, many remembered "Pennies for Kosovo" days in their elementary schools when pocket change was collected to be sent south.

Bosnia's position as neither developed nor undeveloped became even more untenable in the Yugoslav economic decline. The oil shock of the 1970s exposed many of the weaknesses in the Yugoslav version of a managed economy, and Bosnia suffered accordingly. Through the 1970s and 1980s workers in various industries, through their BOALs (Basic Organization of Associated Labor), voted themselves pay raises to be paid for by loans from banks controlled by the industries in which they worked. Thus was inflation pushed ever higher. By the middle and late 1980s, classic hyperinflation had set in, exacerbating rising tensions between republics. Kjell Magnusson (1987: 76) notes that by the early and middle 1980s "almost every aspect of ideology [was] under fire: revolutionary history, the actual practice of 'brotherhood and unity,' self-management and the functioning of the political system." The disintegration of the Soviet Union and the subsequent public revulsion at the exposure of the Potemkin village unreality of applied Marxist ideologies after the fall of the Berlin Wall further fractured the dissolving relationship among the Yugoslav republics. A substitute for communism as an ideology was sought and found by some in radical ethno-nationalism. This ideological shift was to show up in how audiences experienced and reacted to folklore performances.

Recall that during the Tito era, KUDs and professional folklore ensembles were required to perform pan-Yugoslav programs. Only occasionally were exceptions allowed, primarily if the group represented a national minority. The following example illustrates the intensity of audience response to a predominantly Albanian program presented by *Shota*, and illuminates the stakes for the states in managing folklore performances.

The affective potential of these kinds of cultural performances and their potential power to mobilize ethnicity was made stunningly clear to me one evening. A sophisticated Bosnian friend and I sat in the audience at the Djuro Djaković

Worker's University Theater in Sarajevo waiting for a group from Kosovo to perform. Looking around at the sold-out auditorium before the program began, he commented that "there must not be a sweet shop open in Sarajevo tonight!"—a reference to one of the economic specializations of Yugoslav Albanians. As the performance began, even he was surprised at the power of the program to move the audience emotionally. An almost electric hush fell over the audience as familiar songs began to evoke affective responses. In one moment of seemingly heightened perception, I looked around and saw something which until then I had only associated with Western charismatic Christianity. Many men in the audience had stood up, their eyes closed, and were swaying to the beat with their arms and hands held up toward the stage as if basking in the sun. Although I had seen positive audience response before, the intensity of this moment was unprecedented in my experience with folklore performance.

What was not so apparent in viewing these public performances was that they were the result of a sophisticated process of negotiation of identities between the Yugoslav state and its constituent nations and national minorities. Engaged in a complicated minuet of coercion and control over cultural performances, Yugoslavia as the most multinational state in Eastern Europe and Bosnia and Herzegovina, the most multiethnic republic within the Yugoslav state, presented a unique set of circumstances. What may have seemed to the average viewer to be simply a folklore show that romanticized a primarily rural past was really the result of a complex discourse about symbolic national identity. These performances included aspects of negotiation and resistance and had roots antedating the Marxist model and extending back well into the last century. In my view, this negotiation of identity between ethnicity and the state was highly visible in what I have come to call the social lives of dances, a concept I have adapted from ideas presented by Arjun Appadurai (1986) and Jacques Maquet (1971).

By the "social lives of dances," I mean that dances, or indeed other classes of aesthetic goods, objects, and behaviors, act as complex types of symbolic and actual commodities as they circulate in and out of various levels of involvement with the types of political economies in which they find themselves embedded (Maners 1995). It is not so much the social formation of these aesthetic productions that concerns me as it is the role of political economies in their selection and reproduction. While aesthetic objects were certainly valued goods, especially in the formerly socialist states of Eastern Europe, their worth was often determined by the needs of Party ideology (Giurchescu 1987). Through the lens of a particular folklore performance that I witnessed near the end of the Yugoslav era one can see the explicit linkage between dance and political economy in former Yugoslavia and, by extension, to most of pre-1989 Eastern Europe. This linkage of folkloric performance and politics continues right through to today, now harnessed to the new postcommunist ideologies of ethno-nationalism in the other republics of former Yugoslavia.

Clapping for Serbs: When Ideologies Collide

In the fall of 1987, in the seemingly innocuous confines of the performance space of KUD *Slobodan Princip-Seljo* in Sarajevo, I witnessed a moment of *parakrousis* into which then-Yugoslavia was falling. *Parakrousis,* as the Greeks define it, is that one discordant element in an otherwise harmonious presentation that may reveal its underlying conflict. In this case, that discordant, telling note came not from the performers or their performance, but from the audience, the consumers of this manifestation of the state's ideology.

In retrospect, it is not so unusual that this drama would unfold in a realm seemingly so far removed from the political and ideological as folk dance and music adapted to the stage as entertainment. It was just this very aspect of what the Yugoslavs called *folklor* which played a powerful ideological role in the founding of the post–World War II Yugoslav state. *Folklor,* composed of many disparate national elements, was almost by definition ripe for reappropriation and conversion from Yugoslav polysemy to ethnic monosemy.

Having witnessed hundreds of performances of Yugoslav folk material since the 1960s, and specializing in the aesthetic anthropologies of dance and music, I came to the performance that evening with a set of expectations about what I might see. A typical *gradski smotra* (city folklore review) such as this one would normally feature a number of performances of dance suites by the sponsoring amateur group as well as a number of suites by visiting amateur groups from elsewhere in the city. Each would strive to put on the best possible presentation. The quality of a given KUD was often judged by its performances, and budgetary allotments from the *porez kultura* (culture tax) would be adjusted accordingly. It was not at all unknown for a KUD to decline in status and even cease to function if its performances consistently fell below the judges' standards. The substantive aesthetic requirement was that a suite must be *komplet,* that is, appropriate in music, dance, and costuming for the republic or province it was representing. Furthermore, KUDs were not only judged formally. Since audiences were often composed of the dancers' friends and families as well as members of other amateur ensembles, informal judgments were rendered throughout via the traditional method of audience response.

This night, however, there was an odd and disharmonious affect to the program. It began with a suite of colorful Croatian dances from Posavina and Slavonia. Following the Croatian suite, an even more colorful and lively set of urban Muslim dances from Sarajevo appeared with the women dressed in *dimije* (wide satin pantaloons) and *papuče* (backless slippers) and the men in fezes, vests, and baggy trousers.

Everything seemed to be proceeding according to expectation. However, I was puzzled at the audience reaction to the suite. of Serbian dances from the Šumadija region. (Bosnian groups would often alternate this suite with one of Serbian dances *okolina Sarajeva,* dances from the Sarajevo region, immediately recognizable by the women's black *dimija*.) A classic of its genre, choreographed by Branko Marković, I had even seen the Šumadija suite performed by *ansambl kolo* (a professional group) in Belgrade on more than one occasion. The Šumadija suite has a familiar choreography. As a lively tune plays, a line of dancers move in a diagonal line downstage, then pass across the foot of the stage before curving back at another diagonal. They eventually resolve to lines at the sides of the stage. What struck me as odd was nothing about the dance suite per se, but rather the audience's reaction to it. As the suite proceeded, I began to sense a very unusual display of affect by the audience. To my ear, noticeably boisterous pockets of applause were interspersed in the theater with pockets of silence. Many audience members had what appeared to be a nominal response. They neither hissed nor booed, but passively responded by "sitting on their hands."

Struck by something I had never before witnessed at a KUD performance, I turned to a friend seated next to me and asked if she had noticed something strange and if she could explain it. At the conclusion of the suite, she confirmed my perception of the audience's affect. Her interpretation was that the Serbs in the audience were clapping only for Serbs and, in fact, that they were overreacting. Non-Serbs, though, politely applauded as they had for the other suites. Later that evening when we met with some KUD members in the smokey environs of a local small cafe, this opinion was confirmed: Serbs were clapping only for Serbs. Something had changed in the way in which Serbs related to the presentation of Serbian cultural performances, a change not apparent among non-Serbs.

My friends laid much of the blame for this state of affairs at the doorstep of the Serbian Academy of Arts and Sciences (SANU) in Belgrade. The year before it had published an infamous memorandum attempting to reposition Serbia as a victim of Federal Yugoslavia. Thus, had this moment of *parakrousis* occurred two years ago, it might have been interpreted as simply friends clapping for friends. Now, however, it served as a harbinger of the coming crisis. As much as the state had invested in presenting an image of unified Yugoslavia through an elaborate system of folklore performance, that same system which had conveyed the polysemy of the state was now in the process of being deconstructed before our eyes into ethnic monosemy.

In retrospect then, folk music and dance in Bosnia and Herzegovina was a part of not just a critical aesthetic locus but also a critical symbolic focus within the political economy. The main purpose of amateurism in the performance of folklore groups, replicating that of the professional ensembles, was to emphasize the fundamental equality of the Yugoslav nations and nationalities. While KUDs in the other republics and autonomous provinces may have found it hard even to have ethnically mixed ensembles, in Bosnia and Herzegovina this was a given based simply on the demographics of the republic. Bosnia and Herzegovina, as the one non-ethnically based republic in Yugoslavia, had always had the most to lose in any potential reinterpretation of these cultural performances.

After communism lost its legitimacy as an organizing principle, ethno-nationalism replaced nationalism so that bringing us full circle, people could clap for their own just as I had witnessed that evening in Sarajevo. Thus *bricolage* was replaced by *demontaža* as audiences began to deconstruct symbols of Yugoslav national identity into narrower ethnic ones.

At the time of the Dayton Accord, the KUDs of Sarajevo (and at least one in Tuzla and in Mostar) had survived the war. Reflecting the bitter emotions of being shelled by former Serbian neighbors and radical *chetniks* alike, the surviving KUDs of the capital had "ethnically cleansed" their repertoires of Serbian material, including such traditional favorites as those from Serb villages *okolina Sarajeva*.

In the first folklore festival held in post-Yugoslav, but still besieged Sarajevo, a new National Folklore Ensemble performed suites of Bosnian Croatian and Bosnian Muslim traditional dances, Croatian *lindjos*, traditional dances from Herzegovina (*trampas*), and Bosnian oriental dances reflecting Bosnia's Turkish/Ottoman heritage. The mayor of Sarajevo was quoted as saying that the folklore festival was "another way to fight and to resist." Thus these kinds of cultural performances took on yet another new meaning in a changed political, symbolic, and moral economy.

A Reimagined Country: Amateur Folklore and the Idea of Bosnia

In the summer of 1997, I revisited the now independent state of BiH. Met at the airport by an old friend from the *Veterani* of KUD *Slobodan Princip-Seljo,* I soon found myself whisked off to a *teferić* (picnic) at the weekend cabin high on a mountainside. Common to such picnics, we dined on roast goat, drank homemade *rakija*, chatted, sang, and danced kolos until dusk. As we talked, I asked about the KUDs in the post-Yugoslav era. One Veteran told me that while it was politically correct to dismantle things from the old communist days, the KUDs hadn't been. He reminded me that a number of new KUDs had appeared during the war had been established. This is in interesting contrast to the situation reported by Timothy Rice (1996: 186) for Bulgaria, where the former state folklore ensembles were seen as part of the decay of the system and are today in parlous straits.

KUDs had continued to rehearse and perform throughout the war, though in much reduced circumstances. The Gradski Savez-Sarajevo had lost its archives and costume collection to shelling, and the head of the Savez KUD-BiH, Svetan Ninković (a Serb), had been murdered in his home during a particularly dark period during the siege. Some choreographers had also felt the siren song of ethnicity and decamped to Croatia or Montenegro, while male dancers and musicians were drafted into the army and both males and females fled the country as refugees. In the new Bosnia, some KUDs still reflect the sponsorship of various institutions and one KUD successor, *Kolo Bosansko,* sponsored by the Bosnian Cultural Center, aspires to be a professional ensemble while the others soldier on in the spirit of amateurism.

The next morning, while out for a walk, I came across another prewar acquaintance, the eminent choreographer Hajrudin Hadzić. He encouraged me to attend an event on June 7 honoring the 125th anniversary of the Bosnian railways. KUD *Zeljezničar,* sponsored by the railway association in the old days, would be performing a suite of dances he had choreographed which he assured me I would find interesting.

Arriving at the theater that evening, I found myself in a well-dressed crowd of foreign and local dignitaries and interested spectators. After a few speeches (which were translated into English), a chorus performed and I noticed the dancers of KUD *Zeljezničar* beginning to line up at the back of the stage. Before the war, dressed as they were in the traditional garb of Bosnian Serbs, Croats, and Muslims, nothing would have struck me as unusual. Clearly they were going to perform *Sarajevo Zavrazlama* (Sarajevo Medley), a suite composed of Serb, Croat, and Muslim dances. Pre-1992, the performance of this suite would have been unremarkable, though in the late 1980s it would have become subject to reinterpretation. During the war years 1992–95, presenting Serbian material would have been unthinkable and now, in 1997, reflecting the Bosnian government's official policy of cultural diversity (Lausević 1996: 130) in which Muslims and non-Muslims alike were to be equals, such a performance was again, unremarkable.

Thus folklore ensembles and their repertoires become like palimpsests upon which layers of meaning, of nationalism and ethno-nationalism, of construction and deconstruction and reconstruction shimmer through one another upon the page.

18

Serbia

The Inside Story

Mirjana Prošić-Dvornić

Ever since the outbreak of a series of internal wars staged as an ultimate "argument" for the breakup of the multiethnic federal state of Yugoslavia, the combat zones, especially Bosnia and Herzegovina and Kosovo, have been the center of attention. Gale Stokes and colleagues (1996: 136) have surveyed the literature in English which show that there has been a corresponding lack of attention paid to the areas of life in the former Yugoslavia not directly affected by the war. It is significant that this has especially been the case for Serbia despite the crucial role its government has played in instigating these wars.

The same discrepancy by nationality is noticeable in anthropological studies presented at international conferences and appearing in international publications. While anthropologists and ethnologists from other parts of the former Yugoslavia, notably from Croatia, have been very active in international anthropological discourse (see Bennett 1997), scholars from Serbia have not made a significant impact. The UN sanctions in effect from spring 1992 to fall 1996, and the concurrent disastrous economic situation in Serbia, cannot be held solely responsible. In the now truncated Yugoslavia an extremely xenophobic atmosphere created by the official propaganda and isolationism imposed by the regime, the so-called internal sanctions, were just as important in impeding the free flow of information. That is why some of the best writing on the Serbian situation has been that of Serbian (or "Serbian in-laws") scholars and graduate students abroad who have had easier access, by birth or by marriage, to both worlds. The role of scholars with "dual identity" may become even more important in the years to come. Recently Serbian ethnology appears, after decades of influence by western anthropology begun in the 1970s, to have taken a retrogressive path inclining again toward "national science."[1]

Another feature of international coverage of events in former Yugoslavia has been a rather uniform accent on conflicts *among* nations, while the ones taking place *within* a single ethnicity are rarely pointed out. This attitude has created an illusion that the conflicting nations are largely homogeneous, just as their respective rulers would like them to appear. Sometimes, I regret to say, both the media coverage and scholarly contributions echoed the simplistic Manichaean dichotomization exalting one's own nation based on historical myth and clichés, reducing the Others to negative stereotypes, which have been forged in and used by the former Yugoslav republics in media wars against each other. However, this is far from the truth. There certainly have been instances when, for a time, the majority of the (ethnically defined) nation has agreed with and supported its leadership. Nevertheless, constant, fierce, and often irreconcilable differences among groups within the nations have been the *leitmotif* and true expression of the transitional processes following the disintegration of the communist/socialist regime.

Instead of the rather futile, "ethnically engaged" approach, an effort should be made to understand the full complexity of transitional processes currently evolving within this Balkan region. I use "transition" here in the sense defined by Ernest Gellner (1964: 50ff.) and Maurice Godelier (1987); a transition period is a time of instability, ambiguity, and crisis when confrontations and animosities become particularly strained and marked by increasing degrees of intolerance. Hence, it is more appropriate to describe conditions in these newly created states as heteromorphic than it is to subscribe to the simplistic and false representations of individual nations as monolithic entities. Contemporary Serbia needs to be described from more than one viewpoint. Only then can the scope of internal conflicts be grasped in their entirety with all "varied and opposed" voices heard (see Burke 1991: 6, 21, 238). This understanding can shed more light on how confrontations among different communities are created. Thus the reasons for the bloodshed should be ascribed not so much to "ancient hatreds" as to internal struggles for political power and economic gain. Dichotomizing and stereotyping are the same, whether directed inward to justify internal purges or outward against the Other(s). In addition to this, the more balanced picture would also reveal the alternative approaches to the Yugoslav crisis existing in all Balkan

---

1. For example, titles and contents of some anthropology courses offered at the Department of Ethnology and Cultural Anthropology at the University of Belgrade have been changed to reflect the traditional ethnological paradigm.

societies. As they epitomize paradigms opposite to the values promulgated by the regimes (democracy vs. totalitarianism, multiculturalism vs. monoethnicity, modernism/postmodernism vs. traditionalism, etc.), they could serve as nexuses for rebuilding bridges among the nations.

The Dismantling of "Brotherhood and Unity"

Contrary to frequent attempts to present the wars in the former Yugoslavia as the outburst of ancient hatreds, historical evidence shows that the present ethnic/ religious conflicts were preceded only by the atrocities committed during World War II. For centuries before nationalistic ideologies were invented and used as a means of transposing conflicting interests into emotionally charged ethnic griev- ances, the nations of the former Yugoslavia shared a long-term peaceful coexis- tence, particularly in the most mixed ethnic zones (cf. Donia and Fine 1994; Bringa 1995). Although different ethnic, cultural, and religious groups sharing the same *lebensraum* were never fully integrated in the "melting pot" sense of the term, they did successfully communicate among themselves and thrive as groups with well-defined identities.

On the other hand, they have also shared almost a century of periodic out- bursts of hostility, and those have become an important part of their collective historical memories. Most of these negative memories were created when they shared a common Yugoslav state. Yugoslavism as a cultural and political idea with assimilative and integrative implications was born in the nineteenth century. It evolved as an alternative to particularistic ethno-national revivals among the South Slavs. However, it was compromised in the period between the two world wars largely due to Serbian hegemony. This led to national antagonisms, outright animosities, and finally, horrendous atrocities in World War II. Nevertheless, the idea was preserved and revived by the pan-Yugoslav Partisan movement and became the basis of the "Second" or "Tito's Yugoslavia."

This Second Yugoslavia, with the authoritarian nature of its communist/social- ist regime, is generally credited for giving a second life of approximately half a century to a country composed of "unmatchable entities." It is presumed that Yugoslavia survived only because of the regime's firm grip over the "national question." This grip paralleled that held over other aspects of public life, notably the economy and political system. Without it the centrifugal forces of ethnic antagonisms would have caused the unmaking of the multinational state long before the breakdown of the socialist system. Indeed it seemed that the regime, with its alternative (but still Marxist) approach to the "national question," had found a feasible solution. Its unique concept of "brotherhood and unity," which implied harmonious coexistence of linked but different groups of people given a right to preserve individual identities, appeared viable. Actually, as an attempt at providing all constituent nations with the right of self-determination and balancing the possible overbearing power and influence of larger ethnic groups, new nations were created during Titoism. These included Macedonians, Montenegrins, and, finally Muslims after their claim to be recognized as a secular nation rather than as a religious community was formally recognized by the Yugoslav League of Communists in 1968.

Below the surface, however, the attitude of the Communist Party toward nationalism was more complex. Although it appeared that it truly celebrated the revived unity, the commitment hardly went beyond the declarative level. Instead of offering a solution, the regime rather manipulated the situation for its own ends. The memories of former ethnic/national animosities, particularly those from World War II, were never dealt with properly but were suppressed as if the events they recalled had never occurred. Also suppressed were spontaneous expressions of national identity coming from *below*. These ranged from the benign, such as ethnic and regional folk music, celebrating certain national religious or historical holidays, or wearing national insignia (cf. Rihtman-Auguštin 1990, 1992), to serious breeches of the communist order, such as overt, politically linked manifestations of nationalism. The latter included eruptions of Albanian rebellions in Kosovo in the 1960s; followed by the Croatian *Maspok* (Mass Movement), the Serbian Liberal Movement in the early 1970s.

At the same time nationalism was constantly instigated from *above*. Individuals who declared themselves as Yugoslavs in national censuses were classified as "undeclared." Clearly, from the mid-1950s, ethnic identities were favored over pan-Yugoslavism;[2] more important, there was a highly pronounced ambivalence expressed by the government. On the one hand the Party purges in the early 1970s were aimed at eliminating independent republican political elites and minimizing nationalistic conflicts. On the other, while the Party was attempting to maintain control over these nationalistic movements, it was also, gradually, from the late 1950s and early 1960s, transferring power from the federal to the republic governments. Thus a non-unitary, consociational arrangement was being created. The republics, as territorial administrative units, with the sole exception of Bosnia and Herzegovina and its tripartite ethnic structure, were also the homes of one principal nation. This transfer of power favored the idea of creating, or recreating, nation-states and set the stage for the resurgence of individual national agendas. The problem was, however, that the republics, again with a single exception,[3] also housed large "minorities," which opened up the painful subject of ethnic/ territorial re-delineation within republics.

Once the power was vested in the republics, their elites began to instigate

2. From the mid-1970s all Yugoslavs were even required to have dual citizenship: Yugoslav and that of a home republic.

3. That exception was Slovenia, which had the most homogeneous ethnic structure excluding recent, mostly seasonal, influxes of migrant workers from the "underdeveloped south," the same region that supplied raw materials for Slovenia's industries. Was this a case of "internal colonialism?"

nationalism as a means of obtaining support and legitimacy within the borders of their own jurisdictions. The decentralization of the Party/state bureaucracy, and the ramification of the self-management system, with its complex structure of interdependent yet conflicting segments introduced in mid-1970s, brought about the fragmentation of Yugoslav society along national lines (Shoup 1989: 131). The 1974 federal constitution, supposedly designed to prevent the disintegration of the country, actually legalized particularization by granting "national statehood" to the republics and autonomous provinces, Kosovo and the Vojvodina (Shoup 1968: 184ff.; Banac 1992: 171–74). In effect, it provided legal ground for the subsequent secession of republics/states, which were fueled by political rivalry among their power elites.

The 1970s were, thus, both the "golden years" of socialism and the time in which the forces responsible for the final dissolution of "Second Yugoslavia" were affirmed and institutionalized. During that optimistic decade images of progress prevailed. The improved economy, based on favorable foreign credits rather than on increased productive efficiency, enabled living standards to rise considerably. At the same time liberalism, even in the face of Party purges, provided unprecedented freedom in intellectual and social life. By contrast, the following decade brought countless indications that very hard times loomed ahead. In the early 1980s the Yugoslav crisis began to surface in radically changed circumstances. Internally, Tito's death in 1980 and advanced political and economic decentralization left no central authority to take over the leadership and reaffirm unity. Externally, with the post–Cold War global shifts in power structure and consequent loss of its strategic importance, Yugoslavia was deprived of generous foreign financial aid. Instead, it was obliged to settle its debts. Tito could no longer personally resolve growing problems. Tangible economic hardships such as shortages of goods and services, a severe energy crisis, an enormous rise in the cost of living, and inflation of huge proportions became the new reality. These developments initiated the pauperization of the middle class and the enrichment of the few who were favorably positioned politically and socially (see Prošić-Dvornić 1990).

In the early 1980s social and economic grievances, vented through strikes and demonstrations, clearly indicated growing discontent with the system. By the mid-1980s it had become evident that, in spite of all attempts to represent the existing system as irreplaceable, the old socialist ideology had been spent. It could neither compensate for the bleak reality nor cover up its failures. The system had collapsed just as the entire European communist world was beginning to show signs of crumbling. Yugoslav society was entering a dramatic liminal phase in which the crisis could be resolved either through restoration or change. The first solution involved trying to swim against the tide in an attempt to retain communism-after-communism. The other was to shift toward a new, open, civil and plural society governed by democratic institutions and engaged in a free market economy.

The latter solution, however, required giving up totalitarian rule, and eventually, the old political elites relinquishing power. The entrenched bureaucracies were equally incapable and unwilling to remedy any aspect of the crisis. Neither the elites nor the bureaucracies were prepared to give up power or introduce any real change. Since their power stemmed from the authoritarian system, the core had to be preserved unchanged.[4] Therefore they found a solution in the old/new ideology of ethnic nationalism, soon to become common in Eastern Europe as a phase in transition from totalitarianism to democracy. It proved to be an excellent substitute for the failed socialist dogma.[5] Social and economic problems were increasingly translated into ethnic grievances. The blame for the disastrous situation was diverted from the political elites to an outside enemy, notably other nations within Yugoslavia and beyond. Political and national myths were endlessly and purposefully perpetuated.

Forging the War of Stereotypes

The process of dismantling the federal state included government-supported increases of interest in national history and culture aimed at reviving long-suppressed national political identities, as well as closely controlled media use of ethnic/cultural stereotyping. Formerly federated Yugoslav nations were transformed into mutually antagonistic entities, unable to share a common statehood. Some of the differentiating markers were borrowed from a historical inventory of stereotypes. Memories of past conflicts were reactivated in order to construct seemingly insurmountable ethnic barriers. Incorporating "traditions" into modern political myths provided much needed credibility. Such myths cannot "grow

4. The one serious attempt to both preserve the integral federal state and radically reform the system was undertaken by the last Yugoslav government headed by then prime minister, Ante Marković, a Bosnian Croat (March 1989–December 1991). It was met with hostility by the national political elites. They perceived the prime minister's intentions and success as a threat to their own visions and interests. Slovenian and Croatian leaders openly favored independent nation-states. Slobodan Milošević opposed competing pan-Yugoslav programs. The prime minister, however, enjoyed genuine support from the majority of the citizens throughout the country. Milošević felt threatened after the prime minister founded a pan-Yugoslav Reform Party. Marković announced his intentions at a meeting on the Kozara mountain in Bosnia, before more than 100,000 very enthusiastic supporters. This area was inhabited by a Serbian majority that had suffered great losses at the hands of the Ustashi during World War II. It was anathema to Milošević that Marković could be seen gaining support from the Serbian population in the region that was to become, to Milošević's scheme, a stronghold of Serbian nationalistic rebellion. Such an eventuality could seriously jeopardize Milošević's plans. Therefore, he began actions to overthrow the prime minister. In this matter he had the full support of most of the other republics. After the prime minister was eliminated, Milošević took control over federal financial institutions, the army and police, all headquartered in the former Yugoslav capital Belgrade and all of which were Serb dominated.

5. "Nationalism is communism with a passion" (Filip Mladenović, *Naša Borba,* April 8–9, 1995).

freely; they are not wild fruits of an exuberant imagination. They are artificial things fabricated by very skillful and cunning artists" (Cassirer 1961: 282).

The essence of the process was to ascribe remarkably positive traits to one's own group (self-deification), while demonizing the Other(s). Once the objective and ascriptive ethic differences were transposed into the language of political propaganda, they were turned into ruthless, chauvinistic, and bellicose messages. These soon became lethal verbal weapons in the hands of numerous warmongers. By the use of the state-run media, the chief instrument of promoting "politically correct" ways of thinking in authoritarian societies,[6] the "media war" (see Thompson 1994) was soon transposed from virtual to real life combat for "ethnic identities." Former "brotherly" nations were not only represented as enemies, but also as inhuman monsters, worthy only of perishing for the good of mankind. Consequently massacres, ethnic cleansing, forcible population exchanges, prisoners of war camps, rape, senseless destruction of cities and villages, and other atrocities were considered nothing but unfortunate and unavoidable by-products of just struggle (cf. Čolović 1993: 93–98, 123ff.).

One of the most potent metaphors used to differentiate the former Yugoslav peoples was the Balkan versus non-Balkan dichotomy. "The language of orientalism . . . as a powerful set of categories with which to stigmatize societies that are not 'western-style democracies'" (Bakić-Hayden and Hayden 1992: 2) was applied with an aim of redefining cultural (political, ideological) geography. In northwestern parts of the country (Croatia, Slovenia), adjectives like "Byzantine," "Balkan," or "Orthodox"[7] were used for the southeastern areas. Objectively, these adjectives describe the history of the eastern territories. They were indeed part of the Byzantine Empire, their population is still predominantly Orthodox, and they are located on the Balkan peninsula. However, in the context of "name-calling," each of these connoted a specific negative quality such as backward, lazy, poor, violent, or authoritarian, uncivil.[8] Obviously, the purpose of

6. Before the wars it was possible to see the television news of each republic throughout the country. These options did not, however, contribute to a plural and more nuanced vision of reality because of the ethnocentric "we-they" way in which they were presented. For a short while, a non-nationalist approach was attempted by "Yutel," a pro-Yugoslav-station located in Sarajevo and sponsored by the federal government then headed by Marković.

7. Because of the specific Croat/Catholic and Muslim political alliance in Bosnia, epithets like "Islamic" and "Ottoman" were left out.

8. In her recent paper, Dunja Rihtman-Auguštin (1997: 27–35), inspired by Maria Todorova's *Imagining the Balkans*, has shown that the term "Balkan" was not always perceived negatively in Croatia. On the contrary, in the early twentieth century in Croatia for the followers of Starčević's pro-Yugoslav Party of Rights, the idealized Balkans symbolized unity based on free will and equal rights of the participating nations. Even to a Croatian nationalist ideologue of the Croat People's Peasant Party, Ante Radić, the Balkans represented the means of terminating particularism and provincialism, and a chance for modernization and progress (ibid., 30–31). Still later, in the work of the prominent Croatian author, Miroslav Krleža, ideas of "Balkan," as expressed by his characters, reflected ambivalence. "Balkan" did mean backward, politically incongruous, and ill-mannered but it was again represented as a remedy for provincialism (ibid., 34). In the context of the breakup of

clustering societies on the "Balkan pole" was not only to mark them as different, but, more important, also as the *inferior Other*. The message was that for the northwestern, "European" pole a prolonged union with the southeast regions could mean nothing but historical regression. According to the same set of inclusion/exclusion rules, the "Europeans" could perceive themselves only as "civilizing agents" in relation to the demonized "Balkan menace," or a *"cordon sanitaire"* against the "eastern tide of chaos" (see Bakić-Hayden and Hayden 1992: 2 and Hayden 1993: 75–76). This ambivalent orientation, opening up to Europe and excluding the "different South" was noticeable in Slovenia from the beginning of their controversial democratization process in mid-1980s (see Mežnarić 1989) and was epitomized there in a popular graffiti of the time: "Burek? Nein, danke!"[9]

To this, a nationalistic Serbia responded in a manner that seemed to justify the persistent use of "orientalizing metaphors." It stigmatized the other side as "lackeys to foreign masters" and "betrayers of brotherly concord and trust." Worst of all were the ungrounded generalizations. For example, atrocities committed by the Ustasha during World War II were extended to include the entire Croatian nation, which the Serbs labeled as "genocidal." In contrast, Serbian self-representation glorified their nation as a "martyred, celestial people," always ready to "sacrifice its earthly existence for a divine cause," a higher moral order. While the Westerners, the Croats and Slovenes, were seen as sunk into sinful living and ruled by materialism, secularism, and greed, the Serbs and other Slavic Orthodox nations were presented as having preserved the original European spirituality and values embodied in religion, philosophy, and history "with a soul." Therefore, it was the Serbs who had to perform the "noble historic mission" of leading "the sinful West" back to its roots.[10] In this liminal border zone between the northwestern "Europeanism" and southeastern "Balkanism," the inferiority/superiority markers were pivoted to the advantage of the side that was engaged in the delineation procedure.

The Upsurge of Serbian Nationalism

In 1981, despite the renewed Kosovo crisis, which involved Albanian demonstrations openly demanding secession from Yugoslavia and the possibility of a military intervention as a countermeasure, the distorted economy was the primary

---

Yugoslavia, however, the idea of "Balkan" has lost all its charm. Instead, it has become a symbol highly charged with negative emotion.

9. *Burek*—Near Eastern style phyllo dough pastry with cheese or meat filling, a popular dish in the Balkans.

10. Metaphors used by the Serbian side date back to the nineteenth century. They originated in a number of movements ranging from romanticism, to populism, to nationalism, to Pan-Slavism, to Orthodox fundamentalism.

concern of ordinary people. Ethnic conflicts in the southern autonomous province of Kosovo still seemed very remote. Belief persisted that it was a localized, rather than systemic, problem that the government could handle. To the majority, a more tangible threat in the 1970s and the 1980s was the exodus of Serbs and Montenegrins from Kosovo into Serbia proper. Empathy with their grievances against the Albanians was overpowered by the resentment of the "intruders" invading the "natives'" territory.[11]

Several years later the images were transformed. Serbs and Montenegrins from Kosovo were represented as victims, and Albanians as the odious Other— makers of genocidal plans, traitors, infidel rapists of "Our women," and invaders of Serbian soil. This was the first image of the "odious Other," the cause of all evil, that was created by Serbian nationalistic propaganda. Once it was formed it was easy to expand it to include all other potential enemies, real or imagined. These ranged from "ustashas" (Croats), "Turks" and "Mujahedines" (Bosnian Muslims, Albanians), to the Comintern, the Vatican, and the Nazis, as well as the "New World Order." The reason for this dramatic change in attitude was not because the Serbian political elite, contrary to its public declarations, suddenly realized that ethnic conflicts in Kosovo were a burning problem that had to be resolved. Rather this elite saw it as an ideal starting point for reviving Serbian nationalism.

This became evident beginning in 1986 with the rise of an unscrupulous, power-hungry and pragmatic apparatchik, Slobodan Milošević, from the ranks of the Serbian Communist Party. He made it clear from the very beginning that he was not willing to compromise with other republics or accept the need for economic and political reforms. His ambition was to become "Tito after Tito" and to rule over all of the former Yugoslavia with a firm totalitarian hand. In his vocabulary "reform" meant restoration of communist values and centralization of authority. Aware that the socialist formula was not effective any longer, Milošević decided to take advantage of the large Serbian diaspora by trying to bring them all under the ideological umbrella of Serbian nationalism. This substitution of ideologies would allow for the *appearance* of revolutionary transformations while *preventing* or at least *postponing* the inevitable, a change in the *core* system of totalitarian rule.

Although the new Serbian regime was not alone in opting for a nationalistic ideology, it was probably the most dangerous one. It was intimidating not only

---

11. Serbian immigrants from Kosovo during this period were mostly financially well off, thanks to the generous prices Albanians were willing to pay for their property ("monetary" ethnic cleansing?). In addition, they brought with them their own habits, such as ignoring fiscal obligations (taxes, utility bills) that were one of the expressions of the Kosovo Albanians' civil disobedience, but obviously practiced by everyone else. These immigrants were perceived as different, a group apart. The new arrivals tended to stay within their groups and practice a self-ghettoization process. Their squatter settlements in city and town outskirts, mostly consisting of substantial houses but the neighborhoods were given pejorative names, e.g., Katanga (named after a region in southeastern Zaire).

because of the relatively large numbers and widespread distribution of Serbs in the former Yugoslavia but also because of Serbian dominance in the power structures of key federal institutions, such as the Yugoslav People's Army, which could be manipulated to the regime's advantage. The national "reunification" concept, known as Greater Serbia,[12] aimed to include all regions where the Serbs represented the majority of the population. This policy was felt as a threat by the other nations, which were still Yugoslav republics. Fear of Serbian expansionism and renewed hegemony, similar to that experienced in the years between two world wars, spread quickly. The self-defense of one side was taken to mean aggression toward the other, which in turn, led to a rapid escalation of uncertainty and animosity.[13] The more the regime became militant in imposing its will, the more "the Serbian side of the story" was rejected by the others. In turn, Serbian national sentiment increased. Each rejection was interpreted as new evidence of the existence of a master plot against the "celestial nation."

Homogenization "From Above"

Kosovo, because of its historical significance as both the cradle and the grave of the Serbian medieval empire, provided an ideal starting point for the crystallization of Serbian ethnic sentiments. Although Serbia succumbed to the Turkish rule only after the fall of Smederevo in 1459, the Kosovo battle in 1389 is marked as its cataclysmic moment. The Serbian oral tradition of epic poetry transformed this event into myth. Transcriptions were published in the mid-nineteenth century as part of the original nation-building process. This archetypal national myth transformed defeat into moral victory and made the event a sacred component of Serbian ethnicity, a part of the "soul of the Nation" and a symbol of its existence. Resistance to a "foreign yoke" and readiness to die for "the holy cross and golden freedom" were key components amenable to political manipulation. This

12. The idea was fully elaborated for the first time in Ilija Garašanin's Načertanije (Draft), in 1844. The document called for the unification of Bosnia, Herzegovina, Kosovo, Montenegro, Northern Albania, and the Vojvodina, lands that were considered predominantly Serbian and Orthodox. At that time these irredentist plans were not a unique Serbian invention, but rather a trend of the era. Each Balkan state had its own unification plans. The problem with the Balkans is that such plans, striving to recreate the most expansive past state, involve considerable overlapping. The idea of Greater Serbia reappeared in 1911 in a different, militant form and it is associated with a clandestine organization "Union or Death," also known as the "Black Hand," which was involved in the assassination of the Austrian archduke Franz Ferdinand in Sarajevo, which led to World War I. The same idea was expressed in the favorite slogan of Milošević's Socialist Party of Serbia: "All Serbs in one State," reminiscent in a way of Hitler's chilling "Ein Volk, Ein Reich, Ein Führer." The far-right parties and movements also propagated the same idea.

13. A chronology of these events as seen by a historian is given in Banac 1992: 168–87 and an anthropological view is presented in Denich 1993: 47–60. Phases in the process of building up nationalism in Serbia are well articulated in Naumović 1994: 95–119.

is why Albanian demonstrations in Kosovo have been used successfully to link these historical memories to national sentiments and promote the armed struggle over the Kosovo issue.

The Serbian past was transposed into the world of heroic myth with the ultimate goal of paralyzing critical thinking and promoting strong emotions, exaltation, and irrational behavior. Fear, xenophobia, megalomania, and intolerance promoted the transition to aggressiveness and violence. The official propaganda promoted Serbs as a chosen people, blessed with a divine mission "to save mankind from the Evil, incarnated in the Enemy."

The political and ideological shift from communism to nationalism was first tested as a cultural movement, seemingly stemming from nonpolitical circles. Academics, artists, journalists, and clergy were the heralds of this movement of national revival. In the mid-1980s a deluge of titles on the Serbian national tradition saturated the publishing market. Included were the works of contemporary authors on the Serbian past, as well as many reprints. Some of these had been banned as nationalistic during the communist era and now were resurrected. The media dedicated increasing amount of space to "national themes" and opened up many previously tabooed subjects.

A political program titled *Memorandum*, produced in 1986 by a group of members of the Serbian Academy of Arts and Sciences, was staged to appear as the work of independent intellectuals.[14] This event was designed to present the new leadership as democratic and liberal with no intention of exercising censorship over the media, or continuing to oppress the free expression of national affiliation. The latent function of this newly granted freedom was, however, quite pragmatic. In case nationalism turned out to be a futile idea, there would be someone else, the intellectuals, to blame. Later, after political pluralism was introduced in 1990, right-wing parties could also be accused of "instigating chauvinism" and abusing the new freedoms.

Political rallies, a trademark of the new Serbian populism, were another means of promoting Milošević's policies and legitimizing the new Serbian regime. These mass events were initiated as cultural and national revivalist actions designed to bring back "the unjustly obliterated events and personages from Serbian history." Making full use of highly moldable values inherent in tradition blended with romanticized history and combining with religious beliefs, nation-

14. A draft of this document supposedly still lacking final editing somehow, as claimed by its authors, became public. The manner of distribution seems to indicate that the matter had been cleverly staged to provoke reactions and test public attitudes toward nationalism. In 1987 the *Memorandum* served as a basis for the "differentiation procedure" within the Serbian League of Communists. Its supporters led by Milošević won the first, decisive battle in favor of ethnic nationalism. The authors of the document claimed that they were not campaigning for a Greater Serbia (Mihailović, Krestić 1995: 81–97). They accuse their critics as being part of the worldwide anti-Serbian campaign.

alism was employed for political ends. Events carefully staged by the leadership[15] were given emotionally charged meaning and were represented as "spontaneous expression of the people's will." These included the celebration of "Two Centuries of Vuk" (1987);[16] the completion of the new St. Sava church, the largest Orthodox cathedral in Europe (1989);[17] and as a climax, the commemoration of the 600th anniversary of the Battle of Kosovo. The first time this holiday had been celebrated since the days of the Kingdom of Yugoslavia.

In addition to these grand national celebrations other mass gatherings with explicit political goals were also organized in 1988–89. They were known as Meetings of Truth, Happenings of the People, and Meetings of Brotherhood and Unity. They were instrumental in enabling a series of Party purges (Vojvodina, October 1988; Montenegro, January 1989). These purges were staged to eliminate Milošević's political adversaries and annul the previous autonomy of two Serbian provinces, Kosovo and the Vojvodina, and in the process, reestablish a centralized Serbian state. This action too embedded a double opportunity. Taking control over Serbia, its two provinces, and Montenegro gave Milošević command of four of the eight votes in the still existing collective federal presidency created after Tito's death in 1980 and the power to checkmate initiatives coming from the opposing bloc (Slovenia, Croatia, Bosnia-Herzegovina, and Macedonia) advocating a "loose federation" in contrast to centralized government. If Milošević's bloc failed to achieve an all-out takeover, it could still serve as an embryo of a new, rump Yugoslavia constituted on his terms.

Hence mass rallies, designed both as social protests and as nationalistic manifestations, therefore also contained a deliberately built-in ambiguity. As social protest, the "anti-bureaucratic revolution" allegedly aimed to remove "incapable and greedy old elites who were not ready to carry out the demanded radical reforms." They called for restoring Titoism and inaugurating Milošević as Tito's successor. On the other hand, references to Serbian national myth and history clearly defined those meetings as places where nationalism was successfully fostered. This ambivalence gave Milošević additional maneuvering space. If his first

15. The Communist Party of Serbia, in 1991 renamed Socialist, organized free transportation for thousands of workers from all over Serbia to the Kosovo rally. Signs were carefully prepared in advance. This and other rallies centering on the Kosovo issue were interpreted as acts of aggression by the Albanian majority.

16. Vuk Stefanović Karadžić was the first Serbian folklorist who worked in Herder's footsteps. In the first part of the nineteenth century he collected, edited, and subsequently published this Serbian epic poetry. He also reformed the Serbian version of the Cyrillic alphabet, modernized and standardized the Serbian language, "discovered" folk culture, and initiated folklore research. All of these activities were crucial in delineating Serbian ethnicity.

17. The construction of the church begun in 1936, was abandoned in 1941, and resumed only in mid-1980s. This church was dedicated to Saint Sava, the patron saint of the Serbs. The completion of the church marked the return of religion to public life after decades of communism and the partnership of Church, State, and Party in defending national interests (cf. Naumović 1994).

choice to be Tito's successor could not be realized, an alternative would be to unite with the Serbian nationalistic elites and try to implement the concept of Greater Serbia. In the late 1980s and early 1990s, Milošević was successful in convincing the majority of the Serbs of his "good intentions." His attempts to take the lead as a second Tito in reestablishing a centralized Yugoslavia with control over other nations within the former federation was met with contempt by non-Serbs. He was thus unable to persuade them to join him in the fight against Albanian Irredenta. After his last *Meeting of Truth* was banned in Ljubljana in December 1989, he decided it was the time to break all existing ties. The Serbian National Assembly brought sanctions, which involved the severing of economic relations with Slovenia and a boycott of their products. The stage was set to fight the war for "blood and territories."

Inside Diversification "From Above" and "From Below"

The intraethnic homogenization of the masses based on the ideology of nationalism presupposes a strict dichotomization defining the in-group as superior, and the "Others" as inferior. But no matter how aggressively the homogenization process was carried out and how boastful the regime could be about its results, it actually only intensified intraethnic differentiation. Even at its peak the militant nationalistic propaganda never succeeded in eliminating all opposition. The nationalistic leadership, eager to maintain its monopoly, could not tolerate even a neutral and disengaged attitude. It sanctioned all deviation. To this end, the same tactics of creating, denouncing, and punishing the enemies in the "outside world"—the scapegoating of all misfortune—were also applied to intra-group differentiation of "loyal members of the community" from "treacherous opponents."

The latter were out of place and had to be exposed and labeled. Mary Douglas's famous definition that "dirt is the matter out of place," is applicable. The "dirt" included not only "Fifth Columnists" or "Serbs of poor quality," but also "cosmopolites with no sense of belonging, sustained on empty rhetoric" and a great variety of individuals of "objectionable" political views as well as other of different ethnic or religious groups.[18]

In Serbian society a deep schism between nationalistic/totalitarian and demo-

18. This was true for all former Yugoslav nations. The much-used "Balkan stereotype" in the West, for example, turned out to be far more important as an internal differentiating mechanism than as an external one. It was used to stigmatize any member of the society who dared challenge or criticize those in power, or was used against those who simply held opposing views. According to Rihtman-Auguštin, "examples from the Croatian press show that the party in power threatens the people and the opposition with the Balkan black hole, while the opposition attempts to prove that it is the ruling party which is behaving in the Balkan way and leading the nation into that very black hole" (1997: 35).

cratic groups was created soon after Milošević came to power. There were, however, no clear-cut divisions as by education or profession. Followers of both visions could be found throughout the social structure. Still, it can be said that the most zealous supporters of the nationalistic agenda came from the consumers of the neo-folk culture, including the numerous "rural urbanites," caught between two worlds and suffering an identity crisis.[19] Some soccer fans were among the first and loudest heralds of the new nationalistic times. They were also the first to engage in serious Serbo-Croat fights, several months prior to actual clashes between the Serbian minority and police forces in Croatia in August 1990. Certain affluent private entrepreneurs also provided initial financial support to Serbian paramilitary groups.[20] The war economy was not an odious experience to them but rather a welcome shortcut to riches. "Real men living at the edge" who had taken the advantage of wartime chaos for personal promotion became a new type of folk hero. As smugglers and war-profiteers they monopolized illegal trading[21] and manipulated humanitarian aid. Practically overnight a newly rich and politically powerful class developed, setting the rules for the entire society.[22] The "less fortunate" had the option to join paramilitary troops as

19. In one view the authoritarian type of personality, created both by socialist indoctrination and socialization within the preexisting patriarchal cultural model, was most commonly found among these strata. These people were seen as especially vulnerable to mythologized interpretations of reality imposed from above in times of crisis. Many of the communist political elites were recruited from these same strata. They set a model of social behavior marked by conformity. By the early 1970s they created their own subculture built around neo-folk music and stars and singers glamorized by the media. This hybrid of mass culture and folklore was used to launch a nationalistic "kitsch patriotism" (see M. Dragićević-Šešić 1994: 29ff.).

20. For example, Željko Ražnjatović Arkan, a war criminal and the infamous leader of one of the most vicious paramilitary groups in the Balkan wars, is the owner of a renowned café in Belgrade as well as the organizer and financier of the highly popular "Red Star" soccer club fans.

21. The economic blockade, part of the comprehensive mandatory sanctions imposed by the Resolution 757 of the UN Security Council (May 30, 1992), proved to be a double-edged sword. While it did have devastating results on the majority of common citizens, at the same time it opened the door wide for the criminalization of the economy and the rapid enrichment of the ruling clique and a caste of new entrepreneurs. The "war economy" had become not only profitable, but also, among some circles, it came to be regarded as a highly praised patriotic retaliation for the unjust punishment. The UN sanctions also had a symbolic value that could be used for nationalistic propaganda. Two far-right associations, The New Byzantium and The White Rose, in addition to their primary concern, that is fighting for cultural purity, tried, and for a time succeeded, to block international traffic on the Danube. There were also other ways of "defying" the Resolution. One was to disseminate false claims that sanctions "could not hurt a land as rich and as self-sufficient as Serbia even if they were imposed for a thousand years." Another manifestation was to organize and televise festivals centered on gluttony competitions, which involved wasting large quantities of food and drink.

22. It was a culture of conspicuous consumption—expensive imported cars, cellular phones, laptop computers, designer clothes, Rolex watches, wallets swollen with foreign currency, luxurious apartments and houses decorated with marble floors, oriental rugs, Italian furniture, golden faucets, imported whisky, and Cuban cigars. It was one not particularly unusual in the West but a marked departure from the communist past. Many of these consumption practices were common among the

volunteers, or as "weekend warriors,"[23] hoping for some first-hand excitement and plentiful booty.[24] It is not unlikely that after all the Balkan wars are over some of the warriors, especially those who might be indicted as war criminals, will opt to pursue careers as soldiers of fortune.[25]

On the other side were "the different," those who voiced opposing views—for democracy, pluralism, urbanity, and tolerance instead of totalitarianism, nationalism, xenophobia, primitivism, and intolerance. Perceived as most dangerous to the regime and hence most severely attacked were ideas of pacifism. From the beginning there were many different groups brave enough to speak their own minds. Some antiwar protests were spontaneous reactions to specific grievances, as was the case of desperate parents demanding the release of their sons from the Yugoslav Peoples' Army once the war had begun. Others were organized by activists for special groups such as feminist, pacifist, and civil rights organizations. Some acted alone, others with the backing of international groups, such as Amnesty International or Women in Black. A special place belongs to the latter. In the same manner as their predecessors in Israel and Chile they used the black of mourning and silence to express their disgust with violence as a means of conflict resolution. They stood motionless at a busy street corner or square for hours at a time, bravely putting up with rebukes and insults from the passers-by (see Prošić-Dvornić 1994: 186–87).

There were also protests by students and various groups of professionals such

---

communist elite but not overtly publicized. An entirely new hybrid music, the so-called turbo-folk, or techno-rave sound, a mixture of hard rock or rap rhythm and folk melody was created to suit their taste and lifestyle.

23. In 1990 and 1991, from the time of the beginning of the clashes between the Serbian minority and republic/state militia in Croatia, Belgrade streets were flooded with macho-warriors parading in their fatigues, often with weapons. The picture was even more marked when their families accompanied them. Sometimes their young sons, from five or six years of age, to the joy and pride of their parents, also wore fatigues and carried plastic replicas of assault weapons! Later these street parades became much less common.

24. Attitudes toward the war were very ambivalent, and they changed over time. When tanks and other vehicles, carrying soldiers, were leaving the Belgrade garrisons to join army units stationed in Slovenia, spectators cheered. However, when *a* soldier became *the* soldier—oneself, or a family member, cheering often gave way to despair. Beginning with the Slovenian *blitzkrieg* parents organized mass protests demanding immediate release of their sons from their compulsory army service. "It is shameful to win in a civil war!" was one of the memorable slogans. Later, at the onset of the war in Bosnia, parents' protests were backed by feminist and pacifist activists. In addition, mobilization in Serbia produced limited results. The mobilization call was answered by less than 40 percent in Serbia, and in Belgrade and the multiethnic Vojvodina, the turnout did not exceed a single digit. Most of the young people chose to be deserters (Prošić-Dvornić 1994: 179ff.).

25. Serbian soldiers have already made headlines as "international warriors." They were featured in the international media as soldiers of fortune and military instructors of Hutu refugees in Zaire fighting for then president Mobutu Sese Seco against the rebels (H. W. French, *New York Times*, February 12, 1997: A1, A6).

as scientists, journalists, physicians, artists, and classical and rock musicians.[26] All demanded an end to violence, a change of the regime, and reconciliation with the world. At times, these gatherings turned into mass demonstrations in the streets of Belgrade. There was "The Black Band," an attempt to prevent the war in Bosnia. "The Yellow Band" was organized to protest "ethnic cleansing." "The Last Bell" was to signal that time for change was running out, while "Peace in Bosnia—Spring in Serbia," was to impart that there could be no turn for the better in Serbia until the war was stopped and peace negotiated in Bosnia (Prošić-Dvornić 1994: 180–88). Other protests focused on internal matters. The most memorable of these were the Student Protest 1992 (Prošić-Dvornić 1993) and the three-months long civil and student demonstrations in 1996–97, after the election victory of the opposition in thirty-three municipalities throughout Serbia in the November 1996 elections, later annulled by the regime (Prošić-Dvornić 1998).

The regime could not deny the existence of the protesters but they could and did deny them access to the state-run media. Because of its control over the administration and the economy, backed by a strong police force, the government was in a position to be in charge of everything, including the opposition.[27] The regime was aware that the accumulated discontent had to be vented. Protests, as well as freedom of press and speech, were thus allowed, but they were always contained. Mass demonstrations were isolated in space and time as an antistructural, ritualistic, liminal happening having no effect on structural reality. In time the protesters ran out of energy. In addition, the regime gave its own interpretation of these gatherings, discrediting their intentions and goals as "perilous to the society" (Prošić-Dvornić 1998). The participants were, the government proclaimed, "fools brainwashed by enemy propaganda" (Prošić-Dvornić 1994: 189–93). Official metaphors portrayed these individuals as prone to subservience, especially to foreigners, but also as prey to "supernatural forces." After the Dayton Peace Accord had been signed in November 1995, it was President Milošević who became an undeniable "Peacemaker, never in favor of a war option." Hence, the previous set of metaphors used to describe the "Others" among "Us" could no longer apply.

On the other hand, those labeled as "different" did not object to being singled

26. In sharp contrast to folk music, which has been widely used by the regime for chauvinistic, bellicose propaganda, the majority of rock musicians were in the opposition from the very beginning. "I don't want folk music to win!" "Don't count on us," "Under the helmet there is no brain" were some of the rock song titles and verses.

27. From the very beginning of party pluralism it was obvious that the regime had encouraged and maintained full control of far-right political groups. It used them to try out extreme ideas, such as militant chauvinism, or to pursue, through paramilitary forces, ethnic cleansing, or rape as "military tactics." Looking back at the past decade, however, it seems to be reasonable to suppose that a good part of the democratic opposition and some presumably independent media were also under the regime's control. Their function was to control and pacify the opposition-minded public and potentially "dangerous" (i.e., effective) political leaders.

out by the official Serbia. They gladly accepted identification as an antagonistic force and even proclaimed the existence of "Another Serbia." The term signified the broad, independent opposition. It first appeared as a title of a book compiled by the Belgrade Circle[28] containing speeches given at their Saturday sessions. Soon it became a synonym for alternative movements, civil rights advocacy, and resistance to the regime and nationalistic "opposition" parties.[29] One of their most important claims, supported by many freethinking citizens, was that the war in Bosnia was not between different nations. Rather it was seen as a confrontation between various kinds of nationalists who had committed atrocities against civilians.[30]

Many felt that Milošević, like any other dictator, could not continuously control everything. Thus every outburst of discontent seemed to be a step closer to the victory of democratic forces, But after a brutal crack-down and the prolonged apathetic stage which would follow, those in power always made sure that they maintained their totalitarian grip over the entire society. In the process, all newly created democratic institutions, such as the freedom of speech and assembly, an independent media, an autonomous university, and the preservation of human and civil rights, were slowly and systematically destroyed.

The personal rule of Slobodan Milošević, with his wife, Mirjana Marković, the leader of the radical Yugoslav United Left (former Communist Party) and their closest collaborators also allowed right wing movements, at the supposed other end of the ideological spectrum, to flourish. Once Pandora's box was opened in 1990, even the supposedly "undesirable" ideologies such as fascism

28. The Belgrade Circle, founded in January 1991, is an association of independent intellectuals. It has been very active in promoting pacifism and democratic values and it had ardently participated in organizing antiwar protests. Its members were the first to establish contacts with similar organizations in other former Yugoslav republics. They were also the first to visit Bosnian towns, together with international pacifist and human rights activists, and offer unconditional support to Muslims in cities besieged by Serbian forces.

29. "Another Serbia" had its own arsenal of internal "Orientalizing" labels. Within the context of Serbia, it perceived its members as educated, civilized, westernized, and democratic urbanites, and their opponents as xenophobic, nationalistic "cultural hybrids." The latter category was further differentiated into two diametrically different subgroups. On one side were "the descendents of timid, hard-working, sedentary and peace-loving farmers of Serbia Proper and the Vojvodina." On the other side were those, "who originated from restless, violent, militant, Dinaric, city-phobic, transhumant mountain herders, and who inhabited territories mainly outside of the Serbian state." Horrendous deeds such as the destruction of Vukovar, the endless sieges of Sarajevo and Srebrnica, or the shelling of Dubrovnik were attributed to the latter category. Here reciprocal stereotyping reflecting class and cultural bias is clearly expressed.

30. There are many citizens in Serbia, as there are many in other parts of the former Yugoslavia, who support this view. They strongly believe that under different circumstances and power relations the recent history of the Balkans might have taken a very different course. Despite present hostilities among the governments of the newly created states that are presented by the political elites as the "expression of ancient hatreds" there are still many important links that stretch *across* national borders. Serbian peace groups have made great efforts to maintain these ties, which could be the basis for some future renegotiations.

and anti-Semitism, last seen in World War II, appeared, even though many Serbs would have preferred their continued exclusion from public life (Kuljić 1972; Vukotić 1992; Cohen 1996). These ideologies were also familiar from the pre–World War II period. Vojislav Šešelj, the leader of the Serbian Radial Party, started his postcommunist political career as a marginal, neo-folkloric figure. He worked his way up to the office of vice-president of Serbia. His rise epitomizes the gradual grow of fascism in the Serbian government with consequent influences on the wider society. While threatening and terrorizing "the disobedient" within Serbian society, Šešelj has openly established contacts and has advocated collaboration and even union with other pro-fascist forces in Europe ranging from Belarus and Russia to France.

In contrast to the crudeness of the pro-fascist political movements, some right-wing cultural movements were highly aestheticized. Prominent among them, by style of sophistication, was the New Serbian Right founded by a small group of theater people. The movement originated in Sarajevo in the 1980s with camp stylization of symbols from the Third Reich as a way of challenging the established canons of art and politics. In some ways they resembled the movement known as the Neue Slovenische Kunst, the late-twentieth-century version of dadaism. The New Serbian Right retained the camp style, as exemplified in their manifesto and performance, but substituted medieval Byzantine / Serbian Orthodox religious symbols for the German ones and declared themselves sympathizers and/or successors of the pre–World War II Serbian fascist Zbor, led by Dimitrije Ljotić, a Nazi collaborator. Their ideas also reflected those of religious fundamentalism formulated before World War II by Serbian Orthodox theologians, notably Nikola Velimirović and Justin Popović.

Thus the New Serbian Right represented a revived and modernized "Serbianized" variant of Russian Euro-Asians as well as Western traditionalist and revisionist movements. They advocate a return to Byzantine and Orthodox roots, premodern traditions, renewal of religiosity and sacred values (Knighthood, Holy Grail, Honor, and Sacrifice). They wanted to rebuild the "spiritual (Slavic, Orthodox) empire." Old values would, in turn, counterbalance and destroy the evils of the modern world, such as liberalism, atheism, democracy, communism, and egalitarianism. The first and only volume of their journal, Naše ideje (Our ideas)[31] appeared in June 1993. Each of its oversized pages represented a prototype of the New Serbian Aesthetics. The movement is typified by the statement that "New Serbian Culture will turn a stale pool [that is today's non-religious, decadent Western model—M.P-D], into a Jacuzzi with a taste of Studenica [a name of a river and of a medieval monastery—M.P-D]" (N. Popović 1993: 70).[32]

31. The editor of Naše ideje was Dragoslav Bokan, also the leader of the White Eagles, another paramilitary organization that was very active in the 1992 wars in Croatia and Bosnia.
32. New Primitivism, a part of the New Wave Movement, originated in Koševo, a Sarajevo suburb. All these movements spring from the same source, the punk, resonated well with the Yugoslav crisis, degeneration of the society, and a need to reorient the identity of the local youth. However,

Instead of a Conclusion

The vitality of Milošević's regime has derived from its great flexibility and its pragmatism. After every radical turn it has pretended that it had never supported anything contrary to its current action. Imagining a "people with no memory," it has presented a façade that includes the pretense that the life in Serbia has always been peaceful and normal. The regime acts as if the front lines in Bosnia not more than 100 kilometers away never existed. As if the flows of refugees— homeless, displaced people with only memories of the past life and no feasible future—never existed. As if the handicapped young men, survivors of the war in Croatia, missing limbs, in wheelchairs and on crutches, trying to live with their nightmares, desperately wanting to pick up the pieces of their shattered lives, did not exist. As if new areas of ethnic cleansing were not being opened or reopened as in Kosovo.

There is the pretense that society has not suffered from a total implosion, with criminals and war profiteers, pretending to be the new class of entrepreneurs, filling in the void left after the disaster. It is as if no pyramid schemes of any kind have "laundered" and "transferred" the life savings, private and "social," of the entire nation into the hands of the "chosen few." It is as if there have been no unprecedentedly harsh Security Council sanctions and as if there have been no atrocities committed, no villages and cities endlessly held under siege or destroyed, no territories ethnically cleansed, no prisoners held in camps, resembling those of the infamous past in South Africa, the Soviet Union, and Nazi Germany, no raping of "other" women. In the end it is as if several hundred thousand younger and middle-aged educated urbanites have not left Serbia for good to restart their careers and lives somewhere else, mostly overseas. In sum it has seemed as if nothing abnormal or immoral has happened over the years, and as if apathy, despair, hopelessness, and isolation are the normal human condition. The regime has gained increasing control over the years but in the process has destroyed all sound social institutions and even the will of the people to resist. It seems increasingly stable and secure. Can it really last forever?

After twelve long years of Milošević's reign, it is obvious that he has repeatedly used the same strategies with the same disastrous results. After every serious attempt inside Serbia to initiate overall changes and replace, or at least contain, his personal rule, the regime only tightened its grip, making the lives of its citizens even more miserable than before. Every new horrendous military campaign

---

their expressions could vary to a considerable extent. Contrary to the Neue Slovenische Kunst that played with the stylization of totalitarianism, the Koševo group used the aesthetics of primitivism as a formula for creating new authenticity. They insisted upon humorous effects achieved by creating absurdities by juxtaposing elements from different, clashing cultural levels (e.g. traditional and urban, local and imported) and by exaggerating discrepancies between styles. The New Primitives, "barbaric geniuses," used self-parody in order to expose the pretentiousness and triviality of society (cf. Prica 1990: 23ff.).

in areas outside of Serbia Proper, undertaken largely because of the need to restore power within Serbia and put the blame for calamitous reality on somebody else has had the same epilogue; the territorial range of his malice diminished and his outside power contained. However, with each retreat, Serbian ethnic lebensraum, shared for centuries with other entities, also shrunk, bringing more and more discontented refugees into Serbia, under Milošević's rule and mercy. It seems that Serbian lebensraum has remained intact only in Macedonia where Milošević was deprived in time of a chance to "defend" it. In other words, he has lost territories for "his" people wherever he has tried to "protect" them.

Even after seventy-eight days of NATO bombing in Spring 1999, the pattern seems to be repeating itself. There is a growing discontent in Serbia and demands for Milošević's resignation are the leitmotif of all mass gatherings. Manipulation of past events by the state-run propaganda machine desperately trying to present the loss of Kosovo and the fatal destruction of the country as a Serbian victory do not appear to be working. Neither do the promises of fast recovery, or any other imagery striving to portray Milošević as a peace-loving savior. However, after the war, the international media seem to have lost all interest in the area. Without outside attention and substantial support for the efforts to turn a new leaf, there is a serious threat that these protests might fail again. Milošević will thus be left with another chance to restart his monstrous strategy, which is to suffocate the voices of reason and initiate yet another armed conflict. Candidates for the latter are still plentiful: rebellious Montenegro, the predominantly Muslim region of Snajak, the multiethnic Vojvodina, or simply the entire opposition in Serbia.

Will the opposition forces in Serbia, in spite of all odds, have the ability to endure? Will the severe destruction of the country help everyone there see what were the true nature and effects of Milošević's reign? Will the proclamation that Serbia is a terrorist state still be successfully presented as a hostile act from the outside, part of some imagined global anti-Serbian conspiracy aimed at wiping out the entire nation or as a status well deserved by the actions of its uncivil government? Will there still be cries of despair when the actions of the Serbs in power provoke the international community to react in a drastic, even brutal, way against Serbia, while there was mostly silence when the Serbs were harming others? It is evident that even with good will in outside support in place, there could be no radical change before the Serbs are ready to face the deeds of their own leaders, whether freely elected or imposed upon the population. There can be no "fresh start" before the Serbs are ready to say they are truly sorry for the sufferings of the others and not before they ask forgiveness from Vukovar, Sarajevo, Srebnica, Kosovo. . . . Only then will it be possible to demand apologies from the others and start rebuilding their society based on a very different set of values.

PART V

PERSPECTIVES ON INTERVENTIONS

Refugee Women from Former Yugoslavia in the Camps of Rural Hungary

Éva V. Huseby-Darvas

In spring 1992 and summer 1993 I conducted field work in four camps for refugees from the former Yugoslavia (Huseby-Darvas 1993: 6–11, 1994a: 130–38, 1994b: 63–78, 1995: 153–70, and 1996: 11–20). Among other things, I was interested in the experience of women and its effects on perceptions of their ethnic and gender identities, cultural heritage, and social, economic, and familial roles. In visits to camps I ate, sat, and talked with but mostly listened to refugees. While I communicated in Hungarian with ethnic Hungarian refugees, exchanges with Bosnians, Croatians, and others took place with the help of interpreters.[1]

The present work is based on observations in the camps of Nagyatád, in southern Hungary, and Bicske in the west.[2] In the first part of this essay I briefly discuss the refugee problem in general and present some varied perspectives on Hungary's role as host for refugees from former Yugoslavia. Then, based on variations in the two refugee camps, I consider the nature and significance of

---

1. Most interpreters were from Voivodina and were considered more or less official translators in the camps. Occasionally, I was fortunate to find individuals from Bosnia or Croatia who spoke good English. With them I could forgo using official interpreters and heard more candid stories than when I used ethnic Hungarian interpreters from Voivodina or elsewhere from former Yugoslavia.

2. In addition to videos, slides, and photographs, I taped conversations with thirty-seven individuals, six families, and five groups.

refugee demographics. In the second part of this chapter I examine the daily life, dilemmas, and future prospects of refugee women from their own perspectives. I particularly focus on issues of alienation, gender and familial conflict, ethnic competition, and processes of obtaining refugee status.[3]

To a large degree, because of social fragmentation within the camps and angst among the host populations, both the refugee women and their Hungarian hosts have been forced to reevaluate their personal and collective selves and reconstruct their national, ethnic, and gender identities. The quandary faced by refugees from former Yugoslavia, with their unresolved and apparently irresolvable marginalized status, is a transnational concern. Refugee life represents a constant and destabilizing thorn in the side of the international community, which must be addressed in some systematic way. It is clear and understandable that both refugees and their hosts define themselves very differently than they did before the war. The resulting personality transformations certainly need study over the long term. However, it is not premature to say that some refugee-related processes and experiences (e.g., ethnogenesis and long-distance nationalism) have already heightened animosity in former Yugoslavia and make a travesty, or a parody, albeit with tragic overtones, of the Dayton Accord.

The Refugee Predicament and Hungary's Role in the Crisis

> The refusal of states to receive others is an utter impossibility and, to the rest of the world, is likely to appear ruthless and uncivilized; it is a practice adopted by people who use harsh words, such as xenelesia or banishment of strangers, and who have harsh and morose ways. —Plato, *Laws* 12.950

The international refugee crisis has become increasingly volatile since the end of the cold war. At that time the United Nations warned that migration could become the human crisis of our age (Anonymous 1993a: 16). Sadly, the circumstances of refugees throughout the world is, indeed, politicized and often manipulated. In this light, it is rather remarkable that Hungary, during an economically, politically, and culturally difficult transition period, continues to play an active role as a host country. Since the late 1980s it has given refuge to increased numbers of asylum seekers. In the late 1980s there were even reports that likened Hungary to America as a place of asylum, mainly, but not exclusively, for ethnic Hungarians from Romania (Underwood 1989: 4). Hungary's status as a chief refugee center in the region was further cemented with the war in the former Yugoslavia (Bohlen, 1991: A1; Morokvašić 1992: 3–6; Anonymous 1993a).

By July 1992 serious and well-publicized concerns suggested that the entire

---

3. I do not deal here with rape or its results. Ethnic Hungarian health workers told me about incidents of rape and related stories, for example when children were born to victims of rape in the camps. However, none of the refugee women mentioned these topics to me directly.

Hungarian infrastructure supporting refugees would soon crumble. These concerns were well founded, since only 20 percent of the costs to house, clothe, feed, or care for the refugees came from the United Nations and other Western sources. The remaining 80 percent was covered outright by Hungarian sources without much hope of reimbursement (*Hírmondó* 1992). By 1993 Hungary had become safe haven for migrants from a hundred different countries. The great majority asked for temporary asylum and had no desire to settle permanently. They wanted to return home as fast as conditions would allow, or settle in the West. Yet there were regular signs of "refugee overload" and breakdown of refugee support. For example, in mid-October 1992, a spokesperson for the Hungarian Border Guards reported that in the previous year, because of more stringent controls, some 900,000 people without travel documents or money to finance their stay in Hungary were turned back at the border (Oltay 1992). About 800,000 were Romanian citizens of various ethnic groups. Additionally, 27,000 came from the CIS states: 25,000 were Poles; 17,000 were Bulgarians; and the remaining 33,000 came from various Third World countries with some people also beginning to come from former Yugoslavia.

At this time Hungarian refugee agencies declared that the country could not accept Bosnian refugees unless they entered with special permission from the Hungarian government and the International Red Cross. Two days after this declaration and a signed agreement to this effect between the governments of Croatia and Hungary, the latter gave asylum at the Drávaszabolcs crossing point to 206 Bosnian refugees. They were accepted because they either asked to enter Hungary for purposes of family unification, or they had minor children, were ill, or were elderly (Kasriel 1992: 4; Népszabadság 1992). With the addition of these refugees the Nagyatád camp was filled to its capacity of 3,000.

Despite the uncertainty of support for the refugees, in January 1993, Thomas Birath, chief representative of the UNHCR in Hungary, commented on Hungary's role in giving asylum to so many refugees and suggested that "Hungarian [refugee] organizations are doing a very good job" (Népszabadság, January 26, 1993). Later that year he again noted that "Hungary still continues to have (its) border open (to) receive people in need of a safe haven. This policy (has) gained the country respect on an international level" (Birath, 1993). The UNHCR at this time added $1.2 million to the $6 million it had already given to assist Hungary's care of the refugees.[4]

However, as the world, and particularly the West, became increasingly impotent in its handling of the refugee issue and frustrated with its escalating cost, Birath's parting comments were telling. Leaving his Budapest post for good in

4. According to Dr. Ågnes Ambrus, in 1992 the Hungarian government spent $12 million (U.S. dollars) on refugee care, while the UN spent $9.3 million. In 1993 the Hungarian government again spent $12 million, while the UN contributed only $5 million. Evidently the UN did not consider that, though the actual number of refugees may decrease, their cost increases the longer they stay in the camps.

August 1994, he remarked that Hungarian refugee policy is "conflicting" and that "[the Hungarians] should decide what they want to do with refugees and for this it would be important to look around in Europe" (cited by Tömöry 1994: 87). Of course, Mr. Birath did not specify where in Europe to look, as no other country readily opened its gates for the refugees from the former Yugoslavia. To this day it is uncertain if there is a country anywhere in the world that could serve as a worthy example to emulate amid the current refugee problem.

Internal Hungarian support structures for refugees are also often weak or varied. For example, while a number of NGOs have operated in Hungary since 1989, few focused on refugees (see Czakó 1993 on the development and, in some cases, disappearance of local community organizations). Along with a handful of church and grassroots organizations, the organization MENEDÉK, or REFUGE (an acronym for Legal Offices of Hungarian Association for Migrants), was established in early 1995 "to ensure the legal protection of vulnerable migrants as well as to represent migrants in the political process" (Fullerton, Sik, and Tóth 1995). Another group, "The Alba Circle," was formed to help all actual and potential draftees escape from former Yugoslavia (usually via Hungary to Austria), so it has a more specific, though related function. Furthermore, though in theory all migrants are equal, in practice this is not necessarily so. Thus there is ambivalence and inconsistencies in the Aliens Law and Citizenship Law of Hungary, passed in 1993. In particular, in cases of permanent settlement in Hungarian law gives preference to (1) individuals with purposes of family unification and to (2) individuals who declare their Hungarian ethnic affiliation either with a written petition, or with documents showing that one or more of his or her ancestors were Hungarians (J. Tóth 1995: 57; P. P. Tóth 1995: 69–82). Thus, as Judit Tóth (1995: 57–69) suggests, "the effects of moral commitment to ethnic Hungarians crossing the border can also be detected in the laws."

Changing Refugee Camp Populations

Hungarian law is only one factor shaping the demographics of camp populations. In fact, it is difficult to determine the demographic profile of refugees, since it varies over time and from camp to camp. Péter Pál Tóth (1995: 78–79) suggests that 99.2 percent of refugees between 1988 and 1992 had arrived from three countries: Yugoslavia, Romania, and the Soviet Union. In 1992 36 percent of the refugees were ethnic Hungarians. "Excluding refugees from Yugoslavia (among them 11.7 percent were Croatian, 47.5 percent Muslim and 33.6 percent Hungarian), 65 percent of the refugees were ethnic Hungarians. Among the refugees coming from Rumania [sic], 77.2 percent were Hungarians."

However, this overview does not show how the ethnic distribution of migrants also changes constantly. In 1991, for example, Nagyatád's population was 85 percent Croatian and 12 percent Hungarian (Horváth 1995: 145); but by 1994 its ethnic composition was over three-fourths Muslim. In contrast, during my second visit to the Bicske camp in August of 1993 there were a few Russian families, one Romanian family, and three ethnic Hungarian families from Romania. Most refugees were ethnic Hungarians who had fled the Voivodina region of rump Yugoslavia at the outset of the war, for two years received asylum in Sweden, and finally ended up in Hungary after expulsion from Sweden.

Ethnic Hungarians from the Voivodina were threatened with Serb "ethnic cleansing" long before such practices were reported in the Western media (Williams 1993: A12). Serbian threats and vandalism spread fear among Voivodina's ethnic Magyars and "encouraged" them to leave (see Oltay 1993 and Mártonffy 1993). By October 1993, 35,000 of the 350,000 Voivodina Hungarians sought refuge in Hungary or elsewhere (Andrejevich and Reisch RFE/RL, October 13, 1993, also see *Hírmondó*, various issues). A group of Voivodina Hungarians had first made it to Sweden. However, despite long-standing signs of war in their homeland and reports indicating their dire straits, the Swedish government expelled the 798 refugees in summer 1993. They were now expected to leave because, according to the Swedish decree of 1993, the Voivodina was not "a direct war zone" and the refugees were in no direct danger.

A number of these refugees ended up in Hungary, in the refugee camp at Bicske. Not surprisingly, the refugees who either asked for permanent asylum in Hungary or wanted to emigrate to the West often belonged to a double minority. For instance, families of Hungarian-speaking Roma from the northern part of former Yugoslavia had no desire to return. As one Rom in his early fifties told me, the memory of over 200,000 Gypsies put into Croatian-operated concentration camps and murdered during World War II was still "burning in our hearts . . . and we were afraid."

At the time of my 1992 field work, when most refugees from former Yugoslavia were ethnic Croatians (about 65 percent in Nagyatád) and ethnic Hungarians (about 25 percent), it was estimated that only about 15 percent of these asylum seekers actually stayed in the camps. The others stayed with friends or relatives in Hungary. Still others, without relatives or friends among the host population but with money, stayed as paying guests in Hungarian pensions, hotels, and private homes.[5] Many other refugees were not even registered, so it is impossible to establish the precise number of those actually in Hungary. Thus reported estimates of refugees in Hungary vary widely. According to István Morvay, undersecretary of state and director of the Office of Refugees and Migration of the Hungarian Ministry of Home Affairs, there were 50,000 registered refugees and

5. According to newspaper reports, bank deposits had been growing in towns along Hungary's southern borders since 1991 (Tamás Fábián, personal communication). Zoltán Dövényi (1995: 21) suggests that "in Hungary the . . . capital outflux accompanying the refugees is notable. Although there are no exact data available regarding capital influx into Hungary, there appears to be a correlation between capital (leaving) former Yugoslavia and the rapidly increasing number of joint ventures in southern Hungary."

an estimated 50,000 unregistered refugees in Hungary in March 1992 from former Yugoslavia alone (cited in *Hírmondó*, April 12, 1992).

The largest refugee camp in Hungary is located on the outskirts of the town of Nagyatád (Somogy County), population 12,000. This is in the southwestern part of the country, thirteen kilometers from the border with former Yugoslavia. The camp has a total capacity for 3,000 people. Formerly an army camp that had been empty for a year and a half, it reopened in late 1991 as a transitional refugee settlement. Its primary function was to serve as a haven for refugees from Croatia, and increasingly after late spring 1992 for Bosnian refugees, the victims of the Serbian "ethnic cleansing."

Refugees from former Yugoslavia arrived in Nagyatád at various times. One thousand people who were shuffled back and forth between Austria and Hungary in summer 1992 ended up there, as did 610 refugees who arrived in eight buses in November 1991, after the bombing of Vinkovci. They had been refused asylum throughout Western Europe. By the time they arrived in Nagyatád, all were frightened, cold, hungry, and dehydrated. Thus by the third anniversary of its opening it was noted (Gulyás 1994: 7) that the camp resembled a "refugee village." It had an infirmary; elementary, middle, and high schools; a store, and a post office. There was also a Muslim prayer room embellished with over 50 special rugs donated as pre-Ramadan gifts by the Indonesian ambassador, by other embassies, and by Arab students studying in Hungarian universities. The camp also had a library, a club, and television rooms.[6]

The camp is a true, if uncertain, community. Between August 1991 and August 1994, more than thirty babies were born and nearly seventy people died. They were buried in the nearby "refugee cemetery." The camp infirmary also shows some of the contradictions of refugee life. It is a clean but spartan environment. The majority of patients are older women between sixty and ninety-five. Each room contains five to six simple iron cots with mattresses, tables, and nightstands. There is very little space between the beds. Like everything else in the infirmary, the pillows, blankets, and sheets are sparkling clean. But despite the fastidious environment most patients appear totally lost. With empty stares, many seem to be almost catatonic. They give the impression that they are more mentally and spiritually afflicted than physically ill. Many of these women not only suffer from complete displacement from familiar surroundings but also are completely alone in the camp, without kin, neighbors, or friends. Among the most tormenting images I carry with me from the infirmary is an emaciated woman in her seventies, with flowing white hair and a bent back, who walked incessantly back and forth in the narrow, dark corridor with red-rimmed, huge staring dark

---

6. In addition there was a room for crafts supported by funds from the Peruvian ambassador and from other foreign diplomats stationed in Budapest. There were teen activity rooms as well as a playground whose sandbox was built by the "Friends of Nagyatád," a group of young Americans studying or working in Hungary. They visited the camp every five or six weeks with toys, clothing, and candy for the children. They also played with them and taught them English.

eyes, looking at everything but obviously not seeing anything. All I was able to find out from the staff is that she had not spoken since her arrival at the camp.

The camp school and refugee children show similar signs of trauma. Though, of course, the school has a much livelier and more positive atmosphere than the infirmary. Some of the children's crayon and pencil drawings and watercolor paintings that line the school's stairwells and corridors depict peaceful, at times even pastoral, scenes complete with butterflies, dogs, playing children, and houses with smoking chimneys. Still, most of the artwork reflects deeply troubled children with enormous anguish. It depicts war scenes, guns, airplanes with falling bombs, disturbing color compositions with faceless and armless, often amorphous, human-like figures.[7] It is obvious that refugees and camp administrators alike place great emphasis on the school and its activities. The schooling of children is well organized. The children are carefully groomed. They are grouped by age and cared for by deeply concerned teachers. The school has light, spacious classrooms. For those under sixteen there is no shortage of activities, including formal dancing lessons. However, the teachers continue to struggle with a severe shortage of textbooks in their native language.

Views and Impressions of the Nagyatád Refugee Camp

Impressions and perceptions of the camp vary between the refugees, administrators, visitors, and volunteers. For instance, most of the refugees recalled how they first felt safe and clearly grateful when they arrived in the camp. They were given a warm welcome, food, cups of hot tea, and blankets. Now, however, many are frustrated, though only a few were critical of administrative procedures.[8] For instance, a teenage boy came into the room while I was visiting with a Bosnian family. The translator left the room when he noted that the boy and I communicated in English. The teenager told me that he had a pass so he could go leave the camp to buy some ice cream the following day. He wanted to sit with it in the shade under a tree outside the camp gates "just to feel what it is like to be outside." During the same visit, with the help of this teenager as translator, a Bosnian man in his late fifties told me how much it would help with the internal peace and harmony of the camp if the authorities would let them go outside more freely and stay in town longer than rules now permit.[9] He wanted to go out before noon on market days while the market was still open. Though none of the others

7. I am indebted to Gabriella Lonkai (1995) for her insights on children's art at Nagyatád.

8. I am certain that lack of more open complaints had much to do with my use of ethnic Hungarians from Voivodina as guides and translators. As cultural and linguistic mediators between the non-Hungarian-speaking refugees and hosts, they are considered to be in privileged positions and rarely trusted by the refugees.

9. This information was very likely truthful and straightforward, since the man's own teenage son, whose English was impressive, was my translator.

said it quite this way, this man seem to have articulated the sentiment of other refugees when he said: "We could have problems with the camp administration if they find out we are talking with you. In many ways this is like a police state here, a Russian-style police state, and they do with us what they wish. We are at their mercy."

Understandably, administrative perceptions were very different. They often explained camp difficulties by reference to overcrowding and regularly said that the ratio between town dwellers (about 12,000 in the case of Nagyatád) and refugees in the nearby camp (3,000 at maximum capacity) was at a dangerous level, particularly in light of the town's limited telephone, postal, and other services. In 1993 the camp director told me that while relations are generally good between town dwellers and refugees, there are many actual and potential areas of conflict that must be prevented.

For example, the director thought special passes and restrictions on market days were needed to regulate unofficial refugee trading activities. While the refugees get full room and board with three meals each day, they also occasionally receive extra food, like canned liver paté. Some refugees don't eat these canned goods but collect them instead. Then, when they had permits to go to town on market days, they would take them into town to sell or bargain for other goods. These and similar occurrences caused tremendous conflict with the local population, he told me. Many Hungarians are unemployed, underemployed, or trying to make ends meet on very small retirement or disability pensions. They are angered by refugees making profits on goods they are given and "having it better than the townspeople do."

These are frequent sentiments expressed amid the growing economic difficulties in Hungary, problems that are compounded by the increasing number of homeless Hungarians as well.[10] Camp directors were thus in a difficult position, having to mediate between these two sets of legitimate interests. As one Nagyatád director noted in a report:

> At the request of the town, we restricted (refugee's) possibility to leave the camp. This is, on one hand, a protective measure, because the co-existence of two or three thousand asylum seekers in a small town with a population of twelve or thirteen thousand people can cause serious problems. However, on the other hand, our decision can be criticized because the Temporary Shelter is not a prison, and consequently we should not restrict the camp inmates in their free movements. In order to resolve this dilemma, we entrusted the self-government of the asylum seekers with the issuance of the daily permits to leave the camp. (Horváth 1995: 148n)

10. According to the Hungarian Ministry of Welfare, in fall 1994 there were an estimated 20,000 to 25,000 homeless in Hungary (*Hírmondó* 1994).

The "Friends of Nagyatád" have their own perspective on the camp. This is a group of young Americans, studying or working in Hungary, who volunteer to visit the camp once every five or six weeks, to play with and teach English to the children. They collect toys, clothing, candy, gum, and crafts for the children. It is not surprising that their impressions of Nagyatád were strikingly dissimilar from those of both refugees and administrators. One twenty-two-year-old New Yorker spent two years in Hungary working and studying the language. During this period she lived in the Nagyatád camp for several months where she worked with the refugee women and children. Before she left Hungary in August 1994, she reported her experiences to the International Rescue Committee, of which she was a member (see also Miklós 1994 and Tömöry 1994: 87). She specifically protested what she felt to be the refugees' loss of human rights and autonomy in exchange for residence and alleged asylum in the camp. She felt that the director, social workers, guards, police, and other camp staff in direct contact with the Bosnians were often disrespectful, impatient, intolerant, and at times even rude.

This report also suggested how refugee daily life was made more problematic by the lack of privacy in the camp. She cited incidents where camp administrators entered refugee rooms without knocking. Additionally, the only way families achieved a small measure of privacy in the large undivided barracks was to hang sheets between their spaces; obviously not an ideal solution. Further there were broken-down showers, baths, and toilet facilities in the barracks that sharply contrasted with the order and cleanliness elsewhere in the camp. Other difficulties were the greasy, non-nutritious meals. In fact, the refugees were not even consulted about the food that was prepared. The report further deplored the language problem and cultural barriers to communication and the many misunderstandings that resulted between refugees and camp administrators. A related phenomenon also noted in the report was that ethnic Magyar and other Hungarian-speaking refugees enjoy better housing, food, clothing, more lucrative work opportunities, and more frequent passes. These benefits are denied Bosnians and others who don't speak the host population's language.

Another member of the "Friends of Nagyatád," a young man from a small town in Wisconsin, was attending high school in Hungary for a year. He has joined the group with great enthusiasm; however, he was considerably less involved than the young woman from New York, and never actually lived in the camp. He only visited every fifth or sixth weekend for nine months between the late summer of 1993 and the middle of 1994. Despite his less intense relationship with the camp, many of his observations were similar. Like the New Yorker, he too commented on the prison-like, chain-link fence with barbed wire surrounding the camp. They also both objected to the main gate with its guardhouse and guards.[11]

11. Camp administrators claimed that the fence and guards functioned to regulate movement in and out of the camp. They couldn't understand their offensive qualities.

In keeping with the prison motif, people who entered the camp were occasionally searched. According to Mr. János Einwachter, the camp director in 1992, this was primarily for the safety of the refugees and to prevent the entry of alcoholic beverages. In recalling his weekends in Nagyatád to me, the young man from Wisconsin said he enjoyed the children, but that the surroundings made him sad and depressed. Like a number of other American youths, this young man told me that just "looking at the high fences and guard house behind which the refugees had to live" made him think of both a jail and a concentration camp. Another member of the group, a man in his mid-thirties, sent me several desperate-sounding e-mail messages about trying to find groups in the United States and Canada to act as sponsors to help Nagyatád refugees to emigrate. As he wrote "They have a roof over their heads and all their basic needs are met but need to get out of the depressing environment of the camp."

In spite of the difficulties many of the "Friends of Nagyatád," encountered traveling between Budapest and Nagyatád or what they considered as "less than minimum cooperation" from camp administrators while they visited the camp, their ardent involvement is obvious. The Wisconsin teenager summed up the reason for his commitment when he wrote how "the open, beautiful smile on the faces of refugee children made (my efforts) all worthwhile."

Volunteering is a complex matter particularly because it occurs in a culturally alien environment, as the "Friends of Nagyatád" experienced it. Obviously, there were different concepts of what constitutes privacy, and the causes of depression and sorrow as interpreted by refugees, administrators, and American students and other volunteers. Thus the same barbed wire fence can take on very different symbolic properties when seen from different perspectives. Refugees running for their lives from the madness of war see it differently, compared to members of an often-reluctant host population, or the eager, but frequently naive volunteers who were there by choice but essentially taking temporary respite from their safe, affluent North American middle-class backgrounds.[12]

The Dilemma of Refugee Women

By May 1992 eight out of ten refugees from former Yugoslavia in the Hungarian camps were women and their young children.[13] When I asked where their men

12. Visiting the camps and talking with refugees evoked memories of my mid-teen years when, fleeing the aftermath of the Hungarian Revolution, I too lived in camps (Camp Röeder and Camp Kilmer), felt vulnerable and dependent, at the mercy of administrators, and was for a while totally without hope. Still, my circumstances were very different from those of the present-day refugees. The geopolitical and economic circumstances of 1956 and 1957 made Hungarian refugees wanted by the West. We were popular, welcomed, helped, and given choices. This sharply contrasts with refugees' situations in a "postsocialist," globalizing world.

13. Data on the Hungarian camp population is courtesy of János Einwachter and Marica Bacsa of the Nagyatád camp. The unequal gender distribution is very similar to other modern refugee populations, which in 1992–93, according to UNHCR reports, numbered some twenty million worldwide.

were, I was told that some had been killed before the women and children left their homes. In other cases the husbands, fathers, and sons left with their families then returned home to fight. In still other cases, men encouraged women and children to leave while they stayed to fight. Where young or middle-aged men came with their families and stayed on in the camps, the most heated and agonizing topic was the potential return to their towns or villages. They wanted to fight in what, by late spring 1992, appeared to many to be an escalating crisis. The average age of a refugee was thirty-two, which actually reflected the overrepresentation of adults over fifty (again, mostly women) and young children. Few professions were represented, and the majority of adults were agrarian workers—both peasants and commuting worker-peasants from small towns and villages.

The physical structures of the refugee camps were often problematic for women. As discussed above, before August 1991 when it opened as a refugee camp, the Nagyatád camp had been a Hungarian army post. Thus, in spite of some minor changes, the camp bore all the characteristics of 1950s socialist architecture and workmanship. The bathrooms, for example, had been obviously designed only for men. There were no locks on the doors, and there were many more urinals than toilets. The barracks were multistory with four floors in each of the six buildings, and huge rooms that accommodated up to fifty soldiers. For refugee women, most of who had lived in village houses surrounded by orchards, plots, and vineyards, living in the camp was very difficult. In some cases these difficulties were compounded by the frustration of not having anything to do, by homesickness, and by differences between what the refugees perceive and interpret as the behavior and values of the host population and refugee expectations themselves.

For instance, Magda, an ethnic Hungarian in her fifties who fled from her village just across the border, expressed some of these frustrations and their attendant alienation:

> These Hungarians here really don't . . . like to work. But the other day I saw this woman at work in her field and it just about broke my heart. Who is working on my land? They give us everything here, I would be lying if I complained about anything. They are kind to us, feed us, the kids are in school, they set up everything right here in the camp for us, but there are days when I just go crazy. I have had my own orchard. I miss it, I also miss working on the land. Here we are just pacing, walking up and down several times a day, eating, sleeping a bit, and talking. We are talking so much.

A number of studies,[14] more than a decade of my own work on immigrant and refugee women in North America, and my personal background as a refugee all

14. See, for example, Abadan-Unat 1977; Abdo-Zubi 1987; Brettell 1982: 199; Gozdziak 1990 and 1994; Forbes 1992; Markowitz 1988; Marokvašić 1991; Sík n.d.; "Women and Migration,"

illustrate that refugee women's experiences are tremendously complex and in many respects very different than men's. First, there are gender differences in processes and strategies of adaptation. While women often appear to gain considerable independence as refugees, they are frequently the most vulnerable and potentially exploited. Additionally, women are influenced by radical changes in family structure, values, and expectations that directly result from the refugee experience. For example, family violence is mostly aimed at women and separations are more frequent and more visible in the camp environment. The physical and psychological effects of the loss of home, and particularly the loss of traditional support systems of networks of female kin and neighborhood and village community relationships were painfully evident among the women in the camps.

Grieving and post-traumatic stress disorder were common among the refugee women. Older women in the infirmaries were particularly confused about where they were in relation to their homes, when and how they got where they were. The uncertainties of the women's own plight and future appeared overshadowed by the constant worries about the their sons, husbands, fathers, and brothers whose whereabouts were unknown. They also worried about the behavior of their and others' children and teenagers in the camps.

After visiting the camps a number of times, it became clear that confusion, frustration, boredom, and alienation grow in direct proportion to the length of the war in the former Yugoslavia and with the length of stay in the camps. Indeed, while I listened to various refugee accounts, I was not surprised to find an increase in conflicts and other problematic social conditions the longer people stay in the camps. In 1992, amid the many signs of traumatic experiences and family and community disruptions, there were still extraordinary and repeated emphases on social relationships. Kinship, fictive kinship, neighborhood ties, and even newly developed relations were creatively defined and used in the camp setting (Jung 1978). They even shifted across boundaries of ethnic groups and regions. Fifteen months later, during field work in August 1993, by which time the ethnic composition of most camps radically changed because of war-related "ethnic cleansing,"[15] there was clearly less emphasis on all kinds of social relationships.

Despite declining sociability many women still dressed in their best clothes to stroll on camp streets in the afternoons. Many still decorated the walls of their rooms with posters and photographic montages of dead, alive, and missing, extended family members, relatives in the camps and in the West, and portraits of

---

Special issue of the *Anthropological Quarterly* 7 (1976); and Tóth 1992. These works show that while, in some respects, the situation of refugee women in Hungary is *sui generis*, in others it is similar to that of refugee women throughout the world.

15. In the first week in June 1992, 3,273 Bosnian refugees arrived in Hungary. Many were forced from their homes by Serbs, then had to buy new passports from rump Yugoslavia, and even to purchase their own train tickets for their unwanted journey. In unbearable heat, many were shuffled back and forth in trains between west and east central Europe. Ultimately they were "deposited" in Hungary from Vienna as Austria refused to give them asylum.

family houses and home interiors. Many still sat and sipped coffee with their neighbors. Older women gathered together after sunset outside the barracks and visited. Some carved prayer beads. Others knit or crocheted making sweaters and tablecloths, while men sat around drinking coffee and playing cards or chess. Nevertheless, more than the year before, the women's stories in 1993 progressively stressed the trauma of their refugee experience, including lack of reciprocity and related quandaries.

Some of the people I spoke with were "veteran refugees," having spent from one year to two or more in various camps. Many older women complained that it was uncomfortable to live and navigate the stairs in the dilapidated multistoried buildings. Others found that the humiliation of refugee life was even more upsetting than its physical discomforts. The case of a thirty-four-year-old woman illustrates how the lack of reciprocity became an issue in her life. She was an internist before the war in the northern Yugoslavian Voivodina. Together with her husband, a clinical pathologist, and two young daughters, she spent twenty-three months as a refugee in Sweden. This woman observed, "Our lives have taken on a very different direction in the last couple of years. . . . at home we would never accept gifts, not even a good word unless we knew that we could reciprocate. Now . . . we accept anything that is offered to us and that in itself is humiliating to accept. . . . We are constantly aware and we are made aware that we are charity cases. This also contributed to the misery we felt during our twenty-three months in Sweden and feel here in this refugee camp."

Wanting to go home was the leitmotif of stories I heard in 1992 from the majority of refugees from former Yugoslavia, the women in particular. Supporting this point, over 95 percent of the refugees from former Yugoslavia asked only for temporary asylum. In this respect they were similar to refugees worldwide. According to UNHCR, 99 percent of refugees in the world want to go home.[16] People don't give up their culture, home, friends, and belongings lightly (Barringer 1991; Forbes 1992). As a Serbian woman from Bosnia, married to a Muslim man, declared, "We just want to go back home and live in peace. We want the same Bosnia as we had before the war. We want the same relationship between people as before. Over a quarter of all marriages were like ours (mixed) but that never caused problems before."

Yet by 1993, for many refugees the likelihood of return had diminished. As this realization set in, they yearned for a chance to build a viable new existence either in Hungary or in the West. But there is very little encouragement for permanent resettlement. This was also clearly seen in the following remark made by another woman in her late thirties, also from the Voivodina:

> It is a horrible misfortune to be born in this part of the world. . . . Look back in history. Just about when people would be able to forget the last

16. This was according to Sylvana Foa, spokesperson for Sadako Ogata, the United Nations' High Commissioner for Refugees.

feud, then it starts all over again. There is no way to forget this one for a good many centuries. . . . I tell you, we just want to survive. We don't want to perish in this senseless mess. Somehow we hope to raise our children and find jobs and a place somewhere in this world. . . . It is horrible to be a refugee and being torn out of one's own surroundings. And where to go? Are we going to find a place where they will accept us and really take us in, where we can once again feel at home and call our home?

The dilemma of "Where can we go?" has a number of facets. But the gender and familial conflicts and ethnic competition are best understood from the refugee women's interpretation of their own situation. Gender and familial conflict grow in the camps as the roles of women change. Women are given and readily take on several roles that were previously men's domain. Consequently, men have little to do other than occasional warehouse and garden work. As one woman told me, the men in the camp are "often more listless and grumble more than we do, and they get so pathetically depressed." Women are easier to employ. They cook, sew, wash, clean, and also work in the camp infirmaries, schools, and nurseries. Still, despite their greater activity levels, camp women have a very difficult time of it. Transitions from extended to nuclear or stem families are painfully evident. Reports of camp medical personnel suggest that confusion, grieving, and post-traumatic stress disorder are common. Also, there are often attempted suicides in the camps, though comparatively few are "successful."

Several days before I arrived in one of the camps, a sixty-two-year-old ethnic Hungarian refugee woman hanged herself from the pipes of the communal bathroom. She left a note that she could not take life anymore and did not want to be a burden to her family. Four women who shared living quarters with the dead woman and her family said rather matter-of-factly that they understood why she killed herself. They said they also often think and talk about suicide. In addition to worries and anxieties, there is also discord within and between families and generations. Women were especially concerned over the whereabouts of their fathers, sons, husbands, or brothers. They were also anxious about the children's activities and the teenagers' conduct in and beyond the camps. In many families, including even those whose menfolk are not in the camp, domestic violence became more frequent. There were fights between children and their parents or between siblings. According to parents and teachers, in the camp most children either become very aggressive, or turn inward and refuse to communicate. A forty-three-year-old Bosnian teacher compared her students' behavior before and since the war. She said that the advice of the handful of psychologists who come to the camp on rare occasions and work through interpreters makes little if any difference in the everyday realities faced by mothers and teachers. She commented that "these children are excessively nervous and jittery. They are awfully hard to discipline and their attention span is very short. . . . Many lost their parents, grandparents, or other close kin in Bosnia. We are trying to keep them busy and educate them in the meantime. But it is not about education alone. We are trying to make children forget. And here that is our most difficult, nay, irresolvable task."

One widow in her mid-sixties, whose son, daughter-in-law, and grandchildren had all been living in the Nagyatád camp for over five months when our conversation took place, complained of increasing physical abuse from both her son and her grandsons, and of daily verbal abuse by her daughter-in-law. But she said, "My son, he was so good to us before the war: his nerves suffered from having to leave our home. There is nothing to do for us here. . . . We were always busy at home, but here he just sleeps, or sits and thinks all day."

Many conflicts concern gender, familial, and generational issues. One case occurred in summer 1993. At the time there were a few weddings in one of the camps. The parents of one bride, however, were not present at her wedding. Some months back, I was told, the eldest daughter in the family, who was pregnant, ran away to get married, and was hidden in another barracks. The mother was severely beaten by the father, for "not taking care of the daughter" and "allowing shame on the family." The woman was briefly hospitalized after the beating. Camp self-government, comprised entirely of refugee men, tried to mediate between the husband and wife. The wife asked for the help of the camp administrators to move away from her husband to another building. That she did this was one of several unusual elements in the case, and was condemned by many other male and female refugees. The husband promised his wife everything if she would move back, and she eventually did. However, the wife beating was repeated when the second daughter got married less than three months after the first wedding. Although this woman was not pregnant, the father was again furious at his wife because, in his eyes, his daughter married without his approval and below his family's status.

Ethnic Conflict

There is also considerable ethnic conflict and competition in the camps, though it is frequently expressed indirectly. The use of combination bathroom-lavatories is one dispute with an ethnic dimension. However, refugees express this conflict in terms other than ethnicity. They talk of culture or esteem, about which people are more "cultured" and thus of higher rank on some undefined scale that measures being "really European and civilized." They also compare bathroom behavior in terms of healthy and natural ways versus cleanliness and personal hygiene. For example, in one camp there is only one combination bathroom and lavatory on each floor. These are designated for use by men on one floor and by women on the next. But this is less of a problem than personal habits. Bosnian Muslim refugees place their feet on the toilet seat and crouch or squat over it. Ethnic Croatian and Hungarian refugees sit on the toilet seat with feet on the floor. As a result, members of the latter two groups criticize the Bosnians and say that they do not know how to use the lavatories; that they urinate and defecate on the rim or the floor. In turn, the Muslim refugees reproach their Croatian and Hungarian counterparts who, they say, use the lavatories in "repulsively unhealthy and unnatural ways." These types of conflicts extend to other areas of daily life, such as diet, the drinking of alcohol, and clothing.

Economic ventures and daily work opportunities are also a major and continuous source of conflict and competition in which ethnic allegiance and nepotism play important parts. For refugees, there are only two legitimate sources of income. One is the occasional paying job (and here again women most often receive them). The other is remittances from relatives who are guest workers in Western Europe or elsewhere who send money or things of value that can be sold or exchanged. The Bosnian refugees are at a distinct disadvantage in most such situations, while ethnic Hungarians have a clear advantage, since they speak the language of the host population. Consequently, they are most often hired as interpreters, and serve as liaisons between the administration and the self-governing refugee organization, most of whom communicate in their own native language and are not Hungarian speakers.[17]

Often ethnic Hungarian refugees are said to take advantage of their situation by controlling the most lucrative jobs, securing for themselves the best clothes and other supplies from the warehouse, and (in the largest camp) the most frequent passes. Rózsi, a fifty-six-year-old ethnic Hungarian woman from the Voivodina recounted,

You know, the lack of money is a perpetual problem here. There is no money if we want to buy something—cigarettes, fruit, candy, gum. The Bosnians and Croatians curse at the Hungarians. I am really Hungarian too, even though I was born over there, so I let it go in one ear, out the other: I don't let these comments bother me, or I try not to. These Hungarians here do everything for us. But you know, people will be people and even saints are depicted as having their hands turned toward themselves, so even saints look out for themselves first and foremost. There is so much envy and mistrust in the camp. Somebody always questions the fairness of the distribution of food, clothing, and shoes. True, the distribution really could use improvement. Others ask: who knows where some of the (refugee) money goes. True again, a large amount was spent on the refurbishment of this camp before we were moved here. But what did they really do? They could have done a much better job: to make small

17. Teaching Hungarian in the refugee camps was generally unsuccessful. Most Bosnian and other refugees wanted to return home. Those who did not, had no desire to stay in Hungary but hoped eventually to join relatives in Germany, Canada, or elsewhere in the West. Consequently, they were trying to learn either German or English rather than Hungarian.

rooms would have meant so much in cutting down friction between people. You know, a couple of doors, a few walls here and there, and these
large rooms would have been separated into smaller, more livable ones.

Still, curiously, the most successful entrepreneurs are some of the bilingual
Croatian women and not the ethnic Hungarians. These individuals are familiar
with the area of southern Hungary where, for example, both Nagyatád and Cson-
grád are located. For decades they regularly crossed the border to shop at markets
and fairs in the region. In the process they built social networks which they now
skillfully mobilize (see Sík, n.d., on the multiple importance of economic and
social contacts prior to emigration or escape from the homeland). For instance,
in one of the camps an ethnic Croatian woman in her mid-fifties runs a profitable
underground shop with an assortment of cigarettes, candy, fruit, and chewing
gum. She would like to go home and cried as she talked about her house and
showed me her montage of photographs. Still, she told me that as a refugee she
considers herself much more successful both economically and socially than she
was at home as a small-town housewife and seamstress.

There is also status competition between ethnic groups, about who is or should
be more qualified for either temporary political asylum, or refugee status. This is
evident in the following remark of an ethnic Hungarian woman from the Voivodina. Her comment also shows how the refugees see themselves in their hosts'
eyes. In this particular case she said about her Swedish "hosts," "They got rid
of us. They could not fit us into their category of refugee. What kind of refugee
is it who escapes in a car and thus arrives on their shore? Now the Bosnians, they
could easily categorize them as refugees. So they shoved 798 of us out to make
room for a few dozen Bosnians."

These conflicts grow as needed resources dwindle, as warehouses in the camps
become increasingly depleted, as the West turns away from helping with both the
moral and the financial burden.[18] Regardless of how naive and unrealistic this
may sound, there is a growing need for more funds, more usable and practical
clothes,[19] more food that reflects the largely Muslim refugee population's dietary
needs, and more humanitarian attention, more understanding. Most important,
there is need for the Western world to put forth more flexible, open and reasonable immigration policies that fit the postsocialist European refugee crisis.

In Place of a Conclusion

Conclusions are elusive about these refugees' lives. Like for so many others in
the world, the nagging question of "where can we go" is an essential part of their

18. Jane Kramer (1991) noted prophetically, in the West "the panic about immigrants from East
Europe has been mainly . . . financial. . . . As time goes on, the West turns its collective back both
financially and morally to the situation of refugees."

19. Here I refer to a number of totally useless items in the refugee camps, such as riding helmets
and britches, and shoes with high platforms or five-inch high heels.

daily reality. While the accounts of refugee women in Hungary reveal trauma and vulnerability, their experiences are inextricably tied into a much larger, lamentable, and frightening global process. I see contemporary refugees in postsocialist Europe and elsewhere amid what, among others, Benedict Anderson (1992) refers to as "The New World Disorder." In this they are like pawns, who unwittingly and unwillingly play parts in major transnational rites of passage. These rites, however, are no longer transitional phases but are increasingly becoming a permanently ambiguous way of life in which there is considerable ritual degradation and little if any hope for either elevation, integration, or for that matter, reintegration. All refugees exist in a bizarre and sustained liminality, progressively marginalized, cut off from customary social contacts, living in a time out of ordinary time. Their liminality is bizarre because it brings increased fragmentation along gender, ethnic, and age group lines rather than a community spirit, social solidarity, and the equality of communitas. Neither does their liminality lead to a promise of either a new kind of integration or reintegration either in their own homelands or elsewhere.

As a result of the refugees' plight, I am afraid that what Benedict Anderson (1991: 3–14) refers to as "long-distance nationalism" will significantly increase during the following decades both in amplitude and zeal. What about the societies that shelter refugees? Hungary, along with other East-Central European host societies, is interstitial between East and West. Since 1989 the country went from euphoria and great expectations to disappointment and bewildered despair. It grew measurably more resentful of the accumulating refugee presence amid the moral and material detachment of the West (Huseby-Darvas 1993, 1995; Sík 1992; Závecz 1992). To a large degree, because of the fragmentation within the camps and the angst among the host populations,[20] there are ongoing processes of reevaluating both personal and collective selves and reconstructing national, ethnic, and gender identities. I fear that some of these, particularly the processes of ethnogenesis and long-distance nationalism are already leading to even further animosities in that already so very troubled region of our world.

20. Encouraging signs in Hungary that refugees will be better integrated include 1994 election results, waning popularity of rightist politicians, and growth of NGOs helping refugees (Kovács, n.d., Judit Tóth n.d.). Hungarian xenophobia is not quite as rabid as that of, for example, the followers of Jörg Haider in Austria, or German neo-Nazis. Still, the platforms of several Hungarian rightist groups are explicitly anti-foreign (see Huseby-Darvas 1993, 1994b, and 1996). Some observers also aver strong and growing links between Hungarian, German, Austrian, and U.S. neo-Nazis since at least the early 1990s (Hockenos, 1993: 143–63). "Foreigners out!" is a frequent slogan of these groups. In the song "Immigrants' Share," the Hungarian band Mos-Oi sings: "We'll get rid of everyone we don't need, / Including the garbage immigrants. / The immigrants' fate can only be death, / We'll have to drive out all the Blacks, / For the Arabs—to be sure—machine guns are waiting, / Over Palestine atomic clouds are gathering" (cited by Hockenos 1993: 154).

20

Poised for War

Kosova's Quiet Siege

Janet Reineck

This article was first written six years before the war in Kosova, before the
internationalization of the conflict. It is not about the war, or its bloody
aftermath or the subsequent invasion of UN agencies sent to rebuild a region, to
reconfigure a people. It describes Kosova in the 1900s: the cultural and political
backdrop . . . a "quiet siege" . . . unwitnessed, unrevealed.

It's a summer afternoon in Santa Barbara. I am spending the day with a family
of Albanian refugees . . . riding ocean waves, taking in the cool Pacific breezes.

And listening to the tales of torture, starvation, and terror—children's memories of their last days in Kosova.

Besart, a boy of thirteen, smiles beneath his bandages, his face blown half
away by NATO bombs. His sister Luljeta, with her new haircut and manicure,
slumps in a wheelchair, her leg mangled by shrapnel, held together by steel posts.
Their older brother Emrush, in his new Levi's and Reebok's, had rescued the two
from their burning tractor. Silent and brooding, he wasn't able to save their
mother or the scores of relatives who died in agony before his eyes.

"Kosova" is the Albanian appellation for the province. The Serbian is "Kosovo."

It wasn't until today—imprinted with the ghastly wounds and bloody stories of these refugee children—that I comprehended the war. As the twentieth century draws to a close, the world looks pitifully upon Kosova, smoldering in ruin. The bloody war that ripped through Serbia has left a trail of torture and death, and sown the seeds of revenge into the next millennium. Since the conflict ignited in the spring of 1998, I have followed the unfolding of events and the vagaries of international involvement from afar, offering sound-bites on the situation and debating the strategies of American intervention with Balkan scholars. As Kosova friends became displaced refugees strewn about the planet, we kept in touch by e-mail. Serbians mourned innocent family members who fell victim to NATO raids on Belgrade and cursed America: evil incarnate. Albanians described their trail of tears over frozen mountains as they fled Serbian attacks, and their euphoria at NATO's intervention. They confirmed their new name for President Clinton, *pegamer*—the prophet. Now, with the refugee children close by, the war, and its aftermath, are real.

Six years after a version of this chapter was first written (for Kideckel and Halpern 1993), Kosova's "quiet siege" became a screaming bloody battlefield. Thousands are dead, untold numbers are maimed and homeless. In this context, as hundreds of thousands of Albanians struggle to rebuild their lives, and as Serbians wander what is left of their country in search of refuge, a discussion of cultural and societal nuances might seem beside the point.

But as the deluge of recent media reports chronicling the Serbian crackdown on Albanians' bid for independence and the ensuing internationalization of the conflict fail to tell us who the Kosova people really are, how they lived, and how they perceived their lives—before the world turned the spotlight on this island of Balkan enmity.

Like other contributors to this volume, I worked in Yugoslavia when few foreigners had ventured beyond its sun-drenched Adriatic seaports. Since the collapse of the country in 1990, and the massacres and pillage which followed, the country has become infamous. People who used to think of Macedonia as a mythical Greek land, Yugoslavia as one of those pathetic "Iron Curtain" countries, and who had never heard of "Bosnia" or "Kosova," now debate the moral implications of NATO's bombing and wonder about Milošević's fate in a war crimes tribunal.

Armies of diplomats, journalists, and aid workers have pierced through the Balkan veneer and forayed into its political labyrinths. Hundreds of articles and scores of books have chronicled the escalation of violence and the aftermath of savagery. For a brief moment, millions of people all over the world were stunned, fascinated, repulsed, and finally lulled by CNN into crisis fatigue.

As someone who lived in Kosova for seven years, whose life and work have been transformed by it, I present here only a brief overview of prewar Kosova—a quick foray into a complex, deeply entrenched saga. It is a view informed by months and years by the wood stove with old men sadly watching history repeat itself, with teenage boys poised for heroism, and with women helplessly awaiting news of the families' fates.

The Setting

As one travels south through Serbia, lush green rolling hills eventually give way to plains. Further on, something appears on the landscape that immediately strikes the eye: high stone walls surrounding the houses, protecting them from the scrutiny of passers-by. These walls, hiding the lives within from view, tell travelers they have entered the province of Kosova, the home of the Albanians who inhabit former Yugoslavia. Traveling on, there are more tell-tale signs of the Albanian world: women in pastel-colored raincoats with head scarves drawn forward over the forehead; men in white felt skullcaps. These signs: the walls, the scarves, the white hats, are the three most striking visual markers of Albanian ethnic identity. They signify not only ethnic identity but also serve as guideposts to a cauldron of ethnic enmity and conflict: the struggle between Albanians and Serbs for domination over the region.

The struggle between Serbs and Albanians is over a fertile, mineral-rich, diamond-shaped area of land of about 4,000 square miles, the size of Los Angeles county (see Map 6). Bordered to the north and east by Serbia, to the west by Albania, and to the south by Macedonia, the province is chiseled with dramatic alpine ranges and deep gorges which circumscribe its agricultural heartland.

Over 90 percent of the Kosova people are ethnic Albanians. The majority is Sunni Muslim, with a smaller number of Shiite sects. Some 5 percent of the population is Catholic. Unlike Serbs, Croats, and Bosnian Muslims, whose ethnic identity is inextricably linked to their religion, Albanians are quick to point out that they are first Albanians, *then* Muslims or Catholics. While an increasing number of Muslims fast during Ramadan and Catholics attend church every Sunday, and while the nuances of religious life pervade daily ritual and affect worldview, the first religion of Albanians is Albanianism.

The Albanian language is Indo-European. It is thought to be the sole surviving relic of ancient Illyrian, itself a direct offshoot of proto-Indo-European. It is replete with borrowings from Latin, Turkish, Slavic, and Greek. There are two major Albanian dialect groups: Gheg, spoken in northern Albania, Kosova, Montenegro, and western Macedonia; and Tosk, spoken in southern Albania, southern Macedonia, and northwestern Greece.

Of a total of over eight million Albanians on the planet, half live in Albania, one-third in Kosova, and the remainder in Macedonia, Montenegro, southern Serbia, Western Europe, and North America. In 1961, Albanians made up just over 67 percent of Kosova's population; today that figure is over 90 percent, with a

Map 6   Kosova

smaller number of Serbs and Roma, and scattered settlements of Montenegrins, Bosnians, and Croatians. According to the official 1991 census, there were 1,686,661 Albanians in Kosova (as cited in Vickers 1998: xvi), and Yugoslav government projections expected that figure to rise by almost another million by the year 2001.

The reasons for the increase are both political and demographic. A steady exodus of Serbs and Montenegrins from Kosova began in 1966 after the fall of Alexander Ranković, the head of the Yugoslav secret police, who exercised political and social control over Kosova and was responsible for systematic persecution of Albanians. Subsequent to his ousting, Serbian privilege in the region declined. The Serbian exodus accelerated in the 1980s, motivated by their interest in better economic conditions and prospects in Serbia proper, and pressure from the dominant numbers of Albanians. Many Serbs who left Kosova were from families who had settled there during the agrarian reforms between 1918 and 1940. Their exodus resulted in a further weakening of the Slavic presence in Kosova.

A high birthrate among Albanians also accelerated their demographic predominance. Kosova Albanians have the highest birth and infant mortality rates in Europe. By 1988 the birthrate was 29 per thousand (Zickel and Iwaskiw 1994). The average age of Albanians is twenty-four and 50 percent of the population is under twenty, making Albanians the youngest ethnic group in Europe. Currently population growth among Albanians is 17.2 per thousand per year (versus −0.3 in central Serbia). This represents a doubling of the Kosova Albanians' population every thirty years. In fact, as early as 1980 Kosova had become the most densely populated part of Yugoslavia with 146 persons per square kilometer (Library of Congress 1992: 69). The average number of children is 4.5 (the highest in Europe); the average household size is 6.5 (compared to 3 in parts of Serbia).

The Cultural Legacy

One cannot paint a sweeping stroke across the Kosova landscape and say this is Albanian life, this is who the people are and how they live. In cities and towns, the modern coexists in surreal contrast with the traditional. At one extreme is a savvy, modern, educated intellectual class where nuclear families circumvent patriarchal strictures, where young people cultivate international tastes and ideas and don the trappings of the West. At the other extreme is the traditional way of life found in both towns and villages: a patriarchal, religious, conservative world still rooted in the ideology of the corporate extended family.

Specific structural parameters give rise to the traditional cultural order. These components are the residue of ancient customary laws, an amalgam of Catholic and Muslim religious mandates, and economic and ecological parameters. Among Albanians these inherited prescriptions are taken to their logical extreme.

Consider exogamy. While canon law proscribes marriage to anyone related to the seventh degree, Albanians extend this prohibition as far as anyone's memory takes them. Village exogamy is practiced even in villages composed of several unrelated tribes (e.g., Berisha, Krasniqi) comprised of agnatic clans.

Especially among rural Albanians, the extended family—a group including parents, sons and their wives and children, and unmarried daughters—is the rule. The family shares wealth, labor, meals, and reputation. In a family of ten to thirty members, formal harmony is the operational mandate. Patriarchal authority, age and gender hierarchies, and obedience constitute the internal order. Women in extended families are shrouded in *havale*, a symbolic veil over their movement and their behavior—a veil that hides, protects, and circumscribes.

Patrilocality is also the rule. On marriage a girl moves in with her husband's family, outside her native village, away from family and friends. She is considered a visitor in her father's home, a foreigner in her husband's. While acknowledged and respected as the pillar of family continuity, cohesion, and honor, a traditional Albanian woman cultivates acquiescence as her prime directive. As an outsider in her husband's family, she does not achieve the rights of the men indigenous to the house until she reaches old age.

A person's social position and identity is bestowed on them by their family and social group: the *rreth*—both a unit and a concept of group affiliation dominating Albanian consciousness and arresting it in time. Though this force enables an individual to feel secure and rooted, at the same time it is a psychological straitjacket. Since it is very difficult for individuals to challenge it, the *rreth* contributes to the persistence of the status quo in Albanian society.

The power of the *rreth* links the rural and urban worlds of traditional and progressive families. The other force linking disparate social groups in Kosova is their identification with a heroic past—part history, part legend—which tells an otherwise marginalized people that they are unique, that they are victims, that they are destined to suffer and survive in this, their explosive corner of the Balkans. It is a history in dispute, which the political tidal wave has cast into profound, fanatical relief.

Historical Cribnotes

The essence of the dispute over Kosova is that both Albanians and Serbs claim historical rights to the province. Though many Slav scholars refute the claim, Albanians believe they are descendants of the ancient Illyrian tribes, who until the fifth century, dominated much of present-day Albania, Montenegro, Serbia, Macedonia, and northern Greece. While it is clear that Albanians have inhabited parts of western and southern Kosova for many centuries, the length of time they have been in other parts of the province is unclear, making historical claims on territory a source of perpetual enmity and dispute.

With its strategic geographical position (as a link to the sea and bridge to Europe) and its fertile lands and mineral resources, Albanian lands were sought after and conquered by a succession of invaders: Greeks, Romans, Byzantines, Celts, Slavs, Venetians, and for half a millennium, the Ottoman Turks.

Slavs began arriving in the seventh century. During the Middle Ages the Serbian empire dominated this area of the Balkans, ruling from its political and religious heartland in Kosova. The Serbian defeat at the hand of the Ottoman Turks in 1389 at Kosova's Field of Blackbirds (*Kosova Polje*) is at the core of Serbian epic literature and is its quintessential cultural lament. To Serbs, Kosova symbolizes the center of the Serbian medieval kingdom; many of Serbia's most important monuments are located there. It is the principle reason Kosova plays such a crucial emotional role in the identity of contemporary Serbs.

Nearly five centuries of Ottoman rule between 1389 and 1912 left a deep cultural imprint on Albanian life. Although many Albanians remained "closet" Catholics, secretly keeping alive Christian names and customs, the majority chose to adopt Islam and gain the perquisites granted to converts: the right to bear arms, exemption from certain taxes, privileges, and power.

Through the centuries fierce clan and regional loyalties and the absence of incentives for unification prevented the emergence of an Albanian nationalist consciousness to unite them against outside rule. Finally, in 1878, Albanians rose against foreign manipulation, demanding autonomy within the Ottoman Empire, a right to the taxes collected, schooling in the Albanian language, and religious freedom. But because Albanians sought autonomy under Istanbul rather than independence, the European powers saw them as an Ottoman tool. It was not until the revolt of the Young Turks in 1908 and the harsh repressive policies of Ottomanism, that Albanians finally began a unified revolt against the Turks.

In 1912 the Ottomans were finally defeated and Albania was proclaimed a republic. With the withdrawal of the Turks in 1913, the European powers signed the "Treaty of Berlin," creating independent Albania. This new state excluded the ethnic Albanians in Kosova, who then became part of the Kingdom of Serbia and the Kingdom of Montenegro, and in 1918 part of the "Kingdom of Serbs, Croats, and Slovenes." By this time there was a new united Balkan front against the Ottomans and against an autonomous Albania that would claim precious lands. In 1915 the secret "Treaty of London" granted Italy, Greece, and Serbia parts of greater Albania. Serbia and Montenegro divided Kosova and today's western Macedonia between them.

The new Albanian borders, set in 1926, left a half-million Albanians in Yugoslavia. Kosova was now underpopulated from decades of war and emigration, and the Yugoslav government encouraged Serbs to colonize the lowlands. Albanians experienced persecution at the hands of the Serbs and committed atrocities in retaliation. In 1941 Mussolini annexed the Albanian areas of Kosova and Macedonia. Under Tito's orders Albanian communists mounted resistance against

Italy. In 1945 most of Kosova was formally annexed by Serbia, and the remainder divided between Macedonia and Montenegro.

The post–World War II years saw numerous swings in the political fortunes of Kosova Albanians. As the war drew to a close, Yugoslav Partisans mounted a campaign against them under the pretext of eliminating remnants of the "enemy." In 1944, Albanians revolted and martial law was declared. After several years of improved treatment, another era of persecution ensued under Ranković, head of the Yugoslav secret police. In the 1960s a new federalism emerged in Yugoslavia, which promised equal rights to minorities and agitated for greater autonomy. Widespread demonstrations in 1968 in Kosova called for an independent university and republican status. This last demand was rejected, but as compensation Tito offered greater autonomy and economic aid to Kosova. The 1974 constitutional amendments made Kosova a "Socialist Autonomous Province" with its own university, the right to fly the Albanian flag, and the equality of Albanian, Serbo-Croatian, and Turkish languages. Albanians were elected to positions of authority in the administration and police force. But despite huge investments from northern republics, Kosova remained the poorest region in Yugoslavia, with incomes in 1979 about 30 percent of the national average (Vickers 1998: 187). The economic disparity between Slovenia in the north and Kosova in the south was comparable to that between northern Italy and Zaire.

The 1960s and 1970s were decades of tremendous social change in Kosova, change that occurred against a backdrop of poverty, widespread illiteracy, a population explosion, and a deepening national economic crisis. As the economic and social gap between Yugoslavia's more prosperous north and poorer south widened, ethnic tensions increased and in 1981 culminated in massive Albanian demonstrations in Kosova. The Serbian government opted for repression rather than reform. It attempted to tranquilize Kosova with military control, a purge of academics and administrators, and the suppression of all cultural ties to Tirana. The other members of the Yugoslav Federation relinquished the problem to Serbia, deepening the wedge between them. The period was characterized by media propaganda portraying Serbs as the victims of Albanian violence, an image that fueled the fires of fear and resentment.

1989–1995: The Quiet Siege

In the late 1980s the Serb-Albanian struggle reached a climax as Slobodan Milošević, soon-to-be president of Serbia, played the Kosova card in his rise to power. In a rousing speech at a huge 1989 commemoration of the 600th anniversary of the battle of Kosova, an event of mythic proportions in the Serbian worldview (Reineck in Halpern and Kideckel 1983 and Kaser and Halpern 1998), he turned the eyes of the Serbs to their medieval heartland and fueled the fires of nationalism by calling for a return to Serbian hegemony over Kosova.

This ideological campaign climaxed in March of 1989 when a new constitution ended Kosova's fifteen years of nominal autonomy within the Republic of Serbia. The legislation placed effective control of Kosova's police, judiciary, economy, and political life in the hands of the Serbian government. The vast majority of Albanians in public service were dismissed, to be replaced by Serbs, who then launched an organized campaign of repression against them. The move ushered in a period of political upheaval, civil rights abuses, and ethnic violence. Kosova seethed with quiet rage.

To Serbs, this was a much overdue effort to stem the tide of intolerable "Albanian chauvinism and irredentism." They were also pursuing what they saw as their "manifest destiny": control over what they considered Serbia's rightful territory. They justified their claims to this territory with arguments that echoed those being used by their fellow Serbs in Bosnia.

Albanians, shocked by the move, saw it as an illegal regression to pre-1974 statutes. They immediately began to demonstrate and strike, and mounted a campaign for independence from Serbia. Refusing to abide by Serbian rule, but lacking guns or any assurance of outside support for their independence campaign, in 1990 Albanians began a program of "passive resistance." They boycotted the Serbian state institutions and constructed a parallel government and social system complete with taxes, ministries, independent media, trade unions, health, and school systems. The campaign began with the formation of the Democratic League of Kosova (LDK) on December 28, 1989, headed by Dr. Ibrahim Rugova, leader of Kosova's writer's association and an outspoken anticommunist. This was soon followed by the creation of several other parties, which formed a coalition, the Council of Political Parties, also led by Rugova. Their common goal was Kosova's independence from Serbia.

On June 26, 1990, a "Special Emergency Law" was passed by the Serbian legislature to restrain the Albanian move toward independence. The law gave Serbia the legal basis for widespread dismissals of Albanians and the imposition of martial law. On July 2 the Albanians' Assembly responded to the Special Emergency Law by proclaiming Kosova to be an equal and independent unit within Yugoslavia. On July 5 the Serbian Assembly suspended the Kosova Assembly and other organs of the Kosova government. It took control of over sixty Kosova enterprises, including hospitals and energy plants. It suspended Kosova's Constitutional Court, which was considering a challenge to the 1989 constitutional amendments based on the questionable circumstances under which they had been passed. On September 3 the Albanians staged a twenty-four-hour strike.

The Serbian government responded by firing thousands of participants including judges, police, and other government officials who had honored the strike. On September 7, 1990, 111 delegates of the suspended Kosova Assembly dissolved the parliament and drafted a new constitution that declared Kosova a republic.

The remainder of the body disbanded and went into hiding. Later that month the Serbian government nullified the proclamation. All of the Assembly delegates and six members of the Kosova government were apprehended for participation in the events of July 2 and September 7. Many Albanians were arrested and charged with "counterrevolutionary activity." This charge was later changed to "endangering the territorial integrity of Yugoslavia" (Article 136 of the Yugoslav Penal Code), which carried a sentence of fifteen years.

Albanian leaders continued to agitate for independence despite Serbia's denial of Kosova's autonomy. In 1991, Albanians held a referendum in which 87 percent of the populace participated; 99.87 percent voted to declare Kosova an independent republic. In October 1991 the "parallel government" was formed. By the time the Serbian police began rounding up its leaders, most had already fled the country, establishing themselves as a government in exile. May 24, 1992, marked the first elections of the Albanian parallel government, and Dr. Ibrahim Rugova was unanimously chosen as the new "president of Kosova." Serbia did not recognize the elections and prevented the deputies from holding the first meeting of the Albanian Assembly. While Rugova functions as president and routinely visits world leaders with his entourage of cabinet members and ministers, the "Republic of Kosova" is not officially recognized by any foreign government except Albania (Vickers 1998: 254).

Life in the 1990s: Unemployment

Kosova has consistently had the highest unemployment rate in former Yugoslavia. In the 1970s the unemployment rate in Slovenia was 2.4 percent, in Kosova 36.3 percent (*Yugoslav Statistical Yearbook* 1988: 437–39). According to official estimates, in 1988 the unemployment rate in Kosova was 55 percent. In June 1990, Serbia adopted the "Law on Labor in Special Circumstances" in Kosova resulting in the systematic elimination of an estimated 120,000 Albanians from public sector jobs. Out of two million Albanians in Kosova, only an estimated 60,000 are still formally employed.

The first wave of dismissals occurred in July 1990 when Serb police occupied the radio and television stations in Prishtina, cutting off all Albanian language broadcasts in order to censor what the Serbian government considered an enterprise in the service of Albanian nationalism. The 1,350 journalists who refused to sign loyalty oaths to the Serbian state were fired. The only daily newspaper, *Rilindja*, was soon shut down. On September 3, 1990, Albanians staged a three-day general strike, and the some 28,000 workers who participated were fired. The owners of private businesses that closed during the strike faced imprisonment or a fine of $750. Many workers left their jobs in support of coworkers. In vain, President Rugova called on them to remain at work.

The manner in which subsequent dismissals took place and the rationale behind them took many forms. While some Albanians lost their jobs when they refused to sign loyalty oaths, others were fired for negligible infractions of work rules that would have been ignored before 1990. A university professor might be cited for being out of the office at a certain time and return the next day to find he or she had been fired and could not enter the building. Thousands were dismissed on trumped-up charges of misconduct. A history professor with a minimal knowledge of English was asked to proctor the oral examinations of English students—she declined and received a dismissal notice on the basis of noncompliance. Physicians were told to write prescriptions in Cyrillic (which many Albanians cannot read) and in some cases even to speak to Albanian patients in Serbian. Most refused and were fired, some after suffering harsh treatment during physical expulsion from their hospital or clinic. Serbs considered this a fair request to make: Albanians live in Serbia and should speak Serbian.

Many Albanians were fired on the grounds of "technological surplus," that is, an excess of personnel. While Albanians see this as a cover for Serbian aims, it must be understood that corrupt management practices had indeed resulted in decades of excessive, redundant hiring practices. Many Serbs were also fired for this reason. The war in Bosnia and the sanctions imposed against Serbia devastated the economy, causing thousands of Serbs to be laid off also.

But the onslaught against the Albanian workforce was ubiquitous and calculated. Some firings were brutal, most illegal. Many Albanians brought their cases to court. Some appeals were decided in favor of the plaintiffs who were reinstated and compensated; others were prevented from returning to their jobs by managing boards. Some trials were held outside Kosova. Here, plaintiffs were not informed about proceedings, and negative judgments were made as a matter of course. The majority of plaintiffs never received replies to their petitions.

In general, Albanians saw the dismissals as part of a larger strategy of "ethnic cleansing." Serbs saw the move as "ideological and political differentiation" intended to purge the system of dangerous elements. Many Serbs believe that the Albanians had walked off their jobs as a protest or were incompetent and were justly dismissed. In either case, the massive firings had catastrophic effects on Albanian lives, catapulting many families into poverty and wreaking havoc on civil life. Professional people—engineers, actors, professors—have tried to make ends meet by selling cigarettes and vegetables in the marketplace and doing hard labor. University graduates drive taxis, run corner drygoods stores, import consumer goods from Bulgaria, Macedonia, Albania, and Turkey. A small minority has profited handsomely in black market enterprises during the period of sanctions against Serbia, smuggling in fuel, cigarettes, and consumer goods. Some, talented at capitalist ventures and with experience and savings from abroad made small fortunes in new businesses and elegant restaurants and bars. Many Albanians, while in principle supporting separation from the Serbian state, are in business ventures with Serbian suppliers and distributors and serve a Serbian clientele.

But most Albanian families survive on savings, profits from modest businesses, and remittances from family members living abroad. But savings and remittances are running out. The last waves of asylum seekers wait jobless in European countries that plan to expel them eventually. The vast majority of Albanians, their savings now spent, live month to month, joining the ranks of some fifty-seven thousand families surviving on relief (Vickers 1998: 276). There is no unemployment insurance for those fired from their jobs. To receive welfare, applicants must show proof their children attend state schools. Schools in the Albanian parallel system do not qualify. In a system where only working people and their families receive social benefits, many have lost their right to pensions, loans, and health care.

Health Crisis in Kosova: For Every Two Graves, One Is an Infant's

The dismissal of most Albanian doctors and nurses since 1990 has had a devastating effect on health care. Diarrheal diseases, tuberculosis, hemorrhagic fever, scabies, and lice are epidemic. There have been outbreaks of abdominal typhoid and hepatitis B. During the past ten years, one person in four in Kosova had some form of infectious disease. In 1993 alone 221 children died from infectious disease and around 350 people from dysentery or malnutrition. Between 1983 and 1990 a universal vaccination program eradicated polio in Kosova. The elimination of Albanian vaccination teams and the reluctance of Albanians to send their children to Serbs for inoculations resulted in twenty-four cases of polio in the early 1990s (Prishtina's Public Health Institute).

The crisis in 1990 spawned an alternative health care system known as "Mother Theresa," to aid families whose breadwinners are out of work. Hundreds of volunteer doctors and nurses care for the sick in some eighty clinics supplied by international relief organizations. With the dearth of medicine and supplies at state-run institutions because of sanctions and empty state coffers, the Albanian clinics are often better equipped and Serbs also take advantage of their services.

The breakdown of socialism's hold on the economy concurrent with the mass firings have given rise to the privatization of medical care as unemployed Albanian doctors opened clinics in their homes. Patients who can afford their services benefit from better care than they received at state hospitals and Albanian doctors make up to three times the salary of their state-employed counterparts. But the clinics are not equipped for surgery or serious complications and are too expensive for many.

Childbirth now strikes fear in the hearts of Albanian women. In 1990 forty-two Albanian obstetricians left or were fired from their jobs. Albanian mothers were left with the choice of going to a Serbian doctor at the state hospital or paying $100 for a private Albanian doctor. Many women are afraid they will be mistreated at the hands of Serbian doctors. But unable to pay for private care, many Albanian women give birth at home, resulting in a sharp rise in infant mortality and death among women in childbirth.

The Crisis in the Schools

The educational system in Kosova serving some 350,000 children was devastated by the 1990 crackdown. But the crisis actually began in the late 1980s when Belgrade introduced new curricula for humanities courses with strictly Serbian, Communist Party–approved contents. Teachers who did not accept the new texts were faced with dismissal. From the Serbian point of view the move was necessary to still the tide of "Albanian irredentism" and "anti-state propaganda." In 1990 a completely new curriculum was proposed for all schools. Albanian literary figures were replaced with Serbian ones; Serbian history replaced Albanian. Albanian school directors and teachers rejected the plan and were collectively fired for insubordination. There were many instances of brutality against teachers, parents and students who protested (Malcolm 1998: 349). In 1990, Serbian parents, in fear of Albanians, whom the press portrayed as dangerous irredentists, demanded segregation in the schools.

Today most Albanian primary school children still attend classes in state school buildings but are isolated from Serbs, either by occupying different floors or sections of the building, or by attending in different shifts. Given the large numbers of Albanian children, in many schools there are so many shifts that the school day can begin very early and extend well into the evening. Some children set out for school in the dark of night or rise before dawn to make their classes.

In many schools the physical conditions are equally abysmal for Serbian and Albanian children. The only difference is that while Serbian teacher salaries, educational materials, and wood for winter stoves is paid for by the state, Albanians are supported by their compatriots abroad. In mass schools Albanians do suffer inferior physical conditions—the electricity may be turned off before they arrive or they may lack access to water or bathrooms.

While most primary school children still use state buildings, most high schools and all college buildings are off limits to Albanians. When the students were first expelled, Albanian families responded by starting classes in the basements and garages of their homes, a desperate effort that soon evolved into a full-fledged parallel education system. Conditions in the home schools are primitive. Heat is usually inadequate and students sit on the floor or on rough-hewn benches and read textbooks ragged with use. University classes have been hardest hit. There are no laboratories, no technical equipment, no facilities for practical training. With no state support, professors' salaries are paid by student fees of $100 per year.

The international community has made several unsuccessful attempts to reconcile the educational impasse—each promising in vain to reintegrate Albanians into the state system, each leaving the population more hopeless. In 1996, an "education accord" was agreed to under the mediation of an Italian Catholic charity that would have allowed Albanian children to return to the state-operated schools on a normal basis. The Serbian government has yet to live up to this or any other agreement.

International Intervention

In the months and years following the purges, the brutality, and the implosion of Albanian society, the international community seized upon the plight of the Albanians. Other nations, each with its own agenda, had spent considerable time and people power decrying the atrocities. However, all maintained policies of nonintervention. Expressions of polite outrage and haphazard forays into mediation were meted out via twenty-four-hour diplomatic expeditions into the dark and wild belly of southern Serbia.

Arriving in Prishtina, Americans, Germans, Swedes, and other well-meaning outsiders were drawn into the Albanian embrace of seductive hospitality like bees to sweet nectar. Their admonitions against Serbian "special measures" seeped like honey into Albanian hearts and minds. Down a few side streets, past the gypsy beggars and dazzling new pizza parlors, through the pot-holed, muddy field by the soccer stadium, they swarmed to the seat of Albanian "government." This is a tiny bungalow-turned-ideological axis that hummed with whispered dialectics between intellectuals-turned-politicians, and purred with political discourse subsequently blast into the international arena via the Internet. Within the inner sanctum, the diplomats were passionately embraced by President Rugova over Coca-Cola and Turkish coffee. After mountains of mutual admiration and contrived optimism, they were on to the next stop—the home of a torture victim, a parallel school in a nearby basement, a garage-turned-health clinic—feeling very wanted, slightly duped, and helpless to think of a solution.

It was different with the Serbs. Though defiantly perched in imposing gray administration buildings on Main Street a few blocks away, they were much harder to find. Understandably, they were loathe to receive Westerners, especially Americans, who, they believed, had uniformly scapegoated, maligned, misunderstood, and demonized the Serbian nation throughout the Bosnian scourge and now in Kosova. Meetings with Serbian officials required weeks of advance notice, and were often canceled arbitrarily. After all, it was their town, their country, and foiling diplomatic visits was a delectable power play. The discourse between outsider and power holder was reductionist and routine. Foreigners decried the treatment of Albanians on moral and legal grounds. Serbs framed the Albanians as terrorists who merited swift, harsh retaliatory gestures and "preventive measures." It was an impasse at best.

The diplomatic forays, though highly visible and politically charged, were but a transparent veneer on a deeper international presence, which includes foreign relief agencies and private teams of idealistic conflict mediators, educational advisers, feminist activists, human rights advocates, and journalists. Entry to Kosova wasn't easy; obtaining a visa could be an arduous task—a whimsical flexing of power for Serbian embassy officials and border guards. Getting permission to stay in the province requires finding one's way through a bureaucratic labyrinth.

The private teams who managed to gain entrance did their best to apprehend the Kosovar mind, to penetrate Serbian and Albanian social networks, and to enlighten die-hard nationalists. Gravitating toward receptive subjects, they could always find local enthusiasts for their messages. Facilitators create forums for Western-style communication training: role-playing, active listening, brainstorming. All these new ideas were embraced easily, as long as the subjects were young and bright with eyes to the West, eager to stretch their imaginations beyond the mental straitjacket of Balkanism. Sit down to cigarettes and strong brandy with dyed-in-the-wool nationalists on either side, and the game didn't even begin, or else it began on the bloody ground of the Field of Blackbirds and never really left.

The most pervasive, invasive force of international intervention is the armada of international relief agencies, which, to greater or lesser extent, also had a subliminal agenda to influence the Kosovar mind. In 1990 it was the Red Cross, Mercy Corps, Medicins Sans Frontier, and UNHCR, joined later by Doctors of the World, Oxfam, the International Rescue Committee, Catholic Relief Services, the Soros Open Society Foundation, and Handicap International. After the bombing of Albanian villages in spring and summer 1998, and subsequent displacement of some 300,000 Albanians, the number of foreign agencies swelled to forty. They brought medicine and medical training, wheelchairs and birthing clinics, food, clothes, water pumps, seeds and farm tools, computers, English classes, debate clubs, encounter groups. They paid astronomical salaries to cadre of unemployed young locals lucky enough to have excelled in English or French or to be the landlord's son or daughter.

And they brought ideas. Each agency walked a tightrope: appeasing the government by delivering enough aid, money, or infrastructure support to be tolerated, while weaving ideological threads into the fabric of care and relief. They stealthily exposed some of the society's most well-guarded contrivances.

What did their presence mean to the Kosovar? For Albanians they offered solace, the hope of rescue, a link to the world beyond the Balkans. But there was a darker side. The impassioned camaraderie cajoled Albanians into an insidious sense of false security and fueled belief in the promise of independence. It is an ideological bastion that bore no political weight.

The Serbs were, by turns, suspicious, resentful, and on the whole, unimpressed. They perceived the foreigners' attraction to the Albanian cause as misguided, repugnant, insipid. Their relation to the West was also different. Fewer in number, with many very poor and living in villages lacking basic resources, the Kosova Serbs had jobs, their nation was in charge, most stayed home. The outer limits of Serbia enclosed them in what was vaguely perceived as the vanished empire. With the exception of the few who had been educated abroad and a slice of urban youth, their imagination, if it took them beyond their garden walls, took them to the bright lights of Belgrade, not New York. This was changing. After the disintegration of Yugoslavia and the collapse of the economy many saw no need to educate their sons or attempt to have a decent life in what was left of their country. They would have left if they could have, but they didn't embrace the West. They tolerated it.

Kosova Albanians are linked to the West by decades of massive labor migration. Since poverty and oppression after World War II pushed entire communities to the edge of existence, Albanians have survived on remittances from family members abroad. The older generation of migrants slept eight to a room and lived on beans and bread in Zurich, Munich, or Vienna, saving all they had to send back. They stayed for twenty or thirty years. But their honor and their identity stayed home. It still does. Some 450,000 Albanians now live abroad: the new generation of migrants left first to escape the Bosnian front and massive unemployment in Kosova, then to deliver young families from all-out war in Kosova. This time, they've brought their wives; they're raising children in Geneva, Paris, and Stockholm. They may not return. But their souls are in Kosova, as are their relatives, whose fascination with the West only deepens.

In the county of Vitina, western Kosova, the black night was pierced with the twinkle of distant lights from the mountain encampment of UNPROFOR on the Macedonian border. Serbian villagers looked there, to the south, and were uneasy, hoping that Milošević would keep the foreign troops there—outside their sacred borders, out of their internal affairs. For Albanians, the lights were a beacon. They hoped for rescue.

Walk Down a Village Road

Follow the international aid worker into the trenches in the 1990s and you will see Kosova's cruelty and pain, primitive luxury and rough-hewn delicacy—its chaotic harmony and political minefields—etched in profound relief. To the outsider, Kosova is exotic, appalling, and compelling. It is a mild rendition of the Middle East, a cultural island where logic stops and passion takes over. Western feminists come to sit with village families and are appalled by mute, servile brides in satin dresses and gold rings pouring endless glasses of sugar-tea to the companies of men. Journalists relish village hospitality, returning home to hold forth over cocktails on the brutal nature of the nationalist mind and the horrors of oppression.

As program manager for Oxfam and International Rescue Committee during the early 1990s, I headed a team of foreigners and locals, Albanians and Serbs, whose task was, ostensibly, to improve sanitation conditions in schools and provide health education for village women in two adjacent counties of western Kosova. More, it was to resuscitate waning vestiges of community spirit, to ignite sparks of civil society, to propose projects that would enjoin cooperation between Serbs and Albanians.

As an anthropologist speaking Serbian and Albanian whose task in the 1980s had been to observe, decipher, record, but not affect, I knew something of the life, the thoughts, the Kosova slant on experiencing and constructing reality. As humanitarian aid workers, my team and I set out to infiltrate the local ethos. We sought to support the traditions of honor, respect, and solidarity (even though laced with a venomous weight of history). But we also sought to challenge aspects of village life that dealt unnecessary hardship and suffering to its victims in recent years. Such hardships included diarrhea epidemics among children when formula was substituted for breast-feeding, and garbage simmering in disease-infested streams in the absence of trash trucks. There was also an outbreak of polio that resulted when people refused what they believed were contaminated vaccines. The disabled were left stranded for want of wheelchairs, pajamas, or the prospect of dignity. Equally wrenching was the image of Albanian girls spending their adolescence at home over needlepoint and tatting, in fear that an education without future employment would leave them without a husband.

Walk with me into Germova, an ethnically mixed settlement in the county of Vitina. To most it appears to be just another Third World Balkan village. It could be Afghanistan or Nicaragua, except that it is in Europe. Mud, pot holes, water buffalo, horsecarts, and Mercedes. Endemic Balkan nephropathy, a fatal kidney disease that strikes young adults, is rare in the world outside this county, but is rampant here.

It is easy to tell who is who. The two-story, cinder-block facade decorated with palms and dolphins and the requisite satellite dish, the wrought-iron balcony built with deutschmarks sent by a brother in Frankfurt, flashes of scarved women in long skirts or Turkish pantaloons, green-eyed children, white skull-caps on high-cheekbones carved into sunburnt faces mark Albanian turf. Whitewashed adobe houses, pigs, dark eyes, women in knee-length skirts, and men sporting partisan caps (and now, machine guns) mark Serbian.

A new orthodox chapel, paid for by the government, nears completion; an old minaret pokes up tiredly from the Albanian quarter. The school was built in 1950. Its yard has long been given over to pigs, geese, and goats; county officials have been trying unsuccessfully to enforce an ordinance against the neighbor's livestock for twenty years. Serbian children study in one room; Albanians in four others, in two shifts—the demographic microcosm. Two directors, in a school the size of a baseball diamond, have had no contact with each other for eight years. The piles of wood used for heat are kept separately. For the Serbians, wood, teachers' salaries, school maintenance, and scant materials are supplied by the government. Albanians, boycotting an educational system that subverted their culture, pay for these when they can, with donations from emigrants. They have no educational materials and the mere semblance of a blackboard. The well water, rife with nitrites from fecal matter, is used for washing floors. An unfinished concrete shell is testimony to an attempt to build a new outhouse, aborted after a fight broke out over who was to finish it. Inside the classrooms the ceiling is ready to collapse.

It took a month to rebuild the school. It took a year to convince the community it was possible, and worth the trouble. In the end, Albanians did the carpentry and dug the septic pit; Serbs drilled the well. The funds were collected (squeezed) from villagers by their respective leaders and matched by a grant from a group of Dutch lawyers. But with epidemic unemployment, interethnic relations on a razor's edge, and war on the horizon as UNPROFOR's lights twinkled in the distance, the locals were hard-pressed to entertain notions of self-help.

A quick tour of Germova's neighboring villages show examples of Kosova's political, infrastructural and psychological quagmires played out in endless variation. Each village has its own angle on desperation. Down the road from Germova, east toward the Serbian border, we pass Zhiti. The local bus, emblazoned with a huge poster of Milošević on its windshield, delivers Albanian and Serbian farmers who recede, unspeaking, into the respective quarters of their village. Zhiti boasts a new primary school, which only Serbian children are allowed to use. Local Serbs explain that the large number of unruly Albanian children would certainly damage the property. Albanian children, who outnumber Serbs, are therefore relegated to multiple shifts in an unfinished storeroom off someone's house. The official policy that all primary school children—parallel system or not—are allowed to use state buildings, is a sham.

Past Zhiti, up a steep, potholed road all but impassable in the winter, lies the small Albanian village of Balance, its tiny white schoolhouse adorning the peak of a hill just above the mosque. A few months before, the schoolhouse was in ruins; another crumbling postwar adobe. The villagers had gathered funds to renovate, but were afraid that once they began work the county would stop the project, leaving them with no school at all. Oxfam came to build latrines, to bring drinking water, and, in the process, gave the villagers the support to embark on their project. Within a month a new school had been built.

Venturing past Balance, into the next valley, the Albanian Catholic village of Stubila boasts primary and secondary schools in good condition and a small regiment of clergy and nuns educated in Italy. The village was so poor that early on most men took to migration. Now, two-story, finely wrought homes are the rule. Beautiful homes, no work. Every boy hopes to leave the village, to settle abroad. No girls attend high school. Instead, they bide their time, calculating how to land a husband whose prospects are abroad. To counter this trend, we band together: foreign aid workers, school teachers, and community leaders. We visit families one by one. We meet with fathers, uncles, mothers, or the girls themselves, examining together a contradiction: they cry for independence, and say they will die for it, but aren't willing to go to school, to give Kosova the cadres for the future.

The tiny village of Binc is the home of Serbs, Albanians, and Croatians (these the descendants of medieval mining communities). A roadside spigot—the village water source—has been broken for months; repairing it seems too daunting a project for this mixed community. Oxfam was invited to build a latrine and water source for the dilapidated school. Albanians agreed to take part in the project. The Serbs called a village meeting. Fifteen men gathered in the candle-lit schoolhouse on an October night. One was drunk, the others got rowdy, no consensus was reached, and my engineer and I were advised to leave before someone got hurt. Before consensus was reached on how the project was to be undertaken and who was to dig the septic pit, early snows came and the project was aborted. A month later an Albanian man was killed in the village bakery. The community was paralyzed.

Further east, up another green valley, lies the Albanian-Serbian village of Cernica. The state-run health clinic serving this large village is open to all, but the building is in shambles. Its water source is contaminated and piles of toxic garbage from the clinic accumulate nearby. One hundred and twenty Serbian students attend Cernica's primary school in the morning. To separate the two populations, the seven hundred Albanian children are packed into four short afternoon sessions that extend into the evening. Girls from small neighboring mountain villages can no longer attend school; afternoon classes mean they would have to make the hour walk home through darkness. Since any rapprochement from either the Serbian or Albanian director of the school is considered tantamount to treason by their respective compatriots, they have hardly spoken since 1990. Toša, the Serbian director and a sports enthusiast, is proud of the basketball court and modern locker room he has built. He apologizes about denying access to the Albanian children, but, after all, they would surely ruin the facility.

International Rescue Committee helps bring fresh water to Cernica's clinic, create a garbage collection program, construct a leach field for the school's putrid outhouse, begin a women's health education program, a men's discussion group, and English classes. The Soros foundation provides computer and science equipment for a new lab—to be shared by Serbs and Albanians. These few improvements and new ideas are unable to stop villagers from seething with enmity.

Such snapshots from Vitina and Gjilan counties bear witness to some ways each Kosova village manifests the ruin, recalcitrance, and apathy brought on by decades of economic and political corruption and oppression. Each is a political and social time bomb aching to ignite.

Relations with a Martyred Motherland

The violence in Kosova increasingly begs the question: Where does Albania stand? What is Albania prepared to do in the event of full-scale war? Is the underlying plan of the Kosova Albanians to unite with the "motherland?" What is the mutual perception of Albanians on either side of the border? The answer is: ambivalence on both sides. On one hand, Albanians are guided by feelings of brotherhood that transcend historical division. Orthodox, Catholic, or Muslim, speaking Gheg or Tosk, living in Albania or Kosova, on an Adriatic island or in a Bronx slum, the Albanians' most celebrated and powerful self-image and foothold in reality is the experience of themselves as part of a larger Albanian nation. This nation is bound by blood, by ancient history and by what, to its members, is an utterly unique set of cultural laws. It is a profound and enduring sentiment.

But it is not enough, at this junction in history, to dictate unification. After the war the mental landscapes on each side of the border evolved under completely different political and social constraints. Between 1945 and 1991, Enver Hoxha succeeded in creating the most xenophobic, mutilated, deprived state in the western hemisphere—a cruel concoction of primitive Stalinism taken to its logical conclusion. In 1968 when Khrushchev became too revisionist, and Albania's only remaining ally was China, Hoxha sealed off his nation from the rest of the world and threw away the key. He forged an obedient proletariat, an educated urban population, and the semblance of a "modern" state from the wreckage of an Ottoman backwater.

Under Tito, Yugoslav Albanians toed a softer socialist line, suffering brutal repression in the postwar decades under Ranković, struggling for recognition in Yugoslavia, but through it all remaining part of the outside world, traveling back and forth from Europe as migrant laborers, bringing back cars, Western culture, and ideas.

During the Hoxha regime the Kosovar grew to know and idealize an extremely distorted version of "the motherland." Through radio and television, cultural exchanges and books, the regime manufactured and exported an imaginary version of Albania that the Kosovar hungrily consumed and built their dreams upon. Visitors to Albania were shown carefully sanitized portraits of the country: happy women in skirts and blouses delivered from the shackles of tradition to the factory floor, terraced vineyards which had been barren mountainsides, mosques turned into basketball courts. The Kosovar, a fourth-class citizenry adrift in a Slavic sea, were glued to TV Tirana as their compatriots staged spectacular folklore exhibitions, swam in mythical Olympic-sized swimming pools, and ruled their own land. The Kosovar believed. They dreamed of unification. The motherland was where Albanians ruled the day, where the culture was pure and unadulterated, where everyone was equal, and where "if you have a watch, I have a watch." The problem, of course, was that no one had a watch. Neither had they the right to own a radio, or access to the world outside, or a day or an hour of freedom.

Kosova's enchantment with Albania disintegrated in 1992 when the Hoxha regime collapsed. Rushing across the border to visit long-lost relatives, capitalize on their compatriots' business naïveté, or finish medical school closed to them in Kosova, they saw the country as it really was for the first time. They returned to Kosova to testify about the tortured, starving, gasping landscape they once idealized.

Much to their amazement, except among family, intellectual idealists, and politicians, the Kosovar did not receive the heroes' welcomes they envisioned when they first reached Albania. When the people of that country emerged from collective incarceration—shell-shocked and desperate, reeling from the collision of liberation and destitution—they looked around and wondered where the Kosovar had been for forty-five years while they were held hostage under Hoxha's Dark Ages. They found it difficult to take seriously the stories of brutality and repression in Kosova. "Look at those cars, the new homes, the clothes. Now they are tortured by the Serbs. Where were they when we were being tortured by our own government?"

The religion of Albanians is, still, Albanianism. But Albanians on both sides of the border know that the other is fighting for its own survival. Although most Kosova Albanians dream of a greater Albanian state in the future (an impossible idea to Serbs), this is not part of their present political objective. First survival, then unification. Unification, then the reinvention of an Albanian ethos.

1998: The Conflict Ignites

During the 1990s a small number of Albanians began to organize a clandestine paramilitary organization known as the Kosova Liberation Army (Ushtria Çlirimtare e Kosovës). As the violent encounters between Serbs and Albanians increased, Albanians who once espoused passive resistance were radicalized and the ranks of the KLA grew. Most members were young men adrift in a desperate society with no future before them and a dream of independence flaming their patriotism.

With an increase in killings and other atrocities against Serbs, Serbian police and military units prepared for an assault to put down "terrorist" activities. In March 1998, Serbian troops attacked the villages of suspected KLA leaders in the Drenica region of central Kosova, killing over seventy people in two weeks of bloodshed, igniting the powder keg, and bringing international attention to the region. In the following months nearly 300,000 people were driven from their homes in the crackdown by Serbian forces. Dozens of villages were burned. Armed with weapons smuggled in from Albania and Macedonia, the KLA fighters responded to the attacks by waging rag-tag guerrilla warfare against the Serbs.

Serbs defend the bombings and murders as an attempt to counteract terrorist activities. KLA claim that their attacks against Serbs are in retaliation for atrocities committed by Serbs.

Interpreting an Epic Predicament: Serbian and Albanian Views

Serbs and Albanians explain both the roots of the conflict in diametrically opposed ways. These incongruent ideologies are manifest in the way each group envisions the boundaries of its world. Serbs see Kosova as a small enclave within a Greater Serbia stretching from the borders of Hungary in the north to Macedonia in the south, from Romania to the Adriatic. They see the Albanians as barbarian intruders, latecomers, a backward minority in the Serbian homeland, and as the fastest-growing population in Europe, a serious threat to their hegemony over what remains of Yugoslavia.

In contrast, the world of the Kosova Albanians is defined by the immediate borders of the province. They identify with an Illyrian past that places them in the region at the dawn of history, and they see Kosova as an Albanian world—in culture, religion, ethos, and in sheer numbers. By virtue of this cultural integrity and following the example of the former Yugoslav republics, they consider themselves to be a nation with the right to self-determination, the right to break from Belgrade's grasp.

To Serbs, the political takeover of 1989 represented a just response to what they see as Albanian nationalism and separatism. The constitutional changes did not destroy Kosova's autonomy, but were intended to protect Yugoslavia from irredentist forces. Serbs believe that Albanians are disenfranchised from public institutions and social benefits because they chose to boycott the Serbian state; that they have brought on their own social calamity. The "special measures" which brought about massive firings were introduced to prevent a further worsening of the situation. To Albanians, the events were part of Belgrade's plan, already well developed in the 1930s, to take control over the region.

Each group blames their desperate condition on the other. Albanians believe that Belgrade systematically expropriated their mineral wealth and stole from Kosova's coffers at every turn. Serbs maintain that the investments that poured into Kosova in the 1970s and 1980s (almost half of all available Serbian national resources) was misappropriated, mismanaged, and systematically pocketed by Albanians. They believe that the Albanians owe their chronic economic malaise to their own overpopulation, ineptitude, laziness, and corruption, and their current woes to international sanctions, which have crippled Serbia as a whole.

Demographics are key to the contrasting perceptions of reality. Serbs believe that the Slavic presence in Kosova has dwindled for two reasons. First, because Albanian terrorism and abuse forced Serbs to head north. Second, because of

Albanian pro-natalism, Islamic fervor, and cultural backwardness that has resulted in the highest birthrate in Europe. Albanians see the exodus of Serbs and Montenegrins from Kosova as a response to the greater appeal of life in the north. As for large families, most Albanians actually want only three or four children. But their desire for sons and the logistical impediments to birth control cause them often to exceed this number. Most deny that their high birthrate reflects a political agenda.

Cultural stereotypes have much to do with the ideological gap between Serbs and Albanians. Albanians were infamous throughout former Yugoslavia for their "exotic" blend of moral conservatism and cultural fanaticism. To outsiders, the archetypal Albanian man is a sword-wielding, warrior martyr for whom clan loyalties define the social world and blood revenge functions as law. The stereotypical woman is a figure from the past secluded behind oriental veils. The majority of Serbs believe that Albanians are "dangerous subversives" seeking to take possession of Kosova and create a Greater Albania. Most are also in denial about the brutality wielded against the Albanian population. They generally recognize that Albanians have suffered some discrimination during the political overhaul, but believe that the Albanians brought on their own hardship. They believe Albanian joblessness and inadequate schooling and medical care is a result of the Albanian boycott of the Serbian state. The key questions are: what is each side willing to settle for, and what is each willing to do to achieve its political objectives.

Serbs seek to maintain control over Kosova. But while reluctant to give up what they have come to believe is the "cradle of their ethnicity," they are weary of the conflict. In some ways the Albanians were faring better than Serbs, especially in access to goods and assistance. (Albanians were already engaged in private businesses before the collapse of socialism and their political movement inspired a highly developed network of assistance and unprecedented spirit of mutual aid.) It is also clear that the international community supports the Albanians. The Serbs believe the world has been duped by anti-Serb propaganda, but nonetheless feel the heat of international recrimination. While some Serbs are ready to fight to keep Kosova, others are tired of the malaise and would accept a return to 1974 statutes.

Many in the Belgrade opposition believe that Milošević is waging a campaign to maintain his sovereignty in Kosova in the wake of the Bosnian tragedy and his failure to create the Greater Serbian state he championed. The aggression in Kosova is not about preserving the "cradle of Serbian culture." It is about saving face, about defending a precarious political career with an anachronistic, contrived nationalist crusade. As a Beograd Serbian taxi-driver put it: "When we fought in Bosnia, we were fighting for Serbia. If we fight in Kosova, it will be for Milošević's throne, and I wouldn't give a hair on my head for that." While there is much apathy about the Kosova cause among Serbs in Serbia proper, those in Kosova reluctantly believe that they are defending their homeland against the Albanian secessionists and protecting their wives and children against terrorists.

Most Albanians are still willing to lay down their lives for independence. They believe this is their last chance to wrench themselves away from Serbia. If they fail to gain independence now, they will forever be trapped within a state they cannot abide. They believe that no matter what legal structures or civil rights are secured, they will never be accorded equal status within Serbia. It might have been different under a Yugoslav Federation, but not under a lone republic masking itself as Yugoslavia.

Many Serbs and Albanians ache for peaceful resolution to the conflict, even if that compromises epic dreams. They want proper schools for their children. They want a future. They are mired in hate fatigue. But while some popular sentiment supports reconciliation, the two sides have not been able to agree on the terms of a political dialogue. Serbs say they will discuss any of the problems in Kosova except the question of Albanian independence from Serbia. On this there can be no debate. For Serbs, Kosova is, and will always be, part of Serbia. To the Albanians this is an unacceptable premise for dialogue. They insist that a possible independent status be addressed and that representatives from the international community take part. Serbs maintain that Kosova is an internal problem, and as such does not warrant outside intervention. Albanians feel that without international intervention, their cause is lost.

Since 1990 the cultural landscape in Kosova has been assaulted, tortured, impoverished. As villages smolder and snipers rip through the countryside, Serbs and Albanians lie in wait, intoxicated by the promise of sovereignty which laces every thought. Each side had contrived a reality to accommodate its collective passion; both realities resemble dreams. As children die and communities are laid waste, the dreams are becoming bloody nightmares. A Kosovar Albanian now resident in the Bronx perhaps sums the situation up most succinctly:

A friend tells me he may have seen my elderly parents fleeing among the thousands of Albania-bound refugees on a CNN report. There's no way to find out. In the villages under siege, the phone lines are cut, water has become a luxury and the voices of children are silent. I was born and raised there. I recognize the remains of the houses that were leveled. While my family and the rest of the village have left their homes and headed in unknown directions, my two brothers have armed themselves and are trying to defend the village with the rest of the men there who have stayed behind. What should I call them? "Freedom fighters"? Or desperate people who have been pushed against the wall and are defending homes where our ancestors lived for centuries. The Serbs, Russians, Greeks, French and members of our State Department call them terrorists. But they don't know my brothers. If they are terrorists, so are the heroes who liberated this great country two centuries ago. One man could make a world of difference. His name is Bill Clinton. He has been telling us that he won't allow another Bosnia. If Clinton were watching the footage of bombed-out villages and refugees freezing in mountain hideouts, he would realize that Kosova is already Bosnia. (Isuf Hajrizi, *Illyria*, summer 1998).

21

Civil Society and Ethnic Conflict in the Republic of Macedonia

Jonathan Matthew Schwartz

After *Before the Rain*: Tracking Down Civil Society in Macedonia

In November 1994, the Forum Against Ethnic Violence organized a weekend conference in London with the theme "Macedonia: The Next Balkan Tragedy or a Model for Multiculturalism?" The British anthropologists who planned the conference were aware that the choices facing Macedonia are probably not as simple or dramatic as their conference title implies. Milcho Manchevski's film, *Before the Rain*, which predicts violence in Macedonia, had just been released, and that had no doubt affected their thinking. Representatives of several Macedonian nongovernmental organizations (NGOs) were in attendance at the conference as well, and they were working for the better of the two alternatives. It

Thanks are due the Danish Social Science Research Council for a grant to conduct fieldwork in the Republic of Macedonia. Earlier versions of this article benefited from editorial comments by David Kideckel and Joel Halpern. Publication of my book, *Pieces of Mosaic: An Essay on the Making of Makedonija* (Højbjerg: Intervention Press, 1996) was made possible through a grant from the Social Science Research Council. There is some congruence between the ideas of the book and those in the present article. Additional time can, however, lead to different reflections as well as confirm previous observations.

was hoped by all that the diverse and cooperative efforts of these newly created organizations would help the Republic of Macedonia maintain the peace, thereby avoiding a repetition of the tragic experience of Bosnia and Herzegovina. Each NGO had its own specific issue. A representative of Macedonian writers described efforts for dialogue between Greek and Macedonian journalists. A member of the Albanian women's movement in Macedonia described her organization's efforts to mobilize both within her ethnic community and across ethnic boundaries to other Macedonian women's organizations. A director for rural development programs in multiethnic regions of Macedonia described the goals and methods of his organization.

On more than one occasion the speakers on the NGO panel referred to the concept of "civil society" as essential for the processes of peacekeeping and development. There was a general consensus of the participants that the making of Macedonia depended on the various agencies and groups active within civil society. I had the image of several small, resolute tugboats guiding a clumsy ship of state safely into the harbor.

The concept "civil society" is used today in diverse moral and political discourses. It is especially a gloss for NGO initiatives on development and for fostering "transition" from communist to democratic societies (Hann and Dunn 1996). Anthropologists in our time conduct participant-observation among, and as, actors of the civil society. Our entry into sites of conflict, such as those in the former Yugoslavia, is often made possible through endorsement by and affiliation with transnational organizations. No longer soloist fieldworkers in remote villages, we are rather more like members of large, nongovernmental orchestras. An increasingly large branch of the anthropological profession, therefore, might be dubbed "NGOgraphy."

The minimal definition of civil society places it in the realm between the state and individual. Historians and advocates of civil society trace its origins to the age of (European) Enlightenment, when a "Republic of Letters" established autonomy for its members and "citizens" against the intrusions of secular and spiritual authorities. Thus civil society implies group membership for the person inside voluntary associations. Coffee houses, printing houses, informal academies, and salons were the milieus in which civil society was founded and guided. This libertarian image of the public sphere, one could say, has had a renaissance in our epoch. The rebirth of civil society has turned the command economy and communist society into a twentieth-century ancien regime (see Seligman 1992 and Calhoun 1993).

This article will address the development of the institutions and activities of civil society and their relation to the intensification or abatement of ethnic tension in the Republic of Macedonia, which attained its independence from Yugoslavia in September 1991. Since independence, the diverse ethnic, national, and religious identities of the Macedonian peoples have become emphasized in daily behavior. However, as the organizers of the Forum Against Ethnic Violence conference indicate, the promotion of ethno-national identities need not produce difference and dissent if moderated within the context of the civil society's open forum. Self-actualization for the person might mean a rediscovery and self-ascription of one's "true self" (opposed to others who do not share that same identity) but it might also mean emancipation from blind obedience to the exclusiveness of one's ethnic or religious affiliation. Thus, though the ability to give voice to one's ethnic identity is surely one aspect of a civil society's project, especially in the metropolitan, multicultural "mosaics" (Schwartz 1994; Danforth 1995), channeling and shaping such identity is the true challenge of the institutions of civil society.

In the context of the Balkans today ethnic and national movements generally threaten the very existence of civil society. Exclusive ethnic membership obviates common and consensual citizenship. Those who betray their own national, religious group must suffer fatal consequences, as dramatized in Before the Rain. The film's gruesome subject is a (potential) interethnic war between Macedonians and Albanians. Especially harsh punishment is dealt to those who cross ethnic boundaries, as in "mixed marriages." In a discussion of Before the Rain, in Copenhagen, I had to convince an audience of primarily Danish university students that the film was not an actual documentary but a dystopian nightmare. It portrayed what Macedonia might look like if a Bosnian-type war moved south (see Brown 1998). The fictive scenario of Before the Rain is currently unrolling in neighboring Kosovo.

The 1993 film was an intervention by a native artist into the Macedonian present. Its chief moral stance, however, is clearly civil societarian, since it advocates both the freedom to belong to one's own group (i.e., descent) and the freedom to dissent from unquestioned loyalty to that group. The highly stylized, stereotypical, characters of the film inhabit spaces that range from an ancient Byzantine monastery in the Macedonian homeland to a slick photo bureau in cosmopolitan London. The cinematography of the film starkly juxtaposes the icons of the Orthodox Church with the photographs of the London darkroom. Before the Rain underscores, then, the two opposing sets of options facing contemporary Macedonian society: interethnic war or coexistence, violence or negotiation (Gossiaux 1996: 844).

How can we appraise the current efforts of NGOs in maintaining and mobilizing ethnic coexistence, thereby steering society away from violent (un)civil conflict? One of the pervasive and dubious prognoses of Balkan life presents hatred and violence as if they were a rigid, unvarying geopolitical law (e.g., Kaplan 1993). According to this law, ethnic, religious, linguistic, and cultural differences are deeply and permanently rooted. This view suggests that it is unlikely that a handful of well-meaning and committed NGOs can overcome centuries of history. In contrast to this, an anthropological perspective can unmask the essentialist readings of the Balkan, or any other mentality, including our own.

In this essay, I shall consider whether ethnic diversity and civil society can possibly coexist in Macedonia. My basis for the assessment I offer stems from three months of fieldwork in Macedonia in early 1995 where I was preoccupied with issues of "civil society." In my previous field studies (eight visits in the period 1977–90) my focus had been on labor migration (*pechalba*) and on local community life in the Prespa Lake region bordering both Greece and Albania. Furthermore, in five annual visits to Macedonia since the breakup of Yugoslavia, different and more pressing economic and political problems occupied my concerns. That my 1995 project was, at last, able to consider the meaning of NGO activities, was a small positive commentary on the development of Macedonian society.

A critical issue in analyzing the significance of NGOs in the Macedonian transition is their function in mediating between "global" and "local" agents of civil society. The Forum Against Ethnic Violence conference was one such link between the "global" and the "local." However, even though NGO relationships and structures often connected metropolitan donors[1] in Western Europe with mountain villagers in Macedonia, the goals of donors and villagers were often widely disparate. While multiethnic settings in Macedonia were those favored by metropole donor organizations, multiculturalism of the metropolitan variety was seldom a primary interest of the villagers. To villagers, projects geared to improving the water supply and better communication with "the outside world" took precedence over being pieces of "the ethnic mosaic." Significantly, then, the organs of civil society could best develop, not by being explicitly multiethnic, but by forming basic trust among diverse communities in mutually beneficial programs. Ethnic coexistence could be said to emerge from cooperative development. "Too much talk about multiculturalism," as one NGO activist put it, doomed a project's success.

The Breakup of Yugoslavia and the Making of Makedonija

Macedonia's independence from the Yugoslav Federation in autumn 1991 had few of the violent repercussions that occurred in the other Yugoslav republics. A resident of Skopje described how the Yugoslav army (JNA) evacuated its quarters in Macedonia, taking virtually everything with it in autumn 1991, including electric wiring. "Did you dance in the streets when the army left?" I asked my friend. "No," he answered, "but we didn't yell: 'Come back again!' either" (Schwartz 1993: 98). This anecdote also confirmed for my friend that "We Macedonians are a relaxed people."

The breakup of Yugoslavia precipitated, then, the making of Makedonija. Independence from Belgrade meant that persisting national and international prob-

---

1. The George Soros Foundation and the World Council of Churches were two of the more prominent donors represented at this conference.

lems appeared in an amplified form. Symbols of identity, which were quaintly regional and folkloric in the Yugoslav Federation suddenly became nationally potent and sharply contested. Albanian, Bulgarian, Greek, and Serbian borders took on changed meanings for the Republic of Macedonia, the name and identity of which are still contested and awaiting recognition (see Taylor 1992 and Danforth 1995). In official, diplomatic language, the Republic of Macedonia is called by the acronym "FYROM" (Former Yugoslav Republic of Macedonia).[2]

The two million citizens of the Republic of Macedonia have acute problems. Though the lifting of the economic blockade by Greece and the ending of the UN embargo against rump Yugoslavia have eased Macedonia's economic situation, the society's infrastructure is still very pressed, pressure which adds force to ethnic conflicts. The country's citizens, however, have thus far have been spared the worst, and they know it. What is unknown, however, is whether the future will bring conflict or cooperation, lack or plenty. What is also uncertain to Macedonians is the path to achieve a desired future and the specific actions needed to do so. These uncertainties especially implicate the potential role for NGOs.

To an extent the ambiguities of Macedonian belief in destiny or fate (*sudbina*) keeps citizens uncertain. One doesn't know if what happens is a result of one's own intentions and activity, or if "fate" makes events. Modern Macedonian history is characteristically described as "unlucky" by the country's diverse ethnic, linguistic, and religious communities. Fate has been especially cruel to Albanians and Macedonians, the two main communities of the Republic of Macedonia. As small nations and/or large ethnic groups in the Balkans they can both claim a history of injustice. Both national communities demonstrate how they have been unjustly separated from their co-nationals in modern history, that is, after the defeat of the Ottoman Empire. *Sudbina*, it can be noted, has the same etymological root as the word for "judgment" (*presuda*).

As Michael Herzfeld (1987: 139–41; 1992: 134) observes in neighboring Greece, success is often attributed to one's own skill, while failure is blamed on "fate." When speaking about "others," however, the reverse is the case: success is ascribed to kind Fate, while failure is caused by the person's character. Destiny dishes out the goods to others, not to "us" whose work actually makes us more deserving. Now, I do not mean to reify the moral codes of the Balkans, yet there are apparently some regional dispositions for explaining what happens in history. A common proverb in the Balkans, with several ethnic variations, says: "If you burn your mouth on coffee, you blow on your yogurt." History makes people defensive in the extreme, so that even cool water or yogurt needs to be blown upon.

2. Debate over the country's name is due to Greek concerns that the single name, "Macedonia," implies the singularity of Macedonian territory (and hence the irredentism of the government in Skopje). In the 1996 Olympics the Macedonian team marched alphabetically with the other nations whose name began with "F" (i.e., as the "Former Yugoslav Republic of Macedonia").

According to Macedonians, agency and destiny are two forces that motivate and define human affairs, and each new situation requires a reading according to the two. In this way, the past is continually being recycled to interpret the present and divine the future. Is it good fortune or a relaxed, prudent temperament that has prevented civil war and ethnic violence in Macedonia? This is not a simple multiple-choice question. Such a question requires ethnographic fieldwork in diverse locations, and the answers are never crystal clear. Friends and informants in Macedonia, nevertheless, frame their predicament in such terms as those above. Independence—from Belgrade—was not accomplished by a nationalist struggle, but it was welcomed when it arrived. Moral and public revulsion against the Serbian-Croatian war in 1991 encouraged and legitimated independence that seemed to come as a gift dropped from heaven.

There was reluctance on the part of many Macedonian citizens to open the package or, once opened, to accept its contents willingly. Ethnic Albanians in Macedonia looked in the direction of Kosovo for a continued, even stronger alliance against Serbian repression, and increasingly toward Tirana for the full expression of their identity, and they were equally wary of Macedonian irredentism. Macedonians sought international recognition for their independence against the bitter opposition of official Greek policy and the aloof skepticism of Bulgarians, Serbians, and Albanians. The Macedonian majority, moreover, felt threatened by Albanian separatist politics. Both groups were pressing then for political independence and international recognition.

The Albanian and Macedonian ethnic diasporas in Western Europe, North America, and Australia press for international recognition of their homelands. These demands surely form legitimate goals for a civil society within a democratic nation-state. If these demands, however, are aggressively irredentist and nationalist, they incapacitate the development of that very civil society. The Republic of Macedonia may be said to be going through an endurance test, where multicultural civility must prevail over ethno-nationalist seizures.

There remains a wide, though fragile, consensus in the middle of the Macedonian body politic. The elections of October 1994 gave the social democratic coalition a solid mandate, with substantial representation from the Albanian constituency. The Macedonian nationalists (IMRO factions) boycotted the second round of elections, and therefore they are not represented in the parliament. IMRO stands for the "Internal Revolutionary Movement of Macedonians," and the name harks back to the struggle for independence against the Ottoman Turks a century ago (Poulton 1995; Brown 1996). Their organizations thereby evoke in their political rhetoric a "clean" (*chist*) Macedonian nation. Anti-Turkish and anti-Albanian ideology pervades IMRO, and its supporters in the diasporas agitate, moreover, for a "United Macedonia" that (re)incorporates the "lost" parts of "the nation" in Bulgaria and Greece. Albanian nationalists are also mobilized in their diaspora to agitate for separatist goals that, like those of the IMRO, would rip the fragile society apart. Many of these Albanians identify their real nationhood with Kosovo, hardly ever with the Albanian state.

The "Macedonian conflict" has often been contested via census, map, and museum (Wilkinson 1951; Anderson 1991; Danforth 1995; Schwartz 1995). The members of minorities generally feel that the official statistics understate their real numbers. Albanians in the Republic of Macedonia protested the official statistics of the 1994 census, which represented them as some 23 percent of the entire population. They claim to be at least 40 percent. The contested demography in the republic is made more volatile by the situation in neighboring Kosovo. Ethnic Albanians have moved across the border into Macedonia. An estimated 150,000 persons from former Yugoslavia (as of July 1995) are residents of Macedonia, as yet without citizenship; many of them (125,000) are Albanians from Kosovo (Human Rights Watch 1996: 69–74). If this group of Albanians were to become citizens in the Republic of Macedonia, the Albanian population would begin to approach the 40 percent which Albanians insist is now the reality. Civil society and ethnic conflict in the Republic of Macedonia pivot on questions involved with citizenship. Who are citizens? And who are not? Finally, what does this citizenship imply for one's membership in an ethno-national community? Boycotting elections and census-taking can be interpreted as steps toward militant secession, or as appeals for equitable inclusion. The recognition of and tolerance for religious differences is apparently easier for the Macedonian intelligentsia than the endorsement of ethno-national and linguistic autonomy for Albanians. Because religion is regarded as intrinsic to the private sphere and education in the public or collective sphere, tolerance in a Balkan multiculturalist context would be aimed primarily at defending religious identity (Najcevska et al. 1996).

The western rim of the Macedonian Republic borders on both Albania and Kosovo, and there is a majority of Albanians in several of the western municipalities (Tetovo, Debar, and Gostivar).[3] These municipalities have also elected representatives to the parliament in Skopje, and in Tetovo an unofficial university has been organized by Albanian speakers to the chagrin of and attempts at its disestablishment by state officials. Still, Albanians haven't given up on Macedonia completely. Their political factions, though usually divided on accepting or rejecting the wider Macedonian consensus, are represented in the state's parliament.

While the extreme parties of Macedonian nationalism boycotted the second round of the elections and have no seats in the parliament, some of their Party members were elected to municipal governments and they occupy strategic posi-

3. A Kosovo Albanian political faction in Copenhagen has printed in its monthly newsletter a map where the redrawn borders of "Kossova" contain the entire western rim of the present Republic of Macedonia, including the Prespa Lake region (*Shpresa:* organ i komunitetit Shqiptar nä Danimarkä, November 1995). Maps such as these are powerful icons for expressing Balkan national—not ethnic minority—identities.

tions, such as on the police force. Summing up this historical and contemporary context barely scratches the surface of its complexity. Albanians and Macedonians live scattered and divided in others' nation-states and both national communities can rightly claim a history of injustice. Macedonians in northern Greece and Bulgaria are unrecognized. Albanians in the former Yugoslavia are marginalized. Kosovo was and is the poorest region of the former Yugoslavia (Reineck 1993: 90). The structural inequality between regions was exacerbated after the breakup in 1991, when Kosovo no longer received fiscal transfers from the richer republics of Croatia and Slovenia. Serbian seizure of Albanian positions in the regional Kosovo government and infrastructure, moreover, worsened the conflict (see Reineck, this volume).

Persuasive iconoclasm in ethnography seems to be the best approach to the problem at this time. Taking sides with one ethno-national community over another would only reinforce the exclusivist forces of identity. Rather, an appropriate intervention by ethnographers would involve working with the many, usually unheard, groups in the Republic of Macedonia that perceive the dangers of ethno-nationalist politics. Thus independence and transition in Macedonia are precarious sorts of trajectories. The experience of Macedonia suggests that ethnographers ought to speak of "member-citizens," as the persons in "nation-states." The placing of the hyphen between "member" and "citizen" is a corollary to the hyphen between "nation" and "state." Arjun Appadurai (1990: 304) has made the apt semiotic analysis about this hyphen, which in our time, means "that the state and nation(s) are at each other's throats, and that the hyphen which links them is now less an icon of conjuncture than an index of disjuncture."

Ethnic memberships are seldom, if ever, perfectly congruent with political citizenships, though the aim of Macedonian Republic policy is to make citizenship a fundamental form of membership. There are also in the Republic of Macedonia discernible supranational bonds of solidarity and rationality of which the environmental movements are prime examples. Such bonds, which would literally reclaim a common ground, are those which the agencies of the civil society attempt to build upon and strengthen.

The remainder of this essay will thus remove the quotation marks from Macedonia (Schwartz 1993) despite our knowledge that the contests for identity and recognition are still unresolved. Macedonia was, is, and will continue to be polysemous (Schwartz 1995). How the country is envisioned depends on who envisions it and from which vantage points. Loring Danforth's (1995) insightful study of Macedonians in northern Greece and in Melbourne's diaspora indicates how linguistic, national, ethnic, and regional facets all are refractions of "Macedonia." Below I argue that this ambiguity, which is the inevitable result of plurality, is the republic's hidden resource in a transnationalized civilization. Instead of imagining the multiethnic society of Macedonia as a time bomb set to explode unexpectedly, this paper will make a modest wager on the future: an emergent, trusting civil society can hinder the eruption of wide-scale ethnic violence in Macedonia.

When a time bomb actually did explode in Skopje in October 1995, nearly killing President Kiro Gligorov, the political society in the Republic of Macedonia passed one of its hardest tests. The organizations of the civil society assisted the government agencies in maintaining equilibrium. For example, instead of generating a demand for harsh revenge, NGOs helped consolidate a sense of shared concern and belonging. Guesses as to the ethno-nationalist identity of the would-be assassins did not develop into violent conflict. Friends from many ethnic groups in Macedonia conveyed to me by phone and fax their trust that society would hold together. Their responses suggest that problems within Macedonia and across the borders can be resolved through negotiation and changes in policy. Macedonian statesmen and civil society activists, in diaspora and in the homeland, are attempting to avoid imitating Bosnia and Kosovo. Learning from one's neighbors' bitter history might make one's own future less astringent.

Clearly, the Republic of Macedonia's problems are many and varied. Together, they pose a daunting task for the current and future governments. But despite the gravity of the situations I described, the citizens of Macedonia want to avoid any further escalation of tensions. If nothing else, they want to prove to the world that there can be peace in the Balkans, that lessons from Bosnia have been learned (T. Velovski 1995: 73).

Meeting NGOs in Macedonia

In the rural villages and towns of Macedonia NGOs are almost invisible. One has to know of their presence in advance before one can identify them. My fieldwork from February to May 1995 required commuting between Skopje and my main base, Resen, in the Prespa Lake region. Biweekly tours to Skopje (a bus trip that takes four-and-a-half hours) enabled me to maintain explicit contact with organizations of civil society. When I learned, for example, that it was the Institute for an Open Society (a George Soros Foundation agency) which assisted rural, multiethnic regions with various media for cultural communication, I was able to mediate between community and NGO to facilitate the development of a local presence for that organization.

The high school in Resen had no copy machines and lacked new teaching materials. In several conversations with high school teachers and students, I heard repeated the need for a copy machine. I had heard that Soros helped in such situations, so I added "Project Copy Machine" to my fieldwork notes and carried the message from the high school to the office of the Institute for an Open Society. The secretary at the office told me that the high school principal had to send a letter of application for a copy machine, and I took that piece of information to the high school teachers, who brought it to the attention of their supervisor. When

I left Macedonia in May, just before high school graduation, there were still no copy machines. I paid a brief visit to the high school again in October 1996, a year and a half later. One of my first questions to the English teacher was: "Has your school gotten a copy machine?" "Yes, two of them," he answered, "one from the Soros people. It came in time for the next semester." My "Project Copy Machine" had apparently worked.

I tell this anecdote, not to compliment my own efforts, but to illustrate how "civil society" is concretized in practice. Because the Soros Foundation focuses on providing educational and cross-cultural resources, its NGOs in the capitals can help meet specific needs if and only if they hear about them. As long as the Ministry of Education cannot, or does not, ensure that every school has a copy machine for its use, the agencies of civil society can enter the scene if an application is made. Civil society requires actors on the scene in several sites. An anthropologist can be one of the actors. In the long run, which after all is not so long, the question will arise as to the consequences of small-scale projects by NGOs in the civil society. These projects may contribute to improvements in specific localities and meet specific local needs. If, however, these results are so local that the society-at-large cannot be said to benefit from them, one might conclude that civil society activities actually widen the gap between the privileged few and the marginalized many. NGO projects rather should be catalysts for improvement and equality. My "Project Copy Machine" worked only because it was directed at a specific situation with specific actors. The will for results was also present.

The possibilities of NGOs to further civil society in Macedonia can be seen in the activities of two informants, both principals in such organizations. The two men are both from ethnic minorities, though both express a cosmopolitan and multicultural spirit in their work. Whether this is typical or exemplary I cannot say. I suspect that historians and anthropologists tend to meet exemplary persons in the archives and in the field. At some point in their research the "exemplary" conflates with "the typical." The "representative" person is outstanding, because that person seems to embody and articulate a position in a social and cultural milieu.

As indicated, Nehru Sulimanovski and Herbie Elmazi[4] are members of ethnic minorities. Nehru is from the Turkish community of Resen and Herbie from the Albanian community in Skopje. Nehru is in his mid-thirties, married, and has two sons. Herbie is in his late twenties and engaged to be married. Both men expressed in conversations a desire for interethnic coexistence that guaranteed a balance between ethnic membership and civic involvement. Neither of the two considered his ethnic identity as the single most important political force in his life. They disagreed with "nationalist extremism" of all varieties. Both men, as I suggested, described themselves as cosmopolitan. Nehru's activities concerned

---

4. Both men prefer me to use their actual names instead of keeping them anonymous.

the development of a local radio station while Herbie's concerns focused on rural infrastructural development.

"Balkan Blues Cafe": Local Radio, Global Culture, and Civil Society

As part of its agenda to further the development of open societies the Soros Foundation has assisted the formation of local, private radio stations in many rural, multiethnic regions of Macedonia. One of their stipulations for funding transmitting systems is that sending time in a region's minority languages is ensured. The choice of local radio, instead of local newspapers, was highly pragmatic and utilitarian. The effort involved in writing, publishing, distributing, and reading newspapers makes it less attractive than the medium of radio. In contrast, villagers listen regularly and easily to radio in their homes, cafes, barbershops, and orchards. Thus local radio is extremely popular, as much for exchanges of greetings between various people as for its music. The production of local radio is likewise popular, especially among young people, who, crowded in tiny studios, can touch base with the new electronic media and experience a sense of participation in life styles related to it.

The intentions of multiculturalist foundations, however, are not exactly mirrored in local radio production, since local disc jockeys view their activity more as manifestations of modernity than multiculturalism. Still, broadcasting minority folk music in minority languages has an important function in a politics of recognition. Furthermore, interviews and observations of local private radio point to another, equally important, consequence, in the formation of civil society. This consequence may be called the cosmopolitan spirit that local radio engenders. This is particularly obvious in an anecdote describing my initial meeting with Nehru.

One night, early in my fieldwork, I was listening to the tiny radio in my rented apartment. The program "Balkan Blues Cafe" was entertaining. The disc jockey, who spoke Macedonian, English, and Turkish, played evergreens from America, as well as folk music from the Balkan countries. The next morning I had an appointment to notify the municipal authorities in Resen about my research project. At the entry to the town hall, the gatekeeper took me to the office of a municipal worker who spoke English. The man's name was Nehru Sulimanovski, whose job was secretary to the town council. Nehru told me he was a journalist and former editor of the local biweekly newspaper of the Yugoslav Communist League. This newspaper ended with independence. "I do radio work now," he said, and he then told me that he had started Resen's first private radio station, "Radio Delicious" in 1993. Nehru, to my pleasant surprise, was none other than the voice of "Balkan Blues Cafe!"

The Soros Foundation helped provide "Radio Delicious" with the transmitter set. (The name for the station comes from the hybrid apple grown in many Prespa Lake orchards). For a three-year period, Nehru's "Delicious" was the only private radio station in Resen. The publicly financed and administered radio station (Radio "Resen") continued broadcasting after independence, but its role is mainly in the provision of "Information" to the listeners. In contrast, Nehru's station provided programming in Macedonian as well as the minority languages of the region (Albanian, Rom, and Turkish). Nehru also encouraged a group of high school students to air their own program, and for nearly a year, they read their poetry and voiced their opinions on a weekly program. In the guise of modernity, then, "Radio Delicious" thus met the stipulations of the Soros Foundation: ethnic diversity and cosmopolitan spirit. Nehru played all forms of folk music on "Radio Delicious" including Greek and Bulgarian folk music. Angry listeners sometimes called his studio and complained when they heard neighboring nations' music, but Nehru insisted that "all folk music is beautiful."

During my stay in Resen, "Delicious" was joined on the airwaves with a competitor named "Radio Stella." "Stella" appealed to the young people, and it aired a special program on Easter weekend aimed at young listeners. Like Nehru's station, Stella's economy depended on selling advertisement time to Resen's small businesses. "Stella" was a short-lived enterprise, however. By October 1996, it had closed down and was replaced with "Radio Number One," a studio in a Turkish backyard, which I visited. Another station called "Radio Egypt" was also on the air, this one for the Gypsy (Rom) community in Resen.

With or without the aid of the Soros Foundation, local radio stations seemed to thrive in the Republic of Macedonia. In the first few years after independence the government in Skopje had a very laissez-faire attitude toward private radio initiatives. In May 1995, however, the government began to demand licensing of private stations. In the Human Rights Watch Report on Macedonia (1996: 79–83) there were several charges that the government in Skopje closed down more minority stations in its licensing campaign. Nehru in 1995 was also worried that his own station might be closed, not because he was from a minority group, but because his station's frequency was close to one on the neighboring Greek side of the border across Prespa Lake. In 1996 Nehru was still broadcasting. In fact, he had moved his studio from a dilapidated shack in his backyard to better facilities in his father's photo shop in Resen.

Nehru's career includes his work as municipal secretary, his vocation in local radio, and producing videotapes of ethnic weddings in the Lake Prespa region. He has a large collection of wedding videos, in which one can especially see how innovations are added on tradition. Many weddings have moved from village yard to tourist hotel ballroom and, in spite of dwindling economic resources, have become much more urbane and expensive. Further, not only does each ethnic group have its own wedding traditions, but long-term residence in Sweden, Canada, or the United States leaves clear traces of its influence on returned migrants in the weddings they organize. For example, the "best man," at weddings is beginning to replace the role of the traditional *num* (godfather), an obvious importation from North American cities.

Nehru negotiates his own ethnic identity in all his diverse vocations, each involving communication and mediation among Resen's diverse ethnic communities. His approach is pragmatic, not ideological. For example, he and his wife enrolled their sons in the all-Macedonian school in their neighborhood, instead of in the Turkish classes in the elementary school across town. Nehru said that the chance for a better education would be enhanced if their children did their schooling in Macedonian. Nehru's choice is definitely a minority position among the ethnic minorities. It reveals, though, that dissent and descent are both intrinsic to a civil society. At home the language is Turkish, and, as in most of the Turkish households of Resen, a satellite dish enables the family to watch the ten or so TV channels from Istanbul. Balancing identities is a skill and resource. It is by no means a symptom of a split personality.

As Nehru's life indicates, multiculturalness—not an "ism"—in the cities, as well as in the mountain villages, is best seen and understood in everyday practice. Commenting on "the multicultural of daily life" in a Canadian, metropolitan context, Vered Amit-Talai (1995: 140) puts the matter in terms that also make comprehensible the pragmatic approach of Nehru Sulimanovski in "remote" Resen:

> To effectively handle the multicultural of daily life necessarily requires a certain level of pragmatic, comparative consciousness. We are constantly comparing, exploring, pressing, and remaking convergences and distinctions between the activities in which we participate. The articulations which functionalists assumed came as ready made and automatically reproducible functions of social organization are rather a product of the prodigious intellectual effort individuals apply to making sense of the almost impossible complexity of their lives. It is this effort which keeps life from feeling utterly fragmented even in the most dispersed, compartmentalized, anonymous metropolitan setting.

Reciprocal Labor and NGOs: Civil Society and Rural Development

Herbie Elmazi's work also suggests the importance of daily negotiation over ethnic identity and relationships for the development of NGO-inspired civil society. Herbie coordinates rural and social development projects for the Macedonian Center for International Cooperation (MCIC). The Skopje-based Center, funded mainly by the Amsterdam office of the World Council of Churches, is charged to define and sponsor projects that will contribute to the development of mutual trust and autonomy for rural populations. In the Center's mission statement (February 15, 1995) Sasho Klikovski, its director, suggests: "Concentrating on development aid in rural areas and on employment, MCIC considers further development of civic society life the most important component of its program. Specific programs of the Center, supported by its staff of twelve people between twenty-five and thirty-five years of age, are geared to rural development, employment, those to support the handicapped and other marginalized people."

As with grants from the Soros Foundation, the World Council of Churches stipulates that ethnically plural regions take funding priority over ethnically homogenous ones.[5] Additionally, MCIC particularly seeks to develop demonstration projects, for Center staff recognize that a successful project in one or two villages would have a beneficial, contagious effect on neighboring villages. Thus MCIC fieldworkers seek to identify concrete, local problems potentially solved by cooperative efforts that would have diverse benefits. Improved environment, increased employment, interethnic cooperation, and gender equality are all goals of MCIC projects in the civil society. Environmental issues, especially the construction of clean water reservoirs and sewage control, take high priority in the Dolna Reka (Lower River) region in western Macedonia where I accompanied Herbie on a four-day trip in a donated Land Rover.

Herbie was visiting several projects that involved Albanian, Muslim Macedonians (so-called *torbeshe* or "carpet-baggers"), and Orthodox Macedonian populations. The region of the Dolna Reka borders on Albania and consists of very steep mountains and beech forests. In contrast to the plentiful apple orchards of Lake Prespa, the Dolna Reka was a rustic backland with limited agriculture. Like Prespa Lake, however, there was a high rate of emigration (*pechalba*) from its mountain villages. Herbie and his colleague Sasho explained that emigrants who had returned to their homes from abroad were more likely to engage in development projects than those inhabitants who had never lived outside the village. Pechalba is a time of endurance and hardship but today it also provides useful experience for the construction of civil society.

As an observer of these projects in "international cooperation," I also noticed a new variant of a distinct practice of cooperative labor, known in Yugoslavia as the *moba* (Bringa 1995: 70). In times of intense labor demands, such as harvest and home construction, a man will "invite" family members, neighbors, and friends to help out in the work. In the Prespa Lake area cooperative labor is especially utilized in various aspects of apple production: planting apple trees, picking and crating apples, and repacking them for transportation to markets. A lamb dinner is exchanged for the hard labor. Labor teams there worked diligently and amicably, usually on weekends, with never the mention of wages.

Combining such traditional, "Mobaslavian" labor practices within the context of a modern NGO is the catalytic process of Herbie Elmazi's work. One such

5. Actually there are no municipalities of Macedonia that are ethnically pure, so presumably every town is a candidate for funding!

project was for sewage separation. Its village organizers gave us a tour of their completed work. Previously, the mountain stream running through the village carried inhabitants' sewage into their summer pasture, gardens, and walnut groves. In early interviews Herbie heard that this poor drainage system had caused serious illness among livestock and people. Herbie, who had studied several years at an engineering college, proposed a separate PCV piping system to carry the sewage into a steep, forested gully inaccessible to the villagers and their flocks. Clean water could continue to run into the gardens and groves.

It was decided that villagers would cooperatively dig a three-hundred-meter long trench for burying the sewage pipe with each household to contribute six meters of trenching and installation. If one did not provide labor power, it paid the equivalent of six deutschemarks per meter, given in wages for the extra work to local youths. Laying the pipe took only about two weeks, and now only clean water flows into the gardens and groves. Moreover, as hoped, this improvement was now being duplicated by a neighboring, rival village. Herbie was surprised to see that the entire trench had been dug since his last visit even though the PCV piping had not yet arrived.

Another project that Herbie coordinated involved an ethnically mixed village. Its main workplace was a lumber mill and factory that dumped its beechwood sawdust into the stream. Herbie proposed developing an ancillary sawdust compressing plant to produce fuel briquettes. The new addition would provide employment for twelve village women. The gender stipulation was emphasized and understood by the factory's director.

Herbie was particularly interested in the success of this project, for it involved many of the Center's priorities for socio-environmental development and civil society. The Ministry of Labor in Skopje was also a co-financier of the compressor equipment. In a fax to me in Copenhagen in October 1995 the delivery of the machinery from Germany had been delayed, but, Herbie wrote, "everything else is going as planned." In October 1996, the compressor arrived, was installed and operated by four (instead of twelve) women employees.

These success stories contrasted with one from a remote all-Albanian village. Here Herbie proposed the construction of a water storage tank above the village to ensure a water supply during the dry summer. The manual labor for this project was to be performed by terms similar to those of the multiethnic villages of the Dolna Reka, namely, a combination of voluntary labor and wage subsidies. However, as Albanian villagers insisted on wages for the entire project the plan was ultimately suspended. (Village school teachers did accept the Center's offer for new educational materials.) One of the arguments against the water tank was that it conflicted with villagers' work completing a local mosque, a lovely poured concrete building in the shape of a half moon. Cooperative labor was not unknown in the Albanian village, but the men preferred to use it in the building of a mosque. Herbie was disappointed by what he felt was Albanian resistance. He commented that ethnically mixed villages were more conducive to cooperative ventures. I tried to convince him that the Albanians had good reasons for distrusting the opinions of outsiders. Advocates of civil society believe that project participation depends on trust, mutuality, and equality. One cannot expect that the habits of civil society are likely to be found among mountain villagers whose experience is primarily that of marginalization.

In the multiethnic villages where Herbie had better success, the local organizers were proud to show "a guest from Denmark" their new drainage system, which they said, Herbie had "helped" them with. I noticed that the men referred to Herbie's organizing as "help" (*pomosh*), not as "cooperation" (*sorabotka*). That is how the cultural flows of NGOs seem to work. The metropolitan idea of "cooperation" flows into the village as "assistance," just as "dialogue" often turns into "expertise." Still, Herbie's work was a kind of "action anthropology." His understanding of the community, its resources, and its problems pointed to concrete projects and solutions. Thus the members of a community became aware of themselves as agents of change, not just bearers of tradition. Indeed, what emerges from my interpretation is the innovative coupling of local tradition with modern organizational skill. Civil society is as present and active in Skopje offices as it is in the mountain villages of Dolna Reka.

In conclusion, then, the making of Macedonia draws upon volunteer organizations of transnational civil society. However, even though the local and international agencies of civil society have different goals, these goals have to be mutually respected and mutually intelligible if civil society is to develop. Metropolitan "causes" such as gender equity and environmental protection ought not be experienced by the recipients as imports of missionary modernity. Projects for improvement ought to be just that. One should demonstrate that the consequences of a project make life better for the inhabitants, for they are themselves the primary agents of improvement. The Macedonian Center for International Cooperation translates the ideal of civil society into local practice. In this way, its larger goals of multicultural cooperation and gender equity can begin to be achieved.

Whatever Happened to Ethnic Conflict?

After following the two chief informants in this article, one might ask where and when did I confront ethnic conflict in this inquiry into the formation of Macedonian civil society. Have I hidden from the conflicts, or at least hidden them from the text? By foregrounding the conduct of two informants and friends, both members of ethnic minorities, the article has paid little attention to the dramatic scenes of conflict between Albanian and Macedonian groups in the society. However, implicit in this discussion has been the recognition that ethnic conflict can only be diminished when such sentiments are channeled into activities that are cooperative and productive of overall community growth.

The struggle over the Albanian university in Tetovo has crystallized this issue more sharply than any other event. The fatal shooting of an Albanian student on February 17, 1995, in a demonstration outside the university building was one of the two events that received public attention outside Macedonia. The other was the near fatal bombing of President Gligorov on October 3, 1995.

During fieldwork in 1995 I visited the Albanian university in Tetovo, two months to the day after the fatal shooting of Abdusalem Emini. The visit took the form of a "human rights watcher," who was gathering case material in order to advocate the cause of a violated minority group. I had to show my university calling card in order to have a conversation with two of the students and one professor. Because they feared police reprisals, these men would not tell me their full names. This was the only time in many years of fieldwork in Macedonia that informants insisted on secrecy.

The idea of "civil society" is very elastic, and the improvised Tetovo campus is testing the limits of the demands for ethnic autonomy within a precarious, multiethnic society. Civil society, as indicated, is fostered and maintained by voluntary associations of individuals. Mutual respect for "the other" is insepara- ble from the constitution of civil society. I am tempted to say that it is its very "essence." In speaking with informants from diverse ethnic groups about the Albanian university, the typical judgment was that "it is politics." People thus suggested that the demand for a separate Albanian university is not based on legitimate civil needs, but as a method for achieving political power. The men I interviewed in Tetovo were quite candid about this. Ethno-national politics had top priority, even if there was a risk of war.

The name of the village where the university is located is Mala Rekica (Little Stream), four kilometers from the center of Tetovo. One of the students, who had hosted me to lunch in his garden, took me to the site of the demonstration and battle. There were iron railings in rows across a field, about the size of a football gridiron, outside the small building at the lower end of campus. What are the iron railings for? I asked my host. The answer startled me. It was the local cattle market, where animals were tied up before they were weighed, sold, and slaugh- tered.

I have probably exaggerated the quasi-ritual symbolism of the site in my pre- vious interpretations of the ethno-national conflict between Albanians and Mace- donians. Nevertheless, in all the publicity about the shooting of Emini in the Western media, not once was the university campus ever described as a former cattle market. In order to give the image of the Albanian university academic prestige and symbolic capital, and to inscribe it into the discourse of civil society activity, media coverage emphasized the credentials of its rector and professors, several of whom were imprisoned after the demonstration. Many of the profes- sors had their degrees from the university in Prishtina (Kosovo), which was closed by Serbian militia in 1990.[6] The private Albanian language university in Tetovo has, in many respects, been a stand-in for the university in Prishtina. Funding for professors' salaries comes from the many thousand guestworkers in the Albanian diaspora. According to Sessilja Olafsdottir, who spent the summer of 1997 doing her ethnographic fieldwork in Tetovo, several vacant houses, lent by owners in diaspora, are being used as classrooms for university teaching.

In October 1998 I made a second visit to the university and was told by a professor of French that thirty such houses were currently donated as university space. About six thousand students were enrolled, some of whom received scholarship assistance from their home municipalities, that is, those with Albanian leadership. The university is thereby expanding and has a semipublic base. In public opinion the Tetovo university continued to be described as "illegal." Nevertheless, it remains open, regarded with a reluctant tolerance by the Macedonian public. I also saw that the nearby cattle market was very much in use on that clear October day.

The conflict over Tetovo university reveals a highly sensitive point in the conjuncture—or disjuncture—of ethnic affiliation and civil society. Organized Albanian pressure for social and educational equality is surely within the parameters of civil society, and this pressure thereby assumes a form of legitimacy (Human Rights Watch Report 1996). The potential rupture of the entire civil society, however, is seldom reckoned with in global NGO surveys. Because our field experience as ethnographers has a longer and wider duration, we are more circumspect in our accounts. It is not merely to present "both sides in a conflict," but rather to represent the contexts of that conflict.

Organized Albanian pressure for social and educational quality is surely within the goals of any civil society. Nevertheless, the demand for a university faculty in the former cattle market is, at best, bitter irony. University teachers in Skopje, including members of minority groups, told me that starting the university in Tetovo was premature. They were not opposed to the project as such, but it took time and planning to establish a university. Their own university in Skopje was itself in desperate need of reform and financial aid. The professors and students were taking steps to increase the proportion of underrepresented ethnic groups, especially Albanian and Rom communities. NGOs, like the Soros Foundation, were also active in facilitating dialogue across ethnic boundaries.

This comparison between civil society cohesion and ethnonationalist separatism leads to this article's tentative conclusion. Herbie Elmazi and Nehru Sulimanovski express the interests of a wide-ranging civil society in Macedonia concurrently with their affiliations in ethnic communities. Both men cross the threshold into the Macedonian institutions, but the threshold is still open behind

---

6. Serb repression of Kosovo Albanians was the first big step in the breakup of Yugoslavia. See Reineck's contribution in this volume for a more detailed discussion of this situation.

them. The doorway is not sealed. If the concept "civil society" has any practical meaning, it needs to be studied in the context of its practices. This article has attempted to evaluate several practices of civil society in the Republic of Macedonia. Such small events seldom enter into Human Rights Watch reports, which underscore violations of human rights. Peacekeeping anthropology puts in the foreground the activities of civil society members as clues for hope and counterweights to despair.

Redefining *Merhamet* After a Historical Nightmare

Stevan M. Weine

Testimony

The testimony method of psychotherapy was derived by mental health professionals working with survivors of human rights violations. The survivor tells how his or her life was shattered, and the mental health professional records it. Together they make a written, audiotaped or videotaped document of the story, and then look for appropriate ways to share it with others.

Psychiatric workers claim that testimony functions like psychotherapy, as a way of diminishing the suffering that is a consequence of traumas. Yet they also recognize that it is something more than a talking therapy for trauma victims. It can be a means to address phenomenon on the boundaries between the self and history. Survivors speak not only about themselves but also about participating in a way of life that was smashed, and what it could mean for the future of living in the collectives to which they belong.

Testimony and its narrative can assume many different forms—psychotherapy, autobiography, oral history, or even art. Many scholars have claimed that testimony occupies a central position in late-twentieth-century Western culture (De Pres 1976; Felman and Laub 1992; Hartman 1996). Still, there is still much to be learned about testimony.

My colleagues and I have been doing testimony work with Bosnian survivors of ethnic cleansing since they began being resettled in the United States in early 1993 (Weine et al., n.d.; Weine and Laub 1995). The testimony work began in Connecticut and continues in Chicago where our Project on Genocide, Psychiatry, and Witnessing has a testimony project for working with Bosnian refugees of ethnic cleansing. Thus far, more than fifty survivors have participated in the testimony work.

We became interested in doing testimony with Bosnians for several reasons. Based upon the psychotherapeutic claims of Inger Agger and Soren Jensen and of Dori Laub we thought there was a reasonable chance that telling their stories would help survivors reduce the pain associated with their traumatic memories and their traumatic stress symptoms. We also believed that these survivors' stories were important as samplings of the collective memories that are a part of the landscape of Bosnian life. We let the work be influenced by the legacy of Holocaust testimony, a collaborator, the psychiatrist, psychoanalyst, and survivor Dori Laub, was co-founder of the Fortunoff Video Archives for Holocaust testimony at Yale University (see also Hartman 1996). But it was necessary to adapt the method to the very different context of the ethnic cleansing of Bosnia and its survivors. For example, video testimony was dropped. It was too much like being interviewed by a television journalist to provide the atmosphere of safety, trust, and empathy that the survivors needed to be able to tell their stories. Several other modifications to the method enabled us to join with survivors to have them produce their testimonies. But then we also asked how could these testimonies be used to learn not just about individual trauma, but about the trauma to a whole society and its way of life? (See also Weine 1999).

Testimony Inquiry

The Chilean psychiatrists who came up with this testimony method for torture survivors during the Pinochet regime of terror and oppression cited as a major influence the anthropologist Oscar Lewis. Lewis had documented the stories of poor Mexican families in the 1950s. He described five possible approaches to studying families, which he used in combination with each other. One of these comes closest to testimony: "[T]he Rashomon-like technique of seeing the family through the eyes of each of its members. This is done through long, intensive autobiographies of each member of the family. This gives more insight into the individual psychology and feeling and tone as well as an indirect, subjective view of family dynamics. This type of material would probably be most useful to the psychologist" (Lewis 1959).

Lewis did not advocate this approach in isolation, but in combination with others that focused on various aspects of the family as a whole, such as the family economy or a particular family crisis. Could many testimonies by many Bosnians (or a subgroup of Bosnians) provide evidence for an understanding of critical collective aspects of the experience of surviving ethnic cleansing? This would offer a view of "history from below."

Testimony inquiry has much in common with the methodology of oral history as described by Allessandro Portelli (Portelli 1991). In Chicago, it occurs in community settings, such as the Bosnian refugee center, a local cafe, or the survivors' home. The testimony sets a comparatively egalitarian relationship between the survivor and the researcher. The latter is there to listen and learn from the survivors. The survivor is encouraged to raise questions about the researcher (be they Bosnian, Croatian, or American) and all that they represent to them. This unique relationship then also becomes a part of the narrative that the researcher writes, with detailed, close, honest reflection.

The researcher does not seek to avoid the problems of nonobjectivity so much as to exploit their possible benefits. Their inquiry seeks out encounters, collisions, conflicts, and confrontations between the different voices, different sides, including that which is known, and that which is not. The aims of entering into this narrative include to become more aware of how we listen and know; how we live with suffering, oppression, and traumas in our midst; how we can make meaningful changes in psychology and in the cultural concepts that shape the self, family, community, and society.

Bosnian Muslims' *Merhamet*

Something I came to hear in various forms from many survivors made the strongest impression the first time, in the testimony of E., a young doctor from a Sarajevo suburb:

> I remember Bosnia as a beautiful and peaceful country. . . . We all lived together. Before the war, it was unnecessary to know if your neighbor was Serb, Croat, Muslim, or Jew. We looked only at what kind of person you were. We were all friends. But now I think it is like a kind of earthquake. A huge catastrophe. After this war nothing will be the same. People will live, but I think they will not live together. They will not share the same bread like before. Maybe they will be neighbors, but I think the close relationship will not exist any more. Because the Bosnian people, especially the Muslim people, had a bad experience, partly as a result of our attitude.

"What exactly do you mean by 'our attitude'?" I asked.

> We called that the merhamet—that you feel sorry for someone who has bad luck. Philanthropy. You like all people. You want to support every-

one. If you can help, you help. You can even forgive bad things. You can find good in all religions. You will be good and decent to everyone.

Merhamet happens to be the name of the Bosnian Red Cross organization, but E. uses it differently. He makes it sound like something associated with the Tito- ist slogan of "Brotherhood and Unity." I ask E., how do the two compare?

Only Bosnians believed in "Brotherhood and Unity" and agreed with that idea. I think that the politicians knew that, especially Tito. He repeated that slogan very often in Bosnia. When he gave speeches, he'd say, "You must uphold 'Brotherhood and unity.'" And I think that the Bosnian Muslims were good members of brotherhood and unity. They believed in that, and they were big patriots in the former Yugoslavia. And I think that only Muslims and Macedonians tried to avoid any kind of conflict in the former Yugoslavia. They suggested that we all compromise. "For all"— that is one of the main sayings of merhamet. Personally, I believed in Brotherhood and Unity, but now I don't believe in that. Because of mer- hamet I think the Bosnian Muslims forgot a very important thing—that it is not the first genocide against them. . . . But always people forget. Bos- nian Muslims learn the hard way.

From the moment that E. mentioned *merhamet*, it struck me as one of the most compelling ideas I had ever heard about Bosnia and Herzegovina. The pri- mary target of the Serbian nationalists' genocide in Bosnia was the multiethnic way of life. *Merhamet*, which means compassion, forgiveness, altruism, and humbleness, was a central element of that life. As a self and group concept, *merhamet* has been an important cultural value of multiethnic Bosnia and a cen- tral element of the worldview of the Bosnian Muslims.

Maybe it was *merhamet* that was manifest in the way that some survivors seem to approach the traumas of ethnic cleansing with a measure of acceptance. Life brought this ethnic cleansing to them, and they will accept it. That isn't to say that they don't try to meet their own needs or stand up for their rights. But somehow a good number of them were not full of bitterness and hatred. This sense had greatly impressed me and many other outsiders when we first got to know Bosnians, but we didn't know what to call it. After listening to E., I started to think of this as part of what's meant by the attitude of *merhamet*. Perhaps then there was still some *merhamet* left within them after all. Some survivors, when asked what they would do now about *merhamet*, reported that they were sticking with it. They said now we need it more than ever. This was heard both from Bosnian refugees in America and from Bosnians in Sarajevo. But how could they keep *merhamet* alive when its social context had been so dramatically changed?

A Bosnian language dictionary lists *merhamet's* multiple meanings: mercy, pardon, grace, alms, charity, kindness. The sentence it quotes as an example of usage reads, "Do you have any *merhamet* in yourself ?" (Škaljić 1979). Surprisingly, *merhamet* is not named in the English language scholarly literature on Bosnia, although one can find traces in descriptions of Bosnian Muslim identity. For example, anthropologist Tone Bringa writes: "Bosnian Muslims conceptualize their common identity primarily through the knowledge that they share a particular moral environment" (Bringa, 1995). Their social milieu was inclusive not exclusive; heterogeneous not homogeneous. Bosnian national identity was not dependent primary upon ethnicity, but upon a way of life that was multiethnic. Commitment to preserving that way of life was something you did both for the common good, and for the goodness of the self.

The historians Mark Pinson (1993) and Ivo Banac (1993) have outlined the historical basis of Bosnian Muslim identity. There was no historical period of ethnic dominance, and no epic myth of ethnic statehood, Bosnians based identity upon a "centuries-old common life, regardless of confession" as Tito said in 1940 (Pinson 1993). After World War II, Tito's governmental policy of "Brotherhood and Unity" provided the political context for Bosnian Muslim identity and *merhamet*, the mentality of this way of life.

As a historical view, this *merhamet* could then be seen as standing in contrast with a particular strain in the epic culture of the Serbian people that was promoted by some Serbian nationalist intellectual and political leaders over the past decade (Judah 1997). According to this historical view, Serbs as a people, have been victimized, betrayed, and misunderstood by the rest of humanity. This view of Serbian history remembers past injustices, real or exaggerated, and is preoccupied by the fear that violence and injustice will befall them again. The historical view enlivened by Bosnian *merhamet*, on the other hand, lets go of past hurts and injustices, in favor of living together. *Merhamet* is also a departure from the tales of violence motivated by ethnic, religious, and national differences expressed in some Muslim folk epic songs from the eighteenth century and earlier (Serbo-Croatian Heroic Songs 1974).

Survivors' testimonies illustrate just how significantly *merhamet* was contingent upon the silencing of historical memories of World War II that was enforced by the communist government and its policy of "Brotherhood and Unity." Nearly all survivors spoke of the experiences of killings and atrocity from World War II, either their own, if they were old enough, or those of their parents or grandparents. However, these memories were offered hesitantly, and survivors made it clear that this was something they were not used to talking about outside their families. They had always been aware of these memories, but as one survivor told me, "We never put that first." These traumatic memories were silenced, but not erased. They were part of a dark side to Yugoslavia that was not discussed, except in the most rigid, state-scripted, Partisan way.

Merhamet owes its nature, and perhaps its very existence after World War II, to this avoidance of the historical memories of the war except through the narrow frame of Partisan myth. It is discomforting to consider that something that seems so valuable to the Bosnian way of life could be contingent on such an artifice. Yet far greater attention was paid to the Partisan struggle against fascism than to a moral reading of the tensions, conflicts, and violence that stemmed from ethnic nationalisms. The possible limitations associated with *merhamet* were not apparent until these forces surged and culminated in the recent aggression.

Obstacles to *Merhamet* After Ethnic Cleansing

Like many survivors and refugees, E. was struggling to know what to do with *merhamet* now after surviving ethnic cleansing. It all came down to one basic problem:

"You always must have in mind that maybe tomorrow your friend will be your enemy."

I asked, "What will become of *merhamet* now after 'ethnic cleansing'?"

He replied that these crimes would be remembered and passed down through the generations. He did not then know what would become of Bosnia, but he was sure that this aspect of Bosnian life was permanently changed.

How could it not be, given all that has happened? The Second Yugoslavia no longer exists. Nor does the political system organized by Tito's "Brotherhood and Unity." The governments in Serbia and the Republica Serbska, and that of Croatia and Herzeg-Bosna, have inflicted tremendous aggression on the Bosnian Muslims. The international community has limited political will to effectively intervene, the United Nations War Crimes Tribunal has limited capacity and authority to bring perpetrators to justice, and the NATO forces have not been actively enforcing all aspects of the Dayton Peace Accord.

There have been startling demographic changes in Bosnia and Herzegovina and Sarajevo. The Bosnian government estimates that in Bosnia, there were 278,800 killed and missing, 1,250,000 refugees, and 1,300,000 displaced persons. In Sarajevo, the prewar population was 500,000, and now there are about 350,000. An estimated 120,000 displaced persons came to Sarajevo, mostly Muslim and rural. As a consequence of this massive migration, you hear many people saying that Sarajevo no longer belongs to Sarajevans. Bosnians say in characteristic dark humor, that Sarajevo is now "the biggest village in Bosnia."

One million Bosnians are in exile the world over. Of those who are internally displaced, a huge proportion cannot return to their homes. The politics of partition are solidifying the results of the forced ethnic cleansing, with subsequent elections adding further legitimacy. Bosnian survivors know that their own lives will never again be the same. What's more, they live with the likelihood that those who aggressed against them will never be prosecuted. Can it be imagined that these social and individual traumas create ripe conditions for the forgiveness that is a part of *merhamet*? Many survivors express no interest in *merhamet*, preferring to live apart or desiring revenge.

Now, as before, the future of Bosnia is critically dependent upon the political leadership. Certain trends since the signing of the Dayton Accord have given the international community grounds to fear that Bosnian leaders are fostering a Muslim nationalism. There have been changes made in the language spoken, which is not being called Serbo-Croatian any more, but Bosnian. Islam is playing an increasingly important role in the culture; Muslim nations, in the providing of humanitarian, cultural, and military assistance. Human rights organizations have reported the oppression of Croats, Serbs, and so-called mixed persons. To some extent this reflects the West's preoccupation with its own neutrality; its bias toward pointing the finger at all three sides and saying that they are all guilty of the same crimes. But when Bosnian leaders and governmental bodies are taking positions that are more nationalistic than would ever have been allowed in the old system, at the very least, we must recognize that the risks are there.

The Dayton Peace Accord may have established the military and diplomatic structures for halting the ethnic cleansing and the war, but serious questions remain concerning the transition from war mentalities to a culture of peace and the possibilities for a multiethnic way of life. Making peace is more than stopping war and reconstruction is more than building roads. There is a psychological and cultural dimension to making peace. Despite the presence of substantial obstacles, if we are to speak of what ethnic cleansing means to its survivors, and how they are now psychologically prepared to face the future, then it becomes important to address their struggles over what will become of *merhamet*.

Approaching *Merhamet* in Testimony

Testimony can be a place where *merhamet* can be named, reflected upon, understood, and updated by the individual survivor. My belated discovery of *merhamet* in testimony with E. taught me how important it is to first simply give it a name. Survivors will often struggle to give voice to the multiethnic vision or not even mention it. However, there is something about the testimony method, whereby the self's relationship to larger collectives and their history is a central concern, that sets a receptive frame for addressing this phenomenon bridging self and community.

Many Bosnians have shown a desire to use testimony not only to name the trauma that has disrupted their lives but also to name what the years of living together meant and what the multiethnic experiences of those years have left with them. Yet as difficult as it is to speak of the nightmare of genocide, it can be even more painful to speak of the dream that once animated their lives. But for those who are willing, testimony offers a unique opportunity to help Bosnians explore the role that *merhamet* has played in their lives, their communities, their culture, and their history.

In the course of their testimony, individual survivors are encouraged by the listener to attempt the impossible: to reconcile *merhamet* with ethnic cleansing; and to struggle with what kind of attitude toward other ethnic groups and other sides makes sense in the postcommunist, post–ethnic cleansing, postwar, post-Dayton context.

One way this can be approached in testimony is by assisting the survivor in exploring the contingencies of *merhamet*: if the International Tribunal prosecutes the real war criminals; if the Bosnian Serb leaders in Pale would admit their guilt for genocide; if there is a strong enough Bosnian army to protect its people. Some survivors say that after ethnic cleansing there is no contingency that is adequate enough to make *merhamet* work. Still the testimony offers the chance to reflect on *merhamet*'s status post–ethnic cleansing. Not even its strongest detractors would argue that *merhamet* has completely disappeared. Most survivors are not yet so removed from the experience of living together that they have left behind the mentality and the spirit that went with that way of life. Sometimes in testimony it helps to remind the survivor of the years of living together and to give them permission to express feelings that can seem quite contrary after the experience of genocide and war. On the other hand, survivors who speak from a position of *merhamet* when talking about the years of living together are not necessarily revealing where their *merhamet* is now. Even if they praise it, they may still be considering it as something belonging to the past.

You may hear survivors struggling with what to do with *merhamet* now, when they discuss their more recent contacts with Serbs, which force them to reconsider what attitudes they need to take now. It also comes up when survivors give accounts of Serbs who saved their lives during ethnic cleansing. Testimonial evidence of such humane behavior by Serbs can lend support to the mentalities of living together and of *merhamet* (yet it does not erase the harsh truths of ethnic cleansing). Survivors are often insecure and uncertain in possession of this knowledge, especially in a climate where polarizing "war mentalities" abound. The truth that resides in these stories propels them into a gray zone, where they must find nondichotomizing ways of making sense of the history that they have lived through.

Even when survivors use testimony to denounce *merhamet* and to express hatred and the desire for vengeance, there would seem to be healing in naming and sharing these attitudes. It may become possible to see these attitudes standing between the self and history, perhaps even side by side with *merhamet* and other humanistic values. We should not expect that testimony would purge survivors of hatred, any more than it would purge them of their traumatic memories, but it could help them to contextualize their hatreds and to assist them in negotiating with their hatred as a part of a moral struggle with *merhamet*.

Redefining *Merhamet* in the New Landscape

It is obvious that *merhamet* cannot exist as before. However, because it has been near the center of the Bosnian soul, *merhamet* could still be a central force in the evolutionary processes of making peace and rebuilding civil society. But how?

Merhamet would have to be managed in an entirely new way. *Merhamet* is not being nurtured by the multiethnic shared living space as it was before, because those shared living spaces do not now exist, except perhaps to some extent in some parts of Sarajevo. It cannot be nurtured by the same community leaders and intellectuals as before ethnic cleansing because many of those have become refugees or were killed. Bosnia cannot count on a government, such as it had in the Second Yugoslavia, to nurture *merhamet* by keeping the major ethnic groups in line with brute strength. Neither a rump Yugoslavia, nor a Bosnian-Croat Federation, nor a Federation–Republica Serbska structure, are likely to play that role. In fact those governments, including the Bosnian government in Sarajevo, are leaning in the direction of ethnic nationalisms. The West's capacity to fulfill that balancing role is also profoundly limited.

Since Dayton, the West has been placing its emphasis on creating shared institutions that will bring people together once again. But the rehabilitation of *merhamet* is not only an institutional or political problem. It is also a psychological struggle for each and every survivor, and for the communality of survivors. In order to rehabilitate *merhamet* within the survivors' psyche, it would have to be reconciled with such forces as the memories of ethnic cleansing, also with the understandable need to defend against aggression, and with the stronger emphasis on Bosnian Muslim identity. There is of course no linear relationship between individual change and societal change, but it is hard to imagine meaningful transformation at a societal level without an equally meaningful moral struggle at the individual, familial, and communal levels.

Retrospectively we can see that this moral struggle did not occur in Tito's Yugoslavia. After World War II, the dominant political ideology elevated the Partisans' defeat of fascism above all else. Though there was living together, the state did not allow looking at how to reconcile the experiences of living together with the genocidal memories from World War II. In that sense, we can say that *merhamet* was not tested. Citizens of the Second Yugoslavia were never really given the option to consider acting on behalf of their ethnic group, and to reconcile the advantages of taking a pro-ethnic stance against the costs of violence and destruction.

As much as we may admire *merhamet*, we can also see that it is something less than a moral attitude. Perhaps it is more of a sentiment that because it has supported humanistic actions is morally good. That would account for the relatively plastic way that survivors react to the questioning of their *merhamet:* "I don't have merhamet now, but maybe in two years I will," they say.

But now after ethnic cleansing this *merhamet* is being seriously tested. It cannot simply return unchanged. For one, many survivors have said that *merhamet* let the Bosnian Muslims down because it did not prevent the spread of nationalism and genocide. Furthermore, many believe it rendered the Bosnian Muslims defenseless from their enemies. In a sense, this ethnic cleansing has provoked a moral crisis when it comes to *merhamet*. If *merhamet* is to be a critical element in the moral order of the new Bosnia, then it will have to survive the challenge of the new landscape. How is it possible to face this moral crisis? Can a valid *merhamet* survive the conditions of exile and statehood that beset the global Bosnian community?

Some preliminary observations can be made about *merhamet* in the Diaspora. Bosnians in the United States, for example, are comprised of two groups: families from Eastern Bosnia and the Krajina region that were cleansed; and families that left from Sarajevo. Many Bosnians, particularly Sarajevans, who went into exile, were among the strongest endorsers of *merhamet*. Yet those from Eastern Bosnia and the Krajina who were ethnically cleansed and detained in concentration camps, are often not so invested in *merhamet* as a proposition for living together. This is a generalization, but in many ways true. Bosnians in exile who most accepted *merhamet*, often found themselves marginalized and antagonized by those whom had relinquished *merhamet*. They have sworn in disgust, that they cannot be a part of anything Bosnian anymore, and quickened their embrace of an American identity. Among this group are those Bosnians who are a part of mixed marriages, and those who are highly educated. If those who most endorsed *merhamet* continue to distance themselves from the Bosnian community, it may be harder for *merhamet* to establish a foothold in the Diaspora.

In Bosnia itself, the demands for statehood create another set of difficulties for *merhamet*. Dayton would have us speak of a Bosnia and Herzegovina as the defining federal entity, with its constituent parts of a Bosnian-Croat Federation, and a Republica Serbska. But for all intent and purposes, the separate entities have much greater political cohesion than the larger collective entity. At this point in time Bosnia and Herzegovina is comprised of three separate living spaces. Partition looms as a real possibility.

How can Bosnian Muslims in this landscape be *merhametly*? In Sarajevo some kind of *merhamet* may be possible. For example, when the Sarajevo district of Grbavitza was liberated in spring 1996, some Sarajevans distinguished between "city Serbs" or "our Serbs," who they wanted to stay in Sarajevo, and the Serb villagers who torture, raped, enslaved, and killed Sarajevans and therefore must go. They had *merhamet* for those who they perceived to be a part of their way of life. But for those on the other side, they didn't want to recognize that they even existed. Outside of Sarajevo in places such as Tuzla, where some multiethnic living persisted during the war, the Bosnian Muslims were alone on their side, and could thus have little *merhamet* for other groups.

Merhamet could become appropriated by the momentum toward a stronger Muslim identity. One striking symbol of this could be the Muslim Red Cross organization called *Merhamet*, which has developed a reputation for providing humanitarian assistance only to ethnically pure Muslims, and not to mixed persons. If *merhamet* were to now become an attitude that was extended only toward Muslims, it would be a rather dramatic symbolic marker of the success of the Serbian nationalists' efforts to destroy multiethnic Bosnia.

Testimony and *Merhamet*

Testimony provides a way to gather knowledge about *merhamet*, which resides with many survivors in their memories and stories. Further ethnographic studies of *merhamet* are needed to provide a more comprehensive understanding of this critical concept for Bosnian culture. Our testimony work with Bosnians began with the imperative to understand, but also to address the individual and sociocultural challenges to peace, democracy, and pluralism in the Bosnian future. Testimony projects are organized not only to gather historical facts but also to facilitate a moral struggle in survivors and their communities. Chilean testimony projects documented Pinochet's torture and oppression as a part of a reconciliation process. Holocaust testimony projects have provided historical documentation of this cataclysmic event and its survivors' struggles against forgetting. What then can Bosnian testimony accomplish, in the absence of reconciliation, and far more proximate in time to the events themselves?

Bosnian testimony can provide documentation of human rights violations and historical documentatio, and ethnographic stud, pertaining to ethnic cleansing. But there is something more that testimony projects can do. Testimony can create spaces within public life where it becomes possible for survivors to tell and document their stories and to let others interact with these stories. This is what never happened in the communist era of black-and-white, one-dimensional memories. By giving many voices and the community of survivors a voice, testimony can facilitate a moral struggle in individuals, families, and communities.

For this we need testimony projects. These must not in any way be psychiatric in nature. If the testimony projects in Bosnia and Herzegovina were located in higher educational institutions, then the testimonies themselves would be in contact with an interdisciplinary intellectual community of students and scholars. The testimonies could become connected with their ongoing studies, encouraging them to develop intellectually and morally in relation to them. In a testimony project, survivors' voices and stories could also become a focal point for an interdisciplinary intellectual or civic dialogue through connecting the testimonies with artists, journalists, educators, and scholars. Interaction is the key. The testimonies must get involved in university curricular activities, student's studies, and faculty research. There is a very serious need for scholars to work together to address the phenomenon presented by testimony.

To best reflect the multiethnic heritage of Bosnia, these projects should include survivors of ethnic cleansing and war from the three major ethnic communities of Bosnia: Muslims, Orthodox, and Catholics. Listening to the stories of Bosnian Orthodox and Catholics, likely to contain some stories of aggression by Muslims, will be hard for some to tolerate. But there would also be risks in not including their voices. It would send clear signals that the new Bosnia has overtly nonpluralistic, and nondemocratic, designs.

Another critical dimension of testimony-related work for Bosnia concerns teaching youth. The philosopher Richard Rorty has proposed that people learn not to be cruel not by accepting certain truths to be true but through a "sentimental education" (Rorty, 1997). If they hear a story of someone else' humiliation, then they come to feel it as if it was their own, and invest in the other's experience. So education can involve the telling of testimony stories gathered through testimony projects. Once again, stories alone won't do it. They can serve only to provoke sentimental reactions. They can be just as easily coupled with nationalistic ideology and help to propel people to nationalistic points of view.

Which testimony stories, coupled with which ideas can best address the dilemmas in Bosnia? These stories cannot be only of *merhamet* and living together, or of ethnic cleansing, because that would be to ignore half of reality. The stories must encompass both realities and must also communicate the values of democracy, pluralism, and openness. Just as important they must teach a sense of danger that is not simply about identifying the other as something to be feared and hated. Danger does not reside only in the other side, or in politicians, but also in one's own group and in oneself. All may learn to fear and hate given the proper conditions.

By no means should we consider the proposal for a testimony project as some kind of panacea concerning *merhamet*, let alone multiethnic living in Bosnia. Testimony itself guarantees nothing other than banal stories of history, hopelessly small and trivial in comparison with the grand march of history. Yet it is not conceivable that this trauma to the collective memory of Bosnia will be addressed by the Hague War Crimes Tribunal or by any other institution. A testimony project seems to provide an innovative way for attending to survivors' remembrances that offers potential for not only individual healing but a sociocultural form of recovery that is desperately needed. Still, it is perfectly clear that these are not matters that can be resolved here and now but rather issues that must be struggled with over time.

Notes on Contributors

Mart Bax is a professor of political anthropology at the Vrije University, Amsterdam, the Netherlands. His work has mainly focused on the anthropology of religion. He is the author of a number of books and articles, including *Medjugorje: Religion, Politics, and Violence in Rural Bosnia.*

Brian Bennett is a professor of anthropology at Appalachian State University. His early research in Croatia focused on ethnography/community study; he published his results under the title *Sutivan: A Dalmatian Village in Social and Economic Transition*. He has continued to research and publish on socioeconomic change in Croatia and currently does cooperative research and lecturing at the Institute for Anthropological Research, Zagreb, from 1994 to 1995 through a Fulbright lectureship and presently through Rotary International. His recent articles have appeared in *Collegium Antropologicum*, *Drustvena Istrazivanja*, and *Narodna Umjetnost*, both published in Zagreb.

Nikolai Botev currently works at the Population Activities Unit of the United Nations Economic Commission for Europe in Geneva, Switzerland, on a study of population aging and the social and economic status of older persons in Europe and North America. His research interests cover a broad range of topics within the field of social demography, including living arrangements of older persons, cultural and historical factors in population change, and marriage and family formation as well as ethnic demography. He holds a doctorate in demography from the University of Pennsylvania.

Bette Denich began her involvement with Yugoslavia as a graduate student during the mid-1960s when she conducted fieldwork on rapid modernization under the Titoist system. Her recent work centers on the manipulation of collective memory and public discourse in the fomentation of ethnic violence. Denich received her doctorate from the University of California at Berkeley and has taught at several colleges and universities, including Columbia and Harvard. She resides in Cambridge and is currently a research fellow at Boston University.

Elinor Murray Despalatović is the Brigida Pacchiani Ardenghi Professor of History at Connecticut College. She is the author of *Ljudevit Gaj and the Illyrian*

Movement (1975), coeditor with Joel Halpern of *How the People Live* (1981), and the author of numerous articles on Croatian history. Her present research is on Croatian peasant life before World War I.

Hannes Grandits teaches Southeast European history at the Department of Southeast European History, University of Graz-Austria. His main research work is on sociohistorical and historical anthropological questions. He received his doctorate for a study on the changes in family and everyday life in two Croatian communities between 1770 and 1970.

Joel M. Halpern has worked in former Yugoslavia since 1953. His research has mainly concerned sociocultural change, kinship structure, and ethnicity. He has also done research in Bulgaria and, more recently, served as an adviser to the Albanian Academy of Sciences in 1993–94. In addition to articles, monographs, and books in English, he has published on the Balkans in Croatian, German, Serbian, Slovenian, and French. Halpern has been a visiting professor at the Southeast European Institute at the University of Graz (Austria) and is Senior Research Associate there. He has taught at UCLA, Brandeis, and the University of Massachusetts, where he is a professor emeritus. His other fieldwork has been in Indochina (where he served as a foreign service officer), in the Arctic, as well as with American ethnic groups. His Balkan photographs have been widely exhibited.

E. A. Hammel is a professor emeritus of anthropology and demography at the University of California-Berkeley. He has conducted research and published in ethnography, linguistics, archaeology, and biological anthropology, based on fieldwork in California, New Mexico, Peru, Mexico, the former Yugoslavia, and Greece. His most recent work has been on the historical demography and family structures of Serbia and Croatia. He is a member of the National Academy of Sciences and of the American Academy of Arts and Sciences.

Robert M. Hayden is an associate professor of anthropology and an associate professor of law at the University of Pittsburgh. He has done research in and on the former Yugoslavia since 1981, and has also done extensive research in India. His recent book is *Blueprints for a House Divided: The Constitutional Logic of the Yugoslav Conflicts* (Ann Arbor: University of Michigan, 1999).

Éva V. Huseby-Darvas is an adjunct professor of anthropology at the University of Michigan-Dearborn. She was born and raised in Budapest, Hungary, which she fled in 1956. Based on this experience she has been interested in the relationship between women's identity and social change, and the ramifications of migration, nationalism, and ethnicity on individuals and communities. She has conducted research in rural and urban Hungary and North America and has published on women's roles in socialist and postsocialist Eastern Europe and the immigrant and refugee experience and on transforming gender and other roles. She is currently working on a manuscript on long-distance nationalism among groups of American-Hungarians.

Goran Jovanović has graduate degrees in development studies from the University of Geneva, in American Studies from Smith College (Massachusetts), and a master's degree in international relations from the University of Geneva, where he is writing a dissertation on the Yugoslav crisis as expressed in political cartoons. He has also published works on the history and politics of immigration, German historiography, and social theory. He worked for the United Nations Economic Commission for Europe in Geneva. He is currently working as a translator/interpreter at the Cantonal Court and at the Center for Study of Audio-Visual Sources of History. He lives in Geneva with his wife and son.

David A. Kideckel is the chair of the anthropology department at Central Connecticut State University. He is author of *Solitude of Collectivism: Romanian Villagers to the Revolution and Beyond* (Cornell) and editor of *East European Communities: Seeking Balance in Turbulent Times* (Westview). His current research considers changing labor relations in two Romanian regions and its influences on domestic organization and health.

Mirjana Laušević is a native of Sarajevo and received her bachelor's degree from the University of Sarajevo Music Academy. She has a master's and a doctorate from Wesleyan University in ethnomusicology and has been on the faculty of New York University.

Lynn Maners holds a doctorate from UCLA and has specialized in music and dance in the Balkans. One of only a handful of cultural anthropologists to have worked in Bosnia and Herzegovina, he completed fieldwork just before the dissolution of the Yugoslav state. He has recently returned from Sarajevo, where he had resumed his research with folklore ensembles in post-Dayton Bosnia and Herzegovina. He is on the faculty at Pima Community College and the University of Arizona in Tucson, Arizona.

Julie Mertus is a visiting assistant professor and fellow in the Religion and Law Program at Emory University School of Law. A graduate of Yale Law School, she was formerly a fellow in human rights at Harvard Law School, a Fulbright Professor in Romania, and a MacArthur Foundation peace fellow. She has also served as a counsel to Helsinki Watch, as an attorney with the ACLU Reproductive Freedom Project, and a consultant for several international nongovernmental organizations. She is editor of *The Suitcase: Refugees' Voices from Bosnia and Croatia* and *National Truths: (Re)membering Kosovo—The Building of Serbian and Albanian Nationalisms* (University of California Press, 1997), and the author of *Kosovo: How Myths and Truths Started a War* (University of California Press, 1999).

Robert G. Minnich is an associate professor of social anthropology and deputy chair of the department at the University of Bergen, Norway. He is author of *Homesteaders and Citizens: Collective Identity Formation on the Austro-Italian-Slovene Frontier* (Bergen: Norse Publications, 1998). He is currently responsible for the anthropological component of an interdisciplinary and international research project titled "The Austrian-Italian-Slovene Three Border Region: Causes and Consequences of the Geo-political Partition of a Region."

Rajko Muršič is a lecturer in the Department of Ethnology and Cultural Anthropology at the University of Ljubljana. He is author of two monographs written in Slovene: *Non-Verbal Sound Games: From Philosophy Toward Anthropology of Music* (1993) and *CZD: An Ethnological Description of a Rock Group* (1995) and several papers and articles. His main scholarly interests are musical anthropology and philosophy of music, cultural studies (ethnographic studies of subcultures and mass culture phenomena), theory of anthropology, philosophy of science, anthropology of food, political anthropology, ethnology of the Balkans, Eastern Europe and Slavic countries, and studies of contemporary material culture.

Edit Petrović has her master's and doctorate from the University of Belgrade. She has published and has done research in the domain of ethnic relations, the politics of ethnicity, and immigration. Her current research concerns immigrants from former Yugoslavia in Western Canada. She is an adjunct assistant professor with the Department of Anthropology, University of Calgary.

Christian Promitzer is an assistant professor at the Department of Southeastern European History, University of Graz, Austria. His doctoral dissertation is on the history of the almost unknown Slovene minority in Austrian Styria. His main interests are ethnicity, ethnic minorities, and borders and nationalism in Southeastern Europe. He coedited *The Southeast European Educational Initiatives and Co-operations for Peace, Mutual Understanding, Tolerance, and Democracy*, published by the Graz Center for the Study of Balkan Societies and Cultures, 1998.

Mirjana Prošić-Dvornić has a doctorate in ethnology and anthropology from the University of Belgrade, School of Philosophy, where she also worked from 1974 until 1996, advancing from assistant lecturer to professor of anthropology. She also taught at the School of Performing Arts, University of Arts, Belgrade (1985–88). Her research has covered a number of themes including rural and urban Balkan (Serbian) cultures, ethnicity, symbolic systems, rituals and stylistic behavior, gender studies, and the political anthropology and ethnography of everyday life. She has presented papers at many international meetings and has published three books: *Folk Art in Yugoslavia* (with Dj. Petrović), *Folk Costume in Šumadija*, and *Cultures in Transition*, and over seventy studies, articles, and critical reviews.

Janet Reineck was expelled from Yugoslavia by the Serbian government in 1998. She has lived in Kosovo for seven years, most recently as a coordinator of relief and community development programs for Oxfam, the International Rescue Committee, and the Soros Foundation. She has a doctorate in anthropology from the University of California at Berkeley and is currently development coordinator at Direct Relief, a humanitarian aid organization based in Santa Barbara.

Jonathan Schwartz is an associate professor at the Institute of Anthropology, University of Copenhagen. He has published three books in Denmark: *Reluctant Hosts: Denmark's Reception of Guest Workers*, *In Defense of Homesickness: Nine Essays on Identity and Locality,* and *Pieces of Mosaic: An Essay on the Making of Makedonija*. Since 1995 he has been working on a comparative study of the reception of Bosnian refugees in Scandinavia.

Andrei Simić is a professor of anthropology and an associate of the Center for Visual Anthropology at the University of Southern California. He completed his bachelor's in Slavic languages and his doctorate in social anthropology at the University of California, Berkeley. He has conducted research in the former Yugoslavia periodically since 1967. He is the author of more than fifty works dealing with Balkan culture and society, and in 1988 produced a documentary film regarding the preservation of Serbian culture in America.

Stevan M. Weine is codirector of the Project on Genocide, Psychiatry, and Witnessing (with Ivan Pavković, M.D.) and an assistant professor of psychiatry at the University of Illinois at Chicago. His writings on Bosnia have been published in leading professional journals and he is the author of *When History Is a Nightmare: Live and Memories of Ethnic Cleansing in Bosnia-Herzegovina* (Rutgers University Press, 1999).

References

Abadan-Unat
1977. "Implications of Migration on the Emancipation and Pseudo-Emancipation of Turkish Women." *International Migration Review* 6 (1): 31–57.

Abdo-Zubi, Nahla
1987. *Family, Women, and Social Change in the Middle East: The Palestinian Case.* Toronto: Canadian Scholars' Press.

Adamček, Josip
1980. *Agrarni odnosi u Hrvatskoj od sredine XV do kraja XVII stoljeća* (Agrarian relations in Croatia from the mid-sixteenth to the end of the seventeenth centuries). Zagreb: Liber.

Agger, Inger, and Soren Jensen
1990. "Testimony as Ritual and Evidence in Psychotherapy for Political Refugees." *Journal of Traumatic Stress* 3 (1): 115–30.
1996. *Trauma and Healing under State Terrorism.* London: Zed Books.

Akhavan, Payam, and Robert Rouse, eds.
1995. *Yugoslavia, The Former and Future: Reflections by Scholars from the Region.* Washington, D.C.: The Brookings Institution.

Alexander, S.
1979. *Church and State in Yugoslavia since 1945.* Cambridge: Cambridge University Press.

Alilović, Ivan
1980. *Tragom hrvatske kulturne baštine u Hercegovini* (Tracing the Croatian cultural heritage in Hercegovina). Zagreb: Hrvatsko Knjiženo Društvo.

Almond, Mark
1994. *Europe's Backyard War: The War in the Balkans.* London: Mandarin.

Allport, Gordon W.
1976. "Formation of In-groups." In *Ethnic Identity in Society*, ed. Arnold Dashevski. Chicago: Rand McNally.

Alonso, Ana María
1994. "The Politics of Space, Time, and Substance: State Formation, Nationalism, and Ethnicity." *Annual Review of Anthropology* 23: 379–405.

Althusser, Louis
1980. "Ideologija in ideološki aparati države. Idéologie et appareils idéologiques d'état." In *Ideologija in estetski učinek* (Ideology and the aesthetic effect), ed. Zoja Škušek Močnik. Ljubljana: Cankarjeva založba.

Amit-Talai, V.
1995. "Anthropology, Multiculturalism, and the Concept of Culture." *Folk: Journal of the Danish Ethnographic Society* 37: 135–44.

Amnesty International
1991. *Torture and Deliberate and Arbitrary Killings in War Zones*. New York: Amnesty International.

Anderson, Benedict
1983. *Imagined Communities: Reflections on the Origins and Spread of Nationalism*. London: Verso.
1992. *Long-distance Nationalism*. Amsterdam: Casa Publications.
1992. "The New World Disorder." *New Left Review*, no. 193 (May/June): 3–14

Anderson, Kenneth
1990. *Yugoslavia: Crisis in Kosovo*. New York: Helsinki Watch.

Anderton, Douglas L.
1986. "Intermarriage in Frontier Immigrant, Religious and Residential Groups: An Examination of Macrostructural Assimilation." *Sociological Inquiry* 1986: 341–66.

Andrić, Ivo
1961. *Gospodjica*. Zagreb: Mladost.
1990. *The Development of Spititual Life in Bosnia under the Influence of Turkish Rule*, trans. and ed. Želimir Juričić and John Loud. Durham, N.C.: Duke University Press.

Andrić, Nada, et al.
1967. *Beograd u XIX Veku* (Belgrade in the nineteenth century). Belgrade: Muzej Grada Beograda.

Anonymous
1993a. "Menekültek jönnek és maradnak: Nincs visszaút?" (Refugees come and stay: Is there no road to return?) *Uj Magyarország* 3 (179).
1993b. "Information on Asylum Seekers in Hungary as a Consequence of the Armed Conflict in the Former Yugoslavia." Courtesy of Dr. Agnes Ambrus and the Hungarian Refugee Office Budapest. January.

Anthropological Quarterly
1976. Vol. 76. Special Issue, *Women and Migration*.

Appadurai, Arjun
1990. "Disjuncture and Difference in a Global Cultural Economy." In *Global Culture: Nationalism, Globalization and Modernity*, ed. M. Featherstone. London: Sage.
———, ed.
1986. *The Social Life of Things*. Cambridge: Cambridge University Press.

Apter, David
1987. *Rethinking Development*. Newberry Park, Calif.: Sage Publications.

Azcarate y Florez, Pablo de
1945. *The League of Nations and National Minorities, An Experiment*. Washington, D.C.: Carnegie Endowment for International Peace.

Badiou, Alain
1996. "Etika: Razprava o avesti o Zlu. / L'éthique: Essai sur la conscience du Mal." *Problemi* (Ljubljana) 34 (1).

Bakić-Hayden, Milica
1994. "Nesting Orientalisms and Their Reversals in the Former Yugoslavia." Revised version of paper presented at the annual meeting of the American Association for the Advancement of Slavic Studies, Honolulu, Hawaii, November 1993.
1995. "Nesting Orientalisms: The Case of Former Yugoslavia." *Slavic Review* 54 (4): 917–31.

Bakić-Hayden, Milica, and Robert M. Hayden
1992. "Orientalist Variations on the Theme 'Balkans': Symbolic Geography in Recent Yugoslav Cultural Politics." *Slavic Review* 51 (1): 1–15.

Balen, Šime
  1952. *Pavelić*. Zagreb: Biblioteka Društva Novinara.
Ballinger, Pamela
  1996. "The Istrian Esodo: Silences and Presences in the Construction of Exodus."
  In Jambrešić Kirin and Povrzanović 1996.
Banac, Ivo
  1984. *The National Question in Yugoslavia: Origins, History, Politics*. Ithaca, N.Y.:
  Cornell University Press.
  1990. "Political Change and National Diversity." *Daedalus* 119: 141–61.
  1992a. "The Fearful Asymmetry of War: The Causes and Consequences of Yugoslavia's Demise." *Daedalus* (Spring): 141–74.
  1992b. "Post-Communism as Post-Yugoslavism: The Yugoslav Non-Revolution of
  1989–1990." In *Eastern Europe in Revolution*, ed. I. Banac. Ithaca, N.Y.: Cornell
  University Press.
  1994 "Bosnian Muslims: From Religious Community to Socialist Nationhood and
  Post-Communist Statehood, 1918–1992." In *The Muslims of Bosnia-Herzegovina*,
  ed. Mark Pinson. Cambridge: Harvard University Press.
Banks, Marcus
  1996. *Ethnicity: Anthropological Constructions*. London and New York: Routledge.
Banska Vlast Banovine Hrvatske (Government of the Croatian Banovina)
  1940. *Godisnjak 1939–26, kolovoza* (Yearbook 1939–26, August). Zagreb.
Barringer, Felicity
  1991. "Repatriation Is the Trend for Refugee Women Worldwide." *New York Times*,
  November 17, p. 4, col. 3.
Barth, Fredrik
  1969. "Introduction." In *Ethnic Groups and Boundaries*, ed. Fredrik Barth. Boston:
  Little, Brown.
Baskin, Mark A.
  1983. "Crisis in Kosovo." *Problems of Communism* 32 (2): 61–74.
Bataković, Dušan T.
  1996. *The Serbs of Bosnia and Hercegovina: History and Politics*. Paris: Dialogue.
Bateson, Gregory
  1972. "Culture Contact and Schismogenesis." In *Steps to an Ecology of Mind*, 61–
  72. New York: Ballantine.
Bausinger, Hermann
  1990. "Symbolfragen in der Volkskunde" (The question of symbols in European
  ethnology). *Tübinger Korrespondenzblatt* 37: 3–7.
  1996. "Concluding Remarks." In Jambrešić Kirin and Povrzanović 1996.
Bax, M.
  1989. "The Madonna of Medjugorje: Religious Rivalry and the Formation of a Devotional Movement in Yugoslavia." *Anthropological Quarterly* 62 (4): 231–47.
  1990. "The Seers of Medjugorje; Professionalization and Management Problems in
  a Yugoslav Pilgrimage Centre." *Ethnologia Europaea* 21 (2): 82–98.
  1991. "Female Suffering, Local Power Relations and Religious Tourism; A Case-
  Study from Yugoslavia." *Medical Anthropology Quarterly* 5 (4): 371–84.
  1993. "Power and the Definition of the Sacred: Popular Religious Regime-Formation
  in Former Yugoslavia." *Etnološka Tribina* 16: 119–33.
  1995. *Medjugorje, Religion, Politics and Violence in Rural Bosnia*. Amsterdam: VU
  University Press.
  1997. "Mass Graves, Stagnating Identification, and Violence in Bosnia." *Anthropological Quarterly* 70 (1): 11–21.

Belić, Dragan, and Djuro Bilbija
1989. *Srbija i Slovenija: Od Cankarevog doma do "Jugoalata" i Gazimestana* (Serbia and Slovenia: From Cankar's Hall to "Jugoalat" and Gazimestan). Belgrade: Tera. [Cankar's Hall: Where the Slovenes sided with the Albanians in Ljubljana. Jugolat: The site of the first demonstration for Milošević in Serbia. Gazimestan: The site of the battle on Kosovo Field.]

Benderly, Jill, and Evan Kraft, eds.
1994. *Independent Slovenia: Origins, Movements, Prospects.* London: Macmillan.

Bennett, Brian C.
1994. "Among Croatian Friends." *Appalachian Today* 2, no. 1 (Winter): 16–17.
1995a. "Directions for Croatian Anthropology: Reflexive Anthropology." *Collegium Antropologicum* 19 (1): 257–63.
1995b. "An Outline of Socio-cultural Analyses and Discourse on War, Ethnicity, and Change in Croatia and East/Central Europe: Introduction to the Theme and Articles." *Collegium Antropologicum* 19 (1): 1–6.
1997. "25 Years of Economic and Cultural Transition on Hold: War and a State of Ideological Limbo in a Croatian Community." In *Regions in Transition—Applied Anthropology and Demographic Perspectives*, ed. Brian C. Bennett and Pavao Rudan, 1–10. Zagreb: Croatian Anthropological Society.

Bennett, Christopher
1995. *Yugoslavia's Bloody Collapse: Causes, Course and Consequences.* New York: New York University Press.

Bennett, Linda A.
1997. "A Forty-Year Perspective of the Anthropology of Former Yugoslavia." In *Europe in the Anthropological Imagination*, ed. Susan Parman. Upper Saddle River, N.J.: Prentice-Hall.

Benthem van den Bergh, G. van
1989. *The Taming of the Great Powers.* Oxford: Basil Blackwell.

Bentler, P. M., and M. D. Newcomb
1978. "Longitudinal Studies of Marital Success and Failure." *Journal of Consulting and Clinical Psychology* 46: 1953–70.

Berman, Nathaniel
1993. "But the Alternative Is Despair: European Nationalism and the Modernist Renewal of International Law." *Harvard Law Review* 106: 1798.

Bertsch, Gary K.
1971. *Nation-Building in Yugoslavia: A Study of Political Integration and Attitudinal Consensus.* Beverly Hills, Calif.: Sage.
1976. *Values and Community in Multi-National Yugoslavia.* New York: Columbia University Press.

Besarović, R., ed.
1968. *Kultura i umjetnost u Bosni i Hercegovini pod Austrougarskom upravom* (Culture and art in Bosnia Hercegovina under Austro-Hungarian rule). Sarajevo: Arhiv BiH.

Biberaj, Elez
1982. "Kosovo: The Struggle for Recognition." *Conflict Studies* 137/138: 23–43.

Bićanić, Rudolf
1937. "Agrarna kriza u Hrvatskoj 1873–1895 i njezin utjecaj na ekonomsku i socialnu strukturu Hrvatske" (The agrarian crisis in Croatia, 1873–1895, and its effect on the economic and social structure of Croatia). *Ekonomista* 3–5.

BiH Ekskluziv
1994. "Bosna slobodi pjeva" (Bosnia sings in praise of freedom). (March 18): 6.

Bilandžić, Dušan, et al.
1991. *Croatia Between War and Independence*. Zagreb.

Birath, Thomas
1993. "Foreword." In *Asylum and Hope: The New Role of Hungary in International Migration*, ed. Zoltán Hajmanszki, Boldizsár Nagy, and Ágnes Ambrus. Budapest: Pelikán Press.

Blalock, Hubert M.
1967. *Toward a Theory of Minority-Group Relations*. New York: John Wiley & Sons.

Blau, Peter M.
1977. *Inequality and Heterogeneity*. New York: Free Press.

Blau, Peter M., Terry C. Blum, and Joseph E. Schwartz.
1982. "Heterogeneity and Intermarriage." *American Sociological Review* 47: 45–61.

Boehm, Christopher
1984. *Blood Revenge: The Anthropology of Feuding in Montenegro and Other Tribal Societies*. Lawrence: University of Kansas Press.

Bogišić, Valtazar
1874. *Zbornik sadašnjih pravnih običaja u Južnih Slavena* (A compendium of contemporary legal customs among the South Slavs). Zagreb: Jugoslavenska Akademija.

Bohlen, Celestine
1991. "Hungarians Opening Hearts to Refugees from Yugoslavia." *New York Times,* October 18. A1.

Bokan, Dragoslav
1993. "Baja mali Kninđa-Stante paše i ustaše" (Baja mali Kninđa [a Serbian folksinger]—Stop [Turkish] pashas and ustashas). *Naše Ideje* (Our ideas) 1 (June): 71.

Bolčić, Silvano
1994. "O 'svakodnevici' razorenog društva Srbije početkom devedesetih iz sociološke perspektive" (Everyday life in the "destroyed society" of Serbia in the early 1990s: From a sociological perspective). In Prošić-Dvornić 1994b: 139–46.

Bonifačić, Ruža
1995. "Changing of Symbols: The Folk Instrument Tamburica as a Political and Cultural Phenomenon." *Collegium Antropologicum* 19 (1): 65–77.

Bonnafous, Simone
1996. "La géstions de l'incertain par les médias contemporains dans la crise yougoslave" (Dealing with the uncertain in the Yugoslav crisis by the contemporary media). *Mots. Les langages du politique* (Words: The languages of politics, Paris) 47: 7–22.

Botev, Nikolai
1990. "Nuptiality in the Course of the Demographic Transition—The Experience of the Balkan Countries." *Population Studies* 44 (1): 107–26.
1994. "Where East Meets West: Ethnic Intermarriage in the Former Yugoslavia during the Last Three Decades." *American Sociological Review* 59: 461–80.

Botev, Nikolai, and Richard Wagner
1993. "Seeing Past the Barricades: Ethnic Intermarriage in Yugoslavia During the Last Three Decades." In Kideckel and Halpern 1993: 29–38.

Bourdieu, Pierre
1990. *In Other Words: Essays Towards a Reflexive Sociology*. Stanford: Stanford University Press.

Brandt, Miroslav
1996. *Život sa suvremenicama* (Life with contemporaries). Zagreb: P.I.P.

Brettell, Caroline
1982. *We Have Already Cried Many Tears: The Stories of Three Portuguese Migrant Women*. Cambridge, Mass.: Schenkman Publishing.

1994. "Women Are Migrants Too: A Portuguese Perspective." In *Urban Life*, ed. George Gmelch and Walter Zenner.

Brinar, Irena, and Stein Kuhnle
1994. "Perspectives on European Integration in Smaller Democracies: Norway and Slovenia Compared." In Bučar and Kuhnle 1994.

Bringa, Tone
1993a. "Nationality Categories, National Identification and Identity Formation in 'Multinational' Bosnia." In Kideckel and Halpern 1993: 80–89.
1993b. *We Are All Neighbours*. Disappearing World Series (film).
1995. *Being Muslim the Bosnian Way: Identity and Community in Central Bosnian Village*. Princeton: Princeton University Press.

Bromlei, Yu. V., and M. S. Kashuba
1982. *Brak i semia u narodov Yugoslavii* (Marriage and family among the Yugoslav people). Moscow: Nauka.

Brown, K.
1995. "Of Meanings and Memories: The National Imagination in Macedonia." Ph.D. diss., Department of Anthropology, University of Chicago.
1998. "Macedonian Culture and Its Audiences: An Analysis of 'Before the Rain.' " In *Ritual, Performance, Media*, ed. Felicia Hughes-Freeland. London: Routledge.

Bučar, Bojko, and Stein Kuhnle, eds.
1994. *Small States Compared: Politics of Norway and Slovenia*. Bergen: Alma Mater

Bufon, Milan
1995. *Prostor, meje, ljudje: razvoj prekomejnih odnosov, struktura obmejnega območja in vrednotenje obmejnosti na Goriškem* (Territory, borders, and people: Cross-border relations, the structure of the border landscape, and the evaluation of "borderness" in the Gorizia borderland). Trieste: Slovenski raziskovalni inštitut (Slovene research institute).

Burg, Steven L., and Michael L. Berbaum.
1989. "Community, Integration, and Stability in Multinational Yugoslavia." *American Political Science Review* 83: 535–54.

Burke, P.
1991. "Overture: The New History, Its Past and its Future; History of Events and the Revival of Narrative." In *New Perspectives in Historical Writing*, ed. P. Burke. University Park: Pennsylvania State University Press.

Čale Feldman, Lada
1995a. "The Image of the Leader: Being a President, Displaying a Cultural Performance." *Collegium Antropologicum* 19 (1): 41–53.
1995b. "Intellectual Concerns and Scholarly Priorities: A Voice of an Ethnographer." *Narodna Umjetnost* 32 (1): 79–90.
1996. "Theatrical Metamorphoses: Turning Exile into a Fairy Tale." In Jambrešić Kirin and Povrzanović 1996.

Čale Feldman, Lada, Ines Prica, and Reanna Senjković, eds.
1993. *Fear, Death and Resistance, An Ethnography of War: Croatia 1991–1992*. Zagreb: Institute of Ethnology and Folklore Research, Matrix Croatia.

Calhoun, C.
1993. "Civil Society and the Public Sphere." *Public Culture* 10: 267–80.

Calić, Marie-Janine
1993. "Der serbisch-kroatische Konflikt in Kroatien" (The Serb-Croat conflict in Croatia). In *Der ruhelose Balkan. Die Konfliktregionen Südosteuropas* (The unquiet Balkans: The regions of conflict in southeastern Europe), ed. W. Weithmann. Munich: Deutscher Taschenbuch Verlag.

Capotorti, Francesco
   1979. "Study on the Rights of Persons Belonging to Ethnic, Religious, and Linguistic
   Minorities." U.N. Doc. E/CN.4/Sub.2/384/Rev. 1. New York: United Nations.
Carmichael, Cathie
   1995a. "Some Thoughts on the Creation of a Slovenian National Culture." *Glasnik
   Slovenskega etnološkega društva / Bulletin of the Slovene Ethnological Society* 35
   (1): 7–14.
   1995b. "Locating Trieste in the Eighteenth and Nineteenth Centuries." In Šmitek
   and Brumen 1995: 11–12.
Cassirer, E.
   1961. *The Myth of the State*. New Haven: Yale University Press.
Casti, John L.
   1993. *Searching for Certainty: What Science Can Know About the Future*. London:
   Abacus.
Čeribašić, Naila
   1995. "Gender Roles During the War: Representations in Croatian and Serbian Popular Music, 1991–1992." *Collegium Antropologicum* 19 (1): 51–103.
Charaudeau, Patrick, Guy Lochard, and Jean-Claude Soulages
   1996. "La construction thématique du conflit en ex-Yougoslavie par les journaux
   télévisés français (1990–1994)" (The construction of the conflict in the former Yugoslavia in the French TV news). *Mots. Les langages du politique* (Paris) 47: 89–108.
Chaszar, Edward
   1988. *The International Problem of National Minorities*. Indiana: Minority Rights
   Research Program, Indiana University of Pennsylvania.
Chen, Lung-Chu
   1989. *An Introduction to Contemporary International Law*. New Haven: Yale University Press.
Cienfuegos A. J., and C. Monelli
   1983. "The Testimony of Political Repression as a Therapeutic Instrument." *American Journal of Orthopsychiatry* 53 (1): 43–51.
Cigar, Norman
   1996. "The Serbo-Croatian War, 1991." In *Genocide after Emotion: The Postmodern
   Balkan War*, ed. Stjepan G. Meštrović, 51–90. London: Routledge.
Ćirić, Aleksandar
   1991. "Unutrašnji egzodus" (Internal exodus). *Vreme* (Belgrade), December 23,
   1991. Pp. 8–11.
Citron, Suzanne
   1991. "Nacionalni mit: Pretres zgodovine Francije" (National myth: Discussion on
   the history of France [an excerpt from *La mythe national*]). In Rizman 1991: 191–
   220.
Claude, Inis L., Jr.
   1955. *National Minorities: An International Problem*. New York: Greenwood Press.
Clifford, James
   1988. *The Predicament of Culture*. Cambridge: Harvard University Press.
Cohen, Anthony P.
   1994. *Self-Consciousness: An Alternative Anthropology of Identity*. London
   Routledge.
Cohen, Lenard J.
   1995. *Broken Bonds: Yugoslavia's Disintegration and Balkan Politics in Transition*.
   Boulder, Colo.: Westview Press.
Cohen, P. J.
   1996. *Serbia's Secret War: Propaganda and the Deceit in History*. College Station:
   Texas A&M University Press.

Cohen, Roger
    1997. "Nationalism with a Zionist Twist." *New York Times.* August 31. The Week in Review, p. E.
Cole, John W.
    1981. "Ethnicity and the Rise of Nationalism." In *Ethnicity and Nationalism in Southeastern Europe*, ed. S. Beck and J.W. Cole. Amsterdam: Euromed Papers 14.
Collins, R.
    1990. "Violent Conflict and Social Organization. Some Theoretical Implications of the Sociology of War." *Amsterdams Sociologisch Tijdschrift* 16 (4): 63–88.
Čolović, Ivan
    1993. *Bordel ratnika. Folklor, politika i rat* (Warriors' bordello: Folklore, politics, and war). Belgrade: XX vek.
    1994. "Vreme i prostor u savremenoj politickoj mitologiji" (Time and space in contemporary political mythology). In Prošić-Dvornić 1994b: 121–28.
Colson, Elizabeth
    1966. "The Alien Diviner and Local Polities among the Tonga of Zambia." In *Political Anthropology*, ed. M. Swartz, A. Tuden, and V. Turner, 221–28. New York: Aldine.
Connor, Walker
    1991. "Ekonomski ali etno-nacionalizem?" (originally published as "Economic or Ethno-Nationalism?") In Rizman 1991: 297–317.
    1992. "The Nation and Its Myth." In *Ethnicity and Nationalism*, ed. A. Smith. International Studies in Sociology and Social Anthropology 60. New York: E. J. Brill.
    1994. *Ethnonationalism: The Quest for Understanding.* Princeton: Princeton University Press.
Constitution for the Federation of Bosnia-Herzegovina
Ćopić, B.
    1963. *Prolom* (Break). Rijeka: Adria Press.
Ćopić, Bože, ed.
    1991. *Croatia Between War and Independence.* Zagreb: University of Zagreb and OKC-Zagreb.
Craig, M.
    1988. *Spark from Heaven. The Mystery of the Madonna of Medjugorje.* London: Hodder & Stoughton.
Crapanzano, Vincent
    1986. "Hermes' Dilemma: The Masking of Subversion in Ethnographic Description." In *Writing Culture: The Poetics and Politics of Ethnography*, ed. James Clifford and George E. Marcus, 51–76. Berkeley and Los Angeles: University of California Press.
Crnobrnja, Mihailo
    1994. *The Yugoslav Drama.* Montreal: McGill-Queen's University Press.
Csepeli, György, and Endre Sík
    1995. "Changing Contents of Political Xenophobia in Hungary—Is the Growth of Xenophobia Inevitable?" In Fullerton, Sík, and Tóth 1995: 121–28.
Čulinović-Constantinović, Vesna
    1976. "Tradicionalni nevjenčani brak u nasem selu" (Traditional common-law marriage in our villages). *Sociologija Sela* (Rural sociology) 14: 125–37.
Curtis, Glenn E., ed.
    1992. *Yugoslavia, A Country Study.* Washington, D.C.: Library of Congress, Federal Research Division.
Cushman, Thomas.
    1996. "Collective Punishment and Forgiveness: Judgements of Post Communist Na-

tional Identities by the 'Civilized' West." In *Genocide after Emotion: The Postmodern Balkan War*, ed. Stjepan G. Meštrović. New York: Routledge.

Cviić, Christopher.
1990. "The Background and Implications of the Domestic Scene in Yugoslavia." In *Problems of Balkan Security: Southeastern Europe in the 1990s*, ed. Paul S. Shoup, 89–122. Washington, D.C.: Wilson Center Press.
1991. *Remaking the Balkans*. New York: Council on Foreign Relations Press.

Czakó, Ágnes
1993. "A romániai menekültek és a civil szféra változószervezetei" (Romanian refugees and Changing NGOs). In *Utkeresôk*, ed. Endre Sík. Budapest: YIMRG.

Damatta, Roberto
1994. "Some Biased Remarks on Interpretivism: A View from Brazil." In *Assessing Cultural Anthropology*, ed. Robert Borofsky, 119–32.

Danforth, L.
1995. *The Macedonian Conflict: Ethnic Nationalism in a Transnational World*. Princeton: Princeton University Press.

Darby et al.
1968. *A Short History of Yugoslavia*. Cambridge: Cambridge University Press.

Darton, John
1994. "U.N. Faces Refugee Crisis That Never Ends. Forced to Flee: A Special Report." *New York Times,* August 8, A1, A4.

Dedić, Milutin
1981. "Cultural-Artistic Amateurism." *Yugoslav Survey,* May 1981. Pp. 121–40.

Dedijer, Vladimir
1974. *Dnevnik* (Diary). Vol. 3. Belgrade and Sarajevo: Bana.
1992. *The Yugoslav Auschwitz and the Vatican*. Buffalo, N.Y.: Prometheus.

Dedijer, Vladimir, et al.
1975. *History of Yugoslavia*. New York: McGraw-Hill.

Demographic Research Center
1974. *The Population of Yugoslavia*. Belgrade: Institute of Social Sciences.

Denich, Bette
1993. "Unmaking Multi-Ethnicity in Yugoslavia: Metamorphosis Observed." In Kideckel and Halpern 1993: 48–60.
1994. "Dismembering Yugoslavia: Nationalist Ideologies and the Symbolic Revival of Genocide." *American Ethnologist* 21: 367–90.

Denitch, Bogdan
1990. *Limits and Possibilities: The Crisis of Yugoslav Socialism and State Socialist Systems*. Minneapolis: University of Minnesota Press.
1994. *Ethnic Nationalism: The Tragic Death of Yugoslavia*. Minneapolis: University of Minnesota Press.

Despalatović, Elinor Murray
1975. *Ljudevit Gaj and the Illyrian Movement*. New York: Columbia University Press, East European Quarterly.

Deutch, Karl W.
1969. *Nationalism and Its Alternatives*. New York: Alfred A. Knopf.

de Zayas, Alfred-Maurice
1994. *A Terrible Revenge: The Ethnic Cleansing of the East European Germans, 1944–1950*. New York: St. Martins Press.

Dimitrijević, Vojin
1995. "The 1974 Constitution and Constitutional Process as a Factor in the Collapse of Yugoslavia." In Akhavan and Rouse 1995.

Dixon, Ruth B.
    1971. "Explaining Cross-Cultural Variations in Age at Marriage and Proportions Never Marrying." *Population Studies* 25: 215–33.
Djilas, Aleksa
    1985. "The Foundations of Croatian Identity." *South Slav Journal* 8: 27–30.
    1991. *The Contested Country.* Cambridge: Harvard University Press.
    1993. "A Profile of Slobodan Milošević." *Foreign Affairs* 72 (3): 81–96.
Djilas, Milovan
    1958. *Land Without Justice.* New York: Harcourt, Brace, & World.
    1977a. *Der Krieg der Partisanen. Jugoslawien 1941–1945* (The Partisan War: Yugoslavia, 1941–1945). Vienna: Fritz Molden.
    1977b. *Wartime.* New York: Harcourt, Brace, Jovanovich.
    1980. *Druženje s Titom* (Friendship with Tito). Belgrade: CSA.
    1983. *Rise and Fall.* New York: Harcourt, Brace, Jovanovich.
Djukić, Slavoljub
    1990. *Slom srpskih liberala* (The breaking of the Serbian liberals). Belgrade: Filip Višnjić.
    1992. *Kako se dogodio vodja: borba za vlast u Srbiji posle Josipa Broza* (What happened to the leader: The struggle for power in Serbia after Josip Broz). Belgrade: Filip Višnjić.
Djurović, Dragoljub, ed.
    1974. *Ustav Socijalističke Federativne Republike Jugoslavije (The Constitution of the Socialist Federal Republic of Yugoslavia).* Translated by Marko Pavičić. Belgrade: Dopisna Delavska Univerza.
Dominguez, Virginia
    1989. *People as Subject, People as Object: Selfhood and Peoplehood in Contemporary Israel.* Madison: University of Wisconsin Press.
Donia, Robert J., and John V. A. Fine, Jr.
    1994. *Bosnia and Hercegovina: A Tradition Betrayed.* New York: Columbia University Press.
Dövényi, Zoltán
    1995. "Spatial Aspects of the Refugee Issue in Hungary." In Fullerton, Sík, and Tóth 1995: 17–26.
Dragičević-Šešić, M.
    1994. *Neofolk kultura: publika i njene zvezde* (Neofolk culture: Its audience and stars). Srenski Karlovci and Novi Sad: Elementi.
Dragnich, Alex N.
    1989. "The Rise and Fall of Yugoslavia: The Omen of the Upsurge of Serbian Nationalism." *East European Quarterly* 23: 184–198.
    1992. *Serbs and Croats: The Struggle in Yugoslavia.* New York: Harcourt Brace Jovanovich.
Dragojević, Predrag
    1993. "Karikature jugoslovenskog razjedinjenja" (Cartoons of the Yugoslav disintegration). *Likovni život* (Visual arts, Zemun) 44: 62–63.
Drakulić, Slavenka
    1994. *The Balkan Express: Fragments from the Other Side of War.* New York: W. W. Norton.
Dubinskas, Frank
    1983a. "Leaders and Followers: Cultural Pattern and Political Symbolism in Yugoslavia." *Anthropological Quarterly* 56 (2): 95–99.
    1983b. "Performing Slavonian Folklore: The Politics of Reminiscence and Recreating the Past." Ph.D. diss., Stanford University.

Dugandžija, Nikola
1991. "Domet nacionalne zaokupljenosti" (The consequence of national self-absorption). In *Položaj naroda i medjunacionalni odnosi u Hrvatskoj* (National status and relations between nationalities in Croatia). In *Sociologijski i demografski aspekti* (Sociological and demographic aspects), ed. Štefica Bahtijarević and Mladen Lazić. Zagreb: Institut za društvena istraživanja Sveučilišta u Zagrebu.

Dumont, Louis
1986. *Essays on Individualism: Modern Ideology in Anthropological Perspective.* Chicago: University of Chicago Press.

Dunin, Elsie
1966. "Silent Dance of the Dinaric Mountain Area: Analysis of Purpose, Form and Style of Selected Dances." Master's thesis, University of California, Los Angeles.

Dunning, E. G., P. Murphy, and J. Williams, eds.
1988. *The Roots of Football Hooliganism: An Historical and Sociological Study.* London: Routledge & Kegan Paul.

Durham, Edith
1909. *High Albania.* London: E. Arnold.
1928. *Some Tribal Origins, Laws and Customs in the Balkans.* London: Allen & Unwin.

Dyker, David A.
1972. "The Ethnic Muslims of Bosnia—Some Basic Socio-Economic Data." *Slavonic and East European Review* 50 (119): 238–56.

Einwachter, János
1994. "Menekültek a táborban" (Refugees in the camp). In *Jönnek? Mennek? Maradnak?* (Are they coming, going, staying?), ed. Endre Sík and Judit Tóth. Budapest: YIMRG.

Ekmečić, Milorad
n.d. "The Advance of Civilization and National Politics in Bosnia and Hercegovina in the Nineteenth Century" (in Serbo-Croatian). Manuscript.

Elias, N.
1987. *Involvement and Detachment.* Oxford: Basil Blackwell.
1989. *Studien über die Deutschen.* Frankfurt am Main: Suhrkamp.

Elias, N., and E. Dunning
1986. *Quest for Excitement: Sport and Leisure in the Civilizing Process.* Oxford: Basil Blackwell.

Elwert, Georg
1989. "Nationalismus und Ethnizität." *Kölner Zeitschrift für Soziologie und Sozialpsychologie* 41 (3): 440–64.
1995. "Boundaries, Cohesion and Switching: On We-groups in Ethnic, National and Religious Form." In Šmitek and Brumen 1995: 105–21.

Epstein, A. L.
1967. "The Case Method in the Field of Law." In *The Craft of Social Anthropology*, ed. Epstein. London: Tavistock Publications.

Erdheim, Mario
1992. *Die gesellschaftliche Produktion von Unbewußtheit. Eine Einführung in den ethnopsychologischen Prozeß* (The social creation of unconsciousness: An introduction to the ethnopsychological process). Frankfurt am Main: Suhrkamp.

Eriksen, Thomas H.
1993. "Ethnicity, Race and Nation." In *The Ethnicity Reader: Nationalism, Multiculturalism and Migration*, ed. John Rex. Cambridge: Polity Press.

Erlich, Vera
1966. *Family in Transition: A Study of 300 Yugoslav Villages.* Princeton: Princeton University Press.

European Charter for Regional and Minority Languages
    1992.
Falk, Richard
    1993. Comments in "Teaching International Relations and International Organiza-
    tions in International Law Courses." *American Society of International Law Pro-
    ceedings* 87.
Felman, Shoshana, and Dori Laub
    1992. *Testimony: Crises of Witnessing in Literature, Psychoanalysis, and History.*
    New York and London: Routledge.
Ferfila, Bogomil, and Paul Philips
    1994. "Nationalism, the State and Economic Restructuring: Slovenia and the Former
    Yugoslavia." In Bučar and Kuhnle 1994.
Fischer, Gero
    1980. *Das Slowenische in Kärnten: Bedingungen der sprachlichen Sozialisation—
    eine Studie zur Sprachenpolitik* (Slovenes in Carinthia: Conditions for language so-
    cialization—A study of language politics). Klagenfurt and Celovec: Franz Kattnig.
Flere, Sergei
    1988. "Nacionalna identifikacija i preferirana nacionalna identifikacija kod mladih—
    Pitanje Jugoslovenstva" (National identification and preferred national identification
    among the young). *Migracijske Teme* 4: 439–53.
    1991. "Explaining Ethnic Antagonism in Yugoslavia." *European Sociological Re-
    view* 7 (3): 186–93. Special issue, *Eastern Europe.*
Forbes, Susan Martin
    1992. *Refugee Woman.* London: Zed.
"Framework Convention for the Protection of National Minorities"
    1994. Found in the Convention of Bosnia-Herzegovina and in the Dayton Accord,
    Annex 6.
French, H. W.
    1997. "In Zaire's Eccentric War, Serb Trains Refugee Force." *New York Times,* Janu-
    ary, 12. A1, A6.
Fullerton, Maryellen, Endre Sík, and Judit Tóth, eds.
    1995. *Refugees and Migrants: Hungary at a Crossroads.* Budapest: Yearbook of the
    International Migration Research Group-Political Science Institute of the Hungarian
    Academy of Sciences (YIMRG).
Gaber, Slavko, and Tonči Kuzmanić, eds.
    1989. *Kosovo—Srbija—Jugoslavija.* Ljubljana: UK ZSMS, Krt.
Gagnon, V. P., Jr.
    1994. "Reaction to the Special Issue of AEER, War among the Yugoslavs." *Anthro-
    pology of East Europe Review* 12 (1): 50–51.
Geertz, Clifford
    1963 "The Integrative Revolution: Primordial Sentiments and Civil Politics in the
    New States." In *Old Societies and New States,* ed. Clifford Geertz. New York: Free
    Press.
Gelhard, S.
    1992. *Ab heute ist Krieg: Der blutige Konflikt im ehemaligen jugoslawien* (From
    today on it's war: The bloody conflict in former Yugoslavia). Frankfurt am Main:
    Fischer.
Gellner, Ernest
    1964. *Thought and Change.* London: Weidenfeld & Nicolson.
    1983. *Nations and Nationalism.* London: Basil Blackwell.
    1985. *Relativism and the Social Sciences.* Cambridge: Cambridge University Press.

1987. *Culture, Identity and Politics.* Cambridge: Cambridge University Press.
1991. "Nacionalizem." In Rizman 1991: 239–65.
1995a. "On Nations and Nationalism." In Šmitek and Brumen 1995: 85–96.
1995b. "Segmentation—Reality or Myth." *Journal of the Royal Anthropological Institute* 1(4): 821–29.
Ghai, Yash
1996. "Globalization and the Politics of Rights." Presentation at Harvard Law School, Human Rights Program, December 4, 1996, Cambridge, Mass.
Gilliland, Mary Kay
1995. "Interviews with Displaced Persons and Refugees on the Island of Hvar: Themes and Introductory Findings." *Collegium Antropologicum* 19 (1): 103–11.
Giordano, Christian, Ina-Maria Greverus, and Dobrinka Kostova, eds.
1995. *Anthropological Journal on European Cultures* 4 (1). Special issue, *Ethnicity—Nationalism—Geopolitics in the Balkans.*
Giurchescu, Anca
1987. "The National Festival 'Song to Romania': Manipulation of Symbols in the Political Discourse." In *Symbols of Power: The Esthetics of Political Legitimation in the Soviet Union and Eastern Europe,* ed. Claes Arvidsson and Lars Erik Blomqvist. Stockholm: Almqvist & Wiksell International.
Gjelten, Tom
1996. *Sarajevo Daily: A City and Its Newspaper Under Siege.* New York: Harper Perennial.
Glenny, Misha
1992. *The Fall of Yugoslavia.* New York: Penguin.
Godelier, Maurice
1987. "L'analyse des processus de transition." *Information sur les sciences sociales* 26 (2): 265–83.
Goldscheider, Calvin, and Peter R. Uhlenberg
1969. "Minority Group Status and Fertility." *American Journal of Sociology* 74: 361–72.
Gossiaux, J-F.
1996. "Yougoslavie: quand la democratie n'est plus un jeu." *Annales: histoires, sciences sociales* 51 (4): 837–48.
Goudsblom, Johan
1989a. "Human History and Long-term Social Process: Towards a Synthesis of Chronology and Phaseology." In Goudsblom, Jones, and Mennell 1989.
1989b. "The Formation of Military-Agrarian Regimes." In Goudsblom, Jones, and Mennell 1989.
Goudsblom, J. E. L. Jones, and S. Mennell, eds.
1989. *Human History and Social Process.* Exeter: University of Exeter Press
Gozdziak, Elzbieta
1990. "Changing Role of Refugee Women." Manuscript.
1994. "Cyganed out of Refuge: Romanian Gypsies in Poland." In *Selected Papers on Refugee Issues,* vol. 3, ed. Jeffery L. MacDonald and Amy Zaharlick. Washington, D.C: Committee on Refugee Issues, American Anthropological Association.
Grandits, Hannes
1996. "Familie im kroatischen Dorf: Zum Wandel des Alltagslebens im Turopolje und an der Save" (Family in the Croatian village: Changes in everyday life in Turopolje and on the Sava). Ph.D. diss., Department of History, University of Graz.
Grandits, Hannes, and Siegfried Gruber
1996. "The Dissolution of the Large Complex Households in the Balkans: Was the

Ultimate Reason Structural or Cultural?" *The History of the Family: An International Quarterly* 4: 477–98.

Gray, Alan
1987. "Intermarriage: Opportunity and Preference." *Population Studies* 41: 365–79.

Greenfeld, Liah
1992. *Nationalism: Five Roads to Modernity.* Cambridge: Harvard University Press.

Grenville, J.A.S.
1987. *The Major International Treaties, 1914–1945: A History and Guide with Texts.* New York: Methuen.

Greverus, Ina-Marie
1996. "Rethinking and Rewriting the Experience of a Conference on 'War, Exile, Everyday Life.' " In Jambrešić Kirin and Povrzanović 1996.

Gulyás, Attila
1994. "Lassan megtelnek az európai menekülltáborok. A hazatérés reményét táplalni kell" (European refugee camps get filled slowly. The hope of returning home must be nourished). *Magyar Nemzet,* August 3, 1994, p. 7.

Haas, J., ed.
1990. *The Anthropology of War.* Cambridge: Cambridge University Press.

Hajnal, John.
1965. "European Marriage Patterns in Perspective." In *Population in History*, ed. D. V. Glass and D. E. C. Eversley. Chicago, Ill.: Aldine.

Hall, Brian
1994. *The Impossible Country: A Journey Through the Last Days of Yugoslavia.* Boston: D. R. Godine.

Halpern, Joel M.
1967. "The Process of Modernization as Reflected in Yugoslav Peasant Biographies." *Kroeber Anthropological Society Papers. Special Publications* 1: 109–26.
1969. "Yugoslavia: Modernization in an Ethnically Diverse State." In *Contemporary Yugoslavia*, ed. Wayne Vucinich, 316–50. Berkeley and Los Angeles: University of California Press.
1993. "Introduction." In Kideckel and Halpern 1993: 7–15.
1999. "Anthropology and Conflict: Bosnia." In *Cultural Processes and Transformations of the Central and East European Post-Communist Countries*, ed. Rajko Muršič and Borut Brumen, 119–124. Ljubljana: Etnološka stičisča (Ethnological contacts) 9.

Halpern, J. and E. Despalatovic, eds.
1981. *How the People Live: Life in the Passive Regions (Peasant Life in Southwestern Croatia, Bosnia and Hercegovina, Yugoslavia, in 1935)* by Rudolf Bičanić. Research Report No. 21, Department of Anthropology, University of Massachusetts.

Halpern, J., and W. Denny
1997. *The Thin Veneer: The Peoples of Bosnia and their Disappearing Cultural Heritage.* University Gallery, University of Massachusetts, Amherst.

Halpern, Joel M., and E. A. Hammel
1969 "Observations on the Intellectual History of Ethnology and Other Social Sciences in Yugoslavia." *Comparative Studies in Society and History* 2: 17–26.

Halpern, J., and K. Kaser
1994. "Contemporary Research on the Balkan Family, Anthropological and Historical Approaches." Association Internationale d'Etudes du Sud-Est Europeen, Septieme Congres International d'Etudes du Sud-Est Europeen, Thessalonique, Rapports, Athenes.

Halpern, Joel M., and Barbara Kerewsky-Halpern
1979. "Changing Perceptions of Roles as Husbands and Wives in Five Yugoslav

Villages." In *Europe as a Cultural Area*, ed. J. Cuisenier, 159–72. World Anthropology Series. The Hague: Mouton.

Halpern, Joel M., and David A. Kideckel

1983. "Anthropology of East Europe." *Annual Review of Anthropology* 12: 377–402.

Halpern, Joel M., and Peter Kunstädter

1967. "Laos: Introduction." In *Southeast Asian Tribes, Minorities and Nations*, ed. Peter Kunstädter, 233–58. Princeton: Princeton University Press.

Hammel, Eugene A.

1964. "Culture as an Information System." *Kroeber Anthropological Papers* 31: 83–91.

1984. "The Yugoslav Family in the Modern World: Adaptation to Change." *Journal of Family History* (Fall): 217–28.

1993a. "Demography and the Origins of the Yugoslav Civil War." *Anthropology Today* 9 (1): 4–9.

1993b. "The Yugoslav Labyrinth." In Kideckel and Halpern 1993: 39–47.

1994. "Meeting the Minotaur." *Anthropology Newsletter* 35 (4): 48.

1995. "Minotaur Redux." *Anthropology Newsletter* 36 (2): 2.

1996. "Science and Humanism in Anthropology." *Anthropology Newsletter* 36 (7).

1997. "Ethnicity and Politics: Yugoslav Lessons for Home." *Anthropology Today* 13: 5–9.

Hammersley, Martyn

1992. *What's Wrong With Ethnography? Methodological Explorations*. London and New York: Routledge.

Hann, C., and E. Dunn, eds.

1995. *Civil Society: Challenging Western Models*. London: Routledge.

Hartman, Geoffrey

1996. *The Longest Shadow*. Bloomington and Indianapolis: Indiana University Press.

Hasluck, Margaret

1954. *The Unwritten Law in Albania*. New York: Cambridge University Press.

Hayden, Robert

1992a. *The Beginning of the End of Federal Yugoslavia: The Slovenian Amendment Crisis of 1989*. Carl Beck Papers in Russian and East European Studies, no. 1001. Pittsburgh: Center for Russian and East European Studies, University of Pittsburgh.

1992b. "Constitutional Nationalism in the Formerly Yugoslav Republics." *Slavic Review* 51 (4): 654–73.

1993. "The Triumph of Chauvinistic Nationalisms in Yugoslavia." In Kideckel and Halpern 1993: 72–78.

1994a. "Recounting the Dead: The Rediscovery and Reinterpretation of Wartime Massacres in Late- and Post-Communist Yugoslavia." In *Memory and Opposition under State Socialism*, ed. Rubie S. Watson, 167–201. Santa Fe: School of American Research.

1994b. "The Constitution of the Federation of Bosnia and Herzegovina: An Imaginary Constitution for an Illusory 'Federation.'" *Balkan Forum* 2 (3): 77–91.

1995. "The Use of National Stereotypes in the Wars in Yugoslavia." In *Vampires Unstaked: National Images, Stereotypes and Myths in East Central Europe*, ed. A. Gerrits and N. Adler, 207–22. Amsterdam: North-Holland.

1996. "Imagined Communities and Real Victims: Self-Determination and Ethnic Cleansing in Yugoslavia." *American Ethnologist* 23 (4): 783–801.

1999. *Blueprints for a House Divided: The Constitutional Logic of the Yugoslav Conflicts*. Ann Arbor: University of Michigan Press.

Helsinki Watch
1993, 1994. *War Crimes in Bosnia-Herzegovina.* Vols. 1 and 2. New York: Human Rights Watch.
Hercegovina u NOB-U (II) (Hercegovina in the People's Liberation War)
1986. Sarajevo: Berdon.
Herzfeld, M.
1987. *Anthropology through the Looking-Glass: Critical Ethnography on the Margins of Europe.* Cambridge: Cambridge University Press.
1992. *The Social Production of Indifference: Exploring the Symbolic Roots of Western Bureaucracy.* Chicago: University of Chicago Press.
Hilberg, Raul
1985. *The Destruction of the European Jews.* Vol. 2. New York: Holmes & Meier.
Hírmondó
n.d. Electronic-mail communication of a Hungarian-language news bulletin.
Hobsbawm, Eric
1990. *Nations and Nationalism since 1780.* Cambridge: Cambridge University Press.
1992. *Nations and Nationalism: Myths and Realities since 1780.* New York.
Hobsbawm, Eric, and Terence Ranger, eds.
1983. *The Invention of Tradition.* Cambridge: Cambridge University Press.
Hockenos, Paul
1993. "Hungary: Black in the Land of the Magyars." In *Free to Hate: The Rise of the Right in Post-Communist Eastern Europe.* New York and London: Routledge.
Hoffman, George W.
1977. "The Evolution of the Ethnographic Map of Yugoslavia: A Historical Geographic Interpretation." In *An Historical Geography of the Balkans,* ed. F. W. Carter. New York: Academic Press.
Hofwiler, R.
1992. "Armeen, Milizen, Marodeure. Die kämpfenden Parteien und ihre Hintermänner—ein Übersicht" (Armies, militias, and marauders. The contending parties and their supporters—An overview). In *Krieg auf dem Balkan,* ed. E. Rathfelder. Reinbek: Rowohlt.
Hoptner, J. B.
1962. *Yugoslavia in Crisis, 1934–1941.* New York: Columbia University Press.
Horsetzky, Adolf
1913. *Kriegsgeschichtliche Übersicht der wichtigsten Feldzüge seit 1792* (A survey of the military history of the most important campaigns since 1792). Vienna.
Horvat, Branko
1984. *Jugoslavenska privreda (The Yugoslav Economy), 1965–1983.* Zagreb: Cankareva Založba.
Human Rights Watch/Helsinki
1994. *Open Wounds: Human Rights Abuses in Kosovo.* New York: Human Rights Watch.
1995. *Civil and Political Rights in Croatia.* New York: Human Rights Watch.
1996. *A Threat to "Stability": Human Rights Violations in Macedonia.* New York: Human Rights Watch.
Huntington, Samuel
1993. "The Clash of Civilizations?" *Foreign Affairs* 72 (3): 27–49.
Huseby-Darvas, Éva V.
1993. "Needy Guests, Reluctant Hosts? Refugee Women from the Former Yugoslavia in Hungary." *Refugee* 12 (7): 6–12.
1994a. "Nincs hová mennünk. . . . A Balkánról menekült nôk Magyarországon" (We

have nowhere to go. . . . refugee women from the Balkans in Hungary). In *Jönnek? Mennek? Maradnak?* (Are they coming, going, staying?), ed. Endre Sík and Judit Tóth. Budapest: YIMRG.

    1994b. " 'But where can we go?' Refugee Women from the Balkans from the Former Yugoslavia." In *Selected Papers on Refugee Issues*, vol. 3, ed. Jeffery L. MacDonald and Amy Zaharlick. Washington, D.C.: Committee on Refugee Issues of the American Anthropological Association.

    1995. "Puzzling Voices, Pleading Words: Refugee Women's Issues in Hungary." In Fullerton, Sík, and Tóth 1995: 153–71.

    1996. "Ambiguities of Security and Violence in Hungarian Refugee Camps during the 1990s." In *Táborlakók, Diaszpórák, Politikák* (Camp-inhabitants, diasporas, politics), ed. Endre Sík and Judit Tóth. Budapest: YIMRG.

Isaacs, Harold P.

    1975. *Idols of the Tribe: Group Identity and Political Change.* New York: Harper & Row.

Islami, Hivzi

    1989. "Demografski problemi Kosova i njihovo tumačenje" (Demographic problems of Kosovo and their explanation). In Gaber and Kuzmanić 1989: 39–66.

Ivanji, Ivan

    1997. "Persönliche, traurige Gedanken über Kriegsverbrechen" (Sad, personal reflections on war crimes). In *Verschwiegenes Serbien. Stimmen für die Zukunft* (The hidden Serbia: Voices for the future), ed. Irina Slosar, 243–64. Klagenfurt-Salzburg: Wieser.

Izetbegović, Alija

    1990. *The Islamic Declaration.* Sarajevo: N.p.

Jalušič, Vlasta, and Tonči Kuzmanić

    1989. "Posilstvo po albansko (Poskus interpretacije fenomena posilstva na Kosovu)" (Rape the Albanian way: An attempt to interpret the phenomenon of rape in Kosovo). In Gaber and Kuzmanić 1989: 213–25.

Jambrešić, Renata

    1993. "Banija: An Analysis of Ethnonymic Polarization." In Čale Feldman, Prica, and Senjković 1993.

    1996. "Narrating War and Exile Experiences." In Jambrešić Kirin and Povrzanović 1996: 63–82.

Jambrešić Kirin, Renata, and Maja Povrzanović, eds.

    1996. *War, Exile, Everyday Life: Cultural Perspectives.* Zagreb: Institute of Ethnology and Folklore Research.

Janjić, Dušan

    1994. "Od etniciteta ka nacionalizmu" (From ethnicity to nationalism). In Prošić-Dvornić 1994b: 15–33.

    1995. "Resurgence of Ethnic Conflict in Yugoslavia: The Demise of Communism and the Rise of the 'New Elites' of Nationalism." In Akhavan and Rouse 1995.

Janjić, Dušan, and Shkelzen Maliqi, eds.

    1994. *Conflict or Dialogue: Serbian-Albanian Relations and Integration of the Balkans.* Subotica: European Centre for Conflict Resolution.

JAZU (Yugoslav Academy of Arts and Sciences, now the Croatian Academy)

    1897–1918. Archives of ONŽO (Odbor za narodni život i običaje, Committee for Folk Life and Customs), stara zbirka (old collection). Zagreb.

    1898–1927. Zbornik za narodni život i običaje južnih Slavena (Journal of the folk life and customs of the Southern Slavs). III–XXVI.

Jelavich, Barbara

    1990. *History of the Balkans.* 2 vols. Cambridge: Cambridge University Press.

Jelić, I.

   1978. *Hrvatska u ratu i revolucija, 1941–1945* (Croatia in war and revolution, 1941–1945). Zagreb: Ciral.

Jelić-Butić, Fibreta

   1977. *Ustaše i Nezavisna Država Hrvatska, 1941–1945* (Ustaše and the independent state of Croatia, 1941–1945). Zagreb: Liber Školska Knjiga.

   1983. *Hvratska seljacka stranka, 1941–1945* (Croatian Peasant Party, 1941–1945). Zagreb: Ciral.

   1986. *Četnići u Hrvatskoj* (Chetniks in Croatia). Zagreb: Ciral.

Jesih, Boris, et al.

   1994. *Ethnic Minorities in Slovenia.* Ljubljana: Institute for Ethnic Studies.

Jezernik, Božidar

   1995. " 'Evropeizacija' balkanskih mest kot vzrok za njihovo 'balkanizacijo' " ("Europeanization" of the Balkan towns as the cause of their "balkanization"). *Glasnik Slovenskega etnološkega društva, Bulletin of the Slovene Ethnological Society* 35 (2–3): 2–13.

   1998. *Dežela, kjer je vse narobe: Prispevki k etnologiji Balkana* (The land where everything goes wrong: Contributions to the ethnology of the Balkans). Ljubljana: Znanstveno in publicistično središče.

Johnson, Robert A.

   1980. *Religious Assortative Marriage in the United States.* New York: Academic Press.

Jones, F. L.

   1991. "Ethnic Intermarriage in Australia, 1950–52 to 1980–82: Models or Indices?" *Population Studies* 45: 27–42.

Jovanović, Goran

   1996. "Vision ou prévision? Mouvements socio-culturels et artistiques dans la Fédération yougoslave et changements politiques dans les années 80" (Vision or prediction? Sociocultural and artistic movements in the Yugoslav Federation and political changes in the 1980s). *Autres Temps* (Other times, Paris) 48: 77–87.

   1997. "Cartoon in Art, Document of the Time." Third International Cartoon Festival (Ankara). FECO 3: 27–29.

Judah, T.

   1997. *The Serbs: History, Myth and the Destruction of Yugoslavia.* New Haven and London: Yale University Press.

Jung, Carl G., et al.

   1983. *Man and His Symbols.* Garden City, N.Y.: Doubleday.

Jung, Károly

   1978. *Az Emberélet Fordulói: Gombosi Népszokások* (Turning points of life: The customs of Gombos). Szabadka: Fórum Kiadó.

Just, Roger

   1989. "Triumph of the Ethnos." In Tonkin, McDonald, and Chapman 1989: 71–88.

Kacin-Wohinz, Milica

   1996. "Fašizem ob meji: programi raznarodovanja Slovencev in Hrvatov v Julijski krajini" (Fascism on the border: Programs for the denationalization of Slovenes and Croats in the Julian Province). Ljubljana. *Delo,* May 7–11.

Kaeckenbeeck, Georges

   1942. *The International Experiment of Upper Silesia: A Study in the Working of the Upper Silesian Settlement, 1922–1937.* New York: Oxford University Press.

Kalajić, Dragoš

   1993. *Američko zlo* (American evil). Belgrade: BIGZ.

Kaldor, Mary
1996. "Cosmopolitanism Versus Nationalism: The New Divide?" In *Europe's New Nationalism: States and Minorities in Conflict*, ed. R. Caplan and J. Feffer. New York: Oxford University Press.

Kaplan, Robert D.
1993. *Balkan Ghosts: A Journey Through History.* New York: St. Martin's Press.

Karakasidou, Anastasia
1996. *Fields of Wheat, Rivers of Blood.* Chicago: University of Chicago Press.

Karan, Milenko
1986. *Krvna Osveta* (The blood feud). Ljubljana: Partizanska Knjiga.

Kaser, Karl
1986. *Freier Bauer und Soldat. Die Militarisierung der agrarischen Gesellschaft in der kroatisch-slawonischen Militärgrenze (1535–1881)* (Free peasant and soldier. The militarization of the agrarian society of the Croatian-Slavonian military border, 1535–1881). Graz.
1994. "The Balkan Joint Family: Redefining a Problem." *Social Science History* 18 (2): 243–69.
1995a. *Familie und Verwandtschaft auf dem Balkan. Analyse einer untergehenden Kultur* (Family and kinship in the Balkans. An analysis of a disappearing culture). Vienna: Böhlau.
1995b. "Zum Problem der Erhaltung von Gewaltvorstellungen an der ehemaligen österreichischen Militärgrenze in Kroatien" (The problem of the maintenance of violent attitudes in the former Austrian Military Border in Croatia). In *Der Balkan in Europa*, ed. E. Hardten et al. Frankfurt.
1997. "Die Bedeutung des historischen Kapitals in der serbischen Gesellschaft" (The importance of historical capital in Serbian society). Manuscript.

Kaser, Karl, and Joel Halpern
1998. "Historical Myth and the Invention of Political Folklore in Contemporary Serbia." *Anthropology of East Europe Review* 16 (1): 59–68.

Kasriel, Ken
1992. "Hungary begins to 'screen' refugees from Bosnia (Hungary abandons open-door policy toward refugees from Yugoslavia)." *Christian Science Monitor,* July 20, p. 3.

Keesing, Roger M.
1981. *Cultural Anthropology: A Contemporary Perspective.* 2d ed. Fort Worth: Harcourt Brace Jovanovich College Publishers.

Kemura, Ibrahim
1986. *Uloga "Gareta" u društvenom životu Muslimana Bosne i Hercegovine (1903–1941)* (The Garet's Role in the social life of the Muslims of Bosnia and Hercegovina). Sarajevo: Veselin Maslesa.

Kerčmar, Janez
1986. "The Bilingual Education System—An Aid in Maintaining and Developing National Consciousness." *Razprave in gradivo* (Treatises and documents) 18: 114–20. Special Issue, *Education in Multicultural Societies.*

Kideckel, David A.
1983. "Introduction: Political Rituals and Symbolism in Socialist Eastern Europe." *Anthropological Quarterly* 56 (2): 52–54.
1995. "Human Rights in Former Yugoslavia." *Society for the Anthropology of Europe Bulletin* 9 (3): 1.

Kideckel, David A.
1993. "Editor's Notes." In Kideckel and Halpern 1993: 4–5.

Kideckel, David A., ed., and Joel M. Halpern, guest editor
    1993. *War Among the Yugoslavs*. Special issue of *Anthropology of East Europe Review* 11 (1–2).
Klavora, Vasja
    1993. *Blaukreuz: Die Isonzofront, Flitsch / Bovec, 1915–17* (The Blue Cross: The Soča Front, Flitsch / Bovec, 1915–17). Klagenfurt: Hermagoras Verlag.
Klemenčič, Vladimir
    1974. "Odprta meja med Jugoslavijo in Italijo in vloga manjšin" (The open border between Yugoslavia and Italy and the role of minorities). *Teorija in praksa* (Theory and praxis) 9/10: 115–25.
    1994. "Narodne manjšine kot element politične, prostorske, socialne in ekonomske stvarnosti v alpsko- jadransko-panonskem prostoru, 1–8" (National minorities as elements of political, territorial, social, and economic realities in the Alpine-Adriatic-Pannonian region. A collection of reports). In *Manjšine v prostoru Alpe-Jadran— zbornik referatov*. Ljubljana: Delovna skupnost (working group) Alpe-Jadran.
Klopčič, France
    1969. *Velika razmejitev* (The great demarcation). Ljubljana: DZS.
    1984. *O preteklosti drugače* (Differently about the past). Ljubljana: Cankarjeva založba.
Koch, Ulrich, and Goran Jovanović
    1997. "From War to Peace: Sociohistorical Context and Current Challenges for the Public Administration in the Federal Republic of Yugoslavia (Serbia and Montenegro)." *International Review of Administrative Sciences* 63: 493–508.
Koepping, Klaus-Peter
    1995. "Enlightenment and Romanticism in the Work of Adolf Bastian: The Historical Roots of Anthropology in the Nineteenth Century." In Vermeulen and Roldán 1995:75–91.
Kohn, Hans
    1955. *Nationalism: Its Meaning and History*. Princeton, N.J.: D. Van Nostrand Company.
Koljević, S.
    1980. *The Epic in the Making*. Oxford: Clarendon Press.
Kovács, András
    n.d. "Report of the Needs Assessment Mission to Eastern Slavonia Conducted by Menedék Association for Migrants." Manuscript, courtesy of the author and Zsuzsa Berencsi.
Kramer, Jane
    1991. "Letter from Europe." *New Yorker,* July 29, pp. 63–73
Krahwinkler, Harald, ed.
    1994. *Soški protokol* (Soča protocol). Celovec: Mohorjeva založba.
Kremenšek, Slavko
    1978. "Družbeni temelji razvoja slovenške etnoloske misli" (Social basis of the ethnological thought in Slovenia). In *Pogledi na etnologijo/* (Views on ethnology), ed. Angelos Bas and Slavko Kremenšek. Ljubljana: Partizanska knjiga.
Kristeva, Julia
    1991. *Strangers to Ourselves* (Etrangers a nous-meme). New York: Columbia University Press.
Krizman, B.
    1980. *Pavelić izmedju Hitlera i Musolinija* (Pavelich between Hitler and Mussolini). Zagreb: Ciral.
    1983. *Ustaše i treći Reich, II* (The Ustasha and the Third Reich). Zagreb: Ciral.

Kraljevski Zemaljski Statistički Ured u Zagrebu (Royal Statistical Office in Zagreb)
    1905. *Statistički Godišnjak Kraljevina Hrvatske i Slavonije* (Statistical yearbook for the kingdom of Croatia and Slavonia). Vol. 69. Zagreb.
Kučan, Milan
    1989. *Jugoslovanski federalizem od Speransa do razmišljanj o novi ustavi* (Yugoslav federalism from Sperans to Reflections on the New Constitution). In *Sončne in senčne strani federacije* (The bright and dark sides of federation), ed. Ciril Ribičič and Zdravko Tomac. Ljubljana: Komunist.
Kuljić, Teodor
    1978. *Fašizam* (Fascism). Belgrade: Nolit.
Kulundžić, Zvonimir
    1967. *Attentat na Stjepana Radića* (The assassination of Stjepan Radić). Zagreb: Stvarnost.
Kuper, Adam
    1994. "Culture, Identity and the Project of a Cosmopolitan Anthropology." *Man*, n.s., 29: 537–54.
Kuzmanić, Tonči
    1994a. "Wertfrei opravičevanje vojne" (Wertfrei, justifying the war). *Casopis za kritiko znanosti* (Journal of science criticism) 22 (170–71): 97–110.
    1994b. *Strikes, Trade Unions, and Slovene Independence*. In Benderly and Kraft 1994: 159–79.
Lampe, John
    1996. *Yugoslavia as History: Twice There was a Country*. Cambridge: Cambridge University Press.
Lane, Rose Wilder
    1923. *The Peaks of Shala*. New York: Harper & Brothers.
Laslett, Peter
    1983. "Family and Household as Work Group and Kin Group: Areas of Traditional Europe Compared." In *Family Forms in Historic Europe*, ed. R. Wall, J. Robin, and P. Laslett. Cambridge: Cambridge University Press.
Laušević, Mirjana
    1996. "The Ilahiya as a Symbol of Bosnian Muslim National Identity." In *Retuning Culture: Musical Changes in Central and Eastern Europe*, ed. Mark Slobin. Durham: Duke University Press.
Lazić, Mladen
    1995. "Inter-Ethnic Relations in Serbia." In Giordano, Greverus, and Kostova 1995: 63–77.
League of Nations
    1927. *Protection of Linguistic, Racial and Religious Minorities by the League of Nations, Provisions Contained in the Various International Instruments at Present in Force*. IB Minorite (listing documents). Geneva: Le Société.
Leblanc, Gérard
    1996. "Scénarios de l'horreur" (Scenarios of horror). *Mots. Les langages du politique* (Words: The languages of politics, Paris) 47: 47–71.
Lederer, Ivo J.
    1969. "Nationalism and the Yugoslavs." In *Nationalism in Eastern Europe*, ed. P. F. Sugar and I. J. Lederer. Seattle: University of Washington Press.
Lee, Michele
    1983. "Kosovo Between Yugoslavia and Albania." *New Left Review* 140: 62–91.
Lenin, V. I.
    1949. *O pravici narodov do samoodločbe* (On national rights of self-determination). In *Izbrana dela* (Selected works), 291–358. Ljubljana: Cankarjeva zalozba.

Levin, Michael D.
　1993. "Introduction." In *Ethnicity and Aboriginality: Case Studies in Ethnonationalism*, ed. Michael Lavin. Toronto: University of Toronto Press.

Lévi-Strauss, Claude
　1994. *Rasa in zgodovina* (Race and history). In *Rasa in zgodovina. Totemizem danes* (Race and history. Totemism today). Ljubljana: SKUC, Filozofska fakulteta.

Lewis, Oscar
　1959. *Five Families: Mexican Case Studies in the Culture of Poverty.* New York: Basic Books.

Lieberson, Stanley, and Mary C. Waters
　1985. "Ethnic Mixtures in the United States." *Sociology and Social Research* 70: 43–52.

Livada, Svetozar, and Darko Hudelist
　1995. "Kordunski rekvijem" (Kordun requiem). *Erasmus* 13: 15–25.

Livingston, Robert
　1959. "Stjepan Radić and the Croatian Peasant Party, 1904–1929." Ph.D. diss., Harvard University.

Lockwood, William G.
　1975. *European Moslems: Economy and Ethnicity in Western Bosnia.* New York: Academic Press.

Lonkai, Gabriella
　1995. "Egyezményekben definiált jog—rajzokból kiáltó űr" (Judicature defined in agreements—abyss crying out from drawings). Manuscript. Includes colored and black-and-white copies of refugee children's artwork.

Luković, Petar
　1992. "Šta pevaju Srbi i Hrvati" (What Serbs and Croats are singing). *Vreme* (Belgrade), November 30. Pp. 29–32.

Lumens, Valdis O.
　1993. *Himmler's Auxiliaries; the Volksdeutsche Mittlestelle and the German National Minorities in Europe, 1933–1945.* Chapel Hill: University of North Carolina Press.

Macartney, Carlile Aylmer
　1934. *National States and National Minorities.* London: Oxford University Press.

Maček, V.
　1957. *In the Struggle for Freedom.* University Park: Pennsylvania State University Press.

Macklem, Patrick
　1993. "Ethnonationalism Aboriginal Identities and the Law." In *Ethnicity and Aboriginality*, ed. Michael Levin, 9–28. Toronto: University of Toronto Press.

Magaš, Branka
　1993. *The Destruction of Yugoslavia: Tracking the Break-Up, 1980–92.* London: Verso.

Magnusson, Kjell
　1987. "The Secularization of Ideology: The Yugoslav Case." In *Symbols of Power: The Esthetics of Political Legitimation in the Soviet Union and Eastern Europe*, ed. Claes Arvidsson and Lars Eric Blomqvist, 73–84. Stockholm: Almqvist and Wiskell International.

Malcolm, Noel
　1998. *Kosovo: A Short History.* New York: New York University Press.

Mandić, O. Dominik
　1970. "Hrvatski Kockasti Grb" (The Croatian checkerboard coat of arms). *Hrvatska Revija* (Croatian review) 20: 639–52.

Maners, Lynn

1995. "The Social Lives of Dances in Bosnia and Herzegovina: Cultural Performance and the Anthropology of Aesthetic Phenomena." Ph.D. diss., University of California, Los Angeles.

Mappes-Niedick, Norbert

1995. " 'Ethnische Selbstsäuberung?' Der Exodus der Serben aus Kroatien vom 4. bis 8. August 1995" (Ethnic self-cleansing? The exodus of the Serbs from Croatia from August 4 to August 8, 1995). *Südosteuropa* 9–10: 585–92.

Maquet, Jacques

1971. *Introduction to Aesthetic Anthropology.* Addison Wesley. McCabe Module in Anthropology.

Markowitz, Fran

1988. "Rituals as Keys to Soviet Immigrant Jewish identity." In *Between Two Worlds: Ethnographic Essays on American Jewry,* ed. Jack Kugelmas. Ithaca, N.Y.: Cornell University Press.

Marmellaku, Ramadan

1976. *Albania and the Albanians.* London: Hurst.

Marokvašić, Mirjana

1991. "The Invisible Ones: A Double Role of Women in Current European Migration." In *Strangers in the World,* ed. L. Eitlinger and D. Schwartz. Bern: Hans Hubert Publishers.

Marshall, T. H.

1964. *Class, Citizenship, and Social Development.* Westport, Conn.: Greenwood Press.

Martić-Biočina, Sanja

1996. "Cross-cultural Misunderstandings: Examples of Providing Health Services to Refugees from Bosnia-Herzegovina in the Netherlands." In Jambrešić Kirin and Povrzanović 1996.

Martin, David

1946. *Ally Betrayed.* New York: Prentice-Hall.

Mártonffy, Christina

1993. "Voivodina's Hungarians have no quarrel with warring parties, look to Yugoslavia and Serbia for protection. Also: Voivodinan Hungarians caught in Serb-Croat-Muslim crossfire." In *Human Rights Briefing: Newsletter of the Hungarian-America Human Rights Council* 4 (2 [July]): 2, 3, and 8.

Marušić, Branko

1994a. *Povijest Nezavisne Države Hrvatske* (History of the Independent State of Croatia). Zagreb: P.I.P.

1994b. "Prispevki k zgodovini Tolminske" (Contributions to the history of the Tolmin region). In Krahwinkler 1994: 191–200.

Mastnak, Tomaž

1992. *Vzhodno od raja: Civilna družba pod komunizmom in po njem* (East of Eden: Civil society under communism and after). Ljubljana: DZS.

1994. "From Social Movements to National Sovereignty." In Benderly and Kraft 1994: 93–111.

Matković, Hrvoje

1972. *Svetozar Pribićević i samostalna demokratska stranka do Šestojanuarske diktature* (Svetozar Pribićević and the independent democratic party to the sixth of January dictatorship). Zagreb.

1994. *Povijest Nezavisne Države Hrvatske.* Zagreb: P.I.P.

Mazowiecki, Tadeusz

1995. "Situation of Human Rights in the Territory of the Former Yugoslavia, Special

Report on the Media. Report of the (UN) Special Rapporteur Tadeusz Mazowiecki."
Balkan Media 4 (3). *Special Focus*: 3–15.
McCaa, Robert
1989. "Isolation or Assimilation? A Log Linear Interpretation of Australian Marriages, 1947–60, 1975, and 1986." *Population Studies* 43: 155–62.
McNeill, William H.
1977. "Introduction." In Ivo Andrić, *The Bridge on the Drina*. Chicago: University of Chicago Press.
Mennell, S.
1989a. *Norbert Elias. Civilization and the Human Self-Image*. Oxford: Basil Blackwell.
1989b. "Short-term Interests and Long-term Processes: The Case of Civilization and Decivilization." In Goudsblom, Jones, and Mennell 1989.
Mersmann, Birke
1995. "'Was 'bleibt vom Heldentum?' Weiterleben nach dem Krieg" (What remains of heroism? Living after the war). *Historische Anthropologie* 24.
Merton, Robert K.
1972. "Intermarriage and the Social Structure: Fact and Theory." In *The Blending American: Patterns of Intermarriage*, ed. Milton L. Barron. Chicago: Quadrangle Books.
Mertus, Julie
1998. "Prospects for National Minorities Under the Dayton Accords—Lessons from History: The Inter-war Minorities Schemes and the 'Yugoslav Nations.' " *Brooklyn Journal of International Law* 23 (3): 689–723.
1999. *Kosovo: How Myths and Truths Started a War*. Berkeley and Los Angeles: University of California Press.
Mertus, Julie, et al., eds.
1997. *The Suitcase: Refugees Voices from Bosnia and Croatia*. Berkeley and London: University of California Press.
Mežnarić, S.
1989. "Pre-Modern and Modern National Identity and Socialist Polity: The Case of Yugoslavia." Paper presented at the Conference "The Theory of Ethnos: Achievements so Far." Croatian Ethnological Society, Kumrovec, February.
Mihailović, K., and V. Krestić
1995. "Memorandum SANU": Odgovori na kritike" (Memorandum of the Serbian Academy of Arts and Sciences [SANU]: Responses to criticisms). Belgrade: SANU.
Miheljak, Vlado
1989. "Kosovo: Od kontrarevolucije do komunizma (vmes pa še nekaj demonstracij, diferenciacij, aretacij in tankov)" (From counterrevolution to communism [with some demonstrations, differentiations, arrests and tanks in-between]). In Gaber and Kuzmanić 1989: 323–33.
1995. *Slovenci letijo v nebo: 99 razlag tisočletnih sanj* (Slovenes fly to the sky: 99 explanations of the Thousand-Year Dream). Ljubljana: Znanstveno in publicistično središče.
Miklós, Gábor
1994. "A menekültek integrálni kellene: nehéz létfeltételek, kommunikációs gondok a nagyatádi menekülttáborban" (The refugees should be integrated: Difficult living conditions, communications problems in the refugee camp of Nagyatad). *Népszabadság,* August 2, 1994.
Milić, Andjelka
1991. "Socijalna mreža porodičnih odnosa i društveni slojevi" (The social network

of family relations and social strata). In *Srbija Krajem Osamdesetih* (Serbia at the end of the 1980s), ed. Mihailo Popović. Belgrade: Institute for Sociological Research.
1996. "Nationalism and Sexism: Eastern Europe in Transition." In *Europe's New Nationalism: States and Minorities in Conflict*, ed. R. Caplan and J. Feffer. New York: Oxford University Press.

Miller, Nicholas J.
1997. *Between Nation and State: Serbian Politics in Croatia Before the First World War*. Pittsburgh: University of Pittsburgh Press.

Ministry of Information of the Republic of Serbia
1997. "Refugees in Yugoslavia in the Most Difficult Legal Position." *Serbia in the World* 66: 61–63.

Minnich, Robert Gary
1976. "Jugoslavia: kort utredning om den jugoslavisk erfaring med bilaterale avtaler i forsøket på å regulere migrasjon over nasjonale grenser" (Yugoslavia: A short report on the Yugoslav experience using bilateral agreements to regulate migration over state borders). In *Virkninger i avsenderlandet av migrasjon med og uten avtale regulering (Utredning for Rådet for Invandringsspørsmål)* (Effects in sender countries of migration with and without formal inter-state agreements [Report to the Council for Immigration Questions]), ed. R. Grønhaug, 6–21. Bergen: Universitetet i Bergen.
1988. "Speaking Slovene—Being Slovene: Verbal Codes and Collective Self-Images: Some Correlations between Kanalska dolina and Ziljska dolina." *Slovene Studies* 10 (2): 125–47.
1998. *Homesteaders and Citizens: Collective Identity Formation on the Austro-Italian-Slovene Frontier*. Bergen: Norse Publications.

Minow, Martha
1990. *Making All the Difference: Inclusion, Exclusion, and American Law*. Ithaca, N.Y.: Cornell University Press.

Miorner Wagner, Anne-Marie
1996. "Overcoming Despair and Identity Crisis through Music and Dance." In Jambrešić Kirin and Povrzanović 1996.

Mišović, Miloš
1987. *Ko je tražio republiku?* (Who sought a republic?). *Kosovo 1945–1985*. Belgrade: Narodna Knjiga.

Mladenović, O., ed.
1970. *The Yugoslav Concept of General People's Defense*. Belgrade: Medjunarodni Politika.

Moačanin, Fedor
1984. "Vojna krajina do kantonskog uredjenja, 1787" (The military frontier to the time of canton administration, 1787). In *Vojna Krajina. Povijesni pregled, historiografija, rasprave* (Historical review of the military frontier), 23–56. Zagreb.

Mojzes, Paul
1994. *Yugoslavian Inferno: Ethnoreligious Warfare in the Balkans*. New York: Continuum.

Moore, Henrietta
1994. *A Passion for Difference: Essays in Anthropology and Gender*. London: Polity Press.

Moritsch, Andreas
1994. "Uvod" (Introduction). In Krahwinkler 1994: 7–9.
1996a. "Geographische Voraussetzungen der Geschichte der Alpen-Adria-Region" (Geographic preconditions for the Alpine-Adriatic region). Working paper.

1996b. "Dem Nationalstaat entgegen" (Approaching the nation-state). Working paper.

Moritsch, Andreas, and G. Baumgartner
1992. "The Process of National Differentiation within Rural Communities in Southern Carinthia and Southern Burgenland, 1850–1940." *Comparative Studies on Governments and Non-Dominant Ethnic Groups, 1850–1940* 8: 99–143.

Morokvašić, Mirjana
1992. "Yugoslav Refugees, Displaced Persons and the Civil War." *Refugee* 11 (4): 3–6.

Morrison, F.
1996. "The Constitution of Bosnia-Herzegovina." *Constitutional Law Commentary* 13 (Summer).

Moser, Manfred
1982. "Sprachliche und soziale Identität der Slowenen in Kärnten" (Linguistic and social identity of the Slovenes in Carinthia). In *Kein einig Volk von Brüdern: Studien zum Mehrheiten / Minderheitenproblem am Beispiel Kärntens* (No single people: Studies in the majority/minority problem—the case of Carinthia), ed. F. Dotter, 16–34. Vienna: Verlag für Gesellschaftskritik.

Mousavizadeh, Nader, ed.
1996. *The Black Book of Bosnia: The Consequences of Appeasement.* New York: Basic Books.

Mrkalj, Mile
1980. Sjenicak. Karlovac: Historijski arhiv.

Muršič, Rajko
1994. "Proti površni antropologiji: Antropologi in vojskujoči se Jugoslovani" (Against superficial anthropology: Anthropologists and the Yugoslavs in war). *Časopis za kritiko znanosti* 22 (170–71): 111–26.

Mužić, Ivan
1988. *Stjepan Radić u Kraljevini Srba, Hrvata i Slovenaca* (Stjepan Radić in the kingdom of the Serbs, Croats, and Slovenes). Zagreb: Matica Hrvatska.

Nagengast, Carole
1994. "Violence, Terror, and the Crisis of the State." *Annual Review of Anthropology* 23: 109–36.

Najcevska, M., E. Simoska, and N. Gaber
1996. "Muslims, State, and Society in the Republic of Macedonia: The View from Within." In *Muslim Communities in the New Europe*, ed. G. Nonneman, T. Niblock, and B. Szakowski. Reading, Mass.: Ithaca Press.

Naumović, Slobodan
1994. "Upotreba tradicije—politička tranzicija i promena odnosa prema tradiciji u Srbiji 1987–1990" (Instrumentalization of tradition: Political transition and a change of attitude towards tradition in 1987–1990 Serbia). In Prošić-Dvornić 1994b: 95–118.

Nehru, Jawaharlal
1946. *The Discovery of India.* New York: John Day.

New York Times
For the debate between Alan Sokal and Stanley Fish, see the following articles.
1996a. May 18, sec. 1, p. 1, col. 2.
1996b. May 21, sec. A, p. 23, col. 1.
1996c. May 26, sec. 4, p. 6, col. 1.
1996d. June 8, sec. 1, p. 18, col. 6.
1996e. June 22, sec. A, p. 18, col. 5.
1996f. July 16, sec. A, p. 17, col. 1.

Ninčić, Roksanda, and Boris Vekić
1995. "Srbi u Hrvatskoj" (Serbs in Croatia). *Vreme* (Belgrade), August 28, pp. 8–11.
Noelte, Earl
1992. "Comments on Hungary." *Refuge* 12 (4): 4–6.
Nova revija
1987. "Prispevki za slovenski nacionalni program" (Contributions to the Slovene national program). *Nova revija* (New Review) 57.
Oltay, Edith
1993. "UN Concerned about Voivodina Hungarians." *RFE/RL Report*, August 19.
Osmančević, Samir
1994. "Prinzip Hoffnungslosigkeit." *Časopis za kritiko znanosti* 22 (170–71): 57–71.
Pagnini, Deanna L., and S. Philip Morgan
1990. "Intermarriage and Social Distance Among U.S. Immigrants at the Turn of the Century." *American Journal of Sociology* 96: 405–32.
Pajić, Zoran
1993. *Violation of Fundamental Rights in the Former Yugoslavia*. London: David Davies Memorial Institute of International Studies.
1995. "Bosnia-Herzegovina: From Multiethnic Coexistence to 'Apartheid' and Back." In Akhavan and Rouse 1995.
Parin, P.
1991. *Es ist Krieg und wir geben hin* (It is war and we join in). Berlin: Rowohlt.
Paris, Edmond
1961. *Genocide in Satellite Croatia*. Chicago: American Institute of Balkan Affairs.
Pavičić, Stjepan.
1953. *Podrijetlo hrvatskih i srpskih naselja i govora u Slavoniji* (The origins of Croatian and Serbian settlements and dialects in Slavonia). Zagreb: Jugoslavenska Akademija Znanosti i Umjetnosti.
Pavličević, Dragutin
1974. "Bune u bivsoj Banskoj krajini 1883" (Rebellions in the former Banska frontier). *Historijski zbornik* (Historical review, Zagreb). 25–26: 75–133.
1980. *Narodni pokret 1883 u Hrvatskoj* (The national movement of 1883 in Croatia). Zagreb: Liber.
Pawlikowski, Paul
1992. "Serbian Epics." Documentary. Edited by Nigel Williams. London: Bookmark, BBC.
Pesek, Albinca
1995. "Music as a Tool to Help Refugee Children and Their Mothers: The Slovenian Case." In Jambrešić Kirin and Povrzanović 1996.
Pešić, Vesna
1996. *Serbian Nationalism and the Origins of the Yugoslav Crisis*. Washington, D.C.: United States Institute of Peace.
Petrović, Edit
1995. "Ethnicity Deconstructed: The Breakup of the Former Yugoslavia and Personal Reflexions on Nationalism, Identity and Displacement." *Culture* 15 (2): 117–24.
Petrović, Edit, and Andrei Simić
1990. "Montenegrin Colonists in Vojvodina: Objective and Subjective Measures of Ethnicity." *Serbian Studies* 5 (4): 5–20.
Petrović, Ruža
1970. "Ethnically Mixed Marriages in Yugoslavia." *Sociologija* 12 (selected articles): 185–200.
1973. "Nationality Structure of the Yugoslav Population." *Yugoslav Survey* 14 (1): 1–22.

1985. "Etnički mešovitii brakovi u Jugoslaviji" (Ethnically mixed marriages in Yugoslavia). Belgrade: Institut za Sociološka Istraživanja Filosofskog Fakulteta.

1986a. "Ethnically Mixed Marriages in Yugoslavia." *Sociologija* 28 (Suppl.): 229–39.

1986b. "Regionalne razlike u rasprostranjenosti celibata u Jugoslaviji" (Regional differences in the prevalence of celibacy). *Sociologija* 28: 373–83.

1987. *Migracije u Jugoslaviji* (Migrations in Yugoslavia). Belgrade: Institut društvenih nauka (Institute of Social Sciences).

1991. "The Ethnic Identity of Parents and Children." *Yugoslav Survey* 32 (1): 63–76.

Petrović, Ruža, and Marina Blagojević

1989. *Seobe Srba i Crnogoraca sa Kosova i iz Metohije* (Migrations of Serbs and Montenegrins from Kosovo and Metohia). Belgrade: Serbian Academy of Sciences and Arts.

Physicians for Human Rights

1996. *War Crimes in the Balkans, Medicine Under Siege in the Former Yugoslavia, 1991–1995.* PHR: Boston.

Pinson, Mark

1994. "The Muslims of Bosnia-Herzegovina Under Austro-Hungarian Rule, 1878–1918." In *The Muslims of Bosnia-Herzegovina*, ed. Mark Pinson. Cambridge: Harvard University Press.

Pipa, Arshi, and Sami Repishti

1984. *Studies on Kosovo.* East European Monographs, 155. New York: Columbia University Press.

Pirjevec, Jože

1995. *Jugoslavija 1918–1992: Nastanek, razvoj ter razpad Karadjordjevićeve in Titove Jugoslavije* (Yugoslavia, 1918–1992: Origins, development, and disintegration of Karadjordjević's and Tito's Yugoslavia). Koper: Založba Lipa.

Plestina, Dijana M.

1987. "Politics and Inequality: A Study of Regional Disparities in Yugoslavia." Ph.D. diss., University of California, Berkeley.

Podlipnig, Karl

1994. "Gospodarske povezave zgornje Soške, zogrnje Savske, spodnje Ziljske in Kanalske doline skozi stoletja" (Economic connections over the centuries between the upper Soča, the upper Sava, and the lower Gail valleys). In Krahwinkler 1994: 209–14.

Popović, Nevesna

1993. "Putevi i smernice nove srpske kulture" (Paths and directions of the new Serbian culture). *Naše ideje* (Our ideas) 1 (1): 70.

Portelli, A.

1991. *The Death of Luigi Trastulli and Other Stories.* Albany: State University of New York Press.

Poulton, H.

1991. *The Balkans: Minorities and States in Conflict.* London: Minority rights Publications.

1995. *Who Are the Macedonians?* London: Hurst.

Povrzanović, Maja

1995. "Crossing the Borders: Croatian War Ethnographies." *Narodna umjetnost* (Folk arts) (Zagreb) 32 (1): 91–106.

Prica, Ines

1990. " 'Novi val' kao anticipacija krize" ("New Wave" as an anticipation of the crises). *Etnološka tribina* (Zagreb) 13: 23–30.

1993. "People Displaced." In Čale Feldman, Prica, and Senjković 1993.

Pridonoff, Eric L.
1955. *Tito's Yugoslavia.* Washington, D.C.: Public Affairs Press.
Prošić-Dvornić, Mirjana
1990. "Kriza i svakodnevni život na primeru Beograda" (Crisis and everyday life: The case of Belgrade). *Etnološka tribina* (Zagreb) 13: 47–61.
1991. "Sa nama nema neizvosnosti"—politicki predizborni plakat u Srbiji 1990" ("We do not keep you in suspense"—Political election posters in Serbia, 1990). *Narodna umjetnost* (Zagreb) 28: 349–75.
1993a. "Another Serbia": Pacifist and Feminist Movement." In Prošić-Dvornić 1994b.
1993b. "Enough! Student Protest '92: The Youth of Belgrade in Quest of 'Another Serbia.' " In Kideckel and Halpern 1993: 127–37.
1994a. " 'Druga Srbija': mirovni i ženski pokret" ("Another Serbia": Pacifist and feminist movements). In Prošić-Dvornić 1994b: 179–99.
1996. "Laughter in Tears: Today's Humour in Yugoslavia." In *Laughter and Tears in the Balkan Cultures. International Ethnological Symposium,* ed. E. Karpodini-Dimitriadi. Athens: Doukas School.
1998. "The Topsy Turvy Days Were There Again: Student and Civil Protests in Belgrade and Serbia, 1996/1997." *The Anthropology of East Europe Review* 16 (1): 77–98.
———, ed.
1994b. *Kulture u tranziciji* (Cultures in transition). Belgrade: Knjižara Plato.
Puhovski, Žarko
1995. War report. 35. July/August 1995.
Pušić, Vesna
1995. "Use of Nationalism and the Politics of Recognition." In Giordano, Greverus, and Kostova 1995: 43–61.
Radelić, Zdenko
1996. *Hrvatska seljačka stranka, 1941–1950* (The Croatian Peasant Party, 1941–1950). Zagreb: Hrvatski Institut za Povijest (Croatian Institute of History).
Radić, Ante
1897. "Osnova za sabiranje i proučavanje gradje o narodnom životu" (Outline for the collection and study of materials about folk life). *Zbornik za narodni život i običaje južnih Slavena* 2: 1–88.
Ramet, Pedro (*see also* Ramet, Sabrina P.)
1984. "Yugoslavia and the Threat of Internal and External Discontent." *Orbis* 28 (1): 109–20.
———, ed. 1985. *Yugoslavia in the 1980s.* Boulder, Colo.: Westview Press.
Ramet, Sabrina P.
1992. *Nationalism and Federalism in Yugoslavia, 1962–1991.* Bloomington: University of Indiana Press.
1996. *Balkan Babel: The Disintegration of Yugoslavia from the Death of Tito to Ethnic War.* Boulder, Colo.: Westview Press.
Ramet, Sabrina P., and Ljubisa Adamovich, eds.
1995. *Beyond Yugoslavia: Politics, Economics, and Culture in a Shattered Community.* Boulder, Colo.: Westview Press.
Rathfelder, E., ed.
1992. *Krieg auf dem Balkan* (War in the Balkans). Reinbek: Rowohlt.
Rauchensteiner, Manfried
1994. "Vojna ob Soči iz vidika avstrijskega zgodovinarja" (War on the Soč from the perspective of Austrian historians). In Krahwinkler 1994: 15–26.

Rebić, Adalbert (Office for Displaced Persons of the Republic of Croatia)

1995. "Prognanici i izbegljice u svijetu i u nas" (Deportees and refugees, internationally and locally). In *Progonstvo i povratak: psihosocijalne i razvojne odrednice progonstva i mogućnosti povratka hrvatskih prognanika* (Expulsion and return, psychosocial and developmental aspects of deportation and the possibilities for the return of Croatian refugees), ed. Ivan Rogic et al. Zagreb.

Redfield, Robert

1956. *Peasant Society and Culture: An Anthropological Approach to Civilization.* Chicago: University of Chicago Press.

Reineck, Janet

1986. "The Place of the Dance Event in Social Organization and Social Change Among Albanians in Kosovo, Yugoslavia." *UCLA Journal of Dance Ethnology* 10: 27–38.

1990. "The Past as Refuge: Gender, Migration and Ideology Among the Albanians." Ph.D. diss., University of California, Berkeley.

1993. "Seizing the Past, Forging the Present: Changing Visions of Self and Nation among the Kosovo Albanians." In Kideckel and Halpern 1993: 85–92.

Reissmüller, J. G.

1992. *Der Krieg vor unserer Haustür* (War on our doorstep). Stuttgart: DVA.

Reljić, Dušan

1994. "Rückkehr in die Vergangenheit. Medien im ehemaligen Jugoslawien" (Back to the past: Media in former Yugoslavia). *Medium* (Frankfurt am Mein) 2: 18–21.

Remington, R. A.

1979. "Balkanization of the Military: Party, Army and People's Militias in Southern Europe." In *Politics and Modernization in Southeastern Europe*, ed. K. E. Naylor. Boulder, Colo.: Westview Press.

"Report of the Council of the League of Nations" (also known as the "Adatci Report")

1929. In appendix to P. de Azcarate, "Protection of National Minorities," Occasional Paper No. 5, Carnegie Endowment for International Peace, June 1967.

Rezun, Miron

1995. *Europe and War in the Balkans: Toward a New Yugoslav Identity.* Westport, Conn.: Praeger.

Ribičič, Ciril, and Zdravko Tomac

1989. *Sončne in senčne strani federacije* (The Bright and dark sides of federation). Ljubljana: Komunist.

Rice, Timothy

1996. "The Dialectics of Economics and Aesthetics in Bulgarian Music." In *Retuning Culture, Musical Changes in Central and Eastern Europe*, ed. Mark Slobin. Durham: Duke University Press.

Richard, Madeline A.

1991. *Ethnic Groups and Marital Choices: Ethnic History and Marital Assimilation in Canada, 1871 and 1971.* Vancouver: University of British Columbia.

Rihtman-Auguštin, Dunja

1987. *Struktura tradicijskog mišljenja* (Structure of traditional thought). Zagreb: Školska knjiga.

1990. "O dekristijanizaciji narodne kulture" (On the dechristianization of popular culture). *Etnološka tribina* (Zagreb) 13: 9–16.

1992. "Etnologija socijalizma i poslije" (Ethnology: After socialism). *Etnološka tribina* (Zagreb) 15: 81–89.

1994. "Božicni prijepori" (Christmas controversies). *Etnološka tribina* 17: 75–89.

1995a. "National Bias in Anthropology." In Šmitek and Brumen 1995: 97–103.

1995b. "Victims and Heroes: Between Ethnic Values and Construction of Identity." *Ethnologia Europea* 25 (1): 61–67.

1997. "Zašto i otkad se grozimo Balkana?" (Why and since when do we dread the Balkans). *Erazmus* 19: 27–35.

Rizman, Rudi

1989. "O sociološkem razumevanju naroda in nacionalnosti" (On sociological understanding of nation and nationhood). In Gaber and Kuzmanić 1989.

———, ed.

1991. *Studije o etnonacionalizmu* (Studies on ethnonationalism). Ljubljana: Krt.

Robinson, Jacob, et al.

1943. *Were the Minorities Treaties a Failure?* New York: Institute of Jewish Affairs of the American Jewish Congress and the World Jewish Congress.

Rogel, Carole

1994. "In the Beginning: The Slovenes from the Seventh Century to 1945." In Benderly and Kraft 1994: 3–21.

Rogers, Susan, et al., eds.

1995. *European Anthropologies: The Status of the Profession.* Washington, D.C.: American Anthropological Association.

Roksandić, Drago

1991a. *Srbi u Hrvatskoj od 15. stoljeca do naših dana* (Serbs in Croatia from the fifteenth century to today). Zagreb: Vjesnik.

1991b. "Srbi u Hrvatskoj. Pitanja o pola stoljeća povijesti 1941–1990" (Serbs in Croatia: Questions about the half century of history). In *Položaj naroda i medjunacionalni odnosi u Hrvatskoj. Sociologijski i demografski aspekti*, ed. Štefica Bahtijarević and Mladen Lazić. Zagreb: Institut za društvena istraživanja Sveučilišta u Zagrebu.

Ronstrom, Owe

1991. "Folklor: Staged Folk Music and Dance Performances of Yugoslavs in Stockholm." *Yearbook for Traditional Music* 69–77.

Rorty, Richard

1997. "Sentimental Education." In *The Human Rights Reader*, ed. M. R. Ishay. New York and London: Routledge.

Ross Johnson, A.

1973. "Yugoslav Total National Defense." *Survival* 15 (3/4): 54–58.

Roth, Paul A.

1989. "Ethnography without Tears." *Current Anthropology* 30 (5): 555–61.

Roth, Klaus

1995. "Zeit, Geschichtlichkeit und Volkskultur im postsozialistischen Südosteuropa" (Time, historicity, and folk culture in postsocialist Southeast Europe). *Zeitschrift für Balkanologie* (Journal of Balkan studies, Berlin) 31 (1): 31–45.

Rothenberg, Gunter E.

1960. *The Austrian Military Border in Croatia, 1522–1747.* Vol. 42. Urbana: University of Illinois Press.

1966. *The Austrian Military Border in Croatia, 1740–1881.* Chicago: University of Chicago Press.

Rupel, Dimitrij

1994. "Slovenia's Shift from the Balkans to Central Europe." In Benderly and Kraft 1994: 183–200.

Rusinow, Dennison

1974. "Yugoslavia's Return to Leninism." *American Universities Fieldstaff Reports*, Southeast Europe Series 21, no. 1.

1977. *The Yugoslav Experiment, 1948–1974.* Berkeley and Los Angeles: University of California Press.
1980. "The Yugoslav Concept of All-National Defense." *American Universities Field Staff Reports*, Southeast Europe Series, no. 19.
1982. *The Yugoslav Experiment, 1948–1974.* London: M.S.P.C.

Sacirbey, Muhamed
1996. "A Year after Dayton: Has the Bosnian Peace Process Worked?" Remarks at Yale Law School, Conference of the Orville Schell Center for International Human Rights and the Council on Foreign Relations, November 16.

Sahlins, Peter
1989. *Boundaries: The Making of France and Spain in the Pyrenees.* Berkeley and Los Angeles: University of California Press.

Salimović, S.
1994. "Biznis Bosanskog sevdaha: Bosna slobodi pjeva" (The business of the Bosnian *sevdah:* Bosnia sings about freedom). *Večernje Novine* (Evening news) 24 (April 29): 13.

Samary, Catherine
1995. *Yugoslavia Dismembered.* Trans. Peter Drucker. New York: Monthly Review Press.

Sardoć, Dorće
1983. *Tigrova Sled* (In the path of the TIGR movement). Koper: Lipa.

Sardon, Jean-Paul
1991. "Mariage et divorce en Europe de l'Est" (Marriage and divorce in Eastern Europe). *Population* 46: 547–98.

Sartre, Jean-Paul
1946. *No Exit and Three Other Plays.* New York: Vintage Books.

Savezni Zavod Statistiki (Federal Statistical Office)
1961a–1989a. *Demografska Statistika* (Demographic statistics). Belgrade: Savezni Zavod Statistiki.
1965b. *Popis Stanovnistva 1961* (1961 population census). Vol. 1. Belgrade: Savezni Zavod Statistiki.
1963c, 1973c, 1986c, 1990c. *Statistički Godišnjak SFRJ* (Statistical yearbook of Yugoslavia). Belgrade: Savezni Zavod Statistiki.

Schippers, Thomas K.
1995. "A History of Paradoxes: Anthropologies of Europe." In Vermeulen and Roldán 1995: 234–46.

Schopflin, G.
1993. "The Rise and Fall of Yugoslavia." In *The Politics of Ethnic Conflict Regulation: Case Studies of Protracted Ethnic Conflicts*, ed. J. McGarry and B. O'Leary. New York: Routledge.

Schwartz, Jonathan M.
1993. "Macedonia: A Country in Quotation Marks." *Anthropology of East Europe Review* 11 (1 and 2): 93–99.
1994. " 'Mosaic' as Metaphor of (Multi) cultural Space: The Balkans and Canada as Examples." *Migration* 23 (4): 243–60.
1995 "The Petrified Forests of Symbols: Deconstructing and Envisioning Macedonia." *Anthropological Journal on European Cultures* (4): 9–24.
1996. *An Essay on the Making of Macedonia.* Copenhagen: Højbje Intervention Press.

Schwertfeger, Margaret M.
1982. "Interethnic Marriage and Divorce in Hawaii: A Panel Study of 1968 First Marriages." *Marriage and Family Review* 5: 49–59.

Sedmak, Drago
1994. "Ekonomska in politična migracija prebivalstva na Bovškem v letih 1850 do 1940" (Economic and political migration of the Bovec population from 1850 to 1940). In Krahwinkler 1994: 79–128.
Sekulić, Duško, Garth Massey, and Randy Hodson
1994. "Who Were the Yugoslavs? Failed Sources of a Common Identity in the Former Yugoslavia." *American Sociological Review* 59: 83–97.
Seligman, A.
1992. *The Idea of Civil Society.* New York: Free Press.
Sells, Michael A.
1996. *The Bridge Betrayed: Religion and Genocide in Bosnia.* Berkeley and Los Angeles: University of California Press.
Seers, D., et al., eds.
1979. *Underdeveloped Europe.* Sussex: Harvester Press.
Senjković, R.
1995. "Ideologies and Iconographies. Croatia in the Second Half of the 20th Century." *Collegium Antropologicum* (Zagreb) 19 (1): 53–63.
Serbo-Croatian Heroic Songs
1974. Collection by Milman Parry. Translation, with introduction, notes and commentary by Albert B. Lord. Vol. 3. Cambridge: Harvard University Press.
Seroka, Jim, and Vukašin Pavlovic, eds.
1992. *The Tragedy of Yugoslavia: The Failure of Democratic Transformation.* Armonk, N.Y.: M. E. Sharpe.
Sherer, Stan, and Marjorie Senechal
1997. *Long Life to Your Children! A Portrait of High Albania.* Amherst: University of Massachusetts Press.
Shotter, John
1993. *Cultural Politics of Everyday Life: Social Constructionism, Rhetoric and Knowing of the Third Kind.* Buckingham: Open University Press.
1994. "Psychology and Citizenship: Identity and Belonging." In *Citizenship and Social Theory*, ed. Bryan S. Turner. London: Sage.
Shoup, Paul
1968. *Communism and the Yugoslav National Question.* New York: Columbia University Press.
1989. "Crisis and Reform in Yugoslavia." *Telos,* no. 70 (Spring): 130–47. Special Issue, *Perestroika in Eastern Europe.*
Šijaković-Blagojević, Marina
1986. "Obrazovna struktura Jugoslovenskog stanovnistva" (Educational structure of Yugoslavia's population). *Sociologija* 28: 43–62.
Sík, Endre
1992a. "A menekültekkel kapcsolatos elôitéletesség növekedésének elkerülhetetlensége" (The inevitability of growing prejudice related to refugees). In Sík 1992b.
1994. "Reconversion in the Course of Migration: Transylvanian Forced Migrants in Hungary." *Sociological Review,* no. 2: 160–70.
———, ed.
1992b. *Menekülôk, Vándorlók, Szerencsét Próbálók.* Budapest: YIMRG.
Silber, Laura, and Alan Little
1995. *The Death of Yugoslavia.* London: Penguin Books.
Simić, Andrei
1975. *The Ethnology of Traditional and Complex Societies.* Washington, D.C.: American Association for the Advancement of Science.

1979. "Commercial Folk Music in Yugoslavia: Idealization and Reality." *Journal of the Association of Graduate Dance Ethnologists* (UCLA) 2: 37.

1991. "Obstacles to the Development of a Yugoslav National Consciousness: Ethnic Identity and Folk Culture in the Balkans." *Journal of Mediterranean Studies* 1 (1): 18–36.

1993. "The First and Last Yugoslav: Some Thoughts on the Dissolution of a State." In Kideckel and Halpern 1993: 16–22.

1994. "The Civil War in Yugoslavia: Do Ostensibly High Rates of Intermarriage Obviate Hatreds as a Cause?" *Anthropology of East Europe Review* 12 (2): 33–34.

Simić, Andrei, and Glynn Custred
1982. "Modernity and the American Family: A Cultural Dilemma." *International Journal of Sociology of the Family* 12: 163–72.

Simić, Marko
1996. *Po sledeh Soške fronte* (Along the Soča front). Ljubljana: Založba Mladinska knjiga.

Simić, Vladimir
1994. "Iz pravne zgodovine Tolminskega" (From the legal history of Tolmin). In Krahwinkler 1994: 201–8.

Simić, Zvonko
1982. "Narodi, narodnosti, Jugosloveni" (Nations, Nationalities, Yugoslavs). *Nin* (Belgrade), February 21, pp. 8–10.

Singleton, Fred
1976. *Twentieth-Century Yugoslavia*. New York: Columbia University Press.

Širok, Mojca
1996. "Aleksandrinke—Čezmorske dojilje" (Alexandrians—overseas wet nurses). *Mladina* (Ljubljana), March 12–19.

Škaljić, Abdulah
1979. *Turcizmi u srpskohrvatskom jeziku* (Turkicisms in the Serbo-Croatian language). 4th ed. Sarajevo: Svjetlost.

Sluga, Meta, ed.
1979. *Zgodovina Slovencev* (History of the Slovenes). Ljubljana: Cankarjeva založba.

Šmitek, Zmago
1995. "Neevropska etnologija v Sloveniji ali koliko daleč vidimo" (Non-European ethnology in Slovenia or "How Far Can We See?"). In *Razvoj slovenske etnologije od Štreklja in Murka do sodobnih etnoloških prizadevanj* (The development of Slovene ethnology from Štrekelj and Murko to contemporary ethnological efforts), ed. Rajko Muršič and Mojca Ramšak. Ljubljana: Slovensko etnološko društvo (Slovene ethnological society).

Šmitek, Zmago, and Borut Brumen, eds.
1995. *MESS* (Mediterranean Ethnological Summer School). Ljubljana: Slovensko etnološko društvo.

Šmitek, Zmago, and Bozidar Jezernik
1995. "The Anthropological Tradition in Slovenia." In Vermeulen and Roldán 1995: 171–83.

Smith, Herbert L., and Maurice A. Garnier
1987. "Scaling Via Models for the Analysis of Association: Social Background and Educational Careers in France." *Sociological Methodology* 17: 205–45.

Smith, Richard M.
1981. "The People of Tuscany and Their Families: Medieval or Mediterranean?" *Journal of Family History* 6: 107–28.

Smolicz, Jerzy J.
  1979. *Culture and Education in a Plural Society.* Adelaide: University of Adelaide Curriculum Development Center.
Soldo, J.
  1964. *Čitluk i Brotnjo: Istorija.* Zagreb: Privredni Vjesnik.
  n.d. "Mali rat u Brotnju" (The little war in Brotnjo). Manuscript.
Spier, F.
  1993. "Civilisation Theory and Environmental Problems." Lecture held at conference, "Social Functions of Nature." Chantilly, France, March 8–12.
Špoljar-Vržina, Sanja, S. Martić-Biočina, and M. K. Gilliland
  1995. "Beyond the Basic Needs—The Refugee and Displaced Person Families on the Island of Hvar (Croatia)." *Collegium Antropologicum* (Zagreb) 19 (1): 113–19.
Starčević, A.
  1941. *Misli i pogledi* (Thoughts and views). Zagreb: Ciral.
Stein, Gary C.
  1987. "The Biological Basis of Ethnocentrism, Racism and Nationalism in National-Socialism." In *The Sociobiology of Ethnocentrism,* ed. Reynolds, Falger, and Vine, 251–67. London: Croom Helm.
Stojkov, Todor
  1970. "O takozvanom Ličkom ustanku 1932" (On the so-called Lika revolt, 1932). *Casopis za suvremenu povijest* (Magazine for contemporary history) 2: 167–80.
Stokes, Gale
  1993. *The Walls Came Tumbling Down: The Collapse of Communism in Eastern Europe.* Oxford: Oxford University Press.
  ———, ed. *From Stalinism to Pluralism: A Documentary History of Eastern Europe since 1945.* 2d ed. Oxford: Oxford University Press.
Stokes, G., et al.
  1996. "Instant History: Understanding the Wars of Yugoslav Succession." *Slavic Review* 55 (1): 136–60.
Stolcke, Verena
  1995. "Talking Culture: New Boundaries, New Rhetorics of Exclusion in Europe." *Current Anthropology* 36: 1–24.
Stone, J.
  1933. *Regional Guarantees of Minority Rights; A Study of Minorities Procedure in Upper Silesia.* New York: Macmillan.
Stubbs, Paul
  1996. "Creative Negotiations. Concepts and Practice of Integration of Refugees, Displaced People and Local Communities in Croatia." In Jambrešić Kirin and Povrzanović 1996.
Sugar, Peter F.
  1969. "External and Domestic Roots of Eastern European Nationalism." In *Nationalism in Eastern Europe,* ed. Peter F. Sugar and Ivo J. Lederer. Seattle: University of Washington Press.
Sundhaussen, Holm
  1983. *Wirtschaftsgeschichte Kroatiens im nationalsozialistischen Großraum 1941–1945* (The economic history of Croatia in the greater arena of National Socialism). Studien zur Zeitgeschichte (Studies in temporal history) 23. Stuttgart: Deutsche Verlags-Aushalt.
  1993. *Experiment Jugoslawien. Von der Staatsgründung bis zum Staatszerfall.* (The Yugoslav experiment: From the birth of the state to its dissolution). Mannheim, Leipzig, Zurich, Vienna.

1995. *Das Ustascha-Syndrom. Ideologie—historische Tatsachen—Folgen. Das ju-goslawische Disaster* (The Ustashe syndrome: Ideology—historical facts—consequences. The Yugoslav disaster). Ed. Reinhard Lauer and Werner Lehfeldt. Wiesbaden.

Swaan, A. de
1992. "De staat van wandaad. Over the vervagende grenzen tussen oorlogvoering en misdaadbestrijding" (The declining difference between warfare and crime prevention). In *Idem, Twee stukken* (Two essays). Amsterdam: Het Spinhuis.

Szasz, Paul
1996. "A Year after Dayton: Has the Bosnian Peace Process Worked?" Speech at Yale Law School, Conference of the Orville Schell Center for International Human Rights and the Council on Foreign Relations, November 15.

Szporluk, Roman
1991. "Komunizem in nacionalizem" (Communism and nationalism). In Rizman 1991: 345–63.

Tambiah, Stanley
1986. *Sri Lanka: Ethnic Fratricide and the Dismantling of Democracy.* Chicago: University of Chicago Press.
1989. "Ethnic Conflict in the World Today." *American Ethnologist* 16: 335–49.

Tanner, Marcus.
1997. *Croatia: A Nation Forged in War.* New Haven: Yale University Press.

Taylor, C.
1992. *Multiculturalism and the Politics of Recognition.* Princeton: Princeton University Press.

Televizija Sarajevo
1992. "Vojnik Sreće" (The Soldier of Fortune). Music Video.

Temperley, H. W. V., ed.
1920–24. *A History of the Peace Conference of Paris.* London: H. Frowde, and Hodder & Stoughton.

Thompson, Mark
1992. *A Paper House: The Ending of Yugoslavia.* New York: Pantheon Books.
1994. *Forging War: The Media in Serbia, Croatia, and Bosnia-Hercegovina.* London: Article 19.

Todorova, Maria
1994. "The Balkans: From Discovery to Invention." *Slavic Review* 53: 453–82.
1997. *Imagining the Balkans.* New York: Oxford University Press.

Tomasevich, Jozo
1955. *Peasants, Politics and Economic Change in Yugoslavia.* Stanford: Stanford University Press.
1975. *The Chetniks.* Stanford: Stanford University Press.

Tomc, Gregor
1994. "The Politics of Punk." In Benderly and Kraft 1994: 113–34.

Tömöry, Ákos
1994. "Camping of Refugees . . ." *HVG*, August 13. P. 87.

Tonkin, Elizabeth, Maryon McDonald, and Malcolm Chapman, eds.
1989. *History and Ethnicity.* London: Routledge.

Tóth, Judit
n.d. *Lawful Residence in Hungary; Lawful Employment and Drawing Incomes in Hungary; How to Settle in Hungary.* Budapest: Menedék.
1995. "Who Are the Desirable Immigrants in Hungary under the Newly Adopted Laws?" In Fullerton, Sík, and Tóth 1995: 57–68.

Tóth, Olga
1992. "Erdélyi menekült nôk Magyarországon 1989-ben" (Transylvanian refugee women in Hungary in 1989). In Sík 1992b.
Tóth, Péter Pál
1995. "Refugees, Immigrants and New Citizens in Hungary, 1988–1992." In Fullerton, Sík, and Tóth 1995: 69–82.
Treaty Between the Principal Allied and Associated Powers (the British Empire, France, Italy, Japan and the United States), and the Serb-Croat-Slovene State
1992. Signed at St. Germain-en-Laye, Sept. 10, 1919, chap. 1, art. 3, 226 Consol. T.S. 8, 182–91.
Tuchman, Barbara
1984. *The March of Folly.* New York: Knopf.
Tudjman, Franjo
1990a. *Bespuća povijesne zbiljnosti* (Wastelands of historical reality). Zagreb: Nakladni Zavod Matice Hrvatske.
1990b. "Izlaganje Dr. Franje Tudjmana predsjednika Republike Hrvatske" (Address of Dr. Franjo Tudjman, president of the Republic of Croatia). *Glasnik HDZ* (Journal of the Croatian Democratic Union) 15 (August 6): 8–10.
Turner, Bryan S.
1993. "Contemporary Problems in the Theory of Citizenship" In *Citizenship and Social Theory,* ed. Bryan S. Turner. London: Sage.
Turner, Victor
1974. *Dramas, Fields and Metaphors: Symbolic Action in Human Society.* Ithaca, N.Y.: Cornell University Press.
Udovički, Jasminka, and James Ridgeway, eds.
1995. *Yugoslavia's Ethnic Nightmare: The Inside Story of Europe's Unfolding Ordeal.* New York: Lawrence Hill Books.
Underwood, Anne
1989. "Hungary: It's America to Refugees." *Christian Science Monitor,* April 11, p. 4.
United Nations
1950. *Convention for the Protection of Human Rights and Fundamental Freedoms.* Adopted November 4, 213 U.N.T.S. 222.
1993. "World Conference on Human Rights." In *The Vienna Declaration and Platform for Action,* June 1993, DPI/1394–39399-August 1993–20M. New York: United Nations.
1995. *The General Framework Agreement for Peace in Bosnia-Herzegovina.* U.N. Doc. A/50/790-S/1995/999 (Dayton, November 21, 1995) & 35 I.L.M. 89 (1996) (Paris, December 14, 1995).
Ustav Republike Hrvatske (Constitution of the Republic of Croatia)
1991. Zagreb: Centar za informacije i publicitet. For an English text, see www.vlada.hr/dokumenti/dokum2e.html.
Ustav Socialističke federativne republike Jugoslavije (The Constitution of the Socialist Federal Republic of Yugoslavia)
1974. Ljubljana: Časopisni zavod Uradni list SR Slovenije.
Valentić, Mirko
1981. *Vojna Krajina i pitanje njezina sjedinjenja s Hrvatskom, 1849–1881* (The Military Frontier and the question of its unification with Croatia, 1849–1881). Zagreb: Sveučilište u Zagrebu, Centar za poijesne znonosti.
van den Berghe, Pierre L.
1991. "Biologija nepotizma: etničnost kot sorodstvena selekcija" (Biology of nepotism: Ethnicity as a kinship selection). In Rizman 1991: 79–107.

van de Port, Mattijs
    1998. *Gypsies, Wars, and Other Instances of the Wild: Civilization and Its Discontents in a Serbian Town.* Amsterdam: University of Amsterdam Press.
Vaniček, František
    1875. *Specialgeschichte der Militärgrenze.* Aus Originalquellen und Quellenwerken geschöpft (A special history of the Military Border: From original and published sources). 1–3. Vienna: Kaiserlich-Königliche Hof- und Staatsdruckerei.
Varshney, Ashutosh
    1993. "Contested Meanings: India's National Identity, Hindu Nationalism, and the Politics of Anxiety." *Daedalus* 122 (3): 227–61.
Vego, M.
    1981. *Historija Brotnja* (The history of Brotnjo). Čitluk: Svjetlost.
Velat, Dubravka
    1988. *Stanovništvo Jugoslavije u posleratom periodu: Grafički prikaz statistice stanovništva* (The population of Yugoslavia in the postwar period: A graphic view of population statistics). Belgrade: Savezni Zavod za Statisticku.
Velovski, T.
    1995. "Notes from the Field: Republic of Macedonia, March 1995." *Anthropology of East Europe Review* 13 (1): 70–73.
Verdery, Katherine
    1993. "Nationalism and National Sentiment in Post-Socialist Romania." *Slavic Review* 52 (2).
    1996. *What Was Socialism and What Comes Next.* Princeton: Princeton University Press.
Vermeulen, Han F.
    1995. "Origins and Institutionalization of Ethnography and Ethnology in Europe and the USA, 1771–1845." In Vermeulen and Roldán 1995: 39–59.
Vermeulen, Han F., and Arturo Alvarez Roldán, eds.
    1995. *Fieldwork and Footnotes.* London and New York: Routledge.
Vickers, Miranda
    1998. *Between Serb and Albanian: A History of Kosovo.* New York: Columbia University Press.
Višković, Nikola
    1997. "Dilemmata und Skeptizismus betreffend das Internationale Tribunal. Verschwiegenes Serbien" (Dilemmas and skepticism concerning the International Tribunal: Silent Serbia). In *Stimmen für die Zukunft* (Voices for the future), ed. Irina Slosar. Klagenfurt-Salzburg: Wiser.
Vjesnik (Zagreb)
    1992. March 5, p. 6; March 7, p. 2; March 24, p. 2; April 5, p. 2; April 15, p. 2.
Vodopivec, Peter
    1994. "Seven Decades of Unconfronted Incongruities: The Slovenes and Yugoslavia." In Benderly and Kraft 1994: 23–46.
Volkov, A.
    1989. "Etnicheski smeshannie sem'i v SSSR: Dinamika i sostav" (Ethnically mixed families in USSR: Trends and composition). *Vestnik Statistiki* (Moscow) 7: 12–21.
Vucinich, Wayne
    1969a. "Interwar Yugoslavia." In *Contemporary Yugoslavia*, ed. W. Vucinich, 3–58. Berkeley and Los Angeles: University of California Press.
    1969b. "Nationalism and Communism." In *Contemporary Yugoslavia*, ed. W. Vucinich, 236–84. Berkeley and Los Angeles: University of California Press.
Vukotić, Bojana
    1992. "Srpski fasizam i umetnost" (Serbian fascism and art). *Socioloski pregled* (Sociological review, Belgrade) 26 (1–4): 69–78.

Vuković, Zdravko
1989. *Od deformacija SDB do maspoka i liberalizma* (From the deformations of the State Security Service to Maspok and liberalism). Belgrade: Narodna Knjiga.

Walker, Lee, and Paul C. Stern, eds.
1993. *Balancing and Sharing Political Power in Multiethnic Societies.* Washington, D.C.: National Academy Press.

Wallace, Anthony F. C.
1956. "Revitalization Movements." *American Anthropologist* 58: 264–81.

Watkins, Susan C.
1981. "Regional Patterns of Nuptiality in Europe, 1870–1960." *Population Studies* 35: 199–215.

Weine, Stevan M., M.D.
1999. *When History Is a Nightmare: Lives and Memories of Ethnic Cleansing in Bosnia-Herzegovina.* New Brunswick, N.J.: Rutgers University Press.

Weine, S. M., A. Džubur Kulenović, I. Pavković, and R. Gibbons
1999. "Testimony Psychotherapy in Bosnian Refugees: A Pilot Study." *American Journal of Psychiatry* 155: 1720–26.

West, Rebecca
1941. *Black Lamb and Grey Falcon: A Journey Through Yugoslavia.* New York: Viking Press.

West, Richard
1995. *Tito: And the Rise and Fall of Yugoslavia.* New York: Carroll and Graf.

White, Stephen, John Gardner, and George Schopflin, eds.
1987. *Communist Political Systems: An Introduction.* New York: St. Martin's Press.

Wiener, F.
1986. *Die Armeen der neutralen und blockfreien Staaten Europas* (The armies of the neutral European states). Truppendienst, pocket book, vol. 10. Vienna: Carl Ueber-reuter.

Wilkinson, H.
1951. *Maps and Politics: A Review of the Ethnographic Cartography of Macedonia.* Liverpool: the University Press.

Williams, Carol J.
1993. "As Violence Spreads, Hungarians in Serbian Province Fear They Are Next." *Los Angeles Times,* October 12. A12.

Williams, Robin M., Jr.
1994. "The Sociology of Ethnic Conflicts: Comparative International Perspectives." *Annual Review of Sociology* 20: 49–79.

Wilterdink, N.
1991. "Inleiding." In "Alledaags en ongewoon geweld," ed. H. Franke, N. Wilter-dink, and C. Brinkgreve. *Amsterdams Sociologisch Tijdschrift* 18 (3): 7–13.

Woodger, William
1996. "War Reporting: So What's New?" *Serbian Studies* (Washington, D.C.) 10 (1): 15–31.

Woodward, Susan
1995. *Balkan Tragedy: Chaos and Dissolution after the Cold War.* Washington, D.C.: The Brookings Institution.

Wrede, Alphons
1903. *Geschichte der k.u.k. Wehrmacht.* Vol. 5. Vienna: P.K.K. Kriegsarchiv.

Zagar, Mitja
1994. "National Sovereignty at the End of the Twentieth Century: Relativisation of Traditional Concepts—the Case of Slovenia." In Bučar and Kuhnle 1994.

Závecz, Tibor
    1995. "Csökkeno rok//onszenv: A magyar társadalom ítéletei, viselkedései a mene-
    kültekkel kapcsolatban" (Decreasing empathy: Judgments, [and] behaviors of Hun-
    garian society relating to refugees). In Sík 1992b.
Žerjavić, Vladimir
    1992. Opsesije i megalomanije oko Jasenovca i Bleiburga (Obsessions and megalo-
    maniacal claims about Jasenovac and Bleiburg). Zagreb: Globus.
    1993. Manipulations with the Number of Second World War Victims. Zagreb: Cro-
    atian Information Centre.
Zgodovina Slovencev
    1979. Zgodovina Slovencev (The history of the Slovenes). Ljubljana: Cankarjeva
    zalozba.
Zickel, Raymond, and Walter R. Iwaskiw
    1994. Albania: A Country Study. Federal Research Division, Library of Congress.
Zidar, Alojz
    1987. Doživetja tigrovca partizana (The experiences of the Tiger partisans). Koper:
    Lipa (zbirka Primorski portreti).
Žižek, Slavoj
    1991. "Slovenija zdaj! Sanje in realnost" (Slovenia now! Dreams and reality). Mlad-
    ina (Ljubljana) 29 (July 16): 29.

Index

Republic of Dubrovnik, 85–86
Republic of Macedonia, as official name for
    Macedonia, 386
Republic of Slovenia, formation of, 144
Republika Srpska (Bosnia), 240. *See also*
    Banja Luka
Republika Srpska Krajina (Republic of
    Serbian Krajina), 97–98; cartoon depictions
    of, 268–70; Croatian conquest of, 125,
    140–41, 217–18; Croatian view of, 203–7;
    formation of, 125; historical background,
    126–27; map of, 138; refugees from,
    103–4; weakness of, 59
research methodology: bias concerning Serbia
    in, 316–17; congruence of social, cultural
    and historical conditions, 5–7; polarization
    of scholars and, 7; social scientists on
    Yugoslav ethnicity, 17–18
resistance groups, in Bosnia-Herzegovina,
    190–94
ressentiment interpretation: Croatian
    nationalism and, 53–54; nationalist
    ideology, 48–50
režervisti, in Bosnia-Herzegovina, 196–201
Rice, Timothy, 314
right-wing political movements: in Hungary,
    356.20; Serbian encouragement of, 331–33
Rihtman-Auguštin, Dunja, 6–7, 70, 322n.8
Rilindja, 366
Romania: ethnic identity in, 17–18; refugees to
    Hungary from, 340–41
Romantic Movement: influence in Serbia of,
    112; as inspiration for origins of Yugoslavia,
    22, 107–8
Rom KUD, in Bosnia, 305
Rorty, Richard, 412
Royal Serbian Army, 132
rreth affiliation, of Kosovo Albanians, 362
Rugova, Ibrahim (Dr.), 365–66
rural development, in Macedonia, 394–97
"rural urbanites," Serbian nationalism and,
    329
Russia: influence on Yugoslavian dissolution,
    168, 204–5; pan-Slavism supported by, 22;
    post-revolutionary self-determination, 68;
    Serbian relations with, 14, 333

Saddam Hussein, 175
Saint Sava cult: resurgence of South Slav
    nationalism and symbol of, 109; Serbian

nationalism and, 327; as *svetosavlje*
    (national mythology), 174
Šamaržić-Kodar, Darko, 268–70
"SAO Slavonia," 97
Sarajevo: interethnic relations in, 14; objective
    research concerning seige of, 8
Sarajevo Radio and Television, 291n.1
Sarajevo Television, 297
saz (lute), 293n.4
"schismogenesis," ethnopolitics and, 47–50
Schwartz, Jonathan, 12, 17, 382–400
secession, Yugoslavian disintegration and,
    30–31
Second Yugoslavia: dissolution of, 406;
    origins of, 61, 318–20
secularism, as alternative to religious
    ethnopolitics, 38
self-censorship, by media, 291–92
self-determination: creation of national
    minorities and, 235; Croatian ethnographic
    research concerning, 215–18; Dayton
    Accords and role of, 251–52; emergence of
    nationalism and, 71–77; folk concept and,
    68; in Macedonia, 384–85; nationalism in
    Yugoslavia and, 60–61; in Slovenia, 145,
    148–49; of South Slavs, 109–10
self-fulfilling prophecy phenomenon: for
    Bosnian Muslims, 117–18; dissolution of
    Yugoslavia as, 57–59
Sells, Michael, 124
Serbia: antibureaucratic revolution in, 62; bias
    in anthropological research on, 316–17;
    cartoon depictions of, 265–67; economic
    conditions, 33; ethnic identity politics in,
    17; federal institutions in, 63n.15; German
    occupation of, 16; hegemony of, 9, 28,
    60–61; illiteracy rate in, 221; kinship
    networks and national identity in, 112–14;
    Kosovo as part of, 47, 363, 365; Muslims as
    "other" in, 116–24; nationalism in, 9–10,
    112; refugee populations in, 32n.13;
    Slovenian politicians in, 63; Turkish
    influence in, 112, 170–71, 325–26;
    Yugoslavia as name of, 6
Serbian Academy of Arts and Sciences
    (SANU), 313, 326
"Serbian Autonomous Areas," construction
    of, in Croatia, 137
Serbian Autonomous Province of Krajina
    (SAO Krajina), 97
Serbian Communist League, 169–70

DATE DUE

AUG 2 2 2002